Who Can Take the Lord's Supper?

Monographs in Baptist History

VOLUME 21

Ours is a day in which not only the gaze of western culture but also increasingly that of Evangelicals is riveted to the present. The past seems to be nowhere in view and hence it is disparagingly dismissed as being of little value for our rapidly changing world. Such historical amnesia is fatal for any culture, but particularly so for Christian communities whose identity is profoundly bound up with their history. The goal of this new series of monographs, Studies in Baptist History, seeks to provide one of these Christian communities, that of evangelical Baptists, with reasons and resources for remembering the past. The editors are deeply convinced that Baptist history contains rich resources of theological reflection, praxis and spirituality that can help Baptists, as well as other Christians, live more Christianly in the present. The monographs in this series will therefore aim at illuminating various aspects of the Baptist tradition and in the process provide Baptists with a usable past.

Who Can Take the Lord's Supper?

A Biblical-Theological Argument
for Close Communion

Dallas W. Vandiver

PICKWICK *Publications* · Eugene, Oregon

WHO CAN TAKE THE LORD'S SUPPER?
A Biblical-Theological Argument for Close Communion

Pickwick Publications
An Imprint of Wipf and Stock Publishers
199 W. 8th Ave., Suite 3
Eugene, OR 97401

www.wipfandstock.com

PAPERBACK ISBN: 978-1-6667-0313-9
HARDCOVER ISBN: 978-1-6667-0314-6
EBOOK ISBN: 978-1-6667-0315-3

Cataloguing-in-Publication data:

Names: Vandiver, Dallas W., author.

Title: Who can take the Lord's supper? : a biblical-theological argument
    for close communion / by Dallas W. Vandiver.

Description: Eugene, OR: Pickwick Publications, 2021 | Series: Monographs in Baptist
    History | Includes bibliographical references and index.

Identifiers: ISBN 978-1-6667-0313-9 (paperback) | ISBN 978-1-6667-0314-6 (hardcover)
    | ISBN 978-1-6667-0315-3 (ebook)

Subjects: LCSH: Close and open communion. | Lord's Supper—Baptists. | Baptists—
    Membership.

Classification: BX6338 V36 2021 (paperback) | BX6338 (ebook)

09/10/21

To Emily, without whose help and encouragement
this work would not have come to fruition.

[Strict Baptists] allow that their Paedobaptist brethren, on their own principles, do right in forming themselves into churches, and in commemorating the death of their Lord. Though they differ from the Baptists, yet they unite together those whom they deem properly baptized, and walk with them in Christian fellowship. In this the Baptists blame them not. They consider them wrong in their opinion of the first ordinance; yet, with their views, they consider them right in the second; and doubt not their conscientious regard to it. The objection of the strict Baptists to communion with them does not arise from suspicions attaching to their Christian character, to which, they trust, they are always willing to render ample justice; but from the necessary consequence of such communion, as a practical deviation from what they believe was the original constitution of the church.

JOSEPH KINGHORN, *BAPTISM A TERM OF COMMUNION* (1816)

Contents

Preface

I FIRST KNEW I wanted to write this book in 2013 while flying somewhere over the Pacific Ocean on my way back to Texas from Myanmar. When in 2015 I began pursuing a PhD at Southern Seminary, close communion was already my target dissertation topic. In God's kindness, that dissertation is now complete and adapted here.

When, on that trip to Myanmar and back, I read Gentry and Wellum's *Kingdom through Covenant*, I saw ecclesiology emerge from robust biblical theology. While that volume considered several ways in which a progressive covenantal view of Scripture shapes systematic theology, they lacked the space to address Passover and the Lord's Supper. Because their work posits a clear defense of regenerate church membership and believer's baptism, I saw the topic of close communion as a way to further their project.

Specifically, given their treatment of circumcision's relationship to baptism, what would result from a similar consideration of Passover's relationship to the Lord's Supper? Furthermore, how would comparing circumcision's relation to Passover and baptism's relation to the Lord's Supper contribute to a biblically-theologically conceived ecclesiology? And, how would a comparison of the relation of the respective covenantal signs of entry to the signs of participation contribute to the Baptist debate over who can take the Lord's Supper?

These are the questions about which this book is written. I write, having been a member of Southern (Great Commission) Baptist churches since my conversion in 1991. Admittedly, baptistic church leaders and members are the primary audience that will benefit from this book. Those interested in Baptist history will find chapters 1 and 5 to be a unique presentation of and response to the four historical Baptist answers to the question of who can take the Lord's Supper in Baptist churches. Pastors and theological students may be especially interested in the theological method here undertaken, as chapters 2–3 seek to fairly present the scriptural data in its covenantal context before comparing the covenantal signs in chapter 4, answering objections in chapter 5, and presenting ecclesiological conclusions in chapter 6. Finally, those interested in biblical-theological systems will hopefully find this book to be a helpful contribution to the continuing dialogue.

A word about this book's approach may also be helpful. Although this book enters a centuries-old debate among Baptists with an approach to how the whole of Scripture fits together that likewise stimulates debate, its primary burden is to provide a constructive, biblical-theological argument for close communion. I am unaware of any other such constructive argument. Given this approach, the book's interaction with other biblical-theological systems—dispensational and covenantal—primarily occurs in the footnotes to keep the flow of argument more consistent in the body of text.

I pray that Christ's churches are increasingly strengthened and biblically-shaped for the mission of disciple-making to God's glory through reading this book.

Dallas W. Vandiver
Louisville, KY
February 2021

Acknowledgments

I AM GRATEFUL FOR the meticulous and helpful feedback from my doctoral supervisor, Gregg R. Allison, throughout the writing process. Stephen J. Wellum, Hershael W. York, and Jason G. Duesing also provided helpful comments and encouragement through the dissertation defense from which this book originated.

Michael A. G. Haykin's encouragement to pursue publication and Roy M. Paul's gracious guidance in the publication process were instrumental to this work going to press.

Others who helped me think through critical content include Bobby Jamieson, Jonathan Leeman, and John Kimbell. Their fidelity to Scripture and precision of argument are a gift to their churches and others who benefit from their work.

Finally, I am grateful for the brothers and sisters of Clifton Baptist Church of Louisville, KY, who strive to live out the truths contained herein.

Introduction

THE QUESTION OF "WHO is admitted to the Lord's Table is the very core of polity."[1] As Ligon Duncan explains, both ecclesiology "and the doctrine of the sacraments res[t] on a biblical-theological understanding of what constitutes the church."[2] Therefore, the way in which one puts together the biblical-theological storyline of Scripture has significant ramifications on one's definition of the church. Historically, the right preaching of the Word and the right administration of the sacraments have been seen as defining marks of a true church.[3] While baptism is viewed as the entry sign into the church, the Lord's Supper is the continuing ordinance that marks off God's people from the world.[4] Hence, the question of who participates in the Lord's Supper is a very important one. Church polity and organization depends upon who the church views as being inside and who is outside. Across denominations of Christians, the body of Christ receives the bread and the cup (the continuing sign of the new covenant) in different local churches, while those who are not a part of Christ's body do not receive the benefits of the meal Jesus instituted.

What This Book Argues

The question this book seeks to answer is this: "Who may participate in the Lord's Supper"?[5] Or, tailoring the research question more specifically to

---

1. Dever et al., "Church Polity? Really?" Throughout this book, I will use the Lord's Supper synonymously with *communion*, *the Table*, and *the Supper*.

2. Dever et al., "Church Polity? Really?"

3. See Allison, *Historical Theology*, 565–88; Kolb, "Church," in Barrett, *Reformation Theology*, 577–608.

4. Mathison, "Lord's Supper," in Barrett, *Reformation Theology*, 643–74.

5. This book does not seek to answer questions concerning the way in which Christ is present in the ordinances. Thus, I will address these issues only as they relate to the

my approach, this book seeks to provide an answer to the question: "How does a progressive covenantal view of Scripture help us answer the question of who may participate in the Lord's Supper"?[6] I will argue that believer's baptism by immersion should precede communion as prerequisite to it, due to the explicit example of the New Testament, the assumed pattern that all believers are baptized, and a principle of analogy (continuity) from the necessity of circumcision before Passover.

How the Argument Works

I will argue this thesis in three steps. First, I will argue that in the Old Testament, circumcision functioned as the sign of entry into the people of God and was prerequisite to Passover—the sign of fellowship with God and his people. Second, I will argue that the example of Acts 2:41 and the assumed New Testament pattern of all believers being baptized demonstrates that baptism functions as the sign of entry into the new covenant and is prerequisite to the new covenant sign of communion with God and his people—the Lord's Supper. Third, I will argue that a principle of analogy (continuity) exists between the necessity of circumcision before Passover in the old covenant and of baptism before the Lord's Supper in the new covenant. When combined with the New Testament data, this principle of analogy between signs of entry in each respective covenant being prerequisite to signs of

---

primary focus of my research question. Further, I will usually refer to baptism and the Lord's Supper as covenant signs and ordinances, but I will sometimes refer to them as sacraments interchangeably.

6. Progressive Covenantalism refers to view championed by Peter John Gentry and Stephen J. Wellum as a description of how to put the whole Bible together in their work, *Kingdom through Covenant: A Biblical-Theological Understanding of the Covenants* (2012). They argue for a middle position between dispensational theologies and classic covenantal theology whereby (1) they maintain that God brings his saving reign over the earth through successive covenants which are integrally related to each other until all of the prior covenants find their *telos* in Christ and the new covenant he brings; (2) they reject as unhelpful the notion of one covenant of grace with differing administrations, arguing that the idea flattens the distinctions between the covenants; (3) they see all the promises made to OT Israel as fulfilled in Christ; (4) they reject a distinct future for ethnic, national Israel as separate from the one people of God throughout time; and (5) they reject the notion that all the promises to Israel may be directly applied to the church as the replacement of Israel, because Christ is the true Israelite and Davidic king in whom all the promises of God find their amen (2 Cor 1:20). See also Wellum and Parker, *Progressive Covenantalism*. For a covenant theology critique of progressive covenantalism, see Brack and Oliphint, "Questioning the Progress in Progressive Covenantalism," 189–217. For a dispensational critique, see Vlach, "Have They Found a Better Way?," 5–24.

fellowship in those covenants provides a strong argument for the practice of close communion. For the purposes of this paper, I define close communion as the view that all who have been baptized as professing believers and are members in good standing of their respective churches may be admitted to the Lord's Supper under the administration of another local church of like faith and order.

Historical Summary of Research

Protestants have long debated the definition of a true church surrounding the question of who is included in the new covenant and, as corollary, who partakes of the fellowship meal—the Lord's Supper. While this work focuses attention on Baptist views of who may participate in the Lord's Supper, helpful perspective may be gained by noting other denominational views on the question. This section considers the ways in which a variety of Christian traditions answer the question of who may participate in the Lord's Supper, while focusing on Baptists. Rather than initially defining each of the possible views, for clarity's sake, each view is presented in connection with the denomination that holds it.

The Orthodox, Roman Catholic, and Lutheran traditions tend to define their view as closed communion, though by that term they intend communion among all the local congregations that comprise the one Orthodox, Roman Catholic, or Lutheran Church respectively.[7] Communicants in these traditions hold that baptism is prerequisite to receiving the Lord's Supper, which normally entails infant baptism except in cases of an adult convert.[8]

---

7. Harrison and Pless, *Closed Communion?*. Roman Catholic scholar Thomas Baima affirms that "anyone who is baptized and in full communion with the Catholic Church should receive Holy Communion" (Baima, "Roman Catholic View," in Armstong, *Understanding Four Views on the Lord's Supper*, 129–30). Baima claims the Roman Catholic Church may admit someone outside the Church to participate in a limited intercommunion on a case by case basis, depending on who the person is, what church they come from, and that church's standing with the Roman Catholic Church. However, the *Catechism of the Catholic Church* (*CCC*) states that Protestant churches have not "preserved the proper reality of the Eucharistic mystery," which makes "intercommunion with these communities . . . not possible." See USCCB, *Catechism of the Catholic Church*, 1400.

8. Though I hold that infant baptism is not actually New Testament baptism, for the sake of argument, this section speaks of baptism more broadly, in a way that allows infant baptism by sprinkling, immersion, or affusion (pouring over the head) to be considered baptism.

Among these traditions, the Orthodox Church is unique in its practice of closed credo-communion and pedocommunion.[9]

By contrast to closed communion, open communion is defined as allowing all baptized believers in Christ to participate in the Lord's Supper, no matter the mode, subject, or meaning of baptism. Some Presbyterian churches and Reformed churches and all United Methodist churches (UMC) practice an open form of both credo-communion and pedocommunion.[10] However, the majority of Presbyterians,[11] Evangelical Free Church of America (EFCA), Assemblies of God (AG), Disciples of Christ (DOC), and Episcopal Church practice an open form of credo-communion without including infants in the meal.[12] Because open communion normally requires that participants be confessing believers, those open communion advocates who allow/encourage pedocommunion must be distinguished from the dominant perspective.

Due to the non-denominational, autonomous nature of Christian churches, each church has the ability to establish its own policy for admission to the Lord's Supper. While Southland Christian Church of Lexington,

9. Nassif, "Baptism, Eucharist and the Church."

10. Strawbridge, *Case for Covenant Communion*. Strawbridge's volume is a polemical monograph encouraging pedocommunion among pedobaptists, especially Presbyterians. The pedocommunion volume is a companion to the prior polemical publication, Strawbridge, *Case for Covenantal Infant Baptism*. The UMC does not seek to persuade its members of the legitimacy of pedocommunion, but neither does it restrict infants from participating in communion as long as they are baptized. They explain, "All who respond in faith to the invitation are to be welcomed. Holy Baptism normally precedes partaking of Holy Communion. Holy Communion is a meal of the community who are in covenant relationship with God through Jesus Christ. As circumcision was the sign of the covenant between God and the Hebrew people, baptism is the sign of the new covenant (Gen 17:9–14; Exod 24:1–12; Jer 31:31; Rom 6:1–11; Heb 9:15)" (GCUMC, "Holy Mystery," 14–15). Later, they state, "No one will be turned away from the table because of age . . . or mental capacity."

11. Waters and Duncan, *Children and the Lord's Supper*.

12. The EFCA statement reads, "The Lord Jesus mandated two ordinances, baptism and the Lord's Supper, which visibly and tangibly express the gospel. Though they are not the means of salvation, when celebrated by the church in genuine faith, these ordinances confirm and nourish the believer" (EFCA, "Statement of Faith"). While the EFCA practices both infant baptism and believer's baptism, their statement of faith restricts the definition of the church to include believers only. The "Fundamental Principles" of the Assemblies of God do not mention the ordinances at all in the definition of the church. Presumably then, they practice open communion (GCAG, "Sixteen Fundamental Truths"). The Episcopal Church in America is clearer in their affirmation that the Lord's Supper is for baptized believers only. However, one does not have to be an Episcopal to participate (Episcopal Church, "Communion"). For the Episcopal Church, see also Article XXV in Suter and Robinson, "Articles of Religion." For Disciples of Christ, see "Communion and Baptism."

Kentucky, for example, requires believer's baptism by immersion for membership, they are willing to receive those baptized as professing believers from any other Protestant denomination as members and to the Lord's Supper.[13] Thus, their policy is narrow enough compared to the open communion denominations above to be considered a soft form of close communion—all those baptized as professing believers are welcome to participate.

For most of Baptist history, Baptists have offered three answers to the question of who may participate in the Lord's Supper that fall under the headings closed communion (local church members only), close communion (transient intercommunion/denominational communion), and open communion.[14] Each of these positions is defined somewhat uniquely by

13. See http://southland.church/baptism/nicholasville. Hahn, who is cited on the webpage above as the Lead Executive Pastor responsible for explaining the church's doctrine, explained by phone the church's position as "open communion," intending that they receive those baptized by immersion as professing believers from any denomination. However, he explained that they do not explicitly restrict those baptized as infants by another mode. Scott Hahn, personal conversation. For a historical look at the Lord's Supper in the Restoration movement, see Ritchie, "Breaking Bread Together." Ritchie argues that while Campbell emphasized believer's baptism by immersion and even claimed to hold a closed communion position, in practice he was actually closer to open communion.

14. This taxonomy follows that of Gregg Allison as presented in *Sojourners and Strangers*, 401–6. Other Baptists have presented slightly different taxonomies. Thomas White admits that "No consistent terminology to discuss this issue has been used throughout history" (White, "Baptist's Theology of the Lord's Supper," in White et al., *Restoring Integrity in Baptist Churches*, 154–60). Yet, White's three categories match Allison's in their definitions, though not their terminology. They are (1) close communion; (2) transient communion; and (3) open/mixed communion. White's close communion corresponds with Allison's closed position. By mixed communion, White refers to participation in communion by both baptized and unbaptized believers. On this term, it is important to distinguish mixed communion from the Reformed ecclesial notion of a mixed community of covenant keepers and covenant breakers, or regenerate and unregenerate members. Mixed communion merely denotes the baptismal status of the participants of communion rather than the regenerate status of church members. For a description and critique of the pedobaptist view of the church as a mixed community, see Wellum, "Baptism and the Relationship between the Covenants," in Schreiner and Wright, *Believer's Baptism*, 97–161. Emir Caner "sees no less than five competing categories as to who should partake of the Lord's Supper" (Caner, "Fencing the Table," in White et al., *Restoring Integrity in Baptist Churches*, 172–76). Caner's categories are (1) "laissez-faire communion," in which communion is open to all who wish to partake; (2) "open communion," which allows all believers in Christ to partake of communion; (3) "cracked communion," which welcomes any to the Table who have be baptized by immersion as believers no matter who administered the baptism or what the administrators taught the meaning of baptism to be; (4) "closed communion," which corresponds to Allison's close communion and White's transient communion; and (5) "locked communion," which is the same as Allison's closed position and White's close position. It is important to note that Caner finds examples of all five categories within Southern

Baptists in terms of believer's baptism when compared to other denominations. As such, baptism in the following descriptions should be understood as the baptism of a professing believer by immersion.

J. R. Graves, who identified with the Landmark Baptists, promoted the *closed communion view*. Graves et al. argue that the Lord's Supper is available only to baptized members in good standing of the local church administering the ordinance.[15] The closed position is grounded in at least one (sometimes all three) of the following points. First, it denies the existence of the universal church prior to Christ's return in favor of the autonomous, local church, which it defines as a covenanted assembly of baptized believers. Second, this position claims that no church exists without the right preaching of the word and right administration of the ordinances, which entails a rejection of all churches that baptize infants or hold sacramental views of the ordinances. Third, it argues that the connection between the Lord's Supper and excommunication in Scripture requires that believers must only receive the Lord's Supper from the church that can discipline them; otherwise, local church autonomy and purity are threatened.

Throughout their history, various Baptists have advocated the close communion position over against the closed and open positions.[16] *Close communion* allows baptized members in good standing to participate in communion together, where the ordinance is administered by a particular local church of like faith and practice. Some of the most vigorous advocates of close communion in Baptist history include William Kiffin (1616–1701),[17] Abraham Booth (1734–1806),[18] Andrew Fuller (1754–1815),[19] Joseph

---

Baptist life. Nevertheless, he claims that the categories broadly account for all Christian churches. For another similar taxonomy, see Hammett, *Forty Questions*, 259–72.

15. Graves, *Intercommunion*. For a more recent advocate of the closed position, see Kazee, *Church and the Ordinances*. Kazee appears to switch the definitions of closed and close communion (123). However, he clarifies his position to match Graves' by the end of the book. Thanks to Hershael York for recommending this resource. It is noteworthy that not all Landmark Baptists were closed communionists. See chapter 1 for more.

16. For a helpful survey of many of the controversies among Particular Baptists in England, see Naylor, *Calvinism, Communion, and the Baptists*. See also Hilburn, "Lord's Supper."

17. Kiffin, *Sober Discourse*. See also Weaver, "When Biography Shapes Ecclesiology," 31–54.

18. Booth's major defense of close communion is Booth, *Apology for the Baptists*. Other important works on baptism are *Defense for the Baptists* and *Pædobaptism Examined*.

19. Fuller has several helpful statements on the issue of close communion. Chief among them is Fuller, "Admission of Unbaptized Persons," in Belcher, *Fuller's Works*, 3:508–15. This work was published within a year of Fuller's death. Fuller had instructed

Kinghorn (1766–1832),[20] and Thomas Baldwin (1753–1825).[21] Several of the arguments from these historical figures include (1) allowing unbaptized believers to the Table requires Baptists to give up their Baptist principles (Booth and Fuller); (2) baptism is integral for believers according to Jesus' command in Matthew 28:19–20 and the example of Acts 2:41, which testifies that baptism normally precedes communion (cf. Rom 6:1–4; Gal 3:27); (3) allowing the unbaptized to join in communion changes the constitution of the local church from that which Christ established, which may be described as believers marked off from the world by their common belief gospel, their participation in two ordinances, and their mutual commitment to each other for worship and edification (Kinghorn); and (4) Christ instituted the two ordinances as covenant signs that should be held together as positive institutions (Fuller).[22]

Contemporary advocates of *close communion* include Gregg Allison, John Hammett, Thomas White, Mark Dever, Bobby Jamieson, Jonathan Leeman.[23] While these contemporary proponents reject closed communion as unrequired by Scripture, they generally follow the historic Baptist arguments for *close communion*. One emphasis most of the contemporary

---

a friend to publish the letter only if an argument for open communion were published. Robert Hall Jr.'s polemic in favor of open communion made publication of Fuller's letter necessary.

20. For Kinghorn's lengthy debate with Robert Hall Jr., see Kinghorn, *Baptism a Term of Communion* (1816); *Defense of "Baptism a Term of Communion"* (1820); *Arguments Against the Practice of Mixed Communion* (1827). For a helpful secondary source examining the Kinghorn and Hall debate in its Reformation and English Baptist context, see Walker, *Baptists at the Table*.

21. Baldwin, *Baptism of Believers Only* (1806). Thomas Baldwin was pastor of the Second Baptist Church of Boston at the turn of the nineteenth century. He carried on a twenty-year debate with two Congregationalist pastors, Peter and Noah Worcester, that preceded the Kinghorn and Hall debate by around ten years. See Baldwin, *Series of Letters* (1810). For biographical information on Baldwin, see Chessman, *Memoir of Rev. Thomas Baldwin*. Because Baldwin's interlocutors were Congregationalists, their responses are included here rather than in the discussion of open communion Baptists. See N. Worcester, *Friendly Letter* (1791); S. Worcester, *Serious and Candid Letters* (1807); *Two Discourses* (1807).

22. The substance of Fuller's articulation of positive institutions (as opposed to moral duties) can be found in his 1810 publication against the Scotch Baptists, Fuller, *Strictures on Sandemanianism*, Letters IX and X in Belcher, *Fuller's Works*, 2:624. Richard Fuller, a Southern Baptist contemporary of J. R. Graves, argues the close position. See Fuller, *Baptism, and the Terms of Communion*.

23. Allison, *Sojourners and Strangers*, 404; Hammett, *Forty Questions*, 271; White, "Baptist's Theology of the Lord's Supper," 154; Dever, *Church*, 38; *Display of God's Glory*, 52–53; Jamieson, *Going Public*; Leeman, "Congregational Approach to Catholicity," in Leeman and Dever, *Baptist Foundations*, 369. For more on each of these sources see chapters 1 and 5.

authors seem to have gleaned, and tempered, from both the *close and closed* communionists is the appropriateness of connecting the ordinances to each other, to church membership and discipline, and therefore to the local church as the only proper context for celebrating the Lord's Supper.[24] Two contemporary theological developments sometimes marshalled in favor of *close communion* are (1) the connection between union with Christ and the derivative union with Christ's body, the church; and (2) the redemptive-historical epoch of the church as the new covenant people of God with accompanying covenantal signs (ordinances).[25] This book seeks to utilize these areas of theological development in specific application to close communion.

Advocates of *open communion* opposed the close communion advocates in the historic debates. Outside of Baptist life, open communion ordinarily refers to the ability to participate in the Lord's Supper with other believers baptized by any mode.[26] However, under the leadership of Henry Jessey (1601–1663), John Bunyan (1628–1688), and Robert Hall Jr. (1764–1831),[27] *open communion* came to include communion with any who claim

24. Speaking of the baptism of the Ethiopian eunuch, Daniel Akin contends, "Missionary expansion and accompanying baptisms, like those found in the book of Acts, should not be viewed as the pattern once local churches are established" (Akin, "Meaning of Baptism," in White et al., *Restoring Integrity in Baptist Churches*, 71). Instead, Akin et al. argue that the ordinances are given to the local church. See also Allen, "Dipped for the Dead," in White et al., *Restoring Integrity in Baptist Churches*, 85; White, "What Makes Baptism Valid?," in White et al., *Restoring Integrity in Baptist Churches*, 107–18; Lee, "Baptism and Covenant," in White et al., *Restoring Integrity in Baptist Churches*, 133–36; Norman, "Reestablishment of Proper Church Discipline," in White et al., *Restoring Integrity in Baptist Churches*, 210–17; Caner, "Fencing the Table," in White et al., *Restoring Integrity in Baptist Churches*, 165. Caner's proposal explicitly gleans from nineteenth-century Landmarkist Baptist theologian J. M. Pendleton. Further, see Wellum, "Means of Grace: Baptism," in Armstrong, *Compromised Church*, 158–59; Grenz, "Baptism and the Lord's Supper as Community Acts," in Cross and Thompson, *Baptist Sacramentalism*, 76–95.

25. From a progressive dispensational viewpoint, see Saucy, *Church in God's Program*, 66–88, 225–27. From the progressive covenantal position, see Wellum, "Beyond Mere Ecclesiology," in Easley and Morgan, *Community of Jesus*, 183–212. From a covenantal Baptist perspective that identifies each biblical covenant as administrations of the one covenant of grace, see Jones, *Waters of Promise*, 132–53.

26. Pedocommunion is the major exception for allowing unbelieving children of believers to participate. Historically, the context for open communion was usually understood to be the local church, rather than an occasional gathering of Christians from different churches.

27. For more on Jessey, see Duesing, *Henry Jessey*. For Bunyan's views, see Bunyan, "Confession of My Faith," in Offor, *Bunyan's Works*, 2:602–16; Bunyan, "Differences in Judgment," 2:616–48; "Peaceable Principles and True" 2:648–57. For a helpful assessment of the relationship between Bunyan and other open communion advocates, see

to be sincere believers, whether baptized by any mode or not.[28] Charles Spurgeon (1834–1892) notably extended the definition of open communion to include participating in the meal with or without the auspices of an administering local church.[29] Arguments for open communion usually include (1) the church should receive into its communion celebration all those whom Christ has received (Rom 14:1–3); closed and close communion are divisive and unloving; (2) Scripture contains no rule that baptism must precede communion; (3) the Lord's Supper is a sign of union with Christ, which is true of every believer (Spurgeon); (4) to claim that baptism is prerequisite to the Lord's Supper assumes that baptism is necessary for salvation (Hall); (5) while water baptism is not the initiating ordinance or sign of entry into the church, visible sainthood testifies that one belongs to Christ and may receive communion (Bunyan); and (6) close and closed communion restrict the consciences of believers where Christ has not made a pronouncement (Hall). Contemporary advocates of open communion include Robert Saucy, Ray Van Neste, Stanley Fowler, John Piper, Sam Storms, and just over 50 percent of Southern Baptist pastors surveyed by LifeWay in 2012.[30]

From the second half of the twentieth century until the present day, Baptists in England associated with the Baptist Union have sometimes argued for a fourth, *ecumenical view* in answer to the question of who may participate in communion. Paul Fiddes, for example, urges Baptists to welcome all people to communion no matter if their "faith journey" includes

---

George, "Controversy and Communion," in Bebbington, *Gospel in the World,* 38–58. Hall's most important and extensive work on the subject of open communion is Hall Jr., *On Terms of Communion* (1816). For Hall's further engagement with Kinghorn, see Hall Jr., *Reply to the Rev. Joseph Kinghorn* (1818); *Short Statement* (1826).

28. Steve Weaver attributes special responsibility for this view to John Bunyan in Weaver, "When Biography Shapes Ecclesiology," 31–54.

29. In other words, Spurgeon celebrated and encouraged communion with various groups of Christians unhinged from a local church. Morden, "Spirituality of C. H. Spurgeon 2," 34; Morden, *"Communion with Christ and His People,"* 103–4, 166–73.

30. Saucy, *Church in God's Program,* 195; Neste, "Lord's Supper," in Schreiner and Crawford, *Lord's Supper,* 379–86; Fowler, *More Than a Symbol,* 231; Piper, "Baptism and Church Membership"; Storms, "Piper, Grudem, Dever, et al. on Baptism, the Lord's Table, and Church Membership." More interaction with the contemporary advocates of open communion is found in chapter 5. The LifeWay survey concerned each church's actual practice rather than stated theological position. See note 36 below. The survey is presented in Pipes, "Lord's Supper." James Patterson may be correct in assuming that the logic behind the open communion position is that "we live in an increasingly hostile culture where evangelicals from several denominational perspectives may well need to join together in some common causes for the sake of the Gospel. Wisely or unwisely, perhaps the practice of a less restrictive Lord's Supper represents an attempt to articulate a broader Kingdom vision for the battle against secularism and paganism" (Patterson, "Participation at the Lord's Table").

infant baptism in the Roman Catholic Church, Protestant pedobaptism, or no baptism at all.[31] The aim of an ecumenical approach is inclusion, acceptance, and contribution to the mission of the church by offering grace and multiple "ways of belonging" to those often excluded by churches.[32] Anthony Clarke goes further by arguing that the mission of the church should push congregations to blur the lines between the church and the world. Moreover, he proposes that the Lord's Supper may serve as a converting ordinance for some.[33] Clearly, the ecumenical theologies of the Lord's Supper swing the pendulum to the opposite extreme from closed communion.

The Significance of This Book

In light of Baptist history and contemporary trends, this book is significant in at least two ways. Theologically, I will build on the groundwork already

31. Fiddes, *Tracks and Traces*, 55, 135–45, 175–78. Similar is Winter, "Ambiguous Genitives, Pauline Baptism and Roman Insulae," in Cross and Thompson, *Baptist Sacramentalism 2*, 91.

32. Fiddes is especially concerned for children, the mentally handicapped, "half-believers" (i.e., seekers who do not yet profess faith in Christ), and pedobaptists. Fiddes, *Tracks and Traces*, 126, 135–219. See also Fiddes, "Baptism and the Process of Christian Initiation," 49–65. Something of the same ecumenical spirit is at work in the notion that online churches may experience genuine community, even by participating in the Lord's Supper with Kool-Aid and crackers in the privacy of one's own home, as argues Reed, "Computer-Mediated Communication and Ecclesiological Challenges." On virtual communion, see also Ostrowski, "Cyber Communion," 1–8.

33. Clarke, "Feast for All?," in Cross and Thompson, *Baptist Sacramentalism 2*, 114, 116. The move toward ecumenical communion is usually promoted by those who view both ordinances in sacramental terms (not simply outward signs of inward grace as this project is comfortable with, but the signs conveying or communicating grace in some fashion), though the definitions of sacrament vary. In the same volume, Sean A. White surveys a host of twentieth-century Southern Baptist definitions of sacrament but usually speaks vaguely of "means of grace." See White, "Southern Baptists, Sacramentalism, and Soul Competency," in Cross and Thompson, *Baptist Sacramentalism 2*, 197–218. Michael Bird prefers defining sacraments as "effective signs," and occasions on which God works in the believer in Bird, "Re-Thinking a Sacramental View of Baptism," in Cross and Thompson, *Baptist Sacramentalism 2*, 61–76. Paul Fiddes's lengthy description of sacrament includes that "The Triune God . . . uses the world itself as a means or mediation to draw us into participation in God's own communion of life and love." Again, "God makes room within this pattern or dance of relationships [within the Trinity] for us to dwell, and the material signs of the world can be the place where this happens." See Fiddes, "*Ex Opere Operato*," in Cross and Thompson, *Baptist Sacramentalism 2*, 219–38. Fiddes is clearer, even if more troubling, when he states that baptism "actually communicates the presence of the transcendent God. A created thing provides places and opportunities for a transforming encounter" (Fiddes, *Tracks and Traces*, 117).

laid by advocates of progressive covenantalism. While Stephen Wellum and John Meade have made helpful contributions toward understanding the relationship between circumcision and baptism,[34] this work will offer a constructive proposal of how Passover leads to Christ and the Lord's Supper and how the relationship between the ordinances fit into progressive covenantalism. Arguing for *close* communion provides a case study for letting biblical theology drive us to our ecclesiological conclusions.[35]

Practically, this book emphasizes the importance of the local church as God's appointed means and primary context of discipleship for Christians. Especially for Baptists, it emphasizes the significant role the ordinances and the relationships implied by those ordinances (church membership and discipline) are meant to play in Christian growth. Finally, the book encourages healthy churches by urging pastors to practice the ordinances in way that consistently applies the realities of the new covenant. When 61 percent of Southern Baptist pastors surveyed in 2012 allow unbaptized persons to receive the Lord's Supper, while ostensibly adhering to the close communion position of "The Baptist Faith and Message 2000" (BF&M),[36] close communion deserves a fresh articulation.[37]

34. Wellum, "Relationship between the Covenants" in Schreiner and Wright, *Believer's Baptism*, 97–162; Meade, "Circumcision," in Wellum and Parker, 127–58.

35. Some of the theological matters already developed from a progressive covenantal framework include the typological Israel-Christ-Church relationship, the nature of the land promises to OT Israel, and the relationship of the law covenant to Christ and the new covenant. See Parker, "Israel-Christ-Church Typological Pattern"; Martin, *Bound for the Promised Land*; Meyer, *End of the Law*.

36. After surveying 1,066 Southern Baptist pastors in 2012, LifeWay found that 4 percent did not specify who could participate, 4 percent allowed only members of the local church to participate, 5 percent allowed anyone who wants to participate, 35 percent allowed anyone baptized as a believer to participate, and 52 percent allowed anyone who has put their faith in Christ to participate. See Pipes, "Lord's Supper." In the BF&M 2000, Article VII on the ordinances includes that baptism, "Being a church ordinance, it is prerequisite to the privileges of church membership and to the Lord's Supper." See Southern Baptist Convention, "Baptist Faith and Message 2000." According to a 1996 survey cited by Paul Fiddes, "17 percent of churches in the Baptist Union of Great Britain require believer's baptism for membership, 51 percent admit to full membership based on profession of faith, and 24 percent admit to a kind of associate membership without Believers baptism" (Fiddes, *Tracks and Traces*, 140). One can only guess that the percentages of those upholding closed or close communion have dwindled in intervening years. Upon citing the statistics, Fiddes claims that the "openness . . . is based on recognizing people's faith as Christian believers . . . and it itself does not imply any theological view of their baptism as infants." Historically, when faced with a similar argument, Kinghorn and Fuller responded that their interlocutors had effectively approved of Christians leaving off a command of Christ to be baptized and sounded the death knell for true baptism.

37. Other recent dissertations on the communion debate that have not made a

A Summary of What's Ahead

This book argues for the *close communion* position based upon the example of Acts 2:41, the fact that all believers are assumed to have been baptized by the New Testament authors, and a principle of analogy (continuity) from the prerequisite nature of circumcision to participate in Passover. Chapter 1 surveys the arguments from advocates of closed, close, open, and ecumenical communion among Baptists throughout their history. While I include a variety of voices, I focus on the historical figures deemed most influential by successive generations of Baptists. Chapter 1 also serves as a helpful reminder of the need to encourage unity in the gospel with other believers in Christ as far as obedience to Christ will allow. Close and closed communion advocates utilized the biblical-theological analogy of circumcision to Passover; still, this principle of analogy and continuity deserves further development.

---

biblical-theological argument for close communion include Sampler, "Whosoever Is 'Qualified' May Come." Sampler argues that since the nineteenth century, Southern Baptists have viewed the qualifications for church membership as coterminous with those for participation in the Lord's Supper due to the strong connection between the Lord's Supper and church membership. He demonstrates that most Southern Baptists who have written extensively on the topics of communion and membership have claimed believer's baptism as prerequisite. Sampler's solution to the current ecclesial weakness of SBC practice is to change "The Baptist Faith and Message" to reflect the consensus of SBC churches. See Sampler, "Whosoever Is 'Qualified' May Come," 194. Sheila D. Klopfer argues that from 1742 to 1833, Baptists held a view of baptism between mere symbolism and sacramentalism. She proposes that because baptism is an "integrating expression of the church's theology," Baptists should recognize various implications of baptism, including soteriological, ecclesiological, ethical, and eschatological dimensions (Klopfer, "Baptists in America [1742–1833]," vi, 180–204). Stephen Farish summarizes the arguments for close and open communion in three categories: (1) arguments from Scripture; (2) arguments from the theology of baptism and the Lord's Supper; and (3) arguments from the doctrine of the church (Farish, "Open versus Close Communion Controversy," 50). The only recent argument for any view on the question of who may participate in the Lord's Supper is that of Bobby Jamieson. He argues that "baptism and the Lord's Supper are effective signs of church membership: they create the social, ecclesial reality to which they point. Precisely because of their complementary church-constituting roles, baptism must precede the Lord's Supper and the status of church membership which grants access to the Lord's Supper." Jamieson claims to offer "an integrated account of how baptism and the Lord's Supper transform a scattered group of Christians into a gathered local church" (Jamieson, *Going Public*, 2). This project depends significantly on Jamieson, and yet, it will provide much of the biblical-theological argumentation that Jamieson assumes. Whereas Jamieson focuses on the NT, this book will give due attention to the textual and epochal horizons of circumcision and Passover before moving to the NT. Then, this project will have clear data with which to approach a canonical interpretation of Scripture in answer to the research question.

Chapters 2 through 4 supply the biblical, exegetical, and theological material necessary to argue for close communion. Chapter 2 considers the nature and purpose of circumcision and Passover in the Old Testament. From God's installation of circumcision with Abraham, God commanded circumcision to function minimally (1) as a covenant identity marker to demonstrate that one belonged to his people; (2) to point forward typologically to heart circumcision (new birth); and (3) upon the inauguration of the Mosaic covenant, to qualify male covenant members to participate in Passover. Passover then functioned minimally as the celebration and fellowship meal of the Mosaic covenant through which God's people remembered his saving work in Egypt and celebrated fellowship with God as his people.

Chapter 3 considers the nature and connection of the ordinances to the new covenant, each other, the church, and the kingdom. It highlights the way the New Testament authors presume that belief and baptism belong together as aspects of conversion and that Acts 2:41 presents baptized believers participating in the Lord's Supper. Considering the ordinances through a biblical-theological lens, chapter 3 argues that baptism functions as a new covenant sign of entry into the kingdom of Christ, while the Lord's Supper functions as a new covenant sign of participation/communion with Christ primarily and Christ's church derivatively. As such, the Lord's Supper is a proleptic, new covenant ratification meal and an inaugurated kingdom feast. Given the way baptism and the Lord's Supper function as new covenant signs, it follows that Christ appointed them as visible presentations of the gospel that define and mark off the new covenant community from the world.

Chapter 4 makes the most important contribution of the book—a biblical-theological argument on the relationship of the Abrahamic turn old covenant sign of circumcision and the old covenant meal of Passover to baptism and the Lord's Supper. To demonstrate how each of these signs relates to the other, chapter 4 presents the continuities and discontinuities between (1) circumcision and baptism; (2) Passover and the Lord's Supper; and (3) the relationship of the participants in old covenant signs to each other and the relationship of the participants in new covenant signs to each other. The chapter argues that circumcision, which typologically pointed forward to the same reality that baptism signifies retrospectively—regeneration/heart circumcision—was a necessary prerequisite to Passover. Therefore, baptism should be understood to replace circumcision in the sense that baptism serves as the entry sign of the new covenant. Thus, it is reasonable and covenantally consistent to conclude on a principle of analogy (continuity) between the significance and participants of the covenant signs, that just as circumcision was prerequisite to Passover, baptism is prerequisite to the Lord's Supper.

Chapters 5 and 6 summarize and then apply the argument for close communion. Chapter 5 presents each of the three pillars of the thesis in succinct fashion. Following the summary, chapter 5 continues by providing responses to each of the other three historic and contemporary Baptist positions on who may participate in communion and answering possible objections from each position. Chapter 6 applies the thesis to four pastoral and doctrinal issues: baptism, the Lord's Supper, church membership, and church discipline. Each issue will be considered in its relationship to the kingdom of God, the new covenant, the church universal, and the local church. The book concludes by offering counsel for putting close communion into practice on issues such as introducing close communion to the local church, fencing the Table, and excommunication.

Chapter 1

Historical Baptist Arguments
for Who May Participate
in the Lord's Supper

IN ORDER TO DEMONSTRATE the thesis of this book, it is important to understand its continuity or discontinuity with Baptists' arguments about communion from previous generations. By surveying four answers to the question of who may participate in the Lord's Supper, this chapter reveals that this book's thesis is not an entirely new Baptist argument. However, the thesis does contain an emphasis not previously utilized to its full potential—a biblical-theological argument for close communion from a progressive covenantal perspective. Therefore, this chapter presents several Baptist arguments from influential debates on close communion.[1] This section

---

1. According to Peter Naylor, the three primary battles among Particular Baptists in England from 1620 to 1820 are that between William Kiffin and John Bunyan, Abraham Booth and Daniel Turner (Candidus) with John Collett Ryland (Pacificus), and that between Joseph Kinghorn and Robert Hall Jr. This chapter considers the arguments from each of these debates. However, this chapter necessarily expands from these debates in order to cover a fuller array of perspectives, such as closed communion and ecumenical communion. Furthermore, this chapter considers some voices outside of those mentioned as primary (e.g., Thomas Baldwin) due to a variety of factors, such as the influence of the arguments on other better known debates, the unique emphasis present in the author's arguments, and/or the need to provide the variety of grounding that exists for a given view. For Naylor's summary, see Naylor, *Calvinism, Communion, and the Baptists*, 94. Timothy George agrees with Naylor on the significance of those debates already mentioned. However, George traces the open communion position further, to Spurgeon's influential practice. For more on Spurgeon's practice of open communion, see below (George, "Controversy and Communion," 38–58). The focus of this chapter is necessarily limited. Therefore, it does not survey historic Baptist confessions

focuses on the biblical and theological argumentation over who may participate in the Lord's Supper rather than highlighting the many appeals to historical precedent that appear in the literature.[2]

Arguments for Open Communion

Throughout the secondary literature on the early English Baptists, and specifically that on communion controversies, the figures surveyed in this section continually resurface.[3] Henry Jessey (1601–1663)—one of the earliest English Baptists and third pastor of the Jacob-Lanthrop-Jessey church—appears to be the earliest Baptist proponent of open communion.[4] His appeal

---

as it relates to the views on communion presented in those documents. However, it is worth noting that neither the First London Confession of 1644, nor the Second London Confession of 1689 contains a statement on who may be admitted to the Lord's Supper. In an updated edition of the 1644 confession published in 1646, in an appendix, the authors affirm close/strict communion. For more on the ordinances in confessions of faith among English Baptists, see Hilburn, "Lord's Supper," 40–50; Grace II, "Early English Baptists' View of the Lord's Supper," 159–79.

2. Both open and close communion advocates acknowledge that historically, the pattern throughout church history has been that of baptism preceding the Lord's Supper. See Hall Jr., *On Terms of Communion*, 48–55; Kinghorn, *Baptism a Term of Communion*, 160; Baldwin, *Baptism of Believers Only*, 93–100.

3. For controversy over the subjects of the ordinances among American Baptists, see Sampler, "Whosoever Is 'Qualified' May Come"; Klopfer, "Baptists in America (1742–1833)"; "Betwixt and Between Baptismal Theology," 6–20; Farish, "Open versus Close Communion Controversy." For controversy over subjects of the ordinances among British Baptists, see George, "Controversy and Communion"; Walker, *Baptists at the Table*. See especially chapters 4, 11, and 12 in Oliver, *History of the English Calvinistic Baptists*; Naylor, *Calvinism, Communion, and the Baptists*; Hilburn, "Lord's Supper."

4. The J-L-J church was founded in 1613 as an independent congregation of pedobaptists. The group eventually turned Baptist after 1645. Significant for Baptist studies is the fact that as the J-L-J church began to debate the issue of believer's baptism by immersion, they invited William Kiffin (1616–1701) and Hanserd Knollys (1598–1691) to assist them. Much of the discussion in the church occurred in the same year that the 1644 London Confession "inaugurated the Particular Baptist Denomination and movement" (Duesing, *Henry Jessey*, 187). Duesing traces seven distinct influences that led to the change of the J-L-J church from an Independent pedobaptist church to a Baptist church. Most notable is Jessey's conversion to Baptist principles. Although Henry Jessey became a convinced Baptist by 1642, he was not baptized until June 29, 1645, by Hanserd Knollys. See Duesing, *Henry Jessey*, 150–77. John Briggs argues that Jessey's practice of open communion and membership is principally different from that of Bunyan. Jessey's practice was based on "pragmatic concerns," whereby believers who had come to Baptist conviction did not "wish to break fellowship with fellow believers with whom they had shared communion over many years" (Briggs, "Two Congregational Denominations," 99–100). By contrast, Bunyan's open communion and membership stemmed from a concerted desire to affirm a little "c" catholicity.

to Romans 14 and 15—to urge fellow Baptists to receive those who were weak in the faith (lacking light in baptism) because Christ did not give a direct command prohibiting the unbaptized believer from communion—is picked up by every subsequent advocate of open communion. John Bunyan (1628–1688) and Robert Hall Jr. (1764–1831) are the ablest defenders of the open position. Bunyan's arguments that visible sainthood is the ground of communion, that baptism is not a church ordinance or sign of entry into the church, and that the relationship between circumcision and Passover in the Old Testament encourages the practice of open communion each provide and informative background for this book. Robert Hall Jr.'s most notable arguments include (1) his claim that the pattern of the apostolic church should not be followed with respect to the ordinances because error was introduced subsequently and (2) his claim that the local church should have no additional constituting properties besides that which constitutes the universal church. Stanley Fowler presents the surprising argument that despite baptism's sacramental function in the New Testament, local churches may decide to prioritize the unity of the universal church above the doctrine of baptism. While Charles Spurgeon (1834–1892) does not offer any unique theological argumentation for the open position, his practice demonstrates the open position taken to its logical conclusion. The open communion section ends with Daniel Turner's (1710–1798) argument that free communion is grounded in the fact that Jewish and Gentile Christians did not establish separate churches based upon the Jewish Christians' continued practice of circumcision.

Henry Jessey

In *Storehouse of Provision* (1650) Henry Jessey admits that his church's practice of open communion was positive,[5] "procuring more to favor this

---

5. The most thorough study of Jessey's life to date is Duesing, *Henry Jessey*. All subsequent page numbers refer to Duesing's work. Born in 1601, Jessey was influenced by the Puritans in the Church of England and the Puritan influence found at Cambridge. Jessey was converted in September 1622 and soon after pursued a Master of Arts for ministry preparation. In 1637, the J-L-J church prevailed upon Jessey to lead their congregation in London. Through several church transitions, Jessey became convinced of baptism by immersion, though remaining a pedobaptist until 1642. Jessey witnessed the baptism of Blackrock by former church member Richard Blunt on January 9, 1641/1642, an event which also "inaugurated the first Baptist churches in England to practice believer's baptism by immersion" (177). After Jessey endured a vigorous church debate over believer's baptism, he believed the Lord changed his mind through prayer. His change of conviction led to his own experience of believer's baptism at the hands of Hanserd Knollys in June 1645. Although Jessey embraced believer's baptism for himself, he allowed the J-L-J church he pastored to remain ecclesially mixed with

baptism, or not so bitterly to oppose it," resulting in "much blessing the
Lord, for this our course herein."[6] The arguments and objections outlined
here are selected from the thirty-three Jessey covers to provide the clearest
sense of Jessey's position and highlight the arguments most related to the
thesis of this book.

Jessey presents several "grounds of admission" to the Lord's Supper.
First, he provides his methodological privileging of Scripture in the statement, "We must limit what the Lord limits and not limit what he does not
limit."[7] Although the Lord limited participation in Passover to the circumcised and the believers in the New Testament were normally baptized prior
to receiving communion, the New Testament does not limit the Lord's Supper to the baptized. Therefore, Christians have no authority to deprive other
disciples of the Lord's Supper when they conscientiously object to baptism.[8]
Rather, because "the Lord puts no difference between [Christians] in point
of communion; neither should we."[9] Christians are responsible then to receive all those he has received "though they be so weak, as that they hold
up such things to be God's ordinances" (Rom 14:1).[10] Or, to state the matter

----

respect to its view of baptism, thus maintaining a semi-separatist and independent
status. Jessey was also associated with the Fifth Monarchy Movement, characterized
by their (1) willingness to use violence to bring the kingdom; (2) equation of symbols
in Scripture with contemporary referents; and (3) their penchant for deriving political
and ecclesial structures and ideals from Scripture (260). These convictions put Jessey at
odds with Charles II when he was restored to the throne in 1660, which landed Jessey
in prison (324). Jessey petitioned Charles II from prison and was later released only to
die of a fever that was likely rendered more probable by the prison conditions, such that
he died September 4, 1663. For more on Jessey's connection with the J-L-J church, see
Underwood, *History of the English Baptists*, 56–62.

6. Jessey, *Storehouse of Provision*, 101. Although Jessey's view on who can receive
the Lord's Supper is rightly categorized as open communion, his views on membership
are best described as mixed. He explains, "It is granted that church members should
be baptized" (184). Yet, he acknowledges that the individual believers are the judges
of whether or not they have been baptized. Jessey's description of the matter and form
of true churches (22) convinces Jason Duesing that "Jessey's open membership really
did not extend as far as some might have thought" (Duesing, *Henry Jessey*, 219). While
Jessey mentions Independents and Separates as true churches, he omits Presbyterians
and Anglicans. Duesing summarizes, "As a result, to refer to Jessey's view of church
membership as mixed represents more accurately his still very limited circle from
which he would permit for acceptance into church membership." Duesing provides
further discussion of Jessey's church (236–39). For the subsequent history of the Jessey
church after Jessey's death in 1663, see Hilburn, "Lord's Supper," 57–59.

7. Jessey, *Storehouse of Provision*, 94. For this point, see Duesing, *Henry Jessey*, 235.

8. Jessey, *Storehouse of Provision*, 95.

9. Jessey, *Storehouse of Provision*, 96.

10. Jessey, *Storehouse of Provision*.

another way, "There is neither precept, pattern, nor sufficient evidence from the New Testament to reject any professed believer, that walks righteously, soberly, and godly, according to his light, from communion."[11] Without further scriptural requirements for participation in the Lord's Supper being stated in the New Testament, Jessey believes that open position provides a context for obeying all that Scripture expressly requires.

Later, Jessey grounds open communion in the nature of the church. He writes,

> Where there is matter and form, there is a true church. The matter of a true church [is] to be saints visibly. The form [is] a gathering of these out from the world, and joining of them together to worship the Lord in truth, so far as they know, or shall know; and edify themselves. . . . The form giveth the being. The being, when it is lost, then the form is lost. Hence it appears that baptism is not the form; for else, when some are cast out, baptism is lost. And if they be received to have being in the church again they must be baptized again, which is absurd. Therefore, I judge, that the churches called Independents, or Separates, having both the matter, and the form of churches, are true churches.[12]

11. Jessey, *Storehouse of Provision*, 101.

12. Jessey, *Storehouse of Provision*. With this reasoning, Jessey appears to be arguing that no particular mode of baptism can be constitutive of the local church. Jason Duesing interprets Jessey as intending "that baptismal mode could never operate as part of the form or essential nature of the church" (Duesing, *Henry Jessey*, 218). It is admittedly difficult to tell whether Jessey is referring to the inability to claim a particular mode of baptism as part of the form of the church or referring to the inability of considering *any* mode of baptism as part of the form of the church. All Jessey states is, "Hence it appears that baptism is not the form." A hint toward solving this conundrum is found in Jessey's description of baptism, earlier in *Storehouse of Provision*. The question was asked Jessey as to how three unbaptized (in any mode) believers should start a church if they ended up on an island together. Jessey counsels the believers to make sure they are believing in Jesus, specifically that he will be in their midst in worship, that they covenant together to hold Christian fellowship together, and that they then baptize each other. The baptizing would be the means of "entering into covenant" and so "enjoy as well all other ordinances" (Jessey, *Storehouse of Provision*, 71). Later, he claims that baptism's function has not changed since the Apostle's days. Therefore, "there is the same necessity, if we respect the same command which remains in force still from Jesus Christ upon such as are believers, or that are made disciples, that these should be baptized" (79). These references present a strong sense of the requirement of baptism (in some mode) for the existence of a church. Duesing's suggestion that Jessey intends to convey that no particular mode of baptism is part of the form of the church appears on target.

On Jessey's reasoning, because the mode of baptism cannot constitute the form of the church, it must be the case that those who differ on baptismal mode can commune together.

Jessey later continues his discussion of the nature of the church. He provides three arguments for the claim that the Lord's Supper and censures (i.e., church discipline) do not fall uniquely under the administrative auspices of particular local churches. The Lord's Supper belongs to all disciples by virtue of their being disciples because (1) the first disciples received communion with Jesus before Christ's death and the establishment of particular churches; (2) several particular churches could unite in one city to celebrate the Lord's Supper together because they are disciples gathering; and (3) no one should disapprove of a large church gathering for the Lord's Supper in three locations due to "persecution or otherwise."[13] Jessey sometimes insists that all believers should be baptized. Yet, with these three arguments, Jessey presents the local church as gatherings of disciples who may or may not be baptized. Given the implication of Matthew 28:19–20, one becomes a disciple, who is then baptized.[14] Thus, one's identity as a disciple is an important grounding for participation in the Lord's Supper.

Jessey ends with a warning to his opponents:

> If such are debarred from purer ordinances that Jesus Christ hath purchased for them, and thus are driven away; and if they shall mourn and complain to our Lord Jesus that you keep them back from doing his commands which they know; because they yield not to act against their consciences, or with a doubting conscience; and thus being herein refused, and driven out from abiding at, or cleaving to the inheritance, and ways of the Lord, which they would walk in; if they through this your putting them up on a temptation, and by their own weakness, shall turn aside after other gods (as David complained against Saul in another case) or after strange and false ways: will this be for your comfort, or for your grief at the day of our Lord Jesus? (Judge ye.) Or, will it be found a beating and wounding of our fellow-servant, and persecution (by depriving of spiritual goods) and this merely for conscience's sake?[15]

13. Jessey, *Storehouse of Provision*, 79.

14. According to Jessey, "The command lyeth on disciples, that by the Lord's Supper, they hold forth his death till he come again. Therefore, they are bound to do it when they can. . . . If you say, they were baptized, I answer, they are not there [Luke 22] called baptized ones but disciples" (Jessey, *Storehouse of Provision*, 186–87).

15. Jessey, *Storehouse of Provision*, 111.

Responses to Objections

Jessey poses and answers several objections to the open view. To those who claim that Paul's command to receive those Christ has received was originally given to baptized believers (Rom 14:1), Jessey responds simply that the text does not state that all were baptized.[16] Similarly, the New Testament does not explicitly reveal that the apostles were baptized before they participated in the Last Supper.[17] Therefore, the objection that all the believers in the early church are presumed to be baptized is goes beyond what Scripture affirms and locates the grounding of communion in something other than being received by God.[18] The early Baptist utilizes Romans 14 again to answer the charge that "receiving such without baptism, we keep not up to the rule."[19] While Jessey does not grant that a rule exists, he explains that Paul did not charge the Roman Christians with sin for forbearing with their weaker brothers, but rather commended patience. Again from Romans 14, in answering the objection that purity in God's kingdom requires baptism to precede the Lord's Supper, Jessey writes, "The kingdom of God is not found in meat and drink, but rather righteousness, peace, and joy in the Spirit" (v. 17).[20]

Similar to the way Jessey argues from old covenant and new covenant issues in Romans 14–15, Jessey draws an interesting parallel between uncircumcised Gentile believers in Acts 15 and the circumcised Jewish believers. He claims that Gentile Christians then were not to be "burdened with what they cannot bear . . . nor to be refused from being one body with" the circumcised Jewish Christians.[21] So today, those who are "persuaded that the baptizing of infants is God's ordinance [should not] be refused from being one body with us."[22] Jessey also responds to the argument that "none uncircumcised in heart and in flesh should enter into God's sanctuary" entailing that "none unbaptized in heart and in body should be of the church."[23] He replies that if circumcision typified baptism, then all churches should baptize on the eighth day. However, because circumcision "typed

---

16. Jessey, *Storehouse of Provision*, 97. Jason Duesing rightly describes Rom 14:1, "Such as are weak in the faith, receive you," as Jessey's thesis (Duesing, *Henry Jessey*, 228).

17. Jessey, *Storehouse of Provision*, 97.

18. Jessey, *Storehouse of Provision*, 109–10.

19. Jessey, *Storehouse of Provision*, 123.

20. Jessey, *Storehouse of Provision*.

21. Jessey, *Storehouse of Provision*, 178–79.

22. Jessey, *Storehouse of Provision*.

23. Jessey, *Storehouse of Provision*, 184.

the spiritual circumcising by Jesus Christ of persons, both in heart and in outward conversation . . . all these and none but these should be received (so far as we can judge)."[24]

Several objections have to do with the order of the ordinances specifically. Jessey responds to the objection that the necessity of circumcision to participate in Passover is analogous to the requirement for baptism before the Lord's Supper. He states, "Will you argue from circumcision to baptism without a word, in one thing more than in another?"[25] Explanation for the analogy was apparently lacking. To the objection that Jessey's position has no precedent or warrant in Scripture, he lists commands given throughout the New Testament to Christians which seem to be binding without respect to their baptism.[26] Then, he asks, "May we therefore debar believers now from all, or any of these duties, or privileges, for want of any of those qualifications?"[27] If so, Jessey asks, how many commands may be laid aside and how many prerequisites must be met before in order to keep the commands. To the claim that baptism is an initiating ordinance, the pastor asks, "Where does the Scripture once express it thus? It is good to keep the form of sound words warranted in Scripture."[28] Regarding the assertion that the order of the ordinances corresponds to their meaning, Jessey demonstrates that some theological realities symbolized by one ordinance may be as easily claimed to be symbolized by the other.[29]

To the charge that nothing in Scripture commends communion with the unbaptized, Jessey claims it is legitimate to do that for which no scriptural example exists (cf. Matt 12:3–5).[30] He responds similarly, to those who "see plain commands and examples; that when persons repented and believed, they were first baptized, that's the first ordinance they enjoyed: and then, they enjoyed other ordinances."[31] Jessey retorts that all of these

24. Jessey, *Storehouse of Provision*. See chapter 5 for this book's response to Jessey's argument.

25. Apparently, none who objected in this fashion to Jessey, as this book does, explained why the analogy carries warrant for close communion. Jessey, *Storehouse of Provision*, 112.

26. Jessey, *Storehouse of Provision*, 113–15.

27. Jessey, *Storehouse of Provision*, 116. For Jessey, no difference exists between the commands to "Do this in remembrance of me" (Luke 22:19), "Exhort one another daily" (Heb 10:24), and to "earnestly desire spiritual gifts" (1 Cor 14:1). See Jessey, *Storehouse of Provision*, 114–15.

28. Jessey, *Storehouse of Provision*, 117.

29. Jessey, *Storehouse of Provision*, 125–26.

30. Jessey, *Storehouse of Provision*, 100. For similar examples, see Farish, "Open versus Close Communion Controversy," 53–54.

31. Jessey, *Storehouse of Provision*, 185.

passages prove that those who repent and believe should not delay baptism, but they do not prove that those who repent and believe without baptism err by obeying other commands.[32]

John Bunyan

In John Bunyan's *Confession of my Faith and Reason for My Practice in Worship* (1672),[33] he provides at least eight reasons why he will not participate in communion with any but visible saints,[34] by which he means professing believers who demonstrate piety.[35] Following this limitation of the meal he defends his practice of open communion with several arguments. First, although circumcision was an initiating ordinance, baptism is not presented as "a token of the covenant" or "an entry marker" in the New Testament because "Baptism [in water] makes thee no member of the church, neither particular or universal: neither doth it make thee a visible saint; it therefore gives thee neither right to nor being of membership at all."[36] Second, the

32. Jessey, *Storehouse of Provision*, 186. For similar rationale, see Farish, "Open versus Close Communion Controversy," 42–44.

33. John Bunyan is best known for his classic *Pilgrim's Progress* (1678) and his vivid use of allegory and poetry. He was raised among the poor working class of England with little formal education. After his conversion, he was baptized by immersion (ca. early 1650s) by John Gifford. Bunyan joined the Independent congregation at Bedford, which he later pastored from 1672 until his death. As a Calvinist Nonconformist, Bunyan held to the supreme authority of Scripture and landed in prison in two stints from 1660 to 1672 (at the Restoration of Charles II) and in 1676. Bunyan published over sixty books, dealing with issues such as grace, antinomianism, atonement, rejecting Quaker inner light, the relationship of the law to grace, and justification. According to James Leo Garrett Jr., Bunyan's chief contribution to Baptist theology is his case for open communion and open membership, surveyed in this section. See Garrett Jr., *Baptist Theology*, 70; Brackney, *Genetic History of Baptist Thought*, 107–14; Poe, "John Bunyan," in George and Dockery, *Baptist Theologians*, 26–48; Hill, *Tinker and a Poor Man*. Historians have debated Bunyan's status as a Baptist, given his open communion views. This book, along with the aforementioned sources, assumes that Bunyan's affirmation of believer's baptism by immersion as being consistent with the NT is sufficient to consider him as part of the Baptist tradition. For one look at Bunyan's Baptist status, see Poe, "John Bunyan's Controversy with the Baptists," 25–26. The fascinating context of Bunyan's debate with Henry Danvers, Thomas Paul, and William Kiffin is outlined by Duesing, *Henry Jessey*, 219–32. Naylor covers the debate in Naylor, *Calvinism, Communion, and the Baptists*, 94–106.

34. Hilburn has ten arguments from Bunyan. This section combines two of the arguments. See Hilburn, "Lord's Supper," 83–84.

35. Bunyan, "Reason of My Practice in Worship," in Offor, *Bunyan's Works*, 2:602–3.

36. Bunyan, "Reason of My Practice in Worship," in Offor, *Bunyan's Works*, 2:605–6. Given Bunyan's arguments, several clarifications are in order on the purpose of baptism and the Lord's Supper in Bunyan's thought. Baptism, he maintains, is for the believer a

edification of the church should be preserved before the institution of water baptism. If baptism divides, then the duty of the church is to maintain
unity on grounds of visible sainthood.[37] Third, one may have the doctrine
of baptism without the practice. It is the doctrine of baptism—the heart circumcision—that grounds unity.[38] Fourth, the church should commune with
and receive those God communes with and receives (Rom 15:1–7).[39] Fifth,
baptism is an indifferent matter of "outward circumstance," entailing that
failure to participate in it cannot "unchristian" a person.[40] Sixth, love is too
important to break over baptism, because love is that which lets the world
know Christians belong to Christ (John 13:34–35).[41] Seventh, Paul called

means of having God's promises confirmed and visibly confessing faith. Although believers in the New Testament were presumably all baptized, this was owing to their clarity on baptism. Following the precedent is not required today (608–9). After William
Kiffin responded to Bunyan, Bunyan responded with "Differences in Water Baptism
No Bar to Communion" (1673). In that defense, Bunyan further explains the relationship between the believer, baptism, and the church with three points: (1) the believer's
faith is the door to the church rather than faith with baptism or the mutual consent of
the church being required for joining a church (2:619); (2) Christ never commanded
baptism; and (3) baptism is nowhere revealed to be a church ordinance or a practiced
required by primitive churches for inclusion. To this third point, Bunyan writes, "If
baptism respect believers, as particular persons only; if it respects their own conscience
only; if it make a man no visible believer to me, then it hath nothing to do with church-
membership" (2:629). Furthermore, although a community which fails to celebrate the
Lord's Supper is not a church due to the meal's constitutive function, a community that
fails to celebrate baptism loses nothing corporately because baptism is not constitutive
of the local church. Bunyan, "Differences in Judgment about Water Baptism," in Offor,
Bunyan's Works, 2:638–39.

37. Bunyan, "Reason of My Practice in Worship," in Offor, *Bunyan's Works*, 2:609.

38. Bunyan explains, "I am bold therefore to have communion with such (Heb
6:1–2), because they also have the doctrine of baptisms. . . . I distinguish between the
doctrine and practice of water baptism; the doctrine being that which by the outward
sign is presented to us, or which by the outward circumstance of the act is preached to
the believer: viz. The death of Christ; My death with Christ; also his resurrection from
the dead, and mine with him to newness of life" (Bunyan, "Reason of My Practice in
Worship," in Offor, *Bunyan's Works*, 2:609).

39. Bunyan, "Reason of My Practice in Worship," in Offor, *Bunyan's Works*, 2:610.
Bunyan's citation of Rom 15 is interesting given the predominance of citations from
Rom 14:1–7 from Jessey, Hall, and Spurgeon.

40. Bunyan, "Reason of My Practice in Worship," in Offor, *Bunyan's Works*, 2:611.
Harry Poe claims that Bunyan saw strict/close communion as a "functional distortion
of the gospel." By the end of the essay, Poe presents Bunyan as a pastoral example of one
who did not let secondary matters get in the way of evangelism. See Poe, "John Bunyan's
Controversy with the Baptists," 25, 33–34.

41. The tinker's passion is evident: He writes, "Strange! Take two Christians equal in
all points but this, nay, let one go beyond the other far, for grace and holiness; yet this
circumstance of water shall drown and sweep away all his excellencies, not counting

the church at Corinth carnal for dividing over things of more importance than baptism (e.g., which teacher they followed).[42] Eighth, it is wrong to separate from visible saints or to treat them with contempt.[43]

Turning to the offensive, Bunyan claims that strict communion is uncharitable, it denies the validity of the (mistaken) consciences of others, and it shuts those with whom some disagree out of churches. For this book, Bunyan's most significant argument for allowing the conscience of others to weigh on the execution of circumstantial laws regards Hezekiah's Passover (2 Chr 30:13–27). Hezekiah did not forbid uncircumcised Israelites from participating in Passover. Then, as Bunyan interprets the story, God evidenced his approval of Hezekiah's actions in providing forgiveness when Hezekiah prayed for it.[44] Bunyan read the celebration of Passover in Joshua 5 along similar lines. He writes, the "church in the wilderness received members, the way which not prescribed by, but directly against the revealed mind of God."[45] He presumes throughout the explanation that the Israelites held Passover in the wilderness with uncircumcised Israelites. Thus, Bunyan thinks the legislative prohibition against the uncircumcised receiving communion in the Old Testament was not pecuniary. Nevertheless, he calls on strict communion advocates to produce a text—with the force of Exodus 12:48—that legislates baptism as prerequisite to communion in the New Testament.

---

him worthy of that reception, that with hand and heart shall be given to a novice in religion, because he consents to water" (Bunyan, "Reason of My Practice in Worship," in Offor, *Bunyan's Works*, 2:612–13).

42. Bunyan thinks Paul discounted the importance of baptism based on Paul's claim that the Lord did not send him to baptize but to preach the gospel (cf. 1 Cor 1:17). See Bunyan, "Reason of My Practice in Worship," in Offor, *Bunyan's Works*, 2:613.

43. Bunyan, "Reason of My Practice in Worship," in Offor, *Bunyan's Works*, 2:614–15. The substance of these arguments are outlined by Naylor in *Calvinism, Communion, and the Baptists*, 98–100.

44. Bunyan, "Reason of My Practice in Worship," in Offor, *Bunyan's Works*, 2:611. Elsewhere, Bunyan adds, "That if laws and ordinances of old have been broken, and the breach of them born with, when yet the observation of outward things was more strictly commanded than now, if the profit and edification of the church come in competition; how much more, may not we have communion, church communion, when no law of God is transgressed thereby. And note, that all this while I plead not, as you, for persons unprepared, but godly, and such as walk with God" (Bunyan, "Differences in Judgment about Water Baptism," 2:631).

45. Bunyan, "Differences in Judgment about Water Baptism," in Offor, *Bunyan's Works*, 2:625. When explaining how the Hezekiah example relates to strict communion, Bunyan claims that, contra William Kiffin, Passover was not a type of the Lord's Supper; it was a "type of the body and blood of the Lord" (1 Cor 5:7; 2:630).

Response to Objections

Bunyan also responds to several of his opponents' objections. To the argument that Matthew 28:18–20 requires baptism before learning all else Christ commanded, Bunyan claims that this view would require the convert to do nothing until after baptism, "which is absurd."[46] To the pattern of the early church to receive the baptized believers into the church (Acts 2:41), Bunyan answers that the passages merely describes what happened. Even if the example is prescriptive, he appeals to the communion of the uncircumcised in the wilderness as evidence that God would overlook the lack of baptism.[47] To the claim that baptism is a first step of obedience and fruit of faith, Bunyan claims that true faith acts according to its light and "is not bound to any outward circumstance."[48] To the claim that baptism is a foundational doctrine according to Hebrews 6:1–2, he claims that this Scripture refers to the doctrine of baptism but not the act of water.[49] To the argument that Paul recognized the Galatians as Christians in part because they were baptized (Gal 3:27), Bunyan claims that Paul's knowledge of the church is unusual and fails to provide sufficient warrant for excluding the unbaptized from communion. To the argument that baptism is assumed to be understood and practiced by the recipients of Paul's and Peter's epistles, Bunyan retorts that even if this is true, it does not ground strict communion.[50]

---

46. Bunyan, "Differences in Judgment about Water Baptism," in Offor, *Bunyan's Works*, 2:635.

47. Bunyan, "Differences in Judgment about Water Baptism," in Offor, *Bunyan's Works*, 2:636. On this point, see Duesing, *Henry Jessey*, 240–41.

48. Bunyan, "Differences in Judgment about Water Baptism," in Offor, *Bunyan's Works*, 2:637. Poe argues that Bunyan could not approve of what he viewed as an elevation of religious ceremonies as a nonconformist. The strict Baptists argued too similarly to those who demanded subscription to the Book of Common Prayer. See Poe, "John Bunyan's Controversy with the Baptists," 30–31.

49. Bunyan, "Differences in Judgment about Water Baptism," in Offor, *Bunyan's Works*, 2:637.

50. Bunyan, "Differences in Judgment about Water Baptism," in Offor, *Bunyan's Works*, 2:638.

Robert Hall Jr.

Hall's[51] foundational argument for open communion is fourfold.[52] First, the obligation of brotherly love, especially concerning differences between Christians on secondary matters and Paul's encouragement to receive weaker brothers (Rom 14:1),[53] requires mixed communion.[54] Second, the inclusion of pedobaptists within the true church per Christ's reception of them by faith and the corollary punishment entailed by the exclusion of pedobaptists from Baptist church communion entails the appropriateness of mixed communion.[55] Third, strict Baptists falsely bind the consciences of Christians without a clear biblical principle. Fourth, strict Baptists practically imply that pedobaptists are still in their sins.[56]

51. Hall Jr. is distinguished from his father, Hall Sr., a notable Particular Baptist pastor in his own right. Born in 1764, despite his poor health, the younger Hall showed academic promise from an early age through his mastery of Latin and Greek by 1778. He studied at Bristol Academy until 1781 and graduated King's College Aberdeen in 1785. Hall is noted for his oratory skill. Hall ascended to national prominence during his Cambridge pastorate for his views, sermons, and publications on liberty. For an analysis of his writings on this subject, see Parnell, "Baptists and Britons,"102–45. Hall suffered a breakdown and intense spiritual doubts from 1804 to 1809. By 1807 though he began a twenty-year pastorate at Harvey Lane in Leicester. After a difficult case of church discipline at Harvey Lane, on the death of John Ryland, Hall accepted the pastorate at Broadmead Baptist Church in Bristol in 1825. By 1828 however, Hall's health was increasingly poor and forced him to desist pastoral labors completely in 1831. He expired February 21. For more on Hall's life, see McNutt, "Ministry of Robert Hall Jr.," 18–61; Olinthus Gregory, "Brief Memoir of the Rev. Robert Hall," in Gregory, *Works of the Rev. Robert Hall*; Morris, *Biographical Recollections of the Rev. Robert Hall*; Macleod, "Life and Teaching of Robert Hall." That Hall is widely recognized as the ablest proponent of open communion is affirmed in Himbury, "Baptismal Controversies," in Gilmore, *Christian Baptism*, 293.

52. For a similar take on Hall's arguments, see Naylor, *Calvinism, Communion, and the Baptists*, 134–39; Himbury, "Baptismal Controversies," 293.

53. This passage being Hall's emphasis, Geoffrey R. Breed's assertion that Hall grounds mixed communion in shared blessings of the Holy Spirit seems a bit off the mark (Breed, *Particular Baptists in Victorian England*, 22).

54. Hall Jr., *Terms of Communion*, 57. Hall interacts specifically with Abraham Booth over Rom 14:1. Booth argued that receiving the weak in faith does not apply to communion because (1) all to whom Paul wrote were already baptized members of the Roman church; (2) the disputed issue was not baptism; and (3) Christians can receive believers with whom they differ in other ways besides communion. Hall replied that Paul's admonition to receive the weaker brother implies that they were excluded. To Booth's second point, if the principle does not apply to baptism, general axioms of Scripture can be annihilated. To Booth's third argument, Hall answers that surely the means of receiving other believers includes communion (67–68).

55. Hall Jr., *Terms of Communion*, 64–66.

56. Hall Jr., *Reply*, 192–93.

Hall also offers several critiques of the strict Baptist position. First, Hall argues that "no man or set of men, are entitled to prescribe as an indispensable condition of communion what the New Testament has not enjoined as a condition of salvation."[57] For Hall, this statement entails that the only prerequisite for participation in the Lord's Supper is believing in Christ, baptism having no bearing on one's institutional connection to the local church.[58] Second, Hall claims that the order of institution of the ordinances is a moot point, because John the Baptist's baptism did not occur in the Christian dispensation, which entails that even Jesus' disciples came to the Last Supper unbaptized.[59] Third, the ordinances are "independently obligatory."[60] Jesus' command to baptize and teach cannot entail a requirement to baptize before teaching disciples anything else. Fourth, the apostolic pattern should not be applied to the question of strict communion, due to the introduction of pedobaptist error since apostolic times.[61] Fifth, the

57. Hall Jr., *Terms of Communion*, iv. In his 1818 *Reply* to Kinghorn, Hall makes the startling admission that he believes baptism was essential for salvation during apostolic times but ceased being so when error crept into the church's doctrine. If Kinghorn wishes to maintain the connection between baptism and communion from apostolic practice, Hall challenges him to prove why baptism should be viewed in the same manner presently as it was during the apostolic period, as a regenerating ordinance! See Hall Jr., *Reply*, 45–46.

58. Hall Jr., *Reply*, 120–22. Kinghorn had accused Hall of dissenting from the establishment to avoid participating in rites and ceremonies for which he found no biblical basis and, at the same time, allowing the neglect of baptism, about which no one doubts its basis in Scripture.

59. Hall Jr., *Terms of Communion*, 16–23. Hall cites several reasons for denying that John's Baptism belongs to the Gospel age: (1) the command to baptize the nations came afterward; (2) John's baptism was for repentance rather than explicit faith in Christ; (3) Christian baptism is necessarily in the name of Jesus; (4) Christian baptism is associated with the baptism of the Holy Spirit, while John's is not; and (5) Paul baptized John's disciples at Ephesus in Acts 19 after John had already baptized them. Oliver claims this a "novel argument" designed to "cut the Gordian knot," but it would not go unchallenged. See the section on Joseph Kinghorn below (Oliver, *History of the English Calvinistic Baptists*, 242).

60. Hall Jr., *Terms of Communion*, 36. On this third point, Hall takes aim at the thesis of this book. He explains, although a connection existed between circumcision and Passover, "all we demand of the advocates of strict communion is, that instead of amusing us with fanciful analogies drawn from an antiquated law, they would point us to some clause in the New Testament which asserts a similar relation betwixt baptism and the Lord's Supper."

61. Hall Jr., *Terms of Communion*, 39–41. Tyler's argument is similar in principle. He compares the idea of baptism in the NT to the ideal of marriage as designed at creation. Given life in a fallen world, God allows divorce. So also, Christ allows the church to accommodate baptism that is less than ideal. See Tyler, *Baptism*, 138–39.

ordinances do not require connectivity due to their meanings.[62] Sixth, the argument for strict communion from universal pattern of baptism preceding the Lord's Supper throughout church history overlooks the possibility of universal error. Unless the strict Baptist want to similarly associate baptism and regeneration, the argument from history proves nothing.[63]

Throughout *On Terms of Communion*, Hall consistently presents the ordinances as independently binding on Christians. While he appeals to the necessity of exercising brotherly love (cf. Rom 14:1),[64] he explicitly disallows the applicability of Christ's legislation for his church and of the apostolic pattern to the question of who is authorized to participate in the Lord's Supper. Although Hall never states it directly, he always implies that the local church is the context in which the Lord's Supper should be celebrated. Despite the local church context, the unity exhibited in the Lord's Supper seems to be primarily predicated of the universal body of Christ.[65] The only way for the local church to reflect the unity of the universal body of Christ is by separating the ordinances and thereby defining the constitution of the local church in a way that includes pedobaptists—those deemed by the Baptists as unbaptized.[66]

62. Hall dismisses the notion that baptism is the "sacrament of regeneration" and initiation while the Lord's Supper is the "sacrament of nutrition" (Hall Jr., *Terms of Communion*, 43). For Hall, arguing from metaphors is liable to serious error. In a subsequent work, Hall explains, "Since positive duties arise (to human apprehension at least) from the mere will of the legislator, and not from immutable relations, their nature forbids the attempt to establish their inherent and essential connection" (Hall Jr., *Reply*, 62). Interestingly, from the opposite perspective, Andrew Fuller grounds strict communion in the view that Christ instituted baptism and the Lord's Supper as positive institutions in connection. See below in the section on Fuller.

63. Hall Jr., *Terms of Communion*, 52. Alternatively, Hall contends that because infant baptism was prominent by the fourth century and no records exist of churches withdrawing over believer's baptism, then mixed communion must have been the standard (Hall Jr., *Reply*, 219).

64. For more on Romans 14, see Hall Jr., *Reply*, 144–78.

65. Similarly, see Naylor, *Calvinism, Communion, and the Baptists*, 135. Oliver also recognizes the centrality of Hall's doctrine of the church to his argument. On Oliver's reading, Hall accepted the Baptist emphasis on the local church, but he was unwilling to allow the doctrine of the local church to override the unity of the universal church (Oliver, *History of the English Calvinistic Baptists*, 238). In Hall's *Reply*, he articulates his double standard of needing to dissent from the Church of England and yet allowing them to commune with him. Yet, Hall argues for transient or occasional communion rather than mixed membership for pedobaptists. See Hall Jr., *Reply*, 192–93. Therefore, Hilburn misreads Hall when he claims that Hall advocated for mixed membership. See Hilburn, "Lord's Supper," 158.

66. William Brackney writes, "Hall's thinking called for a new view of the church and society: more open, accepting, and inclusive. For him, the church was redefined as an association of people with a common intention to pursue a particular work. Being

Stanley Fowler

In *More Than a Symbol* (2002) Stanley Fowler argues that the New Testament,[67] mainstream seventeenth-century Baptists, and several significant twentieth-century Baptists view baptism as being sacramental.[68] As Fowler surveys history and exegetes the New Testament, he presents an argument for open communion premised on the sacramental nature of baptism. This section surveys his discussion of baptism as a sacrament, followed by his argument for open communion.

The combination of open communion and sacramental baptism is surprising, Fowler admits, because a sacramental view of baptism "seem[s] to demand that Baptists churches practice closed membership."[69] However, most Baptist sacramentalists have practiced at least open, if not ecumenical communion. By referring to baptism as a sacrament and means of grace, Fowler intends the following:

> According to the apostolic witness God has connected various divine gifts (e.g., forgiveness, adoption, the Holy Spirit) to baptism, which amounts to a pledge by God that he will be active in the baptismal event, conveying these gifts to penitent sinners who seal their turning to Christ in confessional baptism. Ultimately, then, it is not that baptism conveys any benefits through any power inherent in itself, but that God, by the Holy Spirit, affects a genuine encounter with the baptizand and in which he unites the baptized believer with Christ and thus with the benefits of Christ.[70]

Baptist, Hall's ecclesiastic perspective favored individuals rather than churches." While Brackney is correct that Hall's view of the local church is more open, Hall does not frame his ecclesiology by privileging the individual over the corporate. Rather, he privileges the universal church over the local, which results in an emphasis on the individual Christian's conscience. See Brackney, *Genetic History of Baptist Thought*, 143.

67. Stanley Fowler (b. 1946) is the long-time Professor of Theology at Heritage Theological Seminary in Cambridge, Ontario. He completed his ThD degree at Wycliffe College, University of Toronto, where he studied initially with John B. Webster and completed the dissertation under William H. Brackney. Fowler's doctoral studies concerned the doctrine of baptism and baptism's place in Baptist history. Thus, his subsequent publications have largely developed his doctoral work. See Fowler, *More Than a Symbol*, xv. Some of Fowler's publications include *Rethinking Baptism*; "Baptists and the Churches of Christ," in Cross and Thompson, *Baptist Sacramentalism 2*, 254–69. Fowler was recently honored with a *festschrift*. See Haykin et al., *Ecclesia Semper Reformanda Est*.

68. Fowler, *More Than a Symbol*, 4.

69. Fowler, *More Than a Symbol*, 105.

70. Fowler, *More Than a Symbol*, 210.

Rather than viewing baptism mechanistically, Fowler describes his sacramental view as connecting faith, baptism, and grace. This combination makes baptism the "normal venue for the introduction of the individual into the sphere of redemption, although this is neither invariably, nor automatically true."[71] Fowler also demurs from a pedobaptist, Protestant sacramental view of baptism, describing the latter as "a sacrament of anticipation" and his view as a "sacrament of fulfillment."[72] Baptist sacramentalism then places "the significance of the rite [of baptism] into the soteriological realm," rather than merely speaking of the necessity of baptism in terms of church order.[73]

Justifying open communion requires some explanation on a sacramental view. Churches have two options: (1) receive persons who "are not validly baptized" on the basis of a profession of faith or (2) "accept infant baptism as valid, although irregular."[74] Fowler rejects both options and proposes another possibility for allowing open communion.[75] He writes,

> In terms of the inner logic, the Baptist practice is more understandable if there is a relative necessity for the occurrence of confessional baptism. If the baptism of confessing believers is the normal means by which God seals the individual's personal, saving union with Christ, then to neglect it is cause for serious concern. If conversion is consciously completed apart from baptism, and baptism is reduced to sheer obedience and pure symbolism, then the narrow Baptist practice is indeed mystifying, especially in its close communion form.[76]

71. Fowler, *More Than a Symbol*, 210.

72. Fowler, *More Than a Symbol*, 221.

73. Fowler, *More Than a Symbol*, 226.

74. Fowler, *More Than a Symbol*.

75. He rejects the first option because it is a "functional denial of a sacramental view of baptism" and it fails to connect the ritual act of baptism with faith in any meaningful sense (Fowler, *More Than a Symbol*, 227). The second view recognizes that baptism and faith are "essential conditions of church membership," which have occurred in an irregular order. Nevertheless, the infant baptism is considered valid because baptism is a once-for-all-time event and pedobaptist churches are valid churches. Fowler rejects the notion that infant baptism is a once for all event because Romans 6 "assumes that baptism is the point at which the work of Christ becomes effective in the individual, not that baptism merely proclaims what may happen to the individual" (229). On the valid church argument, Fowler demurs again, citing the logic of the Second London Confession. Although the document affirms believer's baptism by immersion under the section on ordinances, "this assertion is not used as a litmus test to determine the validity of a church" (230). Thus, pedobaptist churches are true churches not because of their irregular baptism practice, but due to the presence of the Holy Spirit.

76. Fowler, *More Than a Symbol*, 57.

He affirms the legitimacy of Baptist churches requiring "rebaptism of those not baptized as believers, on the basis of its sealing the conversion which is already apparent in other ways."[77] Then, he argues, "Perhaps, it is possible to construct an argument for open membership which is based on giving a higher priority to the biblical principle of the visible unity of Christians than to the biblical principle of baptism as the normative means of union with Christ and the Church."[78] Thus, for Fowler, when a church is faced with the decision of whether the visible unity of Christians or the normative sacramental function of baptism is more important, they may determine to give greater weight to visible unity and allow open communion.

Other Notable Contributions

While Charles Spurgeon did not develop a defense of open communion, he certainly espoused it in his sermons and displayed the logical entailments of the position by his life. Candidus and Pacificus, who wrote just before Abraham Booth's standard, *Apology for the Baptists,* are also notable for contributing an argument based on covenantal signs to the already existing defenses of open communion.

Charles Spurgeon

Because he did not offer any further arguments for his practice than those already surveyed, the discussion of Spurgeon is intentionally brief.[79]

---

77. Fowler, *More Than a Symbol,* 232.

78. Fowler, *More Than a Symbol.*

79. Charles Spurgeon was born to a family of dissenters at Kelvedon in Essex. Although converted in a pedobaptist context at sixteen years old, he soon converted to Baptist principles and joined the Saint Andrews Street Baptist Church. He was called to pastor for the first time in 1851 and transitioned to the New Park Street chapel before he turned twenty. In 1861, the Metropolitan Tabernacle was built to accommodate the large crowds of London who came to see him. Spurgeon is highly praised for his oratory gifts as a prince among preachers. The preacher cared much for practical ministry to the poor and education for children. His theology is largely shaped by the Puritan emphases on Calvinistic doctrine, evangelism, and experiential knowledge of God. Spurgeon held tenaciously to the inspiration and truthfulness of Scripture during what became known as the downgrade controversy (1887 ff.) among the Baptist Union of Britain. In another controversy, he denied the doctrine of baptismal regeneration. He promoted an open communion but closed membership ministry, believing that the Lord's Supper was given to every Christian but that local church membership required a measure of agreement and obedience about baptism that simple participation in the ordinance did not require. Historians often appeal to Spurgeon in contemporary historiography for his spiritual presence view of the Lord's Supper. For biographical information and a survey

Spurgeon is important to include under open communion however, because of the way he followed the open communion principles to their logical conclusion and due to his influence as a pastor. Spurgeon was known to have led the Metropolitan Tabernacle of London to practice open communion and closed membership.[80] Thus, he upheld the necessity of believer's baptism for membership but not for participation in the Lord's Supper.

In a sermon entitled, "The Holy Spirit and the One Church," the preacher states positively, "At the Lord's Table I always invite all churches to come and sit down and commune with us. . . . I think it sin to refuse to commune with anyone who is a member of the church of our Lord Jesus Christ."[81] He describes the role of baptism as "Christ's own way of entering the visible church and . . . the mark of distinction between the Church and the world."[82] Nevertheless, he viewed the Lord's Supper as a symbol of the spiritual unity of all Christians.[83] As a result of these views, Spurgeon

---

of the controversies, see Underwood, *History of English Baptists*, 216–32; Brackney, *Genetic History of Baptist Thought*, 150–56; Garrett Jr., *Baptist Theology*, 264–78. For more on Spurgeon's Puritan spirituality, see Drummond, "Charles Haddon Spurgeon," in George and Dockery, *Baptist Theologians*, 267–88. For a full-sketch of Spurgeon's life and ministry, see Nettles, *Living by Revealed Truth*; Morden, "*Communion with Christ and His People*."

80. Open communion does not necessarily entail open membership. The relationship between who may receive the Lord's Supper, who may become a member, and how the Lord's Supper relates to membership will be explored in chapter 6. At this point, it is important to note that Baptists have at times espoused seemingly contradictory views on communion and membership. For more on the historical relationship of church membership to the open communion debate, see Hilburn, "Lord's Supper," 70–71; Sampler, "Whosoever Is 'Qualified' May Come," 184–86.

81. This sermon, "The Holy Spirit and the One Church," was preached on December 13, 1857. See Spurgeon, *New Park Street Pulpit* 3.2.

82. See Morden, "*Communion with Christ and His People*," 103. Fowler leaves open the possibility that Spurgeon held to a view of baptism as more than a mere symbol. See Fowler, *More Than a Symbol*, 82–83. However, Morden claims that Spurgeon could not be clearer in his rejection of sacramental views (Morden, "*Communion with Christ and His People*," 89).

83. Gregory Wills claims that Spurgeon espoused a broad evangelical unity based upon the common experience of the new birth. Although Spurgeon sought to maintain a regenerate church through believer's baptism, he did not believe participation in the Lord's Supper should be limited beyond the new birth. See Wills, "Ecclesiology of Charles H. Spurgeon," 67. For more on Spurgeon's theology of the Lord's Supper, see Walker, *Baptists at the Table*, 165–81. Interestingly, while Spurgeon strongly denied any sacramental efficacy to baptism, he understood the Lord's Supper as a stronger link between the material and spiritual. On this point, see Morden, "*Communion with Christ and His People*," 181. Others have noted Spurgeon's strong affirmation of Christ's presence at the Lord's Supper. See Grass and Randall, "C. H. Spurgeon on the Sacraments," in Cross and Thompson, *Baptist Sacramentalism*, 55–75.

admitted all professing believers to communion at the church he pastored and participated in communion outside the auspices of a local church.[84] Peter Morden writes,

> When Spurgeon was at Mentone he would hold regular Sunday afternoon communion services in his sitting room at the Hotel *Beau Rivage*. These informal meetings were in addition to the communion services at the Presbyterian church in Mentone which Spurgeon would, when well enough, also attend, occasionally preaching or even taking the whole service.[85]

Holding communion with a variety of Christians in places outside a local church gathering was not unusual for the preacher. Spurgeon was also known to enjoy communion with students at the pastors' college on Friday afternoons.[86] While Spurgeon held to many Baptist distinctives, he tied the Lord's Supper more strongly to the unity of the universal church than that of the local church.[87] In sum, Spurgeon defended those matters essential to the

84. Morden is unaware of an occasion where Spurgeon celebrated communion with Roman Catholics. This observation is not surprising given Spurgeon's emphasis on the new birth as the basis for unity. See Morden, "Spirituality of C. H. Spurgeon 2," 33.

85. Morden, *"Communion with Christ and His People,"* 166. Morden cites Spurgeon, *Autobiography of Charles H. Spurgeon*, 4:216. Commenting on Spurgeon's practice later, Morden describes Spurgeon as holding an "ecumenical" and "catholic" (little "c") approach to the Lord's Supper. See Morden, "Spirituality of C. H. Spurgeon 2," 172. This book classifies Spurgeon as an open communionist because Spurgeon has in mind evangelical believers in Jesus from a variety of denominations rather than those who might claim to be Christian but not evangelical. Another reason to classify Spurgeon with the open communion advocates is his identification with and approval of John Bunyan on this point. In an intriguing illustration from the sermon, "The Wicked Man's Life, Funeral, and Epitaph," preached June 13, 1858, Spurgeon states, "And there lies that loving hand that was ever ready to receive into communion all them that loved the Lord Jesus Christ: I love the hand that wrote the book "Water Baptism no Bar to Christian Communion." I love him for that sake alone, and if he had written nothing else but that, I would say, "John Bunyan, be honored for ever" (Spurgeon, *New Park Street Pulpit* 2.4). It is instructive also that the ecumenical movement did not begin in earnest among Baptists until after Spurgeon's death. See Garrett Jr., *Baptist Theology*, 591–96.

86. Morden, *"Communion with Christ and His People,"* 167. Nettles mentions a similar example in 1883, when Spurgeon met with the elders and deacons to observe communion prior to a congregational prayer meeting. See Nettles, *Living by Revealed Truth*, 270.

87. For example, Spurgeon held to regenerate church membership, believer's baptism, and congregational governance. After surveying several of Spurgeon's sermons, Morden claims that Spurgeon held baptism to be essential to the existence of the local church as it is the public means of confessing one's faith. See Morden, *"Communion with Christ and His People,"* 101; Wills, "Ecclesiology of Charles H. Spurgeon," 67–73. See also Caner, "Fencing the Table," in White et al., *Restoring Integrity in Baptist Churches*, 170–71.

existence and unity of the evangelical movement, but on secondary matters of ecclesiology, he operated with greater liberality.[88]

Candidus and Pacificus

Daniel Turner's *A Modest Plea for Free Communion* (1772)[89] appears largely to follow Bunyan's logic and evidences.[90] However, Turner's argument for

88. Wills, "Ecclesiology of Charles H. Spurgeon," 76.

89. John Collett Ryland (1723–1792) wrote under the name Pacificus—peaceful. Ryland wrote with Daniel Turner in this tract. See note 92. J. C. Ryland came from Dissenting stock, born at Lower Ditchford, near Stow on the Wold. He was converted in 1741 and soon after recommended for ministry and further training at the Bristol Baptist Academy by the church at Bourton Chapel. He served his first pastorate at Warwick Baptist Church (1750–1759). Ryland befriended a number of pedobaptist ministers, including Philip Doddridge and James Hervey when he transferred to the College Lane Baptist Church in Northampton in 1759. Ryland's association with and respect for various pedobaptist ministers appeared in his advocacy of open communion. J. C. Ryland also served as schoolmaster during his pastorate at Northampton, the pastorate continuing until 1786. During his tenure as schoolmaster, J. C. Ryland taught both his son, John Ryland Jr., and Robert Hall Jr., each of which held open communion views as well (Oliver, *History of the English Calvinistic Baptists*, 30–38). For more on J. C. Ryland, see Garrett Jr., *Baptist Theology*, 168–70. Naylor adds that the Northampton church record books reveal that the church did not identify itself as a Baptist congregation until sometime after 1726, and that they advocated for the "mutual toleration and acceptance by Baptists and pedobaptists at communion" from 1697 at least until the church reaffirmed this position in 1783 (Naylor, *Calvinism, Communion, and the Baptists*, 55–56).

90. Daniel Turner wrote under the pseudonym Candidus—meaning candid. Oliver comments that Daniel Turner and John Collett Ryland are an unlikely pair. Whereas J. C. Ryland belonged to the high Calvinist stripe of John Gill and John Brine, Daniel Turner's orthodoxy remained suspect for much of his ministry (Oliver, *History of the English Calvinistic Baptists*, 30–38). Turner was the first student of the London Baptist Education Society as of 1752, "an institution set up to provide training for Particular Baptist ministers and students" (60–61). He served as a pastor who remained in good standing with his contemporaries at the church at Abingdon until 1757. At that time, the committee responsible for the LBES voted to discontinue their support of Turner, probably due to some doctrinal difference. Turner is known for his advocacy of freedom, for individuals and churches, especially through his publication of *A Compendium of Social Religion and the Nature and Constitution of Christian Churches* (1758). In Appendix A, Oliver traces the connection between the Candidus and Pacificus tracts. Joseph Ivimey, in vol. 4 of his *History of the English Baptists* (1830), mentions the Pacificus [John Ryland] tract. However, subsequent historical study has referred to the Pacificus tract by merely citing Ivimey. Oliver claims that a recent search reveals that one copy of the Pacificus tract exists in the Northamptonshire Central Library. Although it is shorter than Turner's tract, the content is nearly verbatim and they were published the same year, virtually requiring collaboration for their existence. See Oliver, *History of the English Calvinistic Baptists*, 357–58. For more on the way Turner was received by other Particular Baptists, see Naylor, *Calvinism, Communion, and the Baptists*, 110–11.

open communion based upon the unity of Jewish and Gentile Christians in the early church deserves mention. Turner believes that "Scripture is in [the open communionists'] favor."[91] He sees the strict Baptist's exclusion of pedobaptists as akin to what would have happened if the early Jewish Christians had excluded Gentile Christians from communion due to their lack of circumcision. The Jewish Christians could have claimed that receiving uncircumcised Gentiles to communion renders circumcision—an initiating ordinance—null.[92] Similarly, the Gentile Christians could have claimed that upholding the need for circumcision subverts the freedom found in the gospel, and on that ground established a separate communion. The apostles eventually declared that circumcision was abolished, but they did so while encouraging the Gentiles to receive the circumcised Jewish believers.[93] Although Turner compares strict Baptists to both the early Jewish and Gentile Christians, he primarily views strict Baptists as holding the same position as the early Gentile Christians. Either way, the Scriptures urge forbearance and peace rather than division (Rom 14–15).[94]

Summary of Strongest Arguments

While the previous section surveys the arguments propounded by the open communion advocates without critique, this section takes a first step toward evaluation by briefly listing the strongest arguments for the view.[95] Those arguments that appeal most strongly to Scripture and sound reason are given privilege in this section and subsequent summaries.

91. Turner [Candidus], *Modest Plea*, 14.

92. Turner [Candidus], *Modest Plea*.

93. Turner [Candidus], *Modest Plea*, 15.

94. Turner [Candidus], *Modest Plea*, 16. Despite the brevity of Turner's pamphlet, contemporary Baptists of continue to commend it. One recent example is Freeman, *Contesting Catholicity*, 328–29.

95. Several other contemporary proponents of open communion include Saucy, *Church in God's Program*, 231; Van Neste, "Lord's Supper," in Schreiner and Crawford, *Lord's Supper*, 379–86; Beasley-Murray, *Baptism in the New Testament*, 392; Tyler, *Baptism*, 137; Wilson, "Why Baptists Should Not Rebaptize Christians," in Shurden, *Baptism and the Lord's Supper*, 40–47; Clifton, "Fencing the Table," in Shurden, *Baptism and the Lord's Supper*, 70–71; Freeman, *Contesting Catholicity*, 377–78; Marshall, *Last Supper and Lord's Supper*, 156. For a thoughtful pedobaptist perspective that claims to require baptism (of any mode) yet allows celebration of the Lord's Supper outside the gathered church, see Billings, *Remembrance, Communion, and Hope*, 153–54. While not a proponent of open communion, Allison provides his own list of strongest arguments for open communion in Allison, *Sojourners and Strangers*, 403–4. Though this section was developed without consultation of Allison's list, significant overlap exists.

The strongest argument for open communion is the appeal to the lack of an explicit New Testament command that baptism precede communion. Open communion advocates have uniformly conceded their willingness to adopt close communion if they could be shown that Scripture requires it.[96] Secondly, most of the authors appealed to Romans 14–15 for the arguments that Christians should receive all those Christ has received and to bear with the weak.[97] If Paul intends this command to require local churches to receive Christians from outside their membership to the Lord's Supper despite issues of conscience regarding the ordinances, then this argument has weight. Third, if the Lord's Supper is given primarily to demonstrate unity amongst all Christians, open communion has a strong case. Fourth, the claim that to exclude a professing Christian from the Lord's Supper is to unchristian, or effectively to excommunicate the Christian, is a significant argument for open communion. Open communion advocates have generally seen a direct connection between one's ability to receive the Lord's Supper and the sincerity of profession of faith in Christ, despite various views on baptism.[98]

Two other arguments deserve mention, though most of the advocates of open communion have not espoused them. John Bunyan's claim that baptism is a personal matter rather than an initiating ordinance into the church, if true, should lead churches to practice open communion. If baptism has no connection to the local church and may be dismissed by those who do not feel compelled to be baptized without error or sin, no more debate would be required. Finally, Robert Hall's argument that the New Testament principles, practices, and patterns are no longer applicable is significant. Hall admits that the New Testament presents new believers being baptized in Acts and assumes baptized believers compose the churches in the epistles. Yet, due to the incursion of error in the Patristic era, he is willing to tolerate pedobaptism, while claiming that the New Testament explicitly teaches believer's baptism by immersion.[99] The irony of Hall's position stems from the

96. For a contemporary appeal to this point, see Van Neste, "Lord's Supper," in Schreiner and Crawford, *Lord's Supper*, 381.

97. For a contemporary expression of this argument, see Van Neste, "Lord's Supper," in Schreiner and Crawford, *Lord's Supper*, 384–85. Subsumed in this argument is the first of the strong arguments for open communion that Allison mentions. He writes, "Because baptism is not necessary for salvation, non-baptized Christians may participate in the Lord's Supper" (Allison, *Sojourners and Strangers*, 403). Allison also refers to Hall's argument that "no man or set of men, are entitled to prescribe as an indispensable condition of communion what the New Testament has not enjoined as a condition of salvation" (Hall Jr., *Terms of Communion*, v).

98. For a contemporary expression of this argument, see Van Neste, "Lord's Supper," in Schreiner and Crawford, *Lord's Supper*, 385.

99. Van Neste makes a similar point, when he claims "The passage [Acts 2:41–42]

fact that his methodology would render moot any explicit New Testament commands for close communion—if one did exist—even while he appeals to the lack of such a command to justify his views. The fact that other open communion advocates have not generally followed either pastor's line of thought reveals that both arguments require caution.

Arguments for Close Communion

Close communion enjoys a long heritage in Baptist thought. This section surveys the writings of several of the early proponents of close communion, including William Kiffin (1616–1701), Abraham Booth (1734–1806), Andrew Fuller (1754–1815), Joseph Kinghorn (1766–1832), and Thomas Baldwin (1753–1825).[100] Similar to the section on open communion, this section surveys a greater number of proponents in order to give voice to their distinctive emphases. Due to the number of advocates surveyed in this section, each section focuses on those aspects of the proponent's thought that are distinctive in order to avoid redundancy where possible. Each of these theologians' arguments overlap with the constructive proposal of this project. However, what follows helps to elucidate the unique contribution of the thesis of this book, because none of the authors surveyed here develop the biblical-theological argument for close communion based on the relationship between the old covenant and new covenant signs. In fact, whenever the close communion proponents surveyed here assert the necessity of baptism for participation in the Lord's Supper based on the necessity of circumcision for participation in Passover, they merely assert the point without argumentation. This book seeks to supply what these Baptist forbears have believed but have not argued.

Several distinctive emphases appear in the following survey of close communion arguments. Kiffin emphasizes that baptism serves as the pledge of covenant entry and initiating sign of identification with Christ, which by nature should precede the Lord's Supper. Booth emphasizes the regulative role of Scripture over all of the church's worship practices and seeks to demonstrate hermeneutical and methodological faithfulness requires close communion. Baldwin emphasizes that distinctions between the old

---

does not speak to the issue where some believers understand baptism differently" (Van Neste, "Lord's Supper," in Schreiner and Crawford, Lord's Supper, 382).

100. Naylor's seminal survey of communion among the English Baptists echoes the fact that the close communionists were largely Particular Baptists. Naylor claims "evidence fails to show that Arminian Baptists [General Baptists] entered into debate on this subject" (Naylor, Calvinism, Communion, and the Baptists, 106).

covenant people of God and new covenant people of God lead to the close communion position. Fuller emphasizes that Christ instituted the ordinances to occur together in connection to each other as positive institutions. Kinghorn emphasizes that if the ordinances are mishandled, as is the case with a mixed communion of the baptized with the unbaptized, the constitution of the local church changes from that which Christ instituted.

William Kiffin

The title page of the 1681 edition of *Sober Discourse* carries a lengthy subtitle:[101] "Wherein is proved by Scripture, the example of the primitive times, and the practice of all that have professed the Christian religion: that no unbaptized person may be *regularly* admitted to the Lord's Supper."[102] In a short forward to Kiffin's *Sober Discourse* entitled, "To the Christian Reader," Kiffin presents his primary argument:

101. Pastor, leather merchant, and respected statesman, William Kiffin, found favor in the eyes of four English kings, during whose reigns he lived. He pastored the Particular Baptist church at Devonshire Square for nearly sixty years as a Dissenter. Although converted under Puritan preaching, his debates over infant baptism with Daniel Featley (1582–1645) solidified his Baptist theology. The shift in theology resulted in Kiffin joining the Jacob-Lanthrop-Jessey church in 1638 and later aligning with the Baptists, as pastor of the Devonshire congregation in 1644. His lucrative career and magisterial influence afforded him freedoms that other Baptists did not enjoy. He was appointed assessor of taxes for Middlesex in 1647 by Parliament, member of Parliament by Lord Cromwell from 1656–1658, and unofficial economic adviser for England by Charles II in 1660, and Alderman by James II in 1687. Yet, Kiffin suffered his own share of losses, being predeceased by three children, his wife, and two grandchildren. Kiffin is one of the noted primary authors of the First and Second London Confessions (1644 and 1677/1689 respectively) (Nettles, *Beginnings in Britain*, 129–45; Ramsbottom, *Stranger than Fiction*; White, "William Kiffin," 91–103; Johnson, "Peculiar Ventures," 60–71). Kiffin's longest writing is that surveyed in this section. See Garrett Jr., *Baptist Theology*, 65–67. Daniel Featley is the "former official of the High Commission and an Anglican clergyman," who in 1645 submitted to British Parliament a work entitled *The Dippers Dipt* in opposition to the First London Confession. In this work, Featley identified all Baptists as revolutionary Anabaptists, in order to convince Parliament not to tolerate Baptists. See Hilburn, "Lord's Supper," 43–44.

102. See Paul and Kiffin, *Some Serious Reflections,* 5. What exactly Kiffin intends by his emphasis of "regularly admitted" remains unclear. Before his more substantial *Sober Discourse* (1681), William Kiffin had already written the preface to Thomas Paul's *Some Serious Reflections* (1673), which was a brief answer to Bunyan's *Confession of My Faith and Reason for My Practice* (1672). In the preface to Paul's work, Kiffin acknowledges that he has greater respect for pedobaptists who follow the ordinances as they see them than for those who allow baptism to remain undone—advocates of open communion. By the time Kiffin took up his pen to write a full length defense of strict communion Bunyan had also published *Differences in Water Baptism No Bar to Communion* (1673).

> If this ordinance of baptism be the pledge of our entrance into covenant with God, and of the giving up our selves unto him in the solemn bond of religion, and we are hereby dedicated unto the service of the Father, Son, and Holy Ghost, then must it of necessity be the first ordinance, before that of the Lord's Supper.[103]

He follows this helpful statement with a summary of the significance of baptism. He calls baptism "the first foundation of our visible profession of Christ; for as repentance is the visible initiating grace; so baptism is called baptism of repentance as the first initiating ordinance."[104] With these matters in place, Kiffin begins the body of his work.

Kiffin opens his *Sober Discourse* with several arguments for close communion. He initially focuses on 2 Thessalonians 3:6, where Paul commends the church for keeping the ordinances as he delivered them.[105] Applied to the case at hand, this verse commends regulating the worship of God by Scripture, which Kiffin aims to do.[106] The author then provides four truths that ground strict communion. They are (1) believers are duty-bound to be baptized in water upon confession of their faith;[107] (2) only those meeting these criteria are to be baptized; (3) any other practice of baptism deviates from the rule of the gospel and precedent of Scripture;[108] and (4) deviat-

---

103. Kiffin, *Sober Discourse*, vi. The first pages of text in the section "To the Christian Reader" are not numbered. This statement is found on page vi when counting the pages with text.

104. This quote is found in the foreword, "To the Christian Reader" in Kiffin, *Sober Discourse*, viii. Kiffin also clearly affirms both divine and human action occurring in baptism by stating "we are sacredly initiated, and consecrated, or dedicated unto the service and worship of the Father, Son, and Holy Ghost; this we take upon us in our baptism" (5). T. Paul adds that the doctrine of baptism includes right administration, right subject, right manner of dipping, and the right end. See Paul and Kiffin, *Serious Reflections*, 19. Elsewhere, Kiffin explains that Baptism functions to represent the preached word to the eye by a symbol, testify to repentance (Matt 3:6; Acts 2:38), evidence regeneration (Titus 3:5), symbolize death to sin and life anew in Christ (Rom 6:4), signify incorporation into the visible church; and sealing up one's invisible union with Christ. See Kiffin, *Sober Discourse*, 31–32, 39.

105. On this point, see Hilburn, "Lord's Supper," 95–96.

106. Kiffin, *Sober Discourse*, 5.

107. This point refutes Bunyan's claim that one can possess the doctrine of baptism without the practice. However, Kiffin never directly addresses Bunyan's argument. Thomas Paul addressed it in the work Kiffin endorsed from 1673. There, Paul explained that while baptism does symbolize spiritual truths, a fundamental part of the doctrine of baptism is the command to "be baptized." See Paul, *Serious Reflections*, 16.

108. Thus, introducing the unbaptized to the Lord's Supper is novel. See Naylor, *Calvinism, Communion, and the Baptists*, 102.

ing is disorderly and will tend to introduce the unregenerate into church membership.[109] Kiffin advocates unity with all true saints so far as possible. However, when disagreement over Scripture requires separation, Christians should "hold communion as far as we agree."[110] Then, he defines unbaptized persons as "all persons that either were never baptized at all, or such as have been (as they call it) christened . . . or sprinkled . . . in their infancy."[111] These foundations set the stage for arguments against open communion. Baptist churches should not allow unbaptized believers to join them in communion because the practice (1) has a tendency of diminishing the role of baptism toward its discontinuation;[112] (2) removes sufficient grounds to separate from the Church of England; (3) rejects the order of the primitive church;[113] and (4) removes the right to require even regeneration as prerequisite to communion.[114]

Response to Objections

Next, Kiffin addresses several methodological objections to strict communion. To the charge that strict communionists lack express warrant from Scripture, his answer is three-fold: (1) Jesus' and the apostles' baptism proves that they did not regard holiness as the sole qualification for the Last Supper; (2) unless it can be proven that baptism was only a duty required

109. Naylor points out that, similar to Andrew Fuller later, Kiffin held that believers in the NT were not baptized into any particular church but into Christ's people. For Fuller's affirmation of the relationship between baptism and the universal church, actualized through the administration of local churches, see Belcher, *Fuller's Works*, 3:512. A baptized believer could belong to a local church only by consent or covenant (Naylor, *Calvinism, Communion, and the Baptists*, 102; Naylor cites Paul, *Serious Reflections*, 3–4). On another note, although Kiffin sought to preserve regenerate church membership by his doctrine of baptism, Poe claims that Kiffin and his allies distorted the gospel. Poe argues, "The Baptists made a functional change in their concept of the gospel by making baptism the logical qualification of faith. Though they did not attribute soteriological significance to baptism as a sacrament, they did attribute to it the test of gospel obedience and the proof of faith" (Poe, "John Bunyan's Controversy with the Baptists," 33).

110. Kiffin, *Sober Discourse*, 6–7.

111. Kiffin, *Sober Discourse*, 9.

112. Kiffin, *Sober Discourse*, 10–13. Indeed, Thomas Paul references John Bunyan's identification of baptism as a pest and plague because it was the subject of contention between Christians. Whereas Bunyan's answer was to discontinue the ordinance if the debate reached the point of dividing Christians, Paul asks who gives Bunyan the right to disparage new covenant blessings (Paul, *Serious Reflections*, 10–11).

113. Kiffin, *Sober Discourse*, 16.

114. Kiffin, *Sober Discourse*, 21.

of the New Testament era, it is still in force;[115] and (3) "This objection supposes that whatever is not forbidden is lawful."[116] To the argument that open communionists allow people to communion who think themselves baptized as infants, Kiffin responds that his fellow Baptists cannot have it both ways. They cannot consistently maintain that infant baptism is not baptism and yet allow a pedobaptist to commune with them on account of the supposed legitimacy of the infant baptism.[117] To the claim that what happened in the church's infant stages is not binding on the contemporary church, Kiffin urges, "Let it be shown where there is another rule."[118] In 1 Corinthians 14:40, Paul grounds the church's edification in their obedience to the apostle's prescribed order. To the claim that union with Christ is the only requirement for participating in the ordinances of Christ, Kiffin makes a lengthy and clear response:

> It is readily granted that union with Christ, signified by a visible profession of faith gives a man right to baptism, and having this union and being baptized, they have right to church fellowship, and the Lord's Supper.... But that by virtue of union with Christ they have a right to the Lord's Supper; and accordingly to partake of the same before they are baptized is denied.[119]

115. Kiffin, *Sober Discourse*, 118.

116. Kiffin, *Sober Discourse*, 120. Poe claims that Kiffin misunderstands Bunyan's hermeneutic at this point. Rather than arguing for the church's ability to establish innovations in worship, Bunyan argued that "making baptism a bar to communion" was an innovation. Thus, Poe claims, Kiffin and Bunyan disagreed over what Christ commanded (Poe, "John Bunyan's Controversy with the Baptists," 31).

117. Kiffin, *Sober Discourse*, 126. This is a common argument. Abraham Booth adds that his opponents admit their inconsistency when they baptize as believers those in their communion who were formerly baptized as infants, whenever the pedobaptist has a change of heart. The act of baptizing pedobaptists after years of communion with them is an admission that the infant baptism was not actually baptism. See Booth, *Apology*, 61. Booth appeals to other inconsistencies in the open communion position stemming from the same argument: (1) they could not reasonably object to receiving a visible Christian who conscientiously objects to taking the Lord's Supper unless they made the same arguments that close communionists make (64), and (2) if an individual Christian's definition of baptism is allowed to be determinative, the Baptists lose their scriptural grounds of dissent from the Church of England (66). As Oliver points out, Booth was concerned that, ironically, "Baptists would become the only branch of the church which did not insist on baptism." See Oliver, *History of the English Calvinistic Baptists*, 73.

118. Kiffin, *Sober Discourse*, 149.

119. Kiffin, *Sober Discourse*, 151. The similitude Kiffin provides is worth citing in full. He writes, "A child, by being the eldest son of his father, has a right to his Father's estate as heir thereof, as soon as his father is dead, but yet for the actual possession thereof, there is required his coming to age, till which time he cannot possess that right;

Finally, to the claim that love and holiness are the disciple's identity marker, Kiffin exclaims, "All true gospel love [is] regulated by gospel rule."[120] Because Christ designed baptism to identify his people, the church should uphold his rule.

Kiffin also addresses several objections based upon specific biblical texts. To the objection that Paul calls believers to receive the weak in faith (Rom 14:1),[121] Kiffin responds, "the weakness involves things of an indifferent nature rather than gospel ordinances."[122] Furthermore, the "receiving here cannot be meant to receive into the church as members, because the Apostle writes this epistle to the church, and these weak members are a part of that church; but the receiving here intended is into the affections of each other."[123] To the charge that 1 Corinthians 12:13 presents only the baptism with the Spirit as that in which all have participated, Kiffin claims most expositors think Paul intends water baptism as well as Spirit baptism. Furthermore, by synecdoche, all drinking of one Spirit stands for eating and drinking of the Spirit in the Lord's Supper. Therefore, Kiffin finds both ordinances present in 1 Corinthians 12:13.[124] Whereas some claimed that

the law requiring this as the order by which he is to come to the enjoyment thereof. So though union with Christ gives a man a right to all the ordinances of Christ, yet are they to be enjoyed in that order which the law prescribeth."

120. Kiffin, *Sober Discourse*, 160. Kiffin writes, "That cannot be called love, which is exercised in opposition to the order prescribed in the Word." Thomas Paul turned this objection around by claiming that obedience in the matter of baptism constitutes part of the believer's holiness. Neglecting baptism in consideration of holiness is too weak a view of holiness (Paul, *Serious Reflections*, 3).

121. For a similar take on Kiffin's treatment of Rom 14, see Duesing, *Henry Jessey*, 231.

122. Kiffin, *Sober Discourse*, 130.

123. Kiffin, *Sober Discourse*, 131. On the same point, Fuller writes, "It is not just to argue from Jewish customs, which though once binding had ceased to be so, to Christian ordinances which continue in full force. The tone which the apostle holds in respect of those Jewish rites which ceased to be obligatory is very different from that which respects commandments still in force." See Belcher, *Fuller's Works*, 3:514; Baldwin, *Particular Communion*, 46. Similarly, Kinghorn contends "We never ought to say to any man, however excellent he may be, 'we love you so much, that as a proof of it, we will give up an institution of the Lord, on your account'" (Kinghorn, *Baptism a Term of Communion*, 39). See also Kinghorn, *Defense of "Baptism a Term of Communion,"* 164. In this work, Kinghorn explains that Paul's command to receive those Christ receives cannot refer to the unbaptized because Hall himself admits "Whatever is affirmed in any part of it [the New Testament], respecting the privilege of primitive believers, was asserted primarily of such only as were baptized, because there were no others originally in the church" (Kinghorn quotes Hall Jr., *Reply*, 184).

124. Kiffin, *Sober Discourse*, 133–34. Several subsequent Baptists followed Kiffin's exegesis here. For their statements, see Booth, *Apology*, 109–10; Baldwin, *Particular Communion*, 41–43; Belcher, *Fuller's Works*, 3:514.

the phrase "as many of you as have been baptized into Christ" implies that not all in the churches were baptized (Rom 6:4; Gal 3:27), Kiffin provides several responses: (1) baptism is viewed in the New Testament as a means of "implanting men into Christ, or the Body of Christ the Church";[125] (2) those who are baptized are coextensive with those who have died to sin and been made alive in Christ (Rom 6);[126] and (3) the phrase "as many" can mean all depending on context (cf. 1 Tim 6:1).[127] To the argument that one who possesses all the foundational pillars of church unity in Ephesians 4:4–6 should be allowed communion, Kiffin replies that the orderly observation of baptism as a positive precept requires that it occur prerequisite to communion as circumcision was prior to Passover.[128]

Abraham Booth

Abraham Booth's *Apology for the Baptists* (1778)[129] is the standard Baptist defense of close/strict communion.[130] In section one, Booth argues that

125. He clarifies that baptism is not "into this or that particular church; but into that one Church of Christ, which is distributed into several parts and particular societies" (Kiffin, *Sober Discourse*, 137–38).

126. Kiffin, *Sober Discourse*, 142.

127. Kiffin, *Sober Discourse*, 144.

128. Kiffin, *Sober Discourse*, 154–58. With this argument, Kiffin assumes that baptism corresponds to circumcision without arguing the point. He also claims that one ordinance does not give a right to the other but must still occur as prerequisite to the other. He writes, "Circumcision was the first ordinance to be administered before they might be partakers of the Passover although it gave not a right to the Passover, yet might not any partake of it before they were circumcised without sin: so also in the New Testament, baptism is the first ordinance to be administered by the direction and appointment of God, without which, the Supper of the Lord may not be received without sin" (158–59).

129. Abraham Booth was born to Anglican parents and raised in Nottinghamshire. However, he was converted and baptized as a General Baptist by age 21 and later became a convinced Particular Baptist. Booth served as pastor of the Prescot-Street Baptist Church in London for thirty-seven years. He was well educated and influential in the founding of Regent's Park College. In his writings, Booth defended orthodoxy against Socinianism, argued against antinomianism, vied for penal substitutionary atonement as a means of particular redemption, and held to a Baptist covenantal theology in line with the Second London Confession (1689). As a Baptist apologist, Booth offered *Paedobaptism Examined* (1784) as a defense of believer's baptism before writing his defense of close communion, *Apology for the Baptists* (1778), that is surveyed in this section. Garrett Jr., *Baptist Theology*, 189–93. For more on Booth's contribution to Baptist theology, see Himbury, "Baptismal Controversies," 297–98; Naylor, *Calvinism, Communion, and the Baptists*.

130. Oliver, *History of the English Calvinistic Baptists*, 70. Throughout the work, Booth references and critiques Bunyan, Candidus, and Pacificus, the latter two being

strict Baptists do not lay undue stress on baptism.[131] Rather than claiming that baptism is a saving ordinance, Booth maintains that both the subject and mode of baptism are essential to the ordinance.[132] Before providing arguments for strict communion, Booth contends for the Scripture's regulative role over Christians and their worship as the ground of strict communion.[133] The regulative rule of Scripture is Booth's primary defense against the claim that those who lack light in baptism should be admitted to communion on grounds of ignorance or misjudgment.[134] From this formative principle, Booth proceeds to his arguments.[135]

In Scripture, Christ commands both of the ordinances; yet they cannot be done at the same time. Therefore, churches should follow the scriptural precedent of baptism occurring first,[136] because churches should receive the precedent of Acts as the mind of Christ. Booth recognizes that Acts 2:41 is the only place to give explicit precedent for the order of belief, baptism, and communion. However, when one considers the matter of immediate baptisms throughout Acts, it requires that baptisms in those cases preceded communion as an implied pattern.[137] The New Testament presumes that all

---

his most recent stimulus for writing.

131. Booth, *Apology*, 5–6. Of this work, Oliver writes, it "was the most detailed work to appear on either side of the communion controversy since the seventeenth century. [Booth] took a broad view of the question, not limiting himself to answering contemporaries. . . . Although he did not allow any previous writer to mold his approach, he displayed a much greater sense of history than any previous eighteenth-century writer on this subject. . . . He wrote with sympathy and respect for pedobaptists, even though he could not receive them to the communion table" (Oliver, *History of the English Calvinistic Baptists*, 71–72).

132. Booth, *Apology*, 21–22. Fowler argues that it is incongruous for Booth "to take such a low view of the meaning of baptism and at the same time exclude from communion persons who are baptized by a defective mode" (Fowler, *More Than a Symbol*, 46). Fowler concludes, "Whatever may be the coherence, or lack thereof, of such a position, what is clear is that Booth and other Baptists like him held tenaciously to a high view of church order but a low view of the efficacy of the ordinances of the church."

133. Booth, *Apology*, 29.

134. Booth is very clear in his application of Scripture's regulative function as he continues. He writes, "It is not the measure of a believer's knowledge, nor the evidence of his integrity; nor is it the charitable opinion we form about his acceptance with God that is the rule of his admission to the sacred Supper; but the precepts of Jesus Christ, and the practice of the apostolic churches." See Booth, *Apology*, 77.

135. For a similar take on Booth's arguments, see Naylor, *Calvinism, Communion, and the Baptists*, 121–23.

136. Booth, *Apology*, 33–34. Booth cites Matt 28 and the practice of baptism soon after profession of faith in Acts as evidence (42–43).

137. Booth, *Apology*, 46.

Christians should be or have been baptized.[138] Given Christ's commands to baptize and participate in the Lord's Supper, those who lay aside baptism, go against Christ.[139]

Booth also appeals to the order of institution of the ordinances and their meaning. Given that Christ was baptized by John before the Last Supper, Christ "must intend" this same order to continue and "tacitly prohibits every unbaptized person having communion at his Table."[140] The meaning of the ordinances is also instructive—baptism is initiatory and communion demonstrates continuing fellowship.[141] Hermeneutically, Booth believes his case is strong. He writes, "If these declarations and facts, and precedents, be not sufficient to determine the point in our favor; it will be exceedingly hard, if not impossible to conclude with certainty, in what order any two institutions that God ever appointed were to be administered."[142]

Next, Booth points to a methodological error in his opponents' position related to covenant signs. The open position, he claims does not derive from Scripture but from inference and analogy.[143] Consistency in the open position would require that open communion advocates "must allow" that those who were not circumcised could have participated in Passover.[144] Booth argues that baptism did not come "in the place of circumcision, as many of our Pedobaptist brethren suppose."[145] However, baptism is "equally

138. He cites Acts 19 and Paul's presumption that the disciples of Jesus would have been baptized. Booth, *Apology*, 88.

139. Booth, *Apology*, 41.

140. Booth, *Apology*, 43.

141. Booth, *Apology*, 48.

142. Booth, *Apology*, 49.

143. Booth, *Apology*, 50.

144. Booth, *Apology*, 51. Booth's point here is interesting in the history of this debate. Years earlier, Bunyan conceded the charge. However, neither Robert Hall Jr. nor Samuel Worcester, the Congregationalist who debated Thomas Baldwin, would concede it. Hall and Worcester simply claimed that the OT law was clear, but no such law is given in the NT. This point is the primary issue of this book.

145. Booth, *Apology*, 82. The only similarity that Booth draws to that of this book is the continuity and analogous role of both circumcision and baptism as entry signs into the people of God. Booth presents a long and amusing parable at this point in which circumcision's definition is confused. He argues that the open communionists' reasoning would require that the incorrect circumcision be accepted (83–86). Later, he considers another view of the way that circumcision and baptism's relationship are sometimes utilized by open communionists. He writes, "And must we indeed consider the administration and neglect of baptism as on a perfect level with being circumcised or uncircumcised, in the Apostolic Times! Must an ordinance of the New Testament, submission to which the Lord requires of all his disciples, be placed on the same footing with an obsolete rite of the Jewish church! How kind it is of our brethren who possess

necessary to communion . . . under the Christian economy, as [circumcision] was to every male, in order to partake of the paschal feast."[146] As similar as this argument is to the thesis of this book, Booth provides no argumentation for why it is true, as this book seeks to do.

Response to Objections

Regarding the texts that Booth's opponents misuse (e.g., Rom 14:1; 15:7; Acts 15:8–9; 1 Cor 9:19–23), Booth charges,

> Unless our opponents can make it appear, that they obtain the grant of a dispersion power to gospel ministers and churches . . . [that] authorizes the ministers of Christ to set aside an ordinance of his, or to invert the order of its administration as they may think it proper; they are far from answering the exigencies of their case, or serving the purpose for which they are cited.[147]

To the argument that baptism may be laid aside to promote edification and unity around the Lord's Supper, Booth claims that one ordinance should not be pitted against another.[148] To Pacificus's and Candidus's claim that the Jewish Christians in the New Testament could have refused to commune with Gentile Christians due to the Gentile's lack of circumcision, Booth notes the supposition that "baptism was no more commanded of believers now than circumcision was of Gentile converts in the apostolic age."[149] In response to Bunyan's argument that the Israelites celebrated Passover in the wilderness without being circumcised, Booth replies that this action was called the

---

this knowledge, and are so well acquainted with Christian liberty, relating to baptism that they are willing to inform us of its true extent. . . . I may however venture an appeal to the intelligent reader, whether this way of arguing does not much better become the pen of . . . any Baptist? Because, as Hornbeck remarks, . . . it is very absurd to explain the design, the command, and the obligation of baptism by the abrogation and abuse of circumcision." See Booth, *Apology*, 140–41.

146. Booth, *Apology*, 82.

147. Booth, *Apology*, 93.

148. Booth, *Apology*, 117. Although he acknowledges that positive commands may on rare occasions be set aside due to natural necessity (e.g., David eating the shew bread) or a moral consideration, Scripture nowhere supports pitting one positive institution against another.

149. Booth, *Apology*, 139. Booth finds Candidus and Pacificus' argument to be contradictory to what he cites Candidus (Daniel Turner) as writing elsewhere. In another work, Turner affirmed baptism's role for incorporating a believer into the visible church. For this discussion, see Booth, *Apology*, 160–61.

reproach of Egypt in Joshua 5:9.[150] To Bunyan's claim that the participation of uncircumcised men in the Passover under Hezekiah legitimates open communion (2 Chr 30), Booth retorts that Hezekiah's request for forgiveness after the act suggests their culpability (v. 19).[151] In short, Booth finds each of his opponents' arguments from Scripture lacking.[152]

150. Booth, *Apology*, 118.

151. Booth, *Apology*, 119.

152. Booth concludes by presenting his designation for the two sides of the debate. The free communionists are "latitudinarian," meaning "the term Baptist when applied to them, is to be understood in such a latitude of signification, as will comport with receiving persons into communion who, in their judgment, are unbaptized" (Booth, *Apology*, 174–75). The strict communion label may be rightly applied to Booth if one intends to convey the rigor and faithfulness with which he and his allies seek to obey and apply Scripture to their practice of who partakes of the Lord's Supper. While the latitudinarian group does "not appear to have had an existence till about the middle of [the seventeenth] century [beginning with Jessey and Bunyan]," the strict group's practice appears to be uniform throughout church history. Oliver explains that Booth's admission of the term "strict Baptist . . . marks the first time a Baptist minister had accepted the description" (Oliver, *History of the English Calvinistic Baptists*, 77). He clarifies, "This acceptance must not however be understood to suggest that Booth considered such a designation to be a distinct denominational title." This was because Booth "always considered himself to be a member of the Particular Baptist denomination, which included open and strict communionists." Thus, Oliver concludes that Booth did not desire to break fellowship with the open communionist Particular Baptists. Alternatively, Booth spoke of Robert Hall Jr. as "the first man in our denomination." Oliver presents Booth as caught in a tension whereby he "showed a real love for all his Christian brethren and a truly catholic spirit." Yet, the pastor "did not . . . feel free to challenge what he perceived to be a divinely-prescribed order in the administration of the sacraments." For an assessment of the impact of the communion controversies from 1772 to 1781, see Oliver, *History of the English Calvinistic Baptists*, 87.

Thomas Baldwin

In Baldwin's initial pamphlet,[153] "Open Communion Examined" (1789),[154] he seeks to establish two things: (1) the Scripture presents baptism as prerequisite to communion and (2) immersion is essential to Gospel baptism.[155] Although Baptists do not view baptism as essential to salvation, they view it as a necessary prerequisite for communion in "regular, visible standing" as a church.[156] In order to demonstrate that baptism is prerequisite to communion, Baldwin presents several arguments: (1) that the church of the New Testament was composed of believers only;[157] (2) that receiving grace and believing is a necessary prerequisite to baptism;[158] and (3) that "a profession

153. Having turned from Congregationalist to Baptist himself, Baldwin was baptized in 1781. Chessman, *Memoir of Rev. Thomas Baldwin*, 19. Besides his lengthy and faithful pastorate (1780–1822), Baldwin served as trustee to a variety of institutions and, at the time of his death, served as President of the Baptist Board of Managers for Foreign Missions, which became the Triennial Convention for foreign missions in 1814. See Chessman, *Memoir of Rev. Thomas Baldwin*, 65. Despite William McLoughlin's statement that "none of [Baldwin's] many published tracts and sermons are worth remembering today," because they are "merely repeated old arguments," he describes Baldwin as having "towered above" his Baptist colleagues in his time. For a brief biography and sketch of the pastor's significance among New England Baptists, see McLoughlin, *New England Dissent*, 2:1114–1116; Sprague, *Annals of the American Baptist Pulpit*, 6:172–179.

154. Baldwin, *The Baptism of Believers Only*, 7. Part I of Baldwin's 1806 publication contains his initial work that examines the topic of open communion. This first tract was published as "Open Communion Examined" (1–51). In response to Baldwin's tract, Noah Worcester (NW from this point), pastor of the Congregational church in Thornton, CT published Worcester, *A Friendly Letter* (1791). Part II of the 1806 publication above is Baldwin's response to N. Worcester, entitled, "A Brief Vindication" in Baldwin, *Baptism of Believers Only*, 53–160. The Appendix to the 1806 work is Baldwin's review of the English Baptist turn pedobaptist, Peter Edwards. N. Worcester's brother Samuel Worcester, the first secretary of the American Board of Commissioners for Foreign Missions, responded to Baldwin with S. Worcester, *Serious and Candid Letters* (1807). Three years later, Baldwin answered S. Worcester's *Serious and Candid Letters* with *A Series of Letters* (1810). For a brief summary of the controversy, see Chessman, *Memoir of Thomas Baldwin*, 61; Sprague, *Annals*, 6:175.

155. Baldwin, *Baptism of Believers Only*, 55.

156. Baldwin, *Baptism of Believers Only*, 13. Baldwin's delineation between matters essential to salvation and matters essential to the ordering of a church are clear; while baptism does not fall in the former category, it does fall in the latter (12).

157. Baldwin, *Baptism of Believers Only*, 15–16. He cites Acts 2:41–42; 5:11–14; 8:12; 18:8; 2 Cor 8:5.

158. Baldwin, *Baptism of Believers Only*, 18–19. He cites Acts 8:37; Rom 4:10–14; 10:10; Gal 3:29. The Baptist anticipates an objection here in defense of infants. According to 1 Pet 2:5–9, those who belong to the church were once not a people and are now the people of God. If infants can belong to the covenant of grace by virtue of their

of faith, in adults, in order to their admission to special communion, is a point generally acknowledged" (Matt 16:13–19).[159] Thus, Baldwin summarizes "We then believe it to be the apostolic order, to baptize none till they profess their faith in Christ; and that till then, they cannot be considered qualified members for a gospel church, nor be received into their fellowship at the Lord's Table."[160] According to Baldwin then, pedobaptists must demonstrate that the apostolic teaching and practice presents something other than a believing church in which belief precedes baptism and baptism precedes communion.[161] After arguing that immersion is essential to baptism,[162] the thesis of Baldwin's third section is that "sincerity is not the term of communion: but being conformed to the apostles' doctrine, and continuing steadfastly therein" (Acts 2:42).[163] Sincerity is an insufficient ground for communion because "whatever we practice that is not according to the will of Christ, is contrary thereto, although we be ever so sincere in doing it."[164]

In his subsequent writings, Baldwin's arguments for close communion are similar to this book's thesis. In an "Appendix" to his *Baptism of Believers*

---

baptism, then "there is no time at which they are not a people" and "the parents convey the right of membership on their infant seed."

159. Baldwin, *Baptism of Believers Only*, 21–22.

160. Baldwin, *Baptism of Believers Only*, 27.

161. Baldwin, *Baptism of Believers Only*, 31. In order to remove the "baptism of the Holy Ghost" from the discussion, Baldwin compares the apparent belief and baptism experience of those in Acts 19:1–6 to the "one baptism" of Ephesians 4:1. He stresses that Paul viewed them as disciples not based on their having the Holy Spirit, whom they did not yet have, but on the basis of their profession and baptism. Baldwin concludes "The baptism of the Holy Ghost ceased when these miraculous gifts cease," which means that Paul refers to water baptism in Ephesians.

162. He states the Baptist sentiment: "The Baptists not only believe that this one baptism is an institution of Christ, but that it is ever to be administered in one mode, and to one kind of subjects. Our opponents suppose (at least many of them) that it may be administered upon a profession of faith, or without it; either by immersion or sprinkling. They acknowledge immersion to believers to be lawful baptism; could we with a good conscience, allow the same of infant sprinkling, much of our dispute would be at an end." Baldwin's indebtedness to the wider, trans-Atlantic debate over open communion is evident in his lengthy quotation from Abraham Booth's *Apology* (without a page number citation) to the same effect (Baldwin, *Baptism of Believers Only*, 32).

163. Baldwin, *Baptism of Believers Only*, 37.

164. Baldwin, *Baptism of Believers Only*, 38–39. Baldwin claims that consistency in the open communion position could not prevent two other errors: The open communion Baptist church would have to allow (1) a converted Roman Catholic to join even if she refused the cup on grounds of conscience; and (2) a Quaker to join even if she refused baptism and the Supper all together on grounds that a sincere Christian faith replaces visible forms.

Only (1806),[165] Baldwin aims to disprove what pedobaptists hold to be basic, namely, "That infants have a right to gospel baptism, because infants under the law had a right to circumcision."[166] Baldwin argues against this principle of continuity along three lines: (1) the Abrahamic covenant (Gen 17) was distinct from the promise given to Abram in Genesis 12 that all the nations would be blessed through his offspring; (2) the change in dispensation from law to grace and from old covenant to new requires that only believers and not their children belong to Christ by faith;[167] and (3) pedobaptists are inconsistent in their application of the covenant terms to their children, given that all circumcised males participated in Passover.[168]

165. Baldwin penned this Appendix in answer to S. Worcester, *Two Discourses* (1807). The first edition of Worcester's work was clearly published prior to Baldwin's 1806 publication.

166. Baldwin resumes this line of argument in depth in later comments on Samuel Worcester's *Two Discourses*. He explains (1) "the promise of blessing to Abraham came twenty-four years before the covenant of circumcision in Gen 17" (Baldwin, *Baptism of Believers Only*, 260). The promise of Gen 12 was "in no sense conditional." (2) The promises that Abraham would have nations spring forth from his loins and have kings come from him "has been literally and fully accomplished." (3) The promise to Abraham regarding the Gentile nations in Christ was renewed with Abraham about twenty years after the covenant of circumcision in Gen 17, that is in Gen 22. It was at this stage, that God repeated the promise, "In thy seed shall all the nations of the earth be blessed." (4) The apostle distinguishes between the "promise" respecting the seed in whom the Gentile nations should be blessed, from that made in the covenant of circumcision respecting the posterity of Abraham." The woman's seed and seed of Abraham refer to Christ. "But primarily, his natural seed, or at most his spiritual seed, and not Christ, was intended, by the seed in the covenant of circumcision. The nations have never been blessed by any other of Abraham's seed but Christ." (5) The apostle makes another distinction in the promises to Abraham by the use of the plural "promises" in Gal 3:16 (cf. Gen 12:3; 22:18). The same distinction is made with reference to the "seed" singular as opposed to "seeds" in Gal 3, according to Baldwin. In a subsequent series of letters, Baldwin clarifies that the promise to Abraham and the Abrahamic covenant are distinct because Paul locates the fulfillment of the Abrahamic promise in Christ (Gal 3:16). See Baldwin, *Series of Letters*, 45–46. He explains, God's promise to "perform the oath which he swore to Abraham" (Gen 22) refers not to the "time when the covenant of circumcision was ratified, but at the time when Isaac was presented as a victim on the altar . . . more than twenty years after the ratification of that covenant." Therefore, "beyond all controversy," the promise of blessing to Abraham's seed refers not to "the natural or even spiritual seed, but Christ." Baldwin's separation of the promise to Abraham and covenant with Abraham appears novel in Baptist history. Others have viewed the Abrahamic covenant as comprising all of the promises and conditions stated throughout Genesis 12–22, understanding the episodes to constitute a whole package.

167. Baldwin, *Baptism of Believers Only*, 195–96. Baldwin presents a very brief explanation of Acts 2:41 with respect to the promise that is "for you and your children." He cites Jer 31:31–34 and explains that this covenant spoken of by Peter in Acts includes only those who know the Lord, because it is enacted on better promises (213–14).

168. Baldwin, *Baptism of Believers Only*, 182. Baldwin cites Exod 12:43–48 to argue

Later, in his *Series of Letters* (1810),[169] Baldwin presents a thoroughgoing Baptist defense of discontinuity between the Mosaic and new covenants, which require differences in the constitution of Israel and the church respectively. Baldwin maintains that covenants must be distinct unless "you can make it appear, that to 'inculcate' the necessity of a renewal of heart, and the actual possession of a renewed heart, are the same thing."[170] Due to the covenantal differences, Baldwin introduces a significant difference in argument regarding baptism in order to argue against baptism replacing circumcision. He writes, "To say that baptism now seals the same covenant, which circumcision formerly did, is to assume what never has, and we believe, never can be proved. Baptism, to my recollection, is never said to be the seal or token of any covenant whatever; but the answer of a good conscience toward God."[171] Instead, because baptism is a positive institution, it "rests on the authority and declaration of the institutor."[172] If this is the case, then "no inference can be made from what is fit and proper under one institution, to what is fit and proper under another," which would include "subjects, qualifications, or requirements."[173] Baldwin claims covenantal continuity in the fact that circumcision guaranteed males the right to participate in Passover as full members of the Mosaic covenant (cf. Exod 12:48–49).[174] Similarly, in the gospel dispensation, according to Galatians 3:28, all who are baptized share in all the benefits of the gospel. In terms of discontinuity though, the distinction between God's visible people and those who share in the covenant of redemption has now vanished because full participation in the covenant is received by faith.[175] The upshot of this biblical-theological argumentation is that the church is composed of believers only, baptism is a covenantal sign given to those believers, and consistency in the application of the signs of the new covenant requires that baptism precede the Lord's Supper.

that baptized infants who fail to participate in the Lord's Supper should be cut off from God's people.

169. This publication was also written in response to S. Worcester, *Serious and Candid Letters.*

170. Baldwin, *Series of Letters*, 88.

171. Baldwin, *Series of Letters*, 89.

172. Baldwin, *Series of Letters*, 119.

173. Baldwin, *Series of Letters*, 119.

174. Baldwin, *Series of Letters*, 121–22.

175. For example, Christians do not have their domestic help baptized. See Baldwin, *Series of Letters*, 120.

Andrew Fuller

Fuller's argument for strict communion is built on the premise that a proper methodology is necessary for arriving at Christ's full teaching on a positive institution.[176] This methodology requires combining Christ's commands to continue baptism and the Lord's Supper in the church with the early church's pattern for participating in those ordinances. While Christ's commands to baptize and take the Lord's Supper supply the grounding for the ordinances being positive institutions, the pattern of New Testament practice elucidates the essential elements of each ordinance from its accidental elements. That each of the ordinances is a positive institution grounds Fuller's arguments for strict communion.[177] Therefore, a brief explication of Fuller's view of positive institutions versus moral duties is in order before moving to the pastor's direct arguments for close communion.

Fuller continually categorizes baptism and the Lord's Supper as positive institutions, which are binding on the church of all ages. They are binding because Christ has legislated them, rather than because of any holy tendency inherent in the action. Fuller writes,

176. Fuller was born and raised in a hyper-Calvinist, Particular Baptist milieu. Fuller's conversion in his teens and subsequent call to ministry occurred in correlation with a controversy over hyper-Calvinism in Fuller's Soham church, during John Eve's (d. 1782) pastorate. Fuller's pastoral ministry began after Eve's resignation with Fuller's initial pulpit supply in Soham, which led to his seven-year pastorate at Soham. Subsequently, Fuller moved to the pastorate at Kettering, where he finished his ministry. After becoming convinced of evangelical Calvinism (i.e., "Fullerism") during his Soham pastorate, Fuller wrote his most famous work, *Gospel Worthy of All Acceptation* (1785). This work, along with William Carey's *Enquiry into the use of Means for the Conversion of the Heathen* sparked a transatlantic missions movement, especially among Baptists. Fuller collaboratively founded the Baptist Missionary Society (BMS) with fellow-pastors and friends from the Northamptonshire Baptist Association, including John Ryland Jr. and John Sutcliff. Fuller's work as the corresponding secretary of the BMS allowed continued correspondence with William Carey and those who joined Carey's mission work in India. Besides writing sermons, Fuller's writing centered around five major controversies: deism, antinomianism, Sandemanianism, Socinianism, and universalism—each as a means to preserving the church's gospel witness. This sketch largely follows Brewster, *Andrew Fuller*. For more on Fuller's life, see Morden, *Life and Thought of Andrew Fuller*; "Andrew Fuller," in Haykin, *At the Pure Fountain of Thy Word*, 1–42; "So Valuable a Life," 4–14; Roberts, "Andrew Fuller," in George, *Baptist Theologians*, 121–39. For synopses of Fuller's controversies, see Haykin, *At the Pure Fountain of Thy Word*.

177. Belcher, *Fuller's Works*, 3:515. Strikingly, Fuller closes his 1814 letter by stating, "I am willing to allow that open communion may be practised from a conscientious persuasion of its being the mind of Christ; and they ought to allow the same of strict communion; and thus, instead of reproaching one another with bigotry on the one hand, or carnal policy on the other, we should confine our inquiries to the precepts and examples of the New Testament.—I am affectionately yours, Andrew Fuller."

> [A moral duty] is commanded because it is right, the other [a positive institution] is right because it is commanded. The great principles of the former are of perpetual obligation, and know no other change than that which arises from the varying of relations and conditions; but those of the latter may be binding at one period of time, and utterly abolished at another.[178]

Furthermore, positive institutions are abolished due to a change of dispensation or covenant—as the way in which circumcision ended with the onset of the new covenant[179]—and remain unknown unless God "expressly reveals" them.[180] Therefore, distinguishing positive institutions from moral duties is vital.

Fuller specifically affirms baptism and the Lord's Supper as positive institutions belonging to the gospel dispensation/kingdom of Christ.[181] Baptism functions to separate the kingdom of Christ from the kingdom of Satan and to distinguish the church from the world, as each professing believer aligns himself or herself with Christ and Christ's church by baptism.[182]

178. Fuller was certainly not the first to argue that baptism and the Lord's Supper are positive institutions. Of those surveyed in this book, he makes the most use of the category. See Belcher, *Fuller's Works*, 2:624. For Abraham Booth on this point, see Booth, *Apology*, 83.

179. For example, in a sermon on Gen 17 to the Kettering congregation, Fuller explains that Christians are not bound to baptize their children as Abraham's descendants were bound to circumcise their children. "In short, we do not think ourselves warranted, in matters of positive institution, to found our practice on analogies, whether real or supposed. . . . Our duty, we conceive, is, in such cases, to follow the precepts and examples of the dispensation under which we live." See Fuller, Discourse XXV, "Abraham and His Seed," from *Expository Discourses on Genesis* in Belcher, *Fuller's Works*, 3:71. See the lengthy note on this page.

180. Belcher, *Fuller's Works*, 2:624.

181. He writes, "Baptism is a divine institution, pertaining to the kingdom of the Messiah, or the gospel dispensation" (Belcher, *Fuller's Works*, 3:339). Fuller appears to see baptism as a structural and institutional marker of the church. While he admits the appropriateness of baptism as a symbol of new life in Christ, he consistently grounds baptism in Christ's command rather than a holy tendency in the act itself. If the latter were true, baptism would be a moral duty and not merely a positive institution (341–42).

182. Belcher, *Fuller's Works*, 3:342. In his letter to William Ward in India, titled "Thoughts on Open Communion," Fuller offers other related points on the relationship between OT law and the command to baptize. He explains that baptism's significance "arises from its being the distinguishing sign of Christianity—that by which they were to be known, acknowledged, and treated as members of Christ's visible kingdom" (Belcher, *Fuller's Works*, 3:504–5). Furthermore, as opposed to the visible church being a mixed community of baptized and unbaptized professing believers, which would allow a "defective" profession of Christianity, one enters the church by verbal and baptismal profession. Entering this way "entitles, us to a place in Christ's visible kingdom."

While baptism is not a moral duty for Fuller, he clearly views positive institutions as signs which reinforce moral duties.[183] With respect to the Lord's Supper as a positive institution, Fuller concludes that the bread and cup with the words of institution in the church are essential to the meal,[184] while the use of unleavened bread, the accompanying agape feast, the time of day or day of the week, and the act of reclining are accidental.[185] Hence, Fuller consistently maintains that the church is duty-bound to follow the examples and principles of the New Testament in similar cases. On this logic, Fuller is unwilling to make any accidental element a "term of communion," because this would be to lay "bonds in things wherein Christ has laid none."[186] Positively though, because the ordinances are instituted "in connection" as positively institutions,[187] whatever is essential to each ordinance remains binding on the church. These hermeneutical categories shed light on Fuller's explicit arguments for close communion.

Fuller's "Letter to a Friend" (1814) is the most strenuous display of argumentation for strict communion in his corpus.[188] Fuller begins his letter

---

Thus, without believer's baptism, "our claim to visible communion must of course be invalid."

183. For example, baptism should reinforce orthodox trinitarian faith, as one marked by the divine name and should issue in a life of repentance. On the trinitarian significance of baptism, see Fuller and Haykin, "Admission of Unbaptized Persons," 68–76. In Fuller's circular letter entitled, "Practical Uses of Christian Baptism" (1802), he argues that baptism should "furnish motives for a faithful adherence to believe Christ's truth and obey his precepts" (Belcher, *Fuller's Works*, 3:339). Thus, Christ established baptism as a positive institution designed to promote piety in individuals and purity in the church (340).

184. Admittedly, Fuller's discussion is lacking in what would comprise essential aspects of the Lord's Supper. The features I listed are chosen because they appear throughout the discussion unquestioned and binding, though never listed as such by Fuller. See Belcher, *Fuller's Works*, 2:634–36.

185. Fuller explains, "There are also circumstances which may, on some occasions, accompany a positive institution, and not on others, which being, therefore, no part of it, are not binding. It is a fact that the Lord's Supper was first celebrated with unleavened bread; for no leaven was to be found at the time in all the Jewish habitations; but no mention being made of this, either in the institution or in the repetition of it by the apostle, we conclude it was a mere accidental circumstance" (Belcher, *Fuller's Works*, 2:634).

186. Belcher, *Fuller's Works*, 2:634.

187. Belcher, *Fuller's Works*, 2:634.

188. Interestingly, in the explanatory letter contained within the parcel to the friend, William Newman, Fuller wrote "I wish none to see it but yourself, and that no mention be made of it. If anything be written on the other side, it may, if thought proper, be printed, but not else" (Belcher, *Fuller's Works*, 3:508). Newman admits that the publication of Robert Hall Jr.'s *On Terms of Communion* (1815) rendered it proper to print the letter. Robert Oliver describes Hall's treatise as the ablest defense of open

by affirming Christian love for all those who belong to Christ.[189] Therefore, his unwillingness to commune with pedobaptists is not for want of love but out of a desire to follow "the revealed will of Christ."[190] Fuller does not refuse to partake of the Lord's Supper with pedobaptists "because I consider them as improper subjects, but as attending to it in an improper manner."[191] The impropriety stems from the fact that baptism and the Lord's Supper appear to maintain an "instituted connection" in the New Testament similar to that between faith and baptism.[192] Fuller recognizes pedobaptists and Baptists argue for open communion on different grounds. The former call Baptists to "give up your principles as Baptists that we may have communion together."[193] The latter see no instituted connection between the ordinances and claim the right for each individual believer to judge the validity of his or her own baptism. Fuller uses the remainder of the letter to address these two Baptist arguments.[194]

Fuller seeks to demonstrate that Christ instituted baptism and the Lord's Supper as connected ordinances by offering several evidences. First, historically, "it does not appear that such a notion [the unbaptized coming to the Lord's Supper] was ever advanced till [Bunyan] or his contemporaries advanced it."[195] Second, Fuller insists that those who claim no connection exists between the ordinances are often looking for a direct statement that baptism is prerequisite to communion, when in Scripture, "the ordinary

---

communion to appear in print in Oliver, *History of the English Calvinistic Baptists*, 244. Interestingly, it was Fuller's "Admission of Unbaptized Persons" letter that Robert Hall described as "the feeblest of all [Fuller's] productions" (Hall Jr., *Reply to the Rev. Joseph Kinghorn*, 68). Newman himself wrote on open communion with help from Abraham Booth before the latter died. Oliver, *History of the English Calvinistic Baptists*, 233.

189. For a similar take on Fuller's letter, see Clary, "Throwing Away the Guns," 95–96.

190. Belcher, *Fuller's Works*, 3:508.

191. Belcher, *Fuller's Works*, 3:508. Fuller cites Hezekiah's prayer for pardon for those who ate Passover while uncircumcised (2 Chr 30:17–19). Interestingly, John Bunyan appeals to the same passage to prove the legitimacy of communing with pedobaptists. See Bunyan, "A Reason of My Practice in Worship," in Offor, *Bunyan's Works*, 2:612.

192. Belcher, *Fuller's Works*, 3:509.

193. Belcher, *Fuller's Works*, 3:510. Similarly, see Hammett, *Forty Questions*, 270.

194. Similarly, in "Practical Uses of Christian Baptism," Fuller explains that if baptism had since its New Testament inception been given only to "those who professed to repent and believe the gospel," two ends would have been achieved: (1) none but professing baptized believers "would have been admitted to the Lord's Supper" and (2) the church would not have been constitutionally mixed to include all the people in a society (Belcher, *Fuller's Works*, 3:342).

195. Belcher, *Fuller's Works*, 3:510.

way in which the mind of Christ is enjoined in the New Testament, is by simply stating things in the order in which they were appointed and are to be practiced; and that this is no less binding on us than if the connexion had been more fully expressed."[196] Fuller then surveys the binding patterns of the ordinances in Scripture. In the New Testament, the participants in the Lord's Supper are always presumed to be, or stated as baptized.[197] Therefore, baptism, "must be necessary to an admission into a particular church, inasmuch as what is particular presupposes what is general."[198]

Besides the binding pattern created by examples in Scripture, Fuller sees an explicit connection between the ordinances in 1 Corinthians 12:13—he argues similarly to Kiffin—and 10:1–5. In 1 Corinthians 10, Paul urges the church not to indulge in sin while partaking of the privileges of Christ that typified baptism and the Lord's Supper. Fuller explains, the "manner in which these allusions are introduced clearly shows the *connexion* between the two ordinances in the practice of the primitive churches."[199] Fuller believes the New Testament connection between the ordinances is as conclusive as that between faith and baptism or the bread and the cup.

196. Belcher, *Fuller's Works*, 3:511.

197. Belcher, *Fuller's Works*, 3:511. Fuller presumes the disciples were baptized because they baptized others (John 4:2; cf. Acts 2:38–47; Acts 19:1–6). The normalcy of baptism is attested by the observation that not to be baptized would have been the anomaly.

198. Belcher, *Fuller's Works*, 3:512. Baptism then is analogous to an oath for entering the military. Although someone could take an oath without being a soldier, all soldiers must take the oath.

199. Belcher, *Fuller's Works*, 3:512.

Joseph Kinghorn

In his 1816 work *Baptism a Term of Communion*,[200] in response to Robert Hall Jr.,[201] Kinghorn warns that if mixed communion is adopted "the constitution of all of our dissenting churches will be altered."[202] If Hall's reasoning is adopted, dissenters would have to "plead not for the liberty of copying the apostolic church," but for the freedom to depart from their example.[203] Thus, Kinghorn deemed the central issue of the debate the relation of the ordinances to the constitution of the local church.[204] This section surveys Kinghorn's arguments for close communion followed by critiques of Robert Hall Jr.'s open communion arguments.

First, Kinghorn contends that baptism is prerequisite to communion because baptism was the visible rite of the profession of faith in Christ.[205] He continues, "If obedience to a rite be not a term of salvation, (which no one supposes) yet it was ordered by the highest authority, as an evidence

200. Joseph Kinghorn was born to David and Elizabeth Kinghorn at Gateshead in Durham county across the Tyne river from Newcastle. After several early apprenticeships, Kinghorn was converted at 14 and baptized at 16. He studied at Bristol Academy under Caleb Evans of Broadmead Church beginning in 1784. After graduating Bristol, Kinghorn was eventually called to pastor St. Mary's of Norwich in 1789, where he remained until his death in 1832. As a single man all of his life, Kinghorn's ministry is most noted for his clarity of thought in publishing *A Defense of Infant Baptism, its Best Confutation* (1795), *Scriptural Arguments for the Divinity of Christ* (1813), and the exchange with Robert Hall Jr. over mixed communion (1816–1827). For more on Kinghorn, see Olive, "Joseph Kinghorn (1766–1832)," in Haykin, *British Particular Baptists*, 2:84–111. The only existing biography of Kinghorn is Wilkin, *Joseph Kinghorn of Norwich*, 1:vii–475. For more on St. Mary's church and its eventual slip into open communion, see Gould, *Open Communion and the Baptists of Norwich*, xiii–liii.

201. Kinghorn recognized that the zealous evangelism of recent years promoted a unified vision of Christianity that tended to blur denominational distinctives. Kinghorn, *Baptism a Term of Communion*, 1. Naylor also discusses this effect of the revivals in connection with George Whitefield. See Naylor, *Calvinism, Communion, and the Baptists*, 126; Briggs, *English Baptists of the Nineteenth Century*, 3:62. For other minor publications that came in answer to Hall in 1816, see Oliver, *History of the English Calvinistic Baptists*, 244–45.

202. Kinghorn, *Baptism a Term of Communion*, 4.

203. Kinghorn, *Baptism a Term of Communion*.

204. For a similar take on Kinghorn's arguments, see Naylor, *Calvinism, Communion, and the Baptists*, 139–47.

205. Kinghorn, *Baptism a Term of Communion*, 18. Kinghorn explains, "It is granted, that baptism is not a term of membership with any particular church: for believers were first baptized, and then either formed into a church, or added to the church which already existed. But it is obvious, that their baptism was the term of professing their faith, by the special appointment of the Lord himself: so that those only who were baptized, would be admitted to the Lord's Supper."

of our submission to the author of salvation," Christian profession must require baptism.[206] Given these distinctions, it follows that "communion which required the profession of faith [during New Testament times] could not dispense with it."[207] To change baptism's function from the New Testament—visible connection to the church—is to change Christ's design for the church.[208] Second, the church must follow the primitive pattern. If one admits that the primitive pattern was strict communion, as Robert Hall did, one must either prove that the church should not follow the primitive pattern or else prove why the church should continue to baptize in a way unreflective of biblical norms.[209] Third, Kinghorn affirms a spiritual unity with pedobaptists, given their common faith in Christ and place in the true church.[210] Yet, pedobaptists intentionally constitute their churches

206. Kinghorn, *Baptism a Term of Communion*, 18.

207. Kinghorn, *Baptism a Term of Communion*, 19.

208. Kinghorn, *Baptism a Term of Communion*, 21. Kinghorn is more explicit and claims one cannot dispense with an institution of the church without changing its constitution, which includes a "profession of faith—baptism—and union with others in our obedience to Christ" (94). In order to prove that mixed communion conforms to the apostolic pattern, pedobaptists must demonstrate from the Scriptures that the early church baptized their infant seed. If infant baptism is a part of the primitive institution of baptism, the baptized children of believers must belong equally to the new covenant and the Christian church, by virtue of baptism's connective function with the church. Kinghorn does not acknowledge the common distinction made by pedobaptists between covenant members and church members. For him, one cannot be a member of the new covenant without being a member of the church. Kinghorn continues, "Without these three things, there can be no New Testament church. In primitive times no church did exist, or could exist without them. If we attempt to collect a church without baptism, we declare that the direct appointment of the Lord on that subject is not needful; and we form a body visibly different from that which distinguished the church in the age of inspiration. If we collect some who are, and others who are not baptized, we cannot maintain that such an assembly resembles the apostolic church in its unity; for they had one Lord, one faith, one baptism" (Kinghorn, *Defense*, 63). Kinghorn does not claim that baptism is necessary for Christian character per se, but that as Christ's appointed means of visible profession of faith, it is a "term" of communion. Kinghorn is not arguing that a new Christian can do nothing else to follow the Lord until baptized. Rather, he claims baptism is preparative "to any other duty or privilege separately considered" (121). Similarly, see Hammett, *Forty Questions*, 271.

209. Kinghorn, *Baptism a Term of Communion*, 25–26. Also critiquing Hall at this point, Timothy George notes the weakness of Hall's exegetical arguments. See George, "Controversy and Communion," 54.

210. Kinghorn, *Defense*, 48. He explains, "He who is unbaptized at present, from opposition to the dictates of the apostles, we suppose will not be considered in a different moral state from the unbaptized in their day. But he who admits the permanency of baptism, who confesses that every conscientious man ought to be baptized, who believes that he has been a subject of that rite in a valid form in his infancy, is not in the situation of those who refused to obey the dictates of inspired men. He pleads that they

on a different principle than do Baptists. Thus, no Baptist church should hold communion with pedobaptists unless they intend to validate their erroneous understanding of the church as consisting of believers and their children. Alternatively, not admitting pedobaptists to communion does not entail excommunication, unworthiness, or that the pedobaptist is an unbeliever. Rather, strict Baptists declare them "unqualified."[211] Fourth, although pedobaptists consider themselves baptized, Kinghorn (1) presumes that pedobaptists would not allow a Baptist to communion if the former believed the latter to be unbaptized and (2) posits the authority of each church to weigh the testimony of its candidates for communion and membership to determine whether they are biblically qualified.[212]

Positively, Kinghorn offers several critiques of open communion. First, Baptists cannot maintain their separation from the established church on solid grounding on open communion principles. The strict communion Baptist relates to the established church and pedobaptist dissenters on the same basis.

---

have been obeyed, and if he does not mean to acknowledge that his infant baptism is unscriptural, he pleads also that their dictates were obeyed in the required order, that he was baptized before he came forward to request communion. We differ from him we acknowledge, and we do not intend to represent the point of difference as less than it has ever been, but the nature of the difference is very distinct from what it would be, if he denied the authority of the apostles. For this reason, we treat him, not as a person who designedly opposes the dictates of the apostles, but as a mistaken good man. But still, neither will his excellencies in other parts of his character, nor our favourable opinion of him on the whole, fulfil the duty he has mistaken, or set aside our obligation to attend to the will of Christ, and support his ordinances as he delivered them."

211. Kinghorn, *Baptism a Term of Communion*, 61. Given the volatility of the matter, the following quote is helpful. Kinghorn writes, "[Strict Baptists] allow that their Pedobaptist brethren, on their own principles, do right in forming themselves into churches, and in commemorating the death of their Lord. Though they differ from the Baptists, yet they unite together those whom they deem properly baptized, and walk with them in Christian fellowship. In this the Baptists blame then not. They consider them wrong in their opinion of the first ordinance; yet, with their views, they consider them right in the second; and doubt not their conscientious regard to it. The objection of the strict Baptists to communion with them does not arise from suspicions attaching to their Christian character, to which, they trust, they are always willing to render ample justice; but from the necessary consequence of such communion, as a practical deviation from what they believe was the original constitution of the church" (67–68).

212. Fiddes misreads Kinghorn at this point. Whereas Kinghorn utilizes a voluntary society of human origin several times as an analogy for the church, Fiddes thinks Kinghorn is describing the church merely as a voluntary society. Rather, Kinghorn's argument is one from the lesser to the greater. If a human society can have terms for entrance, then certainly Christ's society of the church can have terms of entrance. See Fiddes, "Walking Together," in Brackney et al., *Pilgrim Pathways*, 69.

He tells him respectfully, but plainly, that his church is wrong in its very constitution; that it is formed of materials different from those used by the Savior, and that these materials are united together in a way totally diverse from that of his institution. The whole body is, therefore, taken in the aggregate, of a different character from that which is in the New Testament called the Church of Christ.[213]

Second, historically, Kinghorn demonstrates that virtually all churches—pedobaptists included—have held the connection between the ordinances since the early church.[214] Finally, several of Kinghorn's closing critiques of open communion include (1) it tends to the neglect of baptism; (2) it silences appeal to the New Testament; (3) it raises the importance of the Lord's Supper above that of baptism; (4) it turns baptism into a trifle compared to wont of fellowship; (5) it assumes that Scripture should prohibit the unbaptized from communion although the issue could not have arisen in the days of the primitive church; and (6) its defense is similarly unfounded in the New Testament as infant baptism is unfounded.[215]

For Kinghorn then, the connection between the ordinances does not itself constitute the church. The local church is constituted on a profession of faith that is made visible by baptism and on the decision of a group of those professing/baptized believers to walk together in obedience to Christ. The Lord's Supper is subsequent to baptism in its institution and dependent upon baptism in its design, in that communion is one of the commands of the Lord given specifically to the gathered church. Therefore, believer's baptism is prerequisite to communion. Disjoining or separating the ordinances through open communion alters the constitution of the church in two senses. First, mixed communion is contrary to the design and intent

---

213. Kinghorn, *Baptism a Term of Communion*, 127.

214. Kinghorn, *Baptism a Term of Communion*, 160. Thus, the proponents of mixed communion are singular in their sentiments and acting alone, while other churches are operating on the same premise. Even if Hall is correct that the churches of the third and fourth centuries received those baptized as infants and as believers to communion, it is a moot point unless those churches held that infant baptism was a nullity (Kinghorn, *Defense*, 194). For Baptists, who by definition hold to the perpetuity of baptism, to deny strict communion is to deny the arguments for perpetuity (34–35).

215. Kinghorn, *Baptism a Term of Communion*, 164–74. Briggs shares Kinghorn's critique that Hall was downplaying one ordinance in favor of the other such that both are diminished (Briggs, *English Baptists of the Nineteenth Century*, 3:63–64). Earlier in *Baptism a Term of Communion*, Kinghorn summarized Bunyan as arguing, "a person who believes himself to have been baptized, ought to be admitted to the Lord's Supper, by those who may not think his views of baptism correct either with respect to mode or subject" (15). For Kinghorn, Bunyan's argument tended toward the neglect of baptism.

of divine institutions. Second, mixed communion limits the basis of local church unity to spiritual unity. The confusion over the unity of the church exists because open communion blurs the lines between the church and the world by tacitly acknowledging infants who are sprinkled to be covenant seed and part of the church.

Summary of Strongest Arguments

The strongest arguments among the close communion advocates are important for the thesis of this monograph for several reasons.[216] First, this project does not seek to reinvent what earlier Baptists have helpfully argued. Second, this book reiterates two prominent arguments from these earlier Baptists intentionally because (1) those arguments are central to upholding the Baptist distinctive of regenerate church membership and (2) those arguments provide the discontinuous balance to how covenantal signs are applied in the New Testament compared to this book's constructive proposal—an argument based on the principle of continuity between the covenant signs of entry and participation. Third, the fact that Baptists have historically stated the argument for the principle of continuity without arguing for it does two things for this book: (1) it shows that this book's thesis is not novel, because other Baptists have thought similarly that the way one puts the whole Bible together (biblical theology) affects the issue of close communion but (2) it provides justification for the thesis of this book, because connecting the covenant signs across the canon as Baptists have historically done requires more attention than it has received historically. To those arguments we turn.

Several of the historic arguments for close communion deserve mention. First, this book utilizes two historic arguments in the thesis: (1) the New Testament presents a pattern of believers being baptized, and (2) the precedent of Acts 2:41 presents an order of belief, baptism, and the Lord's Supper. Chapter 3 presents the evidence for these arguments more thoroughly.

Close communion benefits from other significant arguments. First, several authors appeal to Christ's authority to command baptism and the

---

216. Contemporary Baptists who argue for close communion include Dever, *Display of God's Glory*, 52–53; *Church*, 38; Hammett, *Forty Questions*, 270–72; Allison, *Sojourners and Strangers*, 404; White, "Baptist's Theology of the Lord's Supper," in White et al., *Restoring Integrity in Baptist Churches*, 154; Wills, "Sounds from Baptist History," in Schreiner and Crawford, *Lord's Supper*, 285–86; Leeman, "Congregational Approach to Catholicity," in Leeman and Dever, *Baptist Foundations*, 369; Jamieson, *Going Public*. For other historical affirmations of close communion, see Dever, *Polity*. Close communion proponents include Benjamin Griffith (101, 111), the Charleston Association (123–24), J. L. Reynolds (391–92), and William Williams (540). A notable, historical volume defending close communion is Fuller, *Baptism, and the Terms of Communion*.

Lord's Supper for his church. If the church practices open communion, it willingly neglects an ordinance of Christ and thereby countervails Christ's authority. What would keep a local church from dispensing with the Lord's Supper as well if the same methodology continues? Second, baptism is presented theologically as the sign of entry and initiation into the (universal) church, that is normally administered by a local church. This sign of entry is followed by the sign of continuation and nutrition—the Lord's Supper. Thus, the meaning of the ordinances seems to require close communion. Third, believer's baptism is a safeguard to regenerate church membership, which entails close communion. If a church allows pedobaptists to receive the Lord's Supper on grounds that although in error the pedobaptist believes he is baptized, this practice allows a greater possibility of those who never profess faith in Christ joining the church and celebrating communion. Fourth, as previously stated, Baptists have historically argued that circumcision corresponds to baptism as a sign of entry into God's covenant people. Because circumcision was explicitly required for Passover, baptism should be understood as required for participating in the Lord's Supper. Fifth, Fuller's contention that Christ instituted baptism and the Lord's Supper in connection entails that the order and meaning of the ordinances leads to a close communion position. Finally, Kinghorn's emphasis on the constitutive nature of baptism for all professing Christians supports the close communion case. If baptism is Christ's means of visible profession whereby the new Christian publicly identifies with the church, and the Lord's Supper is an ordinance given specifically to local churches, baptism must precede communion.

Arguments for Closed Communion

Although J. R. Graves (1820–1893) is the best-known proponent of closed communion, this section also surveys the writings of B. H. Carroll (1843–1914) and Buell Kazee (1900–1976). Closed communion advocates hold that participation in the Lord's Supper is reserved for church members of the administering local church who have been baptized as professing believers. Closed communion is closely associated with the nineteenth-century phenomenon among Baptists in America known as Landmarkism.[217] Not

217. Landmarkism is an ecclesiological movement among Baptists in nineteenth-century America. Three of its proponents have been labeled the "Landmark Triumvirate" for their common adherence to Landmark views—J. R. Graves, James Madison Pendleton (1811–1891), and Amos Cooper Dayton (1813–1865). Garrett Jr., *Baptist Theology*, 213–17. James Patterson acknowledges J. R. Graves' address entitled the "Cotton Grove Resolutions" of 1851 as providing the central tenets of Landmark theology (Patterson, *James Robinson Graves*, 97). In that statement, Graves explains (1) that all

all pastor-theologians associated with Landmarkism have held to closed communion.[218] However, three significant arguments presented by the closed communion advocates below—which provide their distinctive emphasis in contrast to close communionists—are (1) the coextensive relationship between the Lord's Supper and church discipline; (2) the fact that the Lord's Supper is a local church ordinance; and (3) the relationship of the local church with its two signs of baptism and the Lord's Supper to the kingdom of Christ.

---

religious societies that are not organized according to the New Testament should not be considered true churches; (2) "such societies could not be recognized as 'gospel' churches; (3) clergy of such societies could not be recognized as 'gospel' ministers"; (4) pulpit affiliation is not an "appropriate practice"; and (5) "people associated with societies that were not true churches could not be addressed as 'brethren.'" In Graves' view, these tenets allowed local churches an appropriate autonomy and individual Christians the appropriate sovereignty over and accountability for their decisions. If the existence of true churches requires the right administration of baptism, then Baptist churches should reject "alien immersions," defined as the immersion of a professing believer that is not administered by Baptist church and pastor (Garrett Jr., *Baptist Theology*, 228–29). On this logic, the legitimacy of the believer's baptism rests in part on whether or not the person baptizing has been baptized by a Baptist minister. Accordingly, James Milton Carroll (1852–1931), B. H. Carroll's brother, proposed an historical argument for the tenets of Landmarkism in his 1931 work *The Trail of Blood*. In this work, he argues for "baptist successionism" or "perpetuity," affirming the existence of those churches that have baptized believers only upon a profession of faith since the days of John the Baptist (Patterson, *James Robinson Graves*, 101–15). Landmarkism combines each of these ecclesial matters in robust form. However, it is noteworthy that J. M. Pendleton only considered two items essential: (1) the rejection of alien immersions and (2) the rejection of pulpit affiliation with pedobaptist ministers on account of their being unbaptized by immersion as believers. See White, "James Madison Pendleton," 179.

218. Although he is considered part of the Landmark Triumvirate, J. M. Pendleton held to close communion (Garrett Jr., *Baptist Theology*, 226). While Pendleton largely agreed with Graves, he made several qualifications. First, the prerogative to extend the invitation to the Lord's Supper rests with the local church; yet, local churches may welcome other Baptists as a matter of courtesy. Second, while Pendleton held that each church had the responsibility to guard the purity of the Table, he maintained that close communion did no harm. Finally, Pendleton allowed close communion because it did not compromise the Landmark position that neither pedobaptist ministers nor alien immersions are valid. See White, "James Madison Pendleton," 176–79. White notes helpfully that A. C. Dayton died before the communion debate ensued (186). Additionally, while not all Landmark theologians hold/held closed communion, closed communion has been argued by those who did not identify with Landmark theology. See the section on B. H. Carroll below. Note also the volume by Graves's contemporary Jeremiah Bell Jeter (1802–1880) entitled *Baptist Principles Reset*. Therefore, one might say that while Landmark theology lends itself to the closed communion view, it does not require it.

J. R. Graves

Graves's theology was most influential during the nineteenth century among Baptists in the south.[219] Although Graves wrote multiple works on ecclesiological issues, *Intercommunion: Inconsistent, Unscriptural, and Productive of Evil* (1881) is his most sustained argument for closed communion.[220] Graves addresses a variety of connected issues, but this section focuses on two theological arguments for closed communion: (1) the relationship between the church and the kingdom and (2) the nature of the Lord's Supper as a local church ordinance. Then, he answers scriptural objections and presents challenges to his opponents regarding the failures of intercommunion—anything besides local church member only communion.

Graves makes much of the relationship between the church and the kingdom. He defines a local church as "a body of professed believers in Christ, scripturally baptized and organized, united in covenant to hold 'the faith,' and preserve the order of the gospel, and to be governed in all things by the laws of Christ."[221] While many Baptists of Graves's day defined the

219. The page numbers for the subsequent biographical sketch refer to Patterson, *James Robinson Graves*. Graves is best known for his staunch articulation of Baptist identity as the editor of The Tennessee Baptist newspaper. Originally born in Vermont into a Congregationalist family, Graves was converted and baptized into the North Springfield Baptist Church in 1834. Graves relocated to Kentucky in 1841 and was ordained in 1842 (7–11). He married and moved to Nashville in 1845, where he joined the First Baptist Church, pastored by R. B. C. Howell (1801–1868) (34). Due to his connection with Howell, Graves assumed full control of the Tennessee Baptist in 1848, a post he maintained for the next forty years. A steady controversialist already, further conflict ensued between Graves and Howell upon the latter's return to FBC Nashville in 1857. The controversy is complex (123–25). In October 1858, Graves was excluded from church membership on charges of divisiveness and unchristian conduct toward his pastor (141–44). By the end of his life, Graves served as a military chaplain in the Civil War and, after 1867, lived in Memphis, where he continued to work as a Baptist newspaper editor until his death in 1893 (184–88). For more on Graves, see Hall, "When Orphans Became Heirs," 112–27; Smith, "J. R. Graves," in George and Dockery, *Baptist Theologians*, 223–48.

220. Indeed, James Patterson describes this work as Graves' "most definitive statement on the need for restricted communion" (Patterson, *James Robinson Graves*, 173). For clarity's sake, Graves describes himself as a "close-communion Baptist," meaning local church members only communion. Given the inconsistent usage of close and closed throughout the literature, this book utilizes the term "closed" to designate local church members only communion (Graves, *Intercommunion*, 320). Graves allowed for close or denominational communion through the 1850s according to Smith, "J. R. Graves," 241. However, Graves published his change of heart in the Tennessee Baptist in April of 1875 according to White, "James Madison Pendleton," 172.

221. Graves, *Intercommunion*, 139. Harold Smith clarifies that for Graves, "While salvation does not depend on baptism, church and kingdom membership does. Therefore, in order to enter the kingdom of God, the subject must be a Christian who has

universal church as "all existing denominations professing to be churches,"[222] the New Testament's focus is the local church.[223] For Graves, because church means "assembly,"[224] he is willing to speak of a collective of churches that compose the kingdom.[225] While the kingdom has no officers (save Christ the King) or ordinances, kingdom implies organization and visibility.[226] The kingdom is spoken of in future terms in Scripture until Christ's advent. So, it follows that the while the kingdom did exist in heaven before Christ, it did not exist *on earth* before the establishment of local churches.[227] Given that all local, visible Baptist churches constitute the kingdom, Graves denies the existence of the kingdom in heaven during this age.[228] Graves is unwilling to speak of all true Christians or all churches as the universal church, because this church never gathers. In this sense, he denies the existence of an invisible, universal church.[229] Instead, those passages which some utilize to teach the universal church refer to local, visible assemblies.[230] If the New Testament speaks exclusively of the local church rather than the universal church, the Lord's Supper "could not have been delivered as a denomination ordinance, but as a local church ordinance only."[231] Therefore, Graves's view of the local church negates the concept of intercommunion.

The fact that the Lord's Supper is a local church ordinance serves as another argument for closed communion. Graves carefully delineates the essential qualities of a church ordinance: "(1) that it is a rite, the duty of

---

been baptized into a local, visible Baptist church." Smith, "J. R. Graves," 239. Understandably then, "Membership in the kingdom and redemption from sin are two entirely different relations. A person can be a Christian without being in the kingdom."

222. He cites J. M. Pendleton et al. in Graves, *Intercommunion*, 109–11.

223. Graves, *Intercommunion*, 106.

224. Graves, *Intercommunion*, 112.

225. Graves, *Intercommunion*, 107.

226. For a similar take on Graves' theology of church and the kingdom, see Garrett Jr., *Baptist Theology*, 217–23.

227. Graves, *Intercommunion*, 151.

228. Smith, "J. R. Graves," 239.

229. On this point, see Duesing, "A Denomination Always for the Church," in Allen, *SBC and the Twenty-First Century*, 116–17.

230. Graves, *Intercommunion*, 130. Graves has in mind Acts 9:31; 1 Cor 12:28; Matt 16:18; etc. Graves' interpretation of Matt 16:18, "upon this rock I will build my church," is especially interesting. He claims, "the figure here is a metonymy, which means a change of terms, and church is used for kingdom and is the fulfillment of the prophecy of Daniel 2:44" (134). He explains the use of *ekklesia* (church) in Ephesians as a "synecdoche, in which what is logically predicated of the whole may be predicated of each of its parts" (135).

231. Graves, *Intercommunion*, 139.

perpetuating which is committed to the visible churches, as such; (2) the qualifications of its recipients must be decided by the members of the churches as such; (3) any rite which symbolizes church relations can only be participated in by the members of the church celebrating, and is pre-eminently a church ordinance."[232] These marks entail that the Lord's Supper cannot be given to any but a particular, local church without ceasing to be a local church ordinance. The significance of these claims is vast. Graves claims, "It is my conviction that misapprehension of the true nature and limitations of a church ordinance has given rise to all the discussions, mis-understandings . . . and prejudices . . . against us by other denominations, as well as the present disagreement among Baptists."[233] Therefore, Graves argues his point.[234] He holds that the Lord's Supper is a local church ordi-nance because (1) each church possesses "absolute independence" under Christ;[235] (2) each church has sole guardianship of its ordinances (cf. 1 Cor 5:9–11);[236] (3) "all who can be entitled to the Supper must be subject to its discipline";[237] and (4) the Lord's Supper "symbolizes church relations" since apostolic times.[238] Opening the table beyond a local church's member-ship causes the ordinance to no longer truly symbolize one body partaking of one bread; thus, the open table "vitiates and nullifies" the ordinance.[239] Clearly then, for Graves, no other group besides the gathered, local church members should receive the Lord's Supper.

Next, Graves answers several objections to his view regarding breaking bread together (Acts 2:42) and from house to house (2:46), Graves responds,

232. Graves, *Intercommunion*, 166.

233. Graves, *Intercommunion*, 167.

234. Patterson recognizes the following points to be crucial to his argument as well. See Patterson, *James Robinson Graves*, 174.

235. Graves, *Intercommunion*, 168.

236. Graves, *Intercommunion*, 170. Regarding Christ's unique authorization of local churches to administer the ordinances, Graves writes, "That to the church, as such, Christ delivered the ordinances, and constituted each one responsible for the purity of its administrations," to the end that "a scriptural church cannot be constituted without them" (287).

237. Graves, *Intercommunion*, 174. He provides three points of explanation for this argument: (1) Christ has not given anyone the right to commune with a church that does not have "watch and care" over them; (2) Christ does not require that other churches open their tables to nonmembers, since participation in the meal itself "declares he is a member" (1 Cor 10:17); and (3) those churches that do invite nonmembers to com-mune "violate the command of Paul—to allow no disqualified person to participate," given the moral certainty that such an occasion does arise when the table is opened.

238. Graves, *Intercommunion*, 174.

239. Graves, *Intercommunion*, 270.

"[In Acts 2:42] the Supper is undoubtedly referred to, while [in Acts 2:46] it is the noun without the definite article" combined with "the context [that] also determines it to have been a common meal."[240] Although some churches invite Christians from outside their membership for the sake of courtesy, Graves concludes that such a practice "contravenes one of [Christ's] own appointments."[241] Graves charges those who receive the Lord's Supper upon pastoral invitation when they visit a church with the error of eating and drinking unworthily.[242] With respect Paul's so-called visiting communion at Troas (20:7), Graves claims that breaking bread in this instance was not a communion celebration because (1) Paul had not hitherto visited the city; (2) no church yet existed there; (3) no ministers are mentioned; and (4) Luke does not use an article before the phrase "break bread."[243] The meal shared in Acts 20 then should be understood as a normal meal in the context of pastoral training.

For Graves, anything other than closed communion suffers from several faults. Given the one loaf and one body image of 1 Corinthians 10:17, churches that allow non-members to participate do not practice or have church communion, but only denominational communion. Those who do not practice closed communion are not able to properly guard the table, which is their divinely appointed charge.[244] Furthermore, churches with open tables act inconsistently when they exercise church discipline for any reason, because they do not know that someone worse than those they disciplined may be communing with them on any given week.[245] Intercommunion "subverts the divine constitution of the church of Christ," because the visiting Christian and the church claim authority that Christ has not granted.[246] With Christ's authority dismissed through intercommunion, the "independency of each local church" is "destroyed," because churches cannot rightly fence the table or discipline the participants.[247] Practically speaking, Graves charges that intercommunion stirs up strife between local churches and "renders abortive the discipline of the excluding church" in a case of church discipline.[248] Again, intercommunion weakens church

240. Graves, *Intercommunion*, 225.
241. Graves, *Intercommunion*, 183.
242. Graves, *Intercommunion*, 271.
243. Graves, *Intercommunion*, 341–52.
244. Graves, *Intercommunion*, 308.
245. Graves, *Intercommunion*, 309.
246. Graves, *Intercommunion*, 311.
247. Graves, *Intercommunion*, 312–14.
248. Graves, *Intercommunion*, 316.

membership, by providing former church members with the ability not to join a new church and yet still exercise the privileges of membership.[249]

B. H. Carroll

B. H. Carroll offers much of his theology in the form of sermons to the First Baptist Church of Waco.[250] The pastor states his position clearly:

> We believe the Scriptures teach that Christian baptism is the immersion in water, of a believer, by a qualified administrator, to show forth in a solemn and beautiful emblem our faith in the crucified, buried and risen Savior, with its effect in our death to sin, burial from the world and resurrection to newness of life; that this baptism is a prerequisite to the privileges of a church relation, among which is the Lord's Supper, in which the members of the church, by the sacred use of bread and wine are to commemorate together the dying love of Christ; always preceded by solemn, self-examination.[251]

This definition highlights that the group which may participate in the meal is the "members of the church."[252] Presenting Carroll's case for closed commu-

---

249. Graves, *Intercommunion*, 319.

250. The following biography gleans largely from Sampler, "Whosoever Is 'Qualified' May Come," 81–82. After his birth in Carroll County Mississippi, Benajah Harvey Carroll spent most of his childhood in Arkansas before moving to Texas in 1858. He entered Baylor University in 1858, but enlisted in the Confederate Army soon after. After being wounded in 1864, Carroll was converted in 1865 and ordained in 1866. In 1871, he became pastor of the Baptist Church in Waco, Texas, where he remained for twenty-eight years. He resigned in 1898 to become head of the Texas Baptist Education Commission and Dean of the Bible Department at Baylor. He was instrumental in establishing Southwestern Baptist Theological Seminary (SWBTS), first in Waco in 1905 and then in Fort Worth in 1908, where he served as President until his death in 1914. While the majority of his publications are of printed sermons, Carroll's influence on Southern Baptists initially as a Trustee of Southern Seminary during William Whitsitt's presidency and later at SWBTS earned Carroll an important place in Baptist history. For more on Carroll, see Crisp, "B. H. Carroll," 159–65. For a standard look at Carroll's life, see Ray, *B. H. Carroll*.

251. Carroll, "Discussion of the Lord's Supper," in *Christ and His Church*, 143.

252. Interestingly, Garrett cites Spivey, "Benajah Harvey Carroll," in George and Dockery, *Baptist Theologians*, 319, for the claim that B. H. Carroll practiced close communion, allowing baptized members of other Baptist churches to commune (Garrett Jr., *Baptist Theology*, 235–36n111). Spivey cites Carroll's sermon, "The Meaning of the Lord's Supper," as evidence for Carroll's affirmation of close communion among Baptists (328n122). Upon inspection however, no such reference may be found. Carroll's most descriptive answer to who may participate in the Lord's Supper comes in the sermon, "Some Observations on the Lord's Supper" (Carroll in Crowder, *Supper*,

nion requires a brief examination of his ecclesiology, his arguments for why baptism must precede the Lord's Supper,[253] and his answers to objections.

Similar to J. R. Graves, B. H. Carroll emphasizes the particular and local nature of the church in the New Testament. Because the vast majority of New Testament uses of term *ekklesia* ("church") refer to a local, visible company of baptized spiritual saints, Carroll rejects the notion of an invisible church. Instead, wherever a generic sense of the term is used, its use "is prospective and not actual."[254] On this logic, the universal, invisible church does not exist in this redemptive era. Furthermore, it has no ordinances, no officers, and does not assemble in this age.[255] Similarly, because the church "is a particular congregation and not an organized denomination,"[256] Carroll's limitation of the Lord's Supper to disciplinable local church members is understandable.[257] Whereas open communion among Baptists in Carroll's day stressed denominational unity, Carroll stressed "obedience to Christ."[258]

To the question of why baptism is prerequisite to communion, Carroll responds with several arguments. First, baptism was appointed and practiced before communion (John 3:22–23, 4:1; Matt 26:26). Second, the commission commands making disciples, baptizing them, and teaching them to commune (Matt 28:18–20), "For communion is one of the things He had commanded them to observe."[259] Third, "the apostles so understood this order by their practice" because Acts presents Peter calling for repentance, baptism, church fellowship, and breaking bread.[260] Fourth, while Paul's requirement for self-examination may appear sufficient, Carroll argues that Paul was addressing a congregation that Acts 18:1–11 reports had believed

---

7–26). However, Carroll never affirms or implies his approval of close communion in the book. Sampler's dissertation does not acknowledge any debate over the issue. See Sampler, "Whosoever Is 'Qualified' May Come," 81–87.

253. For a helpful synthesis of Carroll's view on who is qualified for both church membership specifically and the Lord's Supper more generally, see Sampler, "Whosoever Is 'Qualified' May Come," 81–87. Sampler describes Carroll's qualifications for church as regeneration and baptism. Carroll presents the qualifications for the Lord's Supper as regeneration, believer's baptism, church membership, and rightly discerning the body.

254. Carroll, *Baptists and Their Doctrines*, 43. He cites Heb 12:23 for example.

255. Carroll, *Baptists and Their Doctrines*, 40–51.

256. Carroll, *Baptists and Their Doctrines*, 25.

257. Summarizing pedobaptist Timothy Dwight approvingly, Carroll explains that communion and church discipline are co-extensive (Carroll, "Discussion of the Lord's Supper," 140).

258. Carroll, "*Discussion of the Lord's Supper*," 149.

259. Carroll, "*Discussion of the Lord's Supper*," 151.

260. Carroll, "*Discussion of the Lord's Supper*." 151.

and been baptized. Fifth, "The Scriptures make baptism an initiatory ordinance . . . the emblem of the beginning of spiritual life."[261] Sixth, the "analogy between the Lord's Supper and Jewish Passover; and some analogy between circumcision and baptism" shows that "no unbaptized man must eat of the Lord's Supper."[262] Carroll concludes by appealing to the universality of the principle that "baptism must precede communion" across "all denominations."[263] This universal principle reveals that the argument over restricted communion is an argument over what counts as baptism.[264]

Carroll next answers objections. Whereas Robert Hall was willing to open communion to Christians who remained unbaptized on account of their weakness of conscience, Carroll urges Hall's allies to also accept Hall's grounds in order to affirm his conclusion.[265] Whereas some argue that the future communion in heaven justifies communion on earth, Carroll answers that the communion of heaven is spiritual rather than of bread and wine.[266] Whereas some claim that closed communion bars Christian union, Carroll cites Charles Spurgeon's lack of union with the British Evangelical Alliance despite Spurgeon's open communion views.[267] Some urge that open communion tends to "perpetuate Baptist churches."[268] However, the pastor cites the history of Bunyan's Bedford church as evidencing a tendency for open communion churches to lose Baptist identity all together. Contra the open communion advocates, Carroll argues that open communion "is the entering wedge of death to our churches." Practicing open communion is so significant and sinful for Carroll that he urges Baptist churches to admonish members who participate in open communion, withdrawing fellowship from them if they persist, and to remove any Baptist pastor who leads his congregation in the practice.[269]

261. Carroll, *"Discussion of the Lord's Supper,"* 152.

262. Carroll, *"Discussion of the Lord's Supper."* Carroll is quick to point out that "baptism did not come in the place of circumcision."

263. Carroll, *"Discussion of the Lord's Supper,"* 153.

264. Carroll, *"Discussion of the Lord's Supper,"* 154.

265. Carroll, *"Discussion of the Lord's Supper,"* 156.

266. Carroll, *"Discussion of the Lord's Supper,"* 159.

267. Carroll, *"Discussion of the Lord's Supper,"* 161.

268. Carroll, *"Discussion of the Lord's Supper,"* 163.

269. Carroll, *"Discussion of the Lord's Supper,"* 165. In the end, Carroll indeed argues that open communion is sin. He lists eight reasons: "(1) It violates the law of God making it a church ordinance. They set their table 'out of the kingdom.' (2) It is a sin, because it gives the bread and wine to the unconverted. (3) It is a sin because given to the unbaptized. (4) I impeach it of the sin of substitution. God's reason for communion is superseded, and it is received to show Christian fellowship and to unite husband and wife. (5) It is treason, in that it makes void the law of discipline. (6) It is sin in being used

Buell Kazee

Kazee argues for closed communion in *The Church and the Ordinances* (1965).[270] Although his position is similar to J. R. Graves, he writes nearly a century later with different emphases. The three primary arguments he presents for closed communion are (1) Baptist churches should not receive those baptized from unscriptural churches; (2) scriptural baptism is necessary to participate; and (3) the Lord's Supper is a fellowship ordinance.

First, the baptism should be received from a scriptural church. For Kazee, Baptist churches should not receive a believer from a church of a different denomination, because churches must be unified in their understanding of salvation and how they interpret salvation.[271] Because baptism and the Lord's Supper are part of the interpretation of salvation, those churches and which make baptism essential for salvation or which do not immerse, are not scriptural churches.[272] Furthermore, their baptisms are understood as "alien" in the sense that those who administrated the baptism held a different theology of baptism than Baptists.[273] For Kazee, Paul's question in Acts 19:3, "into what were you baptized," demonstrates the authority of the churches to determine the validity of baptism for those desiring fellowship with them.[274] Kazee's aim is not sectarian. Instead, he looks forward to the day when all Christians will be united in heaven. Yet, because "error can be subtle and fatal," separation is necessary "wherever we cannot agree on the

---

as a 'means of grace.' (7) It is a sin in that it seeks the destruction of Baptist churches. (8) It is a sin, in that it is founded upon a sickly sentimentality, an affected charity, and upon fallacies and sophisms, and teems with glaring inconsistencies" (166–67).

270. From Lexington, KY, the title page of *The Church and the Ordinances* describes Kazee as a pastor, Bible teacher, conference speaker, and writer (Kazee, *Church and the Ordinances*). At the time of publication Kazee still lived in Lexington. Kazee is known to broader audiences through his skill for banjo playing and folk music. His best known recordings were "The Little Mohee" (A version of On Top of Old Smokey that sold over fifteen thousand copies) and "The Roving Cowboy." See Brennan, "Musical Bio of Buell Kazee." He also published *Faith is the Victory* (1951). Kazee was educated at Georgetown College. As a young adult, he served the congregation at First Baptist Church Morehead, Kentucky, as a Calvinistic Baptist Pastor for twenty-two years. In the Fall of 1952, he began as a full time professor of Old Testament at the Lexington Baptist College. He died in 1976 in Winchester, KY. See Williams, "Buell H. Kazee"; Smith, "Morehead Baptists Appreciate the Labors."

271. Kazee, *Church and the Ordinances*, 110.

272. Kazee, *Church and the Ordinances*, 111.

273. Kazee, *Church and the Ordinances*, 97, 118.

274. Kazee, *Church and the Ordinances*, 112.

vital interpretation of how our experience took place" (e.g., the interpretation of baptism).[275] Therefore, he claims,

> The candidate for baptism and church membership does not submit to the ordinance for any other reason than to receive the symbolic expression of what that church teaches on the matter of salvation. . . . We see, then, that baptism is not something which the candidate for membership brings to the church, that is, something of his own or origination, but rather something he receives from the church, the recognition which the church gives to one who makes a confession in accord with that church's belief.[276]

Clearly then,

> To accept a baptism or a Lord's Supper which declares that we have been saved some other way [sacramental views] or that is administered by those who teach that our salvation is experienced or declared otherwise [e.g., baptismal regeneration], is, indeed, to break fellowship with those whose administration of the ordinances do correctly declare the gospel of a full salvation.[277]

All of this leads Kazee to conclude that only those churches that agree on a theology of the ordinances are true churches. Thus, no one baptized in any church other than a Baptist church may be received as a member or join in communion.

Although the validity of the church matters for who may take the Lord's Supper, Kazee also argues the need for scriptural baptism in order to participate. Immersion of a professing believer by a Baptist church, such that the act is viewed in "purely symbolic" terms constitutes scriptural baptism.[278] Baptism is the "sign of . . . public recognition and identification" as a child of God, as circumcision was for the Israelites.[279] According to Colossians 2:11–13, "circumcision and baptism are directly related in meaning." This is because they both symbolize "death to the flesh and cleansing to the life."[280] So, not only does the validity of the church depend in part on the

275. Kazee, *Church and the Ordinances*, 113.

276. Kazee, *Church and the Ordinances*.

277. Kazee, *Church and the Ordinances*, 126.

278. Kazee, *Church and the Ordinances*, 109, 122.

279. Kazee, *Church and the Ordinances*, 114. Relevant for this book is Kazee's comment, "Not all Israelites were saved people, but they were all types of saved people. Circumcision was associated with Israel in an institutional sense."

280. Kazee, *Church and the Ordinances*, 113.

church's understanding of baptism, the nature of the baptism considered in itself renders a Christian qualified to receive the Lord's Supper.

Kazee's third argument for closed communion is that the Lord's Supper functions as a "fellowship ordinance," such that its participants declare themselves to be in fellowship with each other.[281] He explains,

> [The Lord's Supper] declares that you are in fellowship with the church of which you are a member, otherwise you would have no right to partake of the Supper with even that church. How then can you logically go to another Baptist church where you have no recognition and which has no supervision over your fellowship and participate in the ordinance as if you were a member? Are you not [with your words denying] in such cases that there's a real functioning universal-invisible church as far as baptism is concerned, but recognizing that there is a universal-Baptist Church where all Baptist who are denominationally reputable may join in the Lord's Supper [by your actions]? Are you not making baptism a local church ordinance, while at the same time you are making the Lord's Supper and ecumenical ordinance?[282]

Kazee is clearly writing to an audience that he believes follows his theology in denying the existence of the universal-invisible church. Earlier in the book, he claims that the universal-invisible church cannot exist because, among other reasons, it does not meet, has no officers, and cannot function as a body.[283] Nonetheless, his point is clear. If a church cannot exercise discipline toward every person that receives its communion, that church cannot credibly declare the fellowship of each participant.[284] He writes,

> Let us say it another way. When we accept baptism from a church, we belong to that church. We are under its guidance and care. Not only is [his] approval for baptism give him by that church, but the approval also of our daily walk is its responsibility. If we are out of fellowship with our church, we have no right to participate in the Lord's Supper with it until our fellowship has been restored. The only church which could be in a position to know our spiritual status is the one to which we belong. Logically we could not go to another church and expect it to decide whether or not we are eligible to take the Lord's Supper. While

281. Kazee, *Church and the Ordinances*, 124.

282. Kazee, *Church and the Ordinances*.

283. Kazee, *Church and the Ordinances*, 5–30.

284. Kazee, *Church and the Ordinances*, 122.

our fraternal relationship [extends to] all Baptists, yay, even to all children of God, our covenant relationship in the gospel Proclamation is with the church of which we are members.[285]

For Kazee, only closed communion makes sense.[286]

Summary of Strongest Arguments

Among closed communion advocates, the connection between the Lord's Supper and church discipline appears most consistently.[287] If a church is to lead the congregation to participate worthily and to discern the body of Christ rightly, while at the same time exercising its responsibility for purity through church discipline, closed communion advocates claim these requirements necessitate closed communion. The tight connection between the church's responsibility to seek its own purity through church discipline and the limitations on a local church to guard the purity of the table when non-members participate serves as the strongest argument for closed communion.[288] Indeed, the tight connection between church discipline and the Lord's Supper is the primary distinction between closed communion and close communion. Secondarily, the closed communionists' insistence that

285. Kazee, *Church and the Ordinances*, 125. The timing of Kazee's plea for tighter communion restrictions among Southern Baptist is interesting, given the dramatic growth of Southern Baptists during the 1950s and 1960s. His knowledge of this fact appears as he ends the book. He writes, "Do we not have the greatest number we have ever had? Are not our organizations admired by much of the religious world? Is not efficiency and training our trademark? In spite of all this, do we have to admit worldliness and weakness? If we moved the test of fellowship back to the ordinances where it belongs, we might decimate our numbers, but we might also become purer and stronger."

286. Kazee, *Church and the Ordinances*, 123. Given these distinctions though, Kazee distinguishes between what he describes as closed communion, meaning denominational communion, and close communion, meaning local church only. While he switches the terms from that utilized in this book his position fits with that of J. R. graves above, who, it was noted, also described himself as a proponent of close communion.

287. For a brief, contemporary defense this view, see Riddle, "Piper's Baptism and Membership Proposal." Despite calling the paper a "Neo-Landmark Response," Riddle disagrees with the Landmark movement that "non-Baptist churches are only religious societies and not true churches." Furthermore, he never actually defends the local church only view of the Lord's Supper. I cite him here due to his self-assigned title.

288. Commenting on J. R. Graves' view, Thomas White describes this point by stating, "Close[d] communion can all but ensure the integrity of the Lord's Supper because only members of that local church are allowed to participate. This understanding has the easiest time adhering to Paul's warnings in 1 Cor concerning the oneness of the body and not eating with a person such as the man mentioned in 1 Cor 5" (White, "Baptist's Theology of the Lord's Supper," 159).

the Lord's Supper was given by Christ to the local church specifically serves to highlight the proper administrators of the meal and proper context in which it is to be enjoyed.

Arguments for Ecumenical Communion

For the purposes of this work, ecumenical communion normally refers to the view that all Christians should be received at communion in any given local Baptist church on the basis of a common process of initiation that includes a profession of faith, baptism (by affusion, sprinkling, or immersion on a subject that may be an infant, a child, or an adult),[289] and sometimes confirmation in some unspecified order. While this affirmation is the baseline for ecumenical communion, for the purposes of this project the label also serves as a catch-all for those views that allow an even broader group to participate in communion in a Baptist church.[290] For instance, this

289. One distinction between ecumenical communion and open communion lies in the willingness of ecumenical communion advocates to affirm the validity of a mode and subject of baptism besides the immersion of a professing believer when that "baptism" is considered part of the larger process of initiation. As Curtis Freeman points out, open communion advocates such as Bunyan and Spurgeon did not believe that pedobaptism was truly baptism. Instead, they were willing to hold communion with those they viewed as unbaptized according to the NT's definition of baptism. Ecumenical communionists do not open the Table to those they would describe as "unbaptized." Rather, they open the table to those whose initiation process happens to be different than their own. While the open communion advocates ground unity in a common faith or work of the Spirit without baptism, ecumenical communion advocates ground unity in a common initiation that includes some form of baptism (Freeman, *Contesting Catholicity*, 379).

290. The description above draws from the helpful distinctions made by Haymes et al., *On Being the Church*, 85–86. The authors seem to recognize a difference between open communion an ecumenical communion by distinguishing those churches that have followed John Bunyan's lead from those that additionally have aligned with the World Council of Churches and/or Great Britain's Baptist Union with its efforts and proposals related to promoting "Churches Together in England" (CTE). Interestingly, the authors claim that one difficulty in affirming unity based on a common baptism centers on whether pedobaptists view conversion baptism as re-baptism or not. Finally, the authors' solution to these debates requires accepting one another despite real issues of conscience in such a way that "differences of interpretation and practice of baptism should not be an excuse for division in the church" (87). Similarly, Freeman shows how the *Baptism, Eucharist and Ministry* (BEM) document, which was developed by the World Council of Churches (WCC), does not go far enough in locating unity in a "common baptism" based on Eph 4:5. Instead, the Baptist World Alliance has clarified this proposal to speak of a "whole journey of initiation." If baptism is merely shorthand for the whole conversion process, then the whole conversion process, which may include pedobaptism or credobaptism, should be recognized as legitimate (Freeman, *Contesting*

section includes those who view participation in the Lord's Supper as a converting ordinance. This section demonstrates that adherents of ecumenical communion generally ground their view, at least in part, on some form of sacramental theology.

Paul Fiddes

In Paul Fiddes's work *Tracks and Traces: Baptist Identity in Church and Theology* (2006) he seeks to show that the concept of covenant is essential for a proper understanding of the church.[291] Because he grounds his arguments for ecumenical communion in the idea of covenant, this section surveys Fiddes's teaching on covenant before moving to his arguments for ecumenical communion.[292]

When a local church covenants to walk together in following the Lord, Fiddes claims that God is at work through that human action.[293] Fiddes does not believe it is an accident that the term "covenant" is flexible enough to be employed both in terms of an eternal covenant of grace, whereby the triune God covenants to save sinners through Christ, and in terms of a local church covenant.[294] The dual usage of covenant is important for Fiddes because he argues that "the relation between the local covenant bond and the eternal covenant offered to all humankind will be analogous to the relation between a particular local congregation and 'the invisible company of God's elect.'"[295]

Catholicity, 376). Emir Caner uses the term "Laissez-faire Communion" to refer to the same view that this book calls ecumenical communion (Caner, "Fencing the Table," in White et al., *Restoring Integrity in Baptist Churches*, 173). Caner cites Covenant Church in Houston, TX, as an example of this view.

291. A four-time graduate of Oxford University, Fiddes served at Regent's Park College as a fellow and tutor in theology from 1972 to 1989. At that time, he became principal of the college, a post he held until 2007. Born in 1947 in Upminster, England, Fiddes identifies as a Baptist theologian, who intentionally engages with the wider Christian community through his writings and ecumenical leadership. His writings include a rejection of the doctrine of the impassibility of God (*The Creative Suffering of God*, 1988) and a centrality of participation in God through a critical appropriation of process theology (*Participating in God*, 2000). See Garrett Jr., *Baptist Theology*, 680–81. See also the preface to Fiddes's *Tracks and Traces* and the discussion by Harmon, "Trinitarian Koinōnia and Ecclesial Oikoumenē," 20–22. For further admission of Fiddes's method and way of relating covenant and participation, see Fiddes, "Covenant and Participation," 119–37.

292. For a brief look at Fiddes's contributions to ecumenical theology, see Harmon, "Trinitarian Koinōnia and Ecclesial Oikoumenē," 19–22.

293. Fiddes, *Tracks and Traces*, 18.

294. Fiddes, *Tracks and Traces*, 24–31.

295. Fiddes, *Tracks and Traces*, 32.

By putting the divine covenant and human covenants together in this way, Fiddes argues that the priority of the covenant of grace logically precedes the formation of local church covenants. Similarly, in terms of the covenant of grace, the universal church "pre-exists any local manifestation of it."[296] Therefore, whenever a local church covenants together, in the words of B. R. White, the action "actualize[s] in history" the eternal covenant, and, for Fiddes, serves as the formal entry into the pre-existing universal church.[297] Fiddes summarizes the theological pay off for putting these pieces together, stating, "a theology of covenant is thus of strategic importance in identifying the mission of God and sharing in it. This is also why the Baptist doctrine of the local church should lead it to be thoroughly ecumenical."[298]

Before considering how Fiddes works out his ecumenical vision, two factors on the relationship of the ordinances to the concept of covenant deserve mention. First, by virtue of its covenanting together, a local church officially "comes under the direct rule of Christ and so has been given the 'seals of the covenant'—that is, the power to elect its own ministry, to celebrate the sacraments of baptism and the Lord's Supper, and to administer discipline (the authority to bind and loose)."[299] Second, the ontological and logical priority of the covenant to the sacraments requires that a believer is not baptized into church membership, but must rather, as a distinct act, covenant together with the church to enter its membership.[300] With these theological connections in mind, Fiddes offers three positive arguments for ecumenical communion: (1) the need for different ways of belonging to the church; (2) the sacramental nature of the ordinances and church; and (3) the need to recognize different processes of Christian initiation. These arguments require further explanation.

First, Fiddes acknowledges the ways that believer's baptism often excludes persons from full inclusion into the community, and the Lord's Supper specifically. Those often excluded are believing children, pedobaptists, those who are on their way to faith ("half-believers"), and people with disabilities or mental illness.[301] In order to address the infants, Fiddes encourages the practice of infant blessing. While not unlike child dedication services, Fiddes views infant blessing as a moment of divine activity when

296. Fiddes, *Tracks and Traces*.

297. Fiddes, *Tracks and Traces*.

298. Fiddes, *Tracks and Traces*, 33.

299. Fiddes, *Tracks and Traces*, 33.

300. Throughout this section of Fiddes's book, he interacts heavily with historic Baptist figures and sources. Nevertheless, the position outlined above appears as that which he affirms and not merely what he reports (Fiddes, *Tracks and Traces*, 30).

301. Fiddes, *Tracks and Traces*, 126.

the church and parents pray for the prevenient grace of God for the child.[302] While these infants "are not yet members of the body of Christ . . . we might say . . . that they belong in the sense that they are embraced by the body, like a child enfolded in its mother's arms."[303] In this broader, more open framework of church membership, churches can receive those who are not yet baptized believers as people who rightly belong to "the community which is called 'the body of Christ.'"[304] That reception "declare[s]" a "promise for the child, to be fulfilled in due time."[305] With those children (and those with disabilities), assuming they are exercising a "childlike faith" and "on the journey of being formed as a member," Fiddes argues "they cannot be excluded from the table which identifies members.[306] In sum, "The boundary of baptism . . . creates a space in which many different people can live. It excludes none from fellowship, while it does mean that people will belong to the Christian community in different ways; not all will belong as disciples through baptism, but may belong as those who are 'on the way towards faith' and who are embraced by the body."[307]

Fiddes's second argument for ecumenical communion stems from his sacramental understanding of the ordinances and church.[308] Baptism, he explains, provides a link between grace and nature in the sense that it "actually communicates the presence of the transcendent God. . . . [The water] provides places and opportunities for a transforming encounter."[309] Further,

302. Fiddes, *Tracks and Traces*, 131.

303. Fiddes, *Tracks and Traces*, 133.

304. Fiddes, *Tracks and Traces*, 151.

305. Fiddes, *Tracks and Traces*, 152.

306. Fiddes, *Tracks and Traces*, 184. He further counsels, "Only those believing children who have previously been received [by infant blessing] should be received at the Table, and they should be enrolled in a group preparing for baptism later as a believer, namely the 'catechumenate'" (185).

307. Fiddes, *Tracks and Traces*, 155.

308. For a brief treatment of the relationship between Fiddes's ecumenism and sacramental ecclesiology, see Harmon, "Trinitarian Koinōnia and Ecclesial Oikoumenē," 22–27.

309. Fiddes's descriptive language is striking. He writes, "All this means that if the drama of baptism is properly arranged, the contact with the element of water should arouse a range of experiences in the person baptized and in the community which shares in the act. Immersion into water, with both its shocking and pleasurable sensations can evoke a sense of descent into the womb, or washing away of what is unclean, and encounter with a hostile force, a passing through a boundary marker, and reinvigoration. In all these aspects, water is a place in the material world that can become a rendezvous with the crucified and risen Christ" (Fiddes, *Tracks and Traces*, 117). Fiddes connects his understanding of metaphysics to the relationship between nature and grace. He explains, "In Jesus Christ, God is committed to the utmost extent to

the sacrament of baptism "focuses the presence of God," such that "when the baptismal candidate, or the community which witnesses the baptism, encounters God anew through this particular water, they will be more aware of the presence of God in other situations [besides baptism]."[310] Thus, baptism is intended by God to be a meeting place of grace and faith, where the covenant is forged and the Spirit is sealed with the believer (cf. 1 Cor 12:13).[311] Understandably then, the Lord's Supper is the sacramental instrument by which "Christ takes hold more firmly of [the church members'] own bodies and uses them as a means of his presence in the world."[312] The Lord's Supper also "constitutes the church as community."[313] The Supper's constituting power comes by "enabling the presence of Christ with his people, and that sharing in the table identifies the membership of the church." Furthermore, the church itself "becomes a sacrament" because it is an "extension of the incarnation."[314] On this sacramental basis, Fiddes argues, "We might discern a distinctly Baptist concept here of unity through the body of Christ, both locally and universally."[315] The unity celebrated in the Lord's Supper is that of the universal body of Christ, sacramentally communicated through the elements. Therefore, all those who receive the sacraments as members of the body of Christ from any denomination or tradition should offer and receive the Lord's Supper together because they are already in full communion with each other by virtue of their communion with God in the sacraments.[316]

---

materiality, to human flesh. But with the eternal decision of God to be identified totally (in act and being) with a human son, and with the eternal decree that this son should be the means of creating a new human community, God is also committed to taking on the whole body of the universe. Human flesh is after all entangled with the entire organic structure of the cosmos; it could not exist without this context and community in which it is embedded" (118). Fiddes's interpreters and students have seen fit to describe Fiddes's theology proper by stating that he utilizes a "critical appropriation of aspects of process thought forms." See Harmon, "Trinitarian Koinōnia and Ecclesial Oikoumenē," 22. Although Harmon describes Fiddes's work *Tracks and Traces* as the ecclesiological outworking of Fiddes's relational concept of God, it is beyond the scope of this book to explore Fiddes's metaphysical/theological underpinnings in his other works (23–24).

310. Fiddes, *Tracks and Traces*, 119.

311. Fiddes, *Tracks and Traces*, 145–48.

312. Fiddes, *Tracks and Traces*, 157.

313. Fiddes, *Tracks and Traces*.

314. Fiddes, *Tracks and Traces*, 170.

315. According to one Fiddes interpreter, while Fiddes does not affirm a "one-world church," he does emphasize "churches in full communion with one another," characterized by "unity in diversity, rooted in the triune God's unity in diversity." See Harmon, "Trinitarian Koinōnia and Ecclesial Oikoumenē," 28.

316. Fiddes, *Tracks and Traces*, 195.

Fiddes's third argument, and most thoroughgoing theme throughout the book, grounds ecumenical communion in the idea that initiation into Christianity is a process. He explains, "The very notion of believer's baptism, which requires someone already to profess faith before being baptized means that there will always be a gap between entering upon salvation (conversion) and baptism."[317] For Fiddes, acknowledging a temporal gap entails acknowledging a process of initiation.[318] Acknowledging the process of initiation allows Fiddes to affirm other legitimate processes (e.g., infant baptism) whereby other Christians are initiated. He explains, "Without abandoning their convictions, Baptists might be able to value and affirm someone's *whole* journey of experience, and not just the moment of public profession of faith on which attention is usually fixed; they might be able gladly to recognize how God has used every stage of the journey, including baptism in infancy, for saving purposes."[319]

If churches recognize a "common pattern of Christian initiation rather than a common baptism . . . an ecumenical way forward would be to place whole journeys of Christian beginnings alongside each other."[320] Having an open table and open membership is the result of recognizing the commonalities in the process of initiation, recognizing that an individual or church's judgment about baptism could be wrong, and receiving those Christ has received.[321] Consistency then requires Baptist churches to decline baptizing those previously baptized as infants in order to avoid delegitimizing their initiation processes.[322]

Cross, Gouldbourne, and Haymes

In their 2008 work,[323] *On Being the Church: Revisioning Baptist Identity*, Anthony R. Cross, Ruth Gouldbourne, and Brian Haymes propose a form of

317. Fiddes, *Tracks and Traces*, 136. Believer's baptism for Fiddes is rightly seen as a "disciple's baptism," whereby he or she takes up the responsibilities of "carrying our cross, suffering opposition for the sake of Christ, and sharing in the mission of God in the world."

318. Fiddes, *Tracks and Traces*, 137.

319. Fiddes, *Tracks and Traces*, 141.

320. Fiddes, *Tracks and Traces*, 181–82.

321. Fiddes, *Tracks and Traces*, 183.

322. Fiddes, *Tracks and Traces*, 219.

323. Anthony Cross is an historical theologian, trained at Bristol Baptist College, who completed his PhD on the subject of baptism as an evangelical sacrament at Keele University. He has served as an editor in academic publishing for Paternoster, a Fellow of the Centre for Baptist History and Heritage at Regent's Park College, Oxford, and a member of the faculty at the University of Oxford (2010–2016) (Cross, "Revd Dr

ecumenical communion on several grounds. Following the Baptist Union's suggested phraseology for inviting "all who love the Lord in sincerity and truth" to receive the meal, the authors ask, "Might there be occasions when we want to throw the invitation to table open to all who wish to come?"[324] The authors proceed to ground the ecumenical invitation on six principles: (1) The similarities between Jesus' shared meals with sinners in the Gospels; (2) the need for grace and threat of judgment for all who receive the meal; (3) the assumption that those who have already made the effort to attend a local church's worship demonstrate an interest in Christ by choosing to receive the meal; (4) the idea that the Lord's Supper is a converting ordinance; (5) the similarity between an open invitation to the Lord's Supper and the openness of baptism to those who may not have yet demonstrated discipleship in their lives; and (6) the recognition that most people experience faith as a journey. This section briefly surveys these arguments.

First, the authors suggest that the Lord's Supper echoes all of the meals that Jesus shared with even "promiscuous" companions. They explain, "We might argue that this meal is part of that whole series in which Jesus ate with those who were not necessarily within the household of faith in the fullest way, and yet wanted, to some extent, to be with him." They follow with a question: "Can we be more restrictive" than Jesus? Second, because all who come to the Table do so by grace and "with the challenge of judgment," they suggest the invitation should be commensurate with those realities. Third, rather than making it impossible for those who have not "named the reality of faith in their lives" to share in the meal, churches could open the invitation to any in attendance who might choose to come. The authors presume that in the context of local church worship, participating in the meal is not compulsory for anyone. Therefore, churches could offer the meal to all who are willing on the assumption that those who participate "have some

---

Anthony R. Cross"). His most relevant individual monographs on baptism and Baptist life are *Recovering the Evangelical Sacrament*; *Baptism and the Baptists*; "Baptists and Baptism," 104–21. Ruth Gouldbourne serves as a Senior Research Fellow with the International Baptist Theological Studies Centre of Amsterdam. She earned a PhD in historical theology from the London School of Theology and has served as a Tutor at Bristol Baptist College (1996–2006). See Goodliff, "Reflecting on Ministry"; Gouldbourne, "Revd Dr Ruth M B Gouldbourne." Gouldbourne's research interests also concern Baptist identity. See Gouldbourne, *Reinventing the Wheel*. Brian Haymes is former Principal of Northern and Bristol Baptist Colleges (1986–1994, 1994–2000). He served as President of the Baptist Union of Great Britain (1993) and Minister of Bloomsbury Central Baptist Church (2000–2005), London, according to the back cover of *On Being the Church*. Haymes has also written on issues of Baptist identity. See Haymes, *Question of Identity*.

324. This statement and the discussion that follows is found in Haymes et al., *On Being the Church*, 138–39.

interest in the story we have been telling." Fourth, they question the notion that the church should question the validity of someone's participation in the Lord's Supper due to a lack of baptism. They add, "Might we find ways of taking seriously the idea that the Table is a converting ordinance, and allow those who as yet do not call themselves Christians to receive and explore." Thus, viewing the Lord's Supper as a potentially converting ordinance justifies full inclusion.

Two other arguments round out Haymes, Goldbourne, and Cross's appeal. They recognize a pattern in some churches of admitting people to baptism on a profession of faith without necessarily committing "to helping people live disciple-lives." This openness to baptism, they claim could be extended to the Lord's Supper by allowing those who have not yet professed faith in Christ or discipleship to receive the meal. Finally, they acknowledge the normative role of the Lord's Supper as nourishment for church members and a "place of discipline" for straying members. However, due to the journey-like nature of faith, they propose opening the Table "to those . . . whose faith is barely formed and unexpressed." On this reasoning, the Table would not function as a place of discipline "except insofar as the judgment of God is proclaimed there along with mercy." In the end, the authors promote an open Table at which the only prerequisite is the individual's decision to receive the elements; yet, they maintain a "more restrictive baptism," in which the church looks for signs of authentic commitment before proceeding with that latter sign.

Anthony Clarke

Clarke[325] recognizes a "typical [British] Baptist understanding of the Lord's Supper connects it strongly with baptism."[326] He qualifies this statement by acknowledging "In an ecumenical context baptism as a believer is not

---

325. Clarke affirms an ecumenical communion position in a single essay found in Anthony R. Cross's, *Baptist Sacramentalism 2*. Clarke is the Senior Tutor and Tutorial Fellow in Pastoral Studies and Community Learning at Regent's Park College since 2007. He has served in pastoral ministry in Dagenham and Oxford and studied the interplay between New Testament studies and doctrinal formation. His educational pedigree includes an MA and BD from Oxford and Dmin from Chester University. He has worked closely with Paul Fiddes during his tenure at Regent's Park. Clarke, "Dr Anthony Clarke." See Clarke's works *Within the Love of God*; *For the Sake of the Church*.

326. Clarke, "Feast for All?," in Cross and Thompson, *Baptist Sacramentalism 2*, 93. For a strikingly similar analysis of the same biblical texts for the purpose of encouraging a "radically inclusive Table," see Canoy, "Perspectives on Eucharistic Theology," 179–201.

required," given the participant has "active faith."[327] Then, Clarke presents his intention to "offer an alternative understanding of the relationship between baptism and communion, based on an alternative reading of the key biblical texts and an exploration of some of the wider theological issues, looking to find creative ways to make the Lord's Supper open to all as an experience of grace."[328] Therefore, while Clarke's essay is a reflection on open communion, he clearly intends to push the boundaries of open communion and encourage an ecumenical communion. This section considers his arguments from key New Testament texts and wider theological issues.

Clarke examines passages relating to Jesus' "practice of table fellowship, those that contain Jesus' teaching relating to the great banquet . . . and those that deal more directly with the Lord's Supper."[329] While many have taken Paul's warning against eating the Lord's Supper in an unworthy manner (1 Cor 11:27) as a warrant to fence the Table from unbelievers, Paul's concern has more to do with the strong rich excluding the weak poor.[330] With respect to Paul's instructions, Clarke concludes (1) Paul is not seeking to fence the Table at all, but rather to admonish the rich in Corinth to demonstrate gracious hospitality and (2) Paul commends an attitude of "generous self-giving."[331] Paul's teaching in 1 Corinthians 10:16–17 that those who share in communion together become one body and participate in a "covenant-making event" toward another conclusion:[332] Paul is not arguing for "fixed boundaries" for who participates in communion. Instead, he "leaves open the possibility that individuals can enter the covenant" for the first time through sharing in the Lord's Supper.[333] Finally, because Jesus celebrated the Last Supper with Judas the traitor and the other disciples who had let him down, Jesus presents "more open boundaries" of participation than does Paul.[334]

Jesus' shared meals and his descriptions of the great banquet supply Clarke's final scriptural evidences. Clarke views each example of shared table fellowship as either "prefiguring or echoing" the Last Supper.[335] Given

---

327. Clarke, "Feast for All?," 331.

328. Clarke, "Feast for All?," 93–94. Similar is Canoy, "Perspectives on Eucharistic Theology," 209.

329. Clarke, "Feast for All?," 99.

330. Clarke, "Feast for All?," 101–2.

331. Clarke, "Feast for All?," 102.

332. Clarke, "Feast for All?," 103.

333. Clarke, "Feast for All?," 105.

334. Clarke, "Feast for All?"

335. Clarke, "Feast for All?," 106.

the way Jesus receives the woman at Simon's house (Luke 14:1–14), "We see in Jesus someone who, rather than erecting fences, deliberately dismantles those erected by religious tradition."[336] Bringing together Jesus' shared meals with Paul's teaching "suggests that a radical invitation in our own celebration of communion might best proclaim the life and death of Jesus."[337] Furthermore, the eucharistic function fulfilled by the feeding of the five thousand in John 6 "suggests that the invitation to the Table is open and welcoming," an offer "of sheer grace."[338] In the most detailed exegesis of the article, Clarke contends that the parable of the great banquet (Luke 14:15–24) presents a model for calling all people to participate in the eschatological kingdom feast which may be experienced in the present through communion.[339] From these exegetical arguments, Clarke turns to theological themes.

Clarke's first theological theme is the sacramental nature of communion, which he believes encourages an open Table. As a general principle, not a necessity, he contends "The more we . . . stress communion as a means of grace, the greater the possibility there is for communion to be a space in which faith is found rather than only reaffirmed."[340] By sacramental, Clarke refers to the notion that those who participate in the Lord's Supper "indwell the story" of Jesus and have "the free grace of God . . . mediated through created reality" to them.[341] Thus, although the gospel story is told and the communion meal is "entrusted to" the people of God, neither the story, nor "the Table are restricted to the church."[342] With this understanding, children, for example do not have to wait until they believe and are baptized or until they can express some level of love and child-like faith in the Lord. Instead, children can be received into communion without any prior commitment, "as a way into the story and grace of God."[343]

Clarke recognizes that even those who share his sacramental theology want some connection between baptism and communion that his openness does not provide. Clarke acknowledges that the first believers in Acts were baptized to enter the covenant community before they we "nourished by breaking bread."[344] However, the tradition of baptism before communion,

---

336. Clarke, "Feast for All?"
337. Clarke, "Feast for All?"
338. Clarke, "Feast for All?," 107.
339. Clarke, "Feast for All?," 107–9.
340. Clarke, "Feast for All?," 110.
341. Clarke, "Feast for All?," 111.
342. Clarke, "Feast for All?," 112.
343. Clarke, "Feast for All?"
344. Clarke, "Feast for All?," 113.

stems from the social context of newly forming communities rather than a dominical rule. Therefore, Clarke proposes an alternative to seeing baptism as initiation and communion as nourishment. He writes,

> Baptism is a clear boundary marker in which both faith in Christ is declared and an individual is incorporated into membership of the covenant community. Communion on the other hand, may be a covenantal occasion in that the promises of the covenant are proclaimed and celebrated and the invitation to find God's grace is offered. The church will then be both a baptized and eucharistic community. It will be a baptized community, for this will be the boundary marker that marks the decisive entry of disciples into the community. It will be a eucharistic community, because the Table will be at the heart of the church's experience of God, but not because communion will act as a boundary marker in the same was as baptism. Rather the Table will be a place of grace for all those 'on the way,' which can include those on the way to baptism and those on the way of their Christian journeys post-baptism. In this way the two sacraments can function in complementary ways, baptism declaring the membership of the church and communion proclaiming its openness to the world.[345]

Clarke concludes by contrasting an open and closed Table. Whereas a closed Table communicates that "some will be excluded from the final banquet," the open Table communicates a sense of "provisionality" as it looks to the future banquet at which "some will have chosen not to be there."[346] Thus, in light of the mission of the church, Clarke offers a vision of "radical inclusion" to a Table that is "truly open," in hopes that "we may find the Lord's Supper to be a converting ordinance in an even deeper way" than did John Wesley in a church-state.[347]

Summary of Strongest Arguments

What should be clear from viewing the arguments presented in this section is that ecumenical communion is distinct from open communion.

---

345. Clarke, "Feast for All?," 114.

346. Clarke, "Feast for All?," 115.

347. Clarke, "Feast for All?," 115–16. It is important to note that while Clarke clearly affirms ecumenism, he never describes his view as ecumenical per se. His affirmation of ecumenism and use of the terms "radical inclusion" and "truly open" warrant his placement under the category of ecumenical communion.

Curtis Freeman explains that Jessey and Bunyan would receive persons to communion on the basis of a profession of faith without regard to that person's baptism, on the (implied) principle that "faith rather than baptism is necessary to membership."[348] By contrast, the ecumenical view seeks to maintain the necessity of baptism (defined more broadly that Baptists normally would) for church membership, and, at the same time, to uphold the Baptist doctrines that the subjects of baptism are professing believers and the mode is immersion. The ecumenical communion advocates hold these ideas in tension, by claiming that "the validity of baptism [belongs] to each person's own individual experience and judgment." At the same time, the local church's responsibility is to insist that the "link between faith and baptism is strong and intentional."[349]

While the impulse toward ecumenical communion is not new, some of the arguments promoted in favor of ecumenical communion are more recent.[350] The strongest argument for ecumenical communion, and that which appears to have the most traction among Baptists friendly toward ecumenism, is the notion that Christians may claim a common process of initiation. If one's initiation to Christianity contains similar elements (e.g., belief, baptism, confirmation) even while the order of those elements may be different, churches should not quibble over the order. Instead, the churches should affirm each individual's journey of faith by inviting all to participate in the Lord's Supper together.

Two other arguments for ecumenical communion deserve mention. Several of the authors seek to uphold believer's baptism by immersion and an ecumenically open Table by inviting any who choose to participate in communion to do so. At the same time, they restrict baptism to professing believers whose lives display some level of discipleship. When making this argument, ecumenical communion advocates sometimes claim the Lord's Supper to be a converting ordinance. However, the authors also leverage Pauline texts, sacramental understandings of the ordinances, and the covenant-forming nature of the Lord's Supper to promote this argument. If baptism can be a boundary marker between the church and the world while

---

348. Freeman, *Contesting Catholicity*, 379.

349. Freeman, *Contesting Catholicity*, 379.

350. Briggs recognizes a similar impulse between Bunyan's practice of open communion based on a doctrine of baptism without the practice of baptism and that which ecumenical theologians espouse. In Briggs's words, both groups "seek to focus on the spiritual experience that lay behind baptism rather than the experience itself" (Briggs, "Two Congregational Denominations," 100). While the point stands, the difference between Bunyan's description of the spiritual experience of Christians and the ecumenical theologians' descriptions of sacramental theology remain some distance apart.

the Lord's Supper remains an open meal, the ecumenical view seems to allow for historical faithfulness to Baptist doctrine and an inclusive openness to a world in need of salvation.

Finally, the ecumenical communion advocates surveyed here appeal to Jesus' meals with sinners and parables of banquets in the Gospels to make their case. Indeed, they have a strong case if, as they claim, Jesus' willingness to eat with sinners and his indiscriminate invitations to the final kingdom feast provide determinative instruction to churches on whom should be allowed to participate in the Lord's Supper. One cannot be swayed by their arguments without admitting that the biblical examples they marshal are intended not only to instruct churches on the availability of Christ's salvific work to all people who will believe, but also to give directives on how Christ's community is to relate to the world.

Conclusion

This chapter has surveyed four major answers to the question of who may participate in the Lord's Supper. Two middle positions present themselves—open communion and close communion. Among Baptists, both of these views recognize the scriptural mandate for all who would follow Christ to be baptized by immersion as professing believers. Yet, they come to different conclusions on who may be admitted to the Lord's Supper. On the spectrum of views, this chapter has also presented arguments from two views on either extreme—ecumenical communion and closed communion. Despite the vast difference in how these views answer the question of who may be admitted to the Lord's Supper, both of these groups also affirm that the New Testament teaches believer's baptism by immersion. Therefore, the major differences between the four views do not center on the question of the New Testament teaching on who is to be baptized and by what mode. Rather, the differences emerge in precisely the areas this book seeks to address: the relationship of the ordinances to the new covenant, the relationship of the ordinances to each other, the relationship of the ordinances to individual believers, the relationship of the ordinances to the church (local and universal), and the relationship of the ordinances to the kingdom of God. This book will take up each of these matters in turn in chapter 6.

The most significant fact this survey reveals is the way Baptists have asserted or denied the legitimacy of this book's thesis without biblically arguing their view. This project argues that the necessity of circumcision before Passover under the Mosaic covenant (Exod 12:43–48) should lead new covenant churches to expect baptism to be necessary for participation in the Lord's Supper. John Bunyan flatly denies this line of argumentation. This survey reveals that Bunyan and Booth provide the most thorough argumentation respectively against and for the legitimacy of this book's thesis. Nevertheless, they do not provide an in depth biblical-theological argument on the relationship of circumcision to Passover compared to the relationship of baptism and the Lord's Supper. Thus, while this chapter provides helpful biblical arguments that should not be ignored as this book proceeds, this chapter also serves to reveal the need for the constructive thesis of this book, to which we turn.

Chapter 2

Circumcision and Passover
in the Old Testament

HAVING CONSIDERED SEVERAL HISTORICAL arguments for who may participate in the Lord's Supper, this chapter takes the first step toward presenting
the constructive proposal of this project. While addressing the biblical-
theological debates over the proper recipients of the new covenant signs of
baptism and the Lord's Supper, Stephen Wellum writes, "The only way to
resolve this issue is to think through the relationships between the biblical
covenants," which he and Peter Gentry do in *Kingdom through Covenant*.[1]
Then, Wellum urges, "One must be careful of reading new covenant realities into the old without first understanding the Old Testament rite[s,
of circumcision and Passover,] in [their] own covenantal context." Only
after this step can one "carefully thin[k] through the issues of continuity
and discontinuity."[2] So, to forecast a bit where the constructive proposal is
headed, this chapter thinks through circumcision and Passover in their own
covenantal context. Chapter 3 does the same thing with baptism and the
Lord's Supper, so that chapter 4 can present continuities and discontinuities
between the covenantal signs. Considering the signs in this covenantally
sensitive manner, this book argues, will provide the biblical grounds for affirming close communion.

While several theologians surveyed in chapter 1 mentioned the relationship of circumcision to Passover in their discussion for or against the
necessity of baptism for participation in the Lord's Supper, they did not offer
extended argumentation for their assertions. The aim of this chapter is to

1. Gentry and Wellum, *Kingdom through Covenant*, 78.
2. Gentry and Wellum, *Kingdom through Covenant*.

demonstrate that the Old Testament consistently presents circumcision as prerequisite to participation in the Passover. Making this argument requires four steps: (1) presenting the function and meaning of circumcision in the Abrahamic covenant; (2) tracing the typological development of circumcision in the Mosaic covenant; (3) presenting Passover as a covenantal celebration meal of the Mosaic covenant; and (4) surveying the Old Testament celebrations of Passover with attention to how circumcision relates to those meals. These steps appear crucial to discerning the proper participants of the Lord's Supper.

The Institution of Circumcision in the Abrahamic Covenant

God initiates the covenant with Abram in Genesis 12 and establishes and ratifies that covenant in Genesis 15.[3] Therefore, a summary of the promises given to Abraham when the covenant was established deserves mention, though this section relies heavily on the exegetical work of others.

Summary of the Abrahamic Covenant

After the table of nations recorded in Genesis 10 and the scattering of the nations in Genesis 11, God's call to Abram signals the next step in God's worldwide redemptive plan (cf. Gen 3:15).[4] In Genesis 12:1–3, God promised to make Abram into a great nation, to bless him, to make his name great, and that "in you all the families of the earth will be blessed."[5] Thus, Wellum describes the Abrahamic covenant as "the paradigm of God's dealings with humankind."[6] Given the fallen state of humanity and God's promise of a future, rescuing seed of the woman in Genesis 3:15, the Abrahamic covenant

---

3. The vocabulary utilized here with respect to stages in the elaboration and development of the covenant with Abraham are drawn from Gentry and Wellum, *Kingdom through Covenant*, 230–93.

4. Mathews, *Genesis*, 2:105–6.

5. All Scripture citations are from the ESV unless otherwise indicated. Some in Baptist history (e.g., Thomas Baldwin) have argued that the constellation of God's promises to Abraham recorded in Gen 12; 15; 17; and 22 are not indicative of the one covenant with Abraham. See Baldwin, *Baptism of Believers Only*, 174–94. One contemporary non-Baptist who argues for two covenants with Abraham in Gen 15 and 17 respectively is Williamson, *Sealed with an Oath*, 89.

6. Wellum, "Baptism and the Relationship between the Covenants," in Schreiner and Wright, *Believer's Baptism*, 128.

serves "as the means by which God will fulfill his promises."[7] While God's dealings with Abraham present the patriarch as a new Adam, they also forecast, and eventually serve as the grounds of guaranteeing, the Mosaic, Davidic, and new covenants.[8]

These redemptive-historical observations are significant for this work because they reveal that in the storyline of Scripture, God's covenantal dealings with Abraham encompass, and are the means of God's provision of salvation to, the whole world. God's people at this redemptive stage—those connected with Abraham—eventually testify to their identity through the covenantal sign of circumcision. Abraham's role in redemptive history suggests that circumcision will mark out the people of the Abrahamic covenant from the world. Yet, the worldwide reach of the Abrahamic promises also suggests a worldwide role for the covenant sign, though the relationship of circumcision to foreigners would require further revelation.

In Genesis 15 God reaffirms his promise of descendants for Abram (vv. 1–5) and declares Abraham's right standing before him, on the basis of Abram's faith (v. 6).[9] Verses 7–20 record God's ratification and elaboration of the covenant that was initiated in Genesis 12. God would give Abram land (15:7, 16–20).[10] Yet, his descendants would arrive in that land only after an exodus from slavery (v. 13). In verses 17–18, God ratifies his promises to Abram by passing through the cut carcasses of the animals (cf. v. 9) in the form of a smoking firepot and blazing torch.[11] In so doing, God took upon himself the full obligation for the fulfillment of his promises.[12]

---

7. Wellum, *Relationship between the Covenants*, 129.

8. For a fuller explanation of this point, see Gentry and Wellum, *Kingdom through Covenant*, 130–32.

9. Mathews helpfully demonstrates that Gen 15:6 is not the initiation of Abram's faith but the continuation of it with God's formal declaration of Abram's standing before him. See Mathews, *Genesis*, 2:167.

10. Development of the land promise is beyond the scope of this book. However, for authors that treat the land promise with the same hermeneutical method as this book, see Gentry and Wellum, *Kingdom through Covenant*, 703–16; DeRouchie, "Counting Stars with Abraham and the Prophets," 460–61; Martin, *Bound for the Promised Land*.

11. In Gen 15:17, covenant ratification is God's formal, promissory act whereby he seals the agreement between the two parties and binds them to uphold their obligations. In this case, God takes full responsibility for upholding the covenant stipulations/promises. For a description of covenant ratification, see Gentry and Wellum, *Kingdom through Covenant*, 253–56; Mathews, *Genesis*, 2:172; Stuart, *Exodus*, 551.

12. God's actions here have often been described as a self-maledictory oath based on a comparison with Jer 34:18–20. Each of the following volumes treats this notion in a balanced fashion: Mathews, *Genesis*, 2:172; Gentry and Wellum, *Kingdom through Covenant*, 256.

Circumcision in the Abrahamic Covenant

Genesis 17 serves to codify and confirm the Abrahamic covenant.[13] Although in verse 10, Moses initially describes the covenant as circumcision by synecdoche (the sign for the thing signified), verse 11 makes clear that circumcision is the "sign of the covenant."[14] John Meade delineates five helpful aspects of the rite of circumcision:[15]

> (1) the act of circumcising the flesh of the foreskin (v. 11a); (2) circumcision will be a sign of the covenant between Yahweh and Abraham and his descendants (v. 11b); (3) every male (including offspring and anyone bought with money from a foreigner) shall be circumcised on the eighth day (v. 12a); (4) Yahweh's covenant in Abraham's flesh will be an eternal covenant (v. 13b) and (5) the one who has not undergone circumcision shall be

---

13. Gentry and Wellum, *Kingdom through Covenant*, 275–80; Meade, "Circumcision of Flesh," in Wellum and Parker, *Progressive Covenantalism*, 129; Deenick, *Righteous by Promise*, 19, 41. Each of these authors argues that *heqim berit* refers to confirming or upholding an existing covenant rather than starting a new or, literally, cutting a covenant (*karat berit*).

14. Benton, "Genesis 17:9–14," 13. Circumcision functions as a covenant sign in a way similar to the Noahic sign of the rainbow and the Mosaic sign of the Sabbath. Circumcision's sign function is (1) as a "mnemonic cognition sign," intended primarily to remind Abraham of his covenantal obligations to walk before the Lord and be blameless; (2) a "symbol sign," intended to "represent future reality by virtue of resemblance or conventional association (e.g., Ezek 4:1–3); and (3) as "an identity cognition sign," intended to "rouse knowledge" of one's identity. Although the rainbow (Gen 9:13–17), circumcision, and the Sabbath (Exod 31:13–17) are all covenant signs, the first functions primarily as a reminder to God, while the latter two function primarily as reminders to the covenant people. Although other objects are denoted as signs in the OT (e.g., blood of the Passover lamb; Exod 12:13), the three signs mentioned here are unique in their direct linkage with the term covenant. See DeRouchie, "Circumcision in the Hebrew Bible and Targums," 184–85.

15. Meade provides a helpful and lengthy analysis of the origin of the rite of circumcision in Meade, "Meaning of Circumcision in Israel," 35–45. His study provides three arguments worth noting: (1) the most likely background for biblical circumcision is Egypt; (2) Egyptian circumcision differed from Israelite circumcision in that it was partial (a slit in the foreskin rather than its removal on six to fourteen year olds); and (3) the class of people who seem to have been recipients of the rite were those of the priestly and/ or royal lines. This third point is significant, Meade argues, because it helps make sense of how biblical circumcision could have been associated with the priest-kingly function of Abraham and then the nation of Israel (Exod 19:5–6). For a summary of these points, see Meade, "Circumcision of Flesh," in Wellum and Parker, *Progressive Covenantalism*, 129–31. Jason DeRouchie charts all eighty-five instances of the circumcision word group from the Masoretic text in DeRouchie, "Circumcision in the Hebrew Bible and Targums," 178–81. For additional research on the background of circumcision, see 186–89.

cut off from the people; he has broken Yahweh's covenant (v. 14).[16]

The Genesis narrative reveals little about the significance of the sign. Yet, by noting the biblical-theological context, one may safely conclude several things. First, circumcision functions as a sign of "devotion and consecration" for all of Abraham's household (wife, children, servants).[17] That the scope includes the household is evident in God's promise in verse 7 to "be God to you and your offspring after you" (genealogical principle).[18] Second, the location of the sign on the male reproductive organ makes circumcision a constant reminder of Abraham's inability to produce children apart from God's initiative to fulfill his promises (Gen 15:5; 17:4–7, 16–17; cf. Rom 4).[19] Third, for a foreigner/household slave to reject circumcision is to reject Abraham's (and later Israel's) God.[20] Fourth, whether a male child, or an adult foreigner or slave received the sign of circumcision, the sign functioned as an "initiating-oath sign."[21] The oath signified thereby is primarily the Lord's, entailing the promises of blessing to Abraham. At the same time, the oath belongs to the head of the household and the adult foreigners who submit to circumcision. Fifth, Abraham's circumcision should be considered in light of the storyline of Genesis and the failure of

16. Meade, "Circumcision of Flesh," in Wellum and Parker, *Progressive Covenantalism*, 129.

17. Meade, "Circumcision of the Flesh," in Wellum and Parker, *Progressive Covenantalism*, 131. Duane Garrett contends similarly that circumcision signifies "purification and sanctification." In the OT, being uncircumcised is "equivalent to a Greek calling someone a 'barbarian'" (e.g., David's reference to Goliath as this "uncircumcised Philistine"; 1 Sam 17:36) (Garrett, "Meredith Kline," in Schreiner and Wright, *Believer's Baptism*, 264). For Meade and Garrett, the meaning of circumcision is clearly positive.

18. The genealogical principle refers to God's command to administer the covenant initiation sign of circumcision to the male offspring of Abraham's household and emphasizes the full participation of children within the covenant. For example, see Ross, "Baptism and Circumcision as Signs and Seals," in Strawbridge, *Case for Covenantal Infant Baptism*, 91.

19. Deenick, *Righteous by Promise*, 49.

20. DeRouchie ably defends the thesis that from God's establishment of complete circumcision (as compared to that of the Egyptians) in Gen 17, refusing circumcision as an adult was tantamount to remaining hostile to God. Alternatively, to receive circumcision as an adult was to identify with God and his people. See DeRouchie, "Circumcision in the Hebrew Bible and Targums," 190–203. Thus, for the infant males who received circumcision, the physical sign visually testified to their covenantal peace with God, though they may or may not have borne an internal posture of faith toward God, as Abraham did. For biblical examples of the status of being uncircumcised denoting hostility to God, see Judg 14:3; 15:18; 1 Sam 14:6; 17:26, 36; 31:4; par. 1 Chr 10:4; 2 Sam 1:20.

21. Thanks to Bobby Jamieson for this observation.

Adam and Eve to rule as God's image because of their sin (Gen 1–11). In this context, circumcision functions to mark Abraham and his family as a new nation out of the sinful world who will represent God and his ways to the nations.[22] Even at this stage in redemptive history then, circumcision anticipates the priestly role of blessing God intends for Abraham's family (cf. Exod 19:5–6).[23] Sixth, based on the above points, circumcision functions to mark off Abraham's family as a distinct "political institution," intended to "exemplify true citizenship among all of God's subjects."[24] What is entailed in the citizenship becomes clearer in God's call for Abraham walk before him blamelessly (17:1–2), which carries forward the promise of a seed who would conquer the serpent (Gen 3:15). Finally, as a sign of the covenant, circumcision at one level signifies all the promises God gave to Abraham.[25]

Genesis 15 emphasized the promissory and unconditional elements of the Abrahamic covenant: God placed himself under obligation to fulfill his promises without mention of Abraham's responsibilities. In contrast, Genesis 17:1–2 includes the requirement that Abraham "walk before me and be blameless, that I may make my covenant between me and you." Thus, the Abrahamic covenant should be viewed as containing "unconditional-unilateral and conditional-bilateral elements."[26] The blend of conditionality

22. Beale views the commission to Abraham in Gen 12:2 as a post-fall continuation of God's plan from Gen 1:28 (Beale, *Temple and the Church's Mission*, 95). Peter Gentry highlights the "Adamic role" of Abraham at this point in redemption history, whereby his task becomes the extension of Yahweh's rule over the nations (Gentry and Wellum, *Kingdom through Covenant*, 235–47). Gentry also highlights the call of Abraham as God forming a new creation out of the sinful world (225; cf. Rom 4:16–17).

23. Gentry and Wellum, *Kingdom through Covenant*, 272–75.

24. Leeman, *Political Church*, 216. Leeman writes, "Abraham inherits the Adamic citizenship mandate, a role that combines political and priestly concepts—a vice-regent who is consecrated to God and so rules by being ruled. God's Gen 12 promises to Abraham, institutionalized as a covenant in Gen 15 and 17, point us to nothing less than a political institution, an identity—and behavior-shaping rule structure whose purview embraces an entire public and is directly or indirectly backed by the threat of an authorized force" (cf. Gen 12:3). He explains that true citizenship entails "abiding together as a true and just body politic under God's rule. It is among these people [Abraham's family] that true righteousness and justice should be displayed." These observations form part of the continuity to be teased out in chapter 5.

25. See Gentry and Wellum, *Kingdom through Covenant*, 223–99. While it is true that God's promise to bless the world through Abraham's offspring is, in the fullness of time, revealed to be Christ, reading the Abrahamic covenant as if the progress of revelation had already happened in Gen 17 mistakes the promises and terms of the Abrahamic covenant in its redemptive-historical location for how Christians should read the Abrahamic covenant canonically, given our redemptive-historical location. Contra Gibson, "Sacramental Supersessionism Revisited," 200.

26. Gentry and Wellum, *Kingdom through Covenant*, 705; Fuller, *Unity of the Bible*,

is significant. When combined with God's command that Abraham should circumcise "every male throughout your generations, whether born in your house or bought with your money" (genealogical principle), God's instructions create a covenantal people who must be faithful to walk before him blamelessly yet lack the ability to do so. An inherent tension appears in the fact that although God will be a faithful covenant partner, neither Abraham

---

252, 332–33. Syntactically, DeRouchie recognizes two imperatives ("walk before me and be blameless") in v. 1 plus two cohortatives in v. 2. Because they are joined by a *waw* consecutive, the imperatives contain the condition, which when fulfilled, will result in the fulfillment of the cohortatives. Specifically, "For Abra(ha)m to see realized the confirmation of the covenant and the multiplication of his offspring (v. 2), he must first be blameless, living in accordance with the divine suzerain's will" (cf. Gen 22:16–18) (DeRouchie, "Circumcision in the Hebrew Bible and Targums," 185–86n19). Craig Blaising and Darrell Bock deny (or at least heavily qualify) the blend of conditionality in the Abrahamic covenant. They cite the promise of Gen 18:18 that "Abraham will surely become a great and mighty nation" and in v. 19 that "the Lord may bring upon Abraham what he has spoken about him." They claim, "If the Abrahamic covenant was a bilateral covenant, v. 18 could not be stated in this factual way" (Blaising and Bock, *Progressive Dispensationalism*, 133–34). However, as they explore the requirement for Abraham to walk before God and be blameless (17:1–2), they explain "Abraham's obedience to God's commandments does function as the means by which he experiences God's blessing on a day to day basis. These commandments function as conditions for Abraham's historical experience of divine blessing, for as he obeys God, God blesses him more and more. But these obligations do not condition the fundamental intention to bless Abraham. They condition the how and when of the blessing" (133–34). Several responses may be made to this line of argument. First, I agree that the elements of human conditionality provide the means by which Abraham receives the blessing. In a compatibilistic model of divine sovereignty and human responsibility, the bilateral elements of the covenants may be consistently explained this way. On this point, see Chen, "Historical, Biblical, and Theological Interpretation." Blaising and Bock's denial of the bilateral elements of the Abrahamic covenant may be tied to a denial of compatibilism. Second, given that Blaising and Bock are compelled by Gen 17:1–2 to admit some level of conditionality, it seems tenuous to claim that the Abrahamic covenant is merely unilateral. Third, DeRouchie claims that the "'seed' designation necessitates ethical and spiritual conformity to God's call to 'walk before me and be blameless' (Gen 17:1). Such were the conditions for enjoying the Abrahamic covenant and for participating in its ultimate fulfillment. Only by 'being a blessing' in this way would the worldwide curse be overcome and all the families of the earth be blessed." This entails that physical descendants of Abraham could "lose their covenant privilege and identity" (cf. Rom 9:8) (DeRouchie, "Counting Stars with Abraham and the Prophets," 452). Finally, the bilateral nature of the Abrahamic covenant seems to be the best way to explain the forward-looking, Christological end to which the requirement of blamelessness points. To state it differently, Gen 17:1–2 requires and obedient, human, covenant partner, who is Christ. Blaising and Bock do not deny that Christ provides the fulfillment of the Abrahamic covenant, but their dismissal of the bilateral category introduces a confused element of expectation into the storyline of Scripture. For two different approaches on how the Abrahamic covenant points to Christ, see Deenick, *Righteous by Promise*, 21–47; Gentry and Wellum, *Kingdom through Covenant*, 656–83.

nor his descendants will prove faithful. Yet, God's human covenant partners receive the sign of circumcision of entering covenant with God when they cannot uphold the conditions signified.[27] As Wellum explains, the nation that God would bring from Abraham through Isaac, Jacob, Judah, and David would not yield a blameless and obedient covenant partner until Christ. As such, "every male offspring of Abraham . . . was a type of Christ and thus anticipated his ultimate coming."[28] Chapter 4 explores this connection in more detail.

A further tension created by the sign of circumcision is found in the fact that although Abraham's wife Sarah did not experience the sign of circumcision, she received the blessings of it (Gen 17:15–16).[29] Further, while Abraham's firstborn son of the flesh, Ishmael, did receive the sign as Abraham's biological seed, Ishmael's family would not be a conduit of the blessings to which the sign pointed.[30] Ishmael was considered a full covenant member. Yet, despite God's rejection of Ishmael as a recipient of the covenant promises (Gen 17:19), both he and any foreigners or slaves who were circumcised could "benefit from the divine blessing mediated through [Abraham]" by their proximity to and life with God's chosen recipients of the blessing.[31] Clearly, the genealogical principle of circumcision did not guarantee that all who were circumcised possessed the same hearts of faith or reception of God's promises as Abraham's circumcision did. This observation is best explained by considering what is intended by the notion of the seed of Abraham.

27. In canonical terms, this tension points forward to Christ Jesus, the faithful covenant partner and obedient Son of God (cf. Matt 1:1–2; Rom 4:11; Gal 3:16). This paragraph is heavily indebted to Gentry and Wellum, *Kingdom through Covenant*, 707.

28. Wellum, *Kingdom through Covenant*, 701.

29. This observation is one reason that circumcision should not be considered a "condition" of the Abrahamic covenant. Contra Johnson, "Fatal Flaw of Infant Baptism," in Barcellos, *Recovering a Covenantal Heritage*, 238. While circumcision was required for males to enter the covenant and maintain the covenant status of the households, it is not properly called a condition. See the paragraph above.

30. Deenick, *Righteous by Promise*, 43–44; Meade, "Circumcision of Flesh," in Wellum and Parker, *Progressive Covenantalism*, 131. But see Gen 17:18–21. While God promises to make Ishmael into a great nation, he does not make his covenant with Ishmael. Daniel Fuller explains that Gen 17 "reveals that the seed of Abraham, to whom the covenant blessings were promised, was not coextensive with his physical descendants" (Fuller, *Unity of the Bible*, 331).

31. DeRouchie, "Circumcision in the Hebrew Bible and Targums," 183n11. For more on the significance of circumcision for Ishmael, see DeRouchie, "Counting Stars with Abraham and the Prophets," 450.

The Seed/Offspring of Abraham

In *Kingdom through Covenant* Wellum argues that Abraham's seed has four referents in the canon of Scripture. This section mentions all four. However, explanation of the third and fourth senses is reserved for chapter 4. By understanding which group(s) comprise the seed of Abraham, this section seeks to clarify the relationship between circumcision and the seed(s).

The seed of Abraham refers to (1) the "natural (physical) seed"; (2) "natural yet special seed"; (3) the Messiah who blesses the nations (Gen 12:3; cf. Gen 3:15; Gal 3:16); and (4) those who belong to Christ by faith and regeneration (Gal 3:26–29).[32] For the first category, "Ishmael, Isaac, the sons of Keturah, and by extension Esau, [and] Jacob" belong to the natural (physical) seed (Gen 17:18–20; 25:1–4; 26:3–5; 28:13–15). From this list, only Isaac and Jacob belong to the second category, the natural yet special seed (Gen 17:20–21; cf. Rom 9:6–9).[33] Distinguishing between these referents is crucial to explaining the tension created by the fact that some within the covenant community of Israel believed in the promises of God, while others did not. Thus, the Abrahamic and Mosaic covenant communities were inherently mixed, being composed of those whom God chose to receive his promises and those who would not.

The mixed nature of the covenant community refers to a human and divine reality. As for the human reality, one could be a physical, circumcised descendant of Abraham and yet lack Abraham's faith by which Abraham

32. Wellum, "Relationship between the Covenants," in Schreiner and Wright, *Baptism*, 133–35. For these categories, Wellum is partially indebted to Feinberg, "Systems of Discontinuity," in Feinberg, *Continuity and Discontinuity*, 72. Feinberg claims, "Dispensationalists recognize multiple senses of terms like 'Jew,' 'seed of Abraham,'" etc. Those senses are (1) biological, ethnic, and national; (2) political; (3) spiritual, referring to those "properly related ... to God by faith"; and (4) typological "of the church." Some differences between this approach and Wellum's will be explored in chapter 5. More similar to Wellum than Feinberg is Renihan, "Abrahamic Covenant in the Thought of John Tombes," in Barcellos, *Recovering a Covenantal Heritage*, 167. Contra both Feinberg and Wellum is Waltke, "Kingdom Promises as Spiritual," in Feinberg, *Continuity and Discontinuity*, 268. Waltke claims, "The seed is essentially spiritual not carnal."

33. Wellum, "Relationship between the Covenants," in Schreiner and Wright, *Baptism*, 133. DeRouchie demonstrates that although the initial promises to Abraham in Gen 12 appear to entail blessing for all of his physical descendants, the recipients of the blessing were restricted by divine choice (election) and by human forfeiture. Jacob's selection over Esau is clear in Rom 9:6–9. DeRouchie presents Lot's daughters (Gen 19:32, 34), Onan (38:8–9), and the Pharisees (John 8:39, 42, cf. v. 33) as examples of those who forfeited their seed status. See DeRouchie, "Counting Stars with Abraham and the Prophets," 451–52. See also Deut 32:5, where Moses describes Israel by saying, "They are no longer his children because they are blemished; they are a crooked and twisted generation."

was counted as righteous before God (Gen 15:6).[34] Esau and Ahab are representative of this group. As for the divine reality, one could formally and officially belong to God's covenant people by possessing the sign of circumcision and yet not be one of God's chosen recipients of the promises signified by that sign. Ishmael represents this group.[35] Alternatively, given the nature of circumcision as a sign for males in Israel, females could have the faith of Abraham and thus be recipients of the promises of the covenant without being circumcised (e.g., Sarah; Gen 17:15–19).[36] Males could exercise faith like Abraham and not be chosen by God as those through whom the Messiah would come (e.g., Caleb). Further clarification is needed on the relationship between the first two seed referents.

Genesis 17:5 includes God's promise that Abraham would become "the father of a multitude of nations." While this promise includes the physical fatherhood of the Arabic nation (Ishmael), Israelite nation (Isaac), and Edomite nation (Esau), God's promises entail a more expansive referent. Daniel Fuller explains, because Moses "sees all the peoples of earth as someday blessed through Abraham's seed (12:3), it would seem that the multitude of nations and the kings that Abraham would father [17:6, 16] are in fact to be equated with these worldwide 'peoples.'"[37] That uncircumcised

34. Thus, Gibson is correct that "Abraham is circumcised because God makes a covenant with him, and his descendants are circumcised because God makes the same covenant with them" (Gibson "Sacramental Supersessionism Revisited," 127). Yet, contra Gibson, Abraham is unique in that he is the father of those who believe. While circumcision functions to seal the righteousness Abraham received by faith in God's promises (Rom 4:11), it does not function this same way to his offspring. Paul claims that God was not pleased with the majority of Abraham's descendants, given their unbelief (1 Cor 10).

35. Wellum, "Relationship between the Covenants," in Schreiner and Wright, *Baptism*, 134. Cornelis Venema does not give adequate attention to this category of the seed of Abraham when he writes that circumcision, "was a sacrament that in its deepest meaning stood for fellowship with God" (Venema, "Covenant Theology and Baptism," in Strawbridge, *Case for Covenantal Infant Baptism*, 220). It is true that if a household slave or a foreigner wanting to incorporate into Israel rejected circumcision, they were symbolically and covenantally declaring their hostility to God. Circumcision entailed consecration to God. Nevertheless, the category of physical/biological (not special/chosen) seed of Abraham, requires that not all who possessed circumcision were either believers like Abraham or recipients of the promises. See Deenick, *Righteous by Promise*, 49–50.

36. Chapter 5 includes a discussion of how the onset of the new covenant creates and requires a change in the structure and nature of the new covenant community, with respect to who constitutes the seed of Abraham and who receives the sign of the new covenant—baptism.

37. Fuller, *Unity of the Bible*, 331. Contra Waltke, "Kingdom Promises as Spiritual," in Feinberg, *Continuity and Discontinuity*, 268. While Fuller understands the promise to include both ethnic Israelites and non-ethnic Israelites, Waltke claims "Gen 17:5

foreigners and slaves could be brought in to Abraham's covenantal family by circumcision suggests the "possibility that at least some of those who became attached to Abraham's household, or, in later years to the nation of Israel, could enjoy the covenant blessings without having a genealogy that traced back through Jacob and Isaac to Abraham."[38] Given that the term "nations" (*goy*) used in Genesis 17:6 is more often associated with non-Israelite political communities in the Old Testament, Abraham and Sarah's parenthood of this multitude of nations may be legitimately understood as a "non-biological relationship of authority."[39] Three Old Testament examples substantiate Fuller's and DeRouchie's conclusion: (1) the "mixed multitude" that went up out of Egypt (Exod 12:38; cf. Lev 24:10); (2) the provision for inclusion of foreigners, temporary sojourners, and hired workers to participate in Passover through circumcision (12:43–49; cf. Num 9:14); and (3) Uriah the Hittite's role in Israel (2 Sam 11:3–5; 12:10). These are clear examples of covenantal inclusion and participation for foreigners through the sign of circumcision.[40] The fact that the covenantal sign of circumcision and covenantal meal of Passover could be received by proselytes demonstrates the multinational scope of the Abrahamic blessing through the expansion of God's covenantal people. The existence of these multi-ethnic, natural yet special seed of Abraham in the Old Testament demonstrates that the promise to Abraham carried spiritual significance even before the coming of Christ (cf. Gal 3:16).[41]

Typological Development of Circumcision of the Heart in the Old Testament

This section explains the significance of circumcision as it is progressively developed through the remainder of the Old Testament and understands the later intertextual development of circumcision as indicative of God's

---

does not refer to the Ishmaelites, Edomites . . . but to nations that believe in Christ."

38. Fuller, *Unity of the Bible*, 331.

39. DeRouchie, "Counting Stars with Abraham and the Prophets," 458. DeRouchie argues this point at length. Two entailments are that Abraham's fatherhood of the nations should be understood in terms of adoption and that "Abraham's paternal relationship over the nations is principally an elected rather than formal/biological association." See also Dumbrell, *Covenant and Creation*, 93.

40. DeRouchie, "Counting Stars with Abraham and the Prophets," 455–56.

41. In other words, the Abrahamic covenant, and circumcision specifically, carried spiritual significance in its own redemptive-historical context and not only when viewed retrospectively through the new covenant (Meade, "Circumcision of Flesh," in Wellum and Parker, *Progressive Covenantalism*, 152).

intention when he gave the sign to Abraham in Genesis 17.[42] While circumcision continues to function as a sign of initiation for the people of Israel after the establishment of the Mosaic covenant (Lev 12:3), greater emphasis is placed on the typological significance of circumcision denoted by the phrase "circumcision of the heart." Understanding the theological and functional significance of circumcision is important for grasping how circumcision relates to Passover in the Old Testament and how circumcision relates to baptism in the New Testament.

Circumcision of the Heart
in the Torah

Circumcision appears with unexpected referents—lips (Exod 6:12, 30),[43] fruit (Lev 19:23–25), and ears (Jer 6:10).[44] DeRouchie and Goldingay argue that, given the original, inherent connotation of hostility toward God that accompanied one's unwillingness to be circumcised (cf. Gen 17:14), the metaphorical developments of circumcision in the Old Testament point to an inherent spiritual meaning to the physical rite.[45]

Leviticus 26:41 and Deuteronomy 30:6 provide the most significant development of the circumcision theme in the Torah. In Leviticus 26:41 (cf. Lev 19:23), the Lord's solution to Israel's lack of internal and external

42. See Wellum, *Kingdom through Covenant*, 123n89. By God's sovereign design, the circumcision God gave Abraham was always intended to point to the circumcision of the heart that would come in the new covenant. This becomes evident through the intertextual development of circumcision of the heart in the OT itself, the theme that this chapter traces.

43. Consideration of each mention of circumcision in the Torah is outside the scope of this book. However, this chapter does not knowingly overlook any counterevidence to the thesis. The text regarding Gershom's circumcision (Exod 4:24–26) appears indeterminative. At the least, the account demonstrates the principle necessity of circumcision to avoid God's judgment (cf. Exod 12). For more on Exod 4:24–26, see Howell, "Firstborn Son of Moses," 68–69. Deenick sees a greater significance to Gershom's circumcision. See Deenick, *Righteous by Promise*, 76–80.

44. By describing each of these as uncircumcised, the text refers to a spiritual impurity or lack of ability to produce faithfully. See DeRouchie, "Circumcision in the Hebrew Bible and Targums," 194–96; Fuller, *Unity of the Bible*, 366–67.

45. DeRouchie, "Circumcision in the Hebrew Bible and Targums," 194; Goldingay, "Significance of Circumcision," 15. By claiming an inherent spiritual meaning to the physical rite, I intend the latent referent to circumcision of the heart that is observable retrospectively in the Gen 17 account. As Emadi and Sequiera explain, "OT texts have a *sensus praegnans*—a divinely hidden meaning that is deepened through redemptive-historical progression and literary-canonical development until it reaches its climax in eschatological fulfillment in Christ" (Emadi and Sequeira, "Biblical-Theological Exegesis and the Nature of Typology," 17).

covenant faithfulness and resulting exile occurs when he humbles their uncircumcised hearts.[46] Deuteronomy 29–31 presents the inevitable reality that Israel will fail to keep the covenant and thus be unable to fulfill God's command to circumcise their own hearts (10:16).[47] In Deuteronomy 30:6, the Lord promises "to circumcise your heart and the heart of your offspring." By this act, the Lord effectively removes the sinful obstacle hindering covenant faithfulness and produces a heart that loves and obeys God. This promise provides the theological warrant for understanding part of the meaning of circumcision to be the removal of impurity.[48] While Eugene Merrill describes circumcision of the heart as an internal identification with the Lord,[49] Meade better accounts for the context of covenant fidelity. All the Israelite males were externally circumcised as a mark of consecration and devotion to God as his representative priests, while their lives failed to demonstrate this internal devotion (cf. Exod 19:6). Heart circumcision is the solution to the inconsistency between the sign and the thing signified,

46. Meade provides thorough exegesis on this point. See Meade, "Circumcision of the Heart," 64–68. Meade explains that although the Niphal stem could be translated as a passive (their heart will be humbled) or reflexive (their heart will humble itself), the context suggests the passive reading is best, given the description of Israel's refusal to listen, obey, or walk with the Lord throughout Lev 26. Deenick provides an impressive list of OT examples in which he argues that sinners humble themselves before the Lord so that the Lord acts in favor (e.g., Ahab, 1 Kgs 21:25–29; Judah, 2 Chr 12:7; Manasseh, 2 Chr 33:9; etc.). He favors the reflexive sense despite acknowledging that the curses of Lev 26 look to be the divine means of bringing Israel to humble repentance (cf. Ps 107:12) (Deenick, *Righteous by Promise*, 55–58). Although the events of Leviticus occur prior to Deuteronomy, the context of the mention of heart circumcision—covenant curses from the Lord—is strikingly similar to Deut 30:6, in which the Lord is clearly the agent of heart circumcision. Whether Leviticus intends to highlight human agency in the humility or to make the same point as Deut 30:6, the latter passage would still require that God produces his people's ability to humble their uncircumcised hearts by giving them circumcised hearts.

47. For helpful exegesis of this verse, see Meade, "Circumcision of the Heart," 71–74. Meade observes that "a circumcised or devoted heart would then control and influence the actions and behavior of the whole person" (72). If Israel could change their own sinful posture toward God, such that they obeyed with a proper motive, trust, and love, God's circumcision of their hearts would be unnecessary.

48. The clear implication from the context of Deuteronomy is that the foreskin symbolizes some obstacle or impediment within humanity to their faithful love, devotion, and obedience to the Lord (Meade, "Circumcision of the Heart," 72). Venema's claim that "circumcision specifically reminded the children of Israel of their need to remove the defilement and corruption of sin (Deut 10:16)" appears out of step with other pedobaptists who claim circumcision offered the promise that God would remove their defilement if they believed like Abraham (Venema, "Covenant Theology and Baptism," in Strawbridge, *Covenantal Infant Baptism*, 220).

49. Merrill, *Deuteronomy*, 388.

for, it refers to heart devotion to the Lord that manifests itself in covenant faithfulness.[50] Or, with James Hamilton, circumcision of the heart "results in the ability to love God and live" and "enables people to incline to Yahweh" (cf. Jer 6:10).[51]

Thus, the Torah evidences a typological development of the meaning of circumcision.[52] While the physical sign given to Abraham contained spiritual meaning (consecration and devotion to the Lord as his priest-kings), God's command that Israel should circumcise their own hearts (Deut 10:16), and his promise that he would circumcise their hearts (30:6), reveals a development and escalation in the idea of circumcision. Within the Old Testament itself, in a biblical-theological sense, the physical sign of circumcision points to an inward reality of devotion to God that only God can bring. When the future orientation of the promise of Deuteronomy 30:6 is combined with that of the promise of a prophet like Moses—one who could speak so that the people hear and obey, the text at least suggests

50. Meade, "Meaning of Circumcision in Israel," 135.

51. Hamilton, God's Indwelling Presence, 47. Taking Hamilton and Meade's definitions together, it is difficult to avoid the conclusion that the removal of the foreskin represents the overcoming and/or removal of human sinful resistance to God, whereby God creates within sinful humans the moral inclination to trust and obey him. See chapter 5 below for the relationship between circumcision of the heart, regeneration, and baptism.

52. Brent Parker defines typology as "the study of how OT historical persons, events, institutions, and settings function to foreshadow, anticipate, prefigure, and predict the greater realities in the new covenant age" (Parker, "Israel-Christ-Church Relationship," in Wellum and Parker, Progressive Covenantalism, 47–52). Parker outlines three "fundamental aspects of typology": (1) "the typological patterns develop along the textual, epochal, and canonical horizons or, more specifically, along the backbone of the biblical covenants"; (2) "typology always has an eschatological aspect that is usually described as an escalation or heightening with the arrival of the antitype along the lines of inaugurated eschatology"; and (3) "when a person or entity is identified as typological, this does not include every aspect of the person or entity." As such, types "are prospective in that God has designed and intended certain OT figures, institutions, settings, and events to serve as advance presentations, which are then transcended and surpassed by the arrival of the NT antitype." Therefore, identifying a type in Scripture does not require reading the biblical text allegorically. Instead, for a person, event, institution, etc. to be a biblical type, chronologically subsequent biblical authors must utilize, develop, and intertextually refer to the person, event, or institution at least once across the canonical storyline (e.g., Melchizedek in Gen 14; Ps 110:4; Heb 7). Thus, types are presented by the biblical authors across time in Scripture, but they are discovered exegetically by the reader of Scripture. For further explanation of Parker's approach to typology, see Parker, "Israel-Christ-Church Typological Pattern." See also Emadi and Sequeira, "Biblical-Theological Exegesis," 18.

an eschatological correlation between the promised new mediator and the provision of circumcised hearts from God (Deut 18:15).[53]

Circumcision of the Heart
in the Prophets

According to Deuteronomy 30:6–10, the redemptive historical epoch of God's circumcising action is post-exilic,[54] referring to the "stage when Yahweh would finally act to bring Babylon out of the hearts of the people."[55] This eschatological element receives further development in the prophets, especially Jeremiah and Ezekiel, after God initiates the covenant with David.[56] Significantly, Jeremiah 4:1–4 ties the Abrahamic covenant with its promise of blessing flowing to the nations (v. 2) together with the command to "circumcise yourselves to the Lord; remove the foreskin of your hearts" (v. 4). As Meade explains,

> Jeremiah 4:1–4 supports a developing typology of the circumcision of the Abrahamic covenant. External circumcision under the Abrahamic covenant was a type that already anticipated an antitype—heart circumcision. The association was already made in Deuteronomy 30:4–7, and Jeremiah now forges the relationship between the Abrahamic covenant and heart circumcision

53. For further development of this point, see DeRouchie, "Counting Stars with Abraham and the Prophets," in Wellum and Parker, *Progressive Covenantalism*, 454–55.

54. The return from exile occurs in two stages according to Meade: (1) a geographical return and (2) a spiritual return explained, the latter as an internal transformation within the heart (Meade, "Circumcision of the Heart," 76–77). Meade's two stages of return from exile provide a parallel to the original promise of blessing to Abraham in Gen 12. While exile is not in view in Gen 12, DeRouchie argues that the text presents the blessing coming to Abraham in two stages. "Abra(ha)m must first 'go' to the land in order to become a nation (realized in the Mosaic covenant) and then once there 'be a blessing' in order for all the families of the earth to be blessed (realized through Christ in the new covenant)." By the time Moses foretells Israel's inevitable failure to keep the covenant and eventual exile in Deut 30, it becomes clear that the second stage of fulfilment of the Abrahamic covenant corresponds to the second stage of fulfilment of return from exile. In other words, Israel would become a blessing to the nations when the kingly, blameless seed of Abraham comes and circumcises the hearts of the people. See DeRouchie, "Counting Stars with Abraham and the Prophets," 460. If the Holy Spirit through Moses intended a two-stage fulfillment of the promises to Abram in Gen 12:1–3 that includes a new covenant fulfillment with multiethnic participants, then it is faulty to argue that Israel will experience a distinct eschatological future as an ethnic nation as dispensationalism does (479–80).

55. Meade, "Meaning of Circumcision in Israel," 138.

56. This section assumes the discussion of the Davidic covenant found in Gentry and Wellum, *Kingdom through Covenant*, 389–431.

as part of the means by which the nations will declare themselves blessed in Yahweh [Jer 4:2].[57]

Jeremiah clarifies and develops the eschatological dimension of heart
circumcision in later chapters. Jeremiah 9:25–26 presents Israel as akin to
other pagan nations (Egypt, Edom, etc.), all of them circumcised "merely in
the flesh" and "uncircumcised in heart."[58] Then, Jeremiah 31:31–34 speaks
of the new covenant, whereby God would put his law "within them" and
"write it on their hearts."[59] In Jeremiah 32:38–40, the Lord says "I will give
them one heart . . . that they may fear me forever." And again, "I will make
them an everlasting covenant," entailing that "I will put the fear of me in
their hearts that they may not turn from me." In these latter passages, God
is promising to do for Israel what they cannot do for themselves—transform
them internally to make them able to obey His laws. The references to one
heart, circumcised hearts, and hearts that fear the Lord would seem to be of
a piece. Each of these promises looks toward the dawning of the new covenant age for their fulfillment, rather than being something God promised
to fulfill under the old covenant.

God's promises through Ezekiel add to the typological expectation of
heart circumcision in the new covenant.[60] Ezekiel specifically includes im-

---

57. Meade, "Circumcision of Flesh," in Wellum and Parker, *Progressive Cov-
enantlism*, 140. Jer 9:25–26 further clarifies that external circumcision does not insulate one from God's judgment. A day will come when the Lord will "visit punishment
on all circumcised with the foreskin" (Meade's translation). In note 22, he explains,
"This reading is superior to the ESV's 'circumcised in the flesh' since it incorporates
the background of the practice of incomplete circumcision," referring to the practice of
Egyptian circumcision.

58. DeRouchie, "Circumcision in the Hebrew Bible and Targums," 200.

59. More attention will be given to the way in which the new covenant relates to
heart circumcision and baptism in chapter 4. This paragraph assumes the discussion of
Jer 31 found in Gentry and Wellum, *Kingdom through Covenant*, 492–516; Hamilton,
God's Indwelling Presence, 44–45; Meyer, *End of the Law*, 257–58.

60. In Ezek 36:27, the indwelling promised is not individual per se, but corporate
("in your [plural] midst"). Nevertheless, in Ezek 37:14, God places His Spirit in each of
the dry bones, causing them to come to life, thus implying the hope of God's deposit
of the Spirit into individuals with the coming of this new work. See Hamilton Jr., *God's
Indwelling Presence*, 49–50. Hamilton insists, "Ezek 36:26–27 does not indicate that the
old covenant remnant was indwelt" (135). Nevertheless, he insists they were regenerate.
Although prophetic literature often contains divine words that are partially fulfilled
with more immediacy and more fully or finally fulfilled in the future (e.g., Isa 7:14
and the child born to the "young woman" compared to Matt 1:23 and the virgin Mary
conceiving Jesus by the Holy Spirit), each of the promises contained in Ezek 36:26–27
would appear to be speaking of the new covenant. If this is the case, then the cleansing
of the heart should not be eschatologically separated from the indwelling of the Spirit,
or the indwelling of the Spirit eschatologically separated from the giving of a new heart,

ages of internal cleansing,[61] a new heart, and transformation,[62] by which God guarantees his people's obedience, and a return to the land (36:25–28). In verse 26, the new spirit God gives his people is parallel to the new heart he implants, a heart that would seem to have God's laws inscribed on it (cf. Ezek 16:60; 18:31; Jer 31:33).[63] The newness of heart, will, and mind that results in obedience to God would seem to be an Old Testament way of describing new covenant regeneration—the implantation of a new nature.[64] In verse 27, the result of the Spirit indwelling God's people is that he "causes" or "makes" them to walk obediently to his law, now inscribed on their exchanged hearts (cf. 36:26–27; 37:14).[65] The indwelling presence of God in his people would be part and parcel of the new covenant relationship with God, whereby he would be able to claim them as "my people" and himself as "your God" (36:28). In other words, besides the cleansing, God's renewing work within his people appears to include both his sovereign regeneration of their hearts/minds/wills and his indwelling covenantal presence that makes obedience to God's law possible.[66]

Given the similarity of the Deuteronomic-Jeremiahic theme of a circumcised heart and God's promises through Ezekiel of internal transformation and covenantal presence, one can see that they combine to form a fuller portrait of God's new covenant work. Although God calls his people to circumcise their own hearts, God planned all along to do the renewing work required to form a new people for himself through the Messiah in the

---

and so on. Thus, Hamilton appears inconsistent when he claims that OT believers could have been regenerate but not indwelt since the promises of regeneration and indwelling appear side by side in this text. A possible solution to this dilemma is to see regeneration in the old covenant era as a distinct reality from new covenant regeneration. See chapter 4.

61. Ezek 36:25 "I will sprinkle clean water on you, and you shall be clean from all your uncleannesses, and from all your idols I will cleanse you." See also Jer 31:34, "For I will forgive their iniquity and remember their sin no more."

62. Ezek 36:26 "And I will give you a new heart, and a new spirit I will put within you. And I will remove the heart of stone from your flesh and give you a heart of flesh."

63. Hamilton Jr., *God's Indwelling Presence*, 53.

64. Cooper uses the term regeneration, signifying the internalization of the covenant. Cooper, *Ezekiel*, 315. Block speaks in terms of a "heart transplant" (Block, *Book of Ezekiel*, 2:355). Most helpful for this discussion is his recognition that "'spirit' and 'mind/heart' should be treated as virtual synonyms."

65. The *waw* consecutive appears to be that of result as in the paraphrase "I will put my Spirit in them with the result that I will ensure [עשה] that they obey." See Cooper, *Ezekiel*, 315–16.

66. Hamilton sees a distinction here between regeneration (v. 26) and indwelling (v. 27) whereby he regards them as "separate, though coordinate" works of the Spirit (Hamilton, *God's Indwelling Presence*, 52–53). I agree with this assessment.

new covenant. Thus, the Old Testament itself presents the sign of covenant entry—circumcision—as a type that points forward heart circumcision, available through the Messiah's new covenant work.

Passover and the Mosaic Covenant

Having considered the institution and development of circumcision in the Old Testament, this section turns to the significance of Passover, which is a covenantal meal, given to Israel by God as a continuing celebration of God's redemption. Three steps are necessary to make this case: (1) considering the institution of Passover; (2) presenting the requirement of circumcision as prerequisite to Passover; and (3) relating Passover to the Mosaic covenant.

Institution of Passover

While the following description is not exhaustive, five features of the institution of Passover are noted. First, the context of Exodus 12 suggests that the Passover meal and exodus event should be closely connected.[67] In context, the prescription for the Passover celebration (Exod 12) follows the sequence of plagues on the Egyptians (5–11). As such, Israel's participation in the Passover functions as the Lord's appointed means of preserving them from the final plague of judgment—the death of the firstborn (Exod 12:12–13).[68] Because the death of the firstborn finally moved Pharaoh to free Israel (vv. 29–32),[69] leading to their deliverance through the Red Sea (Exod 14), these events are all of a piece.[70] The Passover event is both temporally connected

67. Pennington describes the event as the "Passover-Exodus" (Pennington, "Lord's Supper," in Schreiner and Crawford, *Lord's Supper*, 50).

68. Exod 12:12 states, "For I will pass through the land of Egypt that night, and I will strike all the firstborn in the land of Egypt, both man and beast; and on all the gods of Egypt I will execute judgments: I am the Lord. The blood shall be a sign for you, on the houses where you are. And when I see the blood, I will pass over you, and no plague will befall you to destroy you, when I strike the land of Egypt."

69. Exod 12:29–32 states, "At midnight the Lord struck down all the firstborn in the land of Egypt, from the firstborn of Pharaoh who sat on his throne to the firstborn of the captive who was in the dungeon, and all the firstborn of the livestock. And Pharaoh rose up in the night, he and all his servants and all the Egyptians. And there was a great cry in Egypt, for there was not a house where someone was not dead. Then he summoned Moses and Aaron by night and said, 'Up, go out from among my people, both you and the people of Israel; and go, serve the Lord, as you have said. Take your flocks and your herds, as you have said, and be gone, and bless me also!'"

70. Carpenter emphasizes the fact that the cluster of God's redemptive acts in Exod 4–19 serves to explain the creation of the nation of Israel in history. See Carpenter, *Exodus*, 1:339–43.

to God's redemption of Israel and the external means by which believing Israelites appropriated that redemption.[71]

Second, the elements of the Passover meal other than the lamb are important, due to their symbolical portrayal of the theological nature of the event. In the context of Exodus, unleavened bread was necessary, because Israel went out in haste without their dough receiving adequate time to be leavened (cf. 12:11, 34, 39).[72] The unleavened bread of the Passover meal serves as a fitting accompaniment to the Feast of Unleavened bread with which it is conjoined (cf. 12:17–20; 13:1–13).[73] Leaven does not appear to have a negative connotation in Exodus. Rather, unleavened bread physically and tangibly demonstrates the immediacy of God's salvation.[74] The common interpretation of the bitter herbs that accompanied the unleavened bread is that they reminded Israel of the bitter oppression they experienced in Egypt.[75] The instructions for Passover served both as a means of Israel's deliverance (when Israel followed the instructions), and as the institution of an ongoing cultic practice. Thus, eating the lamb, unleavened bread, and herbs on their appointed days became the perpetual reminder of God's historical and continuing deliverance (cf. 12:21–28).[76] Yet, failure

71. Robert Walter draws attention to the promises the Lord makes to his people in Exod 6:6–7 to bring them out, deliver, and redeem—all of which they received by faith obedience to God's instructions (Walter, "Passover in the Torah," in Bock and Glaser, *Messiah in the Passover*, 35–37).

72. Exod 12:11 is "In this manner you shall eat it: with your belt fastened, your sandals on your feet, and your staff in your hand. And you shall eat it in haste. It is the Lord's Passover." Verse 39 states, "And they baked unleavened cakes of the dough that they had brought out of Egypt, for it was not leavened, because they were thrust out of Egypt and could not wait, nor had they prepared any provisions for themselves."

73. While the Passover occurred on the fourteenth day of the first month of Nisan, the Feast of Unleavened bread was celebrated from the fourteenth day to the twenty-first day (12:18). Given the Lord's instructions, it is unclear why Walter claims "uncertainty as to whether or not" the feasts occurred at "two separate appointed times" or the same time. The best way to understand the feasts is that while they include distinct rituals and theological significance, they were celebrated together. Carpenter, *Exodus*, 1:39. For mention of Passover and the Feast of Unleavened Bread together, see Lev 23:5–8; Num 28:16–23; Deut 16:1–7; Ezek 45:21; Ezra 6:20–22; 2 Chr 30:2–15; and 35:17. The fact that Passover would mark the first month of the calendar year for Israel reveals the significance of the exodus event (Exod 12:2). In the Jewish calendar, the first month may be called Nisan or Abib (Garrett, *Commentary on Exodus*, 361).

74. Hamilton, *Exodus*, 187.

75. Carpenter, *Exodus*, 1:451; Hamilton, *Exodus*, 182.

76. For this theme, see Vickers, "Past and Future," in Schreiner and Crawford, *Lord's Supper*. Exod 12:21–28 states, "Then Moses called all the elders of Israel and said to them, Go and select lambs for yourselves according to your clans, and kill the Passover lamb. 22 Take a bunch of hyssop and dip it in the blood that is in the basin, and touch

to celebrate Passover (and the Feast of Unleavened Bread) appropriately resulted in removal from the covenant community (12:15).[77] Participation in the physical elements of Passover marked one out as belonging to God's covenant people.

Third, the specific means of Israel's deliverance from the final plague on Egypt was their being covered by the sacrificial blood of the Passover lamb. God instructed "the whole congregation of Israel" (12:3, 6) to slaughter one lamb per "household" (vv. 3–4), whose blood would be placed on the doorposts and lintels of the house and whose roasted flesh would serve as the substance of the meal (vv. 7–10).[78] Yet, the slaughtering of the lamb did not entail mutilation, given God's command not to break any of its bones (v. 46).[79] Because God promised to judge all of Egypt that was not covered by

---

the lintel and the two doorposts with the blood that is in the basin. None of you shall go out of the door of his house until the morning. 23 For the Lord will pass through to strike the Egyptians, and when he sees the blood on the lintel and on the two doorposts, the Lord will pass over the door and will not allow the destroyer to enter your houses to strike you. 24 You shall observe this rite as a statute for you and for your sons forever. 25 And when you come to the land that the Lord will give you, as he has promised, you shall keep this service. 26 And when your children say to you, 'What do you mean by this service?' 27 you shall say, 'It is the sacrifice of the Lord's Passover, for he passed over the houses of the people of Israel in Egypt, when he struck the Egyptians but spared our houses.' And the people bowed their heads and worshiped. 28 Then the people of Israel went and did so; as the Lord had commanded Moses and Aaron, so they did."

77. Exod 12:15 states, "Seven days you shall eat unleavened bread. On the first day you shall remove leaven out of your houses, for if anyone eats what is leavened, from the first day until the seventh day, that person shall be cut off from Israel." For the language of being cut off from the community, see Lev 20:1–6; Exod 30:33, 38; and 32:34–35 (cf. Gen 17:14) (Carpenter, *Exodus*, 1:455). After a survey of reasons Israelites could be cut off from the community, Hamilton summarizes a range of meanings for the significance of being cut off (depending on more specific circumstances) as "(1) an earlier-than-expected death; (2) childlessness; (3) the elimination of the sinner's family and descendants; (4) failure to join and enjoy the hereafter with one's family already in the land of eternal bliss" (Hamilton, *Exodus*, 188). He nearly dismisses the idea that being cut off amounts to being "excommunicated from" (cf. Lev 20:17).

78. Exod 12:7–10 states, "Then they shall take some of the blood and put it on the two doorposts and the lintel of the houses in which they eat it. 8 They shall eat the flesh that night, roasted on the fire; with unleavened bread and bitter herbs they shall eat it. 9 Do not eat any of it raw or boiled in water, but roasted, its head with its legs and its inner parts. 10 And you shall let none of it remain until the morning; anything that remains until the morning you shall burn."

79. This point becomes significant as the canon unfolds and the theme of Christ as the Passover lamb emerges. John claims that the puncturing of Christ's side on the cross and avoidance of his legs being broken fulfills Exod 12:46 (cf. John 1:29) (Hamilton, *Exodus*, 198).

the blood of the lamb, the lamb died as a substitute for the firstborn in the house (vv. 11–12).[80]

Fourth, the lamb's blood marked off God's people from the Egyptians. Ironically, God describes the blood as a "sign" *for Israel*, even while he promises to "see the blood" and "pass over you" (12:13). Thus, the blood that marked off Israel from their enemies served as a comforting, visible symbol to each Israelite. By it, God would distinguish his people from those under judgment.[81] Even while Israel celebrated the feast in households, the whole nation celebrated at the same time—in the evening.[82] Thus, by instructing Israel to participate in the nationally common meal in their respective households, God spared his people from judgment and separated them for himself that they might be his own (Exod 19:4–6). The initial Passover meal and blood on the doors marked off those who would form the old covenant community.[83]

Fifth, the death of the firstborn and the redemption of Israel through that judgment climactically displayed God's saving power and rule over his people's enemies and their gods. God promised not only the death of the firstborn of the Egyptians, but also to "execute judgments" "on all the gods of the Egyptians" (12:12).[84] From the time God summoned Moses to be the

---

80. Bruckner's claim that "representation, if not substitution, is clearly implied" falls short of the evidence (Bruckner, *Exodus*, 113). Bruckner is correct however that the Passover lamb "was not directly connected with sin, although it was 'apotropaic' in the sense of averting God's stroke" (114). Clearly then, the life of the lamb was laid down for that of the firstborn inside each house.

81. Given this context, Walter's reframing of God's action toward those covered by the blood as protecting rather than passing over misses the point that God himself acts as judge of those not covered by the blood that he graciously gave as a means of escape. Note that the Lord says "I will strike all the firstborn in the land" (12:12); "I will execute judgments," "no plague will befall you to destroy you when I strike the land of Egypt" (v. 13); and "The Lord will pass through to strike the Egyptians" (v. 23). The Lord executed these judgments through an emissary called "the destroyer" (v. 23). Nevertheless, retranslating *pesach* to protect rather than pass over is inappropriate due to the context (Walter, "Passover in the Torah," 37). For this interpretation, Walter cites Levine, *Leviticus*, 156. For the argument that the Lord stands by to protect his people who are covered by the blood even while he directs the destroyer on those not covered, see Hamilton, *Exodus*, 185–86.

82. Garrett explains the relationship of household celebrations in light of God's progressive revelation in Deut 16:3, where Israel is told to celebrate Passover in "the place where YHWH choose to have his name dwell," by stating that the whole land would constitute such a place after Israel entered the Promised Land. Furthermore, while the household celebrations would continue, a national celebration also began after the construction of the Temple in Jerusalem (see 2 Chr 30:1–18) (Garrett, *Exodus*, 361–62).

83. Pennington, "Lord's Supper in the Gospels," 53–54.

84. The death of the firstborn "is tied to the ancient Near Eastern idea that the

earthly deliverer of Israel, God promised to display his might over the king of Egypt (Exod 4:21–23; 7:5; 9:14–16; cf. 14:16–18). In the wider context of the Passover-exodus event, the narrative repeatedly portrays God's deliverance of his people as a display of the kingdom of God—God's saving rule, as with the final phrase of the Song of Moses in Exodus 15:18, "the LORD will reign forever and ever."[85] By participating in the Passover and the exodus that followed, Israel experienced God's saving reign over all the nations and displayed their obedience to the LORD as their King (cf. Isa 43:15).

Qualifications for Participation in Passover

After providing the initial instructions for how to celebrate the Passover (12:1–28), the narrative describes the death of the firstborn of the Egyptians (vv. 29–30) and the great exit of the Israelites from Egypt in the night (vv. 31–42). At this point, Moses pauses the narrative to describe the Lord's perpetual instructions for the celebration of Passover and the accompanying Feast of Unleavened Bread throughout Israel's history (12:43—13:16). This section is particularly concerned with the Lord's clear directive that only the circumcised keep the Passover. Exodus 12:43–49 states,

> And the Lord said to Moses and Aaron, "This is the statute of the Passover: no foreigner shall eat of it, but every slave that is bought for money may eat of it after you have circumcised him. No foreigner or hired worker may eat of it. It shall be eaten in one house; you shall not take any of the flesh outside the house, and you shall not break any of its bones. All the congregation of Israel shall keep it. If a stranger shall sojourn with you and would keep the Passover to the Lord, let all his males be circumcised. Then he may come near and keep it; he shall be as a native of the land. But no uncircumcised person shall eat of it. There shall be one law for the native and for the stranger who sojourns among you.

---

defeat of a nation is, in effect, a military victory." Thus, "Any ancient people would have seen this as a defeat of the gods of Egypt" (Garrett, *Exodus*, 363).

85. Those texts which portray God as a warrior for his people (Exod 14:4, 13–14, 17–18; 15:3) and sovereign ruler of all things (Exod 15:1–18; Deut 32:1–43) coalesce around the theme of the kingdom of God. Hafemann also cites Isaiah 43:15 in this regard, which is a clear allusion to the Passover-exodus event. There, God describes himself as the "Creator of Israel, your King." Surely, God's creation of Israel in this context refers to their deliverance from slavery in Egypt and God's kingship to his saving rule that brought their redemption (Hafemann, "Kingdom of God," in Taylor and Storms, *For the Fame of God's Name*, 242).

In Exodus 12:43–48, Moses delivers the Lord's commands to prohibit certain kinds of people from participating and urging qualifications for all who would participate. Four groups were prohibited from participation: (1) foreigners (v. 43); (2) hired workers (v. 45); (3) temporary residents (v. 45); and stranger/sojourner who has either not been circumcised himself or has not circumcised all the males in his household (v. 48).[86] However, Moses states the qualification of circumcision for foreigners and native born Israelites as an open invitation to any who would meet the qualification: "but every slave that is bought for money may eat of it after you have circumcised him" (v. 44).[87] Circumcision was the means of outwardly demonstrating an "inward commitment to [Yahweh] and Israel."[88] Moses describes the qualification of circumcision before Passover as "the statute of the Passover" and as "one law" that applies to the "native" and "the stranger who sojourns among you" (v. 49).[89] Thus, Moses states the qualification for participating in Passover—circumcision—both positively and negatively. In context, even before the

86. Hamilton, *Exodus*, 197.

87. Verse 48 adds, "If a stranger shall sojourn with you and would keep the Passover to the Lord, let all his males be circumcised. Then he may come near and keep it; he shall be as a native of the land. But no uncircumcised person shall eat of it." Given the specificity of the prohibition against the uncircumcised participating in Passover and the positive statement of circumcision's prerequisite nature, James B. Jordan's contention that some of the Gentiles that exited Egypt with the mixed multitude participated in the spiritual food to which 1 Cor 10 refers does not hold as much significance as it first appears (cf. Exod 12:38). The prohibition is given with specific regard to Passover, not the manna in the wilderness, to which Paul refers. The theological and covenantal function of circumcision as a conversion sign of entry must not be overshadowed by the typological function of the manna. For Jordan's argument see Jordan, "Children and the Religious Meals," in Strawbridge, *Case for Covenant Communion*, 65.

88. Garrett, *Exodus*, 366. Several pedocommunion advocates go to great lengths to defend the historicity of infant/child participation in the first and subsequent Passover celebrations. For example, Robert Rayburn argues that the childrens' questions to their parents about the significance of Passover suggests their full participation in the meal. Furthermore, given that the OT calls families to eat the priestly sacrifices (cf. Lev 10:14; 18:11; Deut 12:6–7, 12, 18; 16:11, 14), child participation should be understood as a given. See Rayburn, "Presbyterian Defense of Paedocommunion," in Strawbridge, *Case for Covenant Communion*, 5–7. Rayburn's argument is intended as evidence that just as children participated in Passover, so they should also participate in communion. More will be said on the issue of infant communion in chapter 4. Two points may be mentioned here: (1) the text does not explicitly say one way or the other whether children actually ate the meal and (2) given that infant males received the covenantal entry sign of circumcision, it would be covenantally consistent for them to participate in Passover as well.

89. The Law stipulated a proper care for sojourners among Israel who did not want to participate in Passover. Thus, failure to integrate into the covenant community did not incur immediate judgment. See Exod 22:21; Lev 23:22; Deut 10:18 (Carpenter, *Exodus*, 1:478).

Law is given at Sinai, circumcision functions to bind individuals (and families) to God's people, to bring them into the community so that they can function together as God's priest-kings (Exod 19:4–6).

Carpenter explains that a "covenant level" relationship with God and his people was required in order to join in the meal.[90] In this sense, circumcision continues its function of designating those who were devoted and consecrated to the Lord. Or, to turn the focus toward what the circumcision requirement teaches about Passover, "To eat of it is to declare identity and sharing on a level [the uncircumcised] person is unwilling to do."[91] Circumcision constituted a declaration of identity for a foreigner, Carpenter claims, because the sign was "more theological and religious . . . than it was an ethnic sign."[92] Yet, Carpenter is too quick to dismiss the national aspects of the sign of circumcision. Although the biblical authors develop the meaning of circumcision to the spiritual circumcision of the heart by the end of the Old Testament, the national aspect is crucial to understanding Christ's identity as a son of Abraham (Matt 1:1–2). Furthermore, from the institution of circumcision to the giving of the Law, the responsibility for a purchased slave's circumcision did not only fall on the slave. God instructed Abraham to circumcise every male in his household, including those "born in your house or bought with your money from any foreigner" at the risk of that uncircumcised person being cut off for breaking the covenant (Gen 17:12–14; cf. v. 27). In order to understand the nature of Israel as a covenant community, it must be grasped that the responsibility for circumcision fell both to the head of the household and the foreigner. Infant male children in the household were passive in their reception of circumcision. Significantly, the combination of the command for circumcision in order to belong to the covenant community combined with the requirement of circumcision for Passover forms the material grounding of Israel's status as a mixed community of believers and unbelievers.

Passover as a Celebration of the Mosaic Covenant

In light of the previous points, the Passover should be viewed as a covenantal meal. This fact may be verified by several observations: (1) the Passover/

90. Carpenter, *Exodus*, 1:477.

91. Carpenter, *Exodus*, 1:477.

92. Carpenter, *Exodus*, 1:479. Carpenter points to Ruth's declaration of loyalty to the Lord (1:16) as evidence of a foreigner joining the covenant community. Waltke also holds that circumcision was not an ethnic marker but a spiritual one (Waltke, "Kingdom Promises as Spiritual," in Feinberg, *Continuity and Discontinuity*, 268).

death of the firstborn made the exodus event possible as the initial impetus for their release by Pharaoh; (2) Israel's participation in the Passover was the means by which they could be preserved through the judgment of the firstborn and eventually arrive at Mt. Sinai; (3) God's intention in the Passover-exodus event was always ultimately the inauguration of a covenant at Sinai (Exod 3:12; 4:23; cf. 19:1);[93] and (4) although the instructions for how to celebrate the Passover were given prior to the other covenant stipulations at Mt. Sinai, the command to celebrate the Passover as an ongoing feast/festival (the high point of the Feast of Unleavened Bread) formed part of those stipulations (12:14–20).[94] The lack of requirement for women and children to participate in the Passover, after the celebration moved to Jerusalem, seems to highlight the commensurate responsibility of the heads of household not only to circumcise their male offspring but also to represent the family in the nation's ongoing celebration of being in covenant with God (23:17; 34:23; cf. Deut 16:16).[95]

Although it is incorrect to claim that the Passover meal itself inaugurated the Mosaic covenant, it is correct to say that the Passover meal inaugurated the saving events of the exodus by which God brought Israel into covenant relationship with himself. Furthermore, the Passover served as a yearly covenantal celebration and memorial for Israel's redemption.[96] In this sense, Passover is a covenantal meal.

Mosaic Covenant Ratification Meal

While the Lord clearly intended for Israel to celebrate Passover as an ongoing feast in remembrance of the exodus, Passover is not the only covenantal meal presented in connection with the Exodus event. Exodus 24:1–11 presents the celebratory—and in some ways consummatory—meal of the Mosaic covenant. This section examines several features of this covenant ratification meal.

First, Exodus 24:1–11 is subsequent to God's declaration that he redeemed Israel to be his own people (Exod 19:4-6) and God's delineation of the terms of the covenant with Israel (Exod 20–23). Israel's formal covenant

93. Kline, "Old Testament Origins," 12.

94. Garrett is surely correct that the Lord's instructions to Moses regarding the assemblies and full week of eating unleavened bread were intended for the ongoing celebration of the Passover due to the rush of the first event (Garrett, *Exodus*, 361).

95. Parker, "Paedocommunion, Paedobaptism, and Covenant Theology," 102.

96. Participating in the Passover meal was "one of the ways in which the covenant between God and Israel was maintained in being" (Marshall, *Last Supper and Lord's Supper*, 77).

vow/oath, "All the Lord has spoken we will do" (Exod 24:3, 7) is the nation's response to YHWH's terms, which Moses had written down. Although they had already agreed to the terms of the covenant "in principle" (19:8), Israel had to "solemnly affirm their allegiance to the covenant," having heard its obligations.[97] Therefore, Gentry et al. describe the ceremony that occurs in Exodus 24:1–11 as covenant ratification, meaning that what occurs here formally seals the agreement between the two parties and binds them to uphold their obligations.[98]

Secondly, Moses' sacrifice in Exodus 24:5–6 functions as the covenant-establishing shedding of blood for the Mosaic covenant, as Moses states in 24:8, "Behold the blood of the covenant the Lord has made with you" (cf. Heb 9:18). God's pattern for establishing covenants with people in the Old Testament consistently involves the shedding of blood as a warning of judgment for failure to keep covenant stipulations (cf. Gen 15:7–21). Gentry argues that the shedding of blood in Exodus 24:5 was not for the purpose of cleansing Israel from sin, as cleansing is absent from the context. Rather, "The symbolism is that the one blood joins two parties," making the sacrifices more akin to the fellowship offerings of consecration, prescribed for the making of vows, than to burnt offerings to atone for sin (cf. Lev 7:12–18).[99] Gentry further maintains that although God was making Israel a "kingdom of priests" to the surrounding nations by establishing his covenant with them, as in ordination imagery (Exod 19:4–6; cf. Lev 8),[100] and although Israel was a sinful people in need of cleansing, the absence of cleansing/purification language means that the sprinkled blood on the altar and people testifies to the union/communion established between God (represented by the altar) and the people.[101] Thus, as Garrett concludes, the

97. Garrett, *Exodus*, 542.

98. Gentry and Wellum, *Kingdom through Covenant*, 350. See also Stuart, *Exodus*, 2:551; Kaiser Jr., "Exodus," in Gaebelein, *Expositor's Bible Commentary*, 448–49. Bruckner helpfully discusses the responsive actions of Moses and the people to the revelation of God's law (Bruckner, *Exodus*, 225).

99. Gentry and Wellum, *Kingdom through Covenant*, 551. For a similar take on the purpose of the sacrifices, see Ross, *Recalling the Hope of Glory*, 178–80. For the view that the sacrifices were in part to atone for Israel's sin, see Stuart, *Exodus*, 2:554; Schreiner, *King in His Beauty*, 39.

100. According to Ross, the "burnt offering" (עֹלָה) was an "atoning sacrifice" (see Lev 1; 6:8–13), which signified that the worshiper had surrendered his or her life to God and that God had completely accepted the worshipper. In other words, any barrier that had existed was removed—there was full atonement." Ross understands atonement as God's provision for "the maintenance of a right relationship between the worshipper and God" (Ross, *Hope of Glory*, 200–201).

101. Garrett, *Exodus*, 543. Unlike the Abrahamic covenant in which the smoking firepot (representing YHWH) was the only party to pass between the slain animals,

sacrifices function here to "solemnize a suzerain-vassal relationship and fix the duties of each party,"[102] reminding Israel of the threat of death for failure to keep the covenant.[103]

---

the Mosaic covenant was "fully bilateral, with both YHWH and Israel assuming toward one another a covenant commitment with specific duties." Whereas God unilaterally guaranteed his promises to Abraham and would assume the consequences for failure to uphold his word, the Mosaic covenant "places Israel under covenant obligations—with dire consequences should they fail to keep them."

102. Garrett, *Exodus*, 545. Garrett warns further, "Christians naturally want to see a connection between the blood of Christ and the blood of Old Testament sacrifices. But one must be careful here. The blood of Christ is redemptive (analogous to the Passover lamb) and expiatory (analogous to the sacrifices of the Day of Atonement). The sacrifice enacted here is neither." While the foregoing interpretation faithfully captures much of the emphasis of the burnt offerings and peace offerings in the passage, two factors call for comment. First, because burnt offerings are consistently used to make atonement for the offerer (Lev 1; 6:8–13) and atonement is understood as a sacrifice required to procure acceptance by the Lord (Lev 1:3–4), the burnt offering on Sinai must also signal atonement. Secondly, the inspired author of Hebrews asserts that the blood sprinkled on the people at Sinai not only inaugurated the old covenant, but also made purification for their sin (9:22). One could argue that the author of Hebrews only explicitly describes the articles used in the tabernacle as being sprinkled with blood for purification (v. 21). However, I am swayed by the connecting phrase "In the same way" (v. 21) to believe the author intends the purification rite of blood sprinkling he describes for the tabernacle to be an accurate description of the people being sprinkled with blood at Sinai in 9:19–20. On this reading, "For without the shedding of blood, there is no forgiveness of sins" (v. 22) summarizes the purpose of blood being shed at the inauguration of the Mosaic covenant and the dedication of the tabernacle. Enns cites several passages which associate burnt offerings with the tabernacle in defense of the same conclusion (Exod 29:18, 25, 42; 30:9; 40:29) (Enns, *Exodus*, 490). Kimbell reads the passage similarly. He writes, "Interestingly, covenant institution and atonement are precisely the elements the author of Hebrews holds together in his comments on Exod 24 (Heb 9:15–22). The author makes clear that when the people are sprinkled with blood in Exod 24 they are undergoing a cultic cleansing (*katharizo*) with blood that is directly connected with forgiveness (*aphesis*) (v. 22)" (Kimbell, "Atonement in Lukan Theology," 42n56).

103. While Gentry and Garrett demonstrate a canonical consciousness in their exegesis, they do not interact with Hebrews. Both the term *hôlah* ("burnt offering") and the author of Hebrews' explanation suggest that the burnt offerings and peace offerings at Sinai performed a dual function of sealing communion between two parties as covenant inaugurating blood and providing atonement for the sins of the people. Kaiser points to the similarities with rites of purification in Lev 14:6–7 and Heb 9:19–20 and explains, "The division of blood points to the twofold aspect of the blood of the covenant: The blood on the altar symbolizes God's forgiveness and acceptance of the offering; the blood on the people points to a blood oath that binds them in obedience. In other words, the keeping of the words and laws was made possible by the sacrificial blood of the altar" (Kaiser Jr., "Exodus," 449). Kimbell makes a similar appeal to Heb 9:15–22 and to Targumic texts (see note 54). He outlines several parallels with the consecration of priests (Exod 29:33; Lev 8:34) in which blood was sprinkled on the altar and the people followed by a meal (Kimbell, "Atonement in Lukan Theology," 41).

Thirdly, that a meal followed the shedding of blood in Exodus 24:9–11 verifies that the events recorded in the passage constitute a covenant ratification. As Gentry points out, communal meals often function to ratify covenants in the Old Testament (see Gen 31:44–46, 54; 2 Sam 3:12–13, 20).[104] After the shedding of blood that symbolized the joining of two parties, the meal itself functions to celebrate the union, very much like wedding. As Gentry explains, "It is by virtue of the covenant at Sinai that Yahweh becomes the *goel*, i.e., the nearest relative, and that Israel becomes not just a nation but a 'people' (עַם), i.e., a kinship term specifying relationship to the Lord."[105] When the seventy elders (Israel's representatives) ascended the mountain with Moses, Aaron, and Aaron's sons to eat and drink with their covenant Lord, they did so to celebrate the wedding of God to his people (cf. Hos 1:9; Ezek 16:8–13). The fact that God "did not lay his hand on the chief men of the people of Israel" (Exod 24:11) emphasizes that the holy God of Sinai was welcoming his people into his presence.

Finally, several features of the covenant ratification meal serve to consummate the Mosaic covenant and, in the flow of the biblical storyline, to form patterns of expectations for the consummation of the new covenant. For example, the mountain location of the meal (Horeb/Sinai)[106] is taken up typologically throughout the Old Testament as the place (Moriah/Zion) where the Lord himself will rule the earth in connection with the eschatological day of the Lord (cf. Exod 15:17; Isa 2:1–4; 4:3–6; Mic 4:1–5).[107] Additionally, all who ascended the mountain "saw the God of Israel" (v. 10) and "beheld God" (v. 11). Seeing God and being in his presence functions with the meal as the climax of the establishment of the covenant relationship.[108] Throughout the Old Testament, the privilege of seeing God

104. Gentry and Wellum, *Kingdom through Covenant*, 351.

105. Gentry and Wellum, *Kingdom through Covenant*, 354.

106. Sinai is called the "mountain of God" in Exod 3:1; 18:5; 24:13. See Beale, *Temple and the Church's Mission*, 105.

107. Horton colorfully describes the procession of God's people from Sinai to Zion as a royal parade. As is common in prophetic literature (both of foretelling and event-prophecy of typological patterns) prophecies may be partially fulfilled multiple times in escalating degrees before reaching their culminating fulfillment. In this light, Heb 12:18–24 portrays the new covenant church already participating in the eschatological worship of Mt. Zion made possible by the resurrection of Christ, who faithfully trusted and obeyed the Father's law perfectly and thus completed the procession from Sinai to Zion as the forerunner and first fruits of all who would believe in him (Horton, *People and Place*, 289–96).

108. Schreiner, *King*, 39–40; Kline, "Old Testament Origins of the Gospel Genre," 6. Although I demur from Nicholson at several points, he describes the climactic nature of Israel's representatives seeing God on top of Mt. Sinai well, noting the contrast between God's command not even to touch the mountain in Exod 19:12 (Nicholson,

(his manifest glory) is reserved for God's covenant people and promised as the covenantal blessing for covenant faithfulness.[109] Then, as Beale argues, the color and material of the "pavement of sapphire stone" underneath the throne of God, which was "like the very heaven for clearness," is consistently used in Scripture to portray God's glory as he appears in his heavenly temple (see Ezek 1:26–28; 10:1).[110] Exodus 24:1–11 amounts to a significant eschatological foreshadowing.

Passover and the Mosaic Covenant Ratification Meal

Three points of comparison deserve mention between Passover and the covenant ratification meal on Sinai. First, whereas the Passover meal inaugurated God's saving work in the exodus event, leading to the establishment of the Mosaic covenant, the meal on Sinai ratified and celebrated the newly established covenantal relationship with God. Second, whereas the shedding of blood of the Passover lamb served as the means of Israel's deliverance from the judgment of God, the shedding of blood in Exodus 24:8 and subsequent sprinkling of blood on the people served to formally establish the Mosaic covenant, provide forgiveness of sins, and demonstrate peace and unity between God and the people. Third, whereas the Lord instructed the whole nation of Israel to repeatedly keep the Passover as a covenantal meal celebrating the exodus event, the covenant ratification meal is a one-time event in Israel's history that was enjoyed only by a representative group from Israel.

These comparisons help elucidate the covenantal function of the Passover as compared to the covenant ratification meal on Sinai. Although Passover occurred prior to Israel's historic deliverance as a proleptic symbol of the entire exodus event and the Sinai meal occurred as part of the

---

"Covenant Ritual in Exodus 24:3–8," 84).

109. See Exod 24:16–17; 33:10–11, 18–23; 34:34–38; cf. 1 Kgs 8:10–11. In Isa 24:6–9, the mountain of the Lord is the location at which the LORD himself will act as host, will serve a "feast of rich food" full of marrow and alongside well-aged wine, will "swallow up death forever," and will "wipe away tears from all faces." That this passage refers to the consummation of the new covenant is evident by the fact that the only redemptive-historical moment in which God accomplishes all of these things is described in Rev 19–22 (cf. Isa 65:13, 17–25; Matt 5:8).

110. Beale, *Temple and the Church's Mission*, 44. This image culminates in Rev 21:11, 18–20, where John describes both the glory of God and the New Jerusalem (which reflects God's glory) in similar terms. In Exod 24:10, Beale argues the heavenly temple has "temporarily descended to the top of Mt. Sinai." For a similar connection, see Garrett, *Exodus*, 544–45. While Jesus alludes directly to "the blood of the covenant" in Exod 24:8, in the progress of redemption, it seems clear that John alludes to other aspects of the covenant ratification meal with respect to the new covenant marriage feast.

formal establishment of the Mosaic covenant, the Lord does not command his people to reenact the Sinai meal. Instead, the Lord calls his people to rehearse the experience of their ancestors at Passover as "the ultimate act of old-covenant remembrance."[111] As Brian Vickers explains, the visible elements of unleavened bread and herbs were intended to "be part of [Israel's] collective memory that forms their identity." God called Israelite parents to explain the Passover to their children in personal terms—"I do this because of what the Lord did for me when I came out of Egypt" (Exod 13:8). In this sense, God intended the celebration of the Passover as means by which Israel could "actively call God's grace and salvation to mind, to bring the past into the present with hope for the future."

Because the initial celebration of Passover led to the whole exodus event and the establishment of the Mosaic covenant, the ratification meal on Sinai functions as the climax of entering covenant with God. Because the Passover became Israel's perpetual reminder of the whole exodus redemption and Mosaic covenant, the Sinai meal is unique in Israel's history. Yet, as the section on the ratification meal suggested, the prophetic development of the theme of God's people feasting on the mountain with God eventually builds to create further expectation and hope for Israel. The hope to which the Passover points includes something like a return to the mountain of God, where God's people can see their God and feast in his presence (cf. Isa 25:6–12; 27:13; 40:9; 54:11–17; Jer 3:17–18; 12: 16–17; 30:8–11; Ezek 20:40; Joel 3:17–21).[112] Significantly, after the establishment of the Davidic covenant (2 Sam 7), the means by which God's multi-national (not merely Israelite) people may enjoy God's covenantal presence is the work of the Davidic Messiah (cf. Isa 52:1—55:5).[113]

Israel's Passover Celebrations

Although the Lord clearly required circumcision as prerequisite to Passover at the institution of the Passover meal, Israel's subsequent history fails to demonstrate the people's complete obedience. Nevertheless, by surveying

111. This section is drawn from Vickers, "Past and Future," in Schreiner and Crawford, *Lord's Supper*, 319–21.

112. Gentry and Wellum, *Kingdom through Covenant*, 443–44. For the inclusion of foreigners in the eschatological people of God, who gather at the mountain of the Lord, as a fulfillment of the promise to Abraham in Gen 17:5, see DeRouchie, "Counting Stars with Abraham and the Prophets," 463–64.

113. For an extensive defense of this point, see Gentry and Wellum, *Kingdom through Covenant*, 406–21; DeRouchie, "Counting Stars with Abraham and the Prophets," 465–74.

each of the subsequent celebrations of Passover in the Old Testament, this section demonstrates that the Lord continued to require circumcision as prerequisite to Passover. Thus, circumcision's initiatory function is maintained throughout Israel's history. Additionally, Passover celebrations repeatedly occur in the context of covenant renewal, signaling the way the meal functioned as a celebration of belonging to God's covenant people.

Passover in the Wilderness: Numbers 9:1–14

One year after the people exited Egypt, the Lord commanded Moses to keep the Passover "at its appointed time" and "according to all its statutes and all its rules" (vv. 1–3). Israel followed God's command (v. 5), except for "certain men who were unclean through touching a dead body" (v. 6). When the men explained why they could not keep the Passover at the appointed time, Moses asked the Lord how to respond (v. 8). The Lord made provision for the unclean men to celebrate the Passover in the second month rather than its appointed first month (vv. 10–11). This presumably allowed sufficient time for the men to become ceremonially clean again so that they could participate properly. After making provision for this unusual circumstance, the Lord warned against failing to participate in Passover for all who are ceremonially pure and present with the people in the wilderness.[114] This failure constitutes "sin" that the disobedient Israelite would have to "bear," in part by being "cut off from his people" (v. 13). The passage closes with a clear allusion to Exodus 12:48–49.[115] The Lord commands any strangers sojourning among Israel to keep the Passover "according to the statute of the Passover and according to its rule" (Num 9:14)—a foreigner, slave, or hireling may eat of it "after you have circumcised him" (Exod 12:44, 48).[116]

While Numbers 9:1–14 does not explicitly mention circumcision, the Lord clearly upholds the law of circumcision and the necessity of ritual purity. Further, the Lord accommodates those who entered Passover season unclean by allowing an exceptional time of celebration, without compromising

---

114. Budd writes, "The author is anxious to ensure that the exceptions do not become a rule" (Budd, *Numbers*, 97). The author's conclusion that the allowance for missing the Passover if one is on a journey reflects post-exilic authorship is unwarranted from the text (99).

115. Budd, *Numbers*, 98.

116. Dennis Cole notes that although the Lord made provision for an alternate date for Passover, it does not appear that the Festival of Unleavened Bread was included in the alternate celebration, because Israel moved from their location on the twentieth day of the second month (cf. Num 10:11) (Cole, *Numbers*, 157).

the principle of ritual purity (cf. Lev 7:20).[117] Thus, even if the exception were allowed to be the rule, the exception does not apply to circumcision or purity. The exception is a proviso for all to participate in Passover, given life in a fallen world.[118]

Joshua 5:1–12

After forty years of wandering in the wilderness, on the threshold of the land of Canaan, the Lord instructed Joshua to "circumcise the sons of Israel a second time" (v. 2).[119] The explanation follows: although the exodus generation received circumcision before the first Passover in Egypt, none of the generation born in the wilderness were circumcised (v. 5).[120] The exodus generation, except Joshua and Caleb (Num 14), failed to trust the Lord to give them the land. That generation displayed their lack of trust in a lack of covenant faithfulness as well—the failure to circumcise their offspring (v. 6). Receiving circumcision is described as rolling "away the reproach of Egypt" (v. 9).[121] With the preparations complete, Israel celebrated the Passover at its appointed time, after their crossing of the Jordan (v. 11; cf. Josh 4).

117. Purification rites prescribed by the law included washing with water (Exod 29:4; 30:17–21; Lev 11:24–25; 22:6; 6:27); the rite of the red heifer (Num 19), and the ritual of the birds (Lev 14:2–9). For a helpful description, see Ross, *Hope of Glory*, 205. A purification or sin offering was also necessary for all worship at the sanctuary. It covered "any defilement that had occurred over the preceding weeks or months, as well as any sins committed unwittingly" (198).

118. Bunyan mentions Lev 10:16–20; Num 11:27–28; 2 Chr 30:13–27 (see the section below on this passage); 1 Sam 21:1–6; Matt 12:1–7. Bunyan is keen to supply examples from which to argue that the Lord is concerned with edification of the entire community above outward conformity to the law. In each case, Bunyan claims that an OT law was set aside for the sake of edification (Bunyan, "Reason of My Practice in Worship," in Offor, *Bunyan's Works*, 2:612). A brief response must suffice to a primary example from Bunyan. Jesus' grounds the appropriateness of David eating the shewbread in 1 Sam 21 in the unusual circumstance of urgent need in which David found himself. Jesus grounds his own plucking the heads of grain on the Sabbath in his identity as one greater than David, the Messiah and Lord of the Sabbath. On this point, see Blomberg, *Matthew*, 197. In addition, Mark's account (2:25–28) explains Jesus' action in terms of the law's intention to benefit humanity to the degree that "human need should take precedence over ceremonial laws" (Brooks, *Mark*, 66). Numbers 9, and each of the passages besides (Num 11:27–28 and Lev 10:16–20), seem to present a precedent for occasional and exceptional privileging of legitimate human need for worship and/or life to continue and flourish.

119. The use of a flint knife here parallels Exod 4:25 (Howard, *Joshua*, 147).

120. For a similar take, see Howard, *Joshua*, 148.

121. Deenick appeals to Ps 119:22 to argue that rolling away the reproach of Egypt refers to "Yahweh roll[ing] away the massive burden of slavery in Egypt and the disobedience of the wilderness generation" (Deenick, *Righteous by Promise*, 74). Context

This account provides another clear example of Israel upholding the Lord's law that circumcision is prerequisite to Passover. Nothing in the text, or elsewhere in the Torah, supports Bunyan's contention that the circumcision of Joshua 5 requires that Israel had celebrated the Passover without circumcision each year in the wilderness.[122] Bunyan makes an argument from silence. Moreover, the tenor of the text suggests that the exodus generation's covenantal unfaithfulness to continue circumcision and Passover became part of their disobedience, which resulted in their failure to enter the land (v. 6).[123] Indeed, the sign of the Abrahamic covenant—circumcision—testified to God's promise that his offspring would inherit the promised land (Gen 12:7).[124] Thus, in the context of Joshua 5, the combination of circumcision and Passover reveals the "organic relation" of the Abrahamic and Mosaic covenants.[125] Those who inherit the promised land are the members of the Mosaic covenant community, created in the Passover-Exodus-Sinai event (cf. Exod 19:5–6), who celebrate circumcision and Passover.[126] The clear division

---

suggests that the reproach of Egypt should not be understood as an inadequate, Egyptian method of circumcision (Howard, *Joshua*, 150). McConville and Williams emphasize that the disgrace/reproach is more closely associated with Israel's status as slaves in Egypt, given that they stand on the banks of the Jordan as a people delivered by God. See McConville and Williams, *Joshua*, 28.

122. He writes, "If therefore Moses and Joshua thought fit to communicate with six hundred thousand uncircumcised persons; when by the law not one ought to have been received among them; why may not I have communion, the closest communion with visible saints as afore described" (Bunyan, "Reason of My Practice in Worship," in Offor, *Bunyan's Works*, 2:609).

123. For a similar pairing of Israel's unbelief in Num 14 and the covenant unfaithfulness that followed in the wilderness, see Howard, *Joshua*, 150; McConville and Williams, *Joshua*, 27; Deenick, *Righteous by Promise*, 75. Deenick notes the temporal proximity of Moses' command to Israel that they circumcise their hearts (Deut 10:16) and this national circumcision.

124. McConville and Williams, *Joshua*, 27.

125. Wellum explains that the Mosaic covenant comes "in fulfilment of the promises made to Abraham." Therefore, "The old covenant . . . cannot be understood apart from the Abrahamic covenant" (Gentry and Wellum, *Kingdom through Covenant*, 636).

126. McConville and Williams write, "The point of this passage is to emphasize again the new situation of Israel. Passover had marked their departure from Egypt, an event that set them apart from that nation; now again, they are set apart, on the brink of a campaign against the peoples of the land they have entered" (McConville and Williams, *Joshua*, 29). It is also significant that the group who participated in the Passover in Josh 5 undoubtedly included circumcised sojourners (cf. Exod 12:38; Josh 8:33). The covenantal inclusion of foreigners at this early stage in Israel's history highlights the physical, national, and spiritual associations of the signs of circumcision and meal of Passover. Circumcised foreigners who had celebrated Passover in Josh 5 were considered "Israel" in Josh 8:33 and 35. For more on foreigners' inclusion as Abraham's adopted children, see DeRouchie, "Counting Stars with Abraham and the Prophets," 459.

between the circumcised, Passover keeping covenant community and the unfaithful Israelites bespeaks the function of circumcision and the Passover meal as boundary markers. The Lord's restatement of the requirement that Israel should be circumcised before partaking of Passover forwards the contention that circumcision is prerequisite throughout the Old Testament.

Passover in the Kingdom:
2 Chronicles 30:1–18

When Hezekiah began to reign as king of Israel, he led the restoration of the temple, the sacrifices, and the worship of Israel (2 Chr 29). The priests and Levites were unable to consecrate themselves in time to celebrate Passover in the first month of the year as prescribed due to their late start in cleansing the temple and consecrating themselves (30:3).[127] Therefore, Hezekiah and the leaders of Israel determined to keep the Passover in the second month (vv. 2, 4). Israel appears to have failed in the practice of annual celebration until that point (v. 5).[128] By dispatching couriers, Hezekiah invited the nation to keep the Passover, calling the people to "return to the Lord, the God of Abraham, Isaac, and Israel" (v. 6).[129] The invitation received a mixed response—mocking and humble agreement to participate (vv. 10–11).[130] After gathering in Jerusalem, the assembly removed the idolatrous altars and

127. Although Num 9:9–12 did not specifically stipulate the measures taken in this instance, "These exceptions for individuals were here extrapolated into principles that could apply to the whole nation." Thompson adds that Jeroboam I's feast (1 Kgs 12:32–33) could have put the Israelite calendar behind one month (Thompson, *1, 2 Chronicles*, 352). Ralph Klein argues for an analogical relationship between Num 9 and Hezekiah's practice here. The situation in Numbers allowed for delay due to impurity of a specific kind, a principle that Hezekiah generalizes. Similarly, Numbers allowed for delayed individual celebrations if one was on a journey. The principle is that of delay in the case of absence. Hezekiah applied this principle to the whole nation (Klein, *2 Chronicles*, 433). Hicks claims that Hezekiah specifically violates Num 9, because it allowed for a one-month-delayed participation by those who were already ceremonially pure at that time (see Lev 9:19–21) (Hicks, *1 & 2 Chronicles*, 474). While solving this issue is beyond the scope of this book, Klein's solution seems best.

128. The Chronicler presents Hezekiah as a unifier of Israel, akin to Solomon, in multiple ways throughout the passage (cf. 30:26) (Klein, *2 Chronicles*, 434).

129. His message carries the warning not to "be like your fathers and your brothers, who were faithless to the Lord . . . that he made them as desolation." Furthermore, Hezekiah calls them not to be "stiff-necked" (v. 8). The call to return to the Lord comes four times (v. 6; v. 9 [3x]). Thompson acknowledges several verbal parallels with 2 Chr 7:14 (Thompson, *1, 2 Chronicles*, 353).

130. The author attributes Judah's willingness to comply to the Lord's hand, who gave them one heart to obey the word of the Lord (v. 12) (Thompson, *1, 2 Chronicles*, 354).

celebrated Passover (vv. 14–15). The "shame" experienced by the priests and Levites appears to be grounded in the enthusiastic response of the people contrasted to the priests lack of ceremonial cleansing.[131]

Despite the humble enthusiasm of some in Israel, many of the people also failed to consecrate themselves (v. 17). Although the heads of households were assigned sacrificial duty at Passover (cf. Exod 12:3, 23, 48; Deut 16:1–7),[132] the Levites slaughtered the Passover lamb for all those who were not prepared (2 Chr 30:17).[133] The author explains that the people "ate the Passover otherwise than prescribed. Hezekiah had prayed for them, saying 'May the good LORD pardon everyone who sets his heart to seek God' . . . even though not according to the sanctuary's rules of cleanness" (vv. 18–19). The Lord graciously heard the prayer and "healed the people" (v. 20; cf. 7:14; Lev 15:31). The assembly celebrated the Feast of Unleavened Bread for a total of fourteen days after the Passover (v. 23). Interestingly, the Chronicler specifically mentions "sojourners" from Israel and Judah participating.[134] The author explains the joy in the Passover celebration as unusual—"for since the time of Solomon the son of David king of Israel there had been nothing like this in Jerusalem" (v. 26).

The Passover celebration in this chapter receives much attention because Hezekiah utilizes the exceptional provision for keeping the feast in the second month, which the Lord first allowed in Numbers 9.[135] However, the second reason this account is significant is that the text clearly admits the "majority of the people" "ate the Passover otherwise than prescribed" (v. 18). To explain the situation, commentators emphasize the Lord's attention to the people's hearts rather than their outward conformity. Thompson acknowledges that the law was binding. However, Hezekiah's prayer (vv. 19–20) "was effective in overriding purely ritual considerations," because "the Chronicler was not content with a religion of mere external correctness but delighted in the one who 'sets his heart on seeking God.'"[136] At the same

---

131. Thompson, *1, 2 Chronicles*, 355; Dillard, *2 Chronicles*, 245; Hicks, *1 & 2 Chronicles*, 473. The consensus of opinion on which group failed to consecrate themselves—the priests and Levites or the people of Israel—bears significance on the kind of impropriety this passage represents.

132. Dillard, *2 Chronicles*, 245.

133. Thompson, *1, 2 Chronicles*, 355.

134. Thompson cites Exod 12:48–49 to explain their presence (Thompson, *1, 2 Chronicles*, 356).

135. Flashman, "Passover in the Writings," in Bock and Glaser, *Messiah in the Passover*, 48; Bunyan, "Reason of My Practice in Worship," in Offor, *Bunyan's Works*, 612; Paul and Kiffin, *Some Serious Reflections*, 29.

136. Thompson, *1, 2 Chronicles*, 355. Dillard has, "the Chronicler . . . showed a concern with the spirit of the law where it was in tension with the letter" (Dillard,

time, the text repeatedly emphasizes conformity to the Torah.[137] In fine, the Chronicler's major concern is to emphasize the goodness and mercy of God (vv. 9, 18) toward his people as they turn to the Lord wholeheartedly (cf. 2 Chr 7:14). Yet, the fact remains that Hezekiah would not have prayed to the Lord for "pardon" (ESV) or "atonement" had he believed their actions to be fully in keeping with divine prescription.[138]

Three conclusions follow from this passage. First, ceremonial purity is the focus of the passage rather than circumcision. Nevertheless, the participation of sojourners in the Passover (30:25) without comment from the Chronicler suggests the stipulations for their participation were followed (cf. Exod 12:43–49). While this comment is an argument from silence, it is a strong argument from silence given the concern the Chronicler shows for obedience to the law and how exceptions to obedience were handled in this account. Second, the passage emphasizes the gracious character of God to forgive the sins of his people and receive their imperfect worship. To state the matter differently, this passage illustrates the existence of "weightier matters of the law" to which Jesus refers (Matt 23:23).[139] Yet, third, and without overshadowing the second point, it is illegitimate to ground open communion in God's willingness to pardon sin in this passage, as Bunyan does.[140] Hezekiah's need to ask for pardon requires that he viewed the circumstance as against God's law. Establishing principles and procedures for God's people on the basis of a clear account of sin is highly problematic.[141]

---

2 Chronicles, 245). Surely, Flashman's claim that God "bends His own rules" fails to account for Hezekiah's prayer for pardon (Flashman, "Passover in the Writings," 49).

137. Verse 16 has the priests and Levites taking their posts "according to the law of Moses." Verse 18 refers to a prescription for Passover, that the people failed to follow. Klein observes that the text is cryptic on two counts with regard to law keeping: (1) from where the priests received the blood to sprinkle (cf. 2 Chr 29:22; 35:11) and (2) how sprinkling the blood came about given the spreading of blood on the door posts in the first Passover (cf. Exod 12:8) (Klein, *2 Chronicles*, 438).

138. For the alternate translation, see Klein, *2 Chronicles*, 438.

139. In distinguishing between weightier matters such as justice, mercy, and faithfulness, Jesus does not discount the less weighty matters of tithing mint, dill, and cumin. Instead, he says, "These [less weighty matters] you ought to have done without neglecting the others."

140. Bunyan writes, "The wise king would not forbid them, but rather admitted it, knowing that their edification was of greater concern, than to hold them to a circumstance or two." He summarizes, "What shall we say, all things must give place to the profit of the people of God" (Bunyan, "Reason of My Practice in Worship," in Offor, *Bunyan's Works*, 2:612).

141. Lastly, on Bunyan's argument, the fact remains that the ceremonial purification laws, while punishable by death (Lev 15:31) perform a different function than circumcision in Israel. While the purification laws are fulfilled in the righteous life of Christ

2 Chronicles 35:1–19 and
2 Kings 23:21–23

The Passover celebration during Josiah's reign appears to be kept without the complication that accompanied Hezekiah's Passover. The celebration occurs as part of Josiah's reforms after he discovered the law scrolls in the temple (2 Chr 35).[142] After instructing the priests to prepare themselves (v. 4) and consecrate themselves (v. 6), Josiah and his officials provided animals for sacrificing (vv. 7–9).[143] When the time came to slaughter the Passover lambs, rather than the people of Israel, the Levites sacrificed the lambs (v. 6, 11; cf. Deut 16:5–6) and the priests threw the blood (cf. 30:16).[144] Despite the disparity over who slayed the lamb, Josiah's clear command is to act "according to the word of the Lord by Moses" (v. 6).[145] The Levites set aside more burnt offerings (v. 12) and "roasted the Passover lamb with fire, according to the rule" (v. 13).[146] Interestingly, their celebration includes boiled offerings of animals besides the Passover lamb (v. 13), singers (v. 15; cf. 1 Chr 25),[147] and gatekeepers in their places (2 Chr 35:15; cf. 9:17–29)—none of which are prescribed in Exodus. The Chronicler summarizes the whole event by mentioning "all the service of the Lord" prepared to keep the Passover (35:16), "all the people of Israel who were present" (v. 17), and the

---

and credited to the believer in justification, circumcision's initiatory function into the covenant community is replaced by baptism. Second Chr 30 would have to deal with uncircumcised persons participating in Passover for Bunyan's argument to hold weight. See chapters 4 and 5 below for a fuller discussion of this matter.

142. It is significant that Josiah also removed the idolatrous rivals to the Lord as Hezekiah had (cf. 30:14–15). For a description of Josiah's reforms, see Ross, *Hope of Glory*, 322–23.

143. Possibly, the extra sacrificial animals were for use in the Feast of Unleavened Bread (Thompson, *1, 2 Chronicles*, 383).

144. The flurry of activity that characterized the priests and Levites suggests a significant logistical achievement. The priests and Levites slaughtered lambs all day, offered burnt offerings "until night" (v. 14), and hustled to offer sacrifices for themselves only after serving the people ("carried them quickly to all the lay people," v. 13). Thompson concludes that the total number of animals offered was nearly double to that offered under Hezekiah (30:24), but less than Solomon's temple dedication (7:5) (Thompson, *1, 2 Chronicles*, 383).

145. Thompson thinks this phrase "evidently refers to the principle of sacrificing a Passover lamb rather than to the one who should perform the task" (Thompson, *1, 2 Chronicles*).

146. The text repeatedly mentions the slaughter of the Passover lamb (vv. 1, 6, 11) and the nation's adherence to "the Word of the Lord by Moses" (v. 6; par. vv. 12, 13).

147. The Chronicler references the commands made by David regarding the singers and the divisions of the priests in 35:4, 15. David's commands are found in 1 Chr 24:4, 19–20 30–31; 28:19–21; 2 Chr 8:14 (Thompson, *1, 2 Chronicles*, 382).

claim, "No Passover like it had been kept in Israel since the days of Samuel the prophet" (v. 18).[148] The Chronicler seems to be emphasizing the unique kind of Passover celebration that occurred under Josiah. Josiah's Passover is presented as a feature of national covenant renewal (cf. 2 Kgs 23:1–3).[149]

In the context of 2 Chronicles, Josiah is another David figure who fore-shadows the future Messiah without fulfilling the role.[150] The concluding verse of the paragraph (2 Chr 35:19) notes that Josiah celebrated this Pass-over in the eighteenth year of his reign, the same year he discovered the law in the temple (34:8) and covenanted to walk according to it (34:31). While Josiah wholeheartedly turns to the Lord, the language of 34:32 emphasizes "that Josiah imposes the pledge of obedience on the assembly, suggesting that the people do not fully share the king's faith or convictions about the covenant relationship with Yahweh."[151] Josiah follows the covenant renewal with Israel's ongoing, but neglected, covenant meal—the Passover. In chap-ter 35, the Chronicler presents the Passover as a unified national celebration of God's deliverance, by noting the presence of priests, Levites, the king, Judah, and Israel as "all Israel" (v. 18).[152] Yet, for all Josiah's godly leader-ship, he dies an untimely death soon after for failing to heed God's warning (35:21–24). The Chronicler represents the national decline after Josiah by providing four vignettes for each of the kings who ruled Judah until Jeru-salem and the temple were destroyed by Babylon. The four kings and the nation landed in exile, awaiting a second exodus through a greater David.

While 2 Chronicles 35 does not mention circumcision, it portrays the significance of Passover for Israel and demonstrates the development of the Passover by the eve of exile. Passover functions as a covenant meal, given that it follows naturally from the national covenant renewal of chapter 34

---

148. The Chronicler's historical note bears explanation. Second Kgs 23:22 provides a concurring summary of the time lapse, referring to the period of the Judges instead of mentioning Samuel specifically. The Chronicler is not denying Hezekiah's Passover cel-ebration, nearly ninety years previous. Hill provides a helpful table of the kings of Judah with the estimated dates of their reigns. Hezekiah's reign was approximately 716–687 BC, while Josiah's were 641–609 BC (Hill, *1 & 2 Chronicles*, 665).

149. With some similarity, Hezekiah's Passover is presented as part of his worship reforms (2 Chr 29–30). While Hezekiah's Passover explicitly includes persons from the northern tribes of Israel (2 Chr 30:18), Josiah's Passover includes Israel and Judah (35:18) (Konkel, *1 & 2 Kings*, 638).

150. For a comparison of David, Solomon, Hezekiah, and Josiah, see Konkel, *1 & 2 Kings*, 642–44. Similar to the other kings in Chronicles, Josiah is compared to his father, David. He seeks David's God from his youth (34:3; cf. 34:21, 26) (Hamilton, *God's Glory in Salvation through Judgment*, 347).

151. Hill, *1 & 2 Chronicles*, 623.

152. Hill, *1 & 2 Chronicles*, 628.

and that representative Israelites from the divided kingdom participated together.[153] Nevertheless, two factors emphasize the mixed community tension inherent to the Abrahamic and Mosaic covenants wherein circumcised and ritually clean persons could rightly participate in the Passover: (1) the obligatory (rather than wholehearted) way the people renewed the covenant (34:31–32) and (2) the decline of the nation into unfaithfulness after Josiah's death (cf. 34:33; 36). Besides the significance of the Passover, the celebration occurs in the developed fashion prescribed in brief in Deuteronomy 16:1–7. While family heads continue to play a role, the centralized location of Jerusalem entails a greater dependence on the priests and Levites.

Passover Post-Exile:
Ezekiel 44:7–9; 45:21

Chapters 44–45 are in the middle of Ezekiel's notoriously difficult temple vision (40–48).[154] While the nature of Ezekiel's temple has bearing on how to interpret the passages in question, it is beyond the scope of this section to enter the discussion on the nature of Ezekiel's temple. The reason for analyzing Ezekiel 44:9 and 45:21 are the clear mentions of circumcision, circumcision of the heart, and of Passover. Therefore, the analysis that follows pertains to those issues.

153. Konkel explains, "The last reported covenant renewal was in the days of Joshua" (8:30–35; 24:1–26) (Konkel, *1 & 2 Kings*, 638). Konkel adds that "The covenant of Josiah is the first occasion since that time when the Passover was celebrated as a national festival with official leaders." However, Konkel dismisses Hezekiah's Passover at this point. Hezekiah's Passover was national and involved official leadership. Konkel continues, "The Passover began as a family festival celebrated in each home (Exod 12:1–20)," such that "a central celebration is a monarchic innovation." While he is certainly correct about the institution of Passover, even by Deut 16:1–7, Moses gives instructions for celebrating the Passover in the place the Lord determines for his name to dwell—Jerusalem. Therefore, claiming that the centralized observance of Passover is an innovation denies explicit biblical teaching. The OT does not contain precise legislation for how Passover is to be celebrated in the centralized way. Herein lies mystery, not innovation.

154. Block concludes that just as Ezekiel's valley of dry bones vision should be interpreted as "a declaration of the certainty of the eventual resuscitation of Israel by a new infusion of breath from Yahweh," so also the temple vision "picks up the theological theme [of Yahweh's permanent residence among his people following their return from exile] and describes the spiritual reality in concrete terms, employing familiar cultural idioms of temple, altar, sacrifices . . . and land" (Block, *Ezekiel*, 2:505–6). The vision "presents a lofty spiritual ideal: Where God is, there is Zion." Block believes Ezekiel "lays the foundation for the Pauline spiritualization of the temple," such that "under the new covenant, even Gentile communities may be transformed into the living temple of God (1 Cor 3:16–17)." For a lengthy thematic treatment of the temple in the OT and an in depth discussion of the hermeneutical issues involved, see Beale, *Temple and the Church's Mission*, 23–166.

While 44:7–9 does not concern a Passover celebration, the description of who may enter the Lord's sanctuary has ramifications for the principle that circumcision is prerequisite to Passover. As the Lord's glory fills the temple (44:4; cf. 43:1–9), the Lord speaks directly to Ezekiel: "No foreigner, uncircumcised in heart and flesh, of all the foreigners who are among the people of Israel, shall enter my sanctuary" (v. 9; cf. Jer 9:25–26).[155] The Lord calls such admission a "profaning" of "my temple" (v. 7). The Lord lists his grievances against the people in terms of covenant breaking (v. 7). Yet, after commanding Israel to obey, the Lord holds the Levites responsible for the foreigners' error (v. 10).

The Lord gives the priests and prince further instruction before commanding the Passover to be celebrated on the fourteenth day of the first month, along with the Feast of Unleavened Bread (45:21).[156] While temple purification offerings and instructions and sin offering instructions precede this command, nothing is stated regarding qualifications for participation. Given the description of Passover as a pilgrimage "festival" (HCSB) and that "all the people of the land" should participate in the feast that follows Passover (v. 22), the Passover is surely a national celebration.[157] The national celebration continues the pattern set by Hezekiah and Josiah.[158]

The most intriguing aspect of these two passages is the way in which the Lord requires circumcision of flesh and heart for entrance to the sanctuary and that the sanctuary is the most contextually appropriate location for the Passover to occur. Therefore, although the text does not state the matter so explicitly as Exodus 12:43–49, the exilic prophet appears to place a heightened, though similar requirement on any who would join in the Passover—they must be circumcised not only in flesh but also in heart. The argument for this principle follows.

Ezekiel writes while in exile in Babylon (1:1–3). Early in his prophecy, he promises to make an "everlasting covenant" with his people (16:60). Later,

---

155. Ezek 44:9 is the only verse in the OT that explicitly "refers to foreigners having 'foreskinned' hearts." For this observation, see DeRouchie, "Circumcision in the Hebrew Bible and Targums," 200.

156. After providing rules for the priests (44:15–31), the Lord turns to instructions for allotting land for the priests (45:1–5), for the "holy district" (v. 6), and the prince (vv. 7–10). Then, after commanding the princes to uphold a righteous standard of weights and measures (vv. 11–12) and instructing them on which sacrifices to give and provide for the people (vv. 13–17), the Lord turns to more general sacrificial instructions with the priest in view (vv. 18–25).

157. Exod 34:25 utilizes the same word for Passover—as a pilgrimage festival—as is used in Ezek 45:21 (Block, *Ezekiel*, 2:664).

158. Block, *Ezekiel*, 2:665n26.

the Lord promises to make "a covenant of peace" (34:25).[159] This covenant
includes the fact that both David and the Lord act as the safe-keeping shep-
herd (vv. 11–24) and "they shall know that I am the Lord" when they return
to his land of blessing (v. 27, 30). The covenant of peace and the everlasting
covenant are one and the same, because the Lord promises, "I will make a
covenant of peace with them. It shall be an everlasting covenant" (37:26).[160]
The Lord adds that his sanctuary will be among them "forevermore." Given
that the everlasting covenant of peace is promised for the time after the Lord
rescues them from exile (34:27),[161] the Lord's promises to cleanse them, give
them a new heart/spirit, and place his Spirit in them after gathering them from
the nations, appear to be of a piece (36:24–29; cf. 11:17–21).[162] The circumcised heart that the Lord requires for worshiping in his sanctuary in 44:7–9 is
the same heart the Lord promises to give his people when he establishes the
everlasting covenant of peace, when he delivers them from exile. As Daniel
Block argues, the language prohibiting foreigners here is similar to Jeremiah
9:25–26, in which the Lord indicts Israel for being circumcised merely in the
flesh while retaining uncircumcised hearts, like the nations. Alternatively,
Ezekiel 44:7 and 9 indicate that the door into covenant and worship participation, corresponding to one's priestly status in Israel, is open to any foreigner
who submits to circumcision (Gen 17:27; cf. Exod 12:43).[163]

The context of 45:21 provides the clearest indication that the location at
which the Passover is to be celebrated is the temple. Each of the three preceding verses contains some instruction of cleansing or preparation of the tem-
ple/sanctuary.[164] The development of Ezekiel's own logic is important. Given
Ezekiel's development of the concept of circumcision of the heart (without the
precise verbiage),[165] the requirement that "foreigners" should be "circumcised

---

159. On the connection between the covenant of peace (*shalom*) and the eschatological new covenant, see Block, *Ezekiel*, 2:301–9.

160. For a defense of the covenant of peace being the new covenant, see Gentry and
Wellum, *Kingdom through Covenant*, 480–81.

161. Hamilton, *God's Indwelling Presence*, 51.

162. For a comparison of these passages, see Block, *Ezekiel*, 2:355.

163. For a similar take, grounded in Jeremiah, see DeRouchie, "Counting Stars with
Abraham and the Prophets," 463–64. Block describes several possibilities of the origin
of these foreigners and the duties they were allowed to perform. He suggests they may
have been members of the royal guard, who were allowed to enter the sanctuary. He
marshals the appointment of the Levites to perform the guarding function in 44:10 in
support of his hypothesis (Block, *Ezekiel*, 2:622–23).

164. Verse 18 speaks of purifying the sanctuary. Verse 19 regards the sin offering,
the blood of which the priests were to put on the temple doorposts. Verse 20 gives
instructions for "atonement for the temple."

165. Hamilton describes the promises of a new heart, new spirit, and God's Spirit at

in heart and flesh" bespeaks the same reality Ezekiel develops throughout the book. Because circumcision of the heart and flesh are required for entering the sanctuary for worship, and the sanctuary appears to be the location of the Passover celebration in 45:21, Ezekiel appears to be restating the requirement found in Exodus 12:48–49. Yet, Ezekiel raises the standard by adding that fleshly circumcision is insufficient. Because this circumcision of the heart is redemptive-historically connected to the everlasting covenant of peace after exile, the new covenant is in view. This observation helps explain the significance of the heart/flesh prerequisite on foreigners rather than Israel. The Lord does not say that Israelites must be circumcised in heart and flesh to enter the sanctuary; the foreigners are in view. However, the Lord has already promised that Israel would receive just such a circumcision of the heart, in language of heart cleansing and transplant (11:17–21; 36:25–27). These realities are predicated of the people of God in terms of a new creation, through Ezekiel's valley of dry bones vision and the explanation that follows (37:23–28).[166] Therefore, the prohibition of uncircumcised foreigners entering the sanctuary indicates, ironically, that with the coming of the new covenant and Davidic king, foreigners would also be recipients of the flesh/heart circumcision. Thus, the Lord would provide the means by which foreigners could, together with Israel, celebrate the Passover in the same, renewed spiritual condition as Israel—made alive by the Holy Spirit, Spirit indwelt, heart circumcised, new creations (cf. Isa 52:1).[167]

Ezra 6:19–22

In Ezra 6, Darius decrees that the temple should be rebuilt in Jerusalem, based upon the prior decree of Cyrus and with resources provided by the Persian empire (vv. 1–12). The exiles completed the temple in the sixth year of Darius's reign and dedicated the temple with sacrifices (vv. 12–17).[168] The following year, on the fourteenth day of the first month, "the returned exiles kept the Passover" (v. 19). Ezra documents the priests and Levites purification and active role in slaughtering the Passover lamb "for all the returned

---

work in and indwelling God's people as a "conceptual parallel" to circumcision of the heart (Hamilton, *God's Indwelling Presence*, 53).

166. Dumbrell, *End of the Beginning*, 96; Hamilton, *God's Indwelling Presence*, 48–50.

167. Deenick reaches strikingly similar conclusions about Isa 52:1 (Deenick, *Righteous by Promise*, 82–84).

168. The temple was completed in 516–515 BC. Fensham, *Books of Ezra and Nehemiah*, 92.

exiles" (v. 20).[169] The text describes Israelites who participated in the meal as "the people of Israel who had returned from exile" and "everyone who had joined them and separated himself from the uncleanness of the peoples of the land to worship the Lord" (v. 21). The account concludes by noting the subsequent celebration of the Feast of Unleavened Bread and the favor given to Israel by the king, due to God turning his heart (v. 22).[170]

As with the analysis of the other Passover accounts, the participants in the meal and the function of the meal are the concern of this section. In this post-exilic celebration of Passover, the nation keeps the festival at its appointed time and in the appointed way. Yet, their practice reveals greater continuity with God's prescription in Deuteronomy 16 and the Passover celebrations of Hezekiah and Josiah—they celebrated in a centralized location and the role of the priests and Levites was increased from the Exodus account.[171] The context of Ezra 6 clearly connects the celebration of Passover with the dedication of the second temple in Jerusalem.[172] Whereas Hezekiah's and Josiah's Passover celebrations involved the renewal and restoration of temple worship in Solomon's temple, the post-exile Passover comes on the heels of the return from exile and the second temple's completion. Furthermore, Allen concludes that just as the Passover was instituted to commemorate the Exodus, the returned exiles celebrate their second exodus through the events of chapter 6.[173] The Lord is reconstituting his people. The Lord's presence in the temple, the sacrificial blood covering their sins, and the covenant-participating meal of Passover confirm the Lord's promises to renew them after exile.[174] The con-

169. The progression of responsibility for slaughtering the lamb moves from the head of the house (Exod 12:6), to the Levites out of necessity due to the uncleanness of the people (2 Chr 30:17), to the Levites as a given (2 Chr 35:2; Ezra 6:20). For a clear description of this progression, see Fensham, *Books of Ezra and Nehemiah*, 95.

170. For a discussion of chronology and the king in this verse, see Breneman, *Ezra, Nehemiah, Esther*, 122; Fensham, *Books of Ezra and Nehemiah*, 96–97.

171. Breneman, *Ezra, Nehemiah, Esther*, 121.

172. The temple was completed around one month prior to the Passover celebration. Fensham acknowledges that one reason Passover was not celebrated after the dedication of Solomon's temple was the timing of that temple's completion. It was the wrong time of year (Fensham, *Books of Ezra and Nehemiah*, 95).

173. Leslie Allen contends that the completion of the temple, the sin offerings (the first in seventy years), and the Passover are intended by the author to draw the reader's mind to the exodus theme introduced in 1:4–6. There, Cyrus commanded that the people of Israel could return to Judah to build a house for the Lord with articles of gold and jewelry they were to receive before their exit, reminiscent of the plundering of the Egyptians (cf. Exod 12:35–38). For a prediction of a second exodus after exile, see Isa 43:19–21; 48:21; 51:9–11; 52:11–12 (Allen, *Ezra, Nehemiah, Esther*, 88, 39–40). For the timing of the sacrifices, see Fensham, *Books of Ezra and Nehemiah*, 94.

174. For more on these themes, see Levering, *Ezra and Nehemiah*, 77; Ross, *Hope*

struction of this second temple, the reconstitution of the people, and Lord's presence within it (Hag 2:5) suggests that the second temple is at least a partial fulfillment of Ezekiel's temple vision.[175]

The text does not mention circumcision. However, the description of the participants deserves closer scrutiny. The Israelites who returned from exile were presumably circumcised (v. 21). The group that joined the Israelites may have been sojourners who came back with them from exile and/or sojourners dwelling near Jerusalem during the Israelites' absence.[176] A comparison with Ezra 4:1–4 suggests that proselytes may well be the referent to which Ezra refers.[177] If the group included proselytes, presumably separating from the Gentile uncleanness included circumcision, as it seems to in Numbers 9. One cannot be dogmatic here. At the least, all who participated performed the ceremonial rites for ritual purification (cf. Lev 11).

The New Covenant

The promises of the new covenant in Jeremiah 31:31–34 round out this chapter's consideration of the old covenant signs of circumcision and Passover and should be read in connection with the analysis of Ezekiel 36:26–27 throughout this chapter. Given Israel's inability to keep the Mosaic covenant, the promise of the new covenant establishes the eschatological hope of the Mosaic covenant age because the world-wide scope of the blessing of Abraham and the reversal of sin's effects comes to fruition through an "ideal Israel."[178] Israel's failure to keep the Mosaic covenant lies in the immediate background of Jeremiah 31:31–34. As Thompson explains, "They had not merely refused to obey the law or to acknowledge Yahweh's complete and sole sovereignty, but were incapable of such obedience."[179] Only the Lord's actions could make covenant faithfulness possible, because the change required to uphold God's covenant was humanly impossible (cf. 13:23). Thus,

---

of Glory, 350–51.

175. Hamilton Jr., *God's Indwelling Presence*, 51.

176. Breneman opts for the latter but does not seek to demonstrate the point (Breneman, *Ezra, Nehemiah, Esther*, 122).

177. Allen, *Ezra, Nehemiah, Esther*, 89; Fensham, *Books of Ezra and Nehemiah*, 96. Whereas the people (*goy*) of 4:4 were not allowed to join the returned exiles in building the temple, "all" (*kôl*) who separated themselves from the uncleanness of the peoples (*goy*) of the land were included in the Passover.

178. Wellum defines "ideal Israel" as "a community tied to the [Davidic] servant of the Lord, located in a rejuvenated new heavens and new earth" (Gentry and Wellum, *Kingdom through Covenant*, 645).

179. Thompson, *Jeremiah*, 580.

the Lord promises three things to Israel:[180] (1) to change his people's "inner nature which will make them capable of obedience" by writing his law on their hearts;[181] (2) to be the God of all of his people and to make them his own, entailing a personal and saving knowledge of him (31:34; cf. 7:23; 11:4; 24:7; 30:22; 31:1; 32:38; Ezek 11:20; 36:28);[182] and (3) full forgiveness of sins as the means to that relational knowledge (Jer 31:34). In order to prepare biblically-theologically for chapters 3 and 4, this section presents three promises of the new covenant and three points of theological summary.

First, the new covenant would be structurally different from the old.[183] Rather than mediating his rule through the offices of prophet, priest, and

180. Representing progressive dispensationalists, Ware argues that God promises to make the new covenant with Israel and Judah specifically and exclusively. Yet, Ware recognizes that that same new covenant would "extend beyond Israel to the nations" (Isa 55:3–5). Ware, "New Covenant and the People(s) of God," in Bock and Blaising, *Dispensationalism, Israel, and the Church* 1.1. By contrast, this book follows Wellum's argument that the new covenant is universal in scope (Isa 42:6; 49:6; 55:3–5; 56:4–8; 66:18–24). Across the OT canon, the promises of God are narrowed from Abraham, to Israel, to David as representative of the nation, to a son of David who would fulfill the promises (Isa 9:6–7; 11:1–10; Jer 23:5–6; 33:14–26; Ezek 34:23–24; 37:24–28). Because this son of David would also be a son of Adam (Gen 1:26–28; Exod 4:21–22) and Son of God (Dan 7:14; Ps 2; 110:1), he would represent Israel and all humanity as the new covenant head. See Wellum, "Beyond Mere Ecclesiology," in Easley and Morgan, *Community of Jesus*, 196–97.

181. Thompson, *Jeremiah*, 581; Feinberg, "Jeremiah," in Gaebelein, *Expositor's Bible Commentary*, 576. Jeffery Neill claims, "what is new [about the new covenant] is that the ceremonial law is written on the hearts of God's people" (Neill, "Newness of the New Covenant," in Strawbridge, *Case for Covenantal Infant Baptism*, 147). For problems with viewing the law as divided into ceremonial, civil, and moral, see Rosner, *Paul and the Law*, 36–38. The repetition of "I will" (Jer 31:31–34) indicates God's initiative to unilaterally bring about the new covenant. Yet, the new covenant partners, by having the law written on their hearts, would be divinely enabled to uphold their covenantal obligations. See Ware, "New Covenant and the People(s) of God," in Bock and Blaising, *Dispensationalism, Israel, and the Church* 1.3.4–6.

182. The references are to the covenantal formula: "I will be your God and you shall be my people." See Thompson, *Jeremiah*, 581. The statement in Jer 31:34 that "no longer shall each one teach his neighbor and each his brother saying, 'know the Lord,'" appears to affirm the structural removal of the Levitical priesthood from their mediatorial role and the replacement of that human mediation by the future Messiah" (Neill, "Newness of the New Covenant," in Strawbridge, *Case for Covenantal Infant Baptism*, 148).

183. This and the following paragraphs follow Gentry and Wellum, *Kingdom through Covenant*, 646–50. Ware helpfully describes four new elements of the new covenant as "(1) a new mode of implementation, namely the internalization of the law . . . (2) a new result, namely faithfulness to God . . . (3) a new basis, namely, full and final forgiveness . . . [and] (4) a new scope of inclusion, namely, covenant faithfulness characteristic of all covenant participants" (Ware, "New Covenant and the People[s] of God," in Bock and Blaising, *Dispensationalism, Israel, and the Church* 1.2.4). The theological points that follow present the promises of the new covenant as exegetically

king, the Lord would work effectually within each member of the covenant community so that each would know the Lord, be indwelt by the Spirit, and possess a circumcised heart (cf. Joel 2:28–32).[184] As opposed to the old covenant, where one entered the covenant community by the physical sign of circumcision based upon the genealogical principle of the Abrahamic covenant, the new covenant would entail entry to the covenant based upon one's personal connection with the Messianic Servant of the Lord (Isa 49:6–8).[185]

Second, the new covenant would be different in "nature" from the old.[186] Rather than the covenant community being composed of covenant breakers (Jer 31:32), all within the new covenant community would receive full forgiveness of sins and have the law written on the hearts, enabling their Spirit empowered obedience to the covenant (cf. Ezek 36:26–27).[187] Therefore, Jeremiah signals that the new covenant community would not be mixed with unbelievers and believers together. Rather, in this community the eschatological hope of Deuteronomy 30:6 would be realized.[188]

Third, the new covenant would provide complete forgiveness of sin. Rather than continuing to offer sacrifices to atone for sins (Lev 16), the Servant of the Lord would die as a sacrificial lamb and substitutionary sin offering (Isa 53:4–10), through which covenantal fellowship and knowledge of

---

and redemptive-historically requiring that the new covenant is not merely an extension and continuation of the old covenant. Contra Pratt Jr., "Infant Baptism in the New Covenant," in Strawbridge, *Case for Covenantal Infant Baptism*, 179.

184. Carson, *Showing the Spirit*, 152, cited in Gentry and Wellum, *Kingdom through Covenant*, 647. Contra Neill, "Newness of the New Covenant," in Strawbridge, *Case for Covenantal Infant Baptism*, 134–36. Neill argues that the law written on the heart is not unique to the new covenant community, because, if it were, accounting for any old covenant believer's obedience would be impossible. On this point, see the section on the circumcision of the heart above.

185. Gentry and Wellum, *Kingdom through Covenant*, 648. Feinberg claims the message of the new covenant is "individual, internal, and universal." While he is correct, the plural pronouns entail that the individuals form a covenant community (Feinberg, "Jeremiah," in Gaebelein, *Expositor's Bible Commentary*, 577).

186. Wellum, "Beyond Mere Ecclesiology," in Easley and Morgan, *Community of Jesus*, 199–200.

187. Feinberg, "Jeremiah," in Gaebelein, *Expositor's Bible Commentary*, 576; Ware, "New Covenant and the People(s) of God," in Bock and Blaising, *Dispensationalism, Israel, and the Church* 1.6.3. Contra Neill, "Newness of the New Covenant," in Strawbridge, *Case for Covenantal Infant Baptism*, 133. Neill argues that new covenant breakers must exist due to his interpretation of the warning passages of Hebrews rather than arguing from Jer 31.

188. Thompson, *Jeremiah*, 581. The phrases "the days are coming" (v. 31) and "after those days" (v. 33) emphasize the eschatological period in which the promise of the new covenant would (at least begin to) be fulfilled (Feinberg, "Jeremiah," in Gaebelein, *Expositor's Bible Commentary*, 576).

God would come to all the new covenant members, including Gentiles (Isa 56–57).[189] God's choice not to act against his sinful people (Jer 31:34) due to their covenantal relationship entails "harmony restored between creation and God" as before sin entered the world.[190] Forgiveness would be the "new basis" upon which a saving knowledge of God (cf. Ps 1:6), the law could be written on the heart, and the indwelling Spirit would enable obedience.[191]

The new structure and nature of the new covenant would seem to require new signs of covenant entry and participation. However, knowledge of these signs would only come with the advent of the Messiah.

Summary and Conclusion

As the Old Testament itself develops the theme of circumcision, the tension created by covenant members receiving the sign of circumcision without themselves possessing circumcised hearts moves toward a resolution. By the end of the Old Testament, the prophets create the expectation that all the members of the new covenant would possess heart circumcision, entailing heart cleansing/renewal and the permanent indwelling of the Holy Spirit. Thus, in the Old Testament the physical sign of circumcision functions typologically and prospectively to point toward heart circumcision that God would bring under the new covenant. At the same time, physical circumcision functions mark off the people of God from the surrounding nations as God's representative priest-kings. Circumcision should be understood as a sign of initiation into the covenant community, because the ongoing covenantal meal of God's people required the physical sign of circumcision for participation. Passover should be understood as the sign of participation.

---

189. As Feinberg argues, "The basis of the new covenant is forgiveness of sin" (v. 34). The goal is "I will be their God and they will be my people" (v. 34). See Feinberg, "Jeremiah," in Gaebelein, *Expositor's Bible Commentary*, 577. On the promise of the inclusion of the Gentiles through the Messianic Servant, see Greever, "Nature of the New Covenant," 80–83.

190. Gentry and Wellum, *Kingdom through Covenant*, 650.

191. Ware, "New Covenant and the People(s) of God," in Bock and Blaising, *Dispensationalism, Israel, and the Church* 1.5.

Chapter 3

Baptism and the Lord's Supper
as Kingdom through
Covenant Signs

WHEREAS CHAPTER 2 PRESENTED the old covenant signs of circumcision and Passover in their covenantal relation, this chapter considers the relationship between baptism and the Lord's Supper in the new covenant. Before delving into the more complex matter of how the old covenant signs relate to the new, this chapter surveys the function, meaning, and covenantal relation of the new covenant signs to each other. Two pillars of the thesis find their grounding here: (1) the way in which the New Testament assumes that believers are baptized and (2) the exemplary way that Acts 2:41–42 presents new converts being baptized before they participate in the Lord's Supper. Furthermore, this chapter aims to demonstrate that baptism consistently functions as the sign of entry/initiation to the new covenant and the Lord's Supper functions as the ongoing sign of new covenant participation. Establishing the covenantal functions of the new covenant signs is necessary in order to provide the biblical-theological relationship of the old covenant signs to new covenant signs (chapter 4). These aims can be achieved in three steps: (1) surveying all the baptism passages in the New Testament in order to highlight the assumption of baptism and the sign's covenantal function; (2) surveying all of the Lord's Supper passages in the New Testament to highlight its participants and covenantal function; and (3) presenting the prerequisite relationship of baptism to the Lord's Supper in Acts 2:41–42 (and likely in Corinth in Acts 18:1–11) as exemplary for the church until Christ's return.

Baptism as a Sign of Entry into the Inaugurated Kingdom and New Covenant

By surveying baptism in the Gospels, Acts, Pauline epistles, and general epistles, this section demonstrates that in the New Testament baptism functions as a covenantal initiation sign and mark of entry into the kingdom of God. This section also highlights the assumption that all believers are or soon will be baptized as an aspect of their initial conversion.

Baptism in the Gospels

This section considers John's baptism, Mark 10:38–39, John 3:5, and Matthew 28:18–20 in turn.

John's Baptism

The Gospel writers first mention baptism in connection with John the Baptist (Matt 3:6, 11; Mark 1:4; Luke 3:3; John 1:25–28).[1] John's baptism is one "of repentance for the forgiveness of sins" (Mark 1:4), which he proclaimed in light of the nearness of the kingdom of heaven (Matt 3:2) and in preparation for the Messianic baptism with the Holy Spirit and fire (vv. 11–12). Seven texts speak specifically of baptism with the Spirit in the New Testament.[2] John the Baptist establishes the expectation in the Gospels that Jesus would be the one to baptize with the Spirit, since he himself was anointed by the Spirit as the Messiah at his baptism in order to pour out the Spirit on His followers (John 1:33; cf. Matt 3:11–12; Mark 1:7–8; Luke 3:15–17).[3] In light

---

1. This book follows the research of several scholars who argue that no explicit connection exists between Jewish proselyte baptism and John's baptism or Christian baptism. For example, Everett Ferguson argues that while proselyte baptisms had some similarities to Christian baptisms, differences include several points: "Proselyte baptism required witnesses but was self-administered; baptism by John and Christians had an administrator. In proselyte baptism the candidate was freed from pagan impurity; in Christian baptism one received pardon and regeneration as divine grace. The heart of rabbinic conversion ceremony was circumcision, not baptism; baptism was the central act in Christian conversion. Proselyte baptism was for Gentiles; Christians baptized Jews as well as Gentiles" (Ferguson, *Baptism in the Early Church*, 82). Ferguson writes with a stronger association of baptism to pardon and regeneration than this book affirms. See also Beasley-Murray, *Baptism in the New Testament*, 18–31; Hammett, *Forty Questions*, 56; Köstenberger, "Baptism in the Gospels," in Schreiner and Wright, *Believer's Baptism*, 11n1.

2. Matt 3:11–12; Mark 1:7–8; Luke 3:15–17; John 1:33; Acts 1:4–5; 11:16; 1 Cor 12:13.

3. For more on the baptism of the Holy Spirit, see chapter 5.

of John's pre-Messianic role (3:2; cf. Isa 40:3),[4] his baptism occurred in the overlap of two redemptive-historical ages—the old covenant age of promise and the new covenant age of fulfillment.[5] Other evidence for this claim appears in the way the apostles recognized John the Baptist's ministry as the beginning of the Messianic age (cf. Acts 1:22; 10:37; 13:24).

Given its redemptive-historical location, John's baptism carries some unique aspects. For example, whereas those who received John's baptism looked forward to the Messiah, all who receive baptism after the cross, resurrection, ascension, and sending of the Holy Spirit look back to Jesus' work.[6] Similarly, whereas John's baptism was not explicitly trinitarian,[7] Christian baptism is in the one name of the three persons: Father, Son, and Holy Spirit (Matt 28:19; cf. Acts 18:25; 19:1–6).[8] Finally, for the purposes of this study, because John's baptism occurred prior to the inauguration of the new covenant and kingdom, it necessarily occurred prior to the

4. On the exodus typological aspect of John's ministry in fulfillment of Isa 40, see Köstenberger, "Baptism in the Gospels," in Schreiner and Wright, *Believer's Baptism*, 13–14; Beasley-Murray, *Baptism in the New Testament*, 41.

5. Because Jesus describes John's baptism as being from heaven (Matt 21:25; Mark 11:30), Thomas Baldwin describes John's baptism as beginning the "gospel dispensation" (Baldwin, *Baptism of Believers Only*, 69).

6. John points to this distinction by claiming that the Messiah to come would baptize with the Holy Spirit and fire. The implication is that John's baptism did not entail Holy Spirit baptism (Köstenberger, "Baptism in the Gospels," in Schreiner and Wright, *Believer's Baptism*, 15). See the section on baptism with the Holy Spirit in chapter 4.

7. This statement refers to the lack of baptism in the name of the triune God. Yet, the presence and action of each divine person in Jesus' baptism presents one of the clearest references to the Trinity in the Gospels. See Köstenberger, "Baptism in the Gospels," in Schreiner and Wright, *Believer's Baptism*, 14; Augustine, *Trinity*, in Rotelle, *Works of Saint Augustine*, 70–71.

8. This fact is yet another reason to explain John's baptism as unique in redemptive history. Despite the help it might be to the thesis of this book to claim that John's baptism was explicitly Christian baptism, the lack of trinitarian teaching proves that John's baptism occurred just prior to the period in which progressive revelation included clear teaching on the Trinity. For arguments for and against John's baptism constituting Christian baptism, see Baldwin, *Particular Communion*, 69–76; Worcester, *Friendly Letter*, 36; Hall Jr., *On Terms of Communion*, 114. As to the question of whether the order of institution in the NT is baptism and then Lord's Supper or vice-versa, I disagree with Hall that the Lord's Supper was instituted first. While John's baptism is unique in redemptive history, Jesus' exemplary baptism, the mode of immersion, and the forward looking nature of John's baptism to the coming Messiah suggests that John's baptism served a unique initiatory function for that brief overlap of the ages. As such, although it lacks the clarity that progressive revelation would supply and lacks the force of Jesus' disciple-making commission, John's baptism was sufficient for those who believed explicitly in Jesus even prior to his death and resurrection. Andrew and John were presumably not rebaptized after transitioning from being John's disciples to being Jesus' disciples (cf. John 1:35–42). For a counter argument, see Hall Jr., *Short Statement*, 21.

establishment of the church (cf. Matt 16:19–20; Acts 2:1–2). Therefore, whereas those who received John's baptism identified with the coming Messiah as a group, those who received Christian baptism in Acts identified specifically with Jesus and the local assembly/church composed of his followers (Acts 2:41; 18:8–17; cf. 1 Cor 1:15–16).[9]

John's baptism is significant for this project for three reasons. First, John's baptism functioned as the symbolic response of repentance and confession of sin in light of the imminent appearing of the Messianic king and kingdom. Thus, to receive John's baptism was to publicly proclaim allegiance to the coming Messianic king, which entailed denying allegiance to self and all other authorities. As a result, John's baptism functioned as "an initiatory rite into 'true Israel,' the believing remnant."[10] That baptism functions as a sign of entry into the people belonging to the coming Messianic kingdom is significant.[11] If Israelites were the only recipients of John's baptism (and no Gentiles are recorded in the New Testament), then all those who received baptism came from circumcised households. The move from physical circumcision to baptism points forward to a time after Christ's exaltation when circumcision would no longer be required for entry into God's people, though baptism would continue to be (cf. John 7:37–39; Acts 15).

The second significant point regarding John's baptism is that Jesus was baptized by John. According to the textual clues, John performed baptism by immersing Jesus fully into the Jordan river and raising him up again (Matt 3:16; par. Mark 3:10; cf. Luke 3:21; John 1:32–33).[12] Jesus' explana-

9. Beasley-Murray writes, "Christian baptism is different than John's because it rests on an accomplished fact. [The] new covenant had been made. [The] kingdom was dawning and could be entered" (Beasley-Murray, *Baptism in the New Testament*, 100). Similarly, see Köstenberger, "Baptism in the Gospels," in Schreiner and Wright, *Believer's Baptism*, 31.

10. Köstenberger writes, "In light of the reality and certainty of God's judgment, John called for conversion—a reorientation of one's life, a return to God, and a restoration of one's relationship with him—whereby people's confession of sins resulted in divine forgiveness" (Köstenberger, "Baptism in the Gospels," in Schreiner and Wright, *Believer's Baptism*, 15). Appropriately, Köstenberger refers to John's baptism as having "an eschatological dimension."

11. Beasley-Murray sees at least one similarity between Jesus' baptism and the baptism of Jesus followers: "If [Jesus] had been baptized unto the bringing of the kingdom, there was no reason why people should not be baptized with a view to entering it even while [Jesus] was engaged in his Messianic task" (cf. John 3:22; 4:2) (Beasley-Murray, *Baptism in the New Testament*, 66).

12. Köstenberger explains that *baptizo* is an intensive form of *bapto*, which means to dip or immerse. The Gospel writers' statements that Jesus came up out of the water provide further evidence for immersion. See Köstenberger, "Baptism in the Gospels," in Schreiner and Wright, *Believer's Baptism*, 18n21. Baptists (including this author) generally hold to immersion as the biblical mode of baptism for several reasons. Some

tion that by receiving John's baptism he was "fulfill[ing] all righteousness" functionally identifies Jesus with his people and establishes baptism by immersion as an example for what Jesus would call his followers to do (Matt 3:15; cf. 28:19). Indeed, John emphasizes that Jesus' baptism was divinely intended to reveal the Messiah (John 1:31).[13]

Third, John's baptism serves as the possible means by which Jesus' disciples received baptism prior to their action of baptizing other followers of Christ and celebrating the Last Supper. While the first two points above appear clearly in the Gospels, this third point is disputed.[14] John records the fact that Jesus' disciples baptized others, though Jesus himself baptized no one (4:1–2).[15] Apollos and the Ephesian disciples serve as a test case. Whereas Apollos "knew only the baptism of John," still he "spoke and taught accurately the things concerning Jesus" (Acts 18:25). Due to his lack of full Christian theology (at least in terms of Christian baptism), Priscilla and Aquila "explained to him the way of God more accurately" (v. 26). Yet, Apollos did not require Christian baptism. The Ephesian disciples of John on the other hand were baptized "into John's baptism" and yet, had "not even heard that there is a Holy Spirit" (19:2–3). When Paul explained that John was "telling people to believe in the one who was to come after him, that is, Jesus . . . they were baptized in the name of the Lord Jesus" (vv. 4–5). Putting

---

of these include (1) the examples of Jesus' baptism and the Ethiopian eunuch's baptism with their language of going into the water and coming up out of the water; (2) the meaning of the word baptism; and (3) the symbolism of dying and rising (cf. Acts 8:36–38; Rom 6:3–4). For a carefully argued proposal for the legitimacy of pouring or sprinkling a professing believer as an irregular but legitimate baptism, see Turner, "Immersed into the Church?," 262–69.

13. Jesus' request for baptism in no way suggests his need for repentance or forgiveness. So Köstenberger, "Baptism in the Gospels," in Schreiner and Wright, *Believer's Baptism*, 19, 30.

14. Robert Hall Jr., for example, argues that because John's baptism and the baptism of Jesus' disciples' overlapped in terms of when they were practiced, it is impossible that John's baptism could be attached to a previous dispensation while the disciples' baptism could be associated with the new covenant age (Hall Jr., *Terms of Communion*, 114).

15. Beasley-Murray sees no reason to argue that the disciples were baptized, given the redemptive-historical uniqueness of the period in which the disciples lived. He writes, "The kingdom was being realized in the ministry of the Messiah but not as it would shortly be; so the baptism that belonged to the time of redemption was being adumbrated, but not with the power that it should shortly have. The baptism of the ministry therefore was neither Jewish, nor Johannine, nor Christian; it was a baptism in obedience to the Messianic proclamation, under the sign of the Messianic action and in anticipation of the Messianic deliverance. More than that we cannot say" (Beasley-Murray, *Baptism in the New Testament*, 72). Presumably, Jesus' disciples would not have performed baptisms without themselves being baptized. Although this statement is an argument from silence, it is a common presumption.

these accounts together, Beasley-Murray concludes, "Where submission to the Messiah Jesus is accompanied by the possession of the Spirit, John's baptism needs no supplementing; where both are lacking, baptism in the name of Jesus must be administered."[16] Thus the supposition that Jesus' disciples were baptized with John's baptism prior to the institution of the Lord's Supper, while not determinative for close communion, has some merit.

Mark 10:38–39

Jesus refers to baptism metaphorically in Mark 10:38–39 in response to James and John's request to sit on his right and left hand in glory (10:35–37). Jesus answers their question by asking if they are able "to drink the cup that I drink or to be baptized with the baptism with which I am baptized" (v. 38). Jesus is clearly referring to his impending death in his dual reference to baptism and the cup.[17]

Two points from this passage are significant for this study: (1) Jesus uses baptism to refer to his death as a judgment from God and (2) Jesus associates baptism and the cup together with his death.[18] The association of baptism and death is consistent with Paul's imagery of baptism into Jesus' death (Rom 6:3–4). The association of baptism with the cup places the image of death/burial alongside Jesus' drinking of the cup of God's wrath on the cross as the substitutionary Servant for sinners (Isa 51:17–22; 53; Mark 14:36).[19]

16. Beasley-Murray, *Baptism in the New Testament*, 112. He continues, "Comparing this with the Cornelius episode, it would appear that the baptism of John is viewed as an adequate preparation for Christian discipleship where it is completed in faith by the Spirit. Apollos needs no special baptism, but Cornelius must be baptized. But John's baptism without the Spirit is defective and must be followed by baptism that bestows it." Speaking of baptism bestowing the Spirit goes beyond the evidence. Tyler's use of this passage to justify open communion creates false analogies. He argues that Apollos' experience of the baptism of John is analogous with that of a Christian from a non-Baptist denomination. Because Apollos' baptism was not viewed as defective, so also, Tyler claims, the infant baptism of a genuine believer should be received as sufficient (Tyler, *Baptism*, 141). However, the redemptive-historical relationship of John's baptism to Christian baptism bears unique analogies, given John's temporal context. The comparison fails to convince.

17. Köstenberger, "Baptism in the Gospels," in Schreiner and Wright, *Believer's Baptism*, 16–17.

18. Beasley-Murray, *Baptism in the New Testament*, 75.

19. On the cup of wrath, see also Jer 25:27; Ezek 23:32; and Hab 2:16 (Beasley-Murray, *Baptism in the New Testament*, 73). Robert Stein helpfully connects the metaphorical cup of wrath and the cup of the new covenant in Jesus' blood. He writes, "The [Last Supper] cup's contents represent/symbolize the sacrificial nature of Jesus' death.

John 3:5

Scholars have debated what is meant by the need to be "born of water and Spirit." Although baptism is not mentioned in the passage, Beasley-Murray contends that by the time of John's writing, any mention of being born of water would have been understood as a reference to baptism.[20] However, this connection is tenuous.

Jesus introduces the subject of the new birth or regeneration in John 3:3 by telling Nicodemus, "unless one is born again, he cannot see the kingdom of God." By "born again," Jesus means that to "enter the kingdom" one must be "born of water and spirit" (v. 5). As Hamilton helpfully notes, both nouns are "governed by one preposition (*ex hudatos kai pneumatos*), suggesting they refer to [the] single reality [of] eschatological cleansing and renewal promised by Israel's prophets (see Isa 44:3; Ezek 36:25–26)."[21] Being born is passive,[22] indicating that new birth is God's work rather than humanity's. Jesus explicitly attributes new birth to the Holy Spirit as the divine person on whom the action terminates when he says "that which is born of Spirit is spirit" (v. 6). He adds that the Spirit's regenerating work is elusive like the wind, since only the effects of the new birth can be seen in a born again person (v. 8).

'Blood' refers to the giving up of life (cf. Lev 17:14, NIV: 'For the life of every creature is in its blood'), and the 'blood of the covenant' (Exod 24:8; Zech 9:11; cf. Heb 9:18–22; 10:29) refers to the surrender of the life of the sacrificial victim whose blood (i.e., death) seals a covenant. The death of Jesus, his giving his life as a ransom for many (Mark 10:45), is understood as a sacrificial act sealing a covenant" (Stein, *Mark*, 651). Thus, Mark combines several themes in the image of the cup: (1) Jesus' death functioned to vicariously bear the wrath of God on behalf of sinners; (2) seal the new covenant; and (3) provide forgiveness of sins through that covenant." See the section on the Last Supper in Luke below for more.

20. Beasley-Murray, *Baptism in the New Testament*, 226. Beasley-Murray's claim that baptism is "the occasion when the Spirit gives to faith the regeneration that qualifies it for the kingdom" is stronger than the evidence. In this statement, he makes faith antecedent to the new birth, contra 1 John 5:1 (230). This explanation also pushes too strongly in the sacramental direction.

21. Hamilton, *God's Indwelling Presence*, 131. I concur with this assessment since Ezek 36:25–26 contains both the images to which Jesus refers—water for internal cleansing of idolatrous hearts (v. 25) and a new heart and spirit placed within God's people (v. 26). If the expectation of new hearts/spirits promised in Ezekiel 36:26 is fulfilled in the Spirit's work of regeneration, then expectation of circumcised hearts also finds its fulfillment here (See Eph 2:6; Col 2:11–13). For more on this connection, see chapter 4. See also Hammett, *Forty Questions*, 126; Carson, *Gospel According to John*, 191–96; Caneday, "Baptism in the Stone-Cambell Restoration Movement," in Schreiner and Wright, *Believer's Baptism*, 308–9.

22. Note the passive verbs from γεννάω (to produce, bring forth, give birth)— γεννηθῇ (vv. 3, 5).

Regarding verse 5, Carson argues that although the NIV capitalizes "Spirit" in the phrase "born of water and the Spirit," "the article and the capital 'S' should be dropped . . . [because] the focus is on the imparta-tion of God's nature as 'spirit,' not on the Holy Spirit as such."[23] At the same time, this work of imparting God's nature to a sinner is the work of the Holy Spirit, whom Jesus says works like the wind, which "blows where it will" (v. 8). Therefore, Jesus' first mention of new birth refers to the work of the Spirit of God whereby hard-hearted sinners who are unable to follow God's law are cleansed and given a new nature to enable them to believe the gospel and obey God. The new birth then is a significant conceptual parallel to heart circumcision. While this new birth is aptly pictured in baptism, John's lack of reference to baptism in the context leads to the conclusion that while baptism portrays the new birth, baptism is not the precise occasion of the new birth.

Matthew 28:18–20

Just prior to his ascension, the resurrected Christ commissioned his dis-ciples to make disciples by baptizing them into the one name of the three persons: Father, Son, and Holy Spirit and teaching these new disciples to obey all that he commanded. Jesus grounds his command in his reception of "all authority in heaven and on earth," which he received from God the Father by virtue of his resurrection from the dead on behalf of sinners (Rom 1:4).[24] Jesus' authority as the divine-human Messianic king entails that those who would enter his kingdom must become his disciples by baptism.[25] Be-

23. Carson, *Gospel According to John*, 195–96. Carson answers the objection posed by Hamilton and others that requiring new birth by the Spirit presumes that Nicodemus could experience new birth at that moment. He answers, "The charge is ill-conceived. Jesus is not presented as demanding that Nicodemus experience the new birth in the instant; rather, he is forcefully articulating what must be experienced if he is to enter the kingdom of God." Carson compares the tension here between the mention of new birth and Nicodemus' epochal inability to experience it just yet with the tension of the need to enter the kingdom of God in the other Gospels before Jesus completes His mission. The presence of these tensions in the Gospels is "why all discipleship in all four Gospels is inevitably transitional. The coming-to-faith of the first followers of Jesus was in certain respects unique."

24. Make disciples is the command. Baptizing and teaching are subordinate parti-ciples to the command. See Blomberg, *Matthew*, 431–32. Similar to Dan 7:14, Matthew portrays Jesus as the "exalted eschatological ruler of the world's kingdoms" (Kösten-berger, "Baptism in the Gospels," in Schreiner and Wright, *Believer's Baptism*, 22).

25. Although Doriani acknowledges that Jesus is referring to the conversion of adults in Matt 28:18–20, he still maintains that "baptism is a valuable means of dis-cipling children" (Doriani, "Matthew 28:18–20," in Strawbridge, *Case for Covenantal*

cause baptism is the instrumental, outward, and public means by which one becomes a disciple, Jesus' commission serves to officially institute baptism as the sign of entering his kingdom (saving rule) and joining his people (realm/sphere).[26] Being baptized is a mark of becoming a disciple.[27] As Beasley-Murray explains, baptism "into the Name" of the triune God entails setting a person in a new relation to God and demonstrates a new identity.[28]

Infant Baptism, 41–42). Children, for Doriani, include infants who are not personally capable of submitting to and trusting in Christ as Savior and King. Strawbridge argues similarly from the grounds that children are included in the kingdom by virtue of their belonging to believing parents from Jesus' statement that "to such belongs the kingdom of heaven" (Matt 19:14). See Strawbridge, "Polemics of Anabaptism," in Strawbridge, *Case for Covenantal Infant Baptism*, 284. So also Gallant, "Kingdom of God and Children," in Strawbridge, *Case for Covenant Communion*, 42–43. Pedobaptist Bryan Chappell finds unconvincing the argument for infant baptism based upon the love of Christ for children (Chappell, "Pastoral View of Infant Baptism," in Strawbridge, *Case for Covenantal Infant Baptism*, 27). Köstenberger makes four responses to these lines of argument: (1) Jesus' commission calls for personal responses of repentance and faith rather than reliance on the faith of another for baptism; (2) regeneration occurs in connection with repentance and faith in Scripture and should not be assumed to occur in infants; (3) because baptism is a means of becoming a disciple of Jesus in Matt 28:18–20, viewing baptism as a means of discipling children toward faith in Jesus runs counter to Jesus' order and design of discipleship; and (4) while it is "true that nothing in Matthew excludes children from discipleship and baptism," one must distinguish between children capable of understanding and believing the gospel and incapable infants, for "There is equally nothing in Matthew that suggests that infants ought to be baptized or are capable of conversion" (Köstenberger, "Baptism in the Gospels," in Schreiner and Wright, *Believer's Baptism*, 24–25). Köstenberger also cites Carson. See Carson's argument that Matthew is stressing child-like faith, not that children (of believers) are already apart of the kingdom by virtue of their parentage (Carson, "Matthew," in Gaebelein, *Expositor's Bible Commentary*, 420).

26. The statement that Jesus is given "all" authority "pertains to his mission, to be carried out through the disciples as his emissaries, on the basis of his word." In this sense, by virtue of his cross-work, Jesus is reconstituting image bearers to extend his saving rule to the whole earth (Gen 1:28) (Köstenberger, "Baptism in the Gospels," in Schreiner and Wright, *Believer's Baptism*, 22). For a helpful comparison of definitions of kingdom that includes the notion of saving reign and sphere, see Schreiner, *Kingdom of God*, 18–23.

27. Beasley-Murray argues, "Disciples are made by means of baptism," and the baptism is understood as being by faith in Jesus (Beasley-Murray, *Baptism in the New Testament*, 89). So also Köstenberger, "Baptism in the Gospels," in Schreiner and Wright, *Believer's Baptism*, 33.

28. Beasley-Murray, *Baptism in the New Testament*, 90–91. Significantly, while the convert confesses the name of the triune God in submitting to baptism, the Lord instructs his disciples to call that new convert by his own name as the existing disciple baptizes a new disciple. To state it differently, both divine and human action converge in baptism as the new convert, by divine grace, submits to baptism and as the existing disciple, by divine grace and authority, visibly gives the new disciple a new name and identity. Allison summarizes, "The pronouncement effects the association. Just as

Indeed, disciples must baptize new disciples until Christ returns (28:20), or else find themselves explicitly disobeying Christ.

Given the covenantal location of Jesus' commission, baptism should also be understood as the sign of entry into the new covenant. Two cross-references within Matthew make this point clear. First, Jesus' mention of the "blood of the (new) covenant" at the Last Supper (1) signals the arrival of Jeremiah's new covenant (26:28; cf. Jer 31:31–34) and (2) recalls the covenant ratifying shedding of blood in Exodus 24:8. The fact that Jesus claims his blood "is poured out for many for the forgiveness of sins" provides a second allusion to Jeremiah's prophecy of forgiveness for every participant in the new covenant (31:34). Thus, when Jesus commands his disciples to make more disciples by baptizing them, the command comes after the cross and resurrection event, through which Jesus inaugurated the new covenant. Because this baptism begins when the new covenant begins, it is rightly called the sign of new covenant entry.[29] Second, the command to baptize disciples recalls John the Baptist's baptism for repentance and confession in light of the coming Messiah (Matt 3:6–11). Jesus' inauguration of the new covenant and the association of baptism with cleansing from sin suggests that the baptism Jesus commands in Matthew 28 functions to initiate disciples into the new covenant, where, upon the merits of Christ's work, they receive forgiveness of sins. In sum, baptism in Matthew is the sign of entry to the inaugurated kingdom and the new covenant.

The temporal sequence of events in the commission—making disciples, baptizing, and teaching—requires some hermeneutical care. That the requirement to proclaim the gospel is implicit in the commission is best attested by considering the way the apostolic church carried out the commission. Peter preached the identity and work of Jesus as the Messiah before calling for repentance and baptism, which was followed by church fellowship around the apostles' teaching (Acts 2:36–47). This explanation requires that the order of the participles following the command—baptizing then teaching—should not be taken to mean that no teaching is allowed prior to baptism.[30] Teaching about the good news, the meaning of baptism, and

---

a pastor or justice of the peace communicates 'I now pronounce you husband and wife' to a man and a woman at a wedding ceremony and effects their marriage, so also the one baptizing pronounces the baptismal formula and effects the association of the new Christian with the triune God" (Allison, *Sojourners and Strangers*, 354n144). Craig Keener helpfully suggests that the common formula of baptism "in Jesus' name" in Acts is not intended to deny Matthew's Trinitarian formula. Rather, "both function to identify baptism for followers of Jesus as distinct from other kinds of baptism" (Keener, *Acts*, 1:983).

29. Jamieson, *Going Public*, 61.

30. So Neste, "Lord's Supper," in Schreiner and Crawford, *Lord's Supper*, 382.

some expectations of what follows in discipleship appear to be a normal part of becoming a disciple.[31] When the order of the participles in Matthew 28:19–20 is combined with the practice of the early church, the notion that one might profess to follow Christ and experience church teaching and fellowship for a lengthy period of time without being baptized appears irregular and possibly sinful. "The New Testament does not present anyone as a disciple who is unbaptized."[32]

Baptism in Acts

The narratives of the book of Acts consistently present baptism as the expectation and/or reality for all who follow Christ; it is an assumed part of conversion. Additionally, the examples of Acts reveal that baptism is the sign of entry into the new covenant and inaugurated kingdom. This section demonstrates both themes.

The assumption that all believers are baptized runs throughout Acts. In Acts 2:38, Peter commands those who would receive forgiveness of sins and the promised Holy Spirit to "repent and be baptized."[33] Luke presents

---

31. Consider the Ethiopian eunuch's request "What prevents me from being baptized?" after Philip explained the gospel to him (Acts 8:35–36). The text implies that Philip explained something of the meaning and purpose of baptism as he "told him the good news about Jesus" (v. 35).

32. Beasley-Murray, *Baptism in the New Testament*, 88. The interpretation given above tacitly admits that the order of the participles in Christ's commission is not sufficient on its own to serve as a scriptural basis for close communion. See Neste, "Lord's Supper," in Schreiner and Crawford, *Lord's Supper*, 382.

33. Stein argues convincingly that in the statement "repent and be baptized for (*eis*) the forgiveness of your sins," *eis* is best understood as purposive. His two most helpful comparative examples are (1) "Repent therefore and turn back, that (*eis*) your sins may be blotted out" (Acts 3:19) and (2) "my blood of the covenant, which is poured out for many for (*eis*) the forgiveness of sins" (Matt 26:28). For those concerned that this interpretation leads to baptismal regeneration, he adds, "The desire to refute a mechanistic understanding of baptism that leads to the error of baptismal regeneration need not cause us to divide and separate in time and intent these two components of the conversion experience that are intimately associated by and the NT" (Stein, "Baptism in Luke-Acts," in Schreiner and Wright, *Believer's Baptism*, 49–50). Stein provides thorough and careful exegesis to demonstrate that Luke presents baptism as one of the means of receiving multiple blessings of salvation (36–57), including forgiveness of sins (22:16); reception of the Holy Spirit (9:17–18); and regeneration (11:15–17; 19:3–6). Stein does not endanger justification by faith by these observations, for he also demonstrates that Luke continually associates baptism with belief/faith (8:12–13; 10:43–48) and repentance (11:18). Thus, Luke presents baptism as part of the total conversion process, to the extent that "all these are interrelated and integral components in the experience of conversion in becoming a Christian, and all take place in Acts on the same day" (with the exception of Acts 8:4–24). For a similar, classic account of the same material, see

repentance, faith, and baptism as God's means of internal and external appropriation of Christ's saving work.[34] Acts 2:41 claims that all who received Peter's message were baptized.[35] While it was the responsibility of those who repented and believed to submit to baptism, it was the responsibility of the disciples to baptize.[36] Acts 8:12–13 continues the pattern as the Samaritans

---

Stein, "Baptism and Becoming a Christian in the New Testament," 6–8. Similarly, see Beasley-Murray, *Baptism in the New Testament*, 102–22.

34. Faith is included in this list because Luke identifies the group who responded positively as "all who believed" in v. 44. Allison writes, "The efficient cause, or the only ground, of salvation, is God's gracious, redemptive work in Jesus Christ; his death and resurrection accomplished salvation for sinful human beings. The instrumental cause, or the means, of salvation, is (according to this verse) repentance and baptism; turning from sin and expressing this act by submitting to baptism is the way of appropriating the salvation accomplished . . . by Jesus Christ. Accordingly, the immersion of a repentant woman in water does not save her; it is not and cannot be necessary as the grounds of her salvation. Rather, 'repentance baptism' is the means by which she embraces the forgiveness of sins that Christ has provided for her" (Allison, *Sojourners and Strangers*, 359). For "repentance baptism," Allison cites Stein, "Baptism in Luke-Acts," in Schreiner and Wright, *Believer's Baptism*, 49–50. Hammett, following Demarest, argues that "we interpret the baptism in Acts 2:38 as being for the forgiveness of sins only as it is the outward act reflecting the penitent heart" (Hammett, *Forty Questions*, 127). The term "appropriation" above is intended to express this notion of an external reflective act that expresses faith from the heart. Hammett cites Demarest, *Cross and Salvation*, 296. Caneday explains that Baptists sometimes take issue with the exegetical connection between baptism and forgiveness in Acts 2:38 because they misunderstand the distinction between an instrumental cause and efficient cause of salvation. Baptism in Acts 2:38 is neither an effectual cause (as in baptismal regeneration) nor an action separated from the reception of salvation. Repentance and baptism are distinguishable in the verse but not separable (Caneday, "Baptism in the Stone-Cambell Restoration Movement," in Schreiner and Wright, *Believer's Baptism*, 312–13).

35. Schnabel explains the plausibility of preaching to such a large crowd without amplification and baptizing them all in the same day. On the mass immersions, he claims, "The immersion of three thousand Jews in the large public immersion pools of Jerusalem would not have been unique. Thousands of festival pilgrims who were in the city for Pentecost would all have immersed themselves before entering the gates of the temple complex in the Pool of Siloam or in the Pool of Bethesda" (Schnabel, *Acts*, 167–68). Keener adds to the case, claiming, "Even if only the apostles and a few of their colleagues, a total of perhaps thirty, 'performed' the baptisms . . . they could finish their task in a few hours" (Keener, *Acts*, 1:994–95).

36. Baptism in Acts 2 is given by the apostles because, "They take it as we must that the candidate is not either a liar or hypocrite and that the action is performed not for the automatic fulfillment of the predestined purpose, but as a meeting point for a penitent sinner and the merciful redeemer. If baptism is to be an instrument of surrender by one conquered by the love of Christ, it is equally the gracious welcome of the sinner by the Lord who has sought and found him" (Beasley-Murray, *Baptism in the New Testament*, 102). Keener claims that Luke does not present Matthew's baptismal formula "in the name of the Father, Son, and Holy Spirit" as a "phrase [to be] uttered by a supervisor over one receiving baptism." He grounds this argument in the

and Simon the magician are baptized "when they believe" Philip's gospel message.[37] This is an unusual case given that the apostles had to pray and lay hands on the Samaritans before they received the Holy Spirit (vv. 15–16).[38] Other examples of baptism occurring with or following belief abound:

---

passive use of the verb *baptizo* (cf. Acts 2:38; 8:12, 16; 10:48; 19:5). And, he claims "This indicates that the formula has to do with receiving rather than giving . . . baptism." In other words, the baptizand's confession of the name of Christ fulfills the intention of Matthew's baptismal formula apart from any statement of "I baptize you in the name of Jesus." Keener goes on to speculate that early Christian baptisms were probably "self-dunkings" (Keener, *Acts*, 1:983–84). I do not follow Keener's logic for two reasons. First, he claims that early Christian baptisms would have "evoked" John's baptism and simultaneously maintains that the baptism administrator is unimportant. The irony of this argument is that John's baptism, when seen as a redemptive-historical precedent for Christian baptism, gets its name and association from John who did the baptizing! This observation does not entail that other apostles were so known (but see 1 Cor 1:13–15). Yet, if Christian baptism evokes John's baptism, the association suggests a level of functional importance for the ones doing the baptizing in the early churches. Second, the passive use of *baptizo* may refer to the baptizand's being acted upon in baptism by a human baptizer. The passive voice, without further contextual evidence in the biblical text, is insufficient to ground either the lack of the administrator's use of the Matthean formula or the practice of self-baptism.

37. Luke presents the Samaritans' and Simon's belief and baptism as genuine conversions. However, Peter's subsequent rebuke of Simon (8:22–23), upon the latter's attempt to purchase the power to dispense the Holy Spirit suggests the possibility that Simon was not actually converted when he was baptized. Scholars are divided over how conclusive one can be regarding Simon's spiritual state. Nevertheless, if Simon was baptized upon his profession of faith as a supposed believer when in fact he was not converted, this narrative illustrates the fallibility of human judgment regarding the genuineness of one's profession. See Schnabel, *Acts*, 415; Polhill, *Acts*, 220.

38. Allison notes the way Luke himself portrays the delay in the Samaritan's reception of the Holy Spirit as unusual in 8:16 ("for he had not yet fallen on any of them, but they had only been baptized in the name of the Lord Jesus") (Allison, "Baptism with and Filling of the Holy Spirit," 12). The best explanation of the delay in the reception of the Holy Spirit is the transitional nature of the movement of the gospel message to non-Jews. Whereas baptism and reception of the Spirit normally belong together in Acts (cf. 2:38; 10:44–48), the conversion of Samaritans needed apostolic affirmation, in order for the Jewish Christians to see it as legitimate. More significant is the "divine approval" evident in the sending of the Spirit to the Samaritans, given to the early missionary movement by the Lord. See Polhill, *Acts*, 217–19; Schnabel, *Acts*, 410–11.

the Ethiopian eunuch (v. 36);[39] Saul/Paul (9:18; cf. 22:16);[40] Cornelius's household (10:47–48; cf. 11:15–18; 15:7–11);[41] Lydia and her household

39. The eunuch's faith in Jesus is assumed in his request for baptism. The eunuch's faith is confirmed "by the narrative's emphasis on the eunuch's 'rejoicing,' which is a Lucan hint of salvation (e.g., Luke 19:1–10, esp. v. 6; Acts 8:4–25, esp. v. 8)." Thanks to Gregg Allison for this observation. Schnabel explains, "Philip's explanation of the good news of Jesus included instruction about repentance and faith in Jesus as Messiah and Savior, expressed in immersion in water" in the name of Jesus the Messiah (Acts 2:38). The official's request to be baptized implies that he wants to express his faith in Jesus and become a follower of Jesus" (Schnabel, Acts, 428). So also Parsons, Acts, 122. Both Keener and Parsons note that although a God-fearing Gentile, the eunuch was biologically incapable of becoming a Jew. However, through baptism, he was initiated into the company that followed the promised Jewish Messiah. By using the plural verb (descend) in 8:38, Luke emphatically affirms Philip's presence in the water with the eunuch as the administrator. The text indicates immersion as the mode of baptism here, by referring to "much water," "they both went down into the water," "he baptized him," and "they came up out of the water" (Keener, Acts, 2:595). On Philip as administrator and immersion as the mode, see also Barrett, Acts of the Apostles, 2:434.

40. In Saul's case, he does not appear to have been converted to Jesus initially, upon receiving the revelation of Jesus on the road to Damascus. Rather, Saul was likely converted after hearing Ananias explain what happened to Saul and God's purpose that Saul be filled with the Spirit (9:17–18). This timing is appropriate because it locates Saul's conversion alongside Saul's filling with the Spirit, physical removal of scales from Saul's eyes (symbolizing the removal of spiritual blindness (cf. Luke 19:35–43; 9:45; 24:11), and baptism. On the timing of Saul's conversion, see Allison, "Baptism with and Filling of the Holy Spirit," 13. Saul's baptism is clearly a baptism pursued by faith in Jesus, because Paul was baptized "calling on his name" (Stein, "Baptism in Luke-Acts," in Schreiner and Wright, Believer's Baptism, 44). Keener draws more from Saul's initial (passive) reactions to the revelation of Christ than does Allison (Keener, Acts, 2:662–63).

41. In Cornelius's case, belief is assumed based on three factors: (1) Peter preaches that all who believe receive forgiveness of sins (10:43); (2) Peter explains the need to baptize the household based on the whole household's receiving of the Holy Spirit (11:15; cf. 10:45–46) and belief in Jesus akin to the disciples' belief on the day of Pentecost (11:17); and (3) the Jerusalem church's response to Peter's account that God granted Gentiles (all who received the Spirit and were subsequently baptized) repentance unto life (11:18). See Allison, "Baptism with and Filling of the Holy Spirit," 18; Stein, "Baptism in Luke-Acts," in Schreiner and Wright, Believer's Baptism, 44–45. Also significant is Luke's record of Peter's subsequent account of Cornelius and his household's conversion in Acts 15. Speaking of Cornelius' household, Peter explains "God made a choice among you that by my mouth the Gentiles should hear the word of the gospel and believe" (v. 7). He further explains "God . . . bore witness to them, by giving them the Holy Spirit . . . [and] cleansed their hearts by faith" (vv. 8–9). This passage affirms explicitly that all those in Cornelius' house heard the gospel, received the Holy Spirit, and exercised faith by which God cleansed their hearts.

(16:14–15);[42] the Philippian Jailer and his household (vv. 31–34);[43] Crispus and his household with a group of Corinthians (18:8);[44] and the Ephesian disciples of John the Baptist (19:1–6).[45] These examples clearly indicate that baptism was the assumed and expected response of all who would believe in Jesus in Acts.[46] Baptism commonly accompanies other Lukan descriptions of responses to the gospel—such as repentance (2:38; 11:17; cf. 10:43–48), faith/belief (8:12–13; 18:8; 15:9; cf. Acts 10:43–48), and calling on the name of Jesus (2:38; 22:16). These combinations suggest that when Luke does not

42. Two factors suggest that Lydia believed before her baptism, though the text does not explicitly mention her belief. First, that the "Lord opened her heart to pay attention to what was said by Paul" is Lukan language for divine enablement to see, understand, and believe in Jesus (Luke 24:45; cf. Rom 10:9). Second, Lydia's invitation to the apostles after her baptism begins with the statement "If you consider me a believer in the Lord" (HCSB, TNIV). ESV has "If you have judged me faithful to the Lord." Lydia grounds her ability to show hospitality to Paul and his co-workers in her genuine faith in Jesus. Concerning Lydia's household, the text does not give enough indication to determine who, how old, or how many people belonged to the household and were baptized with Lydia. See Stein, "Baptism in Luke-Acts," in Schreiner and Wright, *Believer's Baptism*, 39; Barrett, *Acts of the Apostles*, 1:784. Jonathan Watt goes beyond the evidence to argue from the various household baptisms in Acts that the burden of proof for denying the presence of infants in the households belongs to Baptists (Watt, "Oikos Formula," in Strawbridge, *Case for Covenantal Infant Baptism*, 84).

43. Chappell is correct that Acts 16:34 states that the jailer believed with a singular verb. So Chappell, "Pastoral View of Infant Baptism," 21. Contra Polhill, *Acts*, 356. However, this fact does not require that the remainder of the jailer's household were baptized only on account of his faith. Given the patriarchal, honor-shame culture in which Luke writes, it is possible that Luke's singular verb indicates the faith of the entire household in line with the husband/father's faith. Thanks to Gregg Allison for this observation. Chappell's observation is also against Stein, who points to two factors that suggest the faith of the whole household: (1) the whole household rejoiced over the jailer's faith (16:34) and (2) the "word" was spoken to the entire household (v. 32). That all in the house had the capacity to hear the word and rejoice over salvation implies a greater capacity in the household members than infants possess. Because Paul's message to the jailer is that he must believe, together with his household (16:31), Paul appears to call the whole household to respond in faith. Given that the whole household was baptized, the text implies that the whole household believed. This analysis largely follows Stein, "Baptism in Luke-Acts," in Schreiner and Wright, *Believer's Baptism*, 63.

44. Crispus's household is a clear case in which not only the head of the household, but also all the individual members of it, are said to have believed before their baptism (Acts 18:8). See Schnabel, *Acts*, 760; Parsons, *Acts*, 252.

45. Beasley-Murray, *Baptism in the New Testament*, 98–100. On the explanation given here, see Peterson, *Acts of the Apostles*, 528–31; Schnabel, *Acts*, 789.

46. For further refutation of the argument that household baptisms in Acts included infants, see Saucy, *Church in God's Program*, 200–202. For arguments against infant baptism more generally, see Beasley-Murray, *Baptism in the New Testament*, 357–78.

mention baptism occurring with any of these other responses, it is still reasonable to assume the believers were baptized (13:12, 48; 14:1, 21; etc.).[47]

Whereas the Abrahamic covenant required circumcision for entry into God's people, Acts consistently presents baptism as the sign of entry into the new covenant and inaugurated kingdom (Acts 15:1–11). Following the eschatological outpouring of the Spirit (Acts 2:1–4, 16–21; cf. Joel 2:28–32), Peter announces that Jesus is the death-defeating Son of David (vv. 30–32), now at the right hand of God (v. 33), whom God "has made . . . both Lord and Christ" (v. 36).[48] The Acts 2 context leads Jamieson to describe baptism as the divine means of "going public" with one's faith and as the "visible embodiment of a person's decisive turn from sin to Christ."[49] Beasley-Murray explains, "Baptism in Acts is the occasion and means to receiving blessings conferred by the Lord of the kingdom." Furthermore, "our act of confession and dedication to Jesus as Lord has as its corollary identification with the people who acknowledge him as Messiah."[50]

At the same time, baptism in Acts is a sign of new covenant entry. Baptism's association with forgiveness (2:38; 22:16) recalls Jeremiah's promise of forgiveness in 31:34. The close association of the reception of the Holy Spirit with baptism (2:38; 9:17–18; 10:43–48; 11:15–18) recalls God's promise that his Spirit would indwell his people (Joel 2:28–32; Ezek 36:26–27). The formation of a Christian community of multi-ethnic, missional believers in the Messiah, who are baptized, forgiven of sin, and receive the Spirit recalls God's promise of a multi-ethnic new covenant community (Acts 2:42–47; 9:31; 13:1–3; 18:5–8; cf. Gen 17:6; Jer 4:1–4).

---

47. Stein, "Baptism in Luke-Acts," in Schreiner and Wright, *Believer's Baptism*. This presumption is not an argument from silence, as is the case in the pedobaptist arguments that infants would have likely been present in the households to be baptized. The observation above is based on explicit biblical connections between repentance, confession, belief/faith, calling on Jesus' name, and baptism elsewhere in Acts. The household baptisms in Acts contain no explicit example of infants being baptized. Whereas the argument above is an implication from clear examples, the household baptism argument is based on a presumed continuity with the old covenant inclusion of children.

48. In context, Acts 1:1 and 8 imply that Luke intends to recount "all that Jesus [continues] to do and teach" through his Spirit empowered church, armed with his word. Then in a crowd of people, some of whom "crucified him" (v. 36), Peter calls those who would cease their opposition to Jesus to repent and be baptized (v. 38). Throughout the remainder of Acts, the internal entry to Christ's kingdom through repentance/belief is coupled with the outward entry through baptism.

49. Jamieson, *Going Public*, 37, 45.

50. Beasley-Murray, *Baptism in the New Testament*, 102–4. "Baptism as incorporation into the people of the kingdom is an element of baptismal teaching that was destined to be developed by Paul in his characteristic doctrine of baptism as incorporation into the body of Christ."

Baptism in Paul's Letters

Paul addresses baptism specifically in Romans, 1 Corinthians, Galatians, Ephesians, and Colossians. This section considers three aspects of Paul's doctrine of baptism that contribute to the thesis: (1) the assumption that all believers are baptized; (2) the function of baptism as the sign of initiation into the new covenant; and (3) the association of baptism with union with Christ.

Throughout Paul's writings, he consistently assumes that all the believers who compose the churches to whom he writes are baptized. Paul grounds his appeal for unity to the Ephesians in their common faith, consisting of "one Lord, one faith, one baptism" (4:5). In Galatians 3:26, Paul assumes that "all" the "sons of God through faith" "were baptized into Christ," and, as a result of that faith-baptism, "have put on Christ" (v. 27). Thus, Paul assumes that if one has not been baptized into Christ, one has not put on Christ. If faith without baptism were normative for Paul's theology or early church practice, then one could be a "son of God" (v. 26) without having "put on Christ" (v. 27), which is inconsistent with Paul's teaching elsewhere (Gal 3:29—4:6; Rom 8:1–17). Paul assumes the Colossians were baptized when he describes their salvation in terms of a circumcision of Christ (2:11), baptism, resurrection through faith (v. 12), new life, and forgiveness (v. 13). Some of the Corinthians experienced physical baptism in water at Paul's hands and some from the hands of other evangelists as part of their conversion (1 Cor 1:13–17). Although Paul did not baptize all those who composed the church at Corinth, he declares that he and they were "were all baptized into one body . . . and we were all made to drink of one Spirit" (12:13).[51] Finally, although Paul had not visited Rome or met those who composed the church there, he grounds his argument for their progressive pursuit of righteous living in their common experience of baptism. He explains, "Do you not know that all of us who have been baptized into Christ Jesus were baptized into his death" (Rom 6:3). By this statement, he assumes that any who are not baptized have not died with Christ (v. 5). Then, Paul claims that he and the Roman Christians were baptized: "we were buried therefore with him by baptism, in order that, just as Christ was raised from the dead by the glory of the Father, we too might walk in newness of life" (v. 4). The association of water baptism with initiation into salvation makes clear that only those who personally trusted in Christ were baptized.[52] The

51. The question of whether water baptism, Spirit baptism, or both are in view is considered below.

52. Gal 3:26–27 shows that all who were baptized had exercised faith. See Schreiner, *Paul*, 375.

evidence also demonstrates that all those to whom Paul wrote were baptized. As such, Paul has no category for an unbaptized Christian.[53]

Baptism in Paul also functions as a sign of initiation into the new covenant people of God. The passages just surveyed communicate the initiatory function of baptism. As Schreiner states of Ephesians 4:5, "Paul can appeal to baptism as a mark of unity . . . because it was a given that all his converts were baptized at conversion."[54] When Paul describes the believer's burial of the old Adamic nature of sin and death and entry to the new realm of life and righteousness in Christ, Paul locates that "realm transfer" in the baptism event (Rom 6:3–5; cf. 5:11–18).[55] The association of baptism with initiation into all the blessings of the new covenant in Paul provides further warrant for identifying baptism as the sign of entry into the new covenant. Baptism portrays a public profession of faith (Gal 3:26–27), union with Christ (Rom 6:3–4), forgiveness/cleansing (Titus 3:4–5),[56] resurrection to new life (Col 2:12), reception of the Holy Spirit (1 Cor 12:13), and belonging to the new creation (Rom 6:5–10).[57]

As the sign of new covenant entry, baptism functions to initiate a new believer into the new covenant community—to add one to many. In Galatians 3:26–28, baptism is "an essential ingredient to the constitution of a new corporate identity in Christ."[58] This function of baptism is evident in verse 28. By virtue of the Galatians having been baptized into Christ and thereby putting on Christ (v. 27), Paul tells them "you are all one in Christ" (v. 28).[59] That identification of "one in Christ" came about through faith

53. Akin, "Meaning of Baptism," in White et al., *Restoring Integrity in Baptist Churches*, 70.

54. Schreiner, *Paul*, 373.

55. Moo, *Romans*, 354. For this source, see Wellum, "Baptism and the Relationship between the Covenants," in Schreiner and Wright, *Believer's Baptism*, 151. As such, baptism is a sign of entry into Christ's inaugurated kingdom as well. In the language of Col 1:13, baptism is the formal time at which the transfer from the "domain of darkness . . . to the kingdom of his beloved Son" occurs. In Col 2, faith with baptism are human means by which one comes out from the power of the "elemental spirits of the world," comes under Christ who is "the head of all rule and authority," and participates in the triumph of Christ over the "rulers and authorities" (see 2:8, 9, 15). That these features of Col 2:8–15 thematically refer to the kingdom may be found in Thompson, *Colossians and Philemon*, 54–58.

56. See the discussion below on washing texts in Paul's letters.

57. Beasley-Murray, *Baptism in the New Testament*, 264; Jamieson, *Going Public*, 44–49.

58. Thanks to Bobby Jamieson for this observation.

59. Stephen Turley's explanation of the verbal pronouncement of Christ as Lord in baptism as a performative speech act helps in understanding the effect of baptism as a sign. He writes, speech acts or "performatives generate reality; they create a state of

as the response by which God justifies sinners and through baptism as the external faith act whereby one publicly pledges allegiance to Christ.[60] As Timothy George explains, "baptism is the event where this divinely given unity is acknowledged, proclaimed, and celebrated."[61] As Turley explains, "By demonstrating an acceptance of the messages communicated through Christian ritual washing, the status of the baptized in relation to the baptizing community is unambiguously established."[62]

The public nature of baptism as the entry sign into the new covenant community is one reason that baptism with the Spirit and baptism with water should not be separated in 1 Corinthians 12:13. Noting the role of rituals in the first century, Turley suggests that Paul's metaphor of baptism with the Spirit makes the most sense when connected with water baptism. For Spirit baptism to be a metonymy, one would need to participate in water baptism as the corresponding outward ritual, because "A person becomes identified with a metaphor by participating in the metaphor's relationship to the

---

affairs the truthfulness of which is an inherent property of the speech itself." Examples include pronouncing a couple man and wife, "utterances that transform a prince into a king, or dub a knight." Turley does not argue that the pronouncement over the baptized creates his or her salvation but that it does constitute the baptized person as a member of the "in Christ" community based on the logic of Gal 3:27–28. Turley, *Ritualized Revelation of the Messianic Age*, 33–35.

60. Throughout Galatians Paul tells his readers that trusting anything else besides or in addition to Christ "profanes the grace of God and renders useless the death of Christ" (George, *Galatians*, 277–78). Paul is not telling the Galatians that they should not trust their circumcision but should rather trust their baptism. He insists that sinners look to Christ alone for salvation. As Timothy George explains, "The baptismal rite, with its evocation of, and association with, the death, burial, and resurrection of Christ, models justification although it can never mediate it." He continues, "For the NT believer's baptism with (or 'in' or 'by;' 1 Cor 12:13) the Holy Spirit is [at least logically] antecedent to baptism with water [cf. Acts 10:46–48], the latter being a confession and public witness of the former. . . . In the opening verses of Gal 3, when Paul reminded the Galatians of the very beginning of their Christian experience, he did not say, 'Were you baptized?' but rather, 'Did you receive the Spirit?' (3:2–3). The objective basis of faith is not the ordinance of baptism but rather that to which baptism bears witness, namely, the whole Christological-soteriological 'event' summarized in the phrase 'God sent his Son' (4:4), together with the gift of the Holy Spirit who through the preaching of the gospel has awakened faith in the elect." Bruce describes baptism as the visible enactment of "one complex experience of Christian initiation." Bruce's explanatory comment that "What is true of the experience as a whole can in practice be predicated of any element of it" seems to go beyond the evidence.(Bruce, *Epistle to the Galatians*, 13). Paul never claims that one is justified by baptism. While baptism represents cleansing/forgiveness, it is more associated with the broader category of union with Christ than it is justification in terms of instrumental means.

61. George, *Galatians*, 283.

62. Turley, *Ritualized Revelation of the Messianic Age*, 48. See also Bruce, *Epistle to the Galatians*, 185.

sign-images it generates." Thus, one does not have to choose whether Paul intends baptism with water or with the Spirit. Turley's comparison helpfully considers both New Testament ordinances—"Just as being a part of the contemporary 'body of Christ' is participating in confession and communion [1 Cor 12:3; 10:16–17], so being 'baptized in the Spirit' is participating in water baptism."[63] Acknowledging the metonymic association of baptism with water and baptism with the Spirit leads allows for a clearer connection between the baptism and one's place within the body of Christ.[64]

Similarly, the way Paul refers to baptism as a completed past action that occurred in association with union with Christ and the reception of the Holy Spirit (1 Cor 12:13) leads Douglas Moo and other scholars to refer to

63. Turley, *Ritualized Revelation of the Messianic Age*, 79. Turley continues, "Thus even if we grant Paul's troping of baptism into a wider Spirit-association in 1 Cor 12:13, water baptism would still be situated within a network of metonymic associations contiguously related to Spirit-baptism, with the mention of the latter legitimately giving rise to association with the former. This accounts for why there is simply no explicit evidence for Paul placing Spirit-baptism in antithesis to water baptism." I understand Turley's insights here as pertaining to the corporate identity one takes on in being united to Christ. In other words, the effectiveness of baptism is found in its constitutive function in forming the body of Christ. Turley seems to recognize a closer relationship between the individual and the community in becoming a Christian, without deemphasizing the necessity of personal faith in Christ.

64. Schreiner contends, "Baptism in 1 Cor 12:13 is linked especially with incorporation into the body of Christ, so that baptism involves induction into the people of God. Here we see the close association between baptism and the Spirit, demonstrating that the reception of water baptism and the reception of the Spirit occur at the same time. There is no need to disassociate water from the Spirit in this text. Paul emphasizes twice in the verse that believers were plunged into and irrigated by the Spirit at conversion" (Schreiner, *Paul*, 373–74). See also Beasley-Murray, *Baptism in the New Testament*, 120; Ciampa and Rosner, *First Letter to the Corinthians*, 594n150. Historically, Bunyan denied that 1 Cor 12:13 referred to both water and Spirit baptism, because "The baptism the Spirit executeth must be the baptism here spoken of because it is a baptism that produces and grounds unity." Presumably, too many differences exist over water baptism for Paul to have spoken of water baptism as a ground of unity (Bunyan, "Differences in Judgment," in Offor, *Bunyan's Works*, 2:623–24). It may sometimes be the case that the Spirit comes to indwell a new believer and incorporates him/her into Christ at precisely the temporal moment of baptism. Nevertheless, a sufficient number of texts in the NT suggest that it is those whom the Spirit regenerates by the word of the gospel who would be morally willing to pursue baptism (1 John 5:1; John 6:37, 44; 1 Pet 1:21–23; Jas 1:18). Therefore, while water and Spirit baptism should not be separated in terms of incorporation into Christ, entering the new covenant, being aspects of conversion, etc., and while baptism should be understood as the formal induction into the body of Christ at a public moment representing baptism with the Spirit, it remains the case that baptism and faith hold an asymmetrical relationship to the reception of the Spirit. While baptism is the public demonstration of Spirit baptism, divinely enabled faith is consistently the human response to which God grants the Spirit (Eph 1:13; Acts 11:17; 19:2; Gal 3:5–6, 14).

baptism as "shorthand for the conversion experience as a whole."[65] As Beasley-Murray explains, "God's gracious giving to faith belongs to the context of baptism, even as God's gracious giving in baptism is to faith."[66] Because baptism in Paul "always assumes faith for its validity,"[67] "Faith and baptism do not enjoy the same logical status of necessity."[68] Thus, baptism's relation to conversion and initiation does not threaten justification by faith. Paul does not present baptism as an "extra condition for salvation" but as faith's initial outward expression, belonging to the cluster of conversion events.[69] Additionally, "As it is the God-ordained mode of faith's appropriation for the believer it can never be said to be of second-rate importance."[70] In sum, Paul presents baptism as a sign of identifying with Christ and thus of entering the new covenant people of God and belonging in the kingdom of Christ.

While the New Testament never presents baptism as effectual of itself or as if "the practice itself unites us to Christ," Paul does describe baptism as the "instrument by which we are united with Christ in his death, burial, and resurrection" (Rom 6:3–4). Wellum argues that union with Christ is "the most fundamental meaning of baptism," in that it "signifies the believer's union with Christ, by grace through faith, and all the benefits that are entailed by that union." "It is for this reason," Wellum concludes, "throughout the New Testament, baptism is regarded as an outward sign that a believer

---

65. Moo, *Epistle to the Romans*, 355. Moo is cited in Wellum, "Relationship between the Covenants," in Schreiner and Wright, *Believer's Baptism*, 150. See also Schreiner, *Paul*, 376.

66. Beasley-Murray, *Baptism in the New Testament*, 273–74. He adds the often quoted statements, "Baptism is the divinely appointed rendezvous of grace for faith" and "Baptism is the crowning act of faith." See also Hammett, *Forty Questions*, 151.

67. Moo, *Epistle to the Romans*, 366. Moo is cited in Wellum, "Relationship between the Covenants," in Schreiner and Wright, *Believer's Baptism*, 151.

68. Wellum, "Relationship between the Covenants," in Schreiner and Wright, *Believer's Baptism*, 152. Carson explains that Gal 3:26 "does not speak to the necessary efficacy of baptism but to its close association with conversion." Also, "Paul can distinguish baptism from conversion," as in 1 Cor 1:15–17, "which shows that in Paul's thought baptism does not have the same logical status as . . . faith. It is impossible to imagine Paul saying he did not come to urge faith but to preach the gospel. Nevertheless, such biblical texts show that baptism and conversion are coextensive in their referents. Those who, so far as can be discerned are converted, are also baptized" (Carson, "Why the Local Church Is More Important," 5).

69. Fowler, *More Than a Symbol*, 205. The cluster of conversion events includes repentance, faith in Christ, "reception of the Spirit, confessing Christ as Lord, justification, adoption, and so on." As such, "It never entered Paul's mind to separate baptism from any of these other realities, but he naturally refers to their baptism as a boundary marker, since it represents the transfer from the old life to the new" (Schreiner, *Paul*, 376). See also Stein, "Baptism and Becoming a Christian," 6.

70. Beasley-Murray, *Baptism in the New Testament*, 180.

has entered into the realities of the new covenant that Jesus sealed with his own blood on the cross."[71] Union with Christ, then, is covenantal language, because all the benefits that Christ affords believers in the new covenant are summed up by it.

Thus, because baptism functions as the sign/instrument of entering union with Christ, it also functions as the sign of entering the new covenant. Although union with Christ is first an individual matter, Paul presents individual union with Christ as forming a correlative and derivative union with the body of Christ.[72] One could say that the vertical union with Christ logically precedes the horizontal union with the new covenant community (1 Cor 12:13). If baptism is the sign of entering into union with Christ, and union with Christ entails union with the body of Christ (the church), then baptism is the sign of entering the church.[73] Consequently, the church must be understood as disciples covenantally united to Christ as his body, who receive the benefits of the new covenant. In circumstances where an established church exists then, baptism should be understood as a corporate or church act—the established assembly of those baptized into union with Christ and each other administer and perform the water baptism of a new disciple into their fellowship.[74] These relationships between baptism and the new covenant, the universal church/body of Christ, and the local church/body of Christ comprise the substance of chapter 6.

Washing Texts in the New Testament

When one considers the washing texts in the New Testament, each passage must be surveyed to determine whether or not the authors had baptism in view. While some scholars see washing as an allusion to baptism each time it is mentioned, some tend to see a reference to spiritual cleansing (Ezek 36:26–27).[75] While the former position would do the most to further the biblical-theological argument of this book, the thesis is strengthened even if

71. Wellum, "Relationship between the Covenants," in Schreiner and Wright, *Believer's Baptism*, 151, 149.

72. Ciampa and Rosner, *First Letter to the Corinthians*, 593–94.

73. Beasley-Murray, *Baptism in the New Testament*, 284; Saucy, *Church in God's Program*, 195.

74. Akin, "Meaning of Baptism," in White et al., *Restoring Integrity in Baptist Churches*, 71.

75. Examples of the former group include Schreiner, *Paul*, 371–78; Beasley-Murray, *Baptism in the New Testament*, 210–15. Examples of those who separate the washing texts from baptism texts include Dunn, *Baptism in the Holy Spirit*, 121–23; Thiselton, *First Epistle to the Corinthians*, 454. The latter group generally explains the washing texts as only referring to spiritual cleansing.

the latter interpretation is adopted. The texts to be considered are Titus 3:5;
1 Corinthians 6:11; Ephesians 5:25; Hebrews 6:1–2; and 10:22. This section
argues that the washing texts sometimes refer to baptism and sometimes
refer more specifically to new covenant regeneration or heart circumcision.
Yet, even when the reference appears primarily to denote internal cleansing
through heart circumcision, the water imagery and the context of conversion in these passages suggests baptism is the outward appropriation and
demonstration of the inward work of the Spirit.

In Titus 3:5, Paul claims, "He saved us by the washing of regeneration
and renewal in the Holy Spirit." The similarity with John 3:5 and Ezekiel
36:25–26 appears in the mention of washing and renewal. Grammatically,
regeneration and renewal are governed by the same preposition,[76] leading to the conclusion that the text refers to a single act of the Spirit that
both cleanses and renews.[77] The term regeneration occurs only here and
Matthew 19:28 in the New Testament. As the latter text refers to the new
creation where Christ will rule, it is no wonder that Paul could elsewhere
describe anyone "in Christ" as a "new creation" (2 Cor 5:17).[78] The conceptual linkage between these concepts of renewal, new life, new nature, and
new creation indicates that new covenant regeneration/heart circumcision
is one of the glorious realities belonging under the banner of union with
Christ. In sum, Titus 3:5 presents a complimentary picture to John 3:5 by
its mention of the Spirit as the agent of regeneration and the dual aspects
of cleansing and new creation-like renewal within the regenerated person.

At the same time, Schreiner's comment accords with the New Testament data more broadly: "Given that baptism was the universal experience
of all believers [in the New Testament], a reference to washing hearkens
back to the inception of the Christian life." Thus, the term "naturally brings
to mind water baptism."[79] On this reading, while washing refers primarily
to spiritual cleansing, baptism "witnesses to the washing or cleansing from
sin" and is the means of externally appropriating it.[80]

76. The statement is, "διὰ λουτροῦ παλιγγενεσίας καὶ ἀ νακαινώσεως πνεύματος ἁγί
ου."

77. This observation is contra those who argue for temporal subsequence between
regeneration and Spirit baptism from this verse. See Dunn, *Baptism in the Holy Spirit*,
166–68. Hammett is correct that the emphasis of Titus 3:5 falls on God's work, and the
human response of faith or baptism are not mentioned (Hammett, *Forty Questions*,
127).

78. Lea and Griffin, *1, 2 Timothy, Titus*, 336.

79. Schreiner, "Baptism in the Bible," in Leeman and Dever, *Baptist Foundations*,
102; Caneday, "Baptism in the Stone-Cambell Restoration Movement," in Schreiner
and Wright, *Believer's Baptism*, 320.

80. Schreiner, "Baptism in the Bible," in Leeman and Dever, *Baptist Foundations*,

Paul's statement in 1 Corinthians 6:11—"You were washed, you were sanctified, you were justified in the name of the Lord Jesus Christ and by the Spirit of our God"—seems to follow the same theological rationale as Titus 3:5.[81] If the sanctification here referred to is definitive rather than progressive, then all three actions belong to the inception of salvation.[82] Ephesians 5:26 is another case in which Paul links washing with being made holy or sanctified. Christ gave himself for the church "that he might sanctify her, having cleansed her by the washing of water with the word." Peter O'Brien argues that Christ's cleansing work is a spiritual washing that occurs through the instrumentality of the gospel as promised in the new covenant.[83] Although the church is never the subject of the verb washed in the New Testament with clear reference to baptism,[84] the reference to washing may refer to baptism as the testifying public witness to that heart cleansing.[85] If this is the case, 1 Corinthians 6:11 and Ephesians 5:26 point to the same conclusion as Titus 3:5—while washing refers primarily to heart cleansing that comes in the new covenant epoch as an application of the gospel to the sinner by the Holy Spirit, washing may well have a secondary referent to the outward sign of that same cleansing—baptism.[86] Furthermore, if one grants that washings may refer to baptism, then, in all three passages, baptism should be understood as the outward entry sign into the new covenant that is assumed to belong to the inception of personal salvation. In other words, these passages appear to support the case made throughout this chapter that baptism is assumed to belong to the cluster of conversion events; at least, they do not provide counter evidence.

Hebrews 6:2 and 10:22 also speak of washings/baptisms occurring in connection with initiation into salvation, albeit with differing levels of specificity. Hebrews 6:1–2 clusters several aspects of becoming a Christian

---

103.

81. Caneday points out Paul's use of the phrase "in the name of the Lord Jesus Christ" in 1 Cor 6:11, "tightly associating baptism and conversion." Just as Ananias told Paul to "Be baptized and wash away your sins," Paul "appeals to the Corinthian believers to recall their conversion, signaled by baptism, as the time of their being washed" (Caneday, "Baptism in the Stone-Cambell Restoration Movement," in Schreiner and Wright, *Believer's Baptism*, 318).

82. Ciampa and Rosner, *First Letter to the Corinthians*, 244.

83. O'Brien, *Letter to the Ephesians*, 422–23. O'Brien presents this verse as following the same logic as others in the NT wherein the word of the gospel is the divine instrument through which regeneration occurs (1 Pet 1:23; Jas 1:18; Rom 10:14).

84. Snodgrass, *Ephesians*, 298; O'Brien, *Ephesians*, 422.

85. Schreiner, "Baptism in the Bible," in Leeman and Dever, *Baptist Foundations*, 102–3.

86. Demarest, *Cross and Salvation*, 296.

together under the banner of "the elementary doctrine of Christ": a "foundation of repentance from dead works and of faith toward God, and of instruction about washings [baptisms], the laying on of hands, the resurrection of
the dead, and eternal judgment." Because the term *baptismon* (translated as
washings or baptisms) is plural, it is difficult to determine whether or not
baptism or some kind of Jewish ritual washing is the referent.[87] If baptism is
entailed in the broader category of ritual washings, then, the passage clearly
connects baptism with repentance, faith, and early Christian teaching. If
baptism is not entailed, the passage is a moot point.

Hebrews 10:22 provides a stronger connection to baptism than 6:2.
After speaking of Jesus as the priest and sacrifice to inaugurate the new
covenant (vv. 11–18; cf. 8:6), the author urges his readers to "Have confidence to enter the holy places by the blood of Jesus" (10:19). The author
frames entry into the holy place in terms of a "new and living way" that was
opened through the curtain of Jesus' flesh (v. 20). Thus, Christian readers
are to understand faith in Jesus as the means of securing the blood of Jesus,
through which they may "draw near [to God] with a true heart" (v. 22).
The salient verse then states, "Let us draw near with a true heart in full
assurance of faith, with our hearts sprinkled clean from an evil conscience
and our bodies washed with pure water" (10:22). Given the author's quotation of the new covenant prophecy of Jeremiah (31:33, 34b) in 10:16–18,
the reference to hearts that are sprinkled clean from an evil conscience also
refers to the new covenant prophecies of Ezekiel 36:25–27.[88] Together, these
prophecies present heart cleansing, forgiveness, and knowledge of God as
benefits of the new covenant. Whereas the Lord promises to "sprinkle clean
water on you" (Ezek 36:25), the author of Hebrews presents the blood of
Christ as that which cleanses the heart, enabling sinners to draw near to
God (Heb 10:19–21; cf. Exod 24:5–8).[89] Furthermore, when the author of
Hebrews mentions a "true heart" and "hearts sprinkled clean from an evil
conscience" in the immediate context of describing the benefits Christ provides the new believer in the new covenant, it is difficult to avoid that the

87. Allen, *Hebrews*, 277; Thompson, *Hebrews*, 133. Schreiner follows a host of commentators in claiming the likely referent is to Christian teaching on the distinctions
between Jewish ritual washings and baptism (Schreiner, *Commentary on Hebrews*, 177).

88. So Turner, "Immersed into the Church?," 130. Having a heart that is sprinkled
clean is the forgiveness that occurs in connection with the writing of the law on the
heart (Jer 31:33). More explicitly, Ezekiel 36:25 promises "I will sprinkle clean water on
you, and you shall be clean from all your uncleannesses, and from all your idols I will
cleanse you." Verse 26 makes clear that the sinful human heart is that which requires
cleansing and transplant.

89. Note that the way by which sinners gain entrance into the holy places is "by the
blood of Jesus" (10:19).

author is referring to heart circumcision (cf. Deut 30:6).[90] In the new covenant, Christ provides believers with hearts that love God and are devoted to God, because Christ's blood cleanses their hearts and consciences.

Not only are believers to draw near with hearts sprinkled clean, but also with "bodies washed with pure water" (10:22).[91] Commentators are divided over whether the reference to the body being washed actually refers to baptism (even by extension from the internal cleansing) or to an internal cleansing in the language of Jewish ritual washings.[92] However, the author of Hebrews contrasts ineffectual Jewish ceremonial washings and sacrifices that could not cleanse the conscience with Christ's effectual blood (9:14–22). Unlike the texts that mention believers being washed in Paul's writings, which suggest internal cleansing of the heart, the author of Hebrews explicitly names the body as that which is washed. Given the assumption that all believers are baptized throughout the New Testament (a point this chapter has demonstrated at length), it seems fair to suppose that the original audience would have understood "bodies washed" as a reference to baptism.[93]

90. Thompson, *Hebrews*, 204.

91. Allen argues that these two participial phrases serve as the grounds that enable sinners to draw near, while the prepositional phrases "with a true heart" and "with full assurance of faith" supply the manner of drawing near (Allen, *Hebrews*, 431). Given the interpretation taken below and the grammar of the verse, it seems preferable to view the phrase "with a true heart in full assurance of faith" as the manner of drawing near, while the "hearts sprinkled clean" and "bodies washed" are the means of drawing near. The grounds by which we draw near is Christ's finished work to which believers lay claim by faith.

92. For a lengthy list of proponents for each side, see Turner, "Immersed into the Church?," 132.

93. Schreiner, *Commentary on Hebrews*, 319; Turner, "Immersed into the Church?," 132. Because the author is describing things that are true of the new covenant believer as the means of access to God, it would be redemptive-historically confusing if the author intends either old covenant washings, or the internal washing of the Holy Spirit on the heart with the phrase "bodies washed with pure water." Contra Allen, *Hebrews*, 431. The "bodies washed" phrase would require a new covenant counter-part, as when Paul speaks of the Corinthians celebrating the feast (of Passover) but clearly intends the Lord's Supper in 1 Cor 5:8, or when he mentions the beneficiaries of the exodus "eating the same spiritual food" as a reference to the Lord's Supper. In other words, even if the author to the Hebrews intends the phrase "bodies washed with pure water" as a reference to old covenant ritual washings, because he is describing a new covenant Christian's experience, he would have to intend a new covenant analogue to this old covenant washing. That analogue would surely be baptism. I do not think the author is referring to old covenant washings, but the argument would lead to baptism nonetheless. As for the latter suggestion that the washing here referenced is, as Allen claims, "a cleansing by the Holy Spirit or the Word of God" and not of baptism, then why does the author distinguish heart cleansing from bodies being washed? The apparent internal and external references would accord well with a holistic newness that starts with the

Given the parallel way in which the author presents heart cleansing and body washing as means of drawing near to the Lord, this passage supports two tentative conclusions. First, the author of Hebrews places internal heart cleansing and external baptism side by side, showing that they belong together (contextually at the entry point of the new covenant). Second, and even more pertinent to the argument of this book, if baptism is indeed the referent of "bodies washed," the author of Hebrews calls new covenant members to approach God with both transformed hearts and baptized bodies. Surely, if this reading is taken, it is not a stretch to suggest that those who draw near to God in the Lord's Supper should approach the Table by the same means.

Baptism in the General Epistles

First Peter 3:21 is the only text that explicitly mentions baptism in the general epistles. This section continues the agenda of this chapter by observing how the New Testament authors assume the believers to whom they write have been baptized in connection with their belief. This section also notes the connection of baptism to the new covenant and inaugurated kingdom.

In 1 Peter 3:21, Peter states, "Baptism, which corresponds to this now saves you, not as a removal of dirt from the body but as an appeal to God for a good conscience, through the resurrection of Jesus Christ." Without explaining baptism's practice, Peter assumes that his readers understand it. By associating baptism with salvation, Peter assumes that his readers understand baptism as belonging to the cluster of conversion events (cf. Acts 2:38).[94] Peter compares the Christians to Noah and his family, a small group in the world, who nonetheless were preserved by God from judgment (v. 20). In fact, baptism is that which "corresponds to" (*antitypos*) Noah's passing through the judgment waters of the flood to salvation on the other side. In the case of Peter's audience, "The basis of their assurance

---

heart through the believer's faith and is externally represented in baptism. As Schreiner explains, "The body stands for the whole person who stands before God clean because of the cleansing work accomplished in the cross" (Schreiner, *Commentary on Hebrews*, 319).

94. While Paul relates baptism to various aspects of salvation, he never claims that "baptism . . . saves." However, the context helps distance Peter's meaning from the notion that baptism itself is effectual for salvation (Beasley-Murray, *Baptism in the New Testament*, 262). Addressing the issue of suffering among the exiles in several regions of Asia Minor (1:1–2), Peter's purpose is to remind his readers not to fear suffering. Jesus suffered and gained victory over the enemy powers, and Peter assures his readers of their ultimate victory, because of Jesus' work (vv. 18–22). First Pet 3:19 is difficult, but defending a particular view is beyond the scope of this study. The interpretation given above generally follows Schreiner, *1, 2 Peter, Jude*, 184–90.

[of salvation] is their baptism, for in baptism, they have appealed to God to give them a good conscience on the basis of the work of the crucified (v. 18) and risen (v. 21) Lord Jesus."[95] Just as new life came on the other side of the flood for Noah's family, so resurrection comes on the other side of the believer's submersion in water—corresponding to Jesus' death, burial, and resurrection.[96]

Concerning baptism's relationship to the new covenant and the kingdom in Peter, kingdom references abound in the immediate context. Peter speaks to those who, through appeal to Christ in baptism, look to Christ's

---

95. Schreiner, *1, 2 Peter, Jude*, 180. While the water was not the instrument of Noah's salvation, it was the form of judgment God used to destroy the wicked and from which God rescued his people (193). Because Peter so explicitly compares baptism to the flood, some have described baptism as a maledictory-oath sign. See Kline, *By Oath Consigned*, 65–70. But see the critique in Garrett, "Meredith Kline," 275. If Peter viewed baptism as submersion under water, then the threat and picture of death reasonably carries over to baptism, which is the view taken here (Rom 6:3–5). See Allison, *Sojourners and Strangers*, 355–56.

96. Schreiner, *1, 2 Peter, Jude*, 194. Given this context, two other brief points need to be made from Peter's mention of baptism: (1) the relation of baptism to faith and (2) the nature of the appeal for or from a good conscience. Peter is not teaching that baptism saves in and of itself. First, Peter describes baptism as "not the removal of dirt from the body" (or flesh; *sarx*), but as an appeal to God. Therefore, baptism does not work to cleanse a sinner as a bath works to remove dirt, where the power of the cleansing lies in the water itself. See Schreiner, *1, 2 Peter, Jude*, 195. So Grudem writes, "We could paraphrase, 'Baptism now saves you—not the outward physical ceremony of baptism but the inward spiritual reality which baptism represents'" (Grudem, *1 Peter*, 172). Instead of water saving, the power that saves is found "as an appeal to God for a good conscience, through the resurrection of Jesus Christ." The power to save is found in the cross and resurrection. Thus, the connection of baptism to "saves" functions as a synecdoche of the sign of faith and conversion standing for the whole conversion process (Jamieson, *Going Public*, 43). As Caneday argues, "In this one verse Peter speaks of both the instrumental and efficient causes of salvation: 'now baptism saves you . . . through the resurrection of Jesus Christ'" (Caneday, "Baptism in the Stone-Cambell Restoration Movement," in Schreiner and Wright, *Believer's Baptism*, 315). The meaning of the appeal (*eperotema*) to God is difficult to determine, because the word is used only here in the NT. The appeal may function as a request to God for cleansing at the deepest level based on Christ's work (Heb 10:22; Acts 22:16), as a pledge and promise to God to maintain a good conscience as when one enters a contract, or as a pledge/confession of God *from* a good conscience. Schreiner opts for the first option, given the comparison to Hebrews. See Schreiner, *1, 2 Peter, Jude*, 195. Beasley-Murray claims that pledge/promise captures the sense best, but he does not decide between the latter two options above. See Beasley-Murray, *Baptism in the New Testament*, 261. Matthew Crawford surveys several key patristic sources (Didache, Cyril, etc.) and demonstrates that they viewed baptism as a pledge/confession from a good conscience, with ongoing obligations. See Crawford, "Confessing God from a Good Conscience," 36–37. Whatever the case, all three interpretations relate baptism to the baptizand's trust of and commitment to Christ.

resurrection as the source of their own eventual resurrection. He tells them that Christ "has gone into heaven and is at the right hand of God" with all powers "subjected to him" (1 Pet 3:22). Schreiner notes the redemptive-historical sense of the phrase "baptism *now* saves you." By contrast to Noah's typological baptism, "'now' refers to the present eschatological age of fulfillment."[97] Thus, these baptized exiles have entered into the saving reign of the resurrected king, David's Lord (cf. Ps 110:1). Because ultimate victory is secured through the resurrection and exaltation of Christ, the baptized can endure trials "for a little while," with God's guarding power, as they wait for the "revelation of Jesus' Christ" at his return (1 Pet 1:5–7).[98]

That baptism functions as a sign of entry into the new covenant is evident in the phrase, "an appeal to God for a good conscience." If Schreiner and Grudem are correct that appeal refers to a request to God for cleansing, then baptism signifies the new covenant by virtue of the promise of forgiveness through the Servant (1 Pet 1:19–20; 2:22–25; cf. Jer 31:34; Isa 53:3–5).[99] If however, appeal is best understood as a pledge either from a good conscience or for a good conscience, baptism would serve as the public oath to depend upon Christ for entry into the new covenant and then walk according to its terms (cf. 1 Pet 2:9–12; 4:1–11).[100]

---

97. Schreiner, *1, 2 Peter, Jude*, 194.

98. Kingdom references abound in 1 Peter, and baptism is the public sign of entry to Christ's kingdom. Christians are exiles in hostile territory (1:1), because they already have an inheritance in heaven (v. 4) and believe in Jesus who "was manifest in the last times for the sake of you" (vv. 20–21). Corporately, Christians are "royal priesthood" (2:9) who have "now... received mercy" (v. 10), and, as a result, become "God's people." If one asks when and how one moves out of the darkness and into this kingdom of Spirit-gifted priests (cf. 4:9–11), the answer has to be that sinners are "born again... by the living and abiding word of God" (1:23), "believed" in God "through [Jesus]" (v. 20–21), and appealed to God with respect to the cleansing of conscience publicly at baptism (3:21).

99. Schreiner, *1, 2 Peter, Jude*, 195; Grudem, *1 Peter*, 172. Similar to Peter's call to "repent and be baptized... for the forgiveness of sins" (Acts 2:38) and Ananias's urging of Paul to rise and be baptized and wash away your sins, calling on his name," the request for cleansing given through Christ and made formal and visible in baptism would function as a sign of entering the new covenant.

100. Beasley-Murray compares baptism to "an oath or pledge of service to join the military" and defines an oath as "a yes answer to the resurrected Lord" (Beasley-Murray, *Baptism in the New Testament*, 261).

Baptism as a Kingdom
and Covenant Sign

Summarizing baptism's relationship to the inaugurated kingdom of Christ and the new covenant serves the thesis of this project by specifying some of the redemptive-historical data that will be used to compare baptism to circumcision in chapter 4. Thus, this section views baptism along both axes in turn.

Throughout the New Testament, baptism consistently functions as the new covenant sign of entry, or, as Jamieson describes it, baptism is an "initiating-oath sign" and act of covenant ratification.[101] Through baptism, the believer is reminded of God's promises to her in Christ, publicly owns the covenant, and assents to personal faith in Christ. God's action to affirm his promises to the believer comes through the responsible participation and administration of the local new covenant community, as they call out the name of the triune God over the new disciple (Matt 28:19).[102] Because the new disciple also personally affirms her trust in Christ in baptism, baptism bears resemblance to the covenant ratification ceremony of Exodus 24:1–11.[103] Indeed, baptism formally seals the agreement between God and the believer and binds each to uphold their obligations.[104]

The believer enters the new covenant in two (logical) "moments" as it were.[105] The first moment occurs when, by the Holy Spirit's initiative through the instrumentality of gospel proclamation, a sinner believes in Jesus, the new covenant head and is justified (Rom 10:14; 2 Cor 4:6).[106] The

101. Jamieson, *Going Public*, 61.

102. This is the sense in which it is appropriate to speak of baptism as a seal. God acts through the administering church to affirm his promise to save through the death and burial of Christ. As Horton explains, "the concern of the sacraments . . . is God's means of action: ratifying, assuring, attesting, confirming, and sealing the covenant promise not only to all people in general [as a public offer before a congregation that may contain unbelievers] . . . but to each recipient in particular" (Horton, *People and Place*, 109). However, when Horton speaks of baptism having a "perlocutionary effect of the gospel promise" as a sign of "our inclusion in the covenant of grace," this book demurs. Instead of the covenant of grace, baptism in the NT is related to the new covenant specifically, which is the culmination of the one plan of God to redeem sinners (116). What Horton claims for adults who are new believers and their children, I am applying only to believers.

103. There, the people affirmed, "All the words the Lord has spoken we will do" (vv. 3, 7).

104. See Gentry and Wellum, *Kingdom through Covenant*, 350; Saucy, *Church in God's Program*, 198; Beasley-Murray, *Baptism in the New Testament*, 376.

105. Leeman, *Political Church*, 362.

106. The logical distinction between these moments provides a crucial part of the

second moment occurs when the believer publicly enters the new covenant community of the local church through the act of baptism. By baptism, the new covenant community of the local church becomes visible and the universal body of Christ is manifested in space and time.[107] The combination of faith and baptism in the formation of the covenant community comes as no surprise. "In a covenantal context, signs do not merely represent or bring to mind an absent thing signified. . . . [Instead,] words and signs together create a covenant."[108] The Lord's intention has always been to purchase a people for himself, who operate in community under his lordship, rather than merely making a covenant with individuals (Tit 2:14; cf. Gen 17:1–11).

In the New Testament generally and most clearly in Acts 2:38–42, these two logical moments occur contemporaneously. Thus, whether a group of people become disciples and plant a church on the same day as in Acts 2, or a pre-existing church adds a new disciple to its fellowship, baptism is a constitutive act, an effective sign. As the entry sign of the new covenant, baptism is one of the divinely-appointed human actions (along with the Lord's Supper) that creates the new covenant community of the local church. In this sense, baptism is the door to both the universal and local church. Normally speaking, baptism "confers membership."[109] Furthermore, it is an "obligation-creating act," whereby the new disciple becomes responsible for and to the other members of the local body of Christ.[110] The obligation is entailed in that (1) baptism is the external means of appropriating union with Christ (Rom 6:3–4; Gal 3:26–27); union with Christ is shorthand for all the blessings of the new covenant (Rom 6:3–4; Col 2:11–14); and all those who by faith in Christ are baptized are derivatively united with each other (Gal 3:26–28), with responsibilities for others who are united to Christ entailed by that union (1 Cor 11:17–34; Eph 4; Rom 12).

Leeman describes baptism provocatively as an official change from "subject" of the kingdom to "citizen" of the kingdom.[111] While all people on earth are rightly under God's rule, baptism is the ceremony by which former rebels publicly confess allegiance to Christ (Matt 28:18–20). As the sign of entering the inaugurated kingdom then, baptism serves as a swearing in

---

grounds for distinguishing the universal and local church (Leeman, *Political Church*, 316–28).

107. Leeman, *Political Church*, 362.

108. Horton, *People and Place*, 101.

109. Baptism is an effective sign "of church membership," in the sense that it "creates the ecclesial reality to which it points" (Jamieson, *Going Public*, 100–101).

110. Horton, *People and Place*, 102. This source is cited in Jamieson, *Going Public*, 72.

111. Leeman, *Political Church*, 215.

ceremony and provides the official passport or stamp of approval on the baptized person, identifying him or her with Christ's kingdom communi-ty.[112] The new identity and new allegiance are entailed by the invocation of the name of the triune God over the person being baptized and the public identification with Christ that results (Matt 28:19; Rom 6:3–4).

Whereas baptism is the new covenant sign of entry, the Lord's Supper is the new covenant sign of participation. The task of the following section is to demonstrate the relationship of the Lord's Supper to the new covenant and the kingdom of Christ.

The Lord's Supper as a Sign of Participation in the Inaugurated Kingdom and New Covenant

The purpose of this section is to consider two aspects of the Lord's Supper: its participants and its covenantal function. This section analyzes these aspects within the Gospel accounts (with a focus on Luke), Acts, 1 Corinthians, and Revelation. The exegesis and theological argumentation that follows demonstrates that (1) the participants of the Lord's Supper are those who are united to Christ by faith that is externally appropriated through baptism; (2) the Lord's Supper occurs within the context of the local church; (3) the Lord's Supper is an ongoing sign of participation in the new covenant; and (4) the meal functions as a new covenant ratification meal and a proleptic kingdom feast in anticipation of the Marriage Supper of the Lamb (Rev 19).

The Institution of the Lord's Supper in the Gospels

Jesus' celebration of the Last Supper is recorded in the Synoptic Gospels. Because Luke's account is the longest, this section begins with that account.

Luke 22:14–20

In Luke's account, Luke 22:14–20 forms part of the culmination of Jesus' journey to Jerusalem (cf. Luke 9:53), where Jesus repeatedly told his follow-ers he would suffer and die for sinners (Luke 9:21–22, 44; 13:33; 18:31).[113]

112. Leeman, *Political Church*, 364.

113. Having arrived in Jerusalem and having been hailed as the "King who comes in the name of the Lord" (19:38), Jesus wept over the coming destruction of Jerusalem (19:41–44) before cleansing the temple (45–48) and proceeding to teach about coming kingdom and answer challenges to his own authority (20:1–21:38).

Luke 22:1 states that the Feast of Unleavened Bread, "which is called the Passover,"[114] was at hand, even while the priests and scribes were seeking to put Jesus to death. Given the festal occasion, Jesus told two of his disciples to locate the upper room that Jesus had apparently pre-arranged for their usage (22:7–13). It was in this upper room that Jesus would inaugurate the new covenant, instruct his disciples to continue to celebrate the transformed Passover meal, and speak of the coming kingdom.

From the beginning of the meal, Jesus sets the Passover celebration in the context of his impending death. Both the allusion to "the hour" (v. 14) and the mention of suffering (v. 15) make Jesus' reinterpretation of Passover around his own death clear.[115] The feast had to occur "before" his imminent suffering of death (v. 15). Nolland contends that verses 15–18 focus primarily on Jesus' celebration of the old covenant meal, albeit with Jesus' death and the consummated kingdom in view, while verses 19–20 focus on Jesus' reinterpretation of the meal around his death.[116] Accordingly, the redemptive-historical transition from the old covenant meal centered on the exodus to the new covenant meal centered on Jesus' death is paramount in Luke's presentation.[117]

For this final Passover, Jesus' disciples were his desired companions; thus, he reclined with the apostles in the manner befitting communion and

114. Several times in the immediate context of the Last Supper, Luke explicitly claims that they were celebrating the Passover (22:7, 8, 11, 13, 15). This fact is noteworthy because scholars debate whether the Apostle John situates the upper room meal the day prior in his Gospel. For the purpose of this paper, Luke's clear indicators of the paschal nature of the Last Supper are sufficient to warrant the Last Supper being described as a Passover celebration. The debate over whether Jesus' Last Supper occurred on Wednesday or Thursday is beyond the scope of this paper. However, four sources which make strong arguments in favor of a paschal interpretation of the Last Supper are Marshall, *Last Supper and Lord's Supper*, 59–61; Köstenberger, "Was the Last Supper a Passover Meal?," in Schreiner and Crawford, *Lord's Supper*, 6–30. The two previous studies depend largely on the classic work: Jeremias, *Eucharistic Words of Jesus*, 41–83. See also Thiselton's excursus entitled "Was the Last Supper a Passover Meal?" in *First Corinthians*, 871–74. Contra Pennington, "Lord's Supper," in Schreiner and Crawford, *Lord's Supper*, 34. Pennington argues that "Jesus intentionally celebrated the Passover meal a day earlier than the official Jerusalem one" without a lamb in light of his approaching death. See below for more on the absence of the mention of a lamb.

115. The "hour" at which Jesus "reclined" (v. 14) with the apostles entailed the time of the completion of his mission to save sinners (cf. Luke 19:10; 22:53) (Stein, *Luke*, 541). Bock's suggestion that the absence of a "qualifier" on the word hour renders it in "no special sense God's hour" is possible, but it overlooks the multiple times that Jesus speaks of his death in the context (Bock, *Luke*, 2:1718n4).

116. Nolland, *Luke*, 3:1044.

117. Pennington, "Lord's Supper in the Gospels," in Schreiner and Crawford, *Lord's Supper*, 41. See also Nolland, *Luke*, 3:1044.

fellowship between Jesus, the host, and his guests.[118] He told them, "I earnestly desired to eat this Passover with you" (v. 15).[119] Jesus' reference to eating and partaking of "this" meal identifies him and the disciples with the exodus generation that celebrated the meal as households (cf. Exod 13:14–16),[120] who were protected from God's judgment by the blood of the substitutionary lamb. As a law-keeping Israelite, Jesus commemorated God's "kingly saving power" of deliverance for his people, which led to the establishing of the Mosaic covenant at Sinai.[121] In the explanation that follows, Jesus shows that his last Passover meal with the disciples would also occur on the eve of the establishment of a new covenant and a demonstration of "kingly saving power" through deliverance from sin.

Verse 16 provides Jesus' clearest typological interpretation of the Passover; he had to eat the Passover before he suffered because he would "not eat *it*, until it is fulfilled in the kingdom of God." Clearly, the "it" cannot be the kingdom of God, because Jesus distinguishes the Passover and the kingdom in the following phrase.[122] The most recent antecedent to the neuter pronoun "it" (*auto*) is the neuter noun "Passover" (*pascha*) in verse 15.[123] The fact that Jesus reinterprets the Passover in this passage requires that the Last Supper itself functions as a partial fulfillment of the first Passover.[124]

---

118. Cf. Matt 26:20. The Gospel writers often speak of reclining at table as representative of fellowship and acceptance (Matt 9:10; par. Mark 2:15; Luke 5:29; Matt 26:7; par. Mark 14:3; Luke 7:37). Further, Luke organizes his Gospel around the theme of Jesus' meals with sinners (e.g. Luke 11:37; 14:15). See Stein, *Luke*, 541.

119. Although some have taken Jesus' eager desire (ἐπιθυμέω) as an unfulfilled wish, Stein et al. rightly affirm that Jesus ate and drank with the disciples. Neither the term "desire" (ἐπιθυμέω), nor the debate over the chronology of the meal require that Jesus refrained from eating. If Jesus refrained from eating, he would be contradicting his whole intention to eat with the disciples (Luke 22:11, 15) (Stein, *Luke*, 541). See also Bock, *Luke*, 2:1719–20. Contra Jeremias, *Eucharistic Words of Jesus*, 207–18).

120. Marshall, *Last Supper and Lord's Supper*, 77.

121. Marshall, *Last Supper and Lord's Supper*, 78.

122. Stein, *Luke*, 541.

123. Bock argues "a Passover meal is the only possible antecedent" (Bock, *Luke*, 2:1720–21).

124. Pennington argues that all four Gospel writers "present Jesus' work as the Passover fulfillment and new exodus," promised in the prophets (see Isa 40:1–11; 65:17–25; 49:8–12). See Pennington, "Lord's Supper in the Gospels," in Schreiner and Crawford, *Lord's Supper*, 49n54. Further, the "water crossings and wilderness feedings in the Gospels (e.g., Matt 14:13–21 and 14:22–33; [John 6:1–15 and 6:16–21]) have long been recognized as an intentional allusion to the exodus events being redone and recast by Jesus." Jesus' recapitulation of these events furthers the typology evident surrounding the Last Supper as a Passover meal. Kline adds, "the exodus typology of Luke's Gospel is forecast earlier in Luke's Gospel when Jesus spoke of his "departure" (*exodus*) with Moses and Elijah at Jesus' transfiguration" (Kline, "Old Testament Origins of the

Jesus' fulfillment language "indicates the end of the old Passover and its replacement by its [inaugurated] fulfillment."[125] By claiming that the Passover would be ultimately fulfilled in the kingdom of God, Jesus explicitly describes the original Passover (Exod 12), the Last Supper (Luke 22:14–20), and a future feast in the consummated kingdom (cf. Luke 13:29; 14:15) as Passover meals.

In verse 17, Jesus likely introduces the first cup of the Passover meal,[126] a facet omitted by the other Synoptics.[127] Jesus' action of giving thanks (*eucharisteō*) before distributing the cup to the disciples has warranted the name "Eucharist" for the Lord's Supper. The communal nature of the meal is evident in Jesus' command to the disciples to "take" a common cup and "divide it among yourselves." As Bock explains, "This act intensifies the oneness that is central to the meal," emphasized by Paul's depiction of the local church that eats together as "one loaf" (1 Cor 10:17).[128] The bread and cup are emblematic of unity. While Jesus does not reinterpret the first cup in

---

Gospel Genre," 10). Most helpful in explaining the typological connection of the Passover to the Last Supper and subsequent Lord's Supper is Parker, "Israel-Christ-Church Relationship," in Wellum and Parker, *Progressive Covenantalism*, 51–52. He explains, "typological patterns are always either completely fulfilled with the coming of Christ, the primary antitype, or they are initially inaugurated by Christ with appropriation directed to the church, living in the 'already-not-yet' tension of the new covenant era." With this in mind, it is appropriate to think of the Last Supper as a partial fulfillment of Passover and the Lord's Supper as an "ongoing or continuing fulfillment." Inserting "inaugurated" before Marshall's term fulfillment is preferable because, as Parker explains, "Some types are completely fulfilled in Christ's first coming while others are initially fulfilled while also having antitypical fulfillment and realization in the church and finally the new creation. Even so, with the arrival of the antitype, namely Jesus Christ, the type is surpassed since the 'antitype fills the role of the type in a way that makes the type unnecessary and effectively obsolete'" (Parker, "Israel-Christ-Church Relationship," in Wellum and Parker, *Progressive Covenantalism*, 52; Parker cites Hoskins, *Jesus as the Fulfillment of the Temple*, 23).

125. Marshall, *Last Supper and Lord's Supper*, 80.

126. Because scholarship is largely dependent on the m. Pesah 10:1–9 and t. Pesah 10:1–14 for the order of the elements in the Passover celebration and the dating of these documents is uncertain, concluding the precise connection between the recorded element of the Last Supper and that of the Passover remains impossible (Nolland, *Luke*, 3:1047–48). See Pennington's fine summary of how the order of the meal in Luke compares to the other Gospels and Jewish tradition (Pennington, "Lord's Supper in the Gospels," in Schreiner and Crawford, *Lord's Supper*, 38–41).

127. Bock, *Luke*, 2:1721. The absence of this verse in the other Synoptics has sparked no end of controversy over whether the short (vv. 15–19a) or long reading (vv. 15–20) is original. For the purpose of this paper, the longer reading of the received text is the source of study. For helpful textual argumentation that the longer reading is to be preferred, see Bock, 1721–22. See also Kimbell, "Atonement in Lukan Theology," 22–32.

128. Bock, *Luke*, 2:1723.

light of his death with the same explicitness he gives to the cup of verse 20, he continues to reveal the relationship of the Passover/Last Supper to the kingdom of God by the explanatory *gar* (γάρ) in verse18.[129] Jesus' reference to the Passover's fulfillment in the kingdom of God (v. 16) is eschatologically parallel to the future coming of the kingdom in verse 18, with both referring to the consummated kingdom meal. After sharing the cup with the disciples, Jesus would abstain from the celebratory and commemorative wine until that feast.[130] In other words, although the cup of verse 18 has more to do with celebrating the old covenant Passover than the ongoing rite of the Lord's Supper that Jesus will institute in verses 19–20, Jesus "implies that [his] end will come before there is occasion for him to have another festive meal of any kind."[131] At the Last Supper then, Jesus presents the old covenant Passover meal as anticipating his death, which would be a greater deliverance than the exodus. Through that death and resurrection (cf. 9:21–22), the future consummation of the kingdom of God would come.

After speaking of the Passover twice in connection with the future coming of the kingdom, Jesus reinterprets the bread and the cup mentioned in verses 19–20 with specific reference to his approaching death. Jesus again gave thanks (*eucharisteō*) before distributing the bread (cf. v. 17). Jesus' breaking of the bread anticipates the way his body would be broken the following day,[132] because Jesus describes the bread as representative of his body,[133] which he would give "for you." This language indicates that Jesus' death functions as a substitutionary sacrifice. Jesus highlights the substitutionary nature of his death again in verse 20 by describing the cup as "poured out for you." Bock correctly observes that the disciples "represented many others for whom Jesus would die."[134] The substitutionary and sacrificial nature of Jesus impending death should not be discounted due to Jesus' association of himself with the bread and cup rather than the lamb because, Kimbell argues, Jesus understood his death as the *telos* of all the Old Testament animal sacrifices. Jesus' death would establish a new

---

129. Contra Nolland, who maintains that the *gar* here merely serves to create a parallel structure with v. 16. The content of v. 18 clearly explains why Jesus will not drink the fruit of the vine again until the consummated kingdom (Nolland, *Luke*, 3:1052).

130. Amos 9:11–15 is one OT portrait of the abundance of wine that will be present in the consummated kingdom (Bock, *Luke*, 2:1724).

131. Nolland, *Luke*, 3:1052.

132. Contra Green, *Gospel of Luke*, 762.

133. Bock is correct that the "to be" verb *estin* "indicates representation, not identification" (Bock, *Luke*, 2:1725).

134. Bock, *Luke*, 2:1719.

covenant community that continued to celebrate a meal of bread and wine in remembrance of him.[135]

Whereas the first cup Luke records celebrates the past redemption of the Passover and places the participants in solidarity with the exodus generation,[136] this second cup (v. 20) recasts God's deliverance in terms of a new covenant inaugurated by Jesus' blood. Therefore, Jesus explanation of the cup harkens back to intertwined Old Testament themes. First, the cup represents his blood that would be shed on the following day in order to cover and atone for the sins of his followers. In this sense, the cup typologically fulfills the purpose of the blood of the Passover lamb (cf. 1 Cor 5:7). Second, Jesus' association of the cup poured out for the disciples with "the new covenant in my blood" is acknowledged by all as an allusion to Exodus 24:8, where the blood Moses sprinkled on the people of Israel to inaugurate the Mosaic covenant is described as "the blood of the covenant."[137] Finally, Jesus' reference to a new covenant must entail the fulfillment of God's promise to make a new covenant with his people whereby all the covenant partners would know the Lord and have their sins forgiven (Jer 31:31–34).[138] Kline summarizes,

> Since the symbol adopted by Jesus as the sign of his covenant blood was the sacramental cup of the transformed Passover meal, Jesus' death answers both to the sacrifice offered in preparation for the Passover and to the ratification sacrifices of the Sinaitic Covenant. Thus, the significance of the blood

135. Kimbell, "Atonement in Lukan Theology," 38.

136. Note God's command to all future generations of Israelites to explain the meal and their identity as a nation in terms of God's redemption (Exod 13:7–9) (Vickers, "Past and Future," in Schreiner and Crawford, Lord's Supper, 320).

137. Matthew's Gospel contains this exact phrase, with the note that some manuscripts add "new" to covenant (Matt 26:28; see par. Mark 14:24). Several examples of those who recognize the reference to Exod 24:8 are Bock, Luke, 2:1728; Marshall, Last Supper and Lord's Supper, 91–92; Green, Luke, 763; Moessner, Lord of the Banquet, 179; Nolland, Luke, 3:1054. More hesitant is Jeremias, Eucharistic Words of Jesus, 194–95.

138. More on the new covenant follows in chapter 4. At this point, it is worth noting that this book understands the God-man Jesus to be the human partner with whom the new covenant is made. In other words, when Jeremiah speaks of "the new covenant I will make with the house of Israel" (31:31), Christ embodies Israel as the promised blessing of Abraham and Son of David. As such, all who come to God through Christ are included in the new covenant. See Parker, "Israel-Christ-Church Relationship," in Wellum and Parker, Progressive Covenantalism, 63–64. Contra Ware, "New Covenant and the People(s) of God," in Bock and Blaising, Dispensationalism, Israel, and the Church 1.1.7.

ceremonies that introduced and consummated the exodus-event fuse in the meaning of the cross.[139]

Of the Synoptic writers, Luke alone records Jesus' command to the disciples to "do this" in remembrance of him (22:19). While the redemptive-historical *telos* of the Last Supper is clearly the Messianic banquet of the consummated kingdom (vv. 16, 18), Jesus' command to repeat the meal he institutes requires the ongoing rite of the Lord's Supper in an intermediary redemptive stage.[140] Although Jesus speaks of the kingdom of God in future terms in verse 18 (cf. 22:29–30), he had already signaled the arrival and inauguration of the redemptive reign of God (Luke 11:20). In the economy of redemption, the inaugurated kingdom had broken in on the old age of the Mosaic covenant. By speaking of the new covenant in his blood in verse 20, Jesus forecasts the formal inauguration of a new, redemptive-historical era by virtue of his death and resurrection. With these factors in view, Jesus command to continue celebrating the meal serves as an indication that Jesus' death and resurrection would bring together both the new covenant phase of God's redemptive plan and the inaugurated kingdom. Until the consummated kingdom feast, all of the celebrations of the meal Jesus instituted are and will be redemptive-historically connected both to the new covenant and the inaugurated kingdom as proleptic anticipations of the consummated kingdom feast.[141]

Matthew and Mark's Accounts

As Luke's account of the Last Supper is the longest, unique aspects of Matthew and Mark's accounts are considered here. Pennington explains that the two distinctive phrases in Matthew's account are "for the forgiveness of sins" (26:28) and "with you" (v. 29).[142] Although Mark and Luke contain new covenant references to "blood of the covenant" (Mark 14:24; Luke 22:20; cf. Exod 24:8), Matthew is the only writer to explicitly includes the forgiveness of sins as a new covenant purpose of the shedding of blood (cf. Jer 31:34).[143]

139. Kline, "Old Testament Origins of the Gospel Genre," 12–13.

140. Pennington, "Lord's Supper in the Gospels," in Schreiner and Crawford, *Lord's Supper*, 63.

141. Green, *Luke*, 761. For this source, see Pennington, "Lord's Supper in the Gospels," in Schreiner and Crawford, *Lord's Supper*, 62.

142. Pennington, "Lord's Supper in the Gospels," in Schreiner and Crawford, *Lord's Supper*, 59.

143. Similar to Luke, Matthew emphasizes the covenant inaugurating nature of Jesus' blood. That Jesus' blood would be "poured out for many" (26:28) recalls the

Pennington notes the theme of forgiveness in Matthew's gospel—from the angel's declaration of Jesus' name (Matt 1:21), to Jesus' exclusive power to forgive (9:1–8), to Jesus' teaching to forgive others (Matt 5:23–24). Matthew reveals the covenantal grounding for God's forgiveness of sinners and of their correlative forgiveness of others in the Last Supper. Jesus' death, foreshadowed in the bread and cup, would make that forgiveness possible.[144]

Jesus' promise not to drink the fruit of the vine again "until that day when I drink it new with you in my Father's kingdom" (26:29) alludes to the Matthean theme of God's covenantal presence with his people through Christ.[145] Whereas Jesus was called "Immanuel, which means God with us" (1:23), he promises his presence with his persecuted disciples by the Spirit (10:19–20), with his church of two or three (18:20), and with his disciples on mission (28:20). The phrase "from now on" signals a period of Jesus' physical absence before the disciples enjoy his presence around the Table in heaven;[146] thus, Jesus' reference to feasting with them in the kingdom of God is a promise to continue with his followers from then to eternity: "To inaugurate a covenant is to form a community."[147] The coalescence of covenant and kingdom (Matt 26:27–29) insinuates that the same group that belongs to the new covenant belongs to the coming kingdom. The dual reference to forgiveness of sins and divine presence with his covenantal people draws specifically on new covenant promises. Not only did the Lord promise to remember his people's sins no more, but he also promised "I will be

---

promise that the Suffering Servant's life poured out (Isa 53:12), would benefit many, and that all of those beneficiaries would then be included in the new covenant people of God (France, *Gospel of Matthew*, 994).

144. Pennington, "Lord's Supper in the Gospels," in Schreiner and Crawford, *Lord's Supper*, 59. Similarly, France writes, "Here then is the essential theological basis for that new community of the restored people of God. . . . It is as people are associated with him and the benefits of his saving death that they are confirmed as members of the newly reconstituted people of God" (France, *Gospel of Matthew*, 995). See also Morris, *Gospel According to Matthew*, 660.

145. The connection between Jesus' presence and feasting in the kingdom recalls Jesus' mention of feasting elsewhere in Matthew. Schreiner writes, "The coming kingdom can be described as a great end-time feast in which the righteous will rejoice but others will be cast out into the darkness (Matt 8:11–12; 26:29; Mark 14:25; Luke 14:15; 22:16, 18, 29–30; cf. Isa 25:6–8)" (Schreiner, *New Testament Theology*, 51).

146. France, *Gospel of Matthew*, 995. Leon Morris writes, "The death of . . . Jesus . . . will inaugurate a whole new religious world" (Morris, *Gospel According to Matthew*, 661–62).

147. Pennington, "Lord's Supper in the Gospels," in Schreiner and Crawford, *Lord's Supper*, 53–54. He writes, "There is no such thing as an 'empty covenant,' that is, one devoid of participants. Rather, a covenant is the formation or re-formation of the people in their relationship to God."

their God" and "they will all know me" (Jer 31:34). The Matthean theme of Jesus being with his people suggests his continuing covenantal presence to bless his gathered church, with that blessing being made especially evident in the sharing of the Lord's Supper.[148]

Because Mark differs from Matthew by the addition of only one phrase in verse 23—"they drank all of it"—the discussion of Mark is appropriately brief.[149] Whereas Matthew includes the command to "drink it, all of you," Mark records the completion of the act. The author envelopes the account of the Last Supper between the promise of Judas' betrayal and Peter's denial.[150] In so doing, Mark highlights the grace of Jesus to include sinners in fellowship with him and promise the benefits of his death to them. He also emphasizes the disciples' solidarity with Christ in their participation of the meal, an inaugural foretaste of the common union with Christ that the new covenant would render actual (cf. 1 Cor 10:16–17).[151] Lane points out that those who drank the cup with Jesus at the Last Supper would become the

148. James Cason concludes that Baptists have traditionally avoided sacramental understandings of the Lord's Supper by noting that Christ promised his presence with the gathered assembly (Matt 18:19–20). He explains, "Baptists met Christ at the Supper but not by means of the elements of the Supper. They met him by means of his scriptural promise to meet with them when they gathered" (Cason, "Gathered Community," 140–42). By grounding their identity as local churches in Christ's promised presence (Matt 18:15–20), Cason argues that Baptists have a fundamentally different polity than Catholics, Lutherans, and Presbyterians. For a fascinating study on the presence of Christ and the kingdom in Matthew, see Schreiner, "People and Place." Schreiner argues that Jesus pulls heaven and earth together in himself as what might be deemed a fully integrated (heavenly and earthly) person (172–75). He argues further that the kingdom of God is a "thirdspace" in Matthew that is both real and imaginary— imaginary in the sense that it exists now but it is not yet fully here temporally. Thus, Schreiner posits a view of Christ's presence in the world that is both temporal and spatial. Schreiner's insights are not couched in classical trinitarian terms; however, one could posit that Christ is present with his church as he promised by virtue of his divine nature (*Extracalvinisticum*). That which is attributed to one nature (Jesus' presence with the gathered church *qua* divine nature) is communicated to the person of the God the Son (*communicatio idiomatum*—properties of either the divine or human nature are rightly predicated of the one person—God the Son). Thus, God the Son is fully present with the gathered church. The additional point which recognizes Schreiner's insights is that the gathered church actually exists in a different metaphysical space—a space that is not fully heavenly and not only earthly where Christ reigns as the exalted king. That Christ's presence with the gathered church is a covenantal presence which entails blessing for Christ's obedient people and judging for those against Christ is clear through the language of binding and loosing (18:18–19).

149. For Passover background specific to Mark's account, see Stein, *Mark*, 649.

150. Pennington, "Lord's Supper in the Gospels," in Schreiner and Crawford, *Lord's Supper*, 61.

151. Pennington, "Lord's Supper in the Gospels," in Schreiner and Crawford, *Lord's Supper*, 55.

nucleus of the "many" belonging to his new covenant community—the beneficiaries of his death as the promised Suffering Servant (cf. Mark 2:10–11;
10:45; Isa 42:25; 53:12; 33:22–24).[152]

John 6

The controversy surrounding the Gospel of John concerns the way in which
Jesus' "bread of" statements (John 6) should be read in connection with the
upper room discourse (chs. 14—17), and the Lord's Supper in particular.[153]
Although Jesus' statement about eating his flesh and drinking his blood
(6:54) has drawn the most controversy within Lord's Supper debates over
the way in which Christ is present in the Lord's Supper, the context of John 6
suggests eating and drinking should be understood as metaphors for believing in Jesus.[154] Throughout the narrative, Jesus is the "bread from heaven"
(v. 32) in whom he calls the crowds to believe (vv. 29, 35). As Köstenberger
explains, 6:54 becomes less enigmatic when one observes that Jesus likens
eating his flesh to "coming" to him and drinking his blood to "believing" in
him in 6:35.[155] Further indication that Jesus intends his disciples (and John

---

152. Lane, *Gospel According to Mark*, 507.

153. Pennington argues that John 6 should be read as thematically connected to
John's upper room discourse and the Synoptic accounts of the Last Supper. While I
agree that the themes are similar, Pennington's essay does not go far enough to describe
the level to which he thinks John 6 is meant to describe the Lord's Supper, and thereby,
the nature of Christ's presence or grace being communicated through it. Pennington
later claims that the Supper is a sacrament whereby the church receives grace, because,
quoting Adolf Schlatter, "Sacraments are acts by which God's love is manifested to us
and his gift is mediated to us." On this view, neither personal nor corporate devotion to
Christ are in view in the Lord's Supper, but rather God is testifying his love to believers.
In my view, while the emphasis on God reminding his people of grace in the Supper is a
helpful corrective to individualism in the ordinances, Pennington overstates his case by
insisting that a believer's obedient participation in the Lord's Supper does not suggest
devotion to Christ. Pennington seems to create a false dichotomy (Pennington, "Lord's
Supper in the Gospels," in Schreiner and Crawford, *Lord's Supper*, 64–67). Contra Pennington's assertion that John 6 be read in connection to the Lord's Supper, see Allison,
"The Theology of the Eucharist," in Schreiner and Crawford, *Lord's Supper*, 184n189.
For Carson, the argument that "we must assume that [John's first audience of] informed
Christian readers might well detect overtones of the eucharist" is unconvincing be-
cause the more natural conclusion would be that John 6 and eucharist passages are each
pointing attention to the way one responds to Christ. See Carson, *Gospel According to
John*, 279.

154. Allison, "Theology of the Eucharist," 183.

155. Köstenberger, *John*, 210. In another parallel, 6:40 has "everyone who looks to
the Son and believes in him" receiving eternal life and being raised up by Jesus. Indeed
Carson offers several reasons why John 6:53–54 should not be read sacramentally: (1)

intends his readers) to believe in him in his sacrificial death on the cross comes from Jesus' promise that all who "eat of this bread" (his flesh that he gives for the life of the world) will live forever (6:51).[156] Therefore, this work concurs with Carson's observation that the allusions to the Lord's Supper in John 6 are secondary, but appropriate only in so far as the Lord's Supper "parabolically [portrays] what it means to receive Jesus Christ by faith."[157] In sum, this section affirms that the Lord's Supper is a parabolic expression of Jesus' summons to eat his flesh and drink his blood (i.e., believe).

---

eating is a metaphorical way to refer to believing throughout the discourse; (2) if vv. 53–54 are primarily interpreted in terms of the Lord's Supper, "We must conclude that the one thing necessary to eternal life is participation in the Lord's Table" (which contradicts previous portions of chapter 6); (3) if the "flesh counts for nothing" (v. 63), then Jesus must intend a spiritual reality as eating's referent; and (4) that on the last day, Jesus must still raise those who have eaten requires that eating/drinking does not "confer resurrection/immortality." For a development of these arguments, see Carson, *Gospel According to John*, 297.

156. It is interesting that the Lord's Supper symbolizes the unity of believers in Paul (1 Cor 10:17; 11:17–34), that Jesus prays for unity amongst future believers (17:20–23), and that the Supper parabolically demonstrates the spiritual reality of believing described in John 6. Therefore, one could genuinely posit that partaking of the Lord's Supper also serves as a distant application of both John 6:53–54 and 17:20–23. Additionally, as Köstenberger and Swain argue, the Spirit "will not come alone," but he will "enable the disciples to enjoy the ultimate covenant blessing: the indwelling presence of the triune God (cf. Lev 26:12; 2 Cor 6:16–18; 1 John 3:24; 4:13; Rev 21:3, 7)" (Köstenberger and Swain, *Father, Son, and Spirit*, 144). Köstenberger claims that Jesus' call to eat the flesh (*sarx*) of the Son of Man "rules out a sacramental interpretation" because of the clear incarnational emphasis—Jesus would die a fully human death for sinners (216). Several scholars point out John's use of *sarx* here as opposed to *soma*, which is most often used in Lord's Supper contexts. See Köstenberger, *John*, 215; Carson, *Gospel According to John*, 295; Beasley-Murray, *John*, 93–94.

157. Carson, *Gospel According to John*, 297. Continuing in the John 6 discourse, v. 56 provides the climax of the whole discussion of eating and drinking (i.e., believing). Those who believe in Jesus abide in Jesus and he in them in what might be called "mutual indwelling." Thus, one should not read John 6 as if Jesus is promising his physical flesh in the church's reception of the Lord's Supper. This comment is appropriate with respect to John 6. However, the presence of Christ at the Supper is beyond the scope of this book. Köstenberger and Swain add that "faith recognizes and receives the incarnate Christ as sustenance for the soul" (Köstenberger and Swain, *Father, Son, and Spirit*, 140). Köstenberger cautions against viewing the mutual indwelling here as "reciprocal," in the sense that "Jesus and the believer fulfill equal roles" (Köstenberger, *John*, 216n79). Similarly, Carson describes the "co-inherence" referred to in v. 56 as requiring that "the believer . . . continues to be identified with Jesus, continues as a Christian . . . [and] continues in saving faith and the consequent transformation of life." Jesus remaining in the believer entails that he continues to identify with the believer in a role of helping, blessing, life-imparting, and "personal presence by the Spirit (cf. 14:23–27)" (Carson, *Gospel According to John*, 298).

The Lord's Supper in Acts

The central issue for consideration in Acts is the nature of "breaking of bread" in Acts 2:42 and 46. That the breaking of bread in Acts refers to a larger meal in a church context that included the Lord's Supper is the consensus.[158] Thus, while the Lord's Supper is not directly mentioned in Acts, this section considers the significance of breaking bread together in the early church.

One of strongest evidences for claiming that "the breaking of bread" (2:42) refers to the Lord's Supper is Luke's use of the same phrase in Luke

---

158. J. Jeremias's classic study presents the breaking of bread as the Lord's Supper and the *koinonia* (fellowship) as a communal meal (Jeremias, *Eucharistic Words of Jesus*, 120). I. H. Marshall follows suit in *Last Supper and Lord's Supper*, 125–27. For a helpful summary of NT scholarship and the argument that the communal meals are the agape feast of Jude 12, see Finger, *Of Widows and Meals*, 48–79. See also Schnabel, *Acts*, 179; Keener, *Acts*, 1:1003–4. For a different take, see Peterson, *Acts of the Apostles*, 160–61. Peterson views the breaking of bread in v. 42 and 46 as separate descriptions of the same reality. Thus, he describes them as "common meals shared by the earliest disciples in their homes." He denies that "the breaking of bread" refers to the Lord's Supper, because "The adoption of this term as a title for the Lord's Supper is not formally attested until the second century AD (cf. Didache 14:1)." Because Luke follows up the clause "breaking of bread" in v. 46 with the phrase "they were partaking of food," he argues that no ground exists for viewing this household common meal as different from that mentioned in v. 42. Given that the household meals occurred in connection with "glad and sincere hearts," he even claims, "In this way, a meal could be given the same sort of significance that Paul ascribed to the community suppers at Corinth (1 Cor 10:16–17; 11:17–34)." In response, it is worth noting the corporate context in which Luke mentions "the breaking of bread" in v. 42 as part of the list of church practices. The house to house eating of v. 46 may well have been for a different, less formal purpose. And, surely claiming that common meals among Christians (even in the same church) carry the same covenantal and ecclesiological significance as the bread and cup of the Lord's Supper misses the dominical authority with which Christ commanded the Lord's Supper, with its specific elements and symbolism (cf. Luke 22:19–20). Furthermore, Peterson's observations may inadvertently work against him. Luke's description of "receiving their food with glad and generous hearts" (v. 46) could describe eating more generally, rather than a formal, Lord's Supper meal. Other evidence against v. 46 referring to the Lord's Supper includes the lack of a definite article before "breaking of bread" and the move from describing essential elements of corporate church life (v. 42) to the overflow of that corporate experience in daily living as a community within Jerusalem (v. 46). Thanks to John Kimbell for the latter two observations. Kimbell's views have changed from what he argued in Kimbell, "Atonement in Lukan Theology," 58. In further response to Peterson's view, Bobby Jamieson's exegesis is helpful. He argues that because "the breaking of bread" in v. 46 is "an adverbial participle modifying the finite verb . . . 'they received their food,'" the construction "suggests the main idea is simply that the church ate all together, not that the Lord's Supper is in view." However, Luke seems to intend the Lord's Supper in v. 42 by using the articular noun (Jamieson, *Going Public*, 118n26).

24:35.[159] Whereas Jesus commanded his disciples to continue to eat the bread and drink the cup in remembrance of him (Luke 22:19), Jesus' disciples knew (i.e., remembered) their resurrected Lord at Emmaus "in the breaking of the bread" (24:35).[160] Although the meal at Emmaus was not a Lord's Supper meal,[161] Luke intends his readers to recall Christ's command to remember him in the breaking of bread (22:19). Thus, when Luke describes the early church's meal together as "the breaking of bread" (Acts 2:42), he intends his readers to understand that the church was doing what Christ commanded at the Last Supper.[162] In this way, Luke 22:35 provides significant warrant for identifying the meal in Acts 2:42 as the Lord's Supper.

In Acts 2:42, the breaking of bread occurs in connection with the activities that characterize the early church meetings—apostles' teaching, fellowship, prayers.[163] The locations at which early Christians broke bread include the temple (2:44–46; 5:12),[164] the homes of those baptized (v. 46),[165] and the home gathering at Troas (20:7, 11; cf. 12:12). The thematic glue of Acts 2:42–47 is unity. The new Christians shared a common devotion to Christ that was evident in their baptism and a common devotion to each other. Together they benefitted from and practiced teaching, prayer, meals, and generous acts of love (cf. 4:32–37). In this context, the Lord's Supper signifies fellowship with Christ and each other.[166] Their fellowship over meals that included the Lord's Supper (which occurred in the context of distributing to those in need; vv. 44–45), generously provided food for mutual enjoyment.[167] Because the Jerusalem church had responded to the

---

159. Kimbell, "Atonement in Lukan Theology," 57. In the book of Acts, Luke presents what the Lord continued to do by the word and Spirit in the church (1:1–2), which suggests that Luke-Acts should be read together.

160. Marshall, *Last Supper and Lord's Supper*, 126. Kimbell argues that the disciples' recognition of Jesus during the meal follows a Lukan theme of remembrance that flows through the resurrection accounts (Kimbell, "Atonement in Lukan Theology," 47–48).

161. Contra Stein, *Luke*, 613; Jeremias, *Eucharistic Words of Jesus*, 120–21n3.

162. Marshall, *Last Supper and Lord's Supper*, 127.

163. Marshall, *Last Supper and Lord's Supper*, 127.

164. Given that the church gathered for corporate worship in Solomon's Portico (5:12), it is possible that the church at Jerusalem could have celebrated the Lord's Supper there. However, if the agape feast usually accompanied the Lord's Supper, bringing a full meal may have been impractical.

165. Schnabel, *Acts*, 179.

166. Fellowship (*koinonia*) denotes partnership and harmony that comes from a shared purpose. See Keener, *Acts*, 1:1002.

167. Keener argues that Luke grounds the breaking of bread in fellowship. As such, Luke's presentation of the shared meal is intended to surpass the "expectations of his contemporaries" in terms of societal position, economic status, gender, and age. While

gospel with repentance, reception of Peter's message, and baptism as their means of connection to Christ (2:38–41), their fellowship with each other must be understood as derivative of that with Christ.

The account of Paul's breaking of bread with the Christians at Troas adds two features relevant to this study (20:7). First, the meal occurred on the first day of the week, seemingly in connection with teaching.[168] Although the reference to the first day of the week is rare in Acts, the celebration of the Lord's Supper in connection with apostolic teaching mirrors Acts 2:42. Second, those who participated with Paul in the breaking of bread

---

evidence of the application of this point is lacking, Paul's admonition to the church at Corinth over its apparently socio-economic inequality in relation to the Lord's Supper may lend support to Keener's claim. If fellowship with Christ is intended to produce gracious and generous fellowship with each other (Acts 2:42–47; 1 Cor 11:17–34), then it stands to reason that one's seating position, one's access to food and drink, etc. should not be hindered by secondary factors of identity beyond union with Christ (Keener, *Acts*, 1:1003–11).

168. J. R. Graves provides a lengthy argument that Acts 20:7 does not record an example of the Lord's Supper. He argues (1) no church yet existed in Troas, because Paul had not yet visited that city; (2) "break bread" is not articular as in Acts 2:42 ("the breaking of bread"); and (3) Luke describes Paul's activity as dialogue rather than teaching (Graves, *Intercommunion*, 341). However, Thomas White notes that Paul's brief, prior visit to Troas is mentioned in Acts 16:8–11. See White, "Baptist's Theology of the Lord's Supper," in White et al., *Restoring Integrity in Baptist Churches*, 158. Furthermore, the presence of Eutychus and those comforted about Eutychus requires that local Christians were gathered, rather than the meeting being merely a missions training discussion. F. F. Bruce notes the use of the pronouns "they" (Christians at Troas) and "we" (Paul's traveling companions) throughout Acts 20:4–13. Bruce et al. generally argue that the Lord's Supper is Luke's referent when he refers to breaking bread. See Bruce, *Acts of the Apostles*, 384. See also Polhill, *Acts*, 118; Barrett, *Acts of the Apostles*, 1:951. While the lack of the article before "breaking of bread" in 20:7 weakens the case that this meal was a Lord's Supper meal, the other contextual factors appear sufficient to claim that the meal was the Lord's Supper. Therefore, both Acts 20:7 and 2:46 lack the definite article before the phrase "breaking of bread." The reason 2:46 does not seem to be a Lord's Supper meal is the apparent transition from those practices that are essential for a church (2:42), to the gathering of the whole church at the temple in v. 46, to the scattering of the church to homes (v. 46). Verse 46 appears to signal a transition from the church gathered to the church scattered. When Luke's commentary of how they received their food in their homes is added to the evidence ("they received their food with glad and generous hearts"), the combined evidence suggests that v. 46 is not properly the Lord's Supper, but rather the ongoing practice of church fellowship outside the time of assembly for worship. Admittedly, it is difficult to make a final determination on the basis of the contextual clues of Acts alone. Bock judges that neither 2:42 nor v. 46 provide sufficient data to prove that the Lord's Supper is in view. Nevertheless, he thinks the case is stronger for the Lord's Supper forming part of the larger meal in 2:42 due to the "broader context for breaking bread" in v. 46. See Bock, *Acts*, 150–51. Thus, Paul's repeated acknowledgement that the Lord's Supper occurred at Corinth "when you come together as a church" (1 Cor 11:17–18), and the corporate nature of the meal in 1 Cor 10:16–17 temper the interpretive decision adopted here.

include Paul's seven traveling companions (cf. 20:4–6), Paul, Eutychus, and the believers who were comforted when Eutychus was restored to life (i.e., other Christians in Troas). Taken together, these two factors suggest that the church at Troas celebrated the Lord's Supper together with Paul and his traveling companions.

The Lord's Supper in Paul's Letters

Paul speaks directly of the Lord's Supper in 1 Corinthians 10:16–17 and 11:17–34. Each of these passages is examined in turn.

1 Corinthians 10:16–17

In 1 Corinthians 10, Paul utilizes Old Testament examples of covenantal unfaithfulness to warn the church against acting unfaithfully toward Christ under the new covenant (10:1–22). He then reminds the church of the significance of partaking the elements of the Lord's Supper as a motivation to avoid the idol feasts.[169] The cup of the Supper is a "participation [*koinonia*] in the blood of Christ," while the bread is "a participation [*koinonia*] in the body of Christ" (v. 16).[170] The following verse stresses the corporate

169. Avoiding idol feasts is the major emphasis of the chapter. So Garland, *1 Corinthians*, 476.

170. This passage is the primary basis for Gregg Allison's covenantal presence view of Christ at the Lord's Supper. While it is beyond the scope of this book to wade into the debates over the presence of Christ at the Supper, Allison's view compliments the arguments of this section on the relationship between the new covenant and the Lord's Supper. Allison describes his view this way: "As the church celebrates the Lord's Supper, Christ and all of the salvific benefits associated with his sacrificial death are present" (Allison, *Sojourners and Strangers*, 396–98). Metaphysically, Allison adds, "included in this understanding is an ontological claim about Christ's presence in observances of the Lord's Supper, a presence that is neither mysterious nor magical but is grounded on the divine attribute of omnipresence. Theologically, divine omnipresence as ontological presence means that God is present in the totality of his being at each point in space. Additionally, divine omnipresence as spiritual or moral presence means that God is present in different ways at different times and places to bless his obedient people and judge those who are against him." The implication of Allison's view is that because covenants include blessings and curses, Christ's covenantal presence will be manifested in blessing on "proper celebrations of the new covenant ordinance of the Lord's Supper" and in judgment on "improper celebrations of it." Allison's textual warrant for the notion of blessing and judgment is Paul's question in 1 Corinthians 10:22, "Shall we provoke the Lord to jealousy?" The key biblical term to describe the corporate fellowship between believers and Christ in the meal is "participation" from 10:16–17. With trinitarian specificity, Allison asserts, "It is this person [the Son] . . . who is present with all his salvific benefits to his church in its celebration of the Lord's Supper," because

unity enacted by sharing the common bread of the Lord's Table. Partaking (*metechein*) of one bread reveals that the church is one body of Christ and shapes the many members into one body (v. 17). In terms of constituting the church, the Lord's Supper should be understood as an effective sign. A defense of these statements follows.

For Thiselton, to participate in the Lord's Supper is to "appropriate the reality or influence" of the body and blood of Christ,[171] which is why participating in the table of idols (demons) is so problematic.[172] While this discussion does not entail that Christ is physically present in the Lord's Supper, it points to a real communion and fellowship (*koinonia*) with Christ that is enjoyed and portrayed in the Supper.[173] Verse 17 emphasizes "that

---

Paul affirms participation "in Christ's body and blood, not in his divine nature." Thus, while Allison affirms the "spiritual presence" of Christ at the Supper, he insists "that our *koinonia* ['participation'] is specifically with Christ and his saving benefits, not in some generic notion of Christ." For a similar but less developed articulation of this view, see Saucy, *Church in God's Program*, 224; Hammett, *Forty Questions*, 256.

171. Thiselton, *First Corinthians*, 772. Paul compares participating in the body and blood of Christ to the way the idol worshipers participate in the altars of sacrifice. The participation is communal, and entails "appropriating the reality or influence that the altar of sacrifice represents or conveys." Confirming this supposition is the fact that Thiselton compares the covenant disloyalty of participating in the altars of idols (1 Cor 10:18) with covenant disloyalty that would fail to keep believing in Christ (Heb 3:14). Hebrews 3:14 states, "For we have come to share [*metachos*] in Christ, if indeed we hold our original confidence firm to the end." Although the terms are different, it seems that both *koinonia* and *metachos* connote covenantal participation in Christ. Paul uses *metachos* in 1 Cor 10:17. See also Garland, *1 Corinthians*, 477.

172. Thiselton, *First Corinthians*, 772. Granted, Thiselton is discussing 10:18 when he provides this definition. However, the fact that Paul uses "participation" to describe that which occurs at the Lord's Table and idol feasts (vv. 16 and 18) suggests that Paul intends the same reality in both instances. On this point, see Allison, *Sojourners and Strangers*, 395–98.

173. Thus, Allison speaks of participating in Christ's body and blood (rather than his divine nature) even while Christ is spiritually present (by the Holy Spirit) (Allison, *Sojourners and Strangers*, 397). Paul's language seems to warrant Calvin's notion that partaking of the Lord's Supper is to spiritually unite with Christ. As Mathison explains, Calvin viewed mystical union with Christ as a "once-for-all union with Christ that occurs when believers are regenerated and engrafted into his body." The spiritual union mentioned here is the fruit of the mystical union, meaning that the spiritual union "can grow and be strengthened throughout the believer's life" (Mathison, "Lord's Supper," in Barrett, *Reformation Theology*, 665). Paul's emphasis on Christ rather than the Spirit is fitting because the elements of the Supper correspond to the Son's economic work—it is the Son who died on the cross in his human nature. The Spirit did not die. Therefore, one should not separate the Spirit's presence from the enjoyment of all the benefits of Christ's work. The Son baptizes believers with the Spirit, and the Spirit unites believers to Christ (12:13), making the church the temple of the Holy Spirit (3:16–17; cf. 2 Cor 6:16–18). In the temple passages, the presence of God is primarily predicated of the gathered local church more generally, rather than being specifically tied to the

the Lord's Supper generates 'partnership,' 'fellowship,' 'communion' with the fellow celebrants."[174] While the ontological ground of unity between those who "partake of the one bread" is Christ in verse 16,[175] partaking of the one bread is twice treated as the ground of the church's status as "one body" in verse 17. Jamieson explains, "This double grounding weighs against seeing the one bread as merely representing the local church's unity. Instead, Paul is asserting that the Lord's Supper in some sense constitutes the local church as one body."[176] Thus, the effectiveness of the sign of the Lord's Supper is "in the formation of the church."[177] The point of Paul's language of participation seems to be that by partaking in the Lord's Supper, the church corporately and visibly enacts their union with Christ—entailing all the benefits of Christ's death and resurrection.[178] Because Paul grounds the unity of the church in their common eating of the one loaf (v. 17), the Lord's Supper deepens the corporate solidarity of the whole church to each other by virtue of each member's individual union to Christ (cf. 1:9; 2 Cor 13:13).[179] "In

---

celebration of the Lord's Supper. But see 1 Cor 6:18–18 for the Spirit's presence within individual believers. See also 1 Cor 5:4 for a specific reference to the "power of the Lord Jesus" being present with the congregation to execute church discipline. Nevertheless, Paul's statement in 10:16 directly connects the act of participating in the Supper to Christ. Partaking in the bread and cup are the means of participating in the body and blood of Christ (albeit by the Spirit via union with Christ) and of proclaiming the Lord's death until he comes (11:26). The meal is eaten "for the glory of God" in the "church of God" the Father (10:31–32; cf. 11:22).

174. Garland, *1 Corinthians*, 477.

175. Thiselton, *First Corinthians*, 767. For this reference, see Jamieson, *Going Public*, 121n31

176. Jamieson, *Going Public*, 120–21.

177. O'Donovan, *Desire of the Nations*, 180, cited in Jamieson, *Going Public*, 121. O'Donovan's point works in the negative as well, as in Billings's observation that the Lord's Supper cannot be a private matter between an individual believer and the Lord. Billings, *Remembrance, Communion, and Hope*, 80.

178. Allison specifically notes the union with Christ categories in the Supper. See Allison, *Sojourners and Strangers*, 396; Ciampa and Rosner, *First Letter to the Corinthians*, 474. In this sense, 1 Cor 10:16–17 and a secondary reading of John 6:5–55 are similar. Union with Christ then serves as the ground for each individual member's incorporation into the body of Christ, the church. Because the body of Christ is visibly represented by the one loaf, the Lord's Supper is a sign of double-connection—to Christ (as the ground) and the church members (as the result). So Thiselton, *First Corinthians*, 762–69; Kistemaker, *Exposition of the First Epistle to the Corinthians*, 342. Contra Ciampa and Rosner, *The First Letter to the Corinthians*, 473–76.

179. Hamilton writes, "This solidarity with Christ entails another: the solidarity of the members of the church with one another in the body of Christ as they partake of the one bread" (Hamilton, "Lord's Supper in Paul," in Schreiner and Crawford, *Lord's Supper*, 80).

sum, the Lord's Supper is an effective sign of the local church's distinct, unified existence as a body," in that it "binds many into one."[180]

The clearest way to account for the mutual enjoyment of participation in Christ and derivative unity among Christians is to recognize that the Lord's Supper is a sign of the new covenant that occurs during the age of the inaugurated kingdom. Paul's reference to participating in the blood of Christ recalls Christ's new covenant inaugurating shedding of blood (cf. 11:25; Luke 22:19–20): "Blood seals the covenant (see Gen 15:9–18; Exod 24:3–8; Zech 9:11; Heb 9:18)."[181] Because Paul describes the church at Corinth as those "on whom the end of the ages has come" (10:11), the church should be understood as belonging to the "already-not yet kingdom of Jesus."[182] The two ages, in context, are that of the old covenant and the new covenant (2 Cor 3), through which comes the inaugurated and later consummated kingdom of Christ.

The relationship of the Lord's Supper to union with Christ and the new covenant has direct bearing on the question of who should participate in the meal: they should be united to Christ and, by virtue of that fact, to each other. Given Paul's association of union with Christ with baptism and the new covenant, surveyed earlier in this chapter (cf. 1 Cor 12:13; Gal 3:26–28), the Lord's Supper appears both parallel to and different from baptism. The two ordinances are parallel in that they are instruments of union with Christ. The ordinances are different in that while baptism is the instrument of Christian initiation to union with Christ and his body, the Lord's Supper is the instrument of continuing participation in Christ and his body.[183] Ja-

---

180. Jamieson, *Going Public*, 122. In an interesting comparison to marriage as a covenant, Jamieson describes "the Lord's Supper's role as an effective sign of the 'one body' unity of a local church" as "a bit like sexual intercourse's role as an effective sign of the 'one flesh' union of marriage." This is because marriage "is entered by solemn, public vows. It creates 'one flesh' where previously there was only an individual man and woman (Gen 2:24). And this union is consummated in sexual intercourse. Until a couple consummates their marriage, they are not yet 'fully' married. Sexual intercourse, therefore, is an effective sign of marriage. It is a covenant ratification and, after the first ratification, renewal—an oath-sign of marriage. Like the Lord's Supper, it should be done regularly (1 Cor 7:5; 11:25). And while the 'one flesh' union of marriage transcends sexual intercourse, the union does not exist without it." On the question of whether those who cannot consummate the marriage are truly married, Jamieson cites Girgis et al., *What Is Marriage?*, 127n5.

181. Garland, *1 Corinthians*, 478.

182. Hamilton, "Lord's Supper in Paul," in Schreiner and Crawford, *Lord's Supper*, 75.

183. Using Calvin's categories, baptism is an instrument of mystical union (Rom 6:3–4), while the Lord's Supper is an instrument of spiritual union. While the former is the external counterpart of initiating union with Christ, the latter is a divine, physical

mieson explains, "It's not surprising, then, that Paul can say we are baptized into one (universal) body at conversion; yet we become one (local) body through participating in the Lord's Supper."[184] Putting these truths together, Paul's theology of baptism and the Lord's Supper suggest that only those who are baptized participate in the Lord's Supper. Indeed, if one goes to the Table without having first confessed Christ through the water, one presumes to receive the benefits of a union that has not yet been formally forged.

1 Corinthians 11:17–34

In 1 Corinthians 11, several features of the text deserve consideration in order to recognize the function of the Lord's Supper as the church's continuing sign of celebration and participation in the new covenant. Those features are (1) the association of the Lord's Supper with the local church; (2) the practical elements of the meal; (3) the relationship between the Lord's Supper and the new covenant; (4) the relationship between the meal and the kingdom; (5) the relationship of the Lord's Supper to unity within the church; and (6) the specific instructions on the manner in which the Lord's Supper is to be celebrated.

First, the Lord's Supper was celebrated by the whole church at Corinth. This point is clear because Paul mentions "when you come together" to eat the meal "as a church" five times (vv. 17, 18, 20, 33, 34).[185] The church's

---

means of deepening one's already existing union with Christ. See Mathison, "Lord's Supper," in Barrett, *Reformation Theology*, 665–66. Similarly, on the Lord's Supper, see Saucy, *Church in God's Program*, 228–29.

184. Jamieson, *Going Public*, 122. In personal conversation, Jamieson explained that he would now want to argue that Paul presents baptism not simply into the universal church at the hands of a local church, but that one is baptized into the local church as well. The social dynamics cited by Turley changed Jamieson's mind. Turley writes, "The *soma*-motif [body-motif] in 10:17 links together baptism with the Lord's Supper. In 1 Cor 12:12–13, Paul writes that the Corinthians were all baptized into [one body] constituted by the Spirit, such that through the ritual washing, their physical bodies were transformed into 'members' (1 Cor 12:12, 14, 18, 19, 20) of the intra-subjective 'body of Christ' (12:27). In 10:17, this same social body . . . appears again through a ritualized act, this time involving one loaf . . . which is identified with Christ in v. 16b" (Turley, *Ritualized Revelation of the Messianic Age*, 159).

185. Hamilton points to three other phrases that signal the church's gathering as the context for the meal: (1) "divisions among you" (v. 18); (2) "in the same place" (v. 20); and (3) "in the eating" (v. 21). He explains, "These phrases indicate that the problem is one that happens once all the members have gathered, rather than one that begins before some members of the church arrive." For a thorough explanation of this point from the grammar, see Hamilton, "Lord's Supper in Paul," in Schreiner and Crawford, *Lord's Supper*, 83. Thiselton says, "This specific eucharistic context denotes not simply

common participation in the meal is also evident in the situational rebuke that forms the occasion for Paul's writing about the Lord's Supper. Commentators have posed various reconstructions of the situation at Corinth, especially based on socio-economic factions. In short, the wealthy were mistreating the poor.[186]

Second, using primarily Lukan language, Paul instructs the church to continue the practice of the Lord's Supper as Christ established it.[187] Paul speaks of Jesus giving thanks over the bread, breaking the bread, explaining the bread as "This is my body" given "for you,"[188] commanding continued practice of the meal in remembrance of him, taking the cup after supper, explaining that 'This cup is the new covenant in my blood,' and commanding the continued practice of drinking the cup in remembrance of him (vv. 23–24). These elements are commonly simplified as giving thanks, bread, cup, and words of institution.[189] Giving thanks is not to be understood as blessing the food but as giving thanks to God or blessing God, as in the

---

assembling together but the meeting you hold as a church" (Thiselton, *First Corinthians*, 856).

186. In any case, one part of the congregation's mistreatment of the other evoked Paul's response (Hamilton, "Lord's Supper in Paul," 77–79; Schreiner, *Paul*, 380–81). For Thiselton's description of a common home during this period based on archeological findings, see Thiselton, *First Corinthians*, 862–64.

187. The Lord's Supper originated "with the Lord himself as a dominical institution." Jesus' command and Paul's reminder to the church at Corinth in 1 Cor 11 demonstrate the ongoing viability, purpose, and requirement of the Lord's Supper for the church (Thiselton, *First Corinthians*, 866).

188. Again, it is beyond the scope of this book to provide a substantive defense of how Christ is present at the Lord's Supper. However, see the section above on participating in the body and blood of Christ in 1 Cor 10 for the clearest statement of my view. The significance of the language "This is my body" for this book is found largely in Paul's continued use of the body metaphor to speak of the Spirit-baptized church (12:13). While I view the phrase "this is my body," as symbolic, Thiselton's memorable explanation is instructive, "The 'surprise' . . . is that my body now replaces the events or objects of redemption from Egypt made participatory and contemporary" (Thiselton, *First Corinthians*, 877). Although commenting on Mark, Stein's comments are also helpful. He writes, "The bread represents the person of Jesus, not simply a part of him, such as his 'flesh' in contrast to his 'blood,' and portrays Jesus as giving himself in death as a ransom for many [Mark 10:45]" (Stein, *Mark*, 650).

189. Because Paul describes what happened at the Last Supper rather than requiring a recital of Jesus' exact words, the implication is that words of explanation of the meal from Scripture should be included in the continuing celebrations of the Lord's Supper, though the exact language may vary so long as it is faithful to the teaching of Scripture. In my view, remaining close to Scripture's own words provides the richest and clearest association of the elements with their divine intention (Thiselton, *First Corinthians*, 868).

Jewish Passover background of reciting the *Hallel* (Pss 113–118).[190] The significance of the breaking of bread (besides that Luke makes the phrase a technical name for the Supper) is its "communal sense of sharing in solidarity and objective fellowship."[191] As with the above explanation of repeating the meal "in remembrance of me" from Luke, Jesus' command must be understood in light of the Passover. He is not merely calling his followers to repeat the meal but also to "make contemporary" their appropriation of redemption pictured by the meal (cf. Exod 13:15; Deut 8:18).[192] *Anamnesis*, in this sense, is a way of describing publicly renewing one's oath of trust and dependence on Christ that was publicly initiated at baptism.[193]

Third, in the same way that Luke describes the cup as the new covenant in my blood, so Paul makes this explicit association. By using the being verb *estin*—the cup "is" the new covenant—Paul utilizes a synecdoche of the covenant sign for the covenant itself. Paul presents Christ's sacrificial blood on the cross as that which inaugurates the new covenant.[194] For Paul, the Lord's Supper is a new covenant meal that entails relationships of humility and love toward others, based on their common participation with Christ (vv. 27–29; cf. 10:16–17). Covenantally understood, participating in the Lord's Supper involves receiving affirmation of God's covenant promises through both individual and corporate reaffirmation of allegiance to Christ.[195] In so

---

190. Thiselton, *First Corinthians*, 871; France, *Gospel of Matthew*, 996; Stein, *Mark*, 650.

191. Thiselton, *First Corinthians*, 875.

192. Thiselton, *First Corinthians*, 879; See also Vickers, "Past and Future," in Schreiner and Crawford, *Lord's Supper*.

193. Jamieson, *Going Public*, 123. Jeremias misdirects the responsibility for remembering by ascribing it to God. Jesus' words and Paul's account of the Last Supper clearly place the responsibility to remember on the individual recipients that compose the church (Jeremias, *Eucharistic Words of Jesus*, 248).

194. Thiselton writes, "the death of Christ also constitutes the ratification and validation of God's promise" (Thiselton, *First Corinthians*, 885). Or again, "In the major Pauline epistles covenant refers to the continuity of God's faithful promises to Israel (Rom 9:4; 11:27), to the ratification of God's promises through the free gift of grace made operative in and through Christ (Gal 3:15, 17; 4:24), and to the glory of the new covenant (2 Cor 3:6, 14) ratified through the blood of Christ and visibly articulated in the Lord's Supper (1 Cor 11:25)."

195. Note Thiselton's list of self-involving aspects of the meal that the participants are to actively engage with based on the call to drink the cup, eat the bread, do both in remembrance of Jesus, and proclaim the Lord's death by those actions. Note also his helpful reminder that the mention of the new covenant entails that the meal serves to reaffirm for the recipients "where they stand with God, namely, in identification with Christ the vindicated Messiah and exalted Lord on the basis of God's promise duly ratified in the events of Calvary" (Thiselton, *First Corinthians*, 885–86).

doing, the church corporately participates in the benefits of Christ's cross and resurrection.

In light of these truths, Jamieson describes the Lord's Supper as a "renewing oath sign" and a repeated "covenant ratification meal."[196] Both designations contain elements of divine and human agency. The Supper is a covenant ratification meal because in it, Jesus as host (through the agency of the church) presents "a visible promise that upon our accepting the things signified by [the bread and cup] at the hands of Christ, we shall enjoy [those benefits]; and the actions and signs signify the same to the eye as the promises do to the ear."[197] Therefore, the Lord's Supper acts as a "sign and seal of the new covenant on God's part in that it visibly extends and confirms his saving promises to us."[198] At the same time, the "self-involving" nature of receiving the elements of the Lord's Supper entails covenant ratification on the individual level as "we solemnly signify our faith in Christ and commitment to him, confirming our union with Christ and one another." As a renewing oath sign, receiving the meal "communicates our commitment to his covenant as surely as if we spoke a verbal oath."[199] As the community created by Jesus' new covenant initiating death, "through their acts of eating and drinking, the Corinthians manifest in space and time the eschatological fulfillment of the Jeremiah-promised new covenant."[200]

Paul's use of Passover imagery in 1 Corinthians is further evidence that he views the Lord's Supper as a reinterpreted Passover meal and thus a covenantal meal. The connection between Passover and the Lord's Supper in 1 Corinthians 5 evidences this claim. When addressing a man who belonged to the church and claimed to be a "brother" (5:11), yet lived in unrepentant sin, Paul commanded that man's removal from the church on grounds that

196. Jamieson, *Going Public*, 114–15. Similarly, see Billings, *Remembrance, Communion, and Hope*, 71. Billings describes the Lord's Supper as a sign of one's own faith and the receiving of a gift from God. On the term covenant ratification meal, see also Ciampa and Rosner, *First Letter to the Corinthians*, 474; Gentry and Wellum, *Kingdom through Covenant*, 350.

197. Jamieson, *Going Public*, 114–15. Jamieson is quoting Edwards, "Thing Desired," in Kistler, *Sermons on the Lord's Supper*, 15.

198. Jamieson, *Going Public*, 114. On this point, see also Vickers, "Past and Future," in Schreiner and Crawford, *Lord's Supper*, 323–24; Hammett, *Forty Questions*, 284–85.

199. Jamieson, *Going Public*, 115. Horton appears to locate the action of ratification only within God's agency and does not recognize an appropriate, grace-enabled, human, corporate ratification on the part of the individual new covenant believers who compose the church (Horton, *People and Place*, 107). By the phrase, "you are proclaiming the Lord's death" (Thiselton's translation), Paul places the whole congregation in the position of witnessing to the benefits of Christ (Thiselton, *First Corinthians*, 887).

200. Turley, *Ritualized Revelation of the Messianic Age*, 151.

"Christ our Passover lamb has been sacrificed" (v. 7). Paul compares the man to "a little leaven" that "leavens the whole lump," using the imagery of God's requirement for unleavened bread at the Passover (Exod 12:14–15). Paul intends the congregation's act to remove the man as a way to "cleanse out the old leaven that you may be a new lump, as you really are unleavened" (1 Cor 5:7). At the end of this instruction, Paul calls the Corinthians "to celebrate the festival, not with the old leaven, the leaven of malice and evil, but with the unleavened bread of sincerity and truth" (v. 8). This reference, and the command "not even to eat with such a one" (v. 11), point to a festive, celebratory meal, a new Passover—the Lord's Supper as the meal from which the man was excluded. Paul instructs the whole congregation in this manner. Furthermore, given that the man is holding on to the leaven of sexual sin (5:1–2), he is disqualified from the meal. Therefore, while daily meals may be included in the prohibition as well, the most natural way to understand Paul's instruction is as a prohibition against participating together in the Lord's Supper.[201]

Fourth, by grounding the Corinthians' present practice of the Lord's Supper in Jesus' celebration of the Last Supper (v. 23), he demonstrates the church's continuing obedience to Jesus' command to "do this in remembrance of me" between the cross and second coming (Luke 22:19; cf. 11:26). In 1 Corinthians, Christ's second coming at least entails the full establishment of his kingdom, "when Christ delivers the kingdom to God the Father" (15:24; cf. v. 23). Combining Paul's recent claim that the Corinthians are those "on whom the end of the ages has come" (10:11) with his eschatological hope of Christ's coming (11:26) reveals part of the meal's eschatological purpose. The Lord's Supper is intended to form the church into the eschatologically new people of God they are in Christ.[202] Their present lives should be a foretaste of their future in the consummated kingdom.[203] The act of taking the meal proclaims the church's hope in Christ's kingdom-consummating return.[204]

Fifth, Paul's emphasizes that Lord's Supper is intended to portray, create, and foster gospel-based unity within the local body, the church at Corinth. Rather than one "going ahead with his own meal" (v. 21), which "despise[s] the church of God and humiliate[s] those who have nothing" (v. 22),[205] the

---

201. Billings, *Remembrance, Communion, and Hope*, 143–45; Hamilton Jr., "Lord's Supper in Paul," in Schreiner and Crawford, *Lord's Supper*, 86–92.

202. Hamilton Jr., "Lord's Supper in Paul," in Schreiner and Crawford, *Lord's Supper*, 89.

203. Turley, *Ritualized Revelation of the Messianic Age*, 152.

204. Billings, *Remembrance, Communion, and Hope*, 170–74.

205. The church belongs to God. To mistreat brothers and sisters in one's

church is to "wait for one another" (v. 33). The divisions in Corinth are anti-gospel; thus, it is no surprise that Paul refers to some members of the congregation proving genuine through their response to the factions (v. 18; cf. 1:10)[206] and describes the Corinthians' meal as "not the Lord's Supper" (v. 20).[207] Hamilton writes, "The issue Paul has with the church at Corinth is simply that their conduct at the Lord's Supper is in conflict with what they are ostensibly proclaiming in the Lord's Supper."[208] The good news of Jesus' death and resurrection for sinners should "reshape" the church's individual and corporate identity. That new identity should be reflected in their humble behavior. However, the fact that the rich could indulge at the expense of the poor demonstrates the church's lack of appropriation of the gospel identity and unity the meal conveys. In Hamilton's words, the Lord's Supper is an "identity-forming proclamation of the Gospel."[209] Where the Supper is marked by class distinctions rather than Christ-like humility and gospel-created unity, the meal ceases to be the Lord's Supper. Paul's rebuke demonstrates that the meal carries within it the inherent symbolism of unity and mutual responsibility within the meal's participants.[210]

Sixth, Paul's positive response to the Corinthian divisiveness begins by reminding them of their common sharing of the benefits of Christ through his death, portrayed in the meal (vv. 23–25; cf. 10:16–17). The Corinthians were to receive the news that Jesus' body was broken for them as a reminder of their common need for forgiveness, which was only possible through Jesus' substitutionary death.[211] Jesus' promised Messianic death and resur-

---

congregation is to despise the group "on which God has set his love" (Thiselton, *First Corinthians*, 864).

206. Hamilton Jr., "Lord's Supper in Paul," in Schreiner and Crawford, *Lord's Supper*, 81.

207. Paul's rebuke, "Do you not have houses to eat and drink in?" suggests that Paul, at this early stage in history, was already able to separate the common meal that often accompanied the Lord's Supper from the Supper itself (Hamilton, "Lord's Supper in Paul," in Schreiner and Crawford, *Lord's Supper*, 77n21).

208. Hamilton Jr., "Lord's Supper in Paul," in Schreiner and Crawford, *Lord's Supper*, 80n30. Expanding on Hamilton's point, Jesus gave his followers the Lord's Supper as a continuing practice "on the night he was delivered up" (v. 23, Thiselton's translation). Therefore, the giving of Jesus' own body for his follower's forgiveness exemplifies one who was "voluntarily to renounce self-direction and autonomy to place his . . . destiny in the hands of God and human persons without any further 'say' in what happens" (Thiselton, *First Corinthians*, 870).

209. Hamilton, "Lord's Supper in Paul," in Schreiner and Crawford, *Lord's Supper*, 83–84. Similarly, see Thiselton, *First Corinthians*, 888.

210. Vickers, "Past and Future," in Schreiner and Crawford, *Lord's Supper*, 326–29.

211. That Jesus gave his body "for (*hyper*) you" entails vicarious, substitutionary atonement. Note Paul's similar usage in 1 Cor 15:3, 29; 2 Cor 5:14; Rom 5:6, 8; 8:32; and

rection purchased and made possible the new covenant unity of Jews and
Gentiles, rich and poor in the church (1 Cor 12:13; cf. Isa 52:13—53:12; Gal
3:26–28). After reminding the church of the gospel, Paul gives the church
four responsibilities regarding how they are to receive the meal together.
While much could be said about these instructions (11:27–34), their bearing on the corporate nature of the meal is paramount for this book. To promote unity within the congregation around the Supper, members are to eat
and drink in a worthy manner (v. 27), examine themselves before the meal
(v. 28), discern the body (v. 29), and receive one another (v. 33). These four
responsibilities are examined in turn.

   Paul declares the need to eat and drink in a worthy manner as a warning: Those who fail to do so "will be guilty of profaning the body and blood
of the Lord" (v. 27).[212] By "worthy manner," Paul's primary target appears
to be the divisive, gospel denying behaviors of the Corinthians toward each
other. In this sense, the Lord's Supper should express the unity the meal
is intended to display and create (cf. 10:16–17).[213] Certainly, Paul is not

---

Gal 3:13. cf. Isa 53:12 (Hamilton Jr., "Lord's Supper in Paul," in Schreiner and Crawford,
Lord's Supper, 89).

   212. Hamilton helpfully connects those whom Paul implies do not prove genuine
(11:19) with those who would be guilty of the body and blood of the Lord. The implication is that those who prove genuine (11:20) will heed Paul's instruction. If they do
not, they will be grouped with those who placed Jesus on the cross (cf. 2:8). Hamilton
compares the warning of judgment here to that of Rev 2:21–23, where those who will
not repent would demonstrate that they are Jezebel's children and would be struck
dead. Similarly, Paul's admonition to judge one's self in order to avoid further judgment is intended as a means to provoke repentance in a straying Christian (Hamilton
Jr., "Lord's Supper in Paul," in Schreiner and Crawford, *Lord's Supper*, 82). Paul claims
that those who eat and drink without discerning the body (v. 29) bring judgment on
themselves. The Lord had already "disciplined" some in the church by bringing sickness
or death on them as a preemptive judgment, that they might avoid condemnation with
the world (v. 32). Although I agree that Paul's warning is intended to preserve the elect,
the context does suggest that those who died of sickness in Corinth received God's
discipline as Christians rather than proving their identity as false professors (Hamilton
Jr., "Lord's Supper in Paul," in Schreiner and Crawford, *Lord's Supper*, 93–94). On this
point, Hamilton cites Schreiner, *New Testament Theology*, 733. Schreiner argues that
the group that is not genuine "are not truly believers." Against Hamilton and Schreiner
regarding those who would prove genuine is Thiselton, *First Corinthians*, 859. But Thiselton's agreement regarding those who would partake of the Lord's Supper while living
a life that disregards Christ and his church is also evident (889–90).

   213. Fee, *First Epistle to the Corinthians*, 559–60. Seeking to balance the corporate
emphasis with individual responsibility is Vickers, "Past and Future," in Schreiner and
Crawford, *Lord's Supper*, 327. By primary target, I suggest that when one broadens out
to the whole letter of Corinthians, Paul does intend to convey the need to come to
the Lord's Supper as one whose life (as a justified and Holy Spirit sealed sinner) does
not betray some persistent and purposeful hypocrisy with repentant gospel living (cf.
5:1–11). Hamilton critiques Fee, because he "focuses too narrowly on the immediate

saying that coming to the Table requires that one be worthy by one's own merit. In order to facilitate approaching the Table worthily, Paul urges, "Let a person examine himself" (11:28). The self-examination required is not intended to induce morbid introspection. Rather, in keeping with the primary emphasis of the passage, Paul calls the church to examine their own hearts with respect to communion with Christ and each other (cf. 10:16–17; 11:17–22).[214] Where that communion is not in accord with the gospel, one should repent and be reconciled before continuing (cf. Matt 5:23–24). "Perhaps then Paul is calling the church in Corinth to judge whether or not they have sufficiently dealt with the leaven of sin in their lives before they partake of the Lord's Supper."[215]

Paul further explains what he intends by participating in a worthy manner with the call to "discern the body" (1 Cor 11:29). Commentators are divided over whether Paul's reference to body here refers to the body of Christ (11:23) or to the church as the body of Christ (10:16–17; 12:13).[216] Yet, Hamilton claims, "No distinction should be drawn between the body

---

context to the exclusion of the broader context." Paul's command to "flee idolatry" (10:14–22) and his reference to not celebrating the feast with leaven (5:8) suggests that a secondary way by which one could come to the table unworthily would be to come in unrepentant sin. The point of Paul's instruction is not to suggest that Christians should wait until they receive the Lord's Supper with the church to think about, confess, and turn from their sin. Rather, the point is that, given the warning that follows, preparing for the Lord's Supper is one of the God-ordained means of reminding sinners to run from their sin to Christ in an ongoing, life-long way in order to grow in holiness. (Hamilton Jr., "Lord's Supper in Paul," in Schreiner and Crawford, *Lord's Supper*, 95). But see also Allison's instructive warning against misrepresenting Paul's intentions for participating in a worthy manner (Allison, *Sojourners and Strangers*, 394).

214. Hamilton Jr., "Lord's Supper in Paul," in Schreiner and Crawford, *Lord's Supper*, 96. Rayburn's suggestion that Paul's summons to partake in a worthy manner and examine one's self only applies to those who were being divisive in the Corinthian church appears to be a case of special pleading. For Paul, all who partake of the bread and cup ostensibly participate in the new covenant benefits of the gospel (1 Cor 10:16–17). Thus, Rayburn is assuming that infants have a right to the meal and then claiming that Paul cannot be calling them to perform a mental function meant to alleviate an error in which they had no part (Rayburn, "Presbyterian Defense of Paedocommunion," in Strawbridge, *Case for Covenant Communion*, 9–10). A similar case of special pleading is J. Meyers, who argues that infants are capable of examining themselves, because this requirement means merely to prove one's self in unity with the congregation (Meyers, "Presbyterian, Examine Thyself," in Strawbridge, *Case for Covenant Communion*, 22). Pedobaptist Cornelis Venema critiques Rayburn's view at this point as well. See Venema, *Children at the Lord's Table?*, 113–25.

215. Hamilton Jr., "Lord's Supper in Paul," in Schreiner and Crawford, *Lord's Supper*, 98.

216. For a survey of views, see the helpful excursus in Thiselton, *First Corinthians*, 891–94.

of Jesus and the church. Both are in view. The one who does not examine himself does not recognize the significance of Christ nor of the body of Christ."[217] The analysis of 1 Corinthians 10:16–17 (provided above) lends credence to this view. Surely, when a Christian is aware of ways in which her behavior is out of step with the Lord such that communion with Christ and his people suffers, she is not discerning the body properly. Discerning the body requires that a Christian come to the Table to renew the pledge of covenant faithfulness to Christ, first, and also to Christ's people. Turley gets at the implication for the way the requirement to discern the body demonstrates that participating in the meal is constitutive of the church. He writes,

> Through eating a ritualized element identified with the physical body of Christ, the Corinthians are transformed into a social body (cf. 11:29), which, according to 12:13, is the very pneumatic body into which each person was baptized. The important point here is that this pneumatically constituted social body in which they were all baptized appears every time the Lord's Supper is celebrated. The *soma*-motif thus links together socially the baptism ritual with the Lord's Supper, providing a ritual relationship (the mutual formation of a social body) analogous to the conceptual reciprocity between Ezekiel 36:25–27 and Jeremiah 31:31–34 [with their respective promises of a new heart and spirit on the one hand and the law written on the heart on the other]: two rituals function together to introduce and reproduce respectively the pneumatic body.[218]

Finally, Paul urges the church, "when you come together, to eat, receive one another" (11:33).[219] Rather than the rich eating their own meals, indulging, and promoting disharmony (cf. vv. 17–22), the church is to come together to eat and welcome each other. These factors clearly present the Lord's Supper as a meal intended to be celebrated in the context of the local church. While Paul is addressing a specific historical situation in his rebuke and commands, the instructions he gives are both historically applicable to the initial audience and theologically timeless.

---

217. Hamilton Jr., "Lord's Supper in Paul," in Schreiner and Crawford, *Lord's Supper*, 97. So also Fee, *First Epistle to the Corinthians*, 564. Opposed is Thiselton, *First Corinthians*, 893–94.

218. Turley, *Ritualized Revelation of the Messianic Age*, 159.

219. Hamilton's translation. See his justification in Hamilton Jr., "Lord's Supper in Paul," in Schreiner and Crawford, *Lord's Supper*, 99. Contra Thiselton, *First Corinthians*, 899.

The Lord's Supper and the Marriage Supper of the Lamb

In Luke 22:16, Jesus provides the warrant for interpreting the Messianic banquet of Revelation 19:6–9 as the typological fulfillment of the Passover. The unity of Scripture's storyline explicitly includes God's redemption of a people for himself through successive covenants, which culminate in the new covenant, are celebrated/ratified by covenant meals, and are finally consummated with the arrival of the kingdom of God. This section focuses on the way in which the Marriage Supper of the Lamb consummates both the new covenant and the kingdom of God.[220]

In Revelation 19:6–9, kingdom and covenant appear side by side, denoting the consummation of both. With the destruction of the wicked complete (19:1–4), the saints begin to worship God because his reign boasts no rivals (v. 6). Throughout the book of Revelation, John portrays the church as a new Israel (Rev 7:1–9; cf. 14:1–5) that experiences a new exodus made possible by the blood of the Lamb (Rev 15:1–4).[221] As a result of Christ's judgment of Babylon (cf. 19:1–4, 11), the authority of the kingdoms of the earth is transferred completely to Christ, "and he will reign forever and ever" (11:15).[222] With the new exodus complete by means of exodus-like plagues on the earth, the declaration of God's rule comprises part of the Song of Moses and Song of the Lamb (15:3–4).[223] At the *parousia* of Christ God brings his final saving deliverance (Passover-exodus) of his people into the peace of his righteous rule (Luke 22:16).

Thus, the time arrives for the "marriage of the Lamb" (19:7). John's depiction of the marriage of the Lamb and his "bride," the church, brims with covenantal overtones. By mentioning the linen garments with which the bride clothes herself (19:8), John alludes to the "robes of righteousness" that God promised to Israel (Isa 61:10),[224] which he would give her in preparation for their marriage and life together in a land called "married"

220. Although John refers to the reign of God before the marriage of the Lamb, we will consider the marriage first (Rev 19:6–7), because of the biblical-theological emphasis on the kingdom arriving through covenant.

221. Schreiner, *King in His Beauty*, 629. Several OT texts unite the promise of an effectual covenant with marriage and eating imagery. In Hos 2:14–23, although Israel was unfaithful to God's marriage-like covenant with Israel when he redeemed them from Egypt, God promised to "betroth her to himself in righteousness," so that she would know the Lord and call him "my husband" in a land brimming with bread, wine, and oil. See also Ezek 16:59–63.

222. Beale demonstrates the linkage between 19:6 and 11:15 by appeal to 11:17. Beale, *Book of Revelation*, 931.

223. Cf. Exod 15:18, "The Lord will reign forever and ever" (Beale, *Revelation*, 933).

224. Beale, *Revelation*, 938–39.

(62:4). Paul describes Christ's relationship to the church in a similar fashion, denoting Christ's present sanctification of his bride as a means to her perfection at his return for their wedding (Eph 5:26–27; cf. 2 Cor 11:12).[225] The marriage imagery in Revelation is meant to convey the consummatory ratification of covenant relationship in fulfillment of the proleptic covenant ratification the church presently experiences.

The kingdom theme remains present with the language of a marriage supper (19:9),[226] because Jesus repeatedly referred to the consummation of the kingdom as involving a wedding feast (Matt 8:11–12; 26:29; Mark 14:25; Luke 14:15; 22:16, 18, 29–30). Schreiner summarizes, "The coming kingdom can be described as a great end-time feast in which the righteous will rejoice but others will be cast out into the darkness."[227] Still, because this meal includes formerly unrighteous sinners who have been forgiven by the blood of their husband, the Lamb, the consummated kingdom feast must also be a covenantal meal. The participants in this meal are both followers/ guests of the Lamb and the bride of the Lamb (12:10–12; 19:7, 9).[228] While the former image emphasizes the Lamb's kingdom rule (cf. Isa 25), the latter emphasizes complete covenant ratification (Exod 24:9–11). At this supper, the resurrected king sits down to enjoy table fellowship with his guests who have arrived at their much anticipated fulfillment meal by virtue of their prior participation in the new covenant (1 Cor 11:26).[229]

---

225. Beasley-Murray, *Revelation*, 273.

226. No consensus has been reached on the timing of this kingdom feast. Patterson distances himself from some interpreters who claim that the marriage supper is only a metaphor. However, as a dispensationalist he makes no formal decision between the millennial reign and the new heavens/new earth. Patterson, *Revelation*, 344. While it is beyond the scope of this paper to determine the timing of the feast, the further mentions of the arrival of the Bride in Rev 21 are noteworthy.

227. Schreiner, *New Testament Theology*, 51.

228. Beasley-Murray, *Revelation*, 275.

229. Seeing God and being in his presence functions with the meal as the climax of the establishment of the covenant relationship (Schreiner, *King in His Beauty*, 39–40). Throughout the OT, the privilege of seeing God (his manifest glory) is reserved for God's covenant people. See Exod 24:16–17; 33:10–11, 18–23; 34:34–38; cf. 1 Kgs 8:10–11. In Isa 24:6–9, the mountain of the Lord is the location at which the LORD himself will act as host, will serve a "feast of rich food" full of marrow and alongside well-aged wine, will "swallow up death forever," and will "wipe away tears from all faces." That this passage refers to the consummation of the new covenant is evident by the fact that the only redemptive-historical moment in which God accomplishes all of these things is described in Rev 19–22 (cf. Isa 65:13, 17–25; Matt 5:8).

The Lord's Supper as a Kingdom
and Covenant Sign

In a redemptive-historical sense, the Lord's Supper functions as a proleptic, covenant ratification meal and inaugurated kingdom feast.[230] Marshall suggests "that Jesus looked forward to a new Passover in the heavenly kingdom of God, but that at the same time he commanded his disciples to celebrate a meal which would be an anticipation of that heavenly feast."[231] That Jesus commands the disciples concerning how they were to observe the Lord's Supper after his departure makes clear that the instructions he gave at the redemptive-historically unique Last Supper establish the necessity of an ongoing Lord's Supper.[232] As Beale explains, "The Lord's Supper "is the antitypical correspondence [partially] fulfilling the type of Israel's meal."[233] When Paul writes that each time the church eats the bread and drinks the wine they "proclaim the Lord's death until he comes" (1 Cor 11:26), the forward looking proclamation of the historical, new covenant inaugurating reality of Christ's death reminds the participants in the Lord's Supper that "the inaugurated form of the Lord's Supper would cease" when Christ returns to consummate the kingdom.[234] By using "fulfillment" language, Jesus' actions at the Last Supper bring the old covenant celebration of the Passover to its initial *telos*, rendering its future celebration as merely an old covenant Passover feast redemptive-historically inappropriate. By Jesus' words of fulfillment and institution of new commands, Jesus instituted a new kind of

230. The Lord's Supper is a covenant ratification meal that looks forward to the consummatory marriage supper of the Lamb. In this sense, the Lord's Supper is a proleptic covenant ratification meal. While inaugurated eschatology is especially associated with the kingdom themes, the new covenant is in a sense already and not yet in terms of the experience of its benefits.

231. Marshall, *Last Supper and Lord's Supper*, 80.

232. Beale contends that Jesus' promise to eat and drink with the disciples when "the kingdom comes" "apparently began to be fulfilled during his resurrection appearances," since Acts 10:41 mentions Jesus eating and drinking with the disciples (Beale, *New Testament Biblical Theology*, 818).

233. Rather than justifying his claim with reference to Luke 22 as this chapter does, Beale shows the correspondence between the Passover meal and Christ as the antitypical Passover lamb from 1 Cor 5:6–8 (Beale, *New Testament Biblical Theology*, 818). Christ is the *telos* of all OT promises, including those of a predictive nature, which come through typological themes. At the same time, Luke clearly describes Passover as being fulfilled in the kingdom feast with Christ (22:16, 18). I have qualified Beale's quotation with the word "partially" to underscore the sense of ongoing fulfillment of Passover through Christ in the Lord's Supper until consummation.

234. Beale, *New Testament Biblical Theology*, 928. So Saucy refers to the Lord's Supper as "provisional." See Saucy, *Church in God's Program*, 225.

celebration that functions as the inaugurated antitype of the Old Testament Passover that centers on his death as the cutting of the new covenant. The Lord's Supper replaces the Passover.[235]

Therefore, the Last Supper and Lord's Supper share a basic continuity, given that Christ established the pattern for his new covenant church to follow in that meal (Luke 22:15–20; 1 Cor 11:17–34). Both meals include at least (1) bread and the fruit of the vine; (2) words of institution/explanation of new covenant redemption; (3) participation in Christ's covenantal presence;[236] (4) the sign and seal of new covenant forgiveness of sins for those who come in faith; (5) a clear picture of unity in the church's eating together and sharing the elements; and (6) anticipation of the consummation of the kingdom of God and new covenant at the return of Christ.

The discontinuities in the Last Supper and Lord's Supper revolve around their respective redemptive-historical moments. Whereas the Last Supper anticipated redemption, the Lord's Supper celebrates redemption accomplished. Whereas the Last Supper anticipated the inauguration of the new covenant in Christ's blood, the Lord's Supper celebrates the present experience of God's new covenant forgiveness and presence as a covenant ratification meal. Whereas the Last Supper looked back to the Passover that it fulfilled and forward to the kingdom feast it anticipated, the Lord's Supper looks back to the cross and resurrection of Christ (with the Passover-exodus event as an interpretive grid) and looks forward to the consummation of the new covenant and the kingdom of God. Whereas the Last Supper occurred during the inaugurated reign of Christ but prior to its corollary new covenant (cf. Matt 12:28; 26:28), the Lord's Supper occurs in the age of the already-not yet new covenant and kingdom (1 Cor 11:26).

Therefore, the present experience of believers as they participate in the Lord's Supper is one of assurance. God reminds them that the new covenant benefits of communion with him through forgiveness of sins are theirs each time they eat and drink together. The new covenant is ratified with Christ and his followers even while it is not consummated. Similarly, as the church participates together in meal that points forward to the saving reign of Christ and as they exercise the authority Christ has given them to bind and

---

235. Marshall, *Last Supper and Lord's Supper*, 80.

236. While the disciples experienced Jesus' covenantal presence to bless by his bodily presence as the God-man, the recipients of the Lord's Supper experience Jesus' covenantal presence to bless through participation in the body and blood of Christ (1 Cor 10:16–17), by virtue of God the Son's divine nature (*Extracalvinisticum*; Matt 18:20), and through the terminating work of the Holy Spirit, who indwells individual new covenant members and the corporate body (John 14:17, 23; 1 Cor 3:18; 6:18–20; 2 Cor 6:16–18; Eph 2:22).

loose related to that meal (Matt 18:15–20; 1 Cor 5:1–12), they participate in an inaugurated kingdom feast.

Because the kingdom feast of Revelation 19:6–9 functions as the consummation of both the new covenant and the kingdom of God, it is the much-anticipated anti-type of all the previous covenantal meals between God and man. At the wedding (Rev 19:7, 9), the church will experience its covenantal goal when it experiences Christ's presence face to face (Rev 21:5) rather than the glorious, inaugurated participation of union with Christ through the Spirit (1 Cor 12:13). At the royal banquet, the church will experience the full fellowship and joy of Christ's complete removal of sin, rather than needing to exercise the keys of the kingdom and fight against personal sin. Indeed, the blessing of new covenant and kingdom consummation at the heavenly banquet will be to eat and drink again with Christ around his table (Luke 22:16, 18).

Baptism's Relationship to the Lord's Supper

Throughout the New Testament, baptism is tied covenantally to the Lord's Supper. While the former is the sign of initiation, the latter is the sign of participation. The data surveyed thus far in this chapter highlights the assumed nature of baptism as connected to faith and entrance into the new covenant community. The data surveyed with respect to the Lord's Supper highlights the function of the meal to unite many new disciples into one body as a remembrance, celebration, and participation in the new covenant benefits of Christ. This section presents the exemplary way in which baptism appears prerequisite to the Lord's Supper and argues for the normalcy of Acts 2:41–42 as prescriptive for the church until Christ comes. This argument is the second pillar of this project's thesis. After considering Acts, this section posits the case of the church at Corinth as a less clear, but probable example, of baptism preceding the Lord's Supper.

The Example of Acts 2:41–42

Clearly, from the beginning of the church's existence as a new covenant reality, baptism preceded participation in the Lord's Supper.[237] Acts 2:41–42 presents the order as it occurred in history: proclamation of the gospel, receiving/believing/repenting, being baptized, being added to the church, and participating in the breaking of bread (the Lord's Supper) together with the

---

237. For the description of the church as a new covenant reality, see chapter 5.

church. This project contends that this order in history is exemplary of the order in which these elements should normally occur until Christ comes. The connection of baptism and the Lord's Supper together in Acts 2:41–42 is significant for understanding the nature of the church. Stanley Grenz writes the church "mediates to its members the framework for the formation of personal identity and values."[238] In other words, the ordinances demonstrate the church's "constituting narrative."[239] As Beasley-Murray explains, "It follows logically that the fellowship with the exalted Lord, that includes within itself a cultic act like the Lord's Supper, is also founded through a cult act like baptism."[240] The fellowship of those who renounced their sinful "killing of God's Messiah" is fostered and represented in the new community's regular practice of breaking bread together.[241]

While Acts describes several unique events in redemption history and the history of the church after Pentecost, several aspects of the account are viewed as binding on the church throughout the new covenant age. As surveyed above, exegetes and theologians regularly group repentance, faith, and baptism together as belonging to the cluster of events that make up conversion.[242] Given this normal pattern throughout Acts and Paul, it is hermeneutically valuable to distinguish those aspects of the formation of the church in Acts 2 that are unique in redemptive history and merely descriptive from those aspects that may contain unique elements but remain prescriptive for the church until Christ returns. Delineating these aspects is the means of providing warrant for the second aspect of the thesis, that the exemplary pattern—belief, baptism, then the Lord's Supper—be the continuing practice of the church.

At least seven aspects of the formation of the church are unique: (1) the whole community of Christ's followers speaking in tongues with flaming tongues of fire on their heads; (2) the mighty rushing wind; (3) the whole

---

238. Grenz, "Baptism and the Lord's Supper as Community Acts," in Cross and Thompson, Baptist Sacramentalism, 91. Grenz's thesis is worth citing at length. He writes, "These acts are an indispensable means whereby the group is placed ritually into the narrative that constitutes them as a community. To this end, baptism and the Lord's Supper serve as symbols of the relationship of believers to God and to one another. These acts symbolize, vividly portray, and ritually enact the participation of the community as a whole in the divine story in the participation of its members in the believing community. In this manner these rights become community acts."

239. Grenz, "Baptism and the Lord's Supper," in Cross and Thompson, Baptist Sacramentalism.

240. Beasley-Murray, Baptism in the New Testament, 99. A "cultic act" in this context is a general reference to an act of worship.

241. Beasley-Murray, Baptism in the New Testament, 98–99.

242. Stein, "Baptism in Luke-Acts," in Schreiner and Wright, Believer's Baptism.

place being shaken; (4) the preacher (an apostle, Peter); (5) the number of responders to the first gospel message after the sending of the Spirit (3,000); (6) the context of a Jewish feast day (Pentecost); (6) the location (in Jerusalem); and (7) the redemptive-historical result: the formation of the new covenant church. Given their redemptive-historical uniqueness, these aspects are not binding, though they remain instructive. For instance, contra some branches of Pentecostal theology, the church should not teach that speaking in tongues is normative for every believer after conversion (cf. 1 Cor 12:30), or that the Spirit comes to believers in a new way for empowerment as a second blessing after conversion (doctrine of subsequence). Yet, these facets of the Acts account are at least instructive to teach the redemptive-historical location of the church, along with the role of the Holy Spirit, the gospel message, and the apostles in the foundation of the church.[243]

At the same time, Luke describes several aspects of the formation of the church in Acts in ways that signal their prescriptive nature for the church until Christ returns. These binding aspects are at least (1) the proclamation of the gospel message is essential to the existence of the church; (2) the required, saving response to the gospel normally includes repentance, receiving the word/belief, and baptism; (3) those who are converted to the church by these means should normally be added to an existing local church;[244] and (4) the practices to which the early church devoted themselves are essential marks of a church: apostles' teaching (now found in Scripture), fellowship, the breaking of bread/Lord's Supper, prayer, and the principle of generosity among the community.[245] If this is so, then, it stands to reason

243. Contra Horton, "Spirit Baptism," in Brand, *Perspectives on Spirit Baptism*, 47–94.

244. Schnabel summarizes the relationship of these first three aspects to the church by stating that Acts 2:42–47 "shows that part and parcel of this public commitment to faith in Jesus was integration into the community of local believers in Jesus" (Schnabel, *Acts*, 187).

245. Concerning the list of practices in Acts 2:42–47, Schnabel summarizes, "Luke's extensive summary of the life of the Jerusalem church is not only a historical statement about the first months of the Christian movement. It is also a theological statement about God's presence in the community of believers, an ecclesiological statement about the priorities of an authentic church, and a missiological statement about the process of church growth" (Schnabel, *Acts*, 185). Schnabel, along with several others, treat the four aspects above as normative for the church. Keener writes, "Presumably, [Luke] also intends [the description of the early church] as a model for Spirit-filled communities of his own day [who were] not restricted by historical particulars (such as meeting in the temple, characteristic of a possible only for, the Jerusalem church)" (Keener, *Acts*, 1:988–91). Keener does see a greater normative role for prophetic gifts. David Peterson has, "Peter's preaching at Pentecost should be understood as being 'theologically normative' for the relation in Acts between conversion, water baptism, and the baptism of the Holy Spirit, whereas later incidents are more historically conditioned and should be

that the order—conversion (repentance/belief/baptism), reception into the church fellowship by that baptism, followed by the Lord's Supper—would remain normative as well.[246] Acts 2:39 adds exegetical strength to this claim by Luke's explanation that the promise applied to his original hearers "and to your children and for all who are far off, everyone whom the Lord our God calls to himself." Thus, subsequent generations throughout "time and space" would have the same promise of forgiveness and reception of the Spirit available to them by the same means as Peter's initial audience.[247] Although verse 39 refers specifically to the promise of verse 38, it suggests that future generations until Christ's return would also enter the fellowship of local churches through belief and baptism, where they would celebrate the Lord's Supper together.

The Example of the Church at Corinth

Much has already been written about baptism and the Lord's Supper in the church at Corinth. What remains to be observed is the force of the example established in the way Paul planted the church. The case can be made that the founding of the Corinthian church presents another example (besides Acts 2:41–42) of baptism preceding the Lord's Supper.

First, Acts 18:8 presents an unqualified affirmation that "Crispus, the ruler of the synagogue," "his entire household," and "many of the Corinthians" (Gentiles) "believed" in Jesus when Paul preached the gospel to them. Second, Scripture clearly claims that Crispus and the Corinthian Gentiles were baptized (Acts 18:8; 1 Cor 1:14). While the text does not state explicitly that Crispus's household was baptized, that fact is assumed given the other household baptisms in Acts. The upshot of this observation—only those

---

circumstantially understood" (Peterson, *Acts of the Apostles*, 155n89). Then, concerning Acts 41–47 on Peterson writes, "Luke was also commending the positive example of the earliest community of Christians to his readers" (158).

246. This argument as stated appeals especially to Baptists. For pedobaptists, the argument above assumes that the missionary context of Acts in which belief and faith normally went together (except from their view in the case of household baptisms) does not adequately account for the genealogical principle they see in Acts 2:39 ("For the promise is for you and your children"), which is carried over from the covenant of grace established in Gen 3:15 and made explicit in 17:7–14. However, the argumentation throughout this chapter is intended to buttress argument that baptism is the response of faith to the gospel.

247. Thanks to John Kimbell for this point. The language of the scope of the promise comes from Barrett, *Acts of the Apostles*, 1:156. Barrett argues that "far" off is a time reference as much as a geographical and ethnic one.

who believed were baptized and all those who believed were baptized—is that it places baptism necessarily prior to the Corinthian church's reception of the Lord's Supper.[248] Third, Paul served as the founding pastor of the church at Corinth. That the church enjoyed subsequent growth in baptized believers is evident from (1) the Lord's evangelism-provoking word of assurance to Paul ("I have many in this city who are my people"; Acts 18:10); (2) the claim that Paul "stayed a year and six months, teaching the word of God among them" (v. 11); and (3) Paul's admission that he "baptized the household of Stephanas" (1 Cor 1:16), which constituted "the first converts in Achaia" (16:15). Fourth, Paul states explicitly that he "delivered" the Lord's teaching about the Supper to the Corinthians when he was with them for that year and a half (1 Cor 11:23).[249] The indication of the text is that Paul not only told the church about the Lord's Supper, but also that they practiced it together. These four points strongly suggest that the founding of the church at Corinth provides an example similar to that of the Jerusalem church (Acts 2:41–42). In both cases, baptism is presented as preceding communion as prerequisite to it.

The fact that Paul's doctrinal statements on both ordinances reveal baptism to be the means of public covenantal identification with Christ (1 Cor 1:14–17) and the Lord's Supper to be the means of corporate participation with Christ, adds theological weight to the historical example (10:16–17; 11:24–25). The implication of these passages is that believers were baptized and that their baptism was prerequisite to church-constituting fellowship in the Lord's Supper (1 Cor 10:16–17), because the meaning of the ordinances would be confused if the order of the ordinances were reversed. Given the way baptism is included as part of the cluster of conversion events in Acts as a pattern, it is probable that all of the churches that began would have experienced baptism before their reception of the Lord's Supper.

248. Paul's pattern was to preach the gospel to the Jews before going also to the Gentiles (Acts 13:46), to baptize those who believed, and to continue teaching and shepherding the new congregation/church for some time (cf. 17:1–9; 19:1–10). Paul affirms his own role in baptizing Crispus in 1 Cor 1:14.

249. Paul writes, "For I received from the Lord what I also delivered to you" (v. 23). Whether his reception of the practice came via direct revelation or apostolic instruction, Paul acknowledges that he previously passed along instructions for how to participate in the Lord's Supper in the phrase "I also delivered to you." Presumably, during Paul's year and a half stay in Corinth (Acts 18:11), after the conversion of Crispus' household, Stephanus' household, and the Gentile Corinthians (v. 8; cf. 1 Cor 1:13–17), Paul taught the church the same content he recounts in 1 Cor 11:23–25 (Hamilton Jr., "Lord's Supper in Paul," in Schreiner and Crawford, Lord's Supper, 85).

Summary and Conclusion

This chapter demonstrates the first two pillars of the book: (1) believers, as those who compose the churches, are baptized and (2) the New Testament (Acts 2:41–42 especially) presents baptism as occurring prior to the Lord's Supper as a normative example for the church to follow until Christ returns. At the same time, this chapter has demonstrated the relationship of the ordinances to the new covenant and the inaugurated kingdom. Baptism is consistently presented as that aspect of conversion that visibly appropriates the gospel and in that way unites the believer to Christ. Thereby, baptism publicly ratifies one's entry into the new covenant community and constitutes that community as distinct from the world. The Lord's Supper is consistently presented as a renewing oath sign that binds many baptized believers into one body. The meal illustrates and effectively deepens union with Christ and unity with each other. Thus, both signs together function to create the new covenant community of the local church.

At the same time, by participating in the benefits of the new covenant, one necessarily belongs under the inaugurated reign of Christ's kingdom. Whereas baptism is the initial pledge of one's allegiance to Christ and Christ's demarcation of the believer as a kingdom citizen, the Lord's Supper is a continuing proclamation of the hope that Christ will return to consummate his reign. Whereas baptism is administered on behalf of Christ through the local church to a believing individual, the Lord's Supper is shared by those whose lives demonstrate loyalty to Christ and distinctness from the world.

In order to present the constructive, biblical-theological proposal of the book, what is needed is a comparison of the new covenant signs of baptism and the Lord's Supper with the old covenant signs of circumcision and Passover. That comparison is the task of chapter 4.

Chapter 4

The Relationship between Old Covenant and New Covenant Signs

THIS CHAPTER IS DEVOTED to biblical-theological synthesis. Reasserting the thesis is helpful at this point: This project argues that believer's baptism by immersion should precede communion as prerequisite to it, due to the explicit example of the New Testament (Acts 2:41–42), the assumption that all believers are baptized, and a principle of analogy (continuity) from the necessity of circumcision before Passover.[1] Chapter 1 surveyed historical arguments for who may participate in the Lord's Supper. Chapter 2 presented the first step of the thesis by demonstrating that God consistently required circumcision of any male who would celebrate the Passover. Chapter 3 demonstrated that the New Testament authors consistently assume all believers are baptized and argued from the example of Acts 2:41–42 that baptism should precede communion as the normative pattern in the new covenant age. The next step, in agreement with Wellum, is to "carefully think through the issues of continuity and discontinuity between covenantal signs."[2] This chapter argues that the continuities and discontinuities between the covenant signs reveal that the new covenant signs are analogically similar to a

---

1. This thesis, and the methodology adopted to demonstrate the thesis, should be sufficient to curtail Pratt's concern that those who deny that the new covenant is a renewal of the old covenant only see as valid for NT practice "those things that are stated or repeated in the New Testament" (Pratt, "Infant Baptism in the New Covenant," in Strawbridge, *Case for Covenantal Infant Baptism*, 179). In other words, this chapter demonstrates one way in which the OT continues to inform the way Christians live in the new covenant.

2. See especially that described in chapter 3, "Hermeneutical Issues in 'Putting Together the Covenants'" (Gentry and Wellum, *Kingdom through Covenant*, 81–126).

sufficient degree to the old covenant signs to suggest that baptism should precede communion.

This argument will be developed in four steps. First, this chapter will trace the continuities and discontinuities of the old covenant signs to their respective, corresponding new covenant signs. Second, it will present the relationship of old covenant signs to new covenant signs in 1 Corinthians 10. Third, it will ground the continuities and discontinuities between the signs in the coming of Christ and the new covenant. Fourth, this chapter will demonstrate the New Testament connection between circumcision and baptism based on an analysis of Acts 2:39, Romans 4:11, and Colossians 2:11–12.

The Relationship between Old and New Covenant Signs of Entry

This section presents the similarities and differences between the old and new covenant signs of entry based upon the biblical data surveyed in chapters 3 and 4.

Continuities between Circumcision and Baptism

Two initial points of continuity between circumcision and baptism are (1) both signs function as boundary markers and initiating oath signs (or signs of entry) into God's covenant people, and (2) both signs entail heart circumcision. From these two larger points of continuity, a variety of sub-points may be deduced.

Signs as Boundary Markers

First, the boundary marking function of circumcision and baptism is similar.[3] Whereas all those (males) who belong to God's covenant people from the inauguration of the Abrahamic covenant through the establishment of the new covenant were marked off from the surrounding nations by circumcision, with the inauguration of the new covenant, Jesus instituted baptism as the public sign of distinction of his (multi-ethnic, male and female) people from the nations (Matt 28:18–20). The consecratory nature of the

---

3. Venema, "Covenant Theology and Baptism," in Strawbridge, *Case for Covenantal Infant Baptism*, 220.

signs retains some consistency across the covenants.[4] In both cases, becoming a member of God's people entails appropriating the divine mandate to represent God to the world by the people's moral life together, exercise of dominion, and ministry of priestly "covenantal allegiance."[5] In both cases, the sign of entry marks off a distinct "political institution," through which God intends to display his character to the world and bless the nations.[6]

Next, the initiating oath sign functions of circumcision and baptism are similar to their boundary marking functions. However, the oath aspect of each sign is more complex than the boundary marking function. The primary oath to which circumcision testified was God's oath to Abraham and his offspring.[7] At the same time, the human partners from the time of Abraham through the Mosaic and Davidic covenants continued to exercise responsible owning of covenantal obligations through circumcision. The heads of households marked off their male offspring, servants, and hirelings by circumcision as a sign of receiving God's covenantal promises and willingness to keep God's covenant (cf. Gen 17:1–2; Exod 24:5–8). Furthermore, the Old Testament continually recognizes the responsibility of foreigners

---

4. For the qualification of "some consistency," see the discontinuities section below. On the theme of the paragraph, see Meade, "Circumcision of Flesh," in Wellum and Parker, *Progressive Covenantalism*, 131; Garrett, "Meredith Kline," in Schreiner and Wright, *Believer's Baptism*, 264.

5. This is not to claim that Israel was called to anything like the commission of Matt 28:18–20. However, the necessity of representing God to the nations as priest-kings who take up Adam's forfeited role is clearly present (Exod 19:4–6; Deut 4:6–7; 1 Pet 2:9–11). Dumbrell explains Israel's role as priestly mediators to the nations as passive in the sense of separation from sin's pollution in the world around it and dedicated service which exemplified "divine forgiveness and to communicate it" (Dumbrell, *Covenant and Creation*, 117). See also Leeman, *Political Church*, 221–27, 303–4; Fuller, *Unity of the Bible*, 355–56.

6. Leeman, *Political Church*, 216. In Exod 19:3b–6 especially, Israel is "the domain over which God rules" (Dumbrell, *Covenant and Creation*, 118). Whereas God commissioned the circumcised nation of Israel to bless the nations (Gen 12:1–3; cf. Gen 1:28), Christ commissions his disciples to extend the blessing of Abraham to all the nations through preaching of the gospel. Christ's blessing would then be received through faith in the Messiah and publically (one could say politically) entered through baptism (Matt 28:18–20). See Beale, *Temple and the Church's Mission*, 95, 174–77. Chamblin explains, "the NT counterpart to OT Israel, considered as 'a body politic,' is the Christian church" (Chamblin, "Law of Moses and the Law of Christ," in Feinberg, *Continuity and Discontinuity*, 188).

7. The connection between God's oath to Abraham and circumcision is one reason that scholars have affirmed that circumcision and baptism function as initial covenant ratification signs. See Garrett, "Meredith Kline on Suzerainty, Circumcision, and Baptism," in Schreiner and Wright, *Believer's Baptism*, 263; Jamieson, *Going Public*, 61; Fowler, *More Than a Symbol*, 239.

to voluntarily submit to circumcision with the covenantal responsibilities entailed by it (Exod 12:43–48).[8]

Baptism also functions as an initiating oath sign from the standpoint of God's promise and responsible human participation in the new covenant.[9] This fact is evident in that all those who would follow Christ as disciples (Matt 16:24; 28:19) trust him alone for forgiveness (Gal 3:26–27; Acts 2:38; 22:16; cf. Eph 2:8–9), submit to the kingship of Christ's saving reign (Matt 28:18–20; Rom 6:3–4; Col 2:11–12; cf. 1:13), identify with Christ and his people (Acts 2:38; 1 Cor 12:13; Eph 4:5), and pledge their allegiance to Christ (Rom 6:3–4; 1 Pet 3:21) receive baptism.[10] Baptism also functions as a reception of God's gracious new covenant oath to save, in Christ. By the church's act of calling the name of the Lord over the new disciple (Matt 28:18–20; Acts 2:28; Gal 3:26–28), baptism serves to assure and remind the believer of all the benefits that come to him or her via union with Christ.[11]

Given the corporate nature of God's covenant people, defined in the boundary marking function of baptism, the initiating oath-sign function of circumcision and baptism function similarly to add people to the covenant community. Whereas circumcision, for the foreigner or hireling, functioned as a conversion to Yahweh and his ways by which the proselyte could participate as a full covenant member (Exod 12:43–48),[12] baptism functions as shorthand for the whole conversion process (Rom 6:3–4; Gal 3:27).[13] By baptism, the Lord visibly incorporates those formerly estranged from God into the new covenant community, the church (1 Cor 12:13). If, as Leeman

---

8. Gibson's analysis at this point is confusing. He claims that circumcision functioned as a symbolic act of faith from the Abrahamic covenant until baptism became such an act in the new covenant (Gibson, "Sacramental Supersessionism Revisited," 200). But, in a significant point of discontinuity, nothing in the OT ever suggests that the infant male being circumcised is an agent of faith toward God in that activity. By contrast, all the biblical examples of baptism present (or at least imply) the person receiving the baptism as an agent exercising faith in Christ.

9. Thus, Waters is correct: "Baptism is the covenant sign of initiation. In this respect, it is for all members of the covenant community. Baptism is administered when someone formally enters the membership of the church. For this reason, baptism is administered only one time" (Waters, *Lord's Supper* 5.3). Yet, given Waters's covenant theology, he misses the other associations of baptism stated in the paragraph.

10. Schreiner, "Baptism in the Epistles," in Schreiner and Wright, *Believer's Baptism*, 67–96; Garrett, "Meredith Kline," in Schreiner and Wright, *Believer's Baptism*, 277.

11. Köstenberger, "Baptism in the Gospels," in Schreiner and Wright, *Believer's Baptism*, 22; Beasley-Murray, *Baptism in the New Testament*, 89–91.

12. Garrett, *Commentary on Exodus*, 366.

13. Moo, *Epistle to the Romans*, 355; Wellum, "Baptism and the Relationship between the Covenants," in Schreiner and Wright, *Believer's Baptism*, 150; Schreiner, *Paul*, 367.

explains, "Abraham and his seed are . . . to exemplify true citizenship among all of God's subjects . . . [and] abid[e] together as a just body politic under God's rule,"[14] and if circumcision was the visible means by which one moved from subject to citizen in that redemptive epoch, then baptism seems to perform a similar function to baptism in the New Testament. Both signs function according to the terms of their respective covenants to establish those who are citizens of God's kingdom in something like an "inauguration ceremony for . . . reinstalled priest-kings."[15] Thus, as initiating oath signs and boundary markers of their respective covenants, circumcision and baptism are constitutive of their respective covenant communities.[16] Clearly, in light of the foregoing affirmations, both circumcision and baptism are continuous in that they are designed to occur once and not repeatedly, to mark one's entrance into the covenant community.[17]

Furthermore, both signs entail obligations toward others within the covenant community. To belong to the covenant community of Israel by circumcision was to be a full covenant member (Gen 17:8–22; Exod 12:43–48),[18] to be responsible to love one's neighbor through manifold ac-

14. Leeman, *Political Church*, 216. With slight variation, see Saucy, "Israel and the Church," in Feinberg, *Continuity and Discontinuity*, 243.

15. Claiming that circumcision and baptism establish those "who are citizens of God's kingdom" is stated to recognize the continuity that does exist, despite the mixed nature of believers and unbelievers in Israel. See the discontinuities section below (Leeman, *Political Church*, 334). Regarding the theme of priest-king, Meade adds, first, "The call to relationship and covenantal responsibility to God in Genesis 17:1–2 becomes signified in the rite of circumcision. Second, just as the king-priest was the son of the god in Egypt, and was consecrated to him through circumcision, Israel as the first born son of Yahweh (Exod 4:22–23) has undergone and will undergo circumcision (Josh 5:2–9) in order to be consecrated to his service. Third, only the priests were obligated to be circumcised in Egypt, but in Israel every male was to be circumcised on the eighth day (Gen 17:12), signifying that Abraham's family consists of priests. Later in the story Israel is called a kingdom of priests and a holy nation (Exod 19:6). The phrase, "holy nation" also means consecrated to God or belonging to God and would complement the meaning of kingdom of priests. As a kingdom of priests, circumcision is the appropriate sign for the people of Israel, for it will remind every male Israelite that he is a priest, specially consecrated to Yahweh and his service." See Meade, "Meaning of Circumcision in Israel," 48. Less helpful is Thomas's language of "covenant inauguration," to describe baptism. The term "inauguration" too closely resembles redemptive-historical categories to be applied to one's personal entry into the covenant. See Thomas, "Not a Particle of Sound Brain," in Waters and Duncan, *Children and the Lord's Supper*, 111.

16. Leeman, *Political Church*, 333. It is as a constitutive sign of local, visible, new covenant churches, that baptism is rightly called an "effective sign" (Jamieson, *Going Public*, 143).

17. Knight III, "1 Corinthians 11:17–34," in Waters and Duncan, *Children and the Lord's Supper*, 81.

18. DeRouchie, "Counting Stars with Abraham and the Prophets," 183n11.

tions (Lev 19:18), to uphold the second table of the commandments (Exod 20:12–17; cf. Rom 13:10), and to be accountable to the community for one's failure to abide by the law (Lev 20:8–21; Deut 13:5–17).[19] As Turley argues, "By demonstrating an acceptance of the messages communicated through Christian ritual washing, the status of the baptized in relation to the baptizing community is unambiguously established."[20] As a boundary marker, baptism publicly identifies a new disciple with the community of Jesus, the church. Additionally, baptism would have been perceived as creating a community marked by moral accountability and obligation toward one another.[21] The New Testament confirms this reading by the manner in which Paul appeals to the churches. He appeals to the Roman Christians' baptism is a basis for putting to death already cancelled sin to death in their lives (Rom 6:3–13), to the Ephesian Christians' baptism as one basis of their unity and love toward each other (4:1–16), and to the Corinthians' baptism as the basis of their unity and need for each other in the body (12:12–33).[22]

Signs and Heart Circumcision

Finally, circumcision and baptism demonstrate continuity in the fact that they each entail heart circumcision. The circumcision of the heart is the removal of the old, sinful nature that impedes loving obedience to Christ from the heart and the act of setting apart the believer to a life of loving obedience. Whereas circumcision pointed toward heart circumcision in the future (prospectively), baptism signifies the reality of heart circumcision in the present (reflectively).

While sharing this continuity of entailing heart circumcision, the way each sign entails heart circumcision is discontinuous. Both circumcision and baptism symbolize cleansing from impurity. On the one hand, Circumcision was a physical removal of flesh that symbolized God's action to remove the sin and impurity.[23] While the Lord called Israel to put off their sin, to love him, and to obey him from the heart in the Old Testament (Deut 10:16), he told them this kind of heart response would ultimately be

19. Chamblin, "Law of Moses and the Law of Christ," in Feinberg, *Continuity and Discontinuity*, 181–87.

20. Turley, *Ritualized Revelation of the Messianic Age*, 48; Wellum, "Relationship between the Covenants," in Schreiner and Wright, *Believer's Baptism*, 159.

21. Turley, *Ritualized Revelation of the Messianic Age*, 81.

22. Paul's use of baptism as a ground of exhorting the church to holy living assumes that water baptism is in view. So Schreiner, *Paul*, 375; Beasley-Murray, *Baptism in the New Testament*, 264.

23. Meade, "Circumcision of the Heart," 72.

possible only by his sovereign work to circumcise their hearts (Deut 30:6; cf. Jer 31:33; Ezek 36:26–27). Because, in the progress of revelation, circumcision points to God's promise to circumcise the heart in the new covenant, circumcision is rightly described as a type of circumcision of the heart.[24]

Baptism on the other hand visibly pictures the reality of circumcision of the heart, reflectively and retrospectively. Colossians 2:11–12 develops this truth more fully than any other text in the New Testament. Yet, the heart cleansing described in Titus 3:5 and John 3:5 are visibly portrayed in baptism.[25] The instrumental role of baptism to outwardly appropriate the work of Christ (Acts 2:38), unite the believer to Christ (Rom 6:3–4; Gal 3:26–27), and so receive the benefits of the new covenant forgiveness supports the notion that baptism pictures the reality (not the prospect) of heart circumcision.[26]

Discontinuities between Circumcision and Baptism

While both circumcision and baptism function as initiating oath signs, the ways in which they do so are discontinuous on a number of levels. First, as previously noted, the human partners responsible for entering covenant with the Lord by circumcision were not the infants who received circumcision. The fathers who circumcised their sons were upholding their place in the covenant, and the foreigners who submitted to circumcision were effectively converting to the Lord to enter the covenant (Josh 5:1–12; Exod 12:43–48).[27] In baptism, however, the human partners receiving baptism do so willingly, as an act of faith in Christ.[28] Whereas entry to the Abraha-

24. Wellum, "Relationship between the Covenants," in Schreiner and Wright, *Believer's Baptism*, 158. See the section on Col 2:11–12 below.

25. Schreiner, "Baptism in the Bible," in Leeman and Dever, *Baptist Foundations*, 102; Garrett, "Meredith Kline," in Schreiner and Wright, *Believer's Baptism*, 268–69.

26. Contra Ross, who makes baptism prospective by claiming that it "signifies and seals that those who believe will be washed from their sins and accounted righteous before God" (Ross, "Baptism and Circumcision as Signs and Seals," in Strawbridge, *Case for Covenantal Infant Baptism*, 96).

27. Howard, *Joshua*, 150; McConville and Williams, *Joshua*, 27; Deenick, *Righteous by Promise*, 75; Garrett, *Exodus*, 366.

28. Thomas admits that "an inconsistency exists if faith is required of the participant as an antecedent to the one (Supper) but not the other (baptism)" (Thomas, "Not a Particle of Sound Brain," in Waters and Duncan, *Children and the Lord's Supper*, 101–2). He argues that both the old covenant and new covenant signs allowed the sign of entry to function legitimately without faith on the part of the recipient, while the sign of participation is "confirmatory (with professing believers in mind)." However, Thomas fails to demonstrate either that infants are baptized in the NT or that belief was prerequisite

mic and Mosaic covenants did not require the assent of the infant being circumcised, in the new covenant God not only requires assent, but graciously "brings about the assent."[29] Assent here entails a whole-hearted surrender and confession of allegiance to Christ on account of his saving work. Not even the circumcision of the physical (special) seed of Abraham is continuous with baptism in terms of the agency and assent exercised in receiving the covenant signs, because the belief would have occurred after circumcision.

A second discontinuity, between the roles of circumcision and baptism as initiating oath signs is found in the content of the divine oath. Whereas God's oath to Abraham is symbolized in the act of circumcision, all the promises of the new covenant in Christ are summed up and symbolized in baptism (Heb 6:13–20; cf. v. 2; 10:22). While the promises of the Abrahamic covenant pointed eschatologically toward Christ's coming and cross-work, the promises of the new covenant are grounded in what Christ already accomplished.[30] Thus, while God's oath to Abraham was the means of providing salvation to the world (cf. Gal 3:8), God's oath to new covenant believers is only possible because Abraham's promises reached their *telos* in Christ.[31] Circumcision, therefore, became a sign of God's unfolding plan of redemption.

Baptism is a sign of Christ's inauguration of the new covenant promises that began to be revealed with Abraham (cf. Gen 3:15) and have now become operative in Christ.[32] In the new covenant, salvific realities that are repeatedly and variously stated in connection with baptism are not prospective as they were with the Abrahamic covenant, awaiting realization in a future epoch (or in the life of a baptized infant).[33] Thus, Paul, for instance,

---

to Passover. He claims that Baptists must demonstrate that belief was prerequisite to circumcision and Passover in order to argue, as the Baptist position maintains, that belief is prerequisite to baptism and the Lord's Supper. However, this argument begs the question. The discontinuities and continuities that this chapter surveys, along with the changes in nature and structure of the new covenant, surveyed below, account for the differences in participants and the covenantal grounding for the differences.

29. Leeman, *Political Church*, 255.

30. Wellum, "Relationship between the Covenants," in Schreiner and Wright, *Believer's Baptism*, 135.

31. DeRouchie, "Counting Stars with Abraham and the Prophets," 477–78.

32. Wellum, "Relationship between the Covenants," in Schreiner and Wright, *Believer's Baptism*, 135–37.

33. On this point, Beasley-Murray writes, "Baptism has been reduced from a sacrament to a sermon, from a gift to an offer, from an event of eternal consequence to an uncertain possibility." Although "the Christian message is a word for today according to 2 Cor 6:2 . . . infant baptism is a gospel for tomorrow. In so changing the time reference, the sacrament itself has been made as uncertain as tomorrow." The corrective is to recognize "In the baptism of the New Testament we have no offer for tomorrow but gift

does not appear to replace circumcision with baptism so much as to sub-stitute "one ritually revealed world with another, no less than the dawn-ing of the Messianic age itself. Hence, Paul can relate the abrogation of the circumcision/uncircumcision hierarchy to the dawning of the new creation (Gal 5:6; 6:15; cf. 2:15–16)."[34] Thus God's promises are presently available and realized by all who believe (Gal 3:11–27).

Third, the human covenant-partner's role in the initiating oath sign requires discontinuity in the recipients and administrators of circumcision and baptism. One could be circumcised as an infant male in an Israelite fam-ily, an adult proselyte, or a slave brought into the household (Gen 17; Exod 12:43–48).[35] However, no examples in the New Testament present infants being baptized. Furthermore, rather than being restricted to males, baptism is given to males and females. Moreover, rather than being baptized for one's association with a household (as in a hireling or slave), baptism always cor-responds to and is reflective of faith, exercised by the person pursuing bap-tism.[36] Thus, whereas the administrators of circumcision were normally the parents (Gen 17:14; cf. Josh 5:7),[37] Jesus charges his disciples (who assemble

---

for today" (Beasley-Murray, *Baptism in the New Testament*, 376).

34. Turley, *Ritualized Revelation of the Messianic Age*, 48. Pedobaptists argue that infants should be baptized in the new covenant based upon what they view as an ex-tension of the genealogical principle in Acts 2:39. They claim that God continues to offer promises to the children of believers in the form of baptism (Venema, "Covenant Theology and Baptism," in Strawbridge, *Case for Covenantal Infant Baptism*, 224–25). With respect to Acts 2:39, Beasley-Murray writes that he is "inclined to believe with Jeremiah that the promise belongs to the hearers' children who will also come to Christ in the same way as their parents do, by hearing the good news and repenting from sin and believing, with that belief being expressed in baptism" (Beasley-Murray, *Baptism in the New Testament*, 342). Again, "Can a baptism in which the sponsors do not exercise a decisive faith, and which has only a prospective faith of the baptized in view, have any decisive effect in the present and be anything more than a prayer that one day the baptism may have power? If not, it must be recognized that the significance of such a baptism is considerably changed from that ascribed to baptism in the New Testa-ment"(351). See also Garrett's critique in Garrett, "Meredith Kline," in Schreiner and Wright, *Believer's Baptism*, 282.

35. As Garrett argues, if baptism were analogous to circumcision in every way, it would "require all persons under [a Christian's] authority to be baptized" (Garrett, "Meredith Kline," in Schreiner and Wright, *Believer's Baptism*, 281).

36. Beasley-Murray, *Baptism in the New Testament*, 273–74; Moo, *Epistle to the Ro-mans*, 366; Hammett, *Forty Questions*, 151.

37. I say "normally," because although Abraham and future parents from Abraham are clearly charged with the task of circumcision in Gen 17, Joshua circumcised the Israelite men before they entered the promised land in Josh 5:3–4. Given the thousands of men present, the statement "Joshua circumcised them" likely communicates by syn-ecdoche Joshua's primary responsibility and leadership as a stand in for the others who helped him, given that the covenant-breaking parents of the men were dead.

as churches and exercise the keys of the kingdom) to baptize new disciples (Matt 28:18–20; cf. 18:15–20).[38] Because baptism is given to all who enter the new covenant, baptism is not given on the basis of "gender distinction . . . nor age division . . . nor class differentiation."[39] Whereas the subjects of circumcision were reminded of their need for circumcised hearts, the subjects of baptism should possess this reality.[40] The subjects of circumcision often lacked the ability to obey God's law due to the dominance of their sinful nature (excluding those who were enabled by the Spirit to believe and obey like Abraham).[41] The subjects of baptism, however, publicly profess

38. Jones writes, "God designed [baptism] to be performed only by representatives of his covenant community because it also marks initiation of a believer's one-time union with it, carrying lasting effects for the community as a whole" (Jones, *Waters of Promise*, 137). See Leeman, *Political Church*, 261, 366; Carson, "Matthew," in Gaebelein, *Expositor's Bible Commentary*, 368.

39. Ware is referring specifically to the lack of human distinctions for who may receive the Spirit (cf. Joel 2:28–29). The broadened scope of those who receive the Spirit is in the NT parallel to the broadened scope of those who receive the sign of covenant entry, baptism (Ware, "New Covenant and the People(s) of God," in Bock and Blaising, *Dispensationalism, Israel, and the Church* 1.6.3). See also Schreiner, "Baptism in the Epistles," in Schreiner and Wright, *Believer's Baptism*, 91; Hammett, *Forty Questions*, 143.

40. See the similar point made by Jones, *Waters of Promise*, 133. They "should" possess circumcised hearts. Given fallible human judgment, it is possible that the person pursuing baptism is deceived about the state of his own heart before the Lord and/ or that those responsible for administering baptism are deceived about the person's spiritual state. This was apparently the case with Simon Magus (Acts 8:9–24). However, Ross overstates the case when he claims, "If baptism is understood to be a sign of faith, or a sign that one has received forgiveness of sins, then it too fails miserably. . . . There are just too many baptized people around who do not have faith, and/or whose lives demonstrate that they are unregenerate, to make credible the claim that baptism is a sign of faith" (Ross, "Baptism and Circumcision as Signs and Seals," in Strawbridge, *Case for Covenantal Infant Baptism*, 92). The biblical examples that would supposedly demonstrate Ross' point are clearly the exceptions: Simon Magus; Demas (2 Tim 4:10); and those who "went out from us because they were not part of us" (1 John 2:19). The clear pattern of the NT is that believers are baptized. To claim that the phenomena of false converts delegitimize a consistent NT pattern usurps the authority of Scripture with one's subjective experience. A kind of neat consistency is found in the claim that baptism signifies God's promise to save all who believe, because even if a baptized infant does not believe, on Ross's view, the significance of baptism would not be overturned. However, a great difference exists between following the pattern of the NT by baptizing a professing believer on the basis of a misjudgment of her spiritual state and baptizing infants based on a sincerely held assumption regarding the baptism of infants in the NT. The former pattern may unintentionally result in a disjunction between faith and baptism. The latter institutionalizes that disjunction to the neglect of the clear teaching of Scripture.

41. Wellum, "Relationship between the Covenants," in Schreiner and Wright, *Believer's Baptism*, 141–42.

their entry into all the promises of the new covenant, including a new heart and the indwelling presence of the Holy Spirit.[42]

As a result of the prior point, a fourth discontinuity concerns the nature of the covenant community formed by the signs of entry. Circumcision was the structural means of perpetuating a mixed community of believers and unbelievers within Israel (Jer 9:25–26). Baptism is the structural and institutional means of perpetuating a regenerate church.[43] The Old Testament command to circumcise infant males, who were incapable of faith, contrasts with the consistent New Testament assumption that those who believe are baptized (Gen 17; Acts 19:1–4).[44]

The eithnic-national, typological, and spiritual aspects of the Abrahamic covenant produce several other points of discontinuity between circumcision and baptism. Regarding the national aspect, circumcision served to mark off the physical seed of Abraham and their households as a national, ethnic entity. Yet, only the physical (special) seed of Abraham—Isaac, Jacob, David, and so on—were those to whom the promised blessing would come (cf. Rom 9:7–8; 2:29).[45] By contrast, baptism does not mark off an ethnic-national community but a multi-ethnic community.[46] Regarding the physical (special) seed of Abraham, circumcision continually presented the nation with another Adam-like figure as history moved toward the coming of Christ.[47] Baptism does not function in the same prospective manner. As a sign of the already established new covenant, baptism points backward to Christ, the last Adam. As the new covenant head, obedient Son, and fulfiller of righteousness, Christ is the *telos* of circumcision. As the Messiah, who as

42. Wellum, "Relationship between the Covenants," in Schreiner and Wright, *Believer's Baptism*, 156–58; Hammett, *Forty Questions*, 143; Allison, *Sojourners and Strangers*, 347–48.

43. Hammett, *Forty Questions*, 143; Wellum, "Relationship between the Covenants," in Schreiner and Wright, *Believer's Baptism*, 138. In a helpful phrase, Fred Malone notes, "A church of regenerate disciples is our goal; a good confession before baptism is our method" (Malone, *Baptism of Disciples Alone*, 8n18).

44. Thus, unbelieving children are not considered either members of the new covenant or the church in any sense. Contra Waters and Duncan, *Children and the Lord's Supper*, 184.

45. As DeRouchie argues, "Some biological 'seed' are not viewed as Abraham's 'children' from a covenantal perspective" (DeRouchie, "Counting Stars with Abraham and the Prophets," 451).

46. Garrett, "Meredith Kline," in Schreiner and Wright, *Believer's Baptism*, 279. Saucy helpfully delineates several aspects of Israel's national identity, including ethnicity, government, and territory. Saucy, "Israel and the Church," in Feinberg, *Continuity and Discontiuity*, 243–44. However, he misses the typological nature of Israel (252–56). See the section on the relationship between the covenants below.

47. Gentry and Wellum, *Kingdom through Covenant*, 130–32.

David's royal Son embodies the nation of Israel, Jesus' circumcision fulfills the national, corporate boundary marking function of Israel.[48] Jesus comes to represent the nation of Israel as a faithful covenant partner.[49]

The typological function of circumcision—both in terms of prospectively raising the expectation of the coming Messiah and signaling eschatological heart circumcision—raises similar discontinuities with baptism.[50] Whereas the typological function of circumcision in both cases points forward to Christ, new covenant baptism is not typological. Rather, it is retrospective both redemptive-historically and logically.[51] Redemptive-historically, the typological fulfillment of circumcision comes with the final "covenantally significant circumcision" of Jesus in the temple (Luke 2:21).[52] Jesus' circumcision is not followed by failure to walk blamelessly before the Lord, as all of the physical seed of Abraham had done. Rather, Jesus undergoes the same kinds of temptations as the other sons of God—Adam, Israel, and David (Luke 1:32; 3:38—4:11)—and emerges a faithful covenant partner. Thus, Jesus demonstrates heart devotion and covenant fidelity to the Lord, matters that circumcision symbolized. By being circumcised, living a perfectly obedient life, being baptized, taking the curse due sinners for their failure to keep the law on the cross (Gal 3:13), and then commanding his disciples to baptize new disciples, Jesus fulfills and puts an end to

48. Johnson, "Fatal Flaw of Infant Baptism," in Barcellos, *Recovering a Covenantal Heritage*, 243.

49. Allison, *Sojourners and Strangers*, 348–49. Similarly, see Parker, "Israel-Christ-Church Typological Pattern," 354–57.

50. On the two-fold nature of circumcision as a type, see Wellum, "Relationship between the Covenants," in Schreiner and Wright, *Believer's Baptism*, 157–58.

51. The logical connection between circumcision and baptism is discussed below in the analysis of Col 2:11–12.

52. Gentry and Wellum, *Kingdom through Covenant*, 701. Douglas Wilson's argument that circumcision continued to have Christian significance after the inauguration of the new covenant fails to convince. See Wilson, *To a Thousand Generations*, 64–66. Paul's mention of circumcision in Col 2:11 and Phil 3:3 can be adequately accounted for if Paul is appealing to the promise of heart circumcision as it was typologically developed in the OT. Paul's positive mentions of circumcision do not require or imply that he recognized an ongoing practice of Christian circumcision. In fact, Gal 6:15 presents a contrary claim. Furthermore, Wilson's claim that Paul's circumcision of Timothy (Acts 16:3) constitutes the continuing practice of "circumcision of adults, who sought in some significant sense to be identified with the Jews" is ill-defined and erroneous. He does not define what "some significant way" means. And, he misses Paul's clear affirmation that in his missionary work, he acted toward the Jews in ways that expressed his freedom in Christ without putting himself under the Jewish law or intending to identify with the Jews in some way that usurped his identity in Christ (1 Cor 9:19–20). For a helpful account of these themes, see Jewett, *Infant Baptism and the Covenant of Grace*, 230.

circumcision.[53] Baptism, while not symbolizing precisely the same realities as circumcision, becomes the redemptive-historically new identity marker that sets apart those connected by faith to Jesus from those who do not belong to Christ. Rather than being a typological marker that looks forward to Christ, baptism is a "reminder of the new eschatological reality that has been obtained with the death and resurrection of Christ."[54] This observation leads to the spiritual aspect of the promises to Abraham—that all the nations would be blessed through the obedient covenant partner, the seed who is Christ (Gal 3:16).

Discontinuity between circumcision and baptism also comes along the axis of the spiritual promises given to Abraham. While not denying a spiritual sense of circumcision within the Old Testament,[55] the spiritual

53. Deenick argues that Christ's reception of the curse of the law on the cross was implied in circumcision, in the sense that, as a maledictory oath-sign, circumcision promised death for those who would not uphold the covenant (Deenick, *Righteous by Promise*, 135, 210). By contrast, Garrett argues that "circumcision is . . . not a metaphor for death at all. It is never used that way in the Bible." Instead, circumcision is a positive action that symbolizes the removal of impurity (Garrett, "Meredith Kline," in Schreiner and Wright, *Believer's Baptism*, 268–69).

54. Schreiner, "Baptism in the Epistles," in Schreiner and Wright, *Believer's Baptism*, 89.

55. Circumcision can be described as having spiritual significance within the OT in at least three ways. First, one could describe the national, boundary marking function of circumcision as having spiritual significance. Throughout the OT, circumcision denotes those who are spiritually associated with the covenant Lord, even if they are merely physical seed (Josh 8:33). The nation of Israel contained the redemptive line of descent that led to Christ (Matt 1:1–2; Luke 3; Gal 3:16). Second, being marked as the physical (special) seed of Abraham should be understood as spiritually significant, because this group believed in the promises of God. Third, because circumcision points to consecration to the Lord and being set apart to him from its inception, physical circumcision has always carried some spiritual (albeit not necessarily salvific) significance. However, Wellum's caution is accurate. He adds "Nowhere is there evidence in the case of the physical seed [e.g., Ishmael] that their circumcision necessarily carried spiritual significance" (Wellum, "Relationship between the Covenants," in Schreiner and Wright, *Believer's Baptism*, 134n76). By this statement, he intends that circumcision in no way made Ishmael part of the nation of Israel or a recipient of God's promises to save. See also Jewett, *Infant Baptism and the Covenant of Grace*, 100. Ishmael is an interesting case for this point. If by spiritual significance, one intends salvific blessing through Christ (which is the most common usage), then Wellum should not be disputed. If, however, one intends blessings from the Lord that are not salvific, and this is a somewhat unusual use of "spiritual," then God's promise to make Ishmael fruitful and multiply him and make a great nation of him would constitute spiritual blessings. See Gen 17:18–22. DeRouchie explains, "Genesis 17 explicitly states that participation in the Abrahamic covenant was determined by one's membership in a promise-holder's household and not necessarily by one's direct biological descent via Sarah (cf. Gen 17:10,12). That is, while the covenant promises were established in the second generation with Isaac and his offspring (and their households) alone (cf. 17:19–21; 21:12–13), Ishmael was a

aspect of the promises to Abraham discussed here pertain to the way in which the nations would receive blessings promised to his seed. Whereas circumcision marked off the physical seed of Abraham until Christ came, baptism marks off the spiritual seed of Abraham through Christ. Galatians describes new covenant believers in Jesus as "children of Abraham" (3:7) and "Abraham's seed" (v. 29). While the former identity comes to new covenant Christians by virtue of faith in God's promises similar to that which Abraham had, the latter comes because the believers "belong to Christ" (v. 29).[56] Whereas old covenant members entered the covenant by virtue of (often passive) circumcision, Paul names faith and baptism (3:26–27) as the active means by which new covenant members enter the new covenant.[57]

---

full-fledged member of the covenant community by virtue of his birth into Abraham's house. Indeed, it was because Ishmael was Abraham's son that God promised to bring forth a nation through him (21:13; cf. 17:20). Not all of Abraham's offspring are considered promise-holders, which is why Ishmael could be called Abraham's 'seed' and yet not a child who would perpetuate the covenant and promise (21:12–13; cf. 17:19–21). (Similarly, we can assume that Esau was circumcised as a son of Isaac, though he too was clearly not part of the line of promise [cf. Gen 25:23; Mal 1:2–5; Rom 9:6, 12, 13, 27].) Nevertheless, while the Abrahamic covenant is not sustained through Ishmael's line, the narrative appears to say that he is a participant in the Abrahamic covenant and thus a recipient of the promises that are part of it, whether for blessing or curse—'and God was with the lad' (21:20)" (DeRouchie, "Circumcision in the Hebrew Bible and Targums," 183n11).

56. DeRouchie, "Counting Stars with Abraham and the Prophets," 475–76.

57. Due to the passive nature of circumcision, Ross argues, "But when we understand baptism as a sign of God's covenant with us, we see that it is more the mark of our duty to God than of our commitment to do that duty. What is signified and sealed by baptism is what God demands of us, not what we have pledged to God" (Ross, "Baptism and Circumcision as Signs and Seals," in Strawbridge, *Case for Covenantal Infant Baptism*, 106). Ross is imbalanced in several ways: (1) even in Israel, circumcision was not always passive, because foreigners could and did receive circumcision as a mark of conversion in order to enter the covenant community (Exod 12:43–49; cf. v. 38; Num 9:14; Josh 5:1–12; 2 Chr 30:25; 2 Sam 11:3–5; 12:10); (2) every example of baptism in the NT presumes faith on the part of the baptized; (3) while the Lord does affirm his promise to the one baptized (presuming faith) and remind the recipient of his/her duty as a kingdom citizen (Matt 28:18–20), the NT regularly presents baptism as an act of obedience, pledge, oath, and sign of a heart devoted to the Lord. See chapter 3. Parker is correct to point out the covenantal inconsistency of pedobaptists on this point when they refuse communion to unregenerate children/infants. Pedobaptists baptize infants because they see no clear reversal of the genealogical principle in the NT and claim implicit NT support for the continuation of the principle based upon the covenant of grace (cf. 1 Cor 7:14; Acts 2:39). However, Parker asks, "Since there is no clear passage that excludes children from the Lord's Supper (1 Cor 11 does not explicitly concern infants), how is it that pedobaptists can 'appeal to texts that imply a continuation of the OT practice of including children of believers within the covenant community' for the case of infant baptism but not for infant communion?" (Parker, "Paedocommunion, Paedobaptism, and Covenant Theology," 105; Parker cites Venema, "Covenant Theology

While faith in Christ is the sole, grace-enabled instrument of justification (Gal 3:6–26; cf. Phil 1:29; Eph 2:8–9), baptism accompanies faith as the external, public, and corporate means of putting on Christ and thereby entering the new covenant community.[58] Furthermore, whereas all the physical seed of Abraham were to be circumcised, in the new covenant epoch, only the spiritual seed of Abraham are to be baptized. Thus, faith in Jesus, reception of the Holy Spirit, and baptism are of a piece as aspects of conversion to Christ and entrance into the new covenant.

Relatedly, circumcision and baptism are discontinuous in that neither the Abrahamic nor Mosaic covenants included God's promise of sufficient grace to maintain covenant fidelity for the circumcised. By contrast, God provides sufficient grace to guarantee covenant faithfulness on the part of those who pursue baptism by saving faith. Under the old covenant one could become a covenant breaker by not being circumcised and failing to circumcise one's offspring (Gen 17:14).[59] Circumcision's typological trajectory reveals a similar prospect of covenant unfaithfulness. The Old Testament makes clear that the Lord gave circumcision to people who would not, in their redemptive historical epoch, be able to carry out the covenant stipulations (Deut 10:16; 30:6).[60] Thus, one's circumcision neither guaranteed nor provided sufficient grace to maintain covenant faithfulness.

Conversely, baptism is given to those who through divine grace are expected to walk in a pattern of covenant faithfulness. Because saving faith in Christ is effectually brought about by the Spirit through the gospel and

---

and Baptism," in Strawbridge, *Case for Covenantal Infant Baptism*, 202). Furthermore, Jewett argues that the active heart responses that the NT associates with baptism (e.g., "receiving the word," "putting on Christ," "believing," or "repenting") require just as much mental/cognitive development, spiritual maturity, and (biblically understood) regenerate hearts as do the commands to "discern the body" or eat "in remembrance of me" (Jewett, *Infant Baptism and the Covenant of Grace*, 198–99; Parker cites this source in Parker, "Paedocommunion, Paedobaptism, and Covenant Theology," 105). See also Jones, *Waters of Promise*, 136–37.

58. Schreiner, "Baptism in the Epistles," in Schreiner and Wright, *Believer's Baptism*, 88–89.

59. Regarding Gen 17:14, Garrett explains "the penalty of being 'cut off' from the people is not applied to the one who first received the mark of the covenant and then violated it. Rather, it applies to the one who does not have the mark of the covenant at all, and who thus never enters into the covenant" (Garrett, "Meredith Kline," in Schreiner and Wright, *Believer's Baptism*, 263). While Garrett is correct with respect to Gen 17:14, he does not seek to account for the exodus generation in his study. Chapter 2 argued that the failure of the wilderness generation to circumcise their offspring was one manifestation of their covenantal infidelity, which led to their inability to enter the promised land (Josh 5).

60. Meade, "Circumcision of the Heart," 72.

exercised by the believer, the new covenant relationship begins by grace alone (John 6:44; Eph 2:8–9; Phil 1:29; 2 Cor 4:6; 1 Pet 1:21–23; Rom 10:17). Because faith and baptism go together in the New Testament, baptism signifies a logically prior work of the grace of God in the human heart (Col 2:11–13; Acts 10:43–48). Finally, God promises to preserve all believers by grace (Rom 8:32–39; John 10:27–30; Jude 24–25) and commands believers to persevere in grace-enabled, faith-fueled obedience (Heb 3:12–14; Gal 5:6; Phil 2:12–13). Because regeneration, faith, and the Spirit's indwelling presence and power are benefits that belong to disciples through entry into the new covenant (which is pictured and formally ratified in baptism), Jesus expects all those who are baptized to be repentant, covenant keepers (Matt 28:19–20).[61] To state the matter differently, because physical circumcision pointed to the need for a circumcised heart, those who were circumcised only physically could not necessarily keep the covenant (Jer 9:25–26). However, because water baptism in the New Testament signifies the presence of a circumcised heart, the baptized are able to walk in a pattern of covenant faithfulness through Christ in a manner appropriate to this eschatological era.[62]

Relationship between Old and New Covenant Signs of Participation

This section surveys continuities and discontinuities between the covenant meals.

61. Parker, "Paedocommunion, Paedobaptism, and Covenant Theology," 109. Duncan and Waters misrepresent the category of disciple by claiming "When the church administers the sacrament of baptism to a child of a professing believer, the church acknowledges that this child is, by calling, a disciple of Christ (Waters and Duncan, *Children and the Lord's Supper*, 191).

62. Against this paragraph, pedobaptists often appeal to the warning passages of the NT to argue that the new covenant community continues to be a mixed community of believers and unbelievers as in the OT. See Booth, "Covenant Transition," in Strawbridge, *Case for Covenantal Infant Baptism*, 193–99; Neill, "Newness of the New Covenant," in Strawbridge, *Case for Covenantal Infant Baptism*, 133; Watt, "*Oikos* Formula," in Strawbridge, *Covenantal Infant Baptism*, 169–70. For a progressive covenantal response, see Cowan, "Warning Passages," in Wellum and Parker, *Progressive Covenantalism*, 189–213; Caneday, "Covenantal Life with God," in Wellum and Parker, *Progressive Covenantalism*, 111–17.

Continuities between Passover
and the Lord's Supper

Several points of continuity relate to the saving event with which each meal is associated.[63] First, the Lord's Supper is presented as a Passover meal, more specifically, the inaugurated fulfillment of the Passover meal (Luke 22:15–16, 18).[64] This fact explains how Paul could command the Corinthians to keep the feast associated with "Christ our Passover lamb" (1 Cor 5:7–11; 10:3–4, 10–17).[65] Within the clear Passover setting of the Last Supper, Jesus' words of institution of the Lord's Supper recall Moses' sprinkling "the blood of the covenant" on the Israelites at the covenant ratification meal on Sinai (Exod 24:8). Therefore, while the Lord's Supper is a kind of Passover meal, Jesus intentionally blends elements of the Passover and the covenant ratification meal on Sinai into the celebration.[66] The blend of substitutionary sacrifice (Matt 26:28; cf. John 1:29; Heb 10:1–20; Exod 12:23–27; 13:14–16) and covenant ratification in the Lord's Supper is the basis for describing the Lord's Supper as a proleptic covenant ratification meal and inaugurated kingdom feast.[67] Whereas the Passover was part of the means of Israel's escape from

63. Jewett's observation is poignant: "As far as the evidence of Scripture is concerned, the parallelism between the covenant meals of Passover and Eucharist is even more overt than that between the initiatory rites of circumcision and baptism" (Jewett, *Infant Baptism and the Covenant of Grace*, 202). Appropriately, this section delineates several such continuities.

64. Parker, "Israel-Christ-Church Relationship," in Wellum and Parker, *Progressive Covenantalism*, 52. Summarizing the Gospel writers' presentation of the Last Supper, Pennington claims, "Jesus and the Evangelists understand the life, death, resurrection, and ascension of the Messiah to be the fulfillment of the Passover and the corresponding inauguration of the new exodus" (Pennington, "Lord's Supper," in Schreiner and Crawford, *Lord's Supper*, 48–49).

65. Hamilton Jr., "Lord's Supper in Paul," in Schreiner and Crawford, *Lord's Supper*, 89–91. In his treatment of the Last Supper, Bock argues "Any application of [Jesus' statement that the Passover would be fulfilled in the kingdom of God in v. 16] to the Lord's Supper is inappropriate, since the Lord's Supper is not a Passover meal" (Bock, *Luke*, 2:1720). However, Bock's progressive dispensational views creep into his exegesis when he claims that "after Jesus' return, some sacrifices will be continued, but as a celebration or memorial, not as a sacrifice for sin [referring to the sacrifices Heb 8–10 renders obsolete]." In sum, writes Bock "The point is that with Jesus' return in the consummation, there will be a celebration of fulfillment that will parallel the original meal." (2:1721). Bock seems to hold that some reinstatement of sacrifices is necessary for the consummated meal to maintain its status as a Passover meal. But this argument is unnecessary given that typological fulfillment by definition contains elements of similarity to maintain the type, while also escalating, surpassing, and rendering the anti-types complete.

66. Contra Venema, *Children at the Lord's Table?*, 87.

67. For recognition of Passover as presenting a substitutionary sacrifice that is fulfilled in Christ, see Duguid, "Christ Our Passover," in Waters and Duncan, *Children and*

Egypt, the meal on Sinai officially inaugurated the Mosaic covenant in a manner that looks forward to the consummation of the new covenant (Exod 24:9–11; Rev 19:6–10; 22:3–5).[68] Unlike the Passover, the Last Supper was not a partial means of God's rescue of his people. But like the Passover, the Lord's Supper continues the pattern set by Jesus at the pre-rescue meal and expects a consummation greater than that of the meal on Sinai (1 Cor 11:26). Without seeing the Passover-exodus and Mosaic covenant ratification meal background for the Lord's Supper, one misses the redemptive-historical significance of the Lord's Supper as an inaugurated fulfillment of Passover within the already/not yet epoch.[69]

Second, both Israel in the old covenant and Jesus' fledgling followers under the new covenant were commanded to continue celebrating their respective feasts as an act of remembrance (Luke 22:19b; cf. Exod 12:14 and 13:9).[70] Therefore, thirdly, both the Passover and the Lord's Supper were instituted by divine instruction prior to the kingly act of redemption—the exodus through the Red Sea in the old covenant and the death and

---

the Lord's Supper, 65.

68. Waters, Lord's Supper 4.8.

69. Venema argues "In the New Testament's understanding of Christ's sacrificial death, it is not the Passover that is most pertinent but the sacrifices that typify atonement for the guilt of sin" (Venema, Children at the Lord's Table?, 88). This emphasis is correct. At the same time, the Passover sacrifices should not be separated too strongly from guilt and sin offerings that belonged to the sacrificial system. Without a once for all atoning sacrifice that fulfills the Passover and Day of Atonement, the new covenant could not be inaugurated. By definition, the new covenant brings full forgiveness of sins. Thus, it requires a perfect sacrifice (Jer 31:34; cf. Lev 16; Heb 10). Christ's substitutionary atonement, his passive obedience specifically, is the means by which God faithfully metes out the covenant curses for Abraham's and Israel's failure to meet the conditions of the covenant (Gal 3:13; cf. Gen 15:17). At the same time, a covenant cannot be ratified without the shedding of blood (Heb 9:18). Christ's blood shed on the cross serves both functions simultaneously. The cup of the Lord's Supper brings both functions together. Similarly, see Estelle, "Passover and the Lord's Supper," in Waters and Duncan, Children and the Lord's Supper, 44–47.

70. Thiselton, First Corinthians, 879; Nolland, Luke, 3:1048; Marshall, Last Supper and Lord's Supper, 90. I do not follow Marshall's further implication that the way the disciples were to remember Jesus was identical to the way Israel was to remember the Passover. While continuity does exist on this point, to suggest that the new covenant community remembered in the same way as the old covenant community seems to discount the Spirit's presence as the down payment of the new covenant. Similar to the concept of remembrance in the Passover though, Jesus calls his followers to make contemporary their appropriation of redemption pictured by the meal and enter a communal sense of identity and solidarity with the disciples and saints throughout the ages. For more on this theme see Thiselton, First Corinthians, 875; Vickers, "Past and Future," in Schreiner and Crawford, Lord's Supper; Billings, Remembrance, Communion, and Hope, 113–36.

resurrection of Jesus in the new covenant.[71] Fourth, both meals are emblematic of God's kingly power and reign over his enemies (Exod 12:12; 15:17; Luke 22:16, 18). The Passover was God's merciful action of sparing his people the judgment he rendered on the king of Egypt and the Egyptian gods.[72] The Lord's Supper is an inaugurated kingdom feast that celebrates Christ's victorious reign as the resurrected Lord (1 Cor 11:26; Luke 22:29–30; cf. Acts 2:29–42) Fifth, both meals anticipate the full arrival of the kingdom of God, including the enjoyment of God's covenantal presence. As Passover led to the covenant ratification meal on Sinai at which the representatives of Israel saw God and feasted in his presence (Exod 24:9–11),[73] the Lord's Supper looks with hope toward the Marriage Supper of the Lamb (Rev 19:6–10; cf. 22:4; Isa 25:6–9; 55:1–5).[74]

Regarding the participants, several continuities may be observed. First, both feasts mark(ed) off the people of God from the surrounding nations as signs of the covenant with which they are associated (Exod 12:12–13; 1 Cor 11:24–25; 1 Cor 5:7–12).[75] As such, both meals are rightly described as covenant meals (2 Chr 34—35; Ezra 6:19-22; Luke 22:19). Second, at least at its inception, the Passover parallels the Lord's Supper in that the covenant community participates in the meal (Exod 12:26; 1 Cor 11:17–22).[76] Third,

71. Pennington, "Lord's Supper in the Gospels," in Schreiner and Crawford, *Lord's Supper*, 57. See also Waters, *Lord's Supper* 4.4.

72. Dempster, *Dominion and Dynasty*, 90–91.

73. Furthermore, the parallels between the Sinai meal and heavenly meal that the Lord's Supper anticipates are multiple: (1) both occur on a "mountain of God"; (2) both are regarded as weddings; (3) both occur in context with the destruction of death and end of pain; (4) both involve God's people seeing God; (5) both involve eating and drinking with God; (6) both represent covenantal fellowship/communion between God and his people; (7) both are covenant ratification meals for their respective covenants; and (8) both celebrate the saving kingly rule (kingdom redemption) of God for his people.

74. Pennington, "Lord's Supper in the Gospels," in Schreiner and Crawford, *Lord's Supper*, 57. Later, Pennington argues "The Lord's Supper is primarily a forward-looking, future-hoping celebration, even as the Last Supper was" (67). While this emphasis helpfully develops the not yet aspect of the Lord's Supper, the claim that the future orientation is primary undervalues the already aspects of life in the inaugurated kingdom under the new covenant. Waters is on target when he argues "The Lord's Supper, therefore, always and simultaneously points in two directions, backward and forward." Waters, *Lord's Supper* 4.10. So also Estelle, "Passover and the Lord's Supper," in Waters and Duncan, *Children and the Lord's Supper*, 42–44.

75. Duguid, "Christ Our Passover," in Waters and Duncan, *Children and the Lord's Supper*, 66.

76. This observation is not intended to affirm that all children, including infants, necessarily participated in the Passover. More generally, Passover was a covenant meal that marked off the whole covenant community even if only the men were required

participation in both covenant meals formally identifies the redeemed community with God's saving acts (Exod 12:3–4; 1 Cor 11:17–34). Not only do
the meals mark off the respective covenant communities, but they each are
intended to form the identity of those communities around the covenant
Lord,[77] as the promise of rescue through divine means is represented to the
covenant community.[78] Fourth, because those in Egypt who did not participate in Passover experienced God's judgment in the death of the firstborn,
and those who do not participate in the Lord's Supper remain under judgment, both feasts function to signify those who are sealed as recipients of
divine mercy compared to those who remain under wrath (Exod 12:29; 1
Cor 5:5, 11).[79]

Most significantly for this book, continuity exists in that the signs of
covenant entry under each respective covenant occur prior to the signs of
participation. The way this principle works out contains some discontinuity as well, but the principle remains: The Old Testament commands the
covenant community (Exod 12:43–49; Num 9; Josh 5), and consistently
demonstrates, that the sign of entry—circumcision—was expected to occur
prior to the sign of participation—Passover (2 Chr 30; 35; Ezra 6:19–22).
Similarly, the New Testament exemplifies that the sign of entry, baptism,
occurred before the sign of participation, the Lord's Supper (Acts 2:38–42;).
Paul presents baptism as the sign of covenant entry (1 Cor 12:13; cf. 6:11),
which occurs logically prior to the sign of covenant participation (10:16–17).
The logical priority of baptism to the Lord's Supper must actually require
temporal priority as well, given that one cannot be baptized and receive the
Supper at the same time. The church at Corinth appears to have operated on
the example of Acts 2:41–42 by initially trusting Christ and being baptized

---

to participate after the initial Passover. For children eating the Passover, compare Lev
10:14; 18:11; Deut 12:6–7, 12, 18; 16:11, 14. See Rayburn, "Presbyterian Defense of
Paedocommunion," in Strawbridge, *Case for Covenant Communion*, 5. Venema is correct that one cannot prove all children and infants actually ate of the first Passover meal,
much less during the subsequent celebrations (Venema, *Children at the Lord's Table?*,
68).

77. Pennington, "Lord's Supper in the Gospels," in Schreiner and Crawford, *Lord's
Supper*, 53.

78. Billings, *Remembrance, Communion, and* Hope, 115–16.

79. Waters, *Lord's Supper* 4.6. Duguid's affirmation that the Lord's Supper marks off
the "visible covenant community" is true in so far as the ordinances make new covenant
members visible (Duguid, "Christ Our Passover," in Waters and Duncan, *Children and
the Lord's Supper*, 74). They are visible boundary markers. However, in context, Duguid intends this statement as affirmation of the visible-invisible distinction within the
new covenant community. This chapter demonstrates, in part, that the visible-invisible
distinction is unhelpful at best and based on an erroneous interpretation of the new
covenant at worst.

before taking the Lord's Supper as a church (Acts 18:1–11; cf. 1 Cor 1:15–17; 11:23). Thus, the New Testament upholds the principle that the sign of entry precedes the sign of participation.

Discontinuities between Passover
and the Lord's Supper

Several discontinuities are also evident, centering on the arrival of the new covenant with Christ's death. First, the relationship between the meal and those who are covered by the blood is different. In the Passover, only the firstborn sons were covered by the blood of a sacrificial lamb (Exod 12:5–7). In the Lord's Supper, Christ's blood covers all the new covenant participants (1 Cor 5:7). Relatedly, while the Passover meal came about through the mediation of Moses (Exod 3–4; 12–14), the Lord's Supper depends upon Christ's role as the new covenant mediator for its validity (Heb 3:1–6). Whereas Moses instructed Israel regarding the Passover lamb, Christ instructed his followers of his own impending death as the fulfillment of the Passover (1 Cor 5:7; cf. 1 Tim 2:4–5).[80]

Whereas Passover meal occurred in anticipation of God's deliverance from Egypt with instructions for its ongoing celebration, the Lord's Supper occurs subsequent to the inauguration of the new covenant (Exod 12; Matt 26–27). Second, this point of discontinuity emphasizes the diachronic relation between the meal and the saving event the meal commemorates. The Last Supper serves as the redemptive-historical transition event between the two meals, because the Last Supper served as the final covenantally significant Passover meal and the inaugural institution of the Lord's Supper.[81] In this sense, Passover was celebrated both pre-redemption (when compared to the whole exodus event) and post-redemption. The Passover led to the covenant inaugurating shedding of blood on Sinai as the Last Supper led to Christ's covenant inaugurating shedding of blood on Calvary (Heb 9:20–23).[82] Passover led to the covenant ratification meal on Sinai, at which representatives of Israel saw God and feasted in his presence (Exod 24:9–11), and the Passover continued in Israel after the meal on Sinai. Whereas only the representatives of Israel were allowed to ascend the mountain into God's presence (Exod 24:9–11), all who enter the kingdom by faith in

---

80. The typological relationship between Moses and Christ as covenant mediators helps account for these similarities and differences. On this theme, see Pennington, "Lord's Supper in the Gospels," in Schreiner and Crawford, Lord's Supper, 52; Parker, "Israel-Christ-Church Typological Pattern," 351.

81. Marshall, Last Supper and Lord's Supper.

82. Hammett, Forty Questions, 193.

Jesus are already assembled on Zion as the temple of God (Heb 12:22–24; 1 Cor 3:16). Whereas Moses sprinkled physical blood on the Israelites to demonstrate their responsibility to uphold their covenant obligations in a bilateral covenant, the church eats and drinks to physically represent their unilateral cleansing and forgiveness received from Christ's sacrifice (Heb 9:20–22; cf. Isa 53).

Thus, the Lord's Supper is uniquely situated in redemptive history as a proleptic covenant ratification meal. By occurring between Christ's ascension and return, it marks the church as the eschatological community of the new covenant (cf. Acts 2:38–42; Joel 2:28–32).[83] As a result, "We can thus regard the Lord's Supper as the feast of fulfillment in the kingdom of God inasmuch as it is an anticipation of the heavenly feast."[84] Participation in this inaugurated kingdom feast displays and enacts benefits of the saving reign of God that come through participation in the new covenant. These benefits of the gospel, experienced in the Supper belong to the church already, but the church will not experience the completion and fulfillment of the new covenant blessings until the consummation.

Third, Passover functioned as a boundary/identification marker for the nation of Israel[85]—all of Abraham's physical seed with foreign converts (Exod 12:23–27; 2 Chr 30:2–7, 25; Ezra 6:21).[86] The ethnic nation constituted the covenant community (Exod 12:43–49). Thus, the celebrations of Passover throughout Israel's history are explicitly tied to the Abrahamic covenant (2 Chr 30:6), to renewal of the Mosaic covenant (34:31–33), and to God's promise to David and Solomon to bring back exiles to the land where they would enjoy the Lord's presence again (Ezra 6:20; cf. 1 Chr 17:11–15, 21–22; 2 Chr 6:24–25; 7:16–17).[87]

The Lord's Supper functions as a boundary/identification marker for all those united to Christ (Acts 2:41–42; 1 Cor 10:16–17; 11:17–34). The Gospels present the Last Supper as the means by which Jesus and his followers

---

83. Waters, *Lord's Supper* 4.7.

84. Marshall, *Last Supper and Lord's Supper*, 80. As Marshall explains, "The Lord's Supper is linked to the Passover in that the Passover is a type of the heavenly banquet while the Lord's Supper is the anticipation of the heavenly banquet," meaning "The middle term of comparison between the Passover and the Lord's Supper is the heavenly banquet." See also Dumbrell, *Covenant and Creation*, 123.

85. Parker, "Paedocommunion, Paedobaptism, and Covenant Theology," 111; Jewett, *Infant Baptism and the Covenant of Grace*, 204.

86. DeRouchie, "Counting Stars with Abraham and the Prophets," 455–56; Duguid, "Christ Our Passover," in Waters and Duncan, *Children at the Lord's Supper*, 62.

87. Green and Pennington recognize the transfer of the boundary marking function of Passover to the new covenant community. See Green, *Gospel of Luke*, 756; Pennington, "Lord's Supper in the Gospels," in Schreiner and Crawford, *Lord's Supper*, 54–55.

re-appropriate the exodus narrative that gave Israel its distinct identity. In the Last Supper though, the new community is gathered around Christ, as the leader/Mediator of the new exodus event.[88] Those who participate in the body and blood of Christ (1 Cor 10:16) do not find their historical genesis in the exodus from Egypt (1 Chr 17:21–22) or mark their ethnic identity by the presence or absence of circumcision (Eph 2:11). Rather, the Lord's Supper marks off the multi-ethnic citizens of Christ's household (v. 19), who individually and corporately compose the new covenant temple of God (v. 20; 1 Cor 3:16–17; 6:19–20; 2 Cor 6:16). Instead of describing the new covenant community as "the one nation on earth whom God went to redeem to be his" (1 Chr 17:21; cf. Exod 19:4–6), those who take the Lord's Supper constitute the "one new man" composed of Jew and Gentile (Eph 2:15).[89]

Fourth, while the Lord progressively revealed instructions for both covenant meals, the progress of revelation concerning Passover occurred over a longer period of history. While the initial instructions for the Passover meal were binding on Israel, the Lord gave subsequent instructions (e.g., male-only participation in Jerusalem rather than households; Deut 16:16) and allowed for accommodations (Num 9). The instructions for the Lord's Supper appear virtually unchanged from Jesus' institution of the meal (cf. 1 Cor 11:17–34; Matt 26:26–29; Mark 14:22–25; Luke 22:14–20).

Appropriately then, fifth, Passover and the Lord's Supper differ in the elements used to celebrate the meals. Whereas the elements of the Passover included roast lamb, unleavened bread, and bitter herbs (Exod 12:8–28; Num 9:11),[90] the Lord's Supper includes bread and the fruit of the vine (Luke 22:19–20; cf. 1 Cor 11:23–25). The new covenant meal lacks an animal sacrifice because "Christ, our Passover lamb has been slain" as the fulfillment of all OT sacrifices (1 Cor 5:7; cf. John 1:29; Heb 10:1–19).[91] The bread continues to be utilized in the Lord's Supper with different significance. Whereas the unleavened bread of the Passover represented the affliction of slavery and the haste with which Israel exited Egypt (Deut 16:3), the bread of the Supper represents Christ's freely given body (Matt 26:26; Mark 14:22; Luke 22:19). Paul extends the significance of the bread in a manner consistent with Christ's initial declaration, "This is my body," by comparing

---

88. Pennington, "Lord's Supper in the Gospels," in Schreiner and Crawford, *Lord's Supper*, 50–51.

89. Greever, "Nature of the New Covenant," 73–89.

90. Venema, *Children at the Lord's Table?*, 69. This discussion is limited to elements prescribed by the biblical text. As such, the cup of wine that emerged in Jewish practice during the intertestamental period is beyond the scope of this book. See Beckwith, "Age of Admission," 147.

91. Parker, "Paedocommunion, Paedobaptism, and Covenant Theology," 112.

the congregation that receives the meal together to the bread (1 Cor 10:17). Given the church's status as new covenant members, the church is also appropriately labeled the body of Christ.[92] Thus, the bread imagery not only stands for Christ but derivatively of those covenantally united to him (cf. 1 Cor 10:16; 11:29). The bitter herbs probably functioned similarly to the bread, as symbolic of the bitter affliction Israel experienced in Egypt.[93] Possibly, no corollary to the herbs exists in the Lord's Supper because the second exodus—Christ's redemptive work (Luke 9:31; cf. Rev 15:1–4)—did not occur in the context of physical slavery. Whatever the case, Christ's blood, represented by the fruit of the vine, carries the imagery of substitutionary death by sacrifice and covenant ratification (cf. Exod 12:14–16; 24:5–11; Heb 9:18–22).[94] Whereas partaking of the elements of Passover did not testify to one's personal forgiveness from sin, taking the cup is such a testimony.[95] The church imbibes wine/juice in the Supper that vividly portrays the bitterness of sin, the love of the Savior, and God's ratification of his promises to save all who trust in Christ (Mark 10:38–39).[96]

Sixth, the demonstration of God's kingly power differs in the Passover compared to the Lord's Supper. Whereas the Passover meal was a demonstration of God's saving reign over Israel's enemies for the purchase of Israel from physical slavery, the Lord's Supper commemorates the demonstration of God's saving reign over the kingdom of darkness and purchase from spiritual slavery to sin (1 Cor 10:1–17; Eph 2:11–12).[97] The first victory was ethnic and national, with specific, historical relation to Israel, though it occurs in expectation of a multinational kingdom (Exod 19:4–6; cf. Gen 17:6; Isa 55:5; 56:1–8). The second victory is cosmic. By Jesus' resurrection he secures the redemption of a new covenant community (Col 1:13–23; cf. 2:11–13). The Lord's Supper occurs after Christ inaugurates his saving reign

92. Those who receive forgiveness by virtue of Christ's new covenant-inaugurating shedding of blood are united with Christ, the beneficiaries of the new covenant promises, and thus covenantally distinguished from the world as the body of Christ. This explanation may help to account for the origin of the image of the church as the body of Christ. Because Christ expected those covenantally united to him to repeatedly feast upon the bread that represents his body (cf. John 6:35), it seems appropriate for Paul to describe the group that eats this bread as his body (covenantally understood, given the reality of union with Christ). The bread of the Lord's Supper is the point of connection between Jesus, the new covenant head, and the body of those covenantally related to him. In this sense, the axiom is true, "you are what you eat!"

93. Carpenter, *Exodus*, 1:451; Hamilton, *Exodus*, 182.

94. Kline, "Old Testament Origins of the Gospel Genre," 12–13.

95. Parker, "Paedocommunion, Paedobaptism, and Covenant Theology," 112.

96. Stein, *Mark*, 651.

97. Parker, "Paedocommunion, Paedobaptism, and Covenant Theology," 113.

over the powers of darkness, as an anticipation of the full celebratory victory banquet in heaven (Rev 19:6–10; cf. Matt 8:10–12; Luke 13:29; 14:12–24).[98]

Seventh, the context in which the meals occur is another discontinuity. Although the Passover was initially celebrated in households as part of the exodus event, the subsequent celebrations were corporate. Only adult males were required to participate (Deut 16:16; cf. 2 Chr 35).[99] The Lord's Supper is observed in the context of the local church's gathered worship (1 Cor 11:17–23; Acts 20:7). The context of the celebration of each meal is directly related to the ethnic, national identity that Passover signified. In one sense, both meals function as "family meals," given the participation of the covenant community.[100] Yet, whereas the relationship between Passover participants required care for one another in the nation (not just the household; cf. Lev 19), the relationship implied by the local church context is much stronger. All who take the Lord's Supper together receive the meal because they are first united with Christ (1 Cor 10:16–17). Thus, the covenantal accountability and responsibility for each other incumbent on those who take the Lord's Supper together derives from their common union with Christ.[101] While the Israelites were accountable for how they treated one another in the nation and could be excluded from the community due to their sin (Deut 13), the covenantal responsibility was civic, political, moral, and national at the same time. In the local church, the covenantal responsibility for one another is not derived from citizenship within a theocratic nation (Exod 19–24); rather, the gospel of Jesus that is proclaimed in the Supper shapes the identity of the church and should lead to humble care and unity on account of that spiritual kinship (1 Cor 11:17–34).[102]

Eighth, closely tied to the context of celebration is the discontinuity of the participants in the meal. Whereas with the Passover it is impossible to prove that every individual in the covenant community participated, the Lord's Supper is specifically given to all who come together as a church by

98. Pennington, "Lord's Supper in the Gospels," in Schreiner and Crawford, *Lord's Supper*, 52.

99. Venema, *Children at the Lord's Table?*, 68.

100. Pennington, "Lord's Supper in the Gospels," in Schreiner and Crawford, *Lord's Supper*, 54. Jesus initiated this new dynamic at the Last Supper. Since that time, "Jesus has called out his disciples from their own families and life stations and is identifying them as his own, true family, for 'whoever does the will of my Father in heaven is my brother and sister and mother' (Matt 12:50)."

101. Hammett, *Forty Questions*, 207; Garland, *1 Corinthians*, 477.

102. Pennington, "Lord's Supper in the Gospels," in Schreiner and Crawford, *Lord's Supper*, 55–56; Hamilton Jr., "Lord's Supper in Paul," in Schreiner and Crawford, *Lord's Supper*, 80; Waters, *Lord's Suppe* 4.10; Knight, "1 Corinthians 11:17–34," in Waters and Duncan, *Children at the Lord's Supper*, 82–92.

virtue of their new covenant membership. While the parental instruction regarding children who ask their parents the meaning of the Passover may indicate that those children who were mentally aware enough to ask such questions ate the Passover (Exod 12:26–27), the Old Testament does not present enough evidence to confirm the matter, much less to demonstrate the participation of infants.[103] During the Passover celebrations in the land, women and children were allowed to remain home rather than make the pilgrimage to Jerusalem for the Passover (Deut 16:1–7). Yet, they were commanded not to keep leavened bread in their homes during the Feast of Unleavened bread (Exod 12:19), lest they be "cut off from the congregation of Israel." Thus, although participation in Passover verified one's covenantal status, it did so representatively—the fathers participating on behalf of the whole household.[104] As Venema argues, "That non-participation in this covenant meal is tantamount to a kind of exclusion from full covenant membership and its privileges is not valid." Rather, if God intended a one to one correspondence between the sign of covenantal participation—Passover— and the reality of being a member of the covenant, "one would expect the Old Testament . . . to require participation of all" the covenant members.[105]

Ninth, it is appropriate then to regard both the Passover and Lord's Supper as renewing oath signs, with differing responsibility for which

103. Contra Rayburn, "Presbyterian Defense of Paedocommunion," in Strawbridge, *Case for Covenant Communion*, 5. See Venema, *Children at the Lord's Table?*, 67–68. Venema's arguments "resonate with the Baptist understanding for limiting the ordinance to believers only." Yet, "The traditional Reformed arguments do not ultimately challenge the core theological rationale for infant communion since they too subscribe to the covenant of grace framework and adhere to the same hermeneutical entailments, namely, the genealogical principle, the mixed assembly of the church, and the continuity of covenantal signs" (Parker, "Paedocommunion, Paedobaptism, and Covenant Theology," 104). Given the similarity of pedobaptist arguments for the continuity of both circumcision and Passover with the new covenant signs, "Only two significant factors prevent traditional pedobaptists from practicing infant communion: their interpretation of 1 Cor 11 and their disassociation of the Lord's Supper from the Passover, either by denying children ate the Passover or by rightly understanding the typological correspondences." (105). Parker's critique of the pedobaptist position on this point follows the same hermeneutical logic as this book.

104. Circumcision's role of creating a covenantal community is similar in this respect. Only Israelite males and those males brought into the community as slaves, hirelings, or converted foreigners received circumcision. Yet, by virtue of the head of household's circumcision, the women in the house were viewed as covenant members. Leaving aside the first three Passover celebrations (Exod 12; Num 9; Josh 5), which all occurred within forty-two years of the exodus, the representative role of the males in circumcision and Passover are similar. These observations underscore the nature of the covenant community as a mixture of believers and unbelievers and of the possibility that one could believe in God's promises and not receive the sign.

105. Venema, *Children at the Lord's Table?*, 68, 70.

human agents renew the covenant with the Lord.[106] The differences in how each meal functions in this manner stem from the differences in each meal's recipients. Given the inherent connection of Passover and the Feast of Unleavened Bread (Exod 12), the celebration should be understood as a renewal of the old covenant members' oaths to uphold their covenantal obligations. Otherwise, the warning of being cut off from the congregation would lack covenantal justification (cf. v. 19).[107] The association of Passover celebrations with national covenant renewal ceremonies buttresses this function of Passover (cf. 2 Kgs 23:1–3; 2 Chr 34–35; Ezra 6). Furthermore, the tie between the Lord's oath to Abraham (Gen 17; 22), symbolized in circumcision, and the requirement of circumcision to participate in Passover, suggests that Passover also functioned as a reminder of the Lord's oath to his people to fulfill the promises to Abraham. In this way, Passover functioned as a renewing oath sign for the nation, received through representatives.

The Lord's Supper functions as a renewing oath sign as well, but the Lord's oath to save all who believe in Christ and the new covenant community's oath of trust in Christ have clearer textual warrant. In the Supper, every new covenant member reaffirms his dependence on the gospel of Jesus (John 6), experience of communion with the Triune God (1 Cor 10:16–17; cf. John 14:17, 21–23), and allegiance to Jesus as king (Luke 22:16, 18, 29–30; 1 Cor 11:26). The Lord also reaffirms his gracious oath to save through Christ those who are anchored to him by faith (Heb 6:13–20). The meal is a means through which God reminds believers of his promises and intends to deepen their experience of union with Christ (1 Cor 10:16–17).[108] The divine act of reaffirming the oath is nowhere clearer in the meal than the words of institution, whereby redeemed sinners hear afresh of Jesus' provision of forgiveness and all the new covenant benefits (cf. Matt 26:26–29; 1 Cor 11:23–25).[109]

106. Renewing oath sign is Jamieson's term for the Supper. However, this paragraph extends his logic and applies it to the Passover. Jamieson, *Going Public*, 123. Similarly, see Duguid, "Christ Our Passover," in Strawbridge, *Case for Covenant Communion*, 62.

107. While the Lord could command his people to follow a command without any apparent moral grounding, the purpose of the yearly was tied to Israel's ability to maintain its sense of covenantal identity (Exod 23:15; 34:18; Lev 23; Deut 16).

108. Clark, "Evangelical Fall from the Means of Grace," in Armstrong, *Compromised Church*, 138.

109. Pennington undervalues the role of the new covenant members' renewing their oath of allegiance to Christ in the meal. He ties the believers' responsible and grateful action of partaking in the meal to the unhelpful category of sacrifice, which he defines, following A. Schlatter, as "acts by which we testify our love to God by our gift." He then claims that the Lord's Supper functions as a means of receiving grace (sacrament) (Pennington, "Lord's Supper in the Gospels," in Schreiner and Crawford, *Lord's*

The tie between membership in the new covenant and participation in the Lord's Supper is one to one. Not only does Jesus command his followers, "Do this in remembrance of me" (Luke 22:19), but Acts and Corinthians record participation in the meal by all the new covenant members (Acts 2:38–42; 18:5–11; 1 Cor 1:15–17; 11:17–34).[110] The gender-inclusive nature of the signs of baptism and the Lord's Supper requires that all the new covenant members participate (Matt 28:19–20; Gal 3:26–28).[111] Only those who are able to look by faith to Christ in remembrance and to discern the body should participate (1 Cor 11:29).[112] Participation in the Lord's Supper by the whole new covenant community evidences changes in the nature and structure of the new covenant.[113]

The tenth discontinuity regarding participants in the covenant meals concerns the manner in which the Scripture presents the sign of covenant entry as prerequisite to the sign of covenant participation. Exodus 12:43–49 commands circumcision as prerequisite to Passover and prohibits Passover without circumcision; subsequent Passover celebrations carry out this command. The New Testament nowhere commands that baptism should be prerequisite to the Lord's Supper;[114] instead, it assumes that baptism belongs

---

Supper, 66–67). This is a false dichotomy.

110. Although the NT does not exemplify or command a catechetical element to the Lord's Supper as is present in the Passover, the presence of children in the congregation (Eph 6:1–4) suggests the appropriateness, in principle, of explaining the meal to one's children, though they should not partake of it.

111. Venema, *Children at the Lord's Table?*, 89. Yet, Waters and Duncan insist that the Lord's Supper is "not for all church members. It is for church members who meet the intellectual and spiritual qualifications set forth by the apostle. When a young church member demonstrates to the satisfaction of the elders of [the] church that he has met these qualifications, then the church, acting through her elders may admit this young person to the Lord's Table" (Waters and Duncan, *Children and the Lord's Supper*, 21). The examples and commands of the NT regarding the Lord's Supper, along with the covenantal transition to the new covenant make clear that the NT has no category for a new covenant (church) member who is non-communing.

112. Parker, "Paedocommunion, Paedobaptism, and Covenant Theology," 112.

113. Parker recognizes "participation" as a corporate expression of union with Christ. As distinct from participation in the old covenant, new covenant participation is "not typological, but is instead a direct covenantal, vital, organic, and spiritual union." (Parker, "Israel-Christ-Church Typological Pattern," 301). Billings writes, both God's promises in the gospel and in the sacraments "portray union with Christ by the Spirit as the source for forgiveness, new life, and new identity in Christ. The material signs and acts of the Supper are to be valued precisely because the gospel promises that what they hold forth are to be valued" (Billings, *Remembrance, Communion, and Hope*, 71).

114. Thus, Thomas is correct to affirm the appropriateness of asking: "is the basis for participation in one sacrament (Baptism, circumcision) the same as the basis for participation in another sacrament (the Lord's Supper, Passover)?" This survey

with faith as the sign of covenant entry and presents baptism as occurring before the Lord's Supper (Acts 2:41–42; cf. 18:1–11; cf. 1 Cor 1:15–17; 11:23).[115] Thus, Venema is correct that "one may not appeal directly to . . . OT restrictions to determine" who should participate in the Lord's Supper, because "no OT precedents are sufficient to determine whether . . . all the members of the new covenant community" should partake of the meal.[116] Yet, when the Old Testament precedents are combined with a full-canonical interpretation of Scripture, the evidence suggests that the sign of entry should precede the sign of participation in the new covenant, as it did in the old.

---

demonstrates that the old covenant required the sign of entry before the sign of participation. The thesis of the chapter is that this principle holds across the canon (Thomas, "Not a Particle of Sound Brain," in Waters and Duncan, *Children at the Lord's Supper,* 105).

115. Duguid appeals to the continuity between the signs of covenant entry as preparatory for each of the meals of participation. However, he misses baptism's continual association with faith on the part of its recipients (Duguid, "Christ Our Passover," in Waters and Duncan, *Children at the Lord's Supper,* 71). Arguing against paedocommunists, Duguid observes that a "crucial difference" exists "between the sacraments within the [OT]. The Passover was not a wordless sign, like circumcision. It was a sign that had explanation and comprehension built into its very structure" (cf. Exod 12:26). However, Duguid never explains the discontinuity between circumcision and baptism regarding the words of baptism into the Trinity that Christ commands (Matt 28:19–20). Duguid cannot consistently maintain that baptism is fully analogous to circumcision in their roles as signs of initiation for their respective covenants. Even granting his claim that circumcision was a "wordless sign," he has to account for the words Jesus associates with baptism, for they imply a covenantal relationship, even union with the Triune God as disciples.

116. Venema, *Children at the Lord's Table?,* 88. Venema is also on target to claim "There are too many substantial differences between the old and new covenant rites to allow any easy inferences" from what is true of Passover to what is true of the Lord's Supper (89). This observation leads Venema to conclude "One needs to look especially at the NT evidence to determine the proper recipients of the new covenant sacrament." The irony of this observation is that as a pedobaptist, Venema does not determine who may be baptized with the same kind of critical methodology as he applies to the question of who may partake of the Lord's Supper. As Parker explains, "At no point in his book does he work out these assertions for the case of infant baptism" (Parker, "Paedocommunion, Paedobaptism, and Covenant Theology," 106). This chapter seeks to provide the very thing Venema excludes. Estelle raises a similar concern to Venema and is liable to critique at the same point (Estelle, "Passover and the Lord's Supper," in Waters and Duncan, *Children at the Lord's Supper,* 40).

The Relation of Signs of Entry
to Signs of Participation

The biblical-theological method that Paul demonstrates in 1 Corinthians 10 is instructive for understanding the storyline of Scripture and the relationship of the signs of entry to the signs of participation. Paul explicitly mentions old covenant types of baptism and the Lord's Supper, in that order.[117] In 1 Corinthians 10:1–4, Paul tells the church "Our fathers were all under the cloud, and all passed through the sea, and all were baptized into Moses . . . and all ate the same spiritual food and drank the same spiritual drink. For they drank from the spiritual Rock that followed them, and the Rock was Christ." Two observations about this passage help solidify this chapter's contention that sufficient continuity exists between the signs of entry and participation to warrant the expectation that baptism should precede the Lord's Supper, as prerequisite to it.

First, Paul's interpretive method is important for understanding the church's relationship to Christ and Israel. Paul's instructions serve to warn the Corinthians that their experience of baptism and the Lord's Supper do not insulate them from judgment,[118] as his flow of argument follows a theological connection from Israel to Christ to the church.[119] Israel experienced the Passover event, followed by the baptism into Moses and spiritual food and drink in the desert, which was Christ (vv. 2–4).[120] Then, Christ was sac-

---

117. Note Paul's use of *typos* in 1 Cor 10:6. See Hamilton Jr., "Lord's Supper in Paul," in Schreiner and Crawford, *Lord's Supper*, 80. Hamilton argues that Paul "learned his interpretive method from Jesus himself." He explains, "Jesus explained his death and resurrection as typologically fulfilling what was celebrated in the Passover—the exodus from Egypt. Taking his cue from this, Paul interprets the events of Israel's history as types of Jesus and those he redeems (e.g., 1 Cor 10:1–13). That is to say, Jesus presents his body, broken for his people, as the new exodus replacement of the bread eaten in the Passover feast commemorating the exodus from Egypt. Just as Israel was instructed to remember what took place at the exodus by celebrating Passover (Exod 12:14; Deut 16:3), so Jesus instructs his disciples to continue to partake of the bread that is his body for his 'remembrance'" (87–88). For a list of interpreters who view the events of Israel's history merely as analogies for the church's experience, see Parker, "Israel-Christ-Church Typological Pattern," 333n100.

118. Hamilton Jr., "Lord's Supper in Paul," in Schreiner and Crawford, *Lord's Supper*, 73–75; Schreiner, *Paul*, 287.

119. Parker, "Israel-Christ-Church Typological Pattern," 322.

120. Being baptized into Moses parallels Paul's language in Gal 3:26–27 and Rom 6:3–4 of being baptized into Christ. Baptized into Moses entails entering the covenant of which Moses acted as mediator. See Parker, "Israel-Christ-Church Typological Pattern," 338–39; Garrett, "Meredith Kline," in Schreiner and Wright, *Believer's Baptism*, 278. Horton explains, "Each generation celebrating the Passover was to recognize its participation in [the] baptism" [into Moses] that the exodus generation experienced

rificed as the Passover lamb, in fulfillment of Israel's Passover celebrations (5:7). Those who participate in Christ (10:16)—the church—are called to cleanse out the old leaven and so reveal their true identity as being unleavened through Christ's sacrificial death (5:8).[121]

Therefore, while Israel experienced a baptism into Moses as a means of entry into the old covenant, the church experiences baptism into Christ as a means of entry to the new covenant (12:13).[122] While Israel received spiritual food in the manna in the wilderness, a provision that pointed to Christ (10:4; cf. John 6),[123] the church receives and participates in Christ

---

historically (Horton, *People and Place*, 103).

121. Those who have been delivered from God's wrath by the blood of Christ, the Passover lamb, and who have been baptized typologically, as Israel was in the Red Sea, receive spiritual food of participation in Christ. Interestingly, Paul typologically connects Israel's experience to that of the church differently (though not in contradiction) in 1 Cor 5 than in 1 Cor 10. In 1 Cor 5:7–10, Paul seems to describe the Lord's Supper as an anti-type of Passover feast. The Passover lamb being celebrated is Christ (v. 7). The Supper is a "festival" the church must still celebrate (v. 7). The unleavened bread pictures the call to holy living by new covenant members, which is in accord with the atoning blood of Christ (v. 8). In 10:3–4, the Lord's Supper is an anti-type of God's miraculous feeding of Israel with manna and water in the wilderness (cf. 10:6; *typos*). In the case of 1 Cor 10, Paul more specifically defines the relationships between type and anti-type, describing the spiritual drink as Christ. Paul's purpose in elucidating the typological connection in chapter 10 is to warn the church that their physical participation in the signs of the new covenant does not guarantee their salvation. If the church participates with Christ and demons simultaneously, God promises judgment like that which Israel received. Some of the foregoing is indebted to Hamilton Jr., "Lord's Supper in Paul," in Schreiner and Crawford, *Lord's Supper*, 74–75, 90. See also Estelle, "Passover and the Lord's Supper," in Waters and Duncan, *Children and the Lord's Supper*, 54.

122. Interestingly, circumcision is not at issue here, because circumcision did not function as a redemptive-historical means of deliverance for Israel in the exodus event. Circumcision predated the baptism into Moses through the Red Sea (Exod 14; cf. Gen 17). This passage demonstrates that while Paul considers circumcision as an old covenant sign of entry (Eph 2:11; Gal 5:3; Acts 16:3), he recognized the exodus event (including the Red Sea) as God's means of creating a new people for himself (cf. Exod 19:4–6). Typologically, the crossing of the Red Sea functions as an indication that baptism is the physical act by which God creates an ideal Israel. By virtue of the church's union with Christ, whose baptism recapitulated Israel's (Matt 3), the baptism that new covenant members experience is the physical means of creating a new people.

123. Pennington's comments on the Gospels provides a helpful comparison to Paul's hermeneutic in 1 Cor 10. Pennington argues that the Gospel writers connect Jesus' "work as the Passover fulfillment and new exodus" with the feeding of Israel in the wilderness (Pennington, "Lord's Supper in the Gospels," 49–50). He explains, "In the Synoptics this is done artfully through a two-step process that first identifies Jesus' water crossing and wilderness feeding as a new exodus, and then second by intra-textually connecting this with the Last Supper." In other words, the Gospel writers present the followers of Jesus as experiencing the new exodus prophesied by Isaiah (40:1–11) by showing Jesus feeding them and then crossing the water (with them or to them; cf. John

when they eat the bread and drink the cup (10:16–17).[124] By presenting God's sustaining of his people in the wilderness through water as typologically fulfilled in Christ, Paul presents the church's experience of Christ as somewhat analogous to Israel's.[125] Yet, the Corinthians participate in Christ in a heightened,[126] eschatological manner, given the dawning of the new covenant.[127] So, Hamilton concludes, "It seems that the undercurrent of Paul's statements to the Corinthians—the narrative framework that results in him saying what he says—is that the Corinthians have experienced the new exodus . . . they have entered into a new covenant."[128]

Second, the order of covenant signs in the passage suggests that one who would enter the new covenant should receive the covenant signs in the order that best represents participation in a new and better exodus. Specifically, the redemptive-historical order of events that occurred in the creation of Israel required that the nation be baptized into Moses before they ate the spiritual food in the wilderness. The order of baptism followed by eating could not have been otherwise. Interestingly, Paul does not utilize the old covenant signs of circumcision and Passover specifically in 1 Corinthians 10. Yet, without the Old Testament sign of covenant entry, he considers the church's experience of becoming God's people as sufficiently similar to Israel's, because given the typology of the exodus, Israel's baptism was always intended to point to the church's baptism.[129] And Israel's eating in the wilder-

---

6:1–15 and 6:16–21). See also Duguid, "Christ Our Passover," 61.

124. By describing the food and water as spiritual, Paul appears to emphasize the "supernatural and miraculous" origin of the items (Parker, "Israel-Christ-Church Typological Pattern," 339–41). The connection of the "spiritual food" to the "spiritual rock," which is Christ "suggests they are 'spiritual' in not just being supernatural, but in pointing to Christ and having a corresponding typological significance with respect to the Lord's Supper." Simply put, the physical elements of manna, water, and the rock from which the water came are intended to highlight Christ as the source of Israel's provision.

125. Turley, *Ritualized Revelation of the Messianic Age*, 153.

126. Parker, "Israel-Christ-Church Typological Pattern," 346.

127. As Christ was disclosed to Israel in the water from the rock, so "Christ is disclosed through the cup of the new covenant in the midst of the Corinthian church (10:16)" (Hamilton Jr., "Lord's Supper in Paul," in Schreiner and Crawford, *Lord's Supper*, 90). Paul's willingness to speak of the Corinthians as those who have been delivered by Christ through a second exodus implies an identity for recipients of the Lord's Supper. They should "identify themselves as redeemed slaves who follow Paul as he follows Christ in giving himself for others."

128. Hamilton Jr., "Lord's Supper in Paul," in Schreiner and Crawford, *Lord's Supper*, 91.

129. Hamilton Jr., "Lord's Supper in Paul," in Schreiner and Crawford, *Lord's Supper*, 91. Hamilton writes, "Christ is the new Passover lamb whose blood covers them

ness was always intended to point to the church's reception of spiritual food at the Lord's Table.[130] While the old covenant community has a different structure and nature than the new covenant community,[131] Paul describes the Corinthians as "brothers" and the Old Testament people of God as "our fathers" (10:1). Despite the discontinuities between the covenant communities, Paul views the two covenant communities as comprising one people of God.[132] Furthermore, Paul presents the historical events that formed the nation of Israel as possessing a "divinely ordained reason for being in Scripture"—the instruction of the new covenant, eschatological people of God (vv. 6, 11).[133] Explicitly, Paul's primary purpose in recounting the example of Israel it to warn the Corinthians against committing Israel's same errors. Nevertheless, the redemptive-historical order of redemption included baptism followed by the eating of spiritual food. Because Paul affirms that the Corinthians were formally constituted as God's people through this order of the covenantal signs (1:13–17; 10:1–4; 12:3, 13; 10:16–17; 11:23),[134] it seems fair to assume that the church should continue to require the sign of entry before the sign of participation.

---

and removes God's wrath; the waters of baptism match the waters of the Red Sea; they have entered into a new covenant; God has tabernacled in them by His Spirit, making them His temple; and they journey through the wilderness toward the kingdom of God, partaking of the Lord's Supper as Israel partook of the manna and celebrated the feasts of God's deliverance." Thus, "They are typologically reliving the story of God's redemption of His people, and Paul is calling them to identify themselves with those who believed and were delivered." Parker writes, "Although the Israelites were never wet as they crossed the sea on dry land (Exod 14:22), since the exodus deliverance initiated Israel as God's covenant people, marking their beginning as a redeemed people from the bondage of Egypt, the correlation with baptism is fitting, for baptism is what initiates and begins the Christian life as one is brought into the new covenant community" (Parker, "Israel-Christ-Church Typological Pattern," 338, 350–51).

130. Parker, "Israel-Christ-Church Typological Pattern," 349. Parker explains, "Thus, there is a historical and theological continuation between Israel and the church as Israel's exodus deliverance and wilderness benefits correspond to and foreshadow the church's deliverance and the church's two ordinances." Similarly, see Pennington, "Lord's Supper in the Gospels," in Schreiner and Crawford, Lord's Supper, 50.

131. On the different structure and nature of the new covenant, see the section below on the relationship between the covenants.

132. Ciampa and Rosner argue that Paul's language "reflects his understanding that the Corinthians are to understand themselves in the light of the new identity formed through their adoption into the covenant people of God. Even the Gentile readers of the letter are now to think of the Israelites of the exodus as their adopted 'fathers' through their inclusion in the covenant community" (Ciampa and Rosner, First Letter to the Corinthians, 446, cited in Parker, "Israel-Christ-Church Typological Pattern," 337).

133. Fee, First Epistle to the Corinthians, 506, cited in Parker, "Israel-Christ-Church Typological Pattern," 344.

134. Parker, "Israel-Christ-Church Typological Pattern," 336.

Relationship between the Old and New Covenants

The only adequate explanation for the discontinuities between the old covenant signs and new covenant signs is the change in structure and nature
that comes with the new covenant. This section seeks to account for the
continuities and discontinuities section above by considering how Christ
brings the new covenant and applies its blessings to all those united to him.
In terms of the four Abrahamic seed referents, this section argues that the
New Testament presents Christ as the typological fulfillment of the seed
of Abraham. Then, all those united with Christ by faith are considered the
spiritual seed of Abraham. Understanding who receives the covenantal
signs requires an understanding of how Christ fulfills the national, typological, and spiritual senses of the seed of Abraham, and, as the covenant head,
forms a multi-ethnic new covenant community.

Christ and the New Covenant

Christ, as the typological seed of Abraham, is the representative Israelite
and Son of David who receives the promises of the new covenant and fulfills
the promises of the Old Testament. Each of these themes will be explored in
turn before putting them together to explain how they affect the nature and
structure of the new covenant community.

First, Christ is the typological seed of Abraham. As discussed in chapter 2, the seed of Abraham has four senses: to (1) the "natural (physical)
seed"; (2) "natural yet special seed"; (3) the true/ultimate seed, who brings
multi-national blessings as Messianic Son of David (Gen 12:3; cf. Gen 3:15;
Isa 55:3; Gal 3:16); and (4) the spiritual seed, meaning those who belong to
Christ by faith and regeneration (Gal 3:26–29).[135] Whereas Genesis 22:17a
speaks of Abraham's seed in the plural, referring to his many descendants,

---

135. Wellum, "Relationship between the Covenants," in Schreiner and Wright, *Believer's Baptism*, 133–35. Wellum rightly refers to the Messiah as the "true/unique seed"
of Abraham. He explains, "Jesus is the unique seed of Abraham both as a physical seed
through a specific genealogical line and as the antitype of all the covenant mediators of
the Old Testament." The fourth sense of Abraham's seed is also described as "spiritual
seed." In this sense, spiritual refers to the spiritual connection to Christ by regeneration and faith and the reception of the blessing promised to Abraham through Christ,
without belonging to Abraham's physical descendants (Gentry and Wellum, *Kingdom
through Covenant*, 632–33). Similar is Allison, *Sojourners and Strangers*, 347. Saucy
declines to mention a typological sense of seed. See Saucy, *Church in God's Program*,
74–75. See also Renihan, "Abrahamic Covenant," in Barcellos, *Recovering a Covenantal
Heritage*, 167. Contra Wellum is Waltke, "Kingdom Promises as Spiritual," in Feinberg,
Continuity and Discontinuity, 268. Waltke claims "the seed is essentially spiritual not
carnal."

the singular verbs and pronominal suffixes of vv. 17b-18 present the seed of Abraham as a collective singular.[136] This collective singular is precisely the clue that Paul picks up in Galatians 3:16 in order to explain how the blessing of Abraham extends to the nations through Christ specifically, rather than through the nation of Israel.[137]

As Wellum explains, Christ came as the last Adam (Luke 3:38), the antitype of Israel (Matt 2:15; cf. Exod 4:22–23), and David's royal Son (2 Sam 7:12–16). After millennia of waiting for a faithful covenant partner who would walk blamelessly before the Lord (Gen 17:1–2) and fully obey the Mosaic law, Christ came as the fulfillment of the national, spiritual, and typological aspects of the promises to Abraham. As a circumcised Jewish male in the line of David, Jesus embodies Israel's corporate and ethnic national identity and fulfills the typological expectation of a seed of Abraham who would bless the nations.[138] Thus, Paul describes Jesus as the seed/offspring to whom all the promises made to Abraham were intended (Gal 3:16).[139]

136. Hamilton Jr., "Seed of the Woman," 261–62. Similarly, see DeRouchie and Meyer, "Christ or Family," 36–48. Against this Israel-Christ-Church progression, Saucy argues, "The participation of the church in the covenant promises made to Abraham rests . . . on the fact that these promises included blessing for all the families of the earth (Gen 12:3). When the apostle speaks of the blessing of Abraham coming on the church, he makes reference specifically to this universal promise and not to the national promises of Israel" (Saucy, *Church in God's Program*, 76).

137. Herman Ridderbos recognizes that some might interpret Paul's reference to Christ from the collective singular, "seed," as misunderstanding the promise made to Abraham. He answers the objection: "From the very beginning, that is, when God spoke to Abraham, a distinction was made between seed and seed. In fact, before the birth of Isaac, God had told Abraham that not in Ishmael but in Isaac should his seed be valid. This could serve therefore to teach Abraham how he had to regard the seed of promise (cf. Gen 17:19–21; 21:12). And this consideration could also give Paul occasion to explain that the concept seed is not to be taken as an indiscriminate quantity but as a unit (concentrated in the person of Christ)" (Ridderbos, *Epistle of Paul to the Churches of Galatia*, 133). By maintaining a distinction between the people of Israel and the nation of Israel, Saucy holds that Christ fulfills the role of the people of Israel but that the nation of Israel will have her covenant promises fulfilled in the future (Saucy, "Israel and the Church," in Feinberg, *Continuity and Discontinuity*, 254).

138. Wellum, "Relationship between the Covenants," in Schreiner and Wright, *Believer's Baptism*, 127–35; Wellum, *God the Son Incarnate*, 133–46; DeRouchie, "Counting Stars with Abraham and the Prophets," 454–55. Contra Malone, *Baptism of Disciples Alone*, 32. As a covenantal Baptist, Malone argues that the church is the typological fulfillment of Israel.

139. Whereas no human partner had been adequate to uphold the covenantal obligations found in the Abrahamic (Gen 17:1–2), Mosaic (Exod 19:1–6), or Davidic covenants (2 Sam 7:14–15), Christ was an obedient Son (Rom 1:1–6). For a defense of how the promises to Eve (Gen 3:15) and Abraham (17:1–23; 22:17–18) lead to a greater son of David being the promised, royal seed, see Hamilton Jr., "Seed of the Woman," 263–68. Christ's death for sinners demonstrates God's faithfulness to uphold

Second, Christ is the one with whom the new covenant is made. Jesus' words of institution before the Last Supper indicate that the meal he instituted inaugurated the new covenant,[140] upon his covenant ratifying shedding of blood the following day (Matt 26:29; Exod 24:8; Heb 9:18–22).[141] As the typological fulfillment of the nation of Israel and the one through whom all the promises find their *telos* (2 Cor 1:20), Christ himself serves as the human partner and true Israelite and Davidic representative of "the house of Israel and the house of Judah" with whom the new covenant is made (cf. Jer 31:31).[142] Isaiah prophesied that Yahweh would provide for himself a covenant keeping representative with the promise to give his servant as "a covenant for the people, a light for the nations" (42:6). As Martin explains, "By being a covenant (Isa 42:6; 49:8; 55:3; 59:21), the servant will supply the means through which people will come into a covenant relationship with the Lord."[143] Thus, the typological development of the seed of Abra-

---

the promises to Abraham (Gen 15) by a divine-human son who would walk blamelessly and yet bare the curse due to sinners (Gal 3:13; cf. Gen 17:1–2). Malone acknowledges that the genealogical principle was necessary to bring about Christ as the true seed of Abraham (Malone, *Baptism of Disciples Alone*, 68).

140. More precisely, "The actual death and resurrection of Jesus . . . inaugurates the new covenant." Yet, "it is the reflection upon" the death and resurrection of Christ "in the Lord's Last Supper that explains and exposits the meaning of those yet to happen events" (Pennington, "Lord's Supper in the Gospels," in Schreiner and Crawford, *Lord's Supper*, 53). Thus, the Lord's Supper is "an occasion to recall and reflect on Jesus death and the inauguration of the new covenant" (Bock, *Luke*, 2:1717–18).

141. Pennington notes the concentration in the Gospels of the term covenant within the narratives of the Last Supper. See Pennington, "Lord's Supper in the Gospels," in Schreiner and Crawford, *Lord's Supper*, 52.

142. Gentry and Wellum, *Kingdom through Covenant*, 646. Although in an OT context, the name Israel could be applied to the whole nation including resident aliens (Deut 29:10–11; Josh 8:33), the narrowing of the redemptive line to Christ required biological descent from Abraham (Gen 17:18) (DeRouchie, "Counting Stars with Abraham and the Prophets," 456). Parker demonstrates that in the OT, the term Israel is covenantally tied to multiple themes in the OT, such as Adam's role as head of the human race, the Davidic king and kingdom, and sonship, among others. Thus, Parker argues that Jesus "not only represents Israel, but also fulfills Israel's identity, calling, and promises in inaugurating the new age, ratifying the new covenant, and bringing forth the dawning of the eschatologically restored Israel—the church" (Parker, "Israel-Christ-Church Relationship," 54–56). Parker demonstrates that Jesus fulfills Israel's role as "the Son out of Egypt" (Matt 2:15; cf. Hos 11:1; Exod 4:22), "true Servant" (Matt 3:16–17; cf. Isa 42:1), "obedient Son in the wilderness" (Luke 4:1–13; cf. Deut 6:13, 16; 8:3), and "true vine" (John 15:1–5; cf. Isa 5:1–5) (Parker, "Israel-Christ-Church Relationship," 57–63).

143. Naselli et al., *Forty Questions about Biblical Theology*, 168. For a progressive dispensationalist affirmation that the new covenant blessings come to Gentiles by their connection to the servant of Isaiah, see Saucy, *Church in God's Program*, 80; Blaising and Bock, *Progressive Dispensationalism*, 158. For the specific connection between the

ham intersects with the typological development of circumcision. While the former marks the ethnic nation from which the Messiah would come, the latter testifies to the integrity of the divine-human covenant partner and his capacity to fulfill spiritual aspects of the promises. Jesus is not only a physical descendant of Abraham; he "has been tempted as we are, yet without sin" (Heb 4:15). As the mediator, head, and sacrificial means of inaugurating the new covenant, Christ is able to extend the spiritual blessings promised to Abraham to all who come to Christ by faith (Gal 3:29).

Third, circumcision ceases to be covenantally significant after Christ's circumcision precisely because he fulfills all the promises of the Abrahamic covenant. Those promises were confirmed and symbolized by the removal of the foreskin. Yet, the ethnic nationality and spiritual integrity of the descendent of Abraham who could bless the nations required typological development (cf. Deut 10:16; 30:6; Jer 9:25–26). Wellum explains,

> Not only does the *a fortiori* quality of typology serve as the crucial means by which Scripture unpacks the unique identity of Christ, it is also the way in which Scripture grounds the uniqueness of the entire era of fulfillment associated with the new covenant. In other words, it is the means by which legitimate discontinuity between the old and new in God's unified plan is established.

Thus, Christ's fulfillment of the Abrahamic covenant grounds not only the shift of covenant signs but also the shift in the nature and structure of the covenant community. Rather than the nation of Israel, "Christ as the antitypical fulfillment of Israel [and the Davidic King], takes on the role of Israel, and by faith union in him, his work becomes ours as his new covenant people."[144]

Christ and Believers

The church's redemptive-historical newness comes as a result of its covenantal union with Christ, given the inauguration of the new covenant. Hebrews 8:6 affirms that the new covenant "has been enacted."[145] As the

---

Isaianic servant of the Lord, the seed of Abraham, and the multi-national community that benefits from the servant/seed's work, see DeRouchie, "Counting Stars with Abraham and the Prophets," 467–69.

144. Gentry and Wellum, *Kingdom through Covenant*, 106–7.

145. The verb here is completed past action (perfect passive tense) (White, "Newness of the New Covenant [Part I]," in Barcellos, *Recovering a Covenantal Heritage*, 340). For this source see Wellum, "Beyond Mere Ecclesiology," in Easley and Morgan, *Community of Jesus*, 201–2.

typological seed of Abraham, the blessings promised to Abraham extend through Christ to all those spiritually connected to him.[146] This connection explains Paul's reference to those who have been united to Christ by faith as "Abraham's offspring, heirs according to promise" (Gal 3:29).[147] Thus, the spiritual seed of Abraham receive that status through spiritual rebirth and adoption via union with Christ.[148]

Thus, the new covenant community is new in both nature and structure. The distinctions that belonged to the circumcised, old covenant community, including "a distinction between the physical/biological (not necessarily true believer) and spiritual/true believer seed of Abraham," gives way with the coming of Christ.[149] By contrast, new covenant members are a regenerate, multinational community of Jew and Gentile blessed by Christ's salvific work (Eph 1:3; 2:11–22; cf. Gen 12:1–3; Gal 3:7–8). Through the cross and resurrection, Christ made provision for the fulfillment of international and universal scope of the promised new covenant (Ezek 44:7–9; 45:21; Isa 56:4–8; 66:18–24).[150] The community is new in its nature because all the members of the new covenant community exercise saving faith (Rom 4:1–5; cf. Gen 15:6), know the Lord (Gal 4:9; cf. Jer 31:33–34), are united with Christ (1 Cor 12:13), are permanently indwelt by the Spirit (Eph 1:13; 2 Cor 1:22; cf. Joel 2:28–32; Ezek 36:26–27), have the law written on their

146. As Christ's people, this "ideal Israel" receives all the benefits that flow from their covenantal connection to Christ (Gentry and Wellum, *Kingdom through Covenant*, 645).

147. Referring to Gal 3:16, Ridderbos argues that Paul "infers that God, when he gave his promise to Abraham and his seed did not intend all of his descendants, but the descendant, the seed, who is Christ, and in Him—as appears from the later v. 29—all who are included in him, namely the believers" (Ridderbos, *Epistle of Paul*, 132–33). By referring to one definite descendant who receives the promise of Abraham, Paul is not being exclusive but inclusive. "Just as in Gen 21:12 the person of Isaac is designated by the word seed in distinction from that of Ishmael, though not, of course, by exclusion of Isaac's descendants, so, according to Paul, the singular of the noun is also a designation of the one Christ in distinction from all other indiscriminate descendants of Abraham together, but not in exclusion of those who are bound with Christ by faith (cf. Gal 3:26–29)" (134).

148. DeRouchie, "Counting Stars with Abraham and the Prophets," 470; Meyer, *End of the Law*, 144–46; Waters and Duncan, *Children at the Lord's Supper*, 186.

149. Greever, "Nature of the New Covenant," 74–80, 83–87.

150. Wellum, "Beyond Mere Ecclesiology," in Easley and Morgan, *Community of Jesus*, 196–97. Through Christ, the Jeremiah's prophecies of a multi-national people of God who possess circumcised hearts is realized (Jer 3:16–18; 4:4) (DeRouchie, "Counting Stars with Abraham and the Prophets," 463).

new/circumcised hearts (Jer 31:33-34; Col 2:11-13; 2 Cor 3:1—4:6),[151] and have their sins forgiven (Acts 2:38; cf. Jer 31:34).[152]

The new nature of the new covenant community also entails a new structure. In the old covenant, all those marked off by circumcision and Passover were considered full covenant members in the national sense,[153] and were thereby constituted as a mixed group of believers and unbelievers by the old covenant signs. Yet, the constitution of the one people of God changes with the inauguration of the new covenant. As Hamilton argues, "In Galatians 3:16 . . . Paul insists on the singularity of the 'seed' before showing how the promises to the singular seed come to the collective seed through baptism into Messiah in 3:27-29."[154] Instead of a priestly and kingly order of authority, as in Israel, the whole new covenant community has personal knowledge of the Lord (Jer 31:34; Gal 4:9).[155] As chapter 3 demon-

151. Thus, it is not the case that only the ceremonial law is written on the heart. Contra Neill, "Newness of the New Covenant," in Strawbridge, *Case for Covenantal Infant Baptism*, 147. Neither is it true that the whole law is written on the heart in a partial manner. Pratt argues for three stages in the fulfillment of Jer 31: "The inauguration of fulfillment in the first coming of Christ, the continuation of fulfilment between the first and second comings of Christ, and the consummation of fulfillment at the return of Christ" (Pratt, "Infant Baptism in the New Covenant," in Strawbridge, *Case for Covenantal Infant Baptism*, 168-71). He claims that the existence of covenant breakers, on his reading, within the new covenant (Heb 10:28-31) and the need to "watch for corruption in our thinking" suggests that "while the internalization of the law of God has begun within believers, it has not yet been completed." Instead, Jesus considers all those who "have learned from the Father and come to me" (i.e., believe; John 6:45; cf. v. 35) as "taught by God." Paul claims that the Thessalonians "have been taught by God to love one another" (1 Thess 4:9) and the Romans "have become obedient from the heart to the standard of teaching to which you were committed" (6:17). Neill and Pratt grant more power to the old nature/sinful flesh than is warranted by Scripture. See Naselli, *Let Go and Let God?*, 262-66.

152. Wellum, "Beyond Mere Ecclesiology," in Easley and Morgan, *Community of Jesus*, 198-200. See also Hammett, *Forty Questions*, 142; Garrett, "Meredith Kline," in Schreiner and Wright, *Believer's Baptism*, 278.

153. Wellum, "Beyond Mere Ecclesiology," in Easley and Morgan, *Community of Jesus*, 200.

154. Hamilton Jr., "Seed of the Woman," 262; Schreiner, "Baptism in the Epistles," in Schreiner and Wright, *Believer's Baptism*, 88-89; Blaising and Bock, *Progressive Dispensationalism*, 190. Strawbridge writes, "Children are to receive the visible covenant signs by right of covenant membership, as first granted to Abraham; their membership has not been revoked" (Strawbridge, "Polemics of Anabaptism," in Strawbridge, *Case for Covenantal Infant Baptism*, 284). But Strawbridge misses the national and typological aspects of the Abrahamic covenant. Children were included in the covenant community in order to lead to Christ, the true seed of Israel. Thus, the membership of children is fulfilled. Now, in the new covenant age, one becomes a member of the covenant community principally by faith and externally by baptism.

155. Dumbrell, *Covenant and Creation*, 264.

strated, the new covenant signs of baptism and the Lord's Supper function respectively as a means of externally appropriating union with Christ in baptism and then participating in Christ and, derivatively, with his body in the Lord's Supper (Gal 3:26–29; 1 Cor 10:16–17). As Turley explains, "As the baptized body is now oriented toward Christ, so those who share in the baptism ritual are reoriented toward one another."[156] Thus, one aspect of the structural difference of the new covenant community is that the new covenant signs constitute the members into local, regenerate assemblies, called churches (cf. Gal 1:2; 1 Cor 1:2; 1 Thess 1:1).[157] The newness in nature and structure does much to explain the abrogation of the genealogical principle. Wellum explains,

> Under the previous covenants, the genealogical principle, that is the relationship between the covenant mediator and his seed was physical. . . . But now, in Christ, under his mediation, the relationship between Christ and his seed is no longer physical but spiritual, which entails that the covenant sign must only be applied to those who in fact are the spiritual seed of Abraham.[158]

---

156. Turley, *Ritualized Revelation of the Messianic Age*, 56. With respect to Gal 3:28, Turley has, "The important point here . . . is that the extent to which a [community] is realized by the Galatians or idealized by Paul is predicated on bodily-established acceptance, specific to ritualized processes" (36). In other words, the realization of community is tied by the NT to the shared, embodied ritual (i.e., physically enacted symbol) of baptism.

157. Contra Ross, "Baptism and Circumcision as Signs and Seals," in Strawbridge, *Case for Covenantal Infant Baptism*, 100.

158. Wellum "Relationship between the Covenants," in Schreiner and Wright, *Believer's Baptism*, 136–37. Contra Neill, "Newness of the New Covenant," in Strawbridge, *Case for Covenantal Infant Baptism*, 155. Neill's appeal to Eph 6 as evidence that the new covenant community continued to include children as in the old covenant goes beyond the evidence. First, the command to obey one's parents implies that the children listening would have matured enough to listen to the letter being read in the congregation. Second, the call to obey "in the Lord" strongly suggests the need to obey for the sake of Christ and as one united to Christ (see Rom 16:2; Phil 4:1; Col 4:7). Thomas follows Neill's same logic when he writes, "Paul makes clear in 1 Corinthians 7:14 that even the children born of marriage where only one partner has become a Christian are considered relationally and covenantally 'holy.' These children are dedicated to and are accepted by God in company with their one Christian parent. Hence they are members of Christ's body, kingdom and (visible) church and enjoy the privileges of the covenant community, including the sacrament of baptism. The right of covenant infant to baptism is not founded on that infant's personal state of grace and regeneration (personal, real, inchoate, or prospective) but rather on the basis of how God defines covenant membership in the covenant of grace in both Old and New Testaments; that is, on the principle of "professing believers and their children" (Thomas, "Not a Particle of Sound Brain," in Waters and Duncan, *Children at the Lord's Supper*, 112). The discontinuities surveyed in this chapter provide an adequate answer to most of Thomas' claims.

The New Testament assumes that every believer is baptized and that baptism is made valid by its connection to faith.

The New Covenant Community

Based upon their union with Christ, the new covenant community is a redemptive-historically new reality.[159] The newness of structure and nature, promised in Jeremiah 31, came about on the basis of Christ's cross and resurrection. The forgiveness Christ provides is then applied to the new covenant community, along with the new covenant blessings of heart circumcision and Spirit baptism. These two blessings are part and parcel of union with Christ, which is externally appropriated, demonstrated, and deepened through the new covenant signs. This section describes the new structure and nature of the new covenant community in terms of these new covenant blessings, which are visibly presented by the new covenant signs.

Heart circumcision and baptism with the Spirit are two eschatological works of the Spirit that make the new covenant community a regenerate

---

However, it is worth noting here that Thomas does not recognize the possible parallel between children who are "made holy" in terms of being set apart in proximity to those who are united to Christ by faith. It is possible that Paul intends something akin to the category of Ishmael here. Ishmael benefitted from his proximity to God's blessed people, though he experienced neither salvation from sin nor did his progeny constitute the seed through which Christ would come. In other words, being "made holy" may simply refer to a child or unbelieving spouse's proximity to the people of God, with the outward benefits entailed therein. Paul does not insinuate a continuation of the genealogical principle on the basis of 1 Cor 7:14. The question of who is baptized and belongs to the new covenant community must be determined by the commands, examples, and covenantal context of the NT. On this point, see Schreiner, "Baptism in the Epistles," in Schreiner and Wright, *Believer's Baptism*, 96. Schreiner argues that if infants belong to the covenant community due to their status as "holy" (v. 14), then so also does an unbelieving spouse, because Paul describes him/her as "sanctified" (v.16). Contra Wilson, "Baptism and Children in the Old and New Testaments," in Strawbridge, *Case for Covenantal Infant Baptism*, 295. Based upon 1 Cor 7:14, Wilson claims, "The children of saints are saints."

159. Parker makes this same point, arguing, "The church is not ontologically new since God has always called out and saved people for himself (the elect), but the nature and structure of the people of God has forever changed due to the coming of Christ and his work on the cross which brings about the fulfillment of OT promises and secures greater soteriological blessings" (Parker, "Israel-Christ-Church Typological Pattern," 301n32). Parker is following Wellum, "Beyond Mere Ecclesiology," in Easley and Morgan, *Community of Jesus*, 195–96. However, Parker appears dismissive of Allison's view that Pentecost marks the inception of the church. See Allison, *Sojourners and Strangers*, 78–82. But if by inception of the church Allison intends the redemptive-historically new beginning of the people of God, as Allison and this book affirm, then Allison's view need not be grouped with a dispensationalist view of the church, as Parker classifies it. For a progressive dispensational view, see Saucy, *Church in God's Program*, 64.

community, unlike Israel. Meade argues that the biblical-theological category of heart circumcision is broader than the systematic category of regeneration. Whereas regeneration "mainly explains why a person believes
in the promises of God under either the old or new covenants," heart circumcision "with its result of Torah obedience and loyalty to Yahweh is tied
firmly to the new covenant era."[160] Given this description, Meade is willing
to call Old Testament believers regenerate, with something like regeneration
1.0, whereas NT believers, due to heart circumcision, experience regeneration 2.0.[161] "In this way, one can affirm that God's Spirit stirred up faith in
the old covenant people, but this same people longed for a greater and better
work of the Spirit to come" (Num 11:17; Joel 2:28–32; Acts 2).[162] One must

160. Meade, "Circumcision of Flesh," in Wellum and Parker, *Progressive Covenantalism*, 157n60.

161. Thanks to Gregg Allison for the terminology of regeneration 1.0 and 2.0. But
note, Hamilton argues that OT believers were regenerate. Yet, he distinguishes between
OT believers who were regenerated/heart circumcised but not indwelt by the Spirit and
the new covenant believers who have both realities at the same time. Another point of
discontinuity for Hamilton is that while he equates circumcision of the heart and regeneration, he claims that OT believers did not have the law written on their hearts. Hamilton Jr., *God's Indwelling Presence*, 45. Hamilton is more inclined than is Meade to see old
covenant believers' ability to obey in terms of heart circumcision (135). For a similar
view to Hamilton, see Ferguson, *Holy Spirit*, 25. Caneday adds that "receipt of the Spirit,
heart circumcision," etc. were "extrinsic to [the old] covenant of shadows." Caneday,
"Covenantal Life with God," in Wellum and Parker, *Progressive Covenantalism*, 123. He
adds, "Many Israelites did obey the law because their hearts were circumcised, and they
were recipients of the Spirit and of eternal life but not by any power of the old covenant."
Similar to Caneday is Fuller, *Unity of the Bible*, 342, who argues that Joshua and Caleb
possessed circumcised hearts as part of the faithful remnant in Israel.

162. Meade, "Circumcision of Flesh," in Wellum and Parker, *Progressive Covenantalism*, 157n60. One example of a covenant theologian who argues that OT believers
had the same experience of the Holy Spirit and heart circumcision as NT Christians
is Neill, "Newness of the New Covenant," in Strawbridge, *Case for Covenantal Infant
Baptism*, 136. However, The OT presents the Spirit's ministry to Israel as a "tribal"
reality rather than a democratized reality. By "tribal," is meant that the Spirit is said
to have "come upon" individual leaders (as representatives of the nation of Israel) for
the purpose of empowering them to perform a specific task. Carson explains, "Despite
remnant themes, the Scriptures picture God working with his people as a tribal grouping whose knowledge of God and whose relations with God were peculiarly dependent
on specially endowed leaders. The Spirit of God was poured out, not on each believer,
but distinctively on prophet, priest, king, and a few designated special leaders such as
Bezalel" (Carson, *Showing the Spirit*, 151). The Spirit "came upon" prophets to speak
(1 Sam 19:20; 2 Chr 15:1; 20:14; Ezek 11:5). The "Spirit of the Lord was upon" judges
whom God raised up by that same Holy Spirit to deliver Israel (e.g., Othniel in Judg
3:10; other judges in 6:34; 11:29; 13:25; 14:6, 19; 15:14). Being filled with the Spirit,
entailing empowerment for ministry, was a reality experienced by OT saints such as
the prophet Micah (3:8). However, the Holy Spirit did not permanently indwell Israel's
leaders, much less every member of the covenant community. Multiple texts support

experience this new covenant regeneration and heart circumcision in order to see the kingdom of God (John 3:3), for in this regeneration, the Spirit works on the heart to cleanse and make new (Titus 3:5; 1 Cor 6:11; Eph 5:25; Heb 10:22; cf. Ezek 36:26–27).[163] This inward cleansing and newness is outwardly reflected in baptism and nurtured in the Lord's Supper, as chapter 3 demonstrated.

Covenantal, dispensational, and Pentecostal theologians agree that the redemptive-historical shift that occurred at Pentecost with the outpouring of the Spirit on Jews and Gentiles signals entry into the new covenant epoch.[164] In each of the prophetic Spirit-baptism texts in the Gospels and Acts (John 1:33; 7:35–37; Matt 3:11–12; Mark 1:7–8; Luke 3:15–17; Acts 1:4–5), the subjects of the baptism will be acted upon by Christ the baptizer as a

---

this claim. For example, because Moses was God's appointed, prophetic leader for Israel God had placed His Spirit "on" Moses (Num 17:17). Yet, when Moses' work became overwhelming, the Lord told Moses to gather seventy elders, so that He could place His Spirit on them as well. When God put His Spirit on them, despite Joshua's initial negative reaction, Moses seemed to give a foretaste of the wider distribution of the Spirit to all of God's people by saying, "Would that all the Lord's people were prophets, that the Lord would put his Spirit on them!" Clearly then, not every old covenant member possessed the Spirit, even though Moses saw that prospect as glorious. Similarly, the contrast between Saul and David in the OT demonstrates the truth that the Spirit did not permanently indwell OT saints. The statement regarding David's anointing in 1 Sam 16:13, that "the Spirit of the Lord rushed upon David from that day forward," is not an exception to the truth that OT saints were not permanently indwelt. Even though the Spirit was apparently "upon" David until his death, the text nowhere states or implies that the Spirit lived within David in a NT sense. Christopher Wright's discussion of the fact that David and Solomon were anointed by the Spirit of God to lead Israel but that the Spirit's anointing did not guarantee their obedience is illuminating (Wright, *Knowing the Holy Spirit*, 90–92). David's plea, that God would "not take your Holy Spirit from me" (Ps 51:11), reveals that although God anointed OT kings with the Spirit to lead Israel, that anointing could be removed as a result of the king's unfaithfulness (1 Sam 16:14). See Hawthorne, *Presence and the Power*, 17–18. Even Ezekiel's experience of the Spirit "enter[ing] into" him was occasional rather than permanent (cf. Ezek 2:2; 3:24). Thus, the Spirit's ministry under the old covenant is especially associated with empowerment without permanent indwelling.

163. For an affirmation that heart circumcision is new covenant regeneration, see Garrett, "Meredith Kline," in Schreiner and Wright, *Believer's Baptism*, 269.

164. See Gaffin, "Cessationist View," in Grudem, *Are Miraculous Gifts for Today?*, Kindle; Carson, *Showing the Spirit*, 158–59; Packer, *Keep in Step with the Spirit*, 164–65. On the question of the normalcy of tongues as the initial sign of having been baptized with the Spirit, see Kaiser, "Spirit Baptism," in Brand, *Perspectives on Spirit Baptism*, 29–30. Jesus' promise to the disciples that the Spirit who had been only with them would be "in them" changed at Pentecost (John 14:17). Thus, God was fulfilling His promises to give His indwelling covenantal presence to all who would call on Him (Joel 2:31–32) so that they could enjoy Him and be empowered by Him. It is no wonder G. K. Beale notices new temple and new creation themes here. See Beale, *Temple and the Church's Mission*, 209–14.

future event. For example, Luke 3:16 states, "He will baptize you with the Holy Spirit." In Acts, Luke purposely signals the fact that he is presenting Pentecost as the fulfillment of Jesus' promise, with the words, "when the day of Pentecost was fulfilled" (2:1) and "they were all filled with the Holy Spirit" (v. 4).[165] Yet, Pentecost also fulfilled Joel 2:28, an eschatological promise related to the then future new covenant that would transform and benefit male and female, young and old, slave and free, who call on the name of the Lord (cf. Acts 2:17–18; Joel 3:1–5; Ezek 36:26–27).[166] Thus, when Paul describes the Corinthians with the parallel expressions "were all baptized into one body" and "were made to drink of one Spirit" (1 Cor 12:13), he is identifying the church in covenantal language. By these descriptions, Paul affirms that all believers in the new covenant age are united to Christ and part of his new creation, while alluding to water baptism (Rom 6:3; Gal 3:27; Joel 2:28–32).[167] After Pentecost, baptism with the Spirit occurs upon entering the new covenant by faith (Eph 1:13; 2 Cor 1:22). This new covenant work is the onset of the Spirit's permanent indwelling, which constitutes the church as the eschatological temple of God (Eph 2:21–22; 2 Cor 6:16–18).[168]

---

165. This is Polhill's translation. Luke's language here is used elsewhere in his writings (Luke 9:51) to denote a redemptive-historical fulfillment and transition as Jesus set His face toward the cross. Here, Luke is drawing attention to the fact that he is describing the promise of the Father mentioned in Acts 1:4–5 (Polhill, *Acts*, 96).

166. Luke highlights the universality of the gift of the Spirit in the subsequent storyline of Acts, often in connection with baptism, as chapter 3 demonstrated. In 2:39, Peter specifically quotes portions of Joel 2:31–32 that reveal the necessity of calling on the Lord in order to receive the Spirit. Allison is correct that Peter's call to be baptized is meant to present the hearers with the means by which they could appropriate the promise of forgiveness and the reception of the Spirit. In this case, the repentance is the internal appropriation that is demonstrated by the external appropriation of water baptism. Thus, one's internal appropriation is no more real than one's external appropriation. Salvation here also is by faith alone, and saving faith is never alone (Allison, "Baptism with and Filling of the Holy Spirit," 12).

167. Ciampa and Rosner, *First Letter to the Corinthians*, 593. Spirit baptism is temporally concurrent with the five new covenant realities of initiation into salvation (regeneration, repentance/faith, justification, adoption, beginning of sanctification) (Grudem, "Perseverance of the Saints," in Schreiner and Ware, *Still Sovereign*, 135). Allison lists effectual calling, regeneration, justification, union with Christ, adoption, and initial sanctification as the other "divine works" occurring at the beginning of salvation (Allison, "Baptism with and Filling of the Holy Spirit," 14).

168. Parker, "Paedocommunion, Paedobaptism, and Covenant Theology," 108. Parker cites Hamilton Jr., *God's Indwelling Presence*, 44; Beale, *Temple and the Church's Mission*, 209–14. Allison explains that every baptism with the Spirit consists of four elements: (1) Christ as the agent who baptizes; (2) the believer as the one baptized; (3) the Spirit as the medium into which believers are immersed; and (4) incorporation into the body of Christ as the purpose of the baptism (Allison, "*Baptism* with and Filling of the Holy Spirit," 5). If this is the mechanism by which baptism with the Spirit works, then

These new covenant blessings of heart circumcision and Spirit baptism are integrally related to the new covenant signs, because the new covenant signs of baptism and the Lord's Supper function to visibly constitute the new structure and nature of new covenant community. One function of water baptism is to externally mirror baptism with the Spirit (1 Cor 12:13).[169] Turley explains,

> While [personal] experience [of the theological reality of baptism in the Spirit] is clearly evident in 1 Corinthians 12:13, [the body-as-society] cannot be appropriated by a subjective experience [of personal faith in Christ] or even a common or shared private experience alone; rather, a ritualized social body as publicly demonstrated and experienced is that which accounts for the formation of a social contract and ethical obligation both theoretically and historically.[170]

Thus, Baptism visibly presents the community's new nature and constitutes the church as a regenerate community in its new structure (i.e., not a mixed community of believers and unbelievers as in the old covenant; see Acts 2:38–42; cf. Titus 3:5).

The Lord's Supper is not exegetically tied to new covenant regeneration or Spirit baptism; yet, a theological relationship exists. Regeneration and Spirit baptism constitute part of the cluster of benefits that transfer to the believer through union with Christ. Union with Christ, I argued in chapter 3, is shorthand for all the blessings of the new covenant, which is symbolized in baptism.[171] The Lord's Supper then is the meal in which all the new covenant blessings are celebrated, encouraged, and deepened.[172] In

---

it is inappropriate to speak of being baptized "by the Spirit" as the acting agent doing the baptizing. John Stott identifies the RSV as an example of this poor translation. If Christ is consistently portrayed as the baptizer in the other six texts, making the Spirit the agent of the baptism is unwarranted in 1 Cor 12:13 (Stott, *Baptism and Fullness*, 14).

169. Schreiner, "Baptism in the Epistles," in Schreiner and Wright, *Believer's Baptism*, 88.

170. Turley, *Ritualized Revelation of the Messianic Age*, 81.

171. Wellum, "Relationship between the Covenants," in Schreiner and Wright, *Believer's Baptism*, 149. In a lengthy development of union with Christ as it relates to typology, Parker explains "Union with Christ is foremost covenantal" (Parker, "Israel-Christ-Church Typological Pattern," 299–300). Again, "being 'in Christ,' which cannot be disassociated from the gift and ministry of the Holy Spirit, who is also linked to the new covenant promises (Ezek 36:24–27; Joel 2:28–29), must be understood in relation to the new covenant." Parker cites Ferguson, *Holy Spirit*, 106.

172. Billings, *Remembrance, Communion, and Hope*, 18–19. Waters helpfully points out ways in which each ordinance signifies the gospel. He writes, "Moreover, baptism and the Lord's Supper have different signification. While each points to Christ, each

a similar way to baptism, the Lord's Supper visibly celebrates the new nature of the new covenant community—the church.[173] But the meal does more. The Lord's Supper visibly constitutes the group of believers who eat the meal together regularly as structurally new from the old covenant community. The Lord's Supper is constitutive of the local church as one body (1 Cor 10:16–17) and as a local manifestation of the universal body of Christ.[174]

Warrant for Linking Circumcision and Baptism

Hermeneutical care is required to argue for the continuing applicability of the principle from the Old Testament that the covenant sign of entry should precede the sign of participation.[175] This section adds warrant to the claim that baptism is sufficiently analogous to circumcision to maintain the principle of continuity and thus to require baptism as prerequisite to the Lord's Supper.

---

does so distinctly. Baptism points particularly to our union with Christ, especially in his death and resurrection (see Rom 6:1–23; Gal 3:27). The Lord's Supper points particularly to the cross of Christ, the redemptive and sacrificial death of Christ for sinners" (Waters, *Lord's Supper* 5.2). More may be said, though. Whereas (assuming immersion) baptism pictures unity with Christ in his burial and resurrection specifically (Rom 6:4–5; Col 2:11–12), the Lord's Supper pictures union with Christ in terms of covenantal peace, similar to that which occurred at the covenant ratification ceremony of Exod 24:5–11, and of continuing to trust and receiving Christ as one's substitutionary sacrifice (Exod 12; Lev 16; John 1:29; Heb 9:18—10:1).

173. Waters explains "Baptism and the Lord's Supper are alike in a number of ways. Christ has instituted both. Each is an ordinance unique to the new covenant. Each is to be observed only within the new covenant community. Each serves to point the recipient to Christ and the benefits of his salvation. Each is to be observed until Christ returns at the end of the age" (Waters, *Lord's Supper* 5.1). On the church as the new covenant community, see Allison, *Sojourners and Strangers*, 78.

174. Turley concludes "The rituals create a composite where baptism provides the ritualized mechanism for establishing Christ-centered obligations while the Lord's Supper provides the ritualized space that facilitate[s] a fulfilling of such obligations" (Turley, *Ritualized Revelation of the Messianic Age*, 172). He continues, "For Paul, the [*soma*] into which the Corinthians were baptized (12:13) was reproduced every time the Lord's Supper was practiced (10:16–17)." Baptism and the Lord's Supper then are the "ritualized mechanisms" by which "a distinct Christian identity was forged."

175. Parker, "Paedocommunion, Paedobaptism, and Covenant Theology," 111; Venema, *Children at the Lord's Table?*, 88; Estelle, "Passover and the Lord's Supper," in Waters and Duncan, *Children at the Lord's Supper*, 40. Although he utilized the circumcision to Passover argument to defend the Baptist position, Abraham Booth warned against viewing OT principles and practices as directly applicable in the Gospel age. See Booth, *Pædobaptism Examined*, 140–41.

Acts 2:39

The issue of who receives the sign of entry into the respective covenants requires consideration of Acts 2:39, which pedobaptists cite in favor of maintaining the genealogical principle and, thus, of baptizing infants.[176] Because "repent and be baptized" are coordinate commands in Acts 2:38, they should normally occur together as a part of the cluster of conversion events.[177] Peter presents the dual results of responding to Christ in this manner as forgiveness of sin and receiving the "promised Holy Spirit." Thus, when Peter explains the "promise" as being "for you and for your children and for all who are far off, for everyone whom the Lord our God calls to himself" (2:39), the promise refers to the eschatological gift of forgiveness of sin and receiving the Spirit upon one's repentance/faith and baptism (cf. 1:4–5).[178]

On the surface, the phrase "for your children" (2:39) resembles the establishment of the covenant with Abraham and his "offspring after [him],

176. Several authors assume that Acts 2:39 is a reaffirmation of the genealogical principle without actually arguing the case. See Strawbridge, "Polemics of Infant Communion," in Strawbridge, *Case for Covenant Communion*, 161–63; Venema, "Covenant Theology and Baptism," 224–25. Others argue for the continuity. Two authors claim "To interpret Acts 2:39 in light of the NT Scriptures, which did not yet exist, as do many Baptists, is to engage in hermeneutical error and can only lead to a serious misrepresentation of the mind of the Spirit" (Beeke and Lanning, "Unto You," in Strawbridge, *Case for Covenantal Infant Baptism*, 57–61). Hübner observes this same hermeneutic in Calvin, Owen, Turretin, and others. See Hübner, "Acts 2:39 in Its Context (Part 1)," in Barcellos, *Recovering a Covenantal Heritage*, 420–48.

177. This observation does not require that baptism occur as temporally close in proximity as possible. However, baptism should be understood as the outward sign of conversion rather than a later step of sanctification. See Stein, "Baptism in Luke-Acts," in Schreiner and Wright, *Believer's Baptism*, 35–66. Beeke and Lanning argue that the coordinate conjunction "and" between the verbs allows that one could be baptized without repenting. However, the fact that the two commands are united by the coordinating conjunction actually emphasizes the importance of both repentance and baptism as leading to the dual benefits of forgiveness and the reception of the Holy Spirit. The authors seem to think that if a causal relationship does not exist between repentance and baptism, then neither the logical or temporal order of the actions is implied (Beeke and Lanning, "Unto You," in Strawbridge, *Case for Covenantal Infant Baptism*, 60).

178. Keener, *Acts*, 1:987. Contra Beeke and Lanning, "Unto You," in Strawbridge, *Case for Covenantal Infant Baptism*, 55. Beeke and Lanning argue "It is clear that Peter speaks of 'the promise' as rhetorical shorthand for the covenant of grace, which embodies the promise of salvation that he calls upon his hearers to embrace (see Acts 2:21)." Further, they claim that the promise is "the same as the promises made to Abraham, to David, to Israel, and even to the Gentiles. It includes the promise of the Holy Spirit and forgiveness of sins" (cf. 2:38). One problem with this interpretation is the assumption of the covenant of grace. Luke's use of "promise" language regularly refers specifically to the eschatological gift of the Holy Spirit (Luke 24:49; Acts 1:4; 2:1–4, 17, 38).

throughout their generations" (Gen 17:7–8) and the promise to "circumcise your heart and the heart of your offspring after you" (Deut 30:6). However, several factors suggest that Acts 2:39 is not a New Testament indication that the genealogical principle continues. The phrase "you and your children (*teknon*) and to all who are far off" appears to present the promise of Acts 2:38 to Peter's initial audience and to subsequent generations of people throughout time and space. As Barrett argues, *teknon* "does not mean little child, but any person, possibly quite adult, viewed in relation to his parents; offspring, or issue."[179] Four contextual features support this interpretation: (1) children (*teknon*) can also refer to distant generations; (2) "far" is often used to denote temporal distance; (3) Peter has already indicated the inclusion in the promise of "your sons and daughters," who will prophesy and receive the Spirit "in these last days" (2:17; cf. Joel 2:28);[180] and (4) the extension of the promise to all those whom "God calls to himself" (2:39). In the book of Acts God's calling comes by means of the expanding missionary work of the church (cf. 11:18; 16:14).[181]

Although the genealogical principle included the circumcision of every male either "born in your house or bought with your money" (Gen 17:12–13), the latter category is clearly absent from Peter's supposed reaffirmation of the principle.[182] Thus, the children who receive the promise appear to be Jews and Gentiles throughout time and space (cf. Joel 3:1–5) who hear the same gospel Peter preached, are called by God, respond appropriately, and so receive the Holy Spirit.[183]

Peter recognized that many of the physical seed of Abraham did not inherit the promises given to Abraham (2:22–24). Peter also recognized that Jesus was the promised offspring of Abraham (3:12–13), a prophet like

---

179. Barrett, *Acts of the Apostles*, 1:156; Schnabel, *Acts*, 165–66.

180. Keener, *Acts*, 1:987. Note also Jeremiah's promises of personal responsibility for sin and of a change to the genealogical principle coming in the new covenant by the statement "They shall no longer say: 'The fathers have eaten sour grapes and the children's teeth are set on edge'" (31:29). Verse 30 explains the change in the promise "everyone shall die for his own iniquity. Each man who eats sour grapes, his teeth shall be set on edge." Thanks to Hershael York for this observation.

181. Jewett, *Infant Baptism and the Covenant of Grace*, 119–22.

182. For a similar argument, see Baldwin, *Series of Letters*, 123–24. Presumably, if the genealogical principle remains continuous across the various administrations of the covenant of grace, and, the promise referred to in Acts 2:39 is the covenant of grace, other male members of the household should be baptized as well. Yet, pedobaptists do not usually argue this point. See Beeke and Lanning, "Unto You," in Strawbridge, *Case for Covenantal Infant Baptism*, 55–56.

183. Parker, "Paedocommunion, Paedobaptism, and Covenant Theology," 110; Barrett, *Acts of the Apostles*, 1:156.

Moses (3:18–22), the Son of David (2:32–36), and the Isaianic servant (3:18, 26) who would bless and restore the world with times of refreshing. Therefore, Peter called Jews and, eventually, Gentiles to repent and have faith in Jesus in order to receive blessing, forgiveness, and restoration instead of destruction/condemnation from God (2:38; 3:16–26; cf. 10:42–48). Luke's biblical-theological and covenantal connections function, in part, to make clear that the recipients of the new covenant signs are the same group that receives the blessings of the new covenant by faith.[184]

Additionally, if baptism were intended to replace circumcision in terms of its recipients, the Jerusalem council of Acts 15 would have provided an appropriate venue in which the apostles could have made that claim.[185] Instead, the apostles flatly rejected the ongoing relevance of circumcision for Gentile Christians by claiming that God had given the Holy Spirit to the Gentiles (vv. 8–10)[186] and that in Christ God was restoring the tent of Da-

---

184. As Acts 3:25–26 states, "You are the sons of the prophets and of the covenant that God made with your fathers, saying to Abraham, 'And in your offspring shall all the families of the earth by blessed.' God, having raised up his servant, sent him to you first, to bless you by turning every one of you from your wickedness." This text explicitly presents the Isaianic servant as the offspring of Abraham who brings the blessing. The means of entering that blessing is explicitly stated as turning from wickedness. The turning of v. 26 is surely the same reality as the repentance of v. 19, which results in having "your sins . . . blotted out." The repentance/turning of vv. 19 and 26 is the same response Peter connects with baptism in 2:38. The point is that the immediate context of Acts 2:39 presents Christ as the "appointed" Messiah (v. 20), upon whom all the covenantal promises of the OT find their fulfillment. By entering into covenant with Christ through repentance/faith and baptism, sinners receive all the blessings promised in the OT (cf. 1 Cor 1:20). Thus, Beeke and Lanning's argument is problematic when they write "To interpret Acts 2:39 in light of the NT Scriptures, which did not yet exist, as do many Baptists, is to engage in hermeneutical error and can only lead to a serious misrepresentation of the mind of the Spirit" (Beeke and Lanning, "Unto You," in Strawbridge, Case for Covenantal Infant Baptism, 57). One problem with this argument is that it fails to account for Peter's own understanding of the flow of redemptive history and interpretation of Pentecost. Furthermore, because Luke is the human author responsible for recording both Acts 2:39 and the context of chaps. 1–3, their argument is self-defeating. One does not have to bring in "the NT Scriptures, which did not yet exist" in order to make a consistent, contextual argument for how Peter, Luke, and the Holy Spirit intended Christians to understand Acts 2:39. As soon as the book of Acts was published, 2:39 could only be rightly understood in light of the whole book of Acts, and all of Luke-Acts for that matter.

185. Saucy, Church in God's Program, 207; Wellum, "Relationship between the Covenants," in Schreiner and Wright, Believer's Baptism, 157. Wellum cites Jewett, Infant Baptism and the Covenant of Grace, 228–32.

186. Although circumcision was not required for entry into the new covenant community, Peter administered baptism to those who evidenced their participation in the new covenant through reception of the Holy Spirit by faith (Acts 10:43–48; 11:15–18; 15:8–9). Barrett recounts, "In the story, the mark of Cornelius's acceptance

vid through Christ in the new covenant (vv. 15–19; cf. Amos 9:11–12).[187] Therefore, Acts 2:39 is best understood not to support infant baptism,[188] but instead to further express the eschatological nature and international scope of the new covenant community until Christ returns.

---

was baptism. . . . Baptism was a bath and could therefore be associated with cleansing; cf. 22:16. This is not however an image that Luke regularly uses (for him baptism is primarily a rite of initiation), and the cleansing of the heart probably means for him the forgiveness of sins (cf. 13:38) and inward renewal with a view to future obedience. Baptism is not viewed as the Christian replacement of circumcision" (Barrett, *Acts of the Apostles*, 2:717).

187. D. Fuller argues that the transition from circumcision to baptism as a covenant marker for the church began with John the Baptist. By calling circumcised Jews to cease dependence on being children of Abraham (Luke 3:8) and be baptized in preparation for the coming Messiah, John was leading his disciples to effectively renounce their dependence on the law and depend on the Messiah for their right standing with God. Fuller's argument here is uncommon. He writes, "A Jew who submitted to John's baptism was acknowledging that as far as salvation was concerned, he was in the same category [as a Gentile convert]; his connection with Abraham as symbolized by circumcision was of no value whatsoever. Therefore, it was appropriate that the church, composed of people who, like Abraham, had a genuine righteousness from God, should have a different sign of that righteousness. It was also fitting that the church, which was in a continuity inaugurated by John the Baptist should adopt as this sign the rite of baptism by which he had signified to disobedient Israel that it had no more favor before God than did Gentile sinners" (Fuller, *Unity of the Bible*, 369–70). Although Fuller's argument somewhat depends on the assumption that Jewish proselyte washings lie in the background of the NT practice of baptism, the tenor of his argument fits with the discussion of John's baptism in chapter 3. See Köstenberger, "Baptism in the Gospels," in Schreiner and Wright, *Believer's Baptism*, 15. Contra Wilson, *To a Thousand Generations*, 61–62. Wilson argues that because Acts 21:21 implies that Jewish Christians continued to circumcise their children, their example of placing a sign of covenant initiation on their infant sons after the coming of Christ implies the legitimacy of infant baptism after the coming of Christ. But this argument fails to account for how Gentile Christians would have made the connection from circumcision to baptism and from infants to believers, given that the new covenant was already inaugurated and the Jerusalem council did not burden the Gentiles with circumcision. Malone calls Wilson's argument novel. See the full critique in Malone, *Baptism of Disciples Alone*, 108–11.

188. Some inconsistency exists on the use of Acts 2:39 to justify and explain pedobaptism. Venema claims that infant baptism "has the same meaning as the baptism of adult believers" (Venema, "Paedocommunion and the Reformed Confessions," in Waters and Duncan, *Children and the Lord's Supper*, 130). Yet, Thomas claims the grounding for infant baptism stems from a different basis in adults than infants. He writes, "The ground of baptism is thereby the same for both adults and for children: covenantal inclusion, the parent on the basis of professed faith; the child on the basis of familial solidarity" (Thomas, "Not a Particle of Sound Brain," in Waters and Duncan, *Children and the Lord's Supper*, 105). It is difficult to see how the one baptism can actually have the same meaning as the other given the different bases.

Romans 4:11

When Paul claims that Abraham received the "sign of circumcision as a seal of the righteousness that he had by faith while he was still uncircumcised," covenant theologians often claim warrant for viewing baptism as symbolizing the same spiritual truths.[189] However, viewing circumcision as forward looking in this manner obscures Paul's argument in Romans 4. Paul is arguing that God counted Abraham righteous on the basis of his faith and not because of the physical sign of circumcision. Paul wants his readers to understand that, given the continuance of circumcision under the Mosaic law, not even Abraham was justified before God by circumcision. Thus, Christians should not view obedience to the law as a means of justification. The sign of circumcision signified and sealed neither Abraham's faith,[190] nor the promise to justify all of Abraham's offspring who believe.[191] Rather, Paul claims that God gave circumcision as a seal of the righteousness Abraham had by faith before Abraham's circumcision.[192] Circumcision was a sign and seal for Abraham specifically (and not his offspring), that God had credited him with righteousness by virtue of his trust in God's promise (Rom 4:1–22).[193]

Thus, it is illegitimate to read Romans 4:11 back onto Genesis 17 as grounds that circumcision for infants sealed a promise that God would save them when they trust in Christ. It was no doubt true that God would justify and save all who trusted his promises (cf. Gen 3:15; 12:1–3; Heb 11; Gal 3:8). However, the initial giving of circumcision did not signify that promise

---

189. David Gibson, for instance, claims, "I take Paul's meaning to be that 'circumcision is the authenticating mark that certifies the truth of God's promise that he will give righteousness to the one who has faith. 'Circumcision' is sign and seal that God justifies the wicked (Rom 4:5). Since the 'sign and seal' have reference to the same reality according to Rom 4:11–12, circumcision should also be understood as a seal of the promise of God's grace to be received by faith, not of the faith that received the promise of grace" (Gibson, "Sacramental Supersessionism Revisited," 196). See also Ross, "Baptism and Circumcision," 97.

190. Salter, "Does Baptism Replace Circumcision?," 20.

191. Gibson, "Sacramental Supersessionism Revisited," 196.

192. Contra Wilson, *To a Thousand Generations*, 44–45, who views the righteousness as that of Christ rather than righteousness that was already imputed to Abraham.

193. Wellum, "Relationship between the Covenants," in Schreiner and Wright, *Believer's Baptism*, 154. Allison writes, "The sign was unique to Abraham, for following him circumcision was administered both to those who believed like Abraham and to those who did not (e.g., Ishmael; 17:20–27) (Allison, *Sojourners and Strangers*, 349). See also Deenick, *Righteous by Promise*, 181–82; Baldwin, *Baptism of Believers Only*, 274.

to Abraham's offspring but rather to Abraham.[194] This line of reasoning, and the biblical-theological section above, require that baptism should not be viewed as a promissory sign and seal to save the person being baptized upon their future faith.[195] Rather, if one wants to argue for continuity between circumcision and baptism in Romans 4:11, it is found in the way the old covenant sign of covenant entry sealed for Abraham and the new covenant sign of entry seals for the new covenant believer the reality of justification.[196]

194. This point helps to clarify some of the confusion present in Ross, "Baptism and Circumcision as Signs and Seals," in Strawbridge, Case for Covenantal Infant Baptism, 91. Ross recognizes the dilemma present in the fact that Abraham possessed righteousness by faith while Ishmael did not. Yet, he seems to suggest that circumcision could not have served as a sign of Abraham's righteousness by faith due to Ishmael's lack of faith and righteousness. He argues further, "whatever meaning circumcision had for Abraham, it had also for Ishmael and for every other male in Abraham's household circumcised on the same day as Abraham (Gen 17:23)" (92). He adds, "If we understand Abraham's circumcision to certify that he had faith, or that God had given him righteousness, then we are at a loss to explain what Ishmael's circumcision meant." The most obvious problem with this view is that Ross appears to deny Paul's clear teaching in Rom 4:11. Paul states that Abraham "received the sign of circumcision as a seal of the righteousness that he had by faith while he was still uncircumcised." He also misses the clear distinction the Lord makes between Ishmael and the seed of promise (Gen 17:18–21). From the establishment of circumcision, God distinguished between a merely physical seed of Abraham and the physical but special seed of promise. Thus, circumcision itself carried different significance for Ishmael than for Isaac. Ishmael's circumcision did not even mark him as part of the ethnic nation to come from Abraham. Ishmael's circumcision signified God's promise to make him "fruitful and multiply him," as he was one of the physical seed of Abraham (v. 20). However, Ishmael's circumcision did not signify God's promise to bring blessing and salvation to the world through him, as it did with Isaac. Ross's solution to Ishmael's lack of righteousness by faith is to view circumcision as a seal of God's promise to give righteousness to those who believe (94). But this interpretation would only solve Ross' invented need for circumcision to seal the exact same spiritual realities for all parties circumcised with Abraham. Again, Paul claims Abraham was already counted righteous by faith before he was circumcised. Circumcision sealed that reality for Abraham specifically.

195. The theology worked out here does not delegitimize Gibson's critique that "in the modern varieties of credobaptism, where baptism is subsequent to conversion, sometimes after several years . . . it appears that the covenant sign of justification has become a functional sign of sanctification." While a proposal for remedying this unfortunate scenario will come in chapter 6, a comment on the relationship of baptism and justification is in order. Paul is teaching that Abraham's justification came prior to his reception of the sign of covenant entry. Whatever the credobaptist errors of practice may be in discerning the sincerity of a professing believer, a simple comparison of Abraham's circumcision to new covenant baptism at this point suggests that at least baptism should flow from faith in Christ rather than occurring before it (Gibson, "Sacramental Supersessionism Revisited," 206).

196. In the NT, the Holy Spirit is the only explicit "seal" of the believer's salvation (Eph 1:13; 2 Cor 1:22). Nevertheless, the continuity explored above and the discussion of Matt 28:28–20 in chapter 3 grounds the affirmation here that baptism can be

Colossians 2:11–12

The only place in the New Testament in which circumcision and baptism are explicitly connected is Colossians 2:11–12.[197] Colossians 2:11–12 presents heart circumcision as the antitypical fulfillment of physical circumcision in the old covenant and baptism as the "external sign of testimony to heart circumcision . . . [for every] member (male and female!) of the new covenant."[198] Specifically, this passage clarifies the prospective, typological role of circumcision from Abraham until Christ's inauguration of the new covenant in comparison to the (at least logically) reflective role of baptism on the prior reality of heart circumcision. This section argues for these theological connections by (1) providing a brief exegesis of the passage; (2) examining the allusions to heart circumcision; (3) presenting the relationship between circumcision and baptism as prospective and reflective of heart circumcision respectively; and (4) explaining the elaborative role of baptism as a new covenant sign.

In Colossians 2:11 Paul describes the Colossians, saying, "you were circumcised with a circumcision made without hands, by putting of the body of the flesh, by the circumcision of Christ." The circumcision in question is not the physical removal of the foreskin, as Paul makes explicit in the phrase, "made without hands." Instead, this circumcision is described as "the putting off of the flesh" and a circumcision "of Christ." Commentators debate whether the phrase "circumcision of Christ" is subjective genitive—circumcision performed by Christ on the human heart[199] or objective genitive—circumcision that Christ received when he died for sin on the cross.[200] "Either way, circumcision finds its fulfillment in being joined to

---

considered a seal (Horton, *People and Place*, 209; Jones, *Waters of Promise*, 134).

197. Beale, *New Testament Biblical Theology*, 803.

198. Meade, "Circumcision of Flesh," in Wellum and Parker, *Progressive Covenantalism*, 157.

199. Representatives of this view are Meade, "Circumcision of Flesh," in Wellum and Parker, *Progressive Covenantalism*, 149; Melick, *Philippians, Colossians, Philemon*, 258; Barcellos, "Exegetical Appraisal of Colossians 2:11–12," in Barcellos, *Recovering a Covenantal Heritage*, 459; Beale, *New Testament Biblical Theology*, 806n13; Salter, "Does Baptism Replace Circumcision?," 24.

200. Representatives of this view are Deenick, *Righteous by Promise*, 135. Deenick argues that the circumcision made without hands also occurs in believers by virtue of union with Christ, though the passage is referring primarily to Christ's own "circumcision" through his death on the cross. See also Thompson, *Colossians and Philemon*, 56–57; Garland, *Colossians and Philemon*, 157; Schreiner, *Paul*, 82.

Christ and experiencing the promises associated with the inauguration of the new covenant age."[201]

Paul's further describes the main verb, "you were circumcised" (v. 11), as "having been buried with him in baptism, in which you were also raised with him through faith in the powerful working of God" (v. 12). The modifying participle of verse 12 suggests an outward, reflective role for baptism of picturing the circumcision of Christ, given that the circumcision was made without hands (v. 11).[202] Thus, the circumcision the church at Colossae had received came somehow through the removal of the body of the flesh, Christ (v. 11), baptism, and faith in God's resurrecting power (v. 12).[203] That Paul intends circumcision of the heart which the Old Testament promised (Deut 30:6) by saying "you were circumcised" deserves further elaboration, as do the means of circumcision.

The descriptions of circumcision as the "putting off the body of the flesh" and the "circumcision of Christ" allude to God's promised eschatological circumcision of Deuteronomy 30:6 (cf. Ezek 36:26–27).[204] Elsewhere in Paul, "the flesh" is regularly associated with a human's covenantal status in Adam that is opposed to God and fails to obey from the heart (Rom 5:12–21; 7:5—8:13; 1 Cor 15:20–23; Gal 5:16–25).[205] In other words,

---

201. Gentry and Wellum, *Kingdom through Covenant*, 702.

202. Garland uses "represents" to describe baptism's relationship to circumcision of the heart (Garland, *Colossians and Philemon*, 157). Thompson describes baptism as "a parabolic enactment of faith, a symbolic narrative" in Thompson, *Colossians and Philemon*, 57. Venema argues, "Baptism now represents the spiritual 'circumcision made without hands, in the removal of the body of the flesh.' . . . The spiritual blessings represented by circumcision in the old covenant are now represented by baptism in the new covenant" (Venema, "Covenant Theology and Baptism," in Srawbridge, *Case for Covenantal Infant Baptism*, 222). The first half of this quotation agrees with the argument of this book. However, Venema's claim that circumcision represented the same reality is redemptive-historically impossible. Heart circumcision is a new covenant benefit. Venema nowhere argues how or why circumcision carried this significance.

203. Ross is correct that "water baptism itself does not accomplish" the heart circumcision or resurrection with Christ (Ross, "Baptism and Circumcision as Signs and Seals," in Srawbridge, *Case for Covenantal Infant Baptism*, 103). However, he provides no evidence for the claim that baptism in v. 12 does not refer to water baptism. He writes, "The baptism in view in v. 12 is just as spiritual as the circumcision in v. 11." Some evidence would be required to justify this claim given that water baptism is in view in Paul's other uses of the term (Rom 6:3–4; 1 Cor 1:14–17; 12:13; Gal 3:26).

204. Thus, it is appropriate to think of the Colossian Christians as an eschatologically renewed Israel by virtue of their union with the Messiah. See Beale, *New Testament Biblical Theology*, 806–7. For the typological connection, see Meade, "Circumcision of Flesh," in Wellum and Parker, *Progressive Covenantalism*, 149; Meyer, *End of the Law*, 265.

205. For an argument that flesh here does not refer to the physical body of Christ

putting off the body of the flesh in Colossians 2:11 is the same reality Paul describes as "the circumcision of the heart" in Romans 2:29 and which the Philippian Christians—"the circumcision" (Phil 3:3)—had experienced.[206] Putting off the body of the flesh is the act of the Spirit, whereby he applies Christ's sin conquering work of the cross and resurrection to the believer and removes the sin-dominated old nature.[207] The circumcision in question happened to the Colossians.[208] The circumcision of Christ then, as applied to the believer, includes the removal of the old, sinful nature that impedes loving obedience to Christ from the heart and the act of setting apart the believer to a life of loving obedience.[209] What remains to be seen is the connection of heart circumcision to baptism.

Meade argues that the "verb plus participle" syntax in "you were circumcised . . . having been buried in baptism" presents baptism as having "an elaborative role to the action of the main verb." In other words, "heart circumcision is the overarching biblical category in which baptism is subsumed."[210] As such baptism is not the antitype of circumcision of the

---

crucified on the cross, see Salter, "Does Baptism Replace Circumcision?," 22–24. Garrett argues that because Paul describes circumcision as "done without hands," the circumcision of Christ should not be understood as a physical act, even a physical act of crucifixion to Christ and a resulting spiritual act of circumcision to believers (Garrett, "Meredith Kline," in Schreiner and Wright, *Believer's Baptism*, 268. Contra the subthesis in Deenick, *Righteous by Promise*).

206. Thus, the flesh is rightly associated with the human nature dominated by sin, apart from Christ, which has been crucified with Christ covenantally when a sinner is united to Christ by faith (Gal 2:20). This crucifixion of the flesh, with Christ in his death, leads to the impartation of new life and the entrance of the justified sinner into the new creation (Col 3:6–9; 2 Cor 4:6; 5:17). Meade, "Circumcision of Flesh," in Wellum and Parker, *Progressive Covenantalism*, 145–48; Schreiner, *Paul*, 81–82, 280–81. Contra Billings, *Remembrance, Communion, and Hope*, 68.

207. Melick, *Philippians, Colossians, Philemon*, 258.

208. Salter, "Does Baptism Replace Circumcision?," 23–24; Meyer, *End of the Law*, 262n67.

209. With Meade, "the circumcision performed by Christ prepares or devotes the church to Christ" (Meade, "Circumcision of Flesh," in Wellum and Parker, *Progressive Covenantalism*, 149). Beale claims, "Paul's reference of the 'removal of the body of the flesh' is likely also part of the allusion to Gen 17, where too 'flesh' is part of the description of the symbolic sinful condition directly preceding circumcision" (Beale, *New Testament Biblical Theology*, 806–8). Beale describes the separation from sinful domination of the world to new life in Christ as two sides of the same coin.

210. Meade, "Circumcision of Flesh," in Wellum and Parker, *Progressive Covenantalism*, 150. Similarly, see also Garrett, "Meredith Kline," 269; Beale, *New Testament Biblical Theology*, 809–10. Contra Beasley-Murray's claim, "It would seem that in the Christian church baptism has replaced circumcision through its mediation of the spiritual circumcision demanded by the prophets" (Beasley-Murray, *Baptism in the New Testament*, 159). But note Meade's biblical-theological nuance. Meade argues that

heart, because, "Identifying the covenantal correspondence between types and antitypes is what ultimately separates a type from two events that are merely analogous to or 'like' one another (cf. 2 Pet 2:1)."[211] If the internal, circumcision of the heart is the antitype of physical circumcision, and Paul does not tie heart circumcision to faith as he does baptism (vv. 11–12), then "baptism through faith elaborates or works out the inner circumcision of the heart."[212]

Baptism's function as an initiating oath sign of entry into the new covenant is maintained by the explanation above. However, Meade's description of heart circumcision as "the sign for all members of the new covenant who are true Jews in God's kingdom" moves against the thesis.[213] After making a similar affirmation about the supposed sign function of heart circumcision, Greever states, "Faith in Jesus Christ would be the mark of membership in this new covenant."[214] Claiming that either the internal circumcision of the

---

describing circumcision of the heart as "spiritual circumcision" is an unfortunate term, because the biblical categories are more precisely "sign, visible, shadow, type, antitype, hidden, and substance" (149).

211. Emadi and Sequeira, "Biblical-Theological Exegesis," 24.

212. Meade, "Circumcision of Flesh," in Wellum and Parker, *Progressive Covenantalism*, 151; Schreiner, "Baptism in the Epistles," in Schreiner and Wright, *Believer's Baptism*, 78–79. The theological relationship between heart circumcision and baptism claimed here makes Melick's argument that "the body of the flesh . . . has been put away at baptism" appear confused (Melick, *Philippians, Colossians, Philemon*, 258–59). Melick is correct if he intends that baptism, as the outward elaboration of heart circumcision is the formal act of putting off the body of the flesh. However, the separation that Melick posits between the circumcision of the heart and baptism throughout his discussion of Col 2 makes this statement appear to give baptism a stronger role than Melick would actually affirm.

213. Meade, "Circumcision of Flesh," 157. While it is true that one's life should demonstrate the reality of possessing a circumcised heart through external works of faith (Jas 2:14; Gal 5:6), these works of faith are not said to be signs. Meade does not argue that good works are signs, but the designation allows for the argument. Bunyan would have concurred, as is evident in his continual insistence that the Lord's Supper is for all who are "visible saints" regardless of baptism (Bunyan, "Reason of My Practice in Worship," in Offor, *Bunyan's Works*, 2:605).

214. Greever, "Nature of the New Covenant," 75–76. Greever's full statement is, "If there was to be a covenantal solution for the Gentiles, as Paul later argues, it would be a different kind of covenant with a different sign. Indeed, it would be a new covenant whose sign was not outward and something handmade but something inward, supernatural, and divinely-made, or as Paul can describe it elsewhere, a circumcision of the heart (Col 2:11). Hence, the mark of membership in this new covenant would not be defined along the same genealogical and ethnic lines as defined within the old covenant, but along the lines of changed hearts that trust and hope in the Lord." But which is it? Does the NT present circumcision of the heart or faith as the sign/mark of the new covenant? Unless Greever intends to distinguish a covenant sign from a covenant mark, and the context suggests he is (unintentionally) equivocating, they cannot

heart or faith in Jesus is "the sign" or mark of the new covenant suggests that one may enter the new covenant formally, officially without the external sign of baptism.[215] While the direction of Meade's argument is to affirm that only those who have received heart circumcision should be baptized, he does not balance this important point with the need for baptism for all who do experience heart circumcision. John Bunyan explicitly agreed with the claim that circumcision of the heart, made evident in works of love, is all that churches should require for participation in communion.[216] Yet, the New Testament regularly presents baptism as part and parcel of one's initial faith in Christ at conversion.

Meade's and Greever's willingness to describe heart circumcision as the sign of the new covenant moves against the normal function of covenantal signs throughout Scripture and in Colossians 2:11–13. As DeRouchie argues, the Old Testament signs of the rainbow, physical circumcision, and the Sabbath functioned in part as an external means of reminding the covenant parties of the promises and obligations.[217] As chapter 2 argued, circumcision also functioned as a forward-looking symbol and an identity marker. Consistent with these functions of signs in the Old Testament, baptism functions as a divine and human initiating oath sign, a symbol of elaborating a now-present reality of internal heart circumcision, and as an identity marker (Matt 28:18–20; Col 2:11–13; Gal 3:26–28).[218] To claim that the internal realities of heart circumcision or the response faith is the sign of the new covenant is to introduce a sign into the biblical storyline that lacks the functions associated with signs throughout Scripture.

---

both be understood as "the mark of membership in the new covenant." Greever further confuses matters by claiming "Circumcision of the heart is the mark of membership for God's [new covenant] people" (87). Even following Greever's own logic of his otherwise clear and helpful article, "the mark" cannot be both heart circumcision and faith in Christ.

215. Meade's and Greever's affirmation on this point is contra Wellum, "Means of Grace: Baptism," in Armstrong, *Compromised Church*, 159. Wellum argues, "Thus Christian baptism . . . signifies nothing less than the fact that the believer has entered into the full realities of the new covenant."

216. Bunyan, "Reason of My Practice in Worship," in Offor, *Bunyan's Works*, 2:607.

217. DeRouchie, "Circumcision in the Hebrew Bible and Targums," 184–85. On the categories of mnemonic meaning of signs, DeRouchie follows Fox, "Sign of the Covenants," 562–67.

218. Beale comments, "Spiritual 'circumcision made without hands' and 'baptism' are ongoing realities designating entrance into the covenant community" (Beale, *New Testament Biblical Theology*, 809). Wellum writes, "In this new era, the new covenantal sign, baptism, has been established to testify to the gospel and to identify one as having become the spiritual seed of Abraham, through faith in Messiah Jesus" (Wellum, "Relationship between the Covenants," in Schreiner and Wright, *Believer's Baptism*, 157).

The heart circumcision that Christ brings in connection with his new covenant work reveals what circumcision's proper *telos* was always intended to be.[219] Both old covenant physical circumcision and new covenant heart circumcision function to initiate one into God's people. Yet, because heart circumcision is internal, it cannot function as a visible sign the way physical circumcision did.[220] Therefore, in accord with all the New Testament data, Paul in Colossians 2:12 presents baptism as the external sign of entry into the new covenant people of God.[221] Although baptism is not the antitype of circumcision, it does function in an analogically similar way.[222] The clear indication is that only those united to Christ, with circumcised hearts,

219. Meade, "Circumcision of Flesh," in Wellum and Parker, *Progressive Covenantalism*, 152. Gibson holds a different view of typology at this point. He carefully and helpfully distinguishes the ways in which covenantal theologians use replacement terminology. He writes, "It is in this way that the reformed use supercessionist terminology in relation to circumcision and baptism. Baptism replaces circumcision, not by fulfilling it, but rather by being the new sign of the same thing that both signify. Using replacement language is simply theological shorthand for the fundamental unity of covenant signs. It is not intended in the sense of baptism 'fulfilling' circumcision nor as a complete description of every aspect of the relationship between the signs. Indeed, reformed texts state that baptism replaces circumcision precisely because they understand that spiritual circumcision fulfills physical circumcision" (Gibson, "Sacramental Supersessionism Revisited," 207). Similar is Beale, *New Testament Biblical Theology*, 809. Beale even claims "Baptism is the redemptive-historical and typological equivalent to circumcision" (816). The approach taken in this book, following *Kingdom through Covenant*, is that types are properly understood as pointing to and fulfilled in Christ, as their *telos*. Therefore, while the sign of baptism does maintain some continuity with circumcision, it should not be said to replace it, even as a new covenant sign of that to which the old covenant sign pointed. See Parker, "Israel-Christ-Church Relationship."

220. Malone, *Baptism of Disciples Alone*, 117–23.

221. As in Acts, Paul presents the Spirit's work on the human heart as that which leads him or her to faith in Christ demonstrated in baptism (cf. Acts 2:41; 8:12; 9:17–18; 10:43–48; 16:31–34; 18:8; 22:14–16). Meade helpfully addresses several counterpoints from Reformed theology to make this argument (Meade, "Circumcision of Flesh," in Wellum and Parker, *Progressive Covenantalism*, 153–56). Melick's claim that Paul does not actually intend water baptism here, but rather "the spiritual meaning that undergirds it" appears to be special pleading (Melick, *Philippians, Colossians, Philemon*, 260). By his interpretation, Melick allows a similar disjunction between a theology of baptism and the practice of baptism similar to that of John Bunyan. Melick claims that no evidence exists for the conclusion that "baptism into Christ actually occurs at water baptism." While Melick's attempt to avoid sacramental interpretations of baptism is laudable so far as he seeks to protect justification by faith alone, he dismisses much NT evidence (Gal 3:27; 1 Cor 12:13).

222. So Beale, *New Testament Biblical Theology*, 808. Analogous means that the signs perform a similar function without existing in a typological relationship. They are "like one another." See Emadi and Sequeira, "Biblical-Theological Exegesis and the Nature of Typology," 24; Wellum, "Relationship between the Covenants," in Schreiner and Wright, *Believer's Baptism*, 157.

expressing faith in Christ, should be baptized. While physical circumcision in the Old Testament pointed prospectively as a type toward circumcision of the heart that God performs on every new covenant member, baptism reflectively/retrospectively signifies circumcision of the heart that produces both faith in Christ and baptism.[223]

In sum, while physical circumcision was a sign that did not equal the thing signified—heart circumcision—baptism is the New Testament sign of possessing the thing signified. In this sense, baptism and circumcision entail the same reality, yet in different ways. While circumcision points to heart circumcision prospectively, as an eschatological promise, baptism signifies heart circumcision reflectively as an inaugurated eschatological reality.[224] This one continuity is insufficient to overturn the other discontinuities surveyed above; therefore, it does not warrant the application of the sign of baptism being given to the children of new covenant members.[225] However, the continuity between circumcision and baptism does suggest that one should not only possess a circumcised heart as prerequisite to participation in the Lord's Supper. Rather, one should also have received the elaborative sign of heart circumcision—baptism—as prerequisite to the Lord's Supper.

Summary and Conclusion

This chapter makes the case that because circumcision was required for participation in Passover, believer's baptism by immersion should be required for participation in the Lord's Supper due to the continuity that exists between circumcision and baptism. As signs of entry into their respective covenants, circumcision and baptism are sufficiently analogous in their

223. Wellum, "Relationship between the Covenants," in Schreiner and Wright, *Believer's Baptism*, 159. Malone writes, "Therefore, circumcision was a prospective sign of the need of heart-circumcision, while baptism is a retrospective sign of that heart-circumcision already received and confessed" (Malone, *Baptism of Disciples Alone*, 117). Similarly, see Renihan, "Abrahamic Covenant," in Barcellos, *Recovering a Covenantal Heritage*, 170; Hammett, *Forty Questions*, 145–48. Venema claims, "Baptism now represents spiritual circumcision made without hands" (Venema, "Covenant Theology and Baptism," in Strawbridge, *Case for Covenantal Infant Baptism*, 222). On this point, he and this book agree. He demurs from the analysis of this chapter on the recipients of baptism and their need to personally exercise saving faith.

224. On this point, I agree with Gibson, at least in the way I have stated it. See Gibson, "Sacramental Supersessionism Revisited," 200. See also Schreiner, "Baptism in the Epistles," in Schreiner and Wright, *Believer's Baptism*, 78–79. Wilson flattens the ways in which circumcision and baptism entail heart circumcision and misses the unique covenantal associations of each sign (Wilson, *To a Thousand Generations*, 73–77).

225. Contra Gibson, "Sacramental Supersessionism Revisited," 201.

covenantal function in comparison to Passover and the Lord's Supper to warrant the continuation of the principle that the sign of entry is prerequisite to the sign of participation.

Chapter 5

Defending Close Communion

THE PURPOSE OF THIS chapter is to provide a response to the alternative answers to the question of who can participate in communion: open communion advocates, closed communion advocates, and ecumenical communion advocates. In order to provide a defense of close communion, this chapter responds to the strongest arguments of each position, surveyed in chapter 1. In order to provide a more thorough application to contemporary Baptist life, this chapter interacts with historical and contemporary Baptist representatives of each view. The chapter begins with a summary of the hermeneutical significance of this book's thesis before responding to the other three views.

Summary of Close Communion Argument

This work argues that believer's baptism by immersion should precede communion as prerequisite to it, due to the explicit example of the New Testament, the assumed pattern that all believers are baptized, and a principle of analogy (continuity) from the necessity of circumcision before Passover. Notable among the arguments against close communion is the charge that while the Jewish law required circumcision as prerequisite to Passover, the New Testament nowhere enjoins this rule upon the church.[1] This project argues that no such rule is required to establish the expectation that baptism should precede the Supper. Instead, the biblical-theological function of covenant signs, when combined with the assumption that believers are baptized in order to enter the church, demonstrates sufficient continuity between the

---

1. Hall Jr., *On Terms of Communion*, 34–35; Allison, *Sojourners and Strangers*, 403.

signs of initiation and the signs of participation to warrant the conclusion of close communion.[2]

In order to argue against the thesis, one could raise a *prima facia* defeater argument borrowed from the pedobaptist pedocommunion debate. Pedocommunion advocates argue that because children, even infants, participated in Passover, the children of believers (covenant children) should be allowed to participate in the Lord's Supper.[3] The pedocommunion argument is distantly similar in that this book also argues that New Testament Christians can and should learn about who may participate in communion by examining who participated in Passover. Pedobaptists who hold to credo-communion rightly critique the pedocommunion position for assuming an "illegitimate totality transfer" in its hermeneutical methodology.[4] However, the pedocommunion argument is less similar to the thesis than it may appear.

Because the pedocommunion debate is intramural among pedobaptists, it begins by making assumptions this book rejects: (1) pedobaptism; (2) the continuation of the genealogical principle; and (3) the whole covenant of grace superstructure. The thesis of this book avoids illegitimately assuming that all the instruction pertaining to the Passover applies directly to the Lord's Supper by carefully distinguishing those aspects of circumcision and Passover that are discontinuous with baptism and the Lord's Supper. Distinguishing these matters was the purpose of chapter 4. Stated differently, this project has sought to establish a biblical-theological principle. The steps taken include (1) considering the covenant signs in their

2. Finn presents this point briefly in Finn, "Baptism as a Prerequisite to the Lord's Supper," 6. For an explanation of how the methodology utilized in this book is needed to provide biblical warrant, see Gentry and Wellum, *Kingdom through Covenant*, 603–4.

3. See the essays cited throughout chapter 5 of this book from Strawbridge, *Case for Covenant Communion*.

4. Estelle, "Passover and the Lord's Supper," in Waters and Duncan, *Children and the Lord's Supper*, 40. Estelle is critiquing Leithart, "Sacramental Hermeneutics and the Ceremonies of Israel," in Strawbridge, *Case for Covenant Communion*, 111–29. Leithart's hermeneutic surpasses merely claiming that because infants participated in Passover, children/infants should participate in the Lord's Supper. Leithart claims, "For Paul, the Passover was not only about the death and resurrection of Jesus but also about the continuing practices in the life of the church. Rather than seeing the bread of the Passover fulfilled in the gift of Jesus as bread (as in John 6), Paul immediately equates the 'unleavened lump' with the church (vv. 6–7). First Cor 5 thus indicates once again that Augustine's notion of the *totus Christus* was central to Paul's reading of the Old Testament" (122). Thus, Leithart misunderstands the typological relation of Passover and Israel to Christ. He would have the church today consider itself as belonging to the person of Christ (*totus Christus*) rather than being covenantally united to Christ and to one another derivatively. For a thorough critique of Leithart's approach, see Parker, "Paedocommunion, Paedobaptism, and Covenant Theology," 91–122.

respective covenantal context; (2) noting the ways in which the instruction about the old covenant signs leads to Christ; and (3) explicating the newness of the new covenant in its relation to the church. This work assumes that by following these steps, the principle of continuity (analogy) that the sign of entry should precede the sign of participation is established and legitimately warranted for continue application in the new covenant age.[5] This principle then grounds close communion as a biblical practice.

Because this book builds on the defense of close communion propounded by multiple, historical Baptists, the relation of this book's thesis to their work deserves comment before moving to defend close communion against the other three views. In so far as Kiffin, Booth, Baldwin, Fuller, and Kinghorn inadvertently expound a biblical theology in their writings, the thesis of this book is largely similar in its conclusions and slightly different in its methodology. Chapter 1 demonstrated that multiple close communion advocates argued that the analogical relationship between circumcision and Passover, when combined with other arguments, warrants the close communion position. Although none of the writers surveyed sought, in any elongated defense, to demonstrate the legitimacy of the analogy between the old covenant and new covenant signs, they affirmed the analogy just the same.[6] Baldwin and Booth even made covenantal arguments for believer's baptism. However, their theology represents the covenantal Baptist view,

---

5. As N. T. Wright argues, the way in which Bible readers today should interpret the Bible is the way in which the Bible itself exemplifies Bible reading. One must know "where we are within the overall drama and what is appropriate within each act." Furthermore, one's understanding of Scripture and how to relate to Scripture should be based on an "overarching narrative which makes sense of the texts" (Wright, *Last Word: Beyond the Bible Wars*, 121). With this biblical-theological hermeneutic in mind, Daniel Doriani's principle of interpretation bears repetition: "Where a clear series of acts by the faithful create a pattern, and God or the narrator approves the pattern, [the pattern of acts] directs believers, even if no law spells out the lesson" (Doriani, "Redemptive-Historical Model," in Meadors, *Four Views*, 89). In practice, Doriani seems to agree largely with Richard Lints' call to utilize three horizons of interpretation: the textual horizon, the epochal horizon, and the canonical horizon (Lints, *Fabric of Theology*, 293). Lints' method takes into account the progress of revelation throughout the biblical storyline and understands Scripture's structure, "symbols, and images" to "be considered part of the very fabric of the meaning" (298). Interpreting Scripture in this manner seeks both to maintain a canonically sensitive and genre attune form of principlizing the text. Additionally, this method aims to detect the relationship between ethical demands and narrative patterns. Then, the principles, ethical demands, and patterns may be understood in light of the canonical storyline of Scripture. See Gaines, "One Church in One Location," 39–46. These methodological aims flesh out Wellum's challenge to undertake an analysis of the covenant signs in their covenantal contexts in order to rightly understand who should participate in each sign. See Gentry and Wellum, *Kingdom through Covenant*, 78–79.

6. Booth, *Apology for the Baptists*, 82.

which often describes the church as the typological fulfillment of Israel.[7] With the authors of the Second London Confession (1689), they affirm one covenant of grace with various administrations.[8]

By arguing from a progressive covenantal view of Scripture, this work has drawn out various typological streams from the Old Testament that the historical close communionists do not address. Those streams include (1) the relationship of baptism to the circumcision of the heart and (2) the way in which Christ typologically fulfills the practice of circumcision and the role of ethnic, national Israel through the Davidic king. Thus, this book rejects replacement theology. Instead, chapters 3 and 4 argued that the church is an eschatological renewal of Israel in union with Christ.[9]

Nevertheless, this project stands largely in continuity with the historical defenses of close communion. This fact explains why this chapter does not repeat all of the arguments from the close communion advocates and why this chapter does not respond to all of the challenges from the other viewpoints. The existing responses are deemed sufficient. The way in which the close communion advocates strove for unity with all Christians, in so far as possible, while upholding their Baptist convictions is exemplary. Now,

---

7. Booth states the argument succinctly: "The different state of things under the old and new economies, and the apostle's distinction between the carnal and the spiritual seed of Abraham, being duly considered, the argument from analogy will run thus: As, under the old covenant, circumcision belonged to all the natural male descendants of Abraham; so, under the new covenant, baptism belongs to all the spiritual seed of Abraham, who are known to be such by a credible profession of faith" (Booth, *Pædobaptism Examined*, 2:265). Jewett references Booth's argument in his addendum II, entitled "Covenant Theology Implies Believer's Baptism." See Jewett, *Infant Baptism and the Covenant of Grace*, 237. Baldwin's argument must be distinguished from Booth's because he distinguishes between natural and spiritual promises to Abraham (Baldwin, *Baptism of Believers Only*, 257–61). Baldwin also distinguishes between the covenants, even acknowledging that "the renewal of the heart" was not "actually possessed" by members of the old covenant (Baldwin, *Series of Letters*, 88). By arguing for close communion, Booth maintained that only those who are baptized as spiritual seed of Abraham may come to the Lord's Supper. Similarly, see Kiffin, *Sober Discourse*, 158–59; Baldwin, *Particular Communion*, 121–22.

8. For the connection to the 1689 London Confession, see Renihan, "Covenant Theology in the First and Second London Confessions of Faith," in Barcellos, *Recovering a Covenantal Heritage*. For affirmation of the church as the typological fulfillment of Israel, see Malone, *Baptism of Disciples Alone*, 32. Regarding the covenants' relation to one another, Malone states, "Covenantal Baptists believe that the Old and New Testament Scripture defines a real unity between the covenants that is not compromised by accepting a biblically defined diversity between the new covenant administration and every other previous historical covenant administration. That is why it is called new" (65). See also pp. 66–94.

9. Parker, "Israel-Christ-Church Relationship," in Wellum and Parker, *Progressive Covenantalism*, 63.

having made the close communion argument, several arguments from the open communion view require a response.

Response to Open Communion Arguments

This section addresses the strongest open communion arguments from chapter 1. The arguments include (1) the lack of scriptural warrant; (2) the call to receive all whom Christ receives; (3) the principle of broad unity; (4) the charge of excommunication; (5) the claim that baptism is personal, not ecclesial; and (6) the allowance for the historical encroachment of error. Each of these arguments is considered in turn.

The first argument to address is the lack of scriptural warrant argument. Although Robert Hall Jr.,[10] Henry Jessey,[11] and John Bunyan[12] argued that the requirement of circumcision before Passover is insufficient scriptural evidence to warrant the requirement of baptism before the Lord's Supper, they fail to demonstrate the inapplicability of the principle. Yet, they call on close communion advocates to demonstrate that Exodus 12:43–48 leads to close communion. This book is, in part, an answer to their challenge. Van Neste picks up on this historical challenge to the close communion position. He adds that while the New Testament presents a pattern of "converts . . . baptized before participating in community observances, [that pattern] is not . . . a law requiring us to bar those who, due to misunderstanding, have improper baptisms. [Instead], we must be careful not to create laws where we have only patterns."[13] The aspect of allowing improper understandings

10. Hall Jr., *Terms of Communion*, 36. Significantly, the biblical-theological argument that the sign of entry should precede the sign of participation provides sufficient evidence, it seems, to demonstrate to Hall that baptism and the Lord's Supper are not "independently obligatory." In the absence of a NT command, evidence of the relation between the ordinances is precisely what Hall claimed would move him to change his position.

11. Jessey, *Storehouse of Provision*, 94.

12. Bunyan, "Differences in Judgment," in Offor, *Bunyan's Works*, 2:625.

13. Van Neste, "Lord's Supper," in Schreiner and Crawford, *Lord's Supper*, 382–83. As a comparison, Van Neste recognizes "more and stronger evidence of a pattern of weekly communion in the NT than of baptism being required for communion." Noting the evidence for weekly communion, he asks, "Why, in practice, have we often overlooked one pattern and treated the other pattern as law?" For his part, he argues "that since [weekly communion] is not directly commanded we cannot say that something less than weekly observance is sin." Hermeneutically, I am prepared to argue that if both weekly frequency and close communion are the pattern of the NT, the contemporary church should take steps to follow those patterns. However, it is not clear how the evidence that Van Neste presents on the pattern of weekly celebration constitutes "more and stronger" evidence.

will be picked up below. As for the necessity of scriptural warrant, clarification is needed.

The first clarification regarding scriptural warrant is that because the New Testament does not command that baptism precede communion as prerequisite to it, this book describes open communion under the category of irregular rather than invoking sin categories.[14] This book posits that the prerequisite nature of baptism should be expected based upon biblical-theological principle. But, second, this book argues that a NT command is not required to warrant the conclusion that baptism is prerequisite to the Lord's Supper.[15] Faithfulness to all that Scripture teaches requires that Christians operate with more categories than law/command on one extreme and *adiaphora* (things indifferent) on the other. This book establishes a canonical principle of continuity that fits, hermeneutically, between those extremes of the spectrum.

As for the third clarification, the thesis depends upon the examples of baptism following belief in Acts, along with the assumption that all believers are baptized in the epistles. These two categories provide significant and clear instruction to the church regarding Christ's plan in the new covenant age. When the data regarding baptism and faith is combined with the example of baptism preceding communion in Acts 2:41, the New Testament alone, without the principle of continuity from circumcision and Passover, strongly suggests that one enters the new covenant community by faith in Christ internally and baptism externally. Then, and only then, is a believer's

---

14. I say "irregular" to distinguish the neglect of a clear canonical expectation and NT pattern from sin, which I take to be the denial of or disobedience to a clear principle or command. Open communion leads to ecclesially weak churches, misunderstands the covenantal nature of the church, leaves itself more vulnerable to sinfulness in its celebrations of the Lord's Supper, and makes church discipline more difficult. In these ways, open communion tends to disorder. Relatedly, if pastors fail to teach or require believer's baptism of those who follow Christ, they are not faithfully calling people to obey all that Christ has commanded (Matt 28:18–20). Therefore, the charge could be, and has historically been levied against open communion advocates, that their view either explicitly or implicitly tends to the neglect of believer's baptism. The scriptural warrant open communionists provide, the strongest arguments of which are outlined in this section, do not overturn the Scripture's clear teaching regarding the ordinances. If this book is successful in establishing a biblical-theological principle for close communion, and yet a pastor or church continues to practice open communion, that would seem to be sin—akin to being convinced of believer's baptism and yet intentionally baptizing an unbeliever. Apart from being convinced of this book's thesis, it may be that open communion qualifies as unintentional sin; one need be cautious with this designation. The complexity of the argument posed in this book makes me hesitate to describe the biblical-theological principle argued herein as clear, even if the book is successful in establishing a canonical principle.

15. For a similar argument, see Jamieson, *Going Public*, 185.

separation from the world and unity with God's people established. Putting these exegetical observations together strongly suggests the practice of close communion (cf. Acts 20:7). Thus, the methodology adopted here seeks to be more canonically sensitive than to posit a law when the evidence does not extend beyond a pattern. But given the conclusion reached by this project's methodology, close communion is established in biblical principle.

The second open communion argument requiring response is that churches should receive all those Christ receives.[16] Similar to this claim is Robert Hall Jr.'s contention that "no man or set of men, are entitled to prescribe as an indispensable condition of communion what the New Testament has not enjoined as a condition of salvation."[17] Because close communion advocates in Baptist history have provided significant responses to this argument based upon Romans 14–15, responses here are limited to biblical-theological observations on strong and weak and the distinction between requirements for salvation versus requirements for communion.

First, Romans 14:1–4 and 15:1 clearly call the church to receive those who are weak in faith and bear with them. Because this letter is written to a church of baptized believers (Rom 6:3–4),[18] who presumably already participate in the Lord's Supper together, the context of clean and unclean food, along with the observance of special days, is important to recognize.[19] The basis of the admonition at the beginning of each chapter was the already occurring division in the church at Rome over how to relate to matters of the law covenant. If, as scholars presume,[20] the church consisted of both Jewish and Gentile Christians, then Paul's instructions are intended to guide the church in a specific matter related to the redemptive-historical transition from the old covenant to the new, through Christ. Paul's instructions not to pass judgment or be a stumbling block (14:13), to pursue peace and build others up (v. 19), and not to destroy the work of God (v. 20; presumably intending the unity of the church), were initially given to help the church honor the Lord through covenantal transition by loving one another as members of the new covenant.

16. For a contemporary expression of this argument, see Wilson, "Why Baptists Should Not Rebaptize Christians," in Shurden, *Baptism and the Lord's Supper*, 40–47.

17. Hall Jr., *Terms of Communion*, iv.

18. Contra Jessey, *Storehouse of Provision*, 97.

19. Longenecker misses this point in his claim that 14:1 applies in the first instance to "all other professing Christ followers" (Longenecker, *Epistle to the Romans*, 1001). While Paul's instructions certainly apply to the way any Christian treats any other Christian, the initial context must not be overlooked. Moo assumes the church context in Rome (Moo, *Epistle to the Romans*, 843–44).

20. Longenecker, *Epistle to the Romans*, 994–96; Schreiner, *Romans*, 662.

Thus, the question that must be answered is whether a sufficient analogy can be established between the strong, presumably Gentile Christians, in Rome who did not observe Jewish laws, and the weak, presumably Jewish Christians, who did.[21] Open communion advocates claim that those who hold that believer's baptism is prerequisite to communion are analogous to the strong (Rom 14), while those who do not understand Scripture to teach believer's baptism explicitly are akin to the weak. On this reading, Paul's exhortations to the church are understood as precluding close communion.[22] However, the issue of food is not sufficiently analogical with baptism for three reasons: (1) whereas food regulations belonged to the law covenant without being the sign of entrance into that covenant, baptism is the sign of entering the new covenant; (2) whereas the law reached its eschatological goal in Christ, resulting, in part, in the declaration that all foods are clean (Mark 7:19), Christ himself commands baptism as an ongoing act of disciple making until he comes (Matt 28:18–20); and (3) whereas Christian liberty allows for the continued observance of OT food laws (Rom 14), Christ has not left the church at liberty to dispense with baptism.[23] Thus, food laws and baptism are not sufficiently analogous, and, as a result, the open communion argument fails to convince.[24]

21. On the identity of the strong and weak, see Moo, *Epistle to the Romans*, 847; Longenecker, *Epistle to the Romans*, 1008.

22. Jessey, *Storehouse of Provision*, 96–97, 102; Hall Jr., *Terms of Communion*, 144–78; Bunyan, "Reason of My Practice in Worship," in Offor, *Bunyan's Works*, 2:610; Turner, *Modest Plea*, 16. Interestingly, Fiddes recognizes that the open communionists' line of argument from Rom 14–15 initially regarded baptism as less important and eventually also downplayed the Lord's Supper. See Fiddes, *Tracks and Traces*, 179.

23. Jamieson writes, "A sensitive conscience regarding food imagines a divine command where none exists, whereas infant baptism results in disobedience to a divine command" (Jamieson, *Going Public*, 179).

24. Daniel Turner's argument is also insufficient. He sees the strict Baptist's exclusion of pedobaptists as akin to what would have happened if the early Jewish Christians had excluded Gentile Christians from communion due to their lack of circumcision. The Jewish Christians could have claimed that receiving uncircumcised Gentiles to communion renders circumcision—an initiating ordinance—null. At points in the tract, Turner supposes that close communion advocates are akin to Jewish Christians who could have started separate churches on grounds that both circumcision and baptism should continue as signs of covenant entry. At other points, Turner presents close communion advocates as akin to Gentile Christians, who could have started new churches on the opposite premise. In defense, it appears mistaken to argue that close communion advocates are, assuming the validity of Turner's comparison for the sake of argument, like both Jewish and Gentile Christians. The fact that the basis of separation is a contradictory view of the role of circumcision undermines Turner's ability to compare close communion advocates to both groups. But more significantly, Turner fails to account for those in the NT who pressed the continuing validity of circumcision and were effectively declared by Paul to be anti-Christian (Gal 1:6–9; 5:1–6). Close

The other side of the Romans 14–15 debate, namely, that a church should require nothing more as prerequisite to communion than Christ requires for salvation, misunderstands at least three issues related to salvation and the church. First, this argument overlooks baptism's function to instrumentally unite the believer to Christ and, by virtue of that union, to formally unite the believer with Christ's body, the church (Gal 3:26–28; Acts 2:38–41). Second, the argument presumes that Christ intends merely to save individual sinners without respect to the individual Christian's divinely intended role in the new covenant community, while the New Testament evidences otherwise. Third, the argument assumes that for baptism to be required for church communion, it has to be salvific in and of itself.[25]

Because Christ not only intends to save individuals but also to incorporate those individuals into his corporate people, he has the right to determine on what basis the corporate people recognizes one another and by what means they become institutionally unified (cf. Acts 2:38–42).[26] Christ calls all those who would follow him to be baptized into covenant relationship with him and, simultaneously, into his people (Matt 28:18–20; Rom 6:3–4; Col 2:11–12). At the same time, the notion that close communion places additional requirements on believers beyond what Christ requires for salvation should not be troubling. Accounting for the covenantal associations of baptism and the corporate nature of the church requires recognition that Christ prescribes formal means whereby his people associate together beyond simply believing in Jesus.[27] As Kinghorn writes, "That may be es-

---

communion is not similar to the argument of the Judaizers because, at least, whereas the Judaizers were pressing for continued adherence to the old covenant despite Christ's fulfillment of the law, close communion advocates argue for the continuing validity of baptism under the new covenant. The Gentile analogy breaks down as well. The Jerusalem council issued specific instructions not to require circumcision of Gentile Christians given the advent of the new covenant era and the Father's gift of the Holy Spirit on the Gentiles (Acts 15:8–19). Paul was willing to continue the practice of circumcision for the sake of gospel witness to Jews (16:3; cf. 1 Cor 9:20), as a matter of Christian freedom (v. 1). His practice testifies to the gradual way in which Jewish Christians laid aside circumcision, given its ethnic basis (Gen 17). Nevertheless, Paul's instructions to the strong Christians in Rom 14 is precisely the instruction needed to assist Gentile Christians in bearing with Jewish Christians during the transition. In short, Turner's argument does not adequately account for the covenantal shift evident in the change from circumcision to baptism (Turner, *Modest Plea*, 14).

25. For this argument, see Hall Jr., *Reply*, 36–46.

26. Jamieson is correct: "In the right circumstances [open communion] allows pedobaptism to make the decisive difference between being included in or excluded from the church. It therefore makes pedobaptism part of the church's constitution, in so far as pedobaptism has become a potential qualification for membership" (Jamieson, *Going Public*, 194). So also Kinghorn, *Baptism a Term of Communion*, 12.

27. For a similar line of argument that is developed differently, see Kinghorn,

sential to the scriptural existence of a church, which is not essential to the salvation of the Christian."[28]

The third argument requiring response is that the Lord's Supper should be open in order to represent the broad unity of the church.[29] However, two counter arguments suggest that predicating the unity symbolized in the Lord's Supper to the universal church is insufficient to warrant open communion. First, universal church unity is not, in the first instance,[30] that which the Lord's Supper symbolizes and enacts. According to 1 Corinthians 10:16–17,[31] the ontological and logical basis of corporate unity with other Christians is individual union with Christ (cf. 12:13). According to verse 16, all who, having been united to Christ, participate in the bread and cup demonstrate their common union with Christ through taking the Supper. Verse 17 emphasizes that reception of the same meal of bread and cup formalizes the horizontal, covenantal union within a local church. Furthermore, Paul's specific indictment of the church at Corinth for their failure to live out gospel unity (during the Supper and otherwise), locates the primary sphere of corporate responsibility and covenantal unity within the local church.[32] Second, given the impossibility for the universal church to gather until the eschaton, when all the saints will gather at the new covenant consummation,[33] the Lord's Supper functions as a foretaste of that heavenly banquet. As a foretaste of the kingdom feast, the Lord's Supper's unitary function and symbolism in the local church should not be isolated from the common union with Christ in which the universal church participates. Nevertheless, unity in the local church is the primary signification and the universal church is secondary (though important!).[34] Given these biblical

---

Baptism a Term of Communion, 18–19; *Defense of "Baptism a Term of Communion,"* 121.

28. Kinghorn, *Baptism a Term of Communion*, 162.

29. See the sermon entitled, "Holy Spirit and the One Church," preached on December 13, 1857, in Spurgeon, *New Park Street Pulpit* 3.2.

30. See chapter 7.

31. The passage states, "The cup of blessing that we bless, is it not a participation in the blood of Christ? The bread that we break, is it not a participation in the body of Christ? Because there is one bread, we who are many are one body, for we all partake of the one bread."

32. Jamieson, *Going Public*, 120–21. Contra Fiddes, *Tracks and Traces*, 145.

33. White, "Universal and Local Church," in Duesing et al., *Upon This Rock*, 218–19. This observation does not entail that the universal church is not already gathered in heaven in a significant, inaugurated sense, per Heb 12:23. White appears to consider Heb 12:23 as entirely future.

34. Finn writes, "Unless it can be shown that the Lord's Supper is a Christian ordinance rather than a church ordinance, then this argument holds little merit. Again,

emphases, Hammett's suggestion is appropriate. In the universal body of Christ, "Our unity should be around the gospel rather than the meal."[35]

The fourth open communion argument requiring response is the charge that close communion is tantamount to excommunication. While excluding a pedobaptist from the Lord's Supper may be considered excommunication in a broad sense of the term, the exclusion does not constitute excommunication in its normal, disciplinary sense. In so far as a close communion church instructs only those baptized by immersion as believers, who are members in good standing of an evangelical church to participate in communion together, and a pedobaptist is, as a result, barred from table fellowship, close communion is an act of ex-communion. Being uninvited to or excluded from the Lord's Table is to be left out ("ex") from the Lord's Supper ("communicated").

At the same time, more is entailed in the normal, biblical discussion of excommunication than is present in the exclusion of the unbaptized due to close communion. The charge of excommunication toward close communion advocates dismisses the lack of an initial, covenanted relationship within a local church from which exclusion would count as excommunication (cf. Matt 18:18; 1 Cor 5:11).[36] Furthermore, the reason for the church's act is not, in Kinghorn's words, that the church views the otherwise godly and faithful,[37] though unbaptized, pedobaptist as "unworthy" to partici-

---

proponents of consistent communion are not ultimately interested in excluding anyone; rather, closed communion Baptists are interested in following the New Testament pattern for the ordinance" (Finn, "Baptism as a Prerequisite to the Lord's Supper," 12).

35. Hammett, *Forty Questions*, 271n19.

36. Chapter 6 will discuss excommunication and church discipline more directly.

37. Kinghorn's language is instructive. He explains, "He who is unbaptized at present, from opposition to the dictates of the apostles, we suppose will not be considered in a different moral state from the unbaptized in their day. But he who admits the permanency of baptism, who confesses that every conscientious man ought to be baptized, who believes that he has been a subject of that rite in a valid form in his infancy, is not in the situation of those who refused to obey the dictates of inspired men. He pleads that they have been obeyed, and if he does not mean to acknowledge that his infant baptism is unscriptural, he pleads also that their dictates were obeyed in the required order, that he was baptized before he came forward to request communion. We differ from him we acknowledge, and we do not intend to represent the point of difference as less than it has ever been, but the nature of the difference is very distinct from what it would be, if he denied the authority of the apostles. For this reason, we treat him, not as a person who designedly opposes the dictates of the apostles, but as a mistaken good man. But still, neither will his excellencies in other parts of his character, nor our favorable opinion of him on the whole, fulfil the duty he has mistaken, or set aside our obligation to attend to the will of Christ, and support his ordinances as he delivered them" (Kinghorn, *Defense of "Baptism a Term of Communion,"* 48).

pate. Instead, the church views the pedobaptist as "unqualified," given the lack of baptism.[38]

Therefore, the close communion church's unwillingness to commune with pedobaptists does not imply that Baptists believe pedobaptists are unregenerate.[39] Close communion advocates understand pedobaptists to be acting sincerely, though erroneously, on what they (pedobaptists) believe to be biblical conviction when they claim that infant baptism is New Testament baptism. Because this misunderstanding on their part does not compromise the gospel, Baptists view any pedobaptist who professes faith in Christ to be regenerate in the same sense as the Baptists who are included in the meal. Nevertheless, given Christ's command to be baptized, a biblical understanding of the recipients of baptism in its relation to faith, the difference in nature and structure of the new covenant, and the principle of continuity from circumcision and Passover, the close communion church humbly appeals to the Scripture as their basis of authority for administering communion.[40]

As a result, Jamieson is correct that close communion churches find themselves in an ecclesial tension. He writes, "Churches that require baptism for membership will, in principle, be forced to withhold their affirmation from people whom they are convinced are genuine followers of Christ, leaving an acute tension between our private judgment and the church's public judgment." Yet, the tension is insufficient to warrant open communion, because "Jesus has bound the church's judgment—and therefore its formal, public affirmation—to baptism." Therefore, despite one's personal affirmation of a pedobaptist's genuineness as a Christian, "the church is

38. Kinghorn, *Baptism a Term of Communion*, 61.

39. Carroll, "Discussion of the Lord's Supper," in Cranfill, *Christ and His Church*, 156–58.

40. Kynes offers a different understanding of humility in defense of open communion. He writes, "I recognize that pedobaptism has been the practice of the overwhelming majority of Christians throughout most of church history. This includes the practice of the Protestant Reformers to which I owe a great theological and spiritual debt. I humbly recognize that I could be wrong about pedobaptism (and the conclusion that the great majority of Christians through history were never really baptized), and for this reason I am hesitant to insist upon my position on baptism as a grounds of church fellowship" (Kynes, "Why I Am a 'baptist' [with a Small 'b']"). Humility in this argument is framed entirely in terms of Kynes' posture toward other Christians. While humility toward others is vitally important (Phil 2:3–8), Kynes argues as if humility toward God did not require him to obey what he sees as Scripture's clear teachings on baptism. He admits being convinced of believer's baptism. In other words, Kynes pits humility toward people in conflict with humility toward God. However, Scripture teaches that humility is evidenced by trembling at the word of the Lord (Isa 66:2). As Kinghorn contends, "We never ought to say to any man, however excellent he may be, 'we love you so much, that as a proof of it, we will give up an institution of the Lord, on your account'" (Kinghorn, *Baptism a Term of Communion*, 39).

simply not authorized [to] admit to the renewing oath-sign . . . anyone who has not [undergone the] initiating oath-sign."[41]

While some have extended the argument regarding excommunication to charge close communion churches with effectively de-churching pedobaptist churches, this charge is also unfounded. Whereas J. R. Graves did refuse to recognize pedobaptist churches as true churches,[42] close communion churches recognize pedobaptist churches as true but irregular.[43] Because the Reformers argued that the basic marks of the church include the right preaching of the Word and the right participation in the sacraments (sometimes implying the necessity of church discipline),[44] Graves understood pedobaptist churches to fall short of the marks that would legitimize their status as true churches. However, the clear presence of gospel preaching and biblical fidelity among various branches of pedobaptists suggests the inadequacy of Graves's logic. Instead, Baptists, who hold that Christ has authority to order his church and yet that genuine Christians (including Baptists) err in their biblical interpretations, distinguish between the being and well-being of a local church.[45] When a church possesses the

41. Jamieson, *Going Public*, 173–74, 176–78. Kinghorn, *Baptism a Term of Communion*, 7.

42. His logic was simple. If right participation in baptism is necessary for a religious society to be a church, and pedobaptist churches do not participate in baptism rightly according to the Bible, then pedobaptist churches are not true churches (Graves, *Intercommunion*, 79).

43. For affirmations of this designation, see Fowler, *More Than a Symbol*, 231. Similarly, Finn writes, "A church can be irregular, meaning that it fails to follow New Testament practice in some specific area(s), but still be a true church where the gospel is rightly preached, the ordinances are observed in such a way that they do not subvert the gospel, believers are nurtured in their faith and the gospel is shared with those on the outside. In fact, I will candidly admit that many otherwise-healthy Baptist churches are 'irregular' in that they do not consistently practice church discipline, a clear aspect of New Testament congregations" (Finn, "Baptism as a Prerequisite," 13).

44. For the Reformation marks of the church, see Allison, *Sojourners and Strangers*, 50–51n67; *Historical Theology* 26.2–3; Kolb, "Church," in Barrett, *Reformation Theology*, 577–608.

45. White spells out this argument in White, "What Makes Baptism Valid?," in White et al., *Restoring Integrity in Baptist Churches*, 113–15. He explains, "The Landmark movement incorrectly added 'rightly administering the ordinances' to the definition of the 'being' of a church. This led to their denying all who baptized infants as true churches." In order to distinguish between the being and well-being of a church, White lists several essential attributes/marks that must be present for a church to exist. For a church to possess being (*esse*), it must be marked by the presence of the gospel, the ordinances, and believers intentionally gathered (the notion of covenanting together to meet, encourage, and hold each other accountable). Those marks which determine a church's well-being (*bene esse*) include (1) the offices (pastor and deacon); (2) church discipline; (3) baptism by immersion of believers; (4) a biblical view of the

gospel and clearly intends to uphold the Scripture's rule over the church's life together, even though it practices the ordinances in an improper way, a true church exists.[46] However, Baptists observe that infant baptism is a structural blight on the purity of the church,[47] which fails to conform to biblical norms for baptism. Thus, the pedobaptist church, while a true church, suffers in its well-being. Or, to state the matter differently, on a scale of less-healthy churches to more-healthy churches, the institutional structure of pedobaptism pushes the church toward the less-healthy side.[48]

The fifth argument to be addressed is the claim that baptism is personal and not ecclesial.[49] Freeman is right to critique Bunyan and Spurgeon

---

Lord's Supper; (5) regenerate church membership; (6) missionary focus; (7) text-driven or expository preaching; etc. Allison provides an even more theological robust way of accounting for the distinction between being and well-being. His presentation distinguishes false churches from true churches. Then, within the true church category, churches may be less pure or more pure. Allison's seven attributes of the church include: doxological, logocentric, pneumadynamic, covenantal, confessional, missional, and spatio-temporal/eschatological. See Allison, *Sojourners and Strangers*, 164–68. For a theologically stimulating presentation of these attributes, see Allison, *Sojourners and Strangers*, 103–60.

46. Contra Freeman, *Contesting Catholicity*, 377, who claims that a consequence of close communion is that its advocates do "not regard communities that observe [infant baptism] to be Christian churches." Instead, White explains, "If the ordinances 'rightly administered' . . . are moved into the category of 'being' of a church, you have Landmarkism. In essence, you have just unchurched all pedobaptist gatherings." White concludes, "The proper practice of these ordinances cannot be added to the 'being' of a church without repeating historical mistakes" (White "What Makes Baptism Valid?," in White et al., *Restoring Integrity in Baptist Churches*, 115).

47. This evaluation stems from the biblical-theological recognition that the new covenant brings a change of nature and structure to the people of God, as discussed in chapter 4. See Wellum, "Beyond Mere Ecclesiology," in Easley and Morgan, *Community of Jesus*, 183–212. Kinghorn explains that the strict communion Baptist relates to the established church and pedobaptist dissenters on the same basis: "He tells him respectfully, but plainly, that his church is wrong in its very constitution; that it is formed of materials different from those used by the Savior, and that these materials are united together in a way totally diverse from that of his institution. The whole body is, therefore, taken in the aggregate, of a different character from that which is in the New Testament called the church of Christ" (Kinghorn, *Baptism a Term of Communion*, 127).

48. Fuller's statement that he does not refuse to partake of the Lord's Supper with pedobaptists "because I consider them as improper subjects, but as attending to it in an improper manner" is relevant here (Fuller, "Letter to William Ward," in Belcher, *Fuller's Works*, 3:508). While this statement applies in the first instance to close communion in a Baptist church specifically, it may be extended to describe the way in which pedobaptists approach the Lord's Table within their own churches (speaking of credocommunion churches specifically).

49. After William Kiffin responded to Bunyan's *Confession*, Bunyan responded with *Differences in Water Baptism No Bar to Communion* (1673). In that defense, Bunyan further explains the relationship between the believer, baptism, and the church with

because they received "Christians into membership not by approving infant baptism but because they believe that faith rather than baptism is necessary for membership."[50] While the connection between baptism and the local church will be more fully explored in chapter 6, three arguments are worth mentioning here: (1) the local church holds the keys of the kingdom and thus authority to baptize; (2) the assumption that believers are baptized and the examples of baptism in Acts demonstrate that baptism was normative means of being added to the church; and (3) baptism instrumentally unites with Christ and formally establishes a derivative union with the body of Christ. Each of these arguments is surveyed briefly.[51]

The first reason baptism should be viewed as the door to the church is that Christ authorized the church to exercise the keys of the kingdom through baptizing converts.[52] Whereas Christ gave Peter the keys to the kingdom in Matthew 16:18, he authorized the church to exercise them to expel unrepentant sinners who claimed to be kingdom citizens in 18:17–20. Then, in Matthew 28:18–20, as the risen king, Jesus authorized his disciples to make disciples by baptizing those new disciples. The result of the baptism would be that the new disciples would be formally and officially recognized as kingdom citizens. Given (1) the local church's use of the authority of the keys to expel those whose profession of allegiance to Christ proves false in 18:17 and (2) the command for the disciples (who would compose the first church in Jerusalem; Acts 2:41) to baptize, baptism appears to be one application of the keys whereby new disciples are brought into the community of

---

three points: (1) the believer's faith is the door to the church rather than faith with baptism or the mutual consent of the church being required for joining a church (619); (2) Christ never commanded baptism; and (3) baptism is nowhere revealed to be a church ordinance or a practiced required by primitive churches for inclusion. To this third point, Bunyan writes, "If baptism respect believers, as particular persons only; if it respects their own conscience only; if it make a man no visible believer to me, then it hath nothing to do with church-membership" (629). Furthermore, although a community which fails to celebrate the Lord's Supper is not a church due to the meal's constitutive function, a community that fails to celebrate baptism loses nothing corporately because baptism is not constitutive of the local church. See Bunyan, "Differences in Judgment about Water Baptism," in Offor, *Bunyan's Works*, 2:638–39.

50. Freeman, *Contesting Catholicity*, 379.

51. Jamieson adds that this argument for open communion "privileges the individual conscience over the authority of the local church" (Jamieson, *Going Public*, 198). In other words, whatever the believer determines to be baptism is to be received as baptism, despite the church's confessional stance. For a sound defense of believer's baptism as a term of communion rather than godly sincerity, see Baldwin, *Baptism of Believers Only*, 101–37. Baldwin was responding to Noah Worcester, *Friendly Letter to the Reverend Thomas Baldwin*.

52. This argument is fully developed in chapter 6.

the king—the church.[53] Second, the consistent assumption that believers are baptized and the example of the early church confirms that the disciples understood baptism for disciples to be a formal means of bringing them into the community. In Acts 2:41, all who became disciples through repentance, faith, and baptism were clearly acting in submission and trust to king Jesus. Then, rather than remaining individual representatives of the kingdom, the new disciples were "added to their number" of the one hundred and twenty existing disciples.[54] Finally, the covenantal associations of baptism clearly present baptism as the means of entering not only union with Christ, but also the derivative union of Christ's body (Gal 3:26–28; 1 Cor 12:13; Col 2:11–12; Rom 6:3–4), even the local church (1 Cor 10:16–17). In light of these three arguments, baptism must be understood as designed by Christ to create an inherent connection with the church.

The sixth open communion argument requiring response is that the historical encroachment of error into the church is a sufficient reason to warrant laying aside baptism as prerequisite to communion.[55] Before defending the ongoing legitimacy, even necessity, of developing ecclesiology from Scripture, an observation on the logical entailments of this open communion argument is relevant. If the principle were carried out, two possibilities could result: (1) the number of denominations and churches would splinter indefinitely according to each charismatic leader's (or individual's) interpretation,[56] or (2) the lack of a coherent theological understanding and

53. For the argument made in this paragraph, see Leeman, *Surprising Offense*, 178–79. For a general support of baptism as one application of the exercise of the keys, see Carson, "Matthew," in Gaebelein, *Expositor's Bible Commentary*, 368. Those historical close communion advocates who argued that baptism is akin to an officer's swearing in ceremony provide a helpful metaphor for considering the relationship of baptism to the kingdom of Christ. So Fuller, "Letter to William Ward," in Belcher, *Fuller's Works*, 3:505. He writes, "Such a declaration is equal to an oath of allegiance in a soldier. He may be insincere, yet, if there be no proof of his insincerity, the king's officers are obliged to admit him into the army. Another may be sincerely on the side of the king, yet, if he refuse the oath and the royal uniform, he cannot be admitted" (Kinghorn, *Baptism a Term of Communion*, 30–31).

54. Interestingly, ecumenical communion advocates agree with this point. See Haymes et al., *On Being the Church*, 90. In Luke's subsequent narrative, he clearly identifies the whole group of disciples as the church in Jerusalem (Acts 4:32—5:13; cf. 8:3–4).

55. This argument is made most significantly by Hall Jr., *Terms of Communion*, 39–41. For a contemporary presentation of this argument, see Tyler, *Baptism*, 139–45.

56. Finn recognizes this possibility and acknowledges that the argument "assumes that an individual pedobaptist's conviction trumps the conviction of an entire church. This is a most dangerous principle" (Finn, "Baptism as a Prerequisite," 11). The irony is that Hall's efforts in making the argument that the encroachment of error legitimizes laying aside baptism was explicitly for the purpose of preventing the atomization of the church (universal). See Hall Jr., *Reply*, 143, 190.

vision for the church would disallow the formal grounding of a local church from Scripture.[57] Thus, this argument effectively removes the Scripture from the hands of Christians and leaves them helpless to establish churches with a clear sense of Christ's authorization.[58]

Another result of the historical encroachment of error argument involves the conscience of the pedobaptist who seeks to join a Baptist church. If the Baptist church refuses to teach or practice infant baptism, as the open communion advocates cited in this book did, then the pedobaptist who joins a Baptist church voluntarily forgoes infant baptism for her children. If one is convinced that pedobaptism is biblical, but is willing to not have her

57. Illustrative of this point is Sampler's proposal that the SBC change the "Baptist Faith and Message 2000" to reflect the open communion practice of the churches. If contemporary practice is the rule of a church or denomination's doctrine, Scripture's formative role for determining ecclesiology is usurped (Sampler, "Whosoever Is 'Qualified' May Come," 190–93). As Jamieson writes, "In principle, by privileging the individual conscience over the local church, open membership [and open communion] actually begins to unravel the theological fabric of a local church's existence as a church" (Jamieson, Going Public, 199). Certainly, Hall does not see these possibilities as entailed by his view, nor does Freeman. See Freeman, Contesting Catholicity, 383. Freeman contends that a consistent ecclesiology can be maintained if Baptist churches recognize "any baptism in which the signs of the common faith which Christians through the ages share." But surely Freeman would not tolerate Roman Catholic baptism as legitimate, given its sacramental status as ex opere operato. Among open communion advocates surveyed in chapter 2, none affirm the acceptability of receiving Roman Catholic baptism as legitimate. However, the way in which they argue varies. Hall speaks of receiving those who are truly Christians and "churchmen," meaning those from the church of England, because he understood the other Protestant denominations as possessing the gospel message. Hall justifies the mixed communion Baptists by claiming that tolerating error is not the same as approving of it or participating in it. For Hall to receive a churchman does not require him to concur with or practice his errors (Hall Jr., Reply, 120–22). Bunyan continually affirms his willingness to commune with visible saints without respect to baptism whatsoever. Thus, if Bunyan would have allowed a Roman Catholic to commune, it would have been without respect to his baptism (Bunyan, "Reason of My Practice in Worship," in Offor, Bunyan's Works, 2:602–03). However, Weaver is correct that baptism for Bunyan became a moot point, given his insistence on faith as the grounds of unity (Weaver, "When Biography Shapes Ecclesiology," 36–42).

58. Kinghorn, Defense, 16. Finn also recognizes this error. He responds that Hall's argument "downplays the fact that there is only one mode of baptism in the NT. The existence of a plurality of 'baptisms' in our own day is no reason to abandon the New Testament pattern. To consistently obey Christ's command is not pugnacity but humility" (Finn, "Baptism as a Prerequisite to the Lord's Supper," 11–12). Wills argues explicitly that the general trajectory toward open communion among Baptists has stemmed from a functional (though not usually a formal) denial of Scripture's authority and sufficiency (Wills, "Sounds from Baptist History," in Schreiner and Crawford, Lord's Supper, 295–312). Although the biblical arguments made for open communion do not necessitate the inability to ground one's ecclesiology in Scripture, it is an example of moving aside what Baptists view as a clear ecclesiological point in favor of a broader principle.

children baptized, is pedobaptism "really a conviction?" If so, why would the pedobaptist be willing to leave it aside? If the pedobaptist chooses to join the Baptist, then she is acting on a "willful inconsistency."[59] One cannot simultaneously affirm that her personal baptism as an infant is biblical and thus does not need to be jettisoned through undergoing believer's baptism while affirming that her infant child need not be baptized.

Positively then, in response to the sixth open communion argument, the church must seek to ground its ecclesiology in Scripture. The description of the church as reformed and always reforming (*ecclesia reformata, semper reformanda*)[60] is only legitimate if the Scripture is understood as the norm of norms that cannot be normed (*norma normata et normativa*).[61] The ability for a local church or a denomination of churches to experience renewal through a recovery of the gospel and (secondarily) various aspects of biblical ecclesiology requires that churches cling to Scripture's authority as God's Word. As Fowler claims, "If Acts and the apostolic epistles do not give us a Christian doctrine of baptism which is valid for the whole inter-advent age, then where do we get such a doctrine?"[62] This final open communion argument fails to answer this question.

Response to Closed Communion Arguments

The strongest closed communion arguments are related: (1) that guarding the purity of the Table and exercising proper discipline in the church requires that only church members receive the meal and (2) that the local church is the only proper context in which the meal should occur, because

59. Jamieson, *Going Public*, 197. Jamieson's analysis is penetrating. He writes, "It's possible to be convinced of pedobaptism and still seek membership in a Baptist church—as long as you're not currently adding to your family. If you are, your 'conviction' goes kaput. But if you're not, you could potentially hold your conviction and stomach a Baptist church's disobedience. Perhaps you could consider it a lesser evil than, say, attending a pedobaptist church that denies the gospel and endorses sin" (196). He continues, "Often, I fear that what seems to be humility—'Who am I to say what is and isn't baptism?'—is much closer to indifference. And indifference is right next door to disobedience. Jesus isn't indifferent to baptism; neither should we be." The substance of Jamieson's argument can be found in Kinghorn, *Baptism a Term of Communion*, 104. Unfortunately, Beasley-Murray proposes the exact situation that Jamieson critiques in Beasley-Murray, *Baptism in the New Testament*, 392–93.

60. For examples of this phrase during the Reformation, see Barrett, "Crux of Genuine Reform," in Barrett, *Reformation Theology*, 47.

61. For examples of the use of this phrase during the Reformation, see Cole, "Holy Spirit," in Barrett, *Reformation Theology*, 411, 416.

62. Fowler, *More Than a Symbol*, 63.

the Lord's Supper is an ordinance of the local church to symbolize its unity. Each of these arguments is considered in turn.

First, closed communion advocates are correct to emphasize that a church's ability to exercise responsible discipline varies in proportion to the members' and pastors' knowledge of and relationships with the recipients of the Supper.[63] Should a professing, baptized believer who is under discipline visit a closed communion church from out of town, the closed communion policy would serve to keep the unrepentant person from partaking of the meal "in an unworthy manner" and "being guilty of the body and blood of the Lord" (1 Cor 11:27). Furthermore, it would keep the church from participating with Christ together with someone who may not turn out to be part of the body of Christ, universal. Because the Lord's Supper is a symbol of unity and an effective sign that, at least normally, formalizes local church unity, the closed policy provides clear lines of demarcation between the church and the world. Therefore, while not affirming the closed communion position, Jamieson is correct that "because the Lord's Supper entails responsibility for the church, it normally entails membership in the local church in which you partake of it."[64]

However, two arguments are put forward here against closed communion: (1) closed communion tends to so emphasize the unity of the local church that it completely denies that the Lord's Supper symbolizes unity of the universal body of Christ and (2) closed communion is not required by Scripture. Paul's exhortations not to eat in an unworthy manner and to eat by discerning the body (1 Cor 11:27–29) each demonstrate the importance of appropriate relationships within the particular local church that receives the meal.[65] The Lord's Supper is clearly a symbol of unity, and that unity creates and reflects the strongest ties among the members of a single church. With 1 Corinthians 10–11 in mind, Hammett concludes,

> I think this point lends some strength to the local-church-only [closed communion] position, though I would reword it to local-church-deepest. The deepest horizontal communion we will experience at the Lord's Supper will naturally be with those with whom we are in the covenantal committed relationship of fellow church member. I am willing to extend that communion to baptized church members from other churches but

63. See Allison's discussion of this argument in Allison, *Sojourners and Strangers*, 402.

64. Jamieson, *Going Public*, 126–27.

65. For the emphasis on the local church as the locus of unity symbolized and enacted by the Lord's Supper, see Ciampa and Rosner, *First Letter to the Corinthians*, 554–55; Hammett, *Forty Questions*, 275.

acknowledge that the horizontal aspect of our communion will not be as deep.[66]

Allison adds further clarity to the issue by stating,

> The close communion view acknowledges that the Lord's Supper (the same is true for baptism) is an ordinance *for* the local church; that is, its celebration *is carried out by the local church*, not by some authoritative ecclesial structure above the local church or by a parachurch movement. At the same time, the position does not hold that the Lord's Supper (or baptism) is an ordinance *of* the local church, that is, that the celebration pertains only to the local church. . . . The baptism is baptism into the body of Christ and thus pertains to all local churches as expressions of that body.[67]

On this point, fencing the Table aids close communion churches in guarding the purity of the Table and the church. The laudable concerns of closed communion advocates may not be as serious a threat if the church fences the Table properly and if other local churches have strong membership

66. Hammett, *Forty Questions*, 271n18. The fact that local church unity is (1) primary in the context of Corinthians and (2) is of the essence of a shared meal in a shared location, help make the point strongly that the unity function of the Supper is primarily local. Yet, as a meal given to the church until Christ returns, the participants should be aware of the unity in Christ that it shares with the saints of old and who exist presently around the world.

67. When this book describes baptism and the Supper as being ordinances "of the local church," the purpose is to affirm that the ordinances belong to the local church in the same sense as Allison claims. Baptism and the Lord's Supper fall under the Christ-authorized jurisdiction of the local church and, as a result, should be administered by local churches. Thus, this book holds to the substance of Allison's view (*Sojourners and Strangers*, 405–6). Allison continues rightly, "Should the baptized believer leave the church in which she was baptized and become a member of another church, she does not need to—indeed, cannot—be rebaptized; her baptism is valid in her new church. Likewise, while the Lord's Supper is administered by a local church, the celebration observed does not avail in that church only. The Lord's Supper proclaims the gospel message [and presents multiple other benefits of the new covenant to the church]; as such, the Lord's Supper does this for all Christ-followers. To exclude baptized Christians who are members in good standing in their local church from participating in the celebrations of the Lord's Supper in a different church symbolizes [that all those new covenant benefits presented in the Supper] do not apply to those excluded people." Allison's statement may cause some open communion advocates to ask how close communion advocates can deny godly pedobaptists the ability to participate in the Lord's Supper without committing the same error as Allison predicates of closed communion. The answer is that Allison's description presumes the exception of believer's baptism. In other words, given that the visitor at a Baptist church has been baptized as an expression of faith, then to deny that person the meal is to commit the error to which Allison points.

practices.[68] A close communion church can instruct the congregation that the Table is open to all those who have been baptized as believers by immersion and are members in good standing of an evangelical church. With this fencing of the Table given, the faithful membership practices of the other churches represented should be trusted as assisting the administering local church in maintaining the purity of its celebration.[69] More will be said about fencing the Table in chapter 6.

Next, closed communion is not required by Scripture. Closed communion lacks biblical warrant because it places too much responsibility for the unrepentant person's unworthy participation on the church. While the church is responsible to guard the ordinances, Paul places the responsibility for rightful participation primarily on the recipients of the Supper rather than the administrators. He says, "Let a person examine himself" (v. 28).

---

68. Cheong admits that his open communion stance makes properly fencing the Table more difficult (Cheong, *God Redeeming His Bride*, 244–45).

69. Jamieson adds, "There is a sense in which [the visiting communicant is] subject to [the administering] church's discipline for one Sunday. He has to make himself known to them in the first place in order to be welcomed to the Table. Further, imagine he had this conversation with an elder before the gathering and then during the gathering started spouting false teaching. The church would be right to bar him from their celebration of the Lord's Supper. In such a scenario, [the visitor] is never really a 'member' of the church in the way we typically use the term. But insofar as he is appealing to the church to participate in their fellowship for just one Sunday, he only does so by consent of the church and thereby submits to the authority of the church" (Jamieson, *Going Public*, 129–30). This scenario need not imply that every visiting Christian is ecclesially aware (or outgoing) enough to seek out a church member or elder to make herself known to the church. Nevertheless, the impulse of the scenario is healthy. Jamieson's concluding reflection is theologically and practically helpful. He writes, "Church membership is a durable relation. Its duties of submission, accountability, mutual care, and so on can only be carried out over time. Elders leading and members following happen through time. If you're only at a church one Sunday, there's no time to be a member, so the theological category of 'membership' doesn't obtain. But that doesn't mean [the effective sign of membership] should be withheld. Instead, a baptized, in-good-standing member of another church should be welcomed to the Table precisely because he would be welcomed as a member if he were staying longer." Regarding the means by which a sister church's healthy membership practices may encourage the purity of administering church's celebration of the Lord's Supper. Benjamin Griffith's counsel could surely be utilized using contemporary communication methods. He writes, "and concerning those that are members of sister churches, their admission is either transient or occasional admission; when any person is dismissed wholly from one church, and transmitted or recommended to another church of the same faith, order and practice . . . such as are and continue members of other regular churches, may, where they are well known, be admitted into transient communion, without a letter of recommendation from the church they belong unto: but from those a church hath no knowledge of, a testimonial letter is necessary, that a church may not be imposed on by any loose or disorderly persons" (Griffith, "Short Treatise," in Dever, *Polity*, 101).

While the local church should follow Paul's example of fencing the Table by calling the congregation to self-examination, the guilt for unworthy participation belongs especially to the participant. Unworthy participation warrants the verdict of "guilty of the body and blood of the Lord" for the participant (v. 27). At the same time, local churches should not be negligent regarding those to whom they serve the elements. Paul tells the Corinthians "not even to eat with such a one" (5:11).

Concerning the closed communion argument that the Lord's Supper is an ordinance of the local church, its advocates are correct.[70] However, they undervalue the unity that can be demonstrated through shared participation in the Lord's Supper by visiting Christians from churches of like faith and practice. Although Paul speaks primarily of the unity of the local church under the symbolism of the body of Christ in 1 Corinthians (10:17; 11:17–22; 12:13, 18–27), the body of Christ metaphor also refers to all those who are united to Christ (Eph 1:22–23).[71] Furthermore, Paul moves back and forth between the local body of Christ at Corinth and the universal church in 1 Corinthians 11:27–28: "Now you are the body of Christ and individually members of it. [28] And God has appointed in the church first apostles, second prophets, third teachers" (cf. 10:32).[72] The role of the apostles in 12:28 appears to mirror the way Paul describes their foundational role in the universal church in Ephesians 2:20. The upshot is that while the Supper primarily reflects and enacts local church unity, each local manifestation of the body of Christ also practices the same meal, on the same gospel grounding. Therefore, in a secondary sense, the Lord's Supper is a symbol of the unity of the universal church. At the same time, the universal church does not gather in a manifest, spatio-temporal way until the eschaton (Rev 19:6–10; Luke 22:16, 18). The universal church cannot, by definition, jointly participate in the Lord's Supper until the Marriage Supper of the Lamb. In sum, close communion does a better job of recognizing the primacy of local church unity that is demonstrated through the embodied participation with physical elements in one place, while continuing to value

---

70. Kazee, *Church and the Ordinances*, 124.

71. Hammett, "Church Membership, Church Discipline," in Hammett and Merkle, *Those Who Must Give an Account*, 12, 15–20. As P. T. O'Brien claims, "the body of Christ' can be used comprehensively of all who are united [with Christ] and also of a particular manifestation of that body, in this case [1 Cor 12] a local congregation" (O'Brien, "Church as a Heavenly Eschatological Entity," in Carson, *Church in the Bible and the World*, 107).

72. Paul's example and encouragement to "Give no offense to Jews or to Greeks or to the church of God" appears to be a reference to the church at Corinth that does not exclude the broader church that belongs to God outside of Corinth (Clowney, *Church*, 112).

the spiritual unity that exists through the gospel with other believers outside the local congregation.

Response to Ecumenical Communion Arguments

The three strongest arguments for the ecumenical position include (1) that a common process of initiation need not require a particular order of baptism, faith, repentance, and/or confirmation; (2) that Baptist identity may be upheld by limiting baptism to professing believers but opening the Table to any who attend worship; and (3) that Jesus' teaching on fellowship meals and parables of banquets in the Gospels apply directly to the church's practice of the Lord's Supper. Each of these arguments is evaluated in turn.

First, the contention that a common process of initiation includes repentance, faith, and baptism occurring in any order, with baptism given to believing or unbelieving subjects, fails to account for the New Testament data. From a macro-level, baptism belongs to the cluster of conversion events (regeneration, repentance, faith, baptism). As the only external sign of conversion, baptism should occur in association with new covenant entry/initiation.[73] From a micro-level, baptism is both logically and (normally) temporally subsequent to saving faith in Christ. New covenant regeneration/ heart circumcision requires the instrumentality of gospel proclamation and makes saving faith possible.[74] Faith is the grace-enabled human response to the gospel by which God declares sinners not guilty but righteous instead (Eph 2:8–9; Phil 1:29; Rom 3:24–28; Gal 3:14, 24). Although faith is the fundamental human response by which the Spirit unites sinners to Christ,[75] God intends for that union to be externally appropriated through baptism and attaches blessings of the new covenant to baptism (Acts 2:38; 22:16; Gal 3:26). In this sense, baptism is an instrument of union with Christ (Gal 3:26–27; Col 2:12–13; Rom 6:3–5)[76] and the mark of becoming a disciple of

73. Stein, "Baptism and Becoming a Christian," 6–17.

74. See Rom 14:17; Jas 1:18; 1 Pet 1:21–23; 1 John 5:1; John 6:44–45; 2 Cor 4:6. For comment on 1 John 5:1 that affirms the new birth enables faith, see Akin, *1, 2, 3 John*, 179.

75. On the importance of the individual and subjective nature of human faith as evidencing the new birth and leading to baptism, see Jewett, *Infant Baptism and the Covenant of Grace*, 228.

76. These affirmations are intended to account for the nuances of the biblical data rather than to flatten the biblical picture of baptism's function. Incidentally these same observations, combined with the much more thorough discussion of baptism's instrumental role in union with Christ, compose part of the theological foundation for countering Fiddes's sacramental theology (Fiddes, *Tracks and Traces*, 117–18).

Jesus (Matt 28:19).[77] These distinctions in the logical and temporal order of initiation events, which are delineated above with a focus on baptism's role at a micro (logical) and macro (temporal) level, demonstrate that the New Testament does not present an openness to varying processes of initiation. Theologically, entering the covenant community happens one way.[78] The subjective, heart posture of faith toward Christ is necessary to validate the baptism as biblical baptism.[79]

77. Beasley-Murray, *Baptism in the New Testament*, 89; Köstenberger, "Baptism in the Gospels," in Schreiner and Wright, *Believer's Baptism*, 33. This way of expressing baptism's role in becoming a disciple is contra White, "What Makes Baptism Valid?," in White et al., *Restoring Integrity in Baptist Churches*, 108. White states, "People must first be made disciples, or become believers, before baptism." The temporal (macro) and logical (micro) distinctions in the order of salvation above are intended to preserve justification by faith, about which White appears concerned.

78. This statement does not require that one cannot be a Christian without baptism, for it is possible that one could be aware of the saving promises of Christ and believe without being aware of Christ's call to baptism. Certainly, some frontier missions situations could present this possibility. Nevertheless, seeking to affirm the legitimacy of becoming a Christian apart from baptism is wrongheaded, for it runs counter to the NT's assumption that all believers are baptized. Furthermore, unless one is in an unusual situation, such as the thief on the cross (Luke 23:43), Christ's expectation is clearly that anyone who would follow him would be baptized as his disciple. Because becoming a Christian carries inherent corporate consequences of belonging to God's people, the statement above understands "Christian" not merely in an individual sense, but to also entail union with Christ's body, the church. Therefore, repentance/belief with baptism is the normative means of becoming a Christian. Fowler's discussion of the normal and necessary means of appropriating the benefits of redemption is helpful here. He writes, "To say that baptism is the normal means of bringing individuals into a redemptive encounter with Christ it to say that it is relatively necessary in two ways: (1) it is a precept of necessity in that it is the dominically-appointed way to express the response of faith in relation to the kerygma. In any case in which the individual understands the gospel and perceives that baptism is the appropriate way to affirm the gospel, the refusal to be baptized would take on great significance not because of the mere absence of baptism, but because of the rejection of what is embodied in baptism [cf. Acts 2:38] and (2) it is what might be termed a holistic necessity, in that we exist as in body persons and therefore respond as more than minds or souls" (Fowler, *More Than a Symbol*, 333–34).

79. Beasley-Murray writes that without the subject of baptism possessing faith in Christ, "Such a misapplication of baptism degrades the conception of membership in the body of Christ and makes the confession of faith and promise of discipleship undertaken in baptism [by the parent or representative of the infant] meaningless" (Beasley-Murray, *Baptism in the New Testament*, 388). Based upon the arguments presented in this book, I conclude that the proper subject is the most important factor for determining whether the baptism is biblical and, therefore, valid. Other factors contribute to determining the validity of baptism though, including mode and administrator. White recognizes that due to the Landmark controversy, Baptist churches have at times rejected a person's baptism as a believer from a pedobaptist church. Rather than advocating for Baptist churches to continue rejecting "alien immersions" as these baptisms are called, White claims, "The determining factor is the ordinance itself"

Part of Fiddes's justification for differing processes of initiation is the claim that believer's baptism presumes one professes faith prior to baptism, allowing for a gap in time between the profession and the baptism. From a biblical perspective, this way of framing the matter obscures what is clear. For the sake of upholding justification by faith, it is possible, and even necessary, to distinguish one's trust in Christ from the heart (Rom 10:9) from one's outward appropriation and pledge of that trust in baptism (1 Pet 3:21; Acts 2:38). Yet, a temporal lapse between faith and baptism in no way entails the legitimacy of reversing the dependence of baptism upon faith.[80] In the New Testament, faith and baptism belong together, as aspects of conversion. Chapter 3 demonstrated that the New Testament data assumes the pattern that all believers are baptized, both in Paul's epistolary addresses to the churches and the examples of Acts. Chapter 4 demonstrated that baptism's function is to reflect heart circumcision that comes to the believer through Christ in the new covenant. These affirmations logically entail a denial of multiple processes of initiation into the church.

(White, "What Makes Baptism Valid?," in White et al., *Restoring Integrity in Baptist Churches*, 117–18). Thus, White encourages churches to determine the validity of a person's baptism on a case by case basis. This counsel is wise. To be sure, the prospect of a Baptist church actually accepting a believer's baptism by immersion from a pedobaptist church is narrow. He even claims, "In the majority of instances, alien immersions have harmed the meaning of baptism enough to render the practice null and void. However, a rare valid exception may exist." He concludes the chapter stating, "Valid baptism, the door to the local church, is performed by an appropriately selected administrator of a true church who immerses a believer in water for the purpose of profession of faith with and in the name of Jesus Christ, the second person of the Trinity, symbolizing the subject's identification with Christ's death burial, and resurrection." With some minor caveats, this description is helpful. Given the preponderance of Bible churches and other baptistic non-denominational churches since White wrote in 2008, I think the possibility of affirming alien immersions (when alien is broadened to include non-SBC churches), is greatly increased. Other questions should be considered with respect to the validity of baptism: (1) What did the baptizing church intend by the baptism? (2) What did the baptizing church's statement of faith affirm and/or deny about baptism? (3) What did the baptismal candidate believe about the gospel and baptism when she pursued believer's baptism in a pedobaptist church? For B. H. Carroll's description of a valid baptism, see Carroll, *Baptists and Their Doctrines*, 33. For a helpful defense of immersion as the biblical mode of baptism see Allen, "Dipped for the Dead," in White et al., *Restoring Integrity in Baptist Churches*, 91–97. Allen calls believer's baptism "the distinctive principle of Baptists" (106). Although Scripture teaches that the immersion of a professing believer by a true church is baptism, this book undergirds what I see as the distinctive principle of Baptists, namely, regenerate church membership. For this claim, see Hammett, "Regenerate Church Membership," in White et al., *Restoring Integrity in Baptist Churches*, 21. Contra Allen, believer's baptism is the logical result of the newness of the new covenant community.

80. Beasley-Murray, *Baptism in the New Testament*, 273–74; Moo, *Epistle to the Romans*, 366.

Furthermore, for a church to affirm that infant baptism followed by confirmation is just as legitimate as believer's baptism leads to logical and practical problems. The argument for multiple processes of initiation requires churches to affirm (at least tacitly) either (1) that the New Testament does not present a defined doctrine of baptism as being for believer's only, and thus deny the Baptist insistence on a believer's church,[81] or (2) that the New Testament affirms the appropriateness of uniting persons in church membership who hold contradictory views of who should be baptized.[82] While Fiddes holds out a common process of initiation as a way to avoid compromising theological convictions,[83] he does not explain how someone

---

81. Contra Freeman, *Contesting Catholicity*, 379–80. Freeman argues that "regenerate membership can be realized without insisting on [a particular order of faith's relation to baptism] as long as the link between faith and baptism is strong and intentional." He supposes that such a link can be established as long as "infant baptism [is] aimed toward conversion of the baptized," such that both infant baptism and believer's baptism "share the common goal of regenerate church membership." This argument practically requires Freeman to claim a link between infant baptism and faith. No such link exists in Scripture, and Freeman does not grant the common pedobaptist appeal to a promissory aspect of infant baptism leading to faith. Certainly, both pedobaptists and Baptists can raise their children with family worship, attending corporate worship, with prayer for the children's salvation, and with intentional conversations about the gospel. However, the infant baptism forges no more of a link to faith than the Baptist's evangelistic efforts. Freeman is refusing to admit that his scheme requires that he give up the Baptist distinctive of regenerate church membership.

82. If the second affirmation pertains, some in the church would believe that infant baptism is not baptism and some would believe that infant baptism is baptism. Fiddes recognizes this possibility among open communion advocates. He considers Daniel Turner's view that infant baptism and believer's baptism are the same in substance. He writes, "To say that infant baptism is the same as pedobaptism on grounds of the intention of the pedobaptist, is to regard an intention as the objective reality" (Fiddes, *Tracks and Traces*, 181). Fiddes thinks he avoids this whole conundrum by proposing that Christians find unity in a common process of initiation rather than in baptism.

83. Fiddes, *Tracks and Traces*, 141. Haymes, Goldbourne, and Cross claim to uphold Baptist convictions in the following solution: "We look to local congregations to teach that [baptism] is the norm for conversion and membership as is explicit in the NT. However, if people should seek membership without baptism, directly or by transfer, we suggest that they be questioned as to why they do not wish to follow the Lord in this respect. In other words, what theological reasons they might have for not being baptized. By so doing we keep up front our convictions about the importance of this sacrament and the theological understandings of being church to which it relates. It would then be for a local congregation to judge whether the candidate is serious about their understanding of sharing the call of God and the practice of discipleship. Thus, we do not rule out the possibility of such a person becoming a local church member" (Haymes et al., *On Being the Church*, 92). Thus, in the end, churches may choose to violate their corporate conscience by receiving someone with a different doctrine of baptism, so long as it is sincerely held. James Leo Garrett recognizes the pull of ecumenism in some Baptist circles. Yet, he argues, "The first principle of healthy

who is convinced of believer's baptism from the New Testament would avoid compromise.

Instead of supplanting the New Testament's doctrine of initiation and becoming entangled in logical and practical problems, churches benefit from recognizing conscientiously held theological differences. Theological triage is a crucial component to upholding the Scripture's authority to determine a church's doctrines and practices and to recognizing the legitimacy of Christians acting in obedience to what they hold to be biblical teaching.[84] Given the constitutive nature of the ordinances for the local church, as demonstrated in this book, baptism should be considered a second tier doctrine—a doctrine upon which genuine Christians may disagree without calling their Christian identity into question. At the same time, second tier doctrines are those about which members of a particular, local church should agree for the sake of unity, covenantal responsibility, and the practical disruption that would result from disagreement. Given baptism's place among other doctrines, the ecumenical vision wherein "baptism is a boundary but it excludes no one" fails to supply churches with the necessary theological foundation on which to build.[85] As a secondary doctrine, baptism gives the church its institutional form and order, which serves to protect and promote the gospel.[86]

---

interdenominational dialogue is to represent one's own beliefs faithfully and accurately. It is not prerequisite to such dialogue to deny one's own beliefs" (Garrett Jr., "Should Baptist Churches Adopt Open Membership?" 2). Open membership, Garrett is clear, would be an appreciation of unity at the expense of truth. Garrett is less clear about the practice of open communion with closed membership in Baptist churches. Historically, both close communion Baptists and open communion Baptists have been willing to uphold their theological convictions regarding what baptism is, even describing infant baptism "a nullity." See Kinghorn, *Defense*, 194. Hall's language is not so strong. However, he clearly affirms that baptism in the NT was believer's baptism and did not include pedobaptism. Thus, throughout his defense of open communion, he argues that infant baptism is an error (Hall Jr., *Terms of Communion*, 39).

84. "Theological triage" is Mohler's term. He argues that determining the order of importance of different doctrines is healthy and necessary; he presents three tiers. First tier theological issues are those matters one cannot fail to believe and still be a Christian (e.g., the Trinity, the full divinity and humanity of Christ, etc.). To the second tier belongs those doctrines over which believers may disagree, but which churches must agree on for life together (e.g., the mode and subjects of baptism, the role of women as elders, etc.). Third tier doctrines are those matters that are important, yet allow for disagreement among Christians even within the same church (e.g., the nature and timing of the millennial reign of Christ, the nature and timing of the rapture, etc.) (Mohler, "Call for Theological Triage").

85. Contra Fiddes, *Tracks and Traces*, 155.

86. By "form" is intended the ritual act by which a church "unites into a distinct body." By "order" is meant that baptism publicly identifies a person with Christ, thus

A similar argument to Fiddes's multiple processes of initiation approach is to claim that infant baptism is valid though incomplete until the infant grows to affirm her personal faith in Christ. Kynes argues,

> Baptism presents a visible and objective declaration of the gospel, and its validity as such is not nullified by the absence of the proper subjective response of faith. In those cases, in which that subjective response is not present at the time of baptism, it remains a valid baptism, though not an effective and completed one. This is similar to the preaching of the gospel. Its validity is not nullified by a failure of the hearers to repent and believe. But when they do, that preaching achieves its appointed end.[87]

This argument fails for three reasons. First, Kynes offers no biblical basis upon which to claim that the lack of a "proper subjective response of faith" does not nullify the baptism. Second, he invents the category of non-effective and incomplete baptism. In the New Testament, baptism is reflective of circumcision of the heart, not prospective. Physical circumcision in the Old Testament was non-effective in terms of guaranteeing, creating, or promising regeneration to the specific, individual, circumcised male. However, baptism assumes circumcision of the heart as a present reality and possession. The whole connection between baptism and the newness of the new covenant is laid aside by Kynes's invented category. Third, certainly, the failure of the hearers to respond in faith does not nullified gospel preaching (cf. Isa 6:9; Matt 13:1–23; 2 Cor 4:1–6). However, baptism is nowhere presented as a divine means of creating faith, as the gospel is (cf. Rom 1:16; 10:17); instead, Christians are called to proclaim the gospel indiscriminately to all people (Acts 1:8; cf. 17:30). But Christians are called to baptize those who voluntarily come under the reign and into covenantal union with Christ (Matt 28:18–20). Therefore, Kynes's argument fails, for

---

making her "fit 'matter' for a church" (Jamieson, *Going Public*, 182). With respect to distinguishing second tier from third tier doctrines, Jamieson cites Hammett, "Nature of the Church," in White et al., *Restoring Integrity in Baptist Churches*, 20. Hammett writes, "But baptism is more than a doctrine; it involves obedience to Christ's command." Thus, the doctrine of baptism is distinguished from the doctrine of the millennium, for instance.

87. Kynes, an Evangelical Free Church pastor, who claims that Scripture teaches believer's baptism, recognizes that this approach has its problems; indeed, some of those are outlined above. Nevertheless, he "offer[s] it as a way of allowing our common grasp of the gospel to overcome our historical and theological differences with regard to baptism that prevent us from welcoming one another in the fellowship of the church." His willingness to open the Lord's Supper and church membership to believing pedobaptist is the basis of the title of his post (Kynes, "Why I Am a 'baptist' [with a Small 'b']").

maintaining it requires him to practically deny the doctrine of believer's baptism he claims to hold.

The second argument of the ecumenical theologians—the claim that Baptist identity may be upheld by opening the Table to any who wish to come, while restricting baptism to those who profess faith—requires a response.[88] Seeking to articulate a defense on grounds of historic Baptist identity is beyond the scope of this book. However, commenting on the way this argument for ecumenical communion intersects with thesis of this book and the Baptist distinctive of regenerate church membership is appropriate. This ecumenical communion argument assumes that the sign of participation may, as a rule, precede the sign of entry. However, the argument is more extreme, for it allows those who do not profess faith to receive the sign of covenant participation, noting the possibility that the Lord's Supper could be a "converting ordinance."[89]

At least two critiques of this argument stem from the thesis of this book. To begin, according to Christ's design, faith is that posture of the heart that renders baptism valid and biblical, and faith with baptism constitute the means of entering the new covenant (Gal 3:26–29). If the order of the signs is reversed, ecumenical theologians would have faith as prerequisite to baptism for the sake of maintaining Baptist identity, but they would not require faith or baptism as prerequisite to the Lord's Supper. This ecumenically friendly suggestion dismisses the appropriate order of covenantal signs and the relationship of each ordinance to union with Christ. Contrary to Clarke, it is not true that Paul "leaves open the possibility that individuals can enter the covenant" by observing the Lord's Supper.[90] First Corinthians presents baptism as the instrument of union with Christ and the church (12:13) in close proximity to the affirmation that the Supper is a participation in Christ and Christ's church (10:16–17).[91]

---

88. Haymes et al., *On Being the Church*, 139.

89. Clarke, "Feast for All?," in Cross and Thompson, *Baptist Sacramentalism 2*, 115–16; Haymes et al., *On Being the Church*, 138. Contra Billings, *Remembrance, Communion, and Hope*, 158. Regarding fencing the table, Billings claims, the church "disrespects the unbelievers when they invite them to the family Table, by acting as if they hold convictions they do not" [hold].

90. Clarke, "Feast for All?," in Cross and Thompson, *Baptist Sacramentalism 2*, 105.

91. Finn also recognizes that the relation of each ordinance to union with Christ is missed by failing to practice close communion. He writes, "In Baptist churches that practice open communion, a pedobaptist may be adequately representing his ongoing union with Christ by participating in communion, but he has never had his initial union with Christ properly represented through immersion. As a result, the theological relationship between the two ordinances is at best disjointed, and at worst it is entirely overlooked. Only consistent [close] communion churches adequately represent the

With regard to Baptist identity, the proposal to reverse the order of the signs while continuing to require a profession of faith as prerequisite to baptism, undermines regenerate church membership in at least two ways. For one, if the sign that marks off the body of Christ from the world is open to whomever may happen to visit the church's meeting, then those who are baptized are baptized into a non-entity. In other words, because the Lord's Supper constitutes the church as a distinct and identifiable group, opening the meal to any who desire to participate evacuates the meal of its covenantal and, as an effective sign for creating a particular local church, its ontological significance. Thus, the proposal would reconstitute Baptist identity into any identifiable group who may happen to attend a "Baptist" church's worship gathering.

The second way reversing the order of the signs hinders Baptist identity applies specifically to regenerate church membership. Refusing to baptize those who do not profess faith guards regenerate church membership only if the group into which one is baptized is regenerate. However, the previous point established that a completely open invitation to the Lord's Supper entails that the group into which one is baptized is not regenerate. Because the requirement that one pursue baptism as a means of professing faith is biblical, biblically faithful Baptists should be thankful for it. Nevertheless, this argument for ecumenical communion does not succeed in maintaining Baptist identity.

The third argument for ecumenical communion is that Jesus' instruction regarding table fellowship is directly applicable to the Lord's Supper and leads to a radically open Table.[92] In response, it is true that Jesus' example of feeding the crowds and his teachings about fellowship meals and parables of banquets contain some secondary relevance for the practice of

---

believer's union with Christ in their observation of both ordinances" (Finn, "Baptism as a Prerequisite," 7).

92. Clarke admits that Jesus' words at Simon's house (Luke 7:36–50) and his instructions not to give invitations in order to be repaid with honor (14:1–14) contain "no direct eucharistic elements . . . or even inferences" (Clarke, "Feast for All?," in Cross and Thompson, Baptist Sacramentalism 2, 106). Yet, he claims Jesus' attitude toward fellowship meals reveals his priority of receiving people "rather than erecting fences." Concerning the parable of the great banquet (14:16–24; par. Matt 22:1–14), Clarke concludes that the whole section from Jesus' lament that Jerusalem would not gather under his wings to the statement "None of those men who were invited shall taste my banquet," is intended to forecast the kinds of people who will be at the Messianic feast in the kingdom. If, Clarke contends, the end time feast will be populated by those normally rejected from religious society, and the Lord's Supper is a present expression of that future feast, should not the church invite a broader group to enjoy the Supper than the religiously affiliated? Others who present this argument include Canoy, "Perspectives on Eucharistic Theology," 203; Haymes et al., On Being the Church, 138.

the Lord's Supper. However, the primary function of the fellowship meal texts is to picture Jesus' grace to receive undeserving sinners by repentance and faith into his people. Furthermore, the closest analogue to the open invitations in the parables of wedding banquets in the Gospels is the call to believe in Jesus as the bridegroom. Spatial constraints prohibit a full response to each passage. However, brief comments on John 6, Luke 7:36–50, and Luke 14:16–24 demonstrate the inadequacy of arguing for ecumenical communion from these texts.

In John 6, Jesus' primary concern in mentioning eating his flesh and drinking his blood in verse 54 is that the crowds might believe in him as the living bread that eternally satisfies.[93] In order to argue that Jesus' open invitation to the crowds has relevance for instructing churches on whom to invite to the Lord's Supper, Clarke assumes that John 6 functions as John's account of the institution of the Lord's Supper.[94] As this work argued in chapter 3, John 6 is better understood as referencing the Lord's Supper in a secondary, parabolic sense.[95] Thus, the context prohibits a direct application of Jesus' open invitation to the church's celebration of the Lord's Supper.

Additionally, the account of the meal at Simon's house is not intended to be applied directly to the Lord's Supper (Luke 7:36–50). Instead, the story demonstrates the problem of self-righteousness and Jesus' gracious bestowal of forgiveness on those who come to him in humility. Whereas Simon attempts to exalt himself socially and morally above the sinful woman who anoints Jesus' feet, Jesus exalts the humble. The church can certainly learn that neither past sins nor social status have legitimate bearing on one's place in Christ's community.[96] However, the context of table fellowship in Simon's house is intended to teach how Jesus came to bring spiritual healing by calling sinners to repentance and bringing them salvation (cf. Luke 5:30–32; 19:10).[97] Similarly, Jesus' instruction at the Pharisee's house (14:13–14), "When you give a feast, invite the poor, the crippled, the lame, the blind," is intended to inspire people to value God's reward over people's social

93. Allison, "Theology of the Eucharist," in Schreiner and Crawford, *Lord's Supper*, 183.

94. Clarke, "Feast for All?," in Cross and Thompson, *Baptist Sacramentalism 2*, 107.

95. Köstenberger claims that Jesus' call to eat the flesh (*sarx*) of the Son of Man "rules out a sacramental interpretation" because of the clear incarnational emphasis— Jesus would die a fully human death for sinners (Köstenberger, *John*, 215–16). Several scholars point out John's use of *sarx* here as opposed to *soma*, which is most often used in Lord's Supper contexts. See also Carson, *Gospel According to John*, 295; Beasley-Murray, *John*, 93–94.

96. Garland, *Luke*, 331–32. See also Bock, *Luke*, 1:708.

97. Garland, *Luke*, 251–52.

reciprocation. Churches rightly apply Jesus' instructions when individual members intentionally value every person made in God's image by their personal and corporate hospitality for Christ's sake. Thus, "the mood is not one of inclusion" for inclusion's sake.[98] Jesus' purpose is to urge those who represent his kingdom toward humble generosity. The specific lesson for the church is again the denial of societal rank, given a common association with Christ (cf. 1 Cor 11:17–22).[99]

The parable of the great banquet also requires clarification (cf. Luke 14:15–24). Jesus introduces the parable after a man, presumably associated with the Pharisees, exclaims, "Blessed is everyone who will eat bread in the kingdom of God" (v. 15). As the statement presupposes that the Pharisees will attend that end time feast,[100] Jesus tells the parable to demonstrate that those who were presumed to have a place at the table must receive the master's invitation when it is given (cf. Matt 22:3–14).[101] Thus, the great banquet in the parable certainly portrays the consummatory kingdom feast (cf. Luke 22:16, 18, 29–30). However, the excuses of those initially invited to the feast, and the resulting open invitation to any who would come, are intended by Jesus to warn the Pharisees. They persist in rejecting Jesus at their own peril. Jesus promises participation in the feast to any who will respond with total allegiance (cf. 14:25–33).[102]

The church today should continue to recognize that Jesus the king has come and calls any who would enter his kingdom to deny themselves, value him above all things, and totally align themselves to his rule—each of these being initially demonstrated in baptism (Acts 2:38–41). Thus, this passage actually assists the close communion argument. The parable teaches that those who refuse to enter the kingdom in the way Jesus prescribes may not participate in the kingdom community's inaugurated kingdom feast (Luke 14:15–33).[103]

Neither Jesus' openness to eat with self-righteous Simon in the presence of the sinful, humble woman, nor his invitation to anyone who would

---

98. Bock, *Luke*, 2:1266.

99. For more that appropriately applies Luke 14 to the Lord's Supper, see Vickers, "Past and Future," in Schreiner and Crawford, *Lord's Supper*, 331–32.

100. Bock, *Luke*, 2:1272.

101. Luke's account is similar to Matthew's, but Matthew is the one to emphasize responding to the invitation in a timely fashion and in a manner appropriate with the master's design. This emphasis occurs through Jesus' mention of the one who apparently snuck into the wedding party without proper wedding clothes and was subsequently thrown into hell (Matt 22:11–14). See Blomberg, *Matthew*, 328–30.

102. Stein, *Luke*, 394–95; Bock, *Luke*, 2:1278; Garland, *Luke*, 592–94.

103. Contra Canoy, "Perspectives on Eucharistic Theology," 208.

respond to eat at his end time feast, suggests the legitimacy of ecumenical communion. Instead, these ecumenical arguments dismiss Jesus' purpose of saving sinners from following their own worldly aims (Luke 9:23–27; 57–62) in order to bring them into his covenant community (22:19–20; Acts 1:4–11). In other words, one must not confuse Jesus' mission with the church's mission.[104] While it was Jesus' unique role as the God-man and typological fulfillment of Israel and David to fulfill the promises to Israel and bring salvation to the nations (Luke 1:54–55, 68–79; 24:47; cf. Luke 3:38—4:11; Exod 4:22–23), the church consists of those who are forgiven for Christ's sake and belong to his new covenant community with all the benefits entailed therein (22:19–20; Acts 2:38–42).

Conclusion

The task of this chapter has been to respond to several arguments put forward by proponents of open, closed, and ecumenical communion respectively. While more arguments could be raised and more could be said in response to the arguments presented, the responses of this chapter have sought to apply the biblical data surveyed in chapters 3 through 5. The task of chapter 6 is to apply the thesis specifically to the doctrine of the church and the practice of close communion.

---

104. This appears to be part of Canoy's error in Canoy, "Perspectives on Eucharistic Theology," 209–10.

Chapter 6

Application to Baptist Ecclesiology

THIS CHAPTER APPLIES THE thesis to the theology and practice of the local church. Regarding ecclesiology, the chapter considers the relationship of the ordinances to the new covenant, kingdom, universal church, and local church. Regarding practice, this chapter applies close communion to the concepts of church membership and church discipline. The chapter closes with practical suggestions for fencing the Table.

The Ordinances and Ecclesiology

The function of the ordinances in relation to the new covenant and inaugurated kingdom lead to further theological implications for the doctrine of the church, which are explored in this section.

The Ordinances and the New Covenant

Baptism's entire cluster of theological associations find their origins in the promises of the new covenant;[1] therefore, this book has argued that baptism is the sign of entry to the new covenant. Because each of the new covenant

---

1. Baptism is associated with the circumcision of the heart (Col 2:11–12; cf. Deut 30:6); heart cleansing (Heb 10:22; Titus 3:5; cf. Ezek 44:7–9); union with Christ (Rom 6:1–5; Col 2:11–13; Gal 3:26); the new birth (Col 2:11–13; Rom 6:5; John 3:5; Titus 3:5; cf. Ezek 36:26–27); forgiveness (Acts 2:38; 22:16; Mark 1:4; cf. Rom 4:11; Jer 31:34); and the divine and human initiating oath sign (Matt 28:18–20; Gen 17:10–11). For summaries of the meaning of baptism, see White, "What Makes Baptism Valid?," in White et al., *Restoring Integrity in Baptist Churches*, 110–11; Allison, *Sojourners and Strangers*, 353–57.

benefits with which baptism is associated comes to the believer by virtue of union with Christ, union with Christ should be understood as a summary expression for the new covenant. Christ intends those who believe in him to externally appropriate/ratify union with him through baptism (Acts 2:38),[2] in what Allison describes as "conversionistic covenantalism."[3] Identification of new covenant members happens through the right application of the new covenant signs, beginning with baptism and continuing through the Lord's Supper.[4] Thus, the redemptive-historical newness of the church is evidenced through the ordinances.[5] More specifically, the ordinances mark the church as a regenerate community, unlike Israel, which was a mixed community of believers and unbelievers.[6]

As a covenantal sign, baptism not only signifies union with Christ, but also the derivative union with Christ's body, the new covenant community (Gal 3:26–28). Therefore, baptism is an "obligation creating act,"[7] one evidence of the church's covenantal nature.[8] As Hammett writes, "In the act of baptism, the church and the one baptized together act to symbolize the

2. Thus, A. B. Caneday is correct to affirm that asking the question of whether someone would be saved who dies after trusting Christ inwardly but before being baptized is unhelpful if it leads to separating what the NT holds together, namely regeneration, repentance/faith, and baptism (Caneday, "Baptism in the Stone-Cambell Restoration Movement," in Schreiner and Wright, Believer's Baptism, 317). See also the section entitled "Is Baptism Necessary for Salvation?" in Allison, Sojourners and Strangers, 357–60. Concerning the pattern of baptism belonging to conversion as compared to the thief on the cross, see Stein, "Baptism and Becoming a Christian in the New Testament," 15. For affirmation of baptism as new covenant ratification, see Fowler, More Than a Symbol, 239; Beasley-Murray, Baptism in the New Testament, 394.

3. Allison, Sojourners and Strangers, 128. By this term, Allison "intend[s] to indicate that the way one enters the new covenant is through conversion to Jesus Christ, attested to by baptism by immersion, and not by means of family associations."

4. Leeman, Political Church, 266.

5. On the mixed nature of pedobaptist churches in contrast to churches seeking a regenerate membership, see Leeman, "Church and Churches," in Leeman and Dever, Baptist Foundations, 348–49; Moore and Sagers, "Kingdom of God and the Church," 78.

6. Carson, "Evangelicals, Ecumenism and the Church," in Kantzer and Henry, Evangelical Affirmations, 371–74.

7. Horton, People and Place, 102.

8. Allison, Sojourners and Strangers, 123–24. Leeman offers nine ways in which the covenantal nature of the church gleans from the covenantal structure of Scripture and the specific covenants of the OT (Leeman, Surprising Offense, 250–66). Covenantal theologians recognize the covenantal nature of the church as well. It is their failure to recognize the newness of the covenant community that leads them to affirm a mixed covenant community of believers and unbelievers. Nevertheless, as chapter 4 demonstrated, their covenantal sensitivity to the NT provides much that is helpful for consideration of the church's covenantal nature. See Waters and Duncan, Children and the Lord's Supper; Strawbridge, Case for Covenant Communion.

meaning of baptism."[9] The covenantal association of baptism, as the sign of entry, and the Lord's Supper, as the sign of participation, give definition to the local church as a covenanted body.

Allison affirms that Christ's covenantal relationship with Christians initiates and is "foundational for and generative of" the "secondary and derivative" covenantal "relationship that exists between church members." Thus, when "Christ-followers make a willful choice by faith and in obedience to their Lord to covenant together as a voluntary organization,"[10] they enact the horizontal union that Christ makes possible.[11] As Webster argues, the "human act of assembly follows, signifies, and mediates the divine act of gathering; it is a moved movement of the congregation."[12] While it is true that "a church is born when gospel people form a gospel polity [organized society]," the human actions depend upon the prior action of the Holy Spirit.[13] Allison explains, "Accordingly, becoming a member, joining with others in a voluntary society called the church does not ultimately constitute the church. Rather, it joins that member to an already existing reality, or it defines the constituents of that particular entity that has already been constituted a church by the Holy Spirit."[14] Therefore, the "socio-historical assembly" of any particular local church is "metaphysically irreducible" to the Lord's prior work.[15]

One function of this book is to ground the claim that baptism and the Lord's Supper are constitutive of the local church in the sense of "defining the constituents of that particular entity."[16] To state it differently, "The basic signs of the church—Scripture and sacraments—are its primary instruments of order," and are thus the means by which the local "church exists

9. Hammett, *Forty Questions*, 149.

10. Allison, *Sojourners and Strangers*, 128.

11. So Billings, *Remembrance, Communion, and Hope*, 80. This is the same reality Leeman describes when he maintains that one enters the new covenant in "two (logical) moments" (Leeman, *Political Church*, 362).

12. Webster, "In the Society of God," in Ward, *Perspectives on Ecclesiology and Ethnography*, 216. For this source, see Jamieson, *Going Public*, 141.

13. Jamieson, *Going Public*, 141.

14. Allison delineates the ordering by which a church is constituted: (1) "God's choice (of us; unilateral election) and covenant making (with us; unilateral new covenant)"; (2) our choice (of God through Christ, as made known through the gospel; 2 Thess 2:13–14) and covenant-making with members of Christ's church" (Allison, *Sojourners and Strangers*, 128). For a similar ordering, see Webster, "In the Society of God," 216–20.

15. Webster, "In the Society of God," in Ward, *Perspectives on Ecclesiology and Ethnography* 217.

16. Allison, *Sojourners and Strangers*, 128.

and enacts its life"[17] as a particular body and institution. Or, in Jamieson's words, "Baptism and the Lord's Supper make the church visible."[18] As Paul explains, "You were all baptized into one body" (1 Cor 12:13) and "We who are many are one body, for we all partake of the one bread" (1 Cor 10:17).

Because Jesus describes the cup of the Lord's Supper as "the new covenant in my blood" and commands the disciples to "Do this in remembrance of me," the church rightly conceives of the meal as the ongoing sign of new covenant participation.[19] Or, as Jamieson describes it, the meal is a "renewing oath sign,"[20] in terms of the individual Christian's reaffirmation of trust in Christ (cf. 1 Cor 10:16; John 6:54), the church's reaffirmation of derivative unity with each other (1 Cor 10:17; 11:17–34),[21] and the Lord's re-affirmation of complete forgiveness through participation in the blood of Christ (10:16; Matt 26:28).[22] The corporate dimension of the Lord's Supper, similar to baptism, entails that the church that participates in the meal "ratifies the [new] covenant" and, by their sharing of the elements, "constitutes the church as a church" (1 Cor 10:16; cf. 11:17–34).[23] The local church should be understood as a eucharistic community.[24] Because the Lord's Supper constitutes those in-

17. Webster, "In the Society of God," in Ward, *Perspectives on Ecclesiology and Ethnography* 219. Stanley J. Grenz explains, "The rights of the church take their meaning from the gospel, for baptism in the Lord's Supper are dramatic community enactments of its constitutive narrative, the biblical story of salvation" (Grenz, "Baptism and the Lord's Supper," in Cross and Thompson, *Baptist Sacramentalism*, 92). He continues, these acts "bear witness to the experience of union with Christ shared by the entire community. The idea of a shared union with Christ embodied in the church . . . suggest that as community acts, baptism in the Lord's Supper function as acts of belonging, albeit each in a distinctive manner."

18. Jamieson, *Going Public*, 142.

19. Marshall, *Last Supper and Lord's Supper*, 89.

20. Jamieson, *Going Public*, 114–15.

21. Hammett, *Forty Questions*, 207. Hammett writes, "Thus at the Lord's Supper we celebrate, recognize, and express our unity, solidarity and commitment to one another in the body of believers and we enjoy fellowship with our Lord as he is present among us."

22. Grenz also recognizes that three agents act in the ordinances: the individual participant, the church, and the Lord. He writes "The Lord's Supper marks the reprise of the great refrain, 'you—I—we belong,' that in baptism the identity-conferring God, the identifying community, and the identity-acknowledging candidate sang together" (Grenz, "Baptism and the Lord's Supper," in Cross and Thompson, *Baptist Sacramentalism*, 93).

23. Jamieson, *Going Public*, 153.

24. Gary D. Badcock explains, "The central idea of eucharistic ecclesiology is that the church is most truly what it is, and can be best understood in its own intrinsic being specifically in the eucharistic celebration" (Badcock, *House Where God Lives*, 96). This description does not require the conclusion that "the Eucharist, rather than the Word of God . . . most clearly and most fully constitutes the church" (97). Instead, the Lord's Supper's constituting role is derivative of the Word of God, for therein lies the formal

dividuals united with Christ into "one body" (1 Cor 10:17), the meal should be understood as an ecclesially effective sign.[25] By the Lord's Supper, the new covenant community becomes visible in time and space.[26] These observations allow further positive and negative statements regarding the church.

Positively, receiving the Lord's Supper together marks the group of Christians as belonging to Christ through his new covenant work and, as a result, belonging to each other in terms of new covenant obligations (1 Cor 12–14; Rom 12–15; Eph 4–6).[27] Negatively, a group of Christians that meets regularly for Bible study, prayer, worship, or the like, but that does not take the Lord's Supper together, is not a church. These statements make sense because at the same time that each Christian reaffirms her trust in Christ in the meal, the local body reaffirms its unity together in the gospel and its shared responsibility for each other's Christian growth. In Jamieson's words, "Church fellowship is joint participation in the benefits of Christ and the life which flows from those benefits, and the Lord's Supper represents and seals fellowship with Christ and with one another."[28]

---

and material authority for predicating a constitutive role to the Lord's Supper (99). As Marshall explains, "The interpretive sayings constituted an essential part of the actions, so that, to use later terminology, the Word is a constitutive part of the sacrament" (Marshall, *Last Supper and Lord's Supper*, 113). Fiddes also describes the church as a eucharistic community in a similar sense offered above (i.e., a constitutive act). However, Fiddes draws the implication that celebrating the Lord's Supper together "enables the presence of Christ" (Fiddes, *Tracks and Traces*, 157). If Fiddes intended that celebrating the Lord's Supper together is the way in which the church formally constitutes as a group gathered in the name of Jesus, his point would be in line with this book. Instead, Fiddes intends that participation in the Lord's Supper results in the church becoming a sacrament and "an extension of the incarnation" (170). This claim is rendered suspect by Fiddes's claim that Christ is not now bodily present in heaven until the second coming and by his willingness to affirm a nature and grace interdependence (170–74).

25. Marshall has, "Paul's present point . . . is that Christians are bound together with their fellow Christians in the Lord's Supper and must express that unity in love and consideration for others" (Marshall, *Last Supper and Lord's Supper*, 121).

26. Horton writes, "The preaching creates the community, while the Supper by evoking personal acceptance through faith, makes that community in some sense visible" (Horton, *People and Place*, 51). For a thoughtful approach to Scripture's relation to the creation of the church, see Webster, *Holy Scripture*, 42–57.

27. Grenz writes, "As the community gathers at the Table, their Lord—through the Holy Spirit—is present among them and communes with them. Moreover, his presence—by the Spirit—constitutes gathered community anew as the fellowship of those who together are in Christ. In this manner, sharing in the one loaf at the Lord's Supper becomes the great communal act of belonging, the great symbol of the fellowship with Christ and each other shared by the participants who belong to each other as the one body of Christ (1 Cor 10:17)" (Grenz, "Baptism and the Lord's Supper," in Cross and Thompson, *Baptist Sacramentalism*, 94).

28. Jamieson, *Going Public*, 123.

The Lord's words of institution at the Last Supper provide the formal warrant for the church's continual celebration of the Lord's Supper until he returns.[29] Given the metonymic nature of the cup (containing the fruit of the vine) for the whole of the new covenant and the association of bread with Jesus' body, the elements of the meal should be understood as inherently covenantal and regulated by Christ, rather than accidental.[30] Bread and the fruit of the vine are symbolic of the gospel itself and explicitly commanded by Christ;[31] thus, they are not expendable, optional, or open for exchange.[32]

29. Marshall writes, "It can, therefore, be assumed that the detailed description of the procedure at the Last Supper was significant. Even if the description was meant primarily as a pattern to be followed at the Lord's Supper, it was still important to follow out this particular pattern" (Marshall, *Last Supper and Lord's Supper*, 83).

30. In churches that believe the NT provides a clear pattern concerning the celebration of the Lord's Supper and yet do not utilize one loaf of bread and a common cup, the reasons vary. However, the size of the church is often enough reason for the church to move from a baked loaf, which is pulled apart for each person to small wafer like crackers, from a common cup to small individual cups. Expediency and sanitation are important to the contemporary Western world. However, some at least do still contend that one common cup and one loaf should be the normative practice of local churches because the bread and cup demonstrate unity (Moore, "Baptist View," in Armstrong, *Understanding Four Views on the Lord's Supper*, 42).

31. Regarding the symbolism of the cup, see Neste, "Lord's Supper," in Schreiner and Crawford, *Lord's Supper*, 374.

32. Paul clearly claims to have taught the Corinthian church to practice the Lord's Supper in virtually the same way as Jesus instituted the meal (cf. Luke 22:19–20 and 1 Cor 11:23–25) (Marshall, *Last Supper and Lord's Supper*, 111; Billings, *Remembrance, Communion, and Hope*, 118). Online churches exemplify one approach to church that precludes a biblical practice of the Lord's Supper in multiple ways, but of special note here, by their allowance of a variety of substitutes for the Lord's prescribed elements. Estes provides four options often used by online churches from instructing the on-line church member take crackers and Kool-Aid, or whatever he may have on hand, and participate alone to having one's online representation (avatar) partake of the elements in one's stead. See Estes, *Sim-Church*, 118–23. Evidence of the inability of online churches to practice the Lord's Supper is Estes' admission that most online churches do not practice the Lord's Supper at all. One study of an online church in the UK found that nearly half of the members believed it was "almost sacrilegious" to participate in communion without physical elements (Ostrowski, "Cyber Communion," 5–6). Reed raises similar issues regarding the elements in Reed, "Computer-Mediated Communication," 188. Hammett argues that some cultures do not have bread or wine and do not grow what is needed to make it; thus, they should use elements that can be poured out and something that can be broken to symbolize unity. He lightly critiques Allison on this point in note 15, for not providing a solution for these cultures while insisting on bread and wine (Hammett, *Forty Questions*, 299). For Hammett's reference, see Allison, *Sojourners and Strangers*, 400. In response to Hammett, giving up the dominically prescribed elements does not appear to be an option for the church. I propose that when possible, churches in the West might take responsibility and assist sister churches across the world by providing them with the needed resources to celebrate the Supper appropriately.

The Supper is the Lord's Table, and the church is not authorized to change it.[33]

The Ordinances and the Kingdom

The kingdom of God refers broadly to God's "dynamic reign and kingly rule" over all that he has made.[34] In various instances throughout the New Testament, the kingdom of God refers more specifically to Christ's saving reign.[35] Thus, the citizens of the kingdom are those who have come under the lordship of king Jesus.[36] As Ladd explains, "The church is the community of the kingdom but never the kingdom itself. Jesus' disciples belong to the kingdom as the kingdom belongs to them; but they are not the kingdom. The kingdom is the rule of God; the church is a society of men."[37] Thus, Allison is correct that "the church owes its existence to the kingdom," and "the church is the community of citizens of the kingdom of God."[38]

33. Marshall, *Last Supper and Lord's Supper*, 112; Allison, *Sojourners and Strangers*, 400.

34. Ladd, *Theology of the New Testament*, 111. The semantic range of the term "kingdom of God/heaven" is broad enough to encompass a more generic sense of God's rule over all that he has made (Pss 93; 97). For the kingdom theme throughout the OT, see Dempster, *Dominion and Dynasty*.

35. For the distinction between God's "kingly and sovereign rule" and his "saving reign," see Gentry and Wellum, *Kingdom through Covenant*, 593–95; Schreiner, *Kingdom of God and the Glory of the Cross*, 18–23. This point explains why Paul can speak of being "delivered from the domain of darkness and [being] transferred to the kingdom of his beloved Son" (Col 1:13)—a sphere change which occurs formally in baptism (2:11–12). God rules over the kingdom of darkness, whose rule, he has already defeated in Christ (v. 20; 2:9, 14–15). Yet, the enemy kingdom will not be fully removed until the second coming (Rev 20; cf. Eph 1:20–21). With respect to this interpretation of Colossians, see Allison, *Sojourners and Strangers*, 96–97. For a substantial treatment of the kingdom of God in the Gospels, see Schreiner, *New Testament Theology*, 41–79.

36. A particular example of this notion of kingdom is found in Jesus' parable of the wheat and the weeds (cf. Matt 13:24–30, 36–43). Allison notes several ecclesiologies that have been posited in church history based on a misunderstanding of this parable, which often result in promoting a doctrine of the church as a mixed group of believers and unbelievers similar to Israel. However, because Jesus identifies the world as the field in which the weeds and wheat grow until judgment (v. 38), the interpretation fails to justify the inclusion of unbelievers as covenant and/or church members (Allison, *Sojourners and Strangers*, 89n60). For a brief survey of these varying ecclesiologies that allowed for a mixture of believers and unbelievers based upon the parable, see Leeman, "Church and Churches," in Leeman and Dever, *Baptist Foundations*, 341–47. For affirmation that "the church is not a society of the regenerate" based on Matt 13, see Waters and Duncan, *Children and the Lord's Supper*, 192–93.

37. Ladd, *Theology of the New Testament*, 111. For more on the kingdom and the church, see Vos and Olinger, *Teaching of Jesus*, 72–86.

38. Allison, *Sojourners and Strangers*, 93–94. For a brief survey of ways in which Southern Baptist theologians have understood the relationship of the kingdom to the

Yet, more may be said about the relationship of the ordinances to the kingdom, and as a result, more may be said about the relationship of the kingdom to the church. As chapter 3 demonstrated, baptism is the sign of entering the kingdom and the Lord's Supper is an inaugurated kingdom feast; accordingly, the ordinances serve to mark off those who have moved from being subjects of God's universal reign to citizens of God's saving reign.[39] Therefore, Jesus' authorization of the church to act as his representatives in the world deserves attention in order to understand how the kingdom, the ordinances, and the church coalesce.

When considered in light of several Matthean contextual features (Matt 16:13–20; 18:15–20), Jesus' commission to make disciples by baptizing and teaching them takes on a more structural, institutional, and defined ecclesial shape (28:18–20). After Peter's divinely revealed confession of Jesus' Messianic identity (16:16), Jesus promises to build his church out of good confessors who make true confessions about him, as Peter did.[40] Matthew 16:18 reads, "I tell you, you are Peter, and on this rock I will build my church." Then, Jesus gives the apostles, represented by Peter, the keys of the kingdom, entailing the authority to bind and loose (v. 19).[41] Leeman argues that the keys should be understood not only in terms of opening

---

church before Allison wrote, see Moore and Sagers, "Kingdom of God and the Church," 73–75.

39. The language describing the change of identity subject to citizen belongs to Leeman, *Political Church*, 215. Similarly, Allison speaks of "children of the kingdom" and "civilian citizens" (Allison, *Sojourners and Strangers*, 97–98).

40. This language stems largely from Leeman. He explains, "There is both a 'what' and a 'who': what is a right confession and who is a right confessor" (Leeman, *Political Church*, 336). Exegetically, this interpretation follows a host of scholars who see Jesus' statement, "You are Peter (*petros*) and on this rock (*petra*) I will build my church" (Matt 18:18) as referring to both Peter and his confession together as the rock on which the church would be built. For this interpretation, Leeman cites Clowney, *Church*, 40; Blomberg, *Matthew*, 251–53; Carson, "Matthew," in Gaebelein, *Expositor's Bible Commentary*, 368. See also Leeman's earlier work on this passage in Leeman, *Surprising Offense*, 178–79. Elsewhere, Leeman describes the power of the keys as pronouncing "on heaven's behalf a judgment concerning the who and what of the gospel: what is the right confession and practice of the gospel, and who is a right confessor [of the gospel]" (Leeman, "Church and Churches," in Leeman and Dever, *Baptist Foundations*, 354).

41. Schreiner contends that binding and loosing refers to what is "forbidden or permitted" (Schreiner, "Biblical Basis for Church Discipline," in Hammett and Merkle, *Those Who Must Give an Account*, 110). In context, binding and loosing amounts to refusing to forgive sins or to forgiving sins. In practice, this interpretation results in the same conclusion that Leeman draws, namely, that the church acts to affirm those whom God has forgiven for the sake of Christ through the gospel by baptizing them and affirming those who are forgiven as belonging to God's people through the Lord's Supper.

the kingdom by proclaiming the gospel of Jesus (cf. Isa 22:22; Rev 3:7).[42] Instead, "Jesus gave Peter and the apostles both the authority to interpret the law, in a teacher-like fashion, and the authority to interpret its claim on actual people, in a judge-like fashion. They were to ensure that the right people belong to the church according to a right confession."[43]

Thus, to exercise the keys "is to render an interpretive judgment over statements of faith and church members."[44] Additionally, to bind and loose on behalf of heaven, as an exercise of the keys is to "make an antici-patory declaration: We, holders of the keys believe that this person might represent Jesus' end-time rule." When one is bound to the community of Christ's citizens, that good confessor is "being formally recognized for all the world to witness."[45]

Matthew 18:15–20 adds three important points to this discussion.[46] First, Jesus extends the authority to bind and loose to the church, rather than

42. Leeman, *Political Church*, 338. Speaking of Matt 16, Allison describes the power of the keys as "preaching the gospel of Jesus Christ, the good news of his cross work and resurrection on behalf of sinful people" (Allison, *Sojourners and Strangers*, 186n23). Rather than point to contextually distant biblical texts and imposing a definition of key, Allison points to Jesus' announcement of his impending death in Matt 16 and the apostolic preaching ministry in the book of Acts. Nevertheless, Allison's interpreta-tion does not appear to be ultimately at odds with Leeman's, at least on hermeneutical grounds. Both similarity and distinction from Allison are evident in Leeman's state-ment, "Strictly speaking, proclaiming the gospel is not the same as exercising the keys, but so closely are proclamation and the keys intertwined that the latter cannot occur without the former. If the keys are likened to speaking a verdict and pounding a gavel, proclaiming the gospel can be likened to reading the law upon which a verdict is based" (Leeman, "Church and Churches," in Leeman and Dever, *Baptist Founations*, 354).

43. Leeman, *Political Church*, 340. As Moore and Sagers contend, "The church is to be made up of those who acknowledge Jesus' kingship now, confessing that one day all men will see by sight what those who are in the church believe by faith. If the church is the manifestation now of the kingdom, and if Jesus' words to Nicodemus are true—that 'unless one is born again he cannot see the kingdom of God' (John 3:3)—surely then only those who have been born again may be admitted to membership in the new covenant community" (Moore and Sagers, "Kingdom of God and the Church," 77).

44. Leeman, *Political Church*, 341. Leeman gives several examples: (1) "when-ever the apostles determined once and for all a doctrinal matter that would bind the churches for all ages [cf. Acts 15]; (2) whenever postapostolic bishops, elders or con-gregations formally adopt a statement of faith or some ethical statement (e.g., a church covenant, standards for divorce) that binds every member and is treated as necessary for membership; (3) whenever a person is brought into membership by confession, removed from membership as an act of discipline or restored to membership following discipline." Given this judicial understanding of the keys, Leeman argues, "The act of teaching the gospel is not the same thing as exercising the keys, but the act of affirming the gospel as the gospel is [such an act]."

45. Leeman, *Political Church*, 344.

46. For a similar, yet historical explanation of Matt 18, see Carroll, *Baptists and*

being merely the prerogative of the apostles, for the human party finally re-sponsible to adjudicate a matter of unrepentant sin among those recognized as kingdom citizens is the church (v. 17).[47] Second, the passage presents adding and/or removing members from the local church as specific applica-tions of the keys (vv. 16–18).[48] Third, Jesus promises his presence with the gathered community of his citizens to authorize their actions of binding and loosing (vv.18–20).[49]

Putting the whole picture together, Jesus deputizes the whole local church as an outpost or embassy of his kingdom. Jesus grants the local church the authority, at least, to either to publicly affirm and therefore add new confessors of the gospel to the church, to deny the legitimacy of the confessor/confession and refuse to add the person to the church, or to re-move the person from the church.[50] Jesus implicitly describes the church (v. 17) as two or three "gathered in my name" (v. 20). Because baptism is the means by which a new disciple comes under Jesus' name (28:19),[51] Jesus is

---

Their Doctrines, 27–31.

47. Hammett, "Regenerate Church Membership," in White et al., *Restoring Integrity in Baptist Churches*, 31; Griffith, "Short Treatise," in Dever, *Polity*, 99.

48. So Hammett, "Regenerate Church Membership," in White et al., *Restoring Integrity in Baptist Churches*, 31. Hammett is correct that congregational authority, that Jesus authorizes in Matt 18, presumes a regenerate church.

49. See the whole discussion of this passage in Leeman, *Political Church*, 344–48. Leeman interpolates v. 20 as "For where two or three witnesses gather to testify to my name and to their shared union under my rule through exercising the keys together, that is, in any such church, my presence and authority is with them such that this church speaks on my behalf" (346; cf. 1 Cor 5:4). That the binding and loosing occurs on behalf of heaven is drawn from the future-perfect tense verbs, translated "shall be bound in heaven" and "shall be loosed in heaven" (ESV) and "shall have been bound" in the footnote (16:19; cf. 18:18). Although scholars are divided over the precise relation of the church's actions to heaven's, the indication is clear that the church acts on behalf of Christ rather than arbitrarily (Schreiner, "Biblical Basis for Church Discipline," in Hammett and Merkle, *Those Who Must Give an Account*, 110–11). Similarly, Craig Bartholomew concludes that the church is territorial in that it is "a sign of the kingdom in a particular place," precisely because the gospel should be "embodied in every place in creation" (Bartholomew, *Where Mortals Dwell*, 123–28). Allison cites this source on a different point in *Sojourners and Strangers*, 148. Christ's promised presence with the gathered assembly is the basis upon which the local church may be described as a sign of the kingdom.

50. The emphasis of Matt 18 is on acting to remove someone previously thought to be a true confessor making a true confession but who has since denied their confession by their unrepentant sin. Thus, the church's action would be to remove someone who was previously baptized.

51. As Michael Horton explains of covenant signs, words and ceremonies go to-gether in Scripture. Because the divine name is given to the new disciple in baptism, the declaration of the triune name "constitutes and certifies a new state of affairs" because

authorizing the local church to baptize. Through baptism, a church binds a new disciple to itself and officially recognizes him or her as a kingdom citizen.[52] Three other affirmations about baptism follow: (1) baptism is the official action by which Christ through the church adds "one to many" and so creates a body politic; (2) baptism is rightly called "the door of the church";[53] and (3) baptism is a boundary marker between the church and the world that signifies the church's eschatological nature.[54]

Given Jesus' deputization of the local church to bind and loose, the local church is the institution uniquely authorized to baptize new disciples.[55]

---

the sign functions as part of the divine speech" (Horton, *People and Place*, 101). On baptism's function of bestowing a new identity from Christ through the church, see Grenz, "Baptism and the Lord's Supper," in Cross and Thompson, *Baptist Sacramentalism*, 93.

52. Summarizing the function of baptism in Matthew from a biblical-theological perspective, Leeman writes, "Through baptism people are formally and publicly reinstated to Adam's original political office and to the body politic of Jesus' church. The keys of the kingdom are exercised first through baptism. Baptism is the recognition of kingdom citizenship and covenant membership. . . . It functions as the public badge or passport or identity papers among Christ's people and the nations now. When the nations come asking who belongs to Jesus and represents his rule on earth, the church points to everyone who has been baptized (and who continues to receive the Lord's Supper)" (Leeman, *Political Church*, 361). On the connection of Matthew 16; 18; and 28, see also Leeman, *Surprising Offense*, 178–83. Contra Venema, "Covenant Theology and Baptism," in Strawbridge, *Case for Covenantal Infant Baptism*, 220. Venema claims, "The sacraments are not administered on the basis of the presumed regeneration of the recipients." Vos's discussion of entering the kingdom contains no discussion of baptism. See Vos and Olinger, *Teaching of Jesus*, 87–97.

53. Jamieson, *Going Public*, 104–5. For a close communion advocate who disagrees that baptism is the "door to the church," see Richard Fuller, *Baptism, and the Terms of Communion*, 176. He writes, "Baptism is an act of personal obedience, by which a believer publicly confesses Christ. It does not initiate any body into any church."

54. On baptism as a sign of inaugurated eschatology, see Moore and Sagers, "Kingdom of God and the Church," 77. Wellum highlights the church's participation in the "age to come" and identity as part of the new creation (Wellum, "Beyond Mere Ecclesiology," in Easley and Morgan, *Community of Jesus*, 202–3).

55. For a similar take, see Mohler Jr., "Church Discipline," in Armstrong, *Compromised Church*, 181–83; Tyler, *Baptism*, 137. Interestingly, when discussing how or why the apostles considered the ordinances to belong to the church, Hammett does not follow Leeman in claiming the power of the keys granted gathered believers that right. He claims instead, "They did not see the commands as pertaining to them alone. It may be that they came to understand that they were the nucleus or representatives of the church, or that the meaning of the sacraments linked them intrinsically to the church. At any rate, the command to observe the Lord's Supper seems to have been transmitted from the apostles to the church early on" (cf. 1 Cor 11:17–22) (Hammett, *Forty Questions*, 40). Apparently, for Hammett, the corporate entailment and meaning of the ordinances is sufficient warrant to keep them in the church's purview and sanction of the church. He does not appeal to the keys, because this theological aspect suffices.

And yet, "Jesus has not prescribed any specific form or ritual by which a group of Christians is invested with the keys." Instead, "These keys which are exercised congregationally are assumed congregationally." In other words, by the action of coming together regularly to celebrate baptism and the Lord's Supper, "A group of Christians assumes responsibility for the keys."[56] Several affirmations follow regarding the local church: (1) As representatives of Christ's future, consummated kingdom, local churches function as outposts/embassies of that kingdom.[57] (2) Because local churches operate under the deputized authority of Christ, they are Christocracies rather than democracies.[58] (3) Local churches exercise the keys of the kingdom when they participate in the Lord's Supper and thereby "publicly unite members of the new covenant."[59] (4) The practice of Lord's Supper physically signifies the spatial location of an embassy of the kingdom of Christ.[60] (5) When one becomes a disciple of Jesus, submission to Christ entails submission to his

---

56. Jamieson, *Going Public*, 153.

57. Carson, "Evangelicals, Ecumenism and the Church," in Kantzer and Henry, *Evangelical Afirmations*, 364. The identity of the church as an outpost of the kingdom verifies Allison's earlier claim that the kingdom creates the church. In Moore and Sagers' words, "In Scripture, the new society created by the 'already' reign of Christ is not some unexplainable force or indefinable group, but rather . . . a colony of the kingdom itself" (Moore and Sagers, "Kingdom of God and the Church," 76). Identifying the local church as a kingdom embassy is Leeman's thesis. As an embassy, the local church "represents the authority, name, reputation, character and glory of one nation inside another nation. The local church does exactly this, only it represents a kingdom not across geographical space, but across eschatological time" (Leeman, *Political Church*, 368).

58. Moore and Sagers, "Kingdom of God and the Church," 77. The power of the keys is a crucial grounding for congregational government, but affirming congregationalism does not require affirming that the church is a pure democracy.

59. Leeman, "Church and Churches," in Leeman and Dever, *Baptist Foundations*, 360.

60. For Patrick Schreiner, "Jesus' body is a microcosm of the two realms [material and ideological] and began the process of reuniting the realms, [such that] the community [of Jesus is] the link between the two spaces" (Schreiner, "People and Place," 176). In other words, "His community is the empirical reality of the new creation." Schreiner continues, "The kingdom is here but hidden in plain sight because metaphysically, it is launched in human bodies. Jesus employs his words and human bodies as seeds upon the earth that will grow up and alter the space of the earth." Horton seems to argue for something similar in Horton, *People and Place*, 30. Horton claims, "The church does not create a transformed world; rather, the church is that part of the world that God has newly created in anticipation of the renewal of the world itself" (33). Leeman writes, "A church is almost like a doorway to another dimension. Through the keys of the kingdom a group of Christians open this doorway to make the invisible visible" (Leeman, *Political Church*, 368).

kingdom embassy—the local church.[61] (6) The kingly authority that is exercised in the congregation's celebration of the Lord's Supper is also displayed in the church's act to exclude an unrepentant, professing Christian from the meal through church discipline (1 Cor 5:1–11). These points help clarify the thesis of this book: If baptism is the formal ceremony that provides the passport to kingdom citizens, the Lord's Supper belongs to those citizens who have had their passport stamped.[62]

Given that baptism is the public ratification and deputization of a new kingdom citizen by the local church, the Lord's Supper is the ratification meal and inaugurated kingdom feast. In the Supper, the church signals its eschatological identity by already enjoying the benefits of Christ's saving reign and looking forward to the consummation of that enjoyment at Christ's return (1 Cor 11:26).[63] To participate in communion is to visibly identify with Christ's bride (Rev 19:6–9) and signify fellowship in the heavenly assembly that is already gathered at Mt. Zion (Heb 12:22–24).[64] Rather

---

61. Submission is appropriate in so far as that church operates under the headship of Christ in obedience to Scripture. Leeman picks up on the biblical-theological principle established in this book when he describes the church as a kingdom embassy responsible for marking off kingdom citizens through the ordinances. He writes, "Every body politic needs some way of publicly registering itself in the eyes of the world. . . . Ancient Israel did the same. Under the patriarchs and while in Egypt, they were marked off by circumcision. Then with the Mosaic covenant and habitation of Canaan, they added Sabbath laws, various cultic celebrations [i.e., worship practices], as well as national borders for publicly registering themselves as a bona fide nation in a manner the other nations of the earth would recognize" (Leeman, "Church and Churches," in Leeman and Dever, *Baptist Foundations*, 359–60). The church, Leeman explains represents Christ's kingdom not so much across geographic space, but more pointedly "across eschatological time." For a local church to practice the ordinances then is to act as border patrol agents of a sort on behalf of heaven. That the church is both covenantal and institutional is contra Cole, *Organic Church*, 111–12, 127–38. Cole argues that the ordinances are appropriately practiced under the sole jurisdiction of individual Christians. Thus, he posits a view of kingdom growth through organic movement and relational encounters without any structural or ecclesial shape. The foregoing arguments of this chapter serve as implicit critiques of Cole's approach.

62. If the local church possesses the power of the keys, then to proceed to the Table "without being a baptized member of a local church is an act of presumption," for the individual Christian places himself above the authority Christ has delegated to the local church to affirm him as a kingdom citizen (Leeman, *Surprising Offense*, 304). Jamieson argues, "The principal means by which the keys are enacted are baptism (initial affirmation) and the Lord's Supper (ongoing affirmation)" (Jamieson, *Going Public*, 153). See also Grenz, "Baptism and the Lord's Supper as Community Acts," in Cross and Thompson, *Baptist Sacramentalism*, 93.

63. On this theme, see Billings, *Remembrance, Communion, and Hope*, 190–91.

64. A classic study of this text and the church is O'Brien, "Church as a Heavenly Eschatological Entity," in Carson, *Church in the Bible and the World*, 88–119. Similar, are Moore and Sagers, "Kingdom of God and the Church," 80–81.

than the church being a mixed community of believers and unbelievers as the Israelite assembly at Sinai was, the church has "salvation (in part), the knowledge of God (in part), deliverance from sin (in part), the power of the Holy Spirit (in part), purity and unity (in part), and eternal life (in part)."[65] These realities characterize the whole, regenerate assembly. Carson explains,

> This means that each local church is not seen primarily as one member parallel to a lot of other member churches, together constituting one body, one church; nor is each local church seen as the body of Christ parallel to other earthly churches that are also the body of Christ—as if Christ had many bodies. Rather, each church is the full manifestation in space and time of the one, true, heavenly, eschatological, new covenant church. Local churches should see themselves as outcroppings of heaven, analogies of 'the Jerusalem that is above,' indeed colonies of the new Jerusalem, providing on earth a corporate and visible expression of 'the glorious freedom of the children of God.'[66]

The Ordinances and
the Universal Church

The universal church may be defined as "all Christ-followers throughout the whole world."[67] Because baptism functions as a sign of entry to the

---

65. Allison, *Sojourners and Strangers*, 152.

66. Carson, "Evangelicals, Ecumenism and the Church," in Kantzer and Henry, *Evangelical Affirmations*, 366. Carson is following O'Brien, "Church as a Heavenly Eschatological Entity," in Carson, *Church in the Bible and the World*, 97. For more on the role of kingdom citizens to function as "priest-kings," in line with the roles of Adam and Israel, see Leeman, *Political Church*, 349. For affirmation of the multi-ethnic composition of the local church in its relation to the heavenly assembly, see Moore and Sagers, "Kingdom of God and the Church," 78.

67. Allison, *Sojourners and Strangers*, 62. Due to the scriptural references to the church as the presently living people of God who are subject to fall prey to idolatry (1 Cor 10:32) and the church as those kingdom citizens whom Christ is presently building into his eschatological assembly (Matt 16:18), I do not hold that the universal church is only the heavenly or eschatological community. Contra Leeman, *Political Church*, 368. Inaugurated eschatology could be rightly employed to explain passages regarding Christ's headship over the church (Eph 1:21–23) or death for the church (5:25) to demonstrate that church in these instances refer to a heavenly/eschatological assembly. However, the heavenly church doctrine does not seem to adequately account for the passages that refer to Christians presently living. Thus, while I affirm that the NT speaks of the local church far more often than the universal church, all three categories are actually helpful to account for the data (i.e., local, universal, and heavenly/eschatological). On the universal and local church, see Hammett, "Church Membership, Church Discipline," in Hammett and Merkle, *Those Who Must Give an Account*,

kingdom of God and local churches manifest the kingdom in space and time, it is important to connect the universal church to the kingdom. If the kingdom is God's saving reign, which was demonstrated during Christ's ministry (Matt 12:28) and inaugurated by Christ's cross and resurrection, then the universal church refers to Christ's kingdom citizens still living. Themes of Christ's covenantal headship and saving reign over the universal church appear side by side in Scripture (Eph 1:21–23; Col 1:13–20). Because baptism is the means by which one is formally recognized as a kingdom citizen and publicly submits to Christ's rule, baptism is the normative means of entering the universal church. Thus, this book agrees with those historical Baptists who tied baptism to the universal church.[68]

At the same time, affirming the covenantal nature of the church, as delineated above, helps identify "the universal church [as] the covenant partner with God in this new covenant relationship"[69] by virtue of each individual Christ-follower's union with Christ.[70] Hammett claims, "One way to relate [water baptism to Spirit baptism] is to see Spirit baptism as marking one's entry into church universal, and water baptism marking one's entry into a local church."[71] It is true that the ordinances are "the hinge between the invisible universal church and the visible local church."[72] However, affirming Hammett's statement suggests that the universal church and local church have two different signs of entry. On this reading, one may enter the universal church without water baptism. Furthermore, the statement potentially, though unintentionally, suggests that the water baptism overseen by a specific local church is performed for the administering local church's sake, such that the sign is not binding for all other local churches. By contrast, Carson's statement about local churches being outcroppings of the future heavenly assembly suggests the opposite.[73] The eschatological nature of the

---

12–13; White, "Universal and Local Church," in Duesing et al., *Upon This Rock*, 208–39.

68. For example, Fuller argues that baptism was not an initiatory rite into a particular church, but rather "into the body of professing Christians" (Belcher, *Fuller's Works*, 3:512). He continues, And, if so, it must be necessary to an admission into a particular church, inasmuch as what is particular presupposes what is general. No man could with propriety occupy a place in the army without having first avowed his loyalty, or taken the oath of allegiance. The oath of allegiance does not, indeed, initiate a person into the army, as one may take that oath who is no soldier; but it is a prerequisite to being a soldier. Though all who take the oath are not soldiers, yet all soldiers take the oath."

69. Allison, *Sojourners and Strangers*, 130.

70. Wellum, "Beyond Mere Ecclesiology," in Easley and Morgan, *Community of Jesus*, 209.

71. Hammett, *Forty Questions*, 69n25.

72. Jamieson, *Going Public*, 142.

73. Allison, *Sojourners and Strangers*, 405–6.

church (Heb 12:28–32) grounds the claim that the local church baptizes in water on behalf of heaven/Christ and with continuing validity for the universal church. Because the universal church cannot baptize and because Christ has authorized the local church to baptize, the baptism performed by the local church on a new believer is the normative means by which a new believer enters the universal church.

Yet, it is precisely this point where the invisible and visible distinction may have some usefulness, albeit predicated of the universal church rather than the local.[74] Baptism is the action by which a new believer becomes visibly aligned with Christ and his people. The New Testament has no category for a Christian who remains aloof from the local church. In cases where one believes in Christ and remains unbaptized, several theological questions should be answered: (1) With respect to the universal church, what is the status of those who trust Christ alone for salvation but lack sufficient biblical teaching to understand Christ's command to be baptized? (2) What is the status of pedobaptists who, although genuinely converted, have not been biblically baptized? (3) What is the status of someone who professes faith in Christ but refuses baptism? Each of these questions is answered in turn.[75]

74. Whereas covenant theologians maintain a distinction between the visible and invisible church in the new covenant age, the newness of the new covenant leads Baptists to reject this distinction. For covenant theologians, the invisible category includes covenant children and possible covenant breakers. Carson is correct to claim that with the onset of the new covenant, "The ancient contrast between the church visible and the church invisible . . . is either fundamentally mistaken, or at best of marginal importance" (Carson, "Evangelicals, Ecumenism and the Church," in Kantzer and Henry, *Evangelical Affirmations*, 367). Thus, the invisible quality of the universal church is different than the category used by covenantal theologians. Instead, the term "invisible" may be used legitimately of the universal church in the sense that the Christ-followers do not gather before the *parousia*. Furthermore, believers may exist across the globe (e.g., unreached people groups) who have little access to Christian teaching, but who nonetheless hear and believe the gospel. The existence of these believers, without baptism and a local church in which to celebrate the Lord's Supper, renders the category legitimate. See also Wellum, "Beyond Mere Ecclesiology," in Easley and Morgan, *Community of Jesus*, 204–5. For examples of the illegitimate use of the visible and invisible distinction throughout church history, see Leeman, "Church and Churches," in Leeman and Dever, *Baptist Foundations*, 346–47.

75. These admittedly complex matters illustrate the angst B. H. Carroll felt in considering the doctrine of the universal church. He wrote, "I repeat that the theory of the co-existence, side by side, on earth of two churches of Christ, one formal and visible, the other real, invisible and spiritual with different terms of membership, is exceedingly mischievous and is so confusing that every believer of it becomes muddled in running the lines of separation" (Carroll, *Baptists and Their Doctrines*, 59). However, because Scripture presents the universal church as a legitimate category, this section seeks to heed the warning and still maintain the doctrine.

Concerning those who do not understand Christ's command to be baptized, their misunderstanding entails at least two possibilities: (1) they are genuine believers who are involved in a local church despite their lack of baptism or (2) they are genuine believers who are not involved in a local church. In the former case, the church is acting in a disorderly fashion. Yet, by the church's unofficial recognition of the Christian as a genuine believer (assuming some continuity of relationship and accountability with the body), the person should be considered a member of the universal church who is acting in unintentional disobedience. Thus, the Christian's status as a member of the universal church does not come about through the normal means of personal faith and baptism under the administration of a local church.

The second possibility is more tenuous. A believer who misunderstands the command to be baptized and is unaffiliated with a local church should be a rare, or at least temporary, circumstance. In the best cases, given life in a fallen world, some reasonable explanations may include health (e.g., aged shut-in), living conditions due to health or age (e.g., nursing home resident), lack of transportation, or rural/frontier missions setting. In cases where someone professes faith in Christ and voluntarily chooses not to associate with a true church, that Christian profession is called into question (1 John 2:19). In the New Testament, conversion to Christ is tied to entrance into Christ's church through baptism. Nevertheless, where a sincere trust in Christ is combined with confusion or lack of teaching and prohibiting factors, the Christian is a member of the universal church. Again, this case must be viewed as exceptional rather than normative.[76]

Because New Testament baptism is the immersion of a believer in water that signals entry into all the benefits of the new covenant, pedobaptists

---

76. Allison speaks to this unusual and troubling situation under the category of the church's spatio-temporal/eschatological nature. Given this characteristic, the church should take into account both the aspects of new covenant life it possesses already and those that are not yet feasible. He writes of Cyprian's statement: "He cannot have God for his father who does not have the church for his mother," that "when understood as a biblically warranted insistence that Christ-followers actually join and engage actively in a local church," the statement has merit (Allison, *Sojourners and Strangers*, 156). Furthermore, "This insistence stands as a much needed corrective to the disturbing trend among American Christians who claim on the one hand to embrace Jesus and on the other hand not to need to become involved in a church." As evidence of the American trend, Allison cites Barna, *Revolution*, 37. Barna writes, "Being in right relationship with God and his people is what matters. Scripture teaches us that devoting your life to loving God with all your heart, mind, strength, and soul is what honors him. Being part of a local church may facilitate that. Or it might not." This book demonstrates that one cannot actually relate rightly to God's people apart from a local church, leaving Barna begging the question.

are in a similar situation to those who believe in Christ and are involved in a local church yet misunderstand the command to be baptized. The difference is that the pedobaptist, presumably, conscientiously holds to the validity of her baptism based on her understanding of Scripture. The ignorant Christian in a baptistic church does not know enough to see that baptism is lacking. Thus, the pedobaptist's membership in the universal church may be affirmed, albeit through irregular means. Indeed, close communion Baptists likely have much more in common with a pedobaptist who fits the above description than an unbaptized Christian in a baptistic church. Spiritual unity between the two is forged across denominational lines by the common trust in Christ and sincere appeal to Scripture to explain their views, despite their separate communions.

Concerning the third group above, it is difficult to imagine a scenario in which a church could affirm the confession of faith from someone who understands Christ's command to be baptized and yet refuses baptism. Apart from some significant health issue that makes baptism impossible, refusing baptism is tantamount to refusing Christ. To profess to believe in Christ and refuse to obey his command to be baptized betrays a heart that maintains its autonomy from Christ (Matt 7:21–23). By virtue of the identity that new covenant members receive in union with Christ, Christians are responsible to freely join a local church for their good and God's glory (Heb 10:24–25; cf. Eph 3:10).[77]

Jesus gives all of his followers two signs that are to continue throughout the new covenant age: baptism and the Lord's Supper. Yet, the question of what unites believers across the universal church naturally arises when one considers the fact that churches disagree over the ordinances. Significantly, Christians share the same signs of baptism and the Lord's Supper even if, through misunderstanding, some Christians claim something to be baptism that is not baptism. The universal church, which is expressed in local churches, practices baptism (though defined differently) as the sign of entry into the people of God. Similarly, the universal church does not yet and cannot gather to participate in the Lord's Supper together, with all of the covenantal responsibilities the meal entails. Yet, the universal church, expressed in each local church, shares the same sign of participation. In this important sense, the universal church is unified around the ordinances.[78]

77. Leeman, *Surprising Offense*, 245.

78. This way of conceiving unity around the Lord's Supper is against the conception of *totus Christus*, wherein the Lord's Supper is the means by which the church becomes a prolonged incarnation of the person of Christ, or that the church is the ontological or mystical body of Christ. For a contemporary presentation of *totus Christus* from a Protestant, see Leithart, "Sacramental Hermeneutics and the Ceremonies of Israel," in

Practicing close communion requires that genuine believers may not be able to participate in the meal together in any given local church. Thus, the issues of the ordinances, unity, and the universal church coalesce. While open and ecumenical communionists claim that unity requires opening the Table to pedobaptist and those with no baptism in any sense, unity across the universal church may be recognized another way. Leeman argues that unity in the universal church may be found in a common adherence to "apostolic doctrine," by which he intends belief in the gospel and the resulting identity as the people of the new covenant. The local church, by distinction, finds its unity in "both apostolic doctrine and apostolic office" with the latter element referring to being "united through the ordinances by their shared affirmation of one another as holy."[79] The universal church is one, in the sense that all those united to Christ throughout the world share the benefits of that union (Eph 4:1–4);[80] holy, in terms of possessing

---

Strawbridge, *Case for Covenant Communion*, 111–29. Speaking of the church in these ways misses the covenantal overtones of the body of Christ metaphor (1 Cor 11:3; Eph 1:22; 4:15; 5:23; Col 1:18; 2:10, 19). See Leeman, *Surprising Offense*, 243. For other critiques of *totus Christus*, see Leeman., "Church and Churches," in Leeman and Dever, *Baptist Foundations*, 340–42; Horton, *People and Place*, 6–9.

79. Leeman, "Church and Churches," in Leeman and Dever, *Baptist Foundations*, 335. Leeman sets this affirmation of universal and local church unity over against his interpretation of Calvin's pedobaptist view that "all true Christians are united in the faith, and all true churches are united by a shared ministry of the Word and ordinances. But, strangely, the local or city churches . . . are not invisibly united in the faith since they are deliberately mixed assemblies." On this view of unity, the unity is predicated of all true believers who belong to the invisible church and of the universal church, but local churches do not share the unity, due to their intentional "designing of the church as a mixed assembly" through infant baptism. While the unity of the universal church centers around apostolic doctrine (i.e., the gospel and its entailments), Duesing adds that the local church is the "vehicle" Christ has ordained "to protect and deliver the gospel to future generations" (Duesing, "Maintaining the Integrity of the Church," in White et al., *Restoring Integrity in Baptist Churches*, 246).

80. Chris Morgan observes that the term "'cooperation' inadvertently grounds our unity in shared goals" rather than the more fundamental union with Christ. But if the universal church is united in apostolic doctrine and the universal church consists of those members of the new covenant currently living, then the universal church is united by their shared possession of circumcised hearts, of the indwelling Holy Spirit, of forgiveness of sin, and justification by God. In other words, the universal church is united by their common union with Christ at an ontological level. However, the universal church is not united in her understanding of the means of initially appropriating union with Christ (i.e., baptism) or deepening union with Christ (i.e., the Lord's Supper) (Morgan, "Baptists and the Unity of the Church," 23). Morgan does not intend to downplay cooperation. Rather, he recognizes the inadequacy of grounding the unity of the universal church in cooperation. As Leeman contends, "Different levels of cooperation are possible based on different levels of doctrinal and ecclesial unity." Several important areas of cooperation, from obeying Christ's commission (Matt 28:18–20) to

definitive sanctification, which comes through justification by faith (1 Cor 6:11); and apostolic, by virtue of its assent and submission to the apostles' doctrine (Eph 2:20).[81]

Close communion recognizes that the universal church extends as far as belief in apostolic doctrine extends. Yet, the view also recognizes that, on the basis of the right confession about Christ, he has given apostolic authority to the local church in the keys of the kingdom. For the keys to be exercised properly, local churches must affirm a believer's initial gospel affirmation through baptism before they can affirm a believer's ongoing gospel affirmation through the Lord's Supper.

Thus, when the question is asked, "who should participate in the Lord's Supper?" the answer cannot be anyone who belongs to the universal church. Normally (except in cases of visiting communion), those who take the Lord's Supper together also have responsibility for maintaining new covenant responsibilities toward all those who celebrate the meal together.[82] Leeman raises a helpful thought experiment at this point by asking what differences exist between the relationship of two Christians who belong to the same church and two Christians who belong to different churches.[83] The upshot is that those who participate together in the Lord's Supper should normally (except in cases of visiting communion) have the ability and knowledge to exercise formative and corrective discipline toward the others. In sum, two factors distinguish the group of Christians belonging to the universal church from a local church: (1) covenantal obligations of mutual encouragement, gospel unity, and accountability symbolized in the ordinances and (2) the authority to exercise the keys in corrective church discipline through the ordinances.

The Ordinances and the Local Church

Wellum argues that while it is legitimate to ask whether one is baptized into the local church or universal church, "One wonders if this kind of question

---

the care of the poor, are spelled out in Leeman, "Congregational Approach to Catholicity," in Leeman and Dever, *Baptist Foundations*, 377–80.

81. The temple imagery of Eph 2:20–22 should not be overlooked (cf. 2 Cor 6:16–18), for the temple theme is one means by which the NT conveys that all the new covenant people of God have the Lord's presence and possess circumcised hearts. For the connection between Eph 2:20 as the eschatological people of God and the fulfillment of Isa 56, see O'Brien, "Church as a Heavenly Eschatological Entity," in Carson, *Church in the Bible and the World*, 102.

82. Billings, *Remembrance, Communion, and Hope*, 145.

83. Leeman, "Church and Churches," in Leeman and Dever, *Baptist Foundations*, 366; Cheong, *God Redeeming His Bride*, 276.

would have been conceivable to the New Testament."[84] Isaak adds that New Testament baptism did not distinguish between a person's identification with Christ's local expression of the church versus the universal church. Rather, the first Christians understood the nature of the church to be a visible manifestation of the whole people of God.[85] Furthermore, personally trusting Christ would have been understood as more than a sign of personal devotion, given that the ancient world was concerned with corporate identity.[86] In the New Testament, baptism not only represented one's position as a Christian but also his association with all those who are part of Christ's visible presence on earth, the church.[87] The covenantal implications of the ordinances require expression in local congregations.[88] Thus, this section argues that the New Testament data presents baptism and the Lord's Supper as the prerogatives of local churches by which they are constituted.[89]

The case can be made that new believers are usually baptized into the fellowship of a church. The connection of baptism to local churches in Acts requires more contextual attention than the assumption of baptism, presented in chapter 3. Acts 2 presents an explicit case in which the baptized believers are "added that day" to the group of one hundred and twenty disciples, who had just received the Holy Spirit (v. 41).[90] Thus, those who believed on the day of Pentecost are clearly baptized into the existing church.[91] Another

84. Wellum, "Means of Grace," in Armstrong, Compromised Church, 169n35.

85. Isaak, "Baptism among the Early Christians," 6.

86. Baptism "is an act of the church. It entails the incorporation of the baptismal candidate into the life of the community" (Grenz, "Baptism and the Lord's Supper," in Cross and Thompson, Baptist Sacramentalism, 93).

87. Saucy, Church in God's Program, 195.

88. Leeman, Surprising Offense, 267.

89. Beasley-Murray, Baptism in the New Testament, 394.

90. That this initial group of one hundred and twenty baptized believers is rightly designated the church is suggested by Luke's own use of the term to refer to the Jerusalem disciples in Acts 5:11. The group Luke references is clearly the same group he describes in 4:32–37, which is clearly the same group described in 2:42–47. The descriptive names such as believers, brothers (and sisters), disciples are often used interchangeably in Acts to highlight a different facet of the same group (e.g., 11:26). For the association of Acts 2 with the disciples' obedience to Christ's commission in Matt 28 and the resulting church membership that resulted from the baptism of the three thousand, see White, "What Makes Baptism Valid?," in White et al., Restoring Integrity in Baptist Churches, 111.

91. Because the church possessed a record of three thousand new converts to Christ who were added to an already existing number, the clear indication is that they were added to the existing Jerusalem church of 120 (cf. Acts 1:15) (Merkle, "Biblical Basis for Church Membership," in Hammett and Merkle, Those Who Must Give an Account, 46–47).

straightforward case is that of the Corinthians (Acts 18:8–11). Within a relatively short period of time, the synagogue ruler, Crispus; Crispus's entire household; and other (Gentile?) Corinthians believed in Jesus and were baptized (v. 8; cf. v. 6).[92] Two textual features suggest that this group of new, baptized believers formed a church: (1) Paul's presence "among them" for a year and a half teaching the word of God suggests the existence of a new church (v. 11), and (2) the Lord's assurance to Paul through a vision that "I have many in this city who are my people" suggests that the initial group of baptized believers grew through more believing baptisms over the time Paul acted as pastor of the new church (v. 10). Though with slightly less specificity than Acts 2, Acts 18:8–11 presents baptism as the initiatory sign of inclusion with God's people, who gather as a local church in the city of Corinth.[93]

The Ethiopian eunuch's case serves as a common proof text for those who see little association of baptism and the church in Acts. Once baptized, the eunuch goes away rejoicing and Philip is carried away by the Spirit (8:39–40). The eunuch is not baptized into any existing group of Christians in a location. Some (at least speculative) evidence exists that the eunuch returned to Africa, proclaimed the gospel, and began church planting.[94] Whatever his missionary efforts proved to be, the eunuch's case is clearly unique in Acts. Luke does not record any others being converted in route to another location. The uniqueness of the situation suggests the usefulness of reading Acts with categories of normative pattern and unusual/

92. Paul's pattern was to preach the gospel to the Jews before going also to the Gentiles, to baptized those who believed, and to continue teaching and shepherding the new congregation/church for some time (cf. 17:1–9; 19:1–10). Paul affirms his own role in baptizing Crispus in 1 Cor 1:14.

93. Acts 16 may be another example. Paul's stay of "some days" (v. 12) in Philippi started with the conversion of Lydia's household (vv. 14–15) and ends with Luke's comment that they visited Lydia, "And when they had seen the brothers, they encouraged them and departed" (v. 40). Those converted with Lydia (and in the intervening time before Paul and Silas were released from prison?) apparently comprised the Philippian church. Luke describes the church at Antioch as "the brothers" and "the disciples" in a span of three verses (cf. 14:27—15:1). Thus, it is reasonable that the Philippian Jailer's household would have been assimilated into that first church at Philippi. Schnabel confidently asserts, "The reference to [the brothers] is evidence that the missionary work of Paul and Silas in Philippi resulted in the founding of a church. The two missionaries evidently had been proclaiming the gospel in Philippi for some time before the incident of the attack of the syndicate that owned the psychic woman. There had been several conversions beyond that of Lydia and her household (vv. 14–15) and of the official in charge of the city jail with his household (vv. 30–34). The emerging community of believers met in Lydia's house" (Schnabel, Acts, 695). Schnabel's confidence exceeds the explicit statements of the text. Nevertheless, his description is likely accurate.

94. Polhill, Acts, 227–28; Dever, "Baptism," in Schreiner and Wright, Believer's Baptism, 336; Keener, Acts, 2:1595.

unique circumstance in mind. Rather than disproving the normative association of baptism with a church in a particular location, the account of the Ethiopian eunuch demonstrates the possibility of special circumstances. As Dever argues, "A clear, apparently sincere conversion of someone who is about to move to an area with little or no Christian presence may lead a pastor to decide to baptize someone who is not moving to membership in his local church."[95]

This book supplies ample biblical data to affirm that the local church is the only appropriate context for celebrating the Lord's Supper. In other words, those who administer the elements should be representatives of a particular local church in a meeting understood as a gathering of the church. Three points substantiate this claim. First, a covenantal relationship of mutual accountability and responsibility under Christ is implied by the meal. The body that celebrates the Lord's Supper together must also be authorized by Christ to carry out church discipline on the participants 1 Cor 5:11).[96] Second, unity is implied by the meal (11:17–22, 27–34). Eating the meal together, at the same time, in the same place, with the same general doctrinal understanding are important means by which the church is able to discern the body (v. 29). Third, only local churches celebrate the Lord's Supper together. Whereas the disciples celebrated the Last Supper with Jesus and all the saints will celebrate the consummatory feast when Christ returns, the Lord's Supper belongs to outposts of the inaugurated kingdom of God. Therefore, the Lord's Supper should not be celebrated at weddings,

---

95. Furthermore, a situation could exist in which, although a faithful church exists where the person or family is moving, the time between conversion and the possibility of baptism in that church would be so long as to apparently separate baptism from conversion. In order to keep these matters together as the NT does, the home church could baptize the person before he/she moves (Dever, "Baptism," in Schreiner and Wright, *Believer's Baptism*, 334). Dever continues, "Other extenuating circumstances which might lead a pastor to decide to proceed with baptizing someone outside the normal course of joining a church would include the case of someone who is apparently converted and seriously ill, someone whose conversion is made more obviously real by the clear and costly repentance that was entailed by it, or perhaps conversions among those coming from anti-Christian families or social circles (as we see examples in the book of Acts). Prayer and consultation among leaders of a congregation should help to give wisdom in such situations."

96. Van Neste writes, "Communion really only makes sense in the setting of believers who know one another and are covenanted together in submission to the Word of God seeking conformity to Christ. Outside of such a setting it is difficult to imagine what 'discerning the body' would mean (1 Cor 11:29). The Corinthian church is rebuked for failing to take note of and care for one another. Furthermore, exclusion from the Table is a significant aspect of discipline. Removing Communion from the local church then makes it difficult to uphold the discipline of the church" (Van Neste, "Lord's Supper," in Schreiner and Crawford, *Lord's Supper*, 376).

Bible college or seminary chapels,[97] Christian para-church ministries, private Christian schools, Sunday School classes, small groups composed of church members from a single church, a group of two or three Christians,[98] home Bible studies unaffiliated with a local church, conferences, private persons,[99] or any other context that falls short of an explicit gathering of a particular local church.[100]

97. In an otherwise very helpful volume, J. Todd Billings, a pedobaptist, argues that "baptized Christians should be invited to the Table regardless of denomination." He adds that an ecumenically open Table would "spurn . . . any possibility of discipline, [which] is completely unsustainable if we are to take Paul at his word" (Billings, *Remembrance, Communion, and Hope*, 151). Yet, he acknowledges participating in Western Theological Seminary's weekly communion service in chapel (122). Although seminaries have codes of conduct by which students should abide, one wonders how discipline akin to what Paul prescribes in 1 Cor 5 could take place in a seminary. Even granting the possibility of expulsion, seminaries are not authorized by Christ to exercise the keys.

98. Saucy's concession is surprising when he writes, "While its normal celebration is for the established church, this does not seem to preclude its observance under other conditions. Christ instituted it for the disciples before the church was inaugurated, and surely the promise of his presence in the midst of two or three (Matt 18:20) may be appropriated in the case of the Supper when necessary. The experience of unity of the body, however, is best served in the larger gathering of the church" (Saucy, *Church in God's Program*, 231). The surprise is based on his earlier claim that unity with fellow believer's in one's own local church is "a central feature" of the meal. If covenanted unity is a central feature, then celebrating the meal outside the context of a gathered church would require that the meal with the small group is not the Lord's Supper, but something else.

99. Billings, *Remembrance, Communion, and Hope*, 193. Helpfully, Van Neste explains, "I understand that it may seem harsh, for example, to say to a shut-in lady, 'No, I will not come and administer this ordinance,' particularly if she has requested it. But I think it is simply not possible any more than it is for her to 'just get up and come to church.' The perceived harshness arises from the assumption that I could bring communion to her if I would. However, my point is that I cannot bring communion to her even if I tried. It cannot be re-created apart from the gathered body. So, as we lament the fact that she cannot attend church, part of that lament is our pity that she thus cannot come to the Lord's Table with us. This can and should lead us to pity and compassion, but we cannot alter the reality" (Van Neste, "Lord's Supper," in Schreiner and Crawford, *Lord's Supper*, 376–77). The logic of this point extends also to the refusal to serve nursery workers and others who are not able to gather with the congregation for worship. I do not think the logic extends to those separated by some spatial constraint such as a sound room, overflow room, or nursing mother's room, for the simple fact that they are participating with the gathered church's celebration and partaking at the same time. I recall hearing Sinclair Ferguson say that churches might strategize even to wheel in hospital beds to the worship gathering in order to enable shut-ins to continue communing with the church. Where such measures are possible, they are certainly commendable.

100. Desiring to remember the broken body and shed blood of Christ in settings outside a church gathering is not wrong, but it fails to "embody" one of the primary purposes of the meal. In Hammett's estimation, it is not sinful to do so but falls short of

Applying Close Communion

Answering the question of who is admitted to the Lord's Supper requires careful consideration of the relationship of baptism to the Lord's Supper and each of the ordinances to church membership and discipline. As Dever explains,

> Baptism and the Lord's Supper are normally the formal acts of being admitted to and continuing in the fellowship of the church. Without a correct understanding of baptism, membership and church discipline are more difficult to practice. Conversely, without a careful practice of church membership and discipline, both baptism and the Lord's Supper can be cheapened.[101]

While the sections above outline the first half of the relationship Dever describes, this section considers the way in which close communion seeks to uphold the biblical nature and function of the ordinances.

Close Communion and
Church Membership

Stanley Fowler describes three views of the relationship between baptism and local church membership among Baptists. "First, some have argued that individuals become members of the local church by the act of baptism so that there is no distinction between those who are being baptized and those who are being received as formal members of the church. . . . Second, some have argued that baptism is prerequisite to but not constitutive of church membership." On this view, conversion and baptism remain connected. Depending on the situation, "the basis of approval" for one's baptism may

---

the purpose for which it was given (Hammett, *Forty Questions*, 297). After a similar list of groups that should not participate in the Lord's Supper, Allison writes, "If a theology of the Lord's Supper adequately establishes that the ordinance symbolizes the unity of all the members of the church, then anything less than whole-body participation would seem to obfuscate that which should be clearly and properly symbolized" (Allison, *Sojourners and Strangers*, 408). Other appropriate terms for assessing celebrations of the Lord's Supper outside the local church include disorderly, misleading, unhelpful, and moving against its purpose. If symbolizing and enacting the unity of the local church is part of the essence of the Lord's Supper, it could be argued that taking the elements outside a church setting is not actually a Lord's Supper meal as infant baptism is not baptism. White provides a similar list of inappropriate contexts and describes participation in the meal outside the gathering of the church as "improper" (White, "Baptist's Theology of the Lord's Supper," in White et al., *Restoring Integrity in Baptist Churches*, 153). See also Wright, "Lord's Supper," in Leeman and Dever, *Baptist Foundations*, 160–61.

101. Dever, "Baptism," in Schreiner and Wright, *Believer's Baptism*, 339.

be given "by the administrator, while church membership requires approval by the church meeting as a whole. . . . Third, some have argued that although all believers ought to be baptized, church membership is for all who credibly profess conversion, and baptism may precede or follow church membership."[102] Freeman recognizes that the third view operates on the "conviction that faith, not baptism, makes the church, thus turning baptism into a recommended but still optional step, rather than a gospel ordinance essential for the church to be the church." Another way of stating the matter is that open communion implies a "decoupling [of] baptism from church membership."[103] Still another view of baptism and church membership is associate membership. On this view, despite being baptized as an infant, one may officially become a member of a Baptist church, possessing all the rights of membership yet without the privilege of exercising them. For example, this category of member may not be able to vote on some (or all) matters of congregational concern (e.g., to vote a pastor into office), become a deacon, or serve in various other capacities.[104] However, this section proposes a modification of Fowler's first view as that which is most consistent with the covenantal functions of baptism and the Lord's Supper.[105]

Church membership may be defined as "(1) a covenant of union between a particular church and a Christian, a covenant whose effective signs are baptism and the Lord's Supper"[106] that "consists of (2) the church's affir-

102. Fowler, More Than a Symbol, 224–25.

103. Freeman, Contesting Catholicity, 371, 373. For Freeman, the answer to this dilemma is found in recognizing that baptism is more than a symbol of human response, "signifying nothing of God's activity." Brandon Jones makes the astute observation that the differences among Baptist understandings of how baptism relates to church membership stem from different theologies of baptism among Baptists. He explains, "The failure of Baptists to present a positive theology of the meaning of baptism exacerbates this issue" (Jones, Waters of Promise, 146).

104. For the distinction between possession of the privileges of membership and exercise of those privileges, see Waters and Duncan, Children and the Lord's Supper, 23. Duncan and Waters posit a category of church members who are indefinitely suspended from the sacrament. In light of the connection between the Lord's Supper and church membership surveyed in this section, it is difficult to account for how indefinite suspension from communion is not actually church discipline (Waters and Duncan, Children and the Lord's Supper, 183n4). For a Baptist rejection of this idea of membership, see Finn, "Historical Analysis of Church Membership," in Hammett and Merkle, Those Who Must Give an Account, 76.

105. For other helpful arguments for church membership besides those presented below, see Merkle, "Biblical Basis for Church Membership," in Hammett and Merkle, Those Who Must Give an Account.

106. Jamieson, Going Public, 148. In this aspect of church membership, Jamieson has altered Leeman's description in order to recognize the way in which the ordinances relate to the vertical and horizontal aspects of the new covenant. See Leeman, Surprising

mation of the Christian's gospel profession; (3) the church's promise to give oversight to the Christian; and (4) the Christian's promise to gather with the church and submit to its oversight."[107] Stated differently, church membership is a way of formalizing what is inherent in the covenantal nature of the church. Therefore, church membership "makes explicit what is implicit in the two ordinances."[108] Jamieson summarizes:

> Both ordinances have vertical and horizontal elements: they commit us to God and to one another. And in ecclesial terms both ordinances are effective signs. They knit the body together: baptism adds one to many, and the Lord's Supper makes many one. So we can say that both ordinances imply a covenant not just between an individual and God but also between an individual and the church. Or, to use an older term, each ordinance is an 'implicit covenant': they implicitly enact a pledge between believer and church and between church and believer. Baptism initiates this covenant, and the Lord's Supper renews it. Seen from this angle, 'membership' names the relation the ordinances imply. . . . To call someone a 'member' is to say that they have been baptized, they partake of the Lord's Supper, and they are welcomed into, and responsible for, the ecclesial life these effective signs entail. . . . The term member, then, describes a person whose ecclesial identity is determined by their ongoing participation in a particular local body. The ordinances [enact] an ecclesial reality, and membership names that reality.

Jamieson clarifies three other features that the category of church membership provides: (1) It "distinguishes the ordinances from the relation they normally imply, when in legitimate though exceptional circumstances, the two are separated" (cf. Acts 8:26–40). (2) It is an inference from Scripture rather than a direct teaching. Finally, (3) "Church membership . . . fulfills a crucial role of protecting the ordinances as practices of the church"

Offense, 217.

107. Leeman, *Surprising Offense*, 217. Merkle defines church membership simply as "a formal commitment to a local church." However, he acknowledges Leeman's definition as a fuller statement of his view (Merkle, "Biblical Basis for Church Membership," in Hammett and Merkle, *Those Who Must Give an Account*, 32).

108. The following is heavily dependent on Jamieson, *Going Public*, 145–47; Leeman, *Surprising Offense*, 249. Less explicit on the relationship between the new covenant and church membership is Kimble, *Forty Questions*, 41–43. Hammett is correct that by using the body metaphor, Paul describes individual Christians as members (Hammett, "Nature of the Church," in Hammett and Merkle, *Those Who Must Give an Account*, 16). Rather than conceiving of church membership as akin to club or team membership, covenantal categories, such as "the body of Christ," are needed.

by ensuring that they maintain the "relational character" in instances when "a professing believer sinfully attempts to participate in them while refusing to enter the relationship of submission and oversight they entail."

Jamieson calls attention to the function of the ordinances in relation to the new covenant and the covenantal nature of the church, both of which are substantiated in chapters 3 and 4. At this point, the question should be answered whether a local church is constituted by a verbal and/or written mutual covenant or by the ordinances. Baptist history reveals multiple examples of the former.[109] Yet, Jamieson rightly responds "This is a false dichotomy," because the local church and church membership are constituted "by the two ordinances which ratify a covenant."[110] From the angle of the kingdom, "Believers or members of the universal church, created by the Word, interpret the what and who of that Word and so establish a local church" by means of the covenant entailed in practicing the ordinances.[111] Because baptism is the sign of entry to the new covenant that is an obligation-creating act, it serves simultaneously as a pledge of loyalty to Christ and (normally) submission to the oversight of the church that administers the baptism. "Joining a church is a public declaration of being rightly related to the king" who rules the church.[112] From the angle of covenant, one should "not separate the act of baptism from a new believer's act of covenanting with a church." Instead, Jones argues "that baptism itself is the means through which the church covenants with, or adds into membership, new believers." Jones continues,

> In light of baptism's covenantal roles, churches should encourage people to consider their baptism, a much more powerful pledge than signing a piece of paper, in times of trial and need. God ordained baptism as a fitting normative means of confirming one's salvation for several reasons, including its symbolic portrayal of the gospel, its evocative use of water that prompts

109. Exemplary are the Covenant of the Broadmead Baptist Church (1640) and of Benjamin and Elias Keach (1697). See George and George, *Baptist Confessions, Covenants, and Catechisms*, 173, 177–79. The Covenant of Great Ellingham Baptist Church in Norfolk, England (1699) includes the statement "We likewise find in Holy Writ, that an explicit covenanting with, and giving up ourselves to the Lord and one another, is the formal cause of a particular gospel church" (182). See also the examples cited in full in Finn, "Historical Analysis of Church Membership," 76–79.

110. Jamieson, *Going Public*, 150. Leeman views the ordinances as the place at which Christ's "charter" for the establishment of his church (Matt 16, 18, 28) "collides" with the new covenant (Leeman, *Surprising Offense*, 247–48).

111. Leeman, "Church and Churches," in Leeman and Dever, *Baptist Foundations*, 359.

112. Moore and Sagers, "Kingdom of God and the Church," 77.

believers to recall their baptisms when they bathe, and its use of God's community to assure his reception of a new believer. For these reasons, baptism has more to offer for one's assurance than more common assurances such as praying the sinner's prayer or church membership without baptism. That is one reason why Scripture repeatedly uses baptism as a shorthand way of referring to the whole process of Christian initiation. Moreover, the covenantal blessings and obligations attached to baptism are the basis of a healthy understanding of what it means to be a member of a church, and baptism is the divinely ordained and fitting means through which a new believer and a church confirm initiation of their covenant with one another.[113]

Similarly, because the Lord's Supper is the sign of participation in the new covenant, participating Christians simultaneously deepen their union with Christ and corporately enact their derivative union with one another.[114] Just as one enters the new covenant in two logical moments—belief and baptism[115]—so also the church is constituted in "two steps": (1) belief in the gospel and (2) constitution as a church through the ordinances.[116] In

---

113. Jones continues, "Baptism is a mutual pledge between God, speaking through the covenant community, and the baptizand who is confirming that he or she is taking on God's new covenant and by extension covenanting together with God's covenant community. Thus, a church should not baptize people who do not intend to covenant together with them or any other local church. A church should explain to prospective baptizands that the act of baptism binds them to the one people of God expressed in that particular local body. This binding includes many blessings and obligations as expressed through the terms of church membership" (Jones, *Waters of Promise*, 146–47). The connection between baptism and local church covenants "does not mean that churches should abolish the practice of having elders who represent the congregation and new members, whether newly baptized or not, sign a written copy of the church covenant. Rather, the covenantal view gives baptism a confirming role as the baptizand's pledge to unite with God's people, the church. Such a pledge carries its own blessings and obligations, including church membership." Pastoral wisdom may allow baptizing those who do not intend to join in unusual circumstances, but Jones's point is well-taken.

114. On deepening union with Christ, Billings writes helpfully of the Spirit moving Christians toward a deeper embrace of the gospel (Billings, *Remembrance, Communion, and Hope*, 201). Because participating in the Lord's Supper enacts new covenant unity to form and maintain a local church, Leeman's statement is, as he admits, an "oversimplification." He writes, "The local church possesses a new covenant unity and a visibly manifest kingdom unity." Both statements are true, but the enacting function of the Lord's Supper is part of why Leeman describes his statement as an oversimplification (Leeman, "Church and Churches," in Leeman and Dever, *Baptist Foundations*, 335).

115. Leeman, *Political Church*, 362.

116. Leeman, "Church and Churches," in Leeman and Dever, *Baptist Foundations*, 363.

other words, "The ordinances initiate and confirm the covenantal relation between Christians we call church membership. Together, they build
Christians into the shape we call a church." Thus, neither a verbal or written church covenant is necessary to constitute a church, for the ordinances
themselves "are acts that speak. They effect a new, mutual relation between
the Christians who participate in them together."[117]

Nevertheless, in order to clarify the covenantal bond that exists between the members of a local church, it is appropriate (and often helpful) for
churches to verbally covenant together and form a written church covenant.
The written covenant stipulates the way the congregation agrees to live together under the authority of Christ, encourage and bear with one another,
and hold each other accountable.[118] While Scripture does not require the
writing of church covenants,[119] they are helpful in so far as they concretize
the church's covenantal nature, which is inherent in the New Testament,
and assist the church in casting aside notions of the church as a voluntary
society or contractual arrangement.[120] Written church covenants also benefit new members who transfer from other churches by teaching them the
covenantal entailments of their communion celebrations.[121] The ongoing
practice of the ordinances in a local church then require explanation from
the pastors and teachers of the church in order for the congregation to

117. Jamieson, *Going Public*, 150.

118. Leeman, *Surprising Offense*, 248. On the benefits of written church covenants
and the process of forming and adopting one, see Hammett, "Regenerate Church Membership," in White et al., *Restoring Integrity in Baptist Churches*, 34–37.

119. Allison, *Sojourners and Strangers*, 124–25.

120. Leeman recognizes two factors that assist a church in determining its membership structures: "societal complexity" and "societal favor and disfavor" (Leeman,
Church Membership, 124–25). Within the realm of prudence, Leeman proposes that
church covenants may be less useful in less complex societies, where Christians experience societal disfavor. In these cases, the covenantal nature of the church may be more
readily understood by the congregation. They are more useful in more complex societies where Christians are generally favored. For a lengthier presentation of the same
arguments, see Leeman, *Surprising Offense*, 285–92. Allison adds that "in [societies
without a church-state structure] . . . church covenants play an important formative and
disciplinary role" (Allison, *Sojourners and Strangers*, 127). Allison is also correct that
the biblical support for church covenants is "indirect" (125n3). Thus, the covenantal
nature of the church is the primary ground upon which I contend for the helpfulness
of church covenants. So also Jamieson, *Going Public*, 144–45, 153. More hopeful on
the ability to glean a basis for church covenants from biblical precedent (cf. Neh 8–10)
is Hammett, "Regenerate Church Membership," in White et al., *Restoring Integrity in
Baptist Churches*, 35–36.

121. Leeman, *Surprising Offense*, 299. For "twelve practical steps to meaningful
church membership," see Dever, "Practical Issues of Church Membership," in Hammett
and Merkle, *Those Who Must Give an Account*, 96–101.

attach the appropriate biblical and covenantal functions to them. Churches need to know "that the ordinances are vows and what those vows enact."[122]

This description of membership illumines the need for baptism as prerequisite to the Lord's Supper. Christ has assigned baptism as the means by which a church confirms the good confession of a new believer, and he has provided no other means by which a new Christian may be recognized or added to the group. One may profess faith in Christ and display fruit that demonstrates a circumcised heart. Nevertheless, Christ commands those who would enter covenant with him, and derivatively with his people, to be baptized (Matt 28:18–20; cf. 18:15–20). Baptism is the external, reflective means Christ has given as the sign that one trusts in Christ and possesses a circumcised heart (Col 2:11–12) and as the instrument of entering the body of Christ (1 Cor 12:13).[123] Thus, Jamieson is correct that "we can't remove baptism from membership because without baptism membership doesn't exist," because "baptism is the vow that creates the union of membership."[124]

However, this book does not argue merely that baptism is prerequisite to church membership, but that baptism is prerequisite to sharing in the Lord's Supper. Rather that argue for closed membership and an open Table, this book argues for close communion, which implies a closed membership. In other words, while a Christian baptized as a professing believer may belong to another evangelical church of like faith and order, occasional communion with another church is appropriate. In that sense, the Lord's Supper is a close communion, allowing non-members to participate. However, the close communion position implies closed membership—only those immersed as professing believers and are members in good standing in their church.

By considering the relationship of the ordinances to membership, outlined above, the need for close communion is clarified. Because the ordinances normally entail covenantal promises and obligations toward the group with which a Christian celebrates the Lord's Supper, this section argues that church membership is a conceptual way of naming the relationships that the ordinances create. But if ordinances and membership are normally coextensive, then churches should uphold the same requirements for participation in the Lord's Supper as they do for membership, given a

122. Jamieson, *Going Public*, 152.

123. Hammett, "Nature of the Church," in Hammett and Merkle, *Those Who Must Give an Account*, 18.

124. Jamieson, *Going Public*, 154. Because baptism belongs only to those who have experienced heart circumcision/regeneration, pedobaptism is not baptism. See Hammett, "Regenerate Church Membership," in White et al., *Restoring Integrity in Baptist Churches*, 27–28.

limited knowledge of the occasional communicants. One could argue that the allowance for exceptions in the term "normal" implies that Spurgeon's congregation was operating consistently to call for open communion and closed membership.[125]

It is true that the position is logically consistent, given the open communionists' expectation that those who are unbaptized would only join in celebrating the Lord's Supper occasionally and, therefore, exceptionally. However, the logical consistency of the position does not override the biblical principle that the sign of entry should precede the sign of participation. Because the New Testament continually assumes that baptism belongs with faith as the external means of conversion, and because of baptism's relationship to circumcision of the heart, a church is no more at liberty to open the Table to the unbaptized than it is to open its membership to the unbaptized. The covenantal associations of baptism and the Lord's Supper with the new covenant remain intact even when the normative church membership relationships do not pertain.[126]

The position of open communion and closed membership should be rejected because it misunderstands the relation of membership to communion. Church membership refers to those persons who most often take the Lord's Supper together as an expression of and means to unity, entailing all of the covenantal responsibilities for one another. The associate member view should also be rejected because it misunderstands the function of the new covenant signs to make the new covenant community visible.[127]

---

125. For instance, with respect to church membership, Jamieson writes, "I'm not denying that a church has the ability to extend membership to unbaptized persons. But ability is not authority. If a church extends membership to an unbaptized person, the person really does become a member of that church with all the privileges and responsibilities that entails. But in doing so, the church departs from Jesus' authorizing warrant and operates outside its heavenly constitution [cf. Matt 18:18-20]" (Jamieson, *Going Public*, 154-55). In my view, a similar dynamic is at work when a church opens the Table to the unbaptized. The difference is that the degree to which the church experiences the results of acting out of line with the church's authority is less in open communion than in open membership. In open communion-closed membership, the church voluntarily and occasionally enacts a constitution in which those who have not formally entered the new covenant and inaugurated kingdom through believer's baptism are affirmed as equally initiated into the church. In open communion-open membership, the church voluntarily and repeatedly enacts a constitution in which those who have not formally entered the new covenant and inaugurated kingdom through believer's baptism are affirmed as equally initiated into the church. These observations explain Kinghorn's argument that open communion alters the constitution of the church from that which Christ established (Kinghorn, *Baptism a Term of Communion*, 8-9).

126. Jamieson, *Going Public*, 125-26.

127. Tyler is correct to affirm that the category of associate member misunderstands the nature of the whole congregation as a priesthood of believers. However, his

Baptism is a sign of possessing the realities of the new covenant, and the sign of entry should occur prior to the sign of participation. Therefore, the thesis of this book precludes not only the broader category of open communion but also the narrower categories of open or associate membership. The Lord's Supper normally functions to define those who are members and distinguish them from the world. While intercommunion provides an exception to the constitutive function of the meal for the local church, it remains an exception. "After all, to disagree on the subjects and meaning of baptism may well be to disagree on the fundamental shape and purpose of the church and on who is to constitute it."[128] Thus, "Whatever determines the conditions of membership, defines also the terms of communion."[129] As Kinghorn and Fuller observed long ago, to change the definition of baptism is to change the nature of the church from a regenerate community to a mixture of "baptized" believers and their unbelieving children. Baptist churches must recognize the newness of the church's structure and nature as a new covenant community and conform their practices to that which upholds the redemptive-historical newness of the church. Close communion appears to be the best option for fulfilling these tasks.

The issue of close communion and church membership brings the question of proper inter-denominational relationships to the fore. If a pedobaptist cannot be a church member in a Baptist church, does this position require that the Baptist church thinks the pedobaptist would be partaking of the Supper in an unworthy manner? The discussion of 1 Corinthians 11:27 throughout this book suggests that this is the wrong question to ask, due to the category confusion that it assumes. In context, those who partake in an unworthy manner are already members of the church (12:27). The unworthiness is predicated to them due to their anti-gospel divisiveness toward each other. Therefore, a visiting pedobaptist who partakes of communion in a Baptist church cannot, by definition commit this error.

Furthermore, Baptist churches should not view pedobaptists as engaging in willful sin by their refusal to be baptized by immersion as professing believers. As Van Neste argues, "Their problem is one of scriptural interpretation. They seek to obey the command of baptism,"[130] but they read the biblical teaching differently and erroneously. While the pedobaptist does

---

conclusion that open membership should be acceptable is unwarranted (Tyler, *Baptism*, 145).

128. Dever, "Baptism," in Schreiner and Wright, *Believer's Baptism*, 341.

129. Reynolds, "Church Polity in the Kingdom of Christ," in Dever, *Polity*, 391. For this source, see Allison, *Sojourners and Strangers*, 405.

130. Van Neste, "Lord's Supper," in Schreiner and Crawford, *Lord's Supper*, 383.

not commit willful sin, failing to obey a positive command of Scripture, even due to interpretive error must be deemed unintentionally sinful.[131]

Helping a church understand the importance of close communion is helping them understand the role and importance of the ordinances in Scripture. Close communion is a principle derived from biblical theology in the function of covenant signs and systematic theology concerning the assumption of baptism as belonging to the cluster of events that make up conversion. Therefore, the pastors/elders who intend to strengthen the discipling relationships entailed by church's membership can start by teaching and celebrating the importance of baptism. "The command to be baptized is clearly taught in Scripture, is simple to obey, and is significant for the boundaries of the church." As the church recognizes these truths through patient and persistent teaching and preaching, then requiring "baptism for membership [should be understood as requiring] no more than Scripture does of Christians."[132] This observation assists the pastors' resolve to conform the church's structures to that which facilitates faithfulness to all that Christ commands. At the same time, recognizing that Christ requires believer's baptism and applying that principle to membership should embolden the church to recognize infant baptism as a misunderstanding of Scripture and a failure (even if unintentional) to follow Christ's commands. If the church can humbly relate to otherwise faithful and godly pedobaptists

131. So Dever, "Baptism," in Schreiner and Wright, *Believer's Baptism*, 340. Contra Van Neste, "Lord's Supper," in Schreiner and Crawford, *Lord's Supper*, 384. Van Neste raises the matter of cessationism by analogy. If the cessationist is wrong and God intends for Christians to "earnestly desire the spiritual gifts, especially that he may prophesy" (1 Cor 14:1), then one would think that failure to obey this command would be sin. Van Neste claims not because "even if he is wrong [he] is striving to obey the Scripture and should not be identified as one whose heart is hardened and refuses to obey the commands of Christ." The problem with Van Neste's analysis is that, due to the complexity of sin and life in a fallen world, it is possible to claim that the cessationist is committing unwitting sin without being required to also claim that the cessationist has a hard heart and refuses to obey Christ. Consider David's request for forgiveness for "hidden faults" in Ps 19:12.

132. Dever, "Baptism," in Schreiner and Wright, *Believer's Baptism*, 341. Dever's statement provides an apt reply to Hall's contention that the ordinances are "independently obligatory" and thus close communion hinders those who are unbaptized from obeying the Lord's command to come to the Lord's Supper. In short, pastors may present brothers or sisters who are interested in joining the church with Scriptures and/or theological books to read on baptism to have the candidates consider the evidence for believer's baptism. A church that practices close communion is not harming the true Christian who is unbaptized by urging the Christian toward baptism before receiving the Supper. Instead, the church is encouraging the Christian to undergo the sign of entry before the sign of participation. For Hall's argument, see Hall Jr., *On Terms of Communion*, 36–37.

with these truths in mind, they will be better equipped and have a greater resolve to approve a change in the bylaws and/or statement of faith requiring believer's baptism as prerequisite to the Lord's Supper and membership. These affirmations suggest that the process of receiving new members through baptism or by transfer of membership requires pastoral care.

For example, a church should be careful to distinguish the baptism of a professing believer who was sprinkled as an infant from rebaptism.[133] Baptists do not understand pedobaptism to be what Scripture intends by the word baptism. Therefore, to be biblically baptized by immersion as a professing believer for the first time is not rebaptism; it is biblical baptism.[134] The sign of entry—baptism—only happens once, and baptism belongs with saving faith as an aspect of conversion throughout the New Testament.[135] A pedobaptist who wishes to join with a Baptist church must recognize her pedobaptism is not actually a baptism. Without the pedobaptist's conscientious affirmation of this point, the church should not baptize the individual. To do so would introduce confusion for the person seeking membership and for the church. For someone baptized as an infant to receive believer's baptism while maintaining the legitimacy of one's infant sprinkling suggests one can formally enter the new covenant community two times and by two different means, which is untenable.

133. Rebaptism refers to the immersion in water of a professing believer performed a second time after the profession of faith. Sometimes rebaptism is requested by those who think of baptism, incorrectly, in terms of a rededicatory act or as somehow doing something to the baptizand that would prevent her from falling into sin post-baptism. In local church ministry, pastors sometimes hear language like "my baptism did not take." However, rebaptism is not a biblical category and should be rejected. The reasons for rebaptism often include a misunderstanding of the role of ongoing repentance and faith in the life of a believer after conversion. Accordingly, churches should not rebaptize someone who is convinced that her initial baptism was an act of professing faith in Christ. Similarly, see Allison, *Sojourners and Strangers*, 362. For a helpful discussion of the category of rebaptism as it relates to administrator, subject, and mode, along with implications for the ecumenical movement of calling pedobaptists to be baptized, see Jones, *Waters of Promise*, 149–52.

134. This point helps to answer a similar issue that arises among those baptized as professing believers while children or youth in Baptist churches, who later determine that they were not actually converted until sometime after their "baptism." For example, a twenty-year-old who believes in Jesus after having been immersed at twelve, on grounds of what she thought at the time to be faith in Christ but now admits not to have been saving faith, should be baptized as a twenty-year-old. By sincerely rejecting the former profession of faith, she implicitly rejects the baptism. While the immersion at twelve-years-old included biblical symbolism and the church's affirmation of the twelve-year-old as a kingdom citizen, the act was not baptism because it was not connected with the subjective heart response of faith. Therefore, to baptize the twenty-year-old is not rebaptism, because the first act with water is declared null.

135. Jones, *Waters of Promise*, 136.

Continuing the discussion of receiving new members, pedobaptists sometimes claim that, "because Christ has not given the church infallible knowledge of any person's heart . . . it is impossible that the visible church should be, in this age, entirely composed of regenerate persons."[136] However, this argument dismisses the responsibility of local churches to speak on behalf of heaven and exercise the keys of the kingdom, albeit fallibly.[137] The impossibility of a fully regenerate church due to fallible human perception and self-deceit in no way warrants giving up the responsibility to seek a regenerate church membership.[138] Thus, it is incumbent upon local churches to utilize proper means to know persons seeking baptism, to responsibly and caringly listen to their testimonies, and to watch their lives for some evidence of conversion.[139] At minimum, a clear profession of faith in Christ and a desire to follow him in baptism would constitute such evidence.[140]

136. Waters and Duncan, *Children and the Lord's Supper*, 193.

137. As Dever understands, "Not even all these stages [outlined below] can prevent the occasional baptism of someone who proves to be unregenerate. Hypocrisy cannot finally be prevented, but it can be discouraged" (Dever, "Baptism," in Schreiner and Wright, *Believer's Baptism*, 335). Similarly, see Baldwin, *Baptism of Believers Only*, 59, 68.

138. White explains, "While Baptists and dissenting groups throughout history may desire to move the believers' church into a mark for the 'being of the church,' Augustine's arguments are well-heeded. He argued against the Donatists that a truly regenerate church was not possible. While the Donatists and Baptists were and are right to seek after truly regenerate congregational membership, that requirement of such would result in constant evaluation of which churches are true and which are faulty. The effort and desire to have a regenerate church membership and the attainment of regenerate church membership adds greatly to the well-being of a church. Refusing to strive for a regenerate church is where Augustine erred. Giving up on seeking regenerate church membership harms the well-being of the church" (White, "What Makes Baptism Valid?," in White et al., *Restoring Integrity in Baptist Churches*, 115). For more on Augustine's controversy with the Donatists over their conceptions of the church, see Kelly, *Early Christian Doctrines*, 409–17.

139. This point applies to the transfer of members from one church to another as well. The practice, common among SBC churches (at least in the deep south) of receiving new member candidates through a come-forward ("altar call" style) invitation at the close of the service is at best ecclesially weak. At worst, when someone coming to transfer membership is immediately voted in by the congregation, the church is actually abdicating its responsibility to exercise the power of the keys to affirm the transfer member candidate as making a credible profession of the gospel. Hammett wisely suggests that where the come forward invitation persists, churches "have no basis for voting on such a person." At least, the church should "make a clear separation between welcoming someone who applies for membership and the official granting of membership itself" (Hammett, "Regenerate Church Membership," in White et al., *Restoring Integrity in Baptist Churches*, 37–41).

140. For a description of how the baptismal candidate's interview process should work, who should conduct it, and how to know when the person is ready to be baptized,

Following a process of discerning the professing believer's readiness to be baptized, the candidate should be presented before the whole congregation; that believer then becomes "part of the covenanted community" with the elders and congregation.[141] Prudentially, between the membership interview and the baptism, the other elders and members of the congregation should seek to know the candidate. Before the candidate is presented before the whole congregation for a vote into membership, the elders should minimally not sense any significant issues related to the new believer's profession of faith.[142] Churches in some areas may also require a new member or baptism class prior to the new believer being baptized.[143] The prudential nature of these decisions varies based upon the church's cultural context. Through its forms of communication, a church may helpfully inform the congregation of the new believer's request for baptism and membership and supply the congregation with a written testimony.[144]

---

see Dever, "Baptism," in Schreiner and Wright, *Believer's Baptism*, 333–35; Leeman, *Surprising Offense*, 300–303. Jamieson is correct to point to the adding of three thousand to the church at Jerusalem on the day of Pentecost as evidence that "in principle an unknown Christian does not need to prove his mettle by demonstrating 'fruit' over time or undergoing a lengthy catechetical process before being admitted to church membership" (Jamieson, *Going Public*, 128).

141. White explains, "The gathered believers should see the person's baptism and accept him or her into fellowship. It is a church ordinance" (White, "What Makes Baptism Valid?," in White et al., *Restoring Integrity in Baptist Churches*, 113). See also Dever, "Baptism," in Schreiner and Wright, *Believer's Baptism*, 335. The statement above alters Dever's statement to emphasize that baptism is the means whereby the church adds one to many. See Jamieson, *Going Public*, 104–5.

142. Appropriately, Allison "advocate[s] for baptism very soon after a person has embraced the gospel. This position assumes that the new convert has given a credible profession of faith and thus has demonstrated a sufficient genuineness of having grasped onto Christ so as to be saved. It further assumes that biblical teaching on baptism—its importance, meaning, and practice—has been communicated to new the Christian and understood, but this instructional process is not a lengthy one. Because the church will never achieve a complete guarantee that a person's conversion is absolutely genuine, to aim at such assurance—and, correlatively, postpone baptism until such a point is reached—is unrealistic" (Allison, *Sojourners and Strangers*, 362). Moreover, "To withhold baptism for the purpose of seeking an exaggerated level of assurance of conversion is wrong." Allison argues this point based upon the pattern of belief and baptism going together in Acts, as this book affirms. For appropriate warnings regarding relaxing standards of membership, see Hammett, "Regenerate Church Membership," in White et al., *Restoring Integrity in Baptist Churches*, 25–27.

143. For the usefulness of new member classes and of presenting a clear statement of faith in those classes, see Leeman, *Surprising Offense*, 294–99.

144. Some churches will choose to have the baptizand share a brief testimony at the baptism service.

After these processes, the time will come for the congregation to publicly vote on the new believer/new member candidate. Given that no significant questions arise with respect to the credibility of the new believer's profession of faith, the church will appropriately vote to affirm the new believer as a member contingent upon his or her baptism.[145] With these appropriate safeguards in place, the church should baptize the new believer.[146] Normally, the baptism should occur in the context of a congregational gathering. Whether the gathering is specifically a baptism service or the baptism occurs in conjunction with the other Lord's Day elements of worship, the congregation should act as covenant witnesses to the sign of new covenant ratification.[147] While the Scripture does not require that the church utilize formal questions addressed to the candidate during the baptism, such questions do manifest the covenantal nature of baptism. As when a couple exchanges vows in a wedding, to enter covenant together, the church's representative may ask questions such as (1) "Are you trusting in Christ and Christ alone for your salvation?" and/or (2) "Do you promise, depending on God's grace, to follow Christ and to join with this church in

145. Fiddes surmises, "It was probably the fact that the adoption of believer's baptism as the moment of entry into the local church that diminished the usage of a written covenant among Baptists for a period in the seventeenth century" (Fiddes, *Tracks and Traces*, 30). Although Fiddes's claim is possible, this study demonstrates the legitimacy of recognizing baptism as serving the dual purpose as an initiating oath sign. Through baptism, the believer ratifies the covenant with the Lord and formalizes the covenantal relationship with the local church responsible for administering the baptism. While the official, congregational act of covenanting is represented in the vote, the congregation exercises its rightful, Christ-authorized role by baptizing the new converts.

146. Scripture does not prescribe the person who should administer the baptism. However, "The church's leaders at least need to act in a supervisory capacity—ensuring that proper instruction about baptism has been provided, that the candidate(s) has/have articulated a credible profession of faith, that the one performing the baptism is prepared to do so in the proper manner, and that all the necessary preparations for the baptismal celebration have been made" (Allison, *Sojourners and Strangers*, 363). While my preference is to have an elder/pastor administer the baptism as one who has been already set apart by the church for the task of shepherding, Allison is correct that "nothing in Scripture prevents a member of the church . . . from engaging in the act of baptism."

147. For more on the importance of baptism being performed by representatives of the covenant community and in their presence, see Jones, *Waters of Promise*, 137. For more on possible confusion over the nature of baptism that could result from planning merely baptismal services, see Dever, "Baptism," in Schreiner and Wright, *Believer's Baptism*, 336. At the same time, heeding the warning does not require totally abstaining from well-planned baptism services. Given the lack of baptisteries in certain parts of the world and the variety of buildings in which churches meet, it could be appropriate to meet for a baptism service.

so doing as long as the Lord has you here?"[148] The baptizand would respond simply, "I do," to each question prior to the baptism.

148. The first question is the one used at Clifton Baptist Church in Louisville, KY. The second question is adapted from Dever, "Baptism," in Schreiner and Wright, *Believer's Baptism*, 338. Dever's questions are (1) "Do you make profession of repentance toward God and of faith in our Lord Jesus Christ?" The person responds, "I do." Then, (2) "Do you promise, depending on God's grace, to follow him forever in the fellowship of this church?" The person responds, "I do." The adaption above is intended to communicate a similar notion of joining Christ and his covenant community. Nevertheless, Dever's wording seems to imply that the baptizand is agreeing to remain in the church that baptizes him or her "forever." Although the verbal interaction between the baptizer and the baptizand, are not biblically necessary, they can be helpful to clarify the covenantal implications of baptism, as being similar to wedding vows. However, Jamieson is correct that "the covenant of membership [into which baptism introduces a Christian] is not permanent. Christians can change churches for a number of legitimate reasons, like moving to another city. Leaving a church is not necessarily equivalent to divorce. Yet, the covenant of membership is like certain biblical covenants in that the subordinate party—the Christian—may not unilaterally terminate the covenant. One may join or leave a church only with the consent of the church. So this definition of membership uses the term covenant somewhat analogically or metaphorically, yet with substantial parallels to biblical uses of the word" (Jamieson, *Going Public*, 148–49). Jamieson does not intend to communicate that the church has coercive authority over the Christian to bind her from going elsewhere. Instead, Jamieson is emphasizing the life on life responsibilities that the church members have for one another. Furthermore, claiming that the church must give consent for someone to leave and/or join another church helps the members understand that they cannot turn their back on Christ and their church family without the church graciously pursuing them in hopes of their repentance. For example, should a church member choose to enter an adulterous affair, that member could not individually and arbitrarily resign her membership in order to evade corrective church discipline. See the sections on membership and discipline below. For further discussion of how membership relates to an individual acting autonomously to leave a church, with implications for membership and prolonged, voluntary non-attendance, see Leeman, *Surprising Offense*, 314–18, 21. Hammett's proposal that churches renew their covenants yearly undervalues the church's role to dismiss members to a sister church through a transfer of letter, because a church member could choose not to re-sign the covenant and move on without the church's consent. The supposed benefit of Hammett's proposal is that it places the primary responsibility for continuing in membership with a church on the individual and allows for a church member to move to cease membership without excommunication. When the member chooses not to sign the covenant again, the decision "simply recognizes what the reality has been" (Hammett, "Regenerate Church Membership," in White et al., *Restoring Integrity in Baptist Churches*, 36–37). While the individual Christian's voluntary covenanting with a church is a crucial part of membership, Hammett's proposal does not adequately account for the church's responsibility to continue affirming and overseeing the church member's discipleship. Even with Hammett's caveat that those who do not sign should be visited by the church before allowing their removal from membership to be final, the proposal appears to place the authority of the keys in the individual's hand rather than the church's.

Within the church context of baptism, as the sign of covenant entry, "It is best not to isolate the administration of either baptism or the Lord's Supper from the preaching of God's Word,"[149] which functions with the covenant signs to explain them and render them legitimate. Certainly, then, baptism functions corporately in the following ways: (1) it "confers membership;[150] (2) it acts as a public swearing in ceremony to the kingdom of Christ; (3) it effectively binds the new believer into the covenant community;[151] and (4) it officially recognizes the change of the new believer from subject to citizen of Christ's kingdom in something akin to an embassy's stamp on a passport.[152]

If church membership names the covenantal relation that exists between the group of Christians who regularly participate in the ordinances together, church discipline refers to Christ's corporate means of maintaining integrity of the local church in their new covenant obligations.[153]

Close Communion and Church Discipline

This section considers the process of church discipline in its relation to the Lord's Supper. Church discipline refers to the process that Christ has instituted to maintain the church's holiness. In a broad sense, church discipline refers to both informal conversations between church members in which they speak truth each other in love (cf. Eph 4:15) and corrective measures for calling those practicing unrepentant sin to repentance (Matt 18:15–20).[154]

149. Dever, "Baptism," in Schreiner and Wright, *Believer's Baptism,* 337.

150. Jamieson, *Going Public,* 101.

151. Although exceptional cases exist in which a believer may be baptized apart from entering the membership of the local church that administers the baptism, great care should be taken to limit the confusion these exceptional cases create with respect to the individual Christian's ongoing discipleship and the need for the local church. Churches can help clarify the covenantal significance of baptism by baptizing believers in a congregational meeting, where the congregation acts both as witnesses to the believer's new covenant pledge of faith in Christ and as the local body among which the one another commands of the NT should be applied. Alternatively, it is unwise and breeds ecclesial confusion for churches to baptize new Christians without the congregation's affirmation and (virtually without exception) the direct leadership of the elders (e.g., baptizing a teenager in the ocean on a mission trip). For examples of this principle, see Leeman, *Surprising Offense,* 200–201.

152. Leeman, *Political Church,* 120. See Dever's helpful comments on planning a baptism in a Lord's Day service in Dever, "Baptism," in Schreiner and Wright, *Believer's Baptism,* 337–38.

153. Similar is Hammett, "Nature of the Church," in Hammett and Merkle, *Those Who Must Give an Account,* 13.

154. Leeman, *Church Discipline,* 27. For the distinction between formative and

Given the regenerate nature of the church, a church member's intentional and persistent sin calls his allegiance to Christ into question. Furthermore, for the church to remain a regenerate body, the church must act to remove a church member whose actions suggest his profession of faith is false. The normal process of church discipline involves four steps: (1) private confrontation over an issue of unrepentant sin to call the church member to come back to Christ (v. 15); (2) confrontation of the unrepentant party with one or two witnesses (v. 16); (3) telling the matter to the church members to give them opportunity to pray for and confront the unrepentant party; and (4) a congregational vote to remove the unrepentant person from membership (v. 17).[155] The purpose of church discipline is that the removal will be a means of ultimate restoration to Christ and the church (1 Cor 5:4–6; cf. 2 Cor 2:5–11).[156] Carson explains, "Church discipline is not only illustrated in Scripture; it is virtually mandated by the nature of the church."[157] In other words, "Without discipline, the ordinances even biblically observed can

---

corrective discipline, see Leeman, *Surprising Offense*, 319–22. Within the category of formative discipline Cheong distinguishes between "informal and formal" discipline. The former refers to conversations around truth and the latter is the official teaching ministry of the church (Cheong, *God Redeeming His Bride*, 65–66; Schreiner, "Biblical Basis for Church Discipline," in Hammett and Merkle, *Those Who Must Give an Account*, 105–6). For examples of the types of sin that should receive discipline in the NT, see pp. 123–24.

155. For a thorough treatment of church discipline in Matt 18, see Allison, *Sojourners and Strangers*, 184–90; Schreiner, "Biblical Basis for Church Discipline" in Hammett and Merkle, *Those Who Must Give an Account*; Norman, "Reestablishment of Proper Church Discipline," in White et al., *Restoring Integrity in Baptist Churches*, 199–219; Mohler Jr., "Church Discipline," in Armstrong, *Compromised Church*. For an historical look at church discipline throughout the history of the church, with a focus on Southern Baptists, see Wills, "Historical Analysis of Church Discipline," in Hammett and Merkle, *Those Who Must Give an Account*, 131–55. For an immensely helpful look at implementing church discipline in a church plant or established church and biblical wisdom for practicing church discipline, see Davis, "Practical Issues of Church Discipline," in Hammett and Merkle, *Those Who Must Give an Account*, 157–85; Cheong, *God Redeeming His Bride*.

156. Leeman lists five related purposes of church discipline: (1) expose sin; (2) warn the member of judgment to come for unrepentant sinners; (3) save the member and others harmed by the sin; (4) protect; and (5) "present a good witness for Jesus" (Leeman, *Church Discipline*, 33). For more on the redemptive purpose of church discipline and the connection of 2 Cor 2:5–11 to 1 Cor 5 and Matt 18, see Schreiner, "Biblical Basis for Church Discipline," in Hammett and Merkle, *Those Who Must Give an Account*, 117–21.

157. Carson, "Evangelicals, Ecumenism and the Church," in Kantzer and Henry, *Evangelical Affirmations*, 374.

become nothing more than . . . a ceremonial sign of something that does not really exist, a check written on a bankrupt account."[158]

Throughout the New Testament, Christ promises his power, presence, and authority with the assembled church to render its verdict in church discipline cases.[159] Four observations regarding church discipline clarify the relationship of exercising the keys to the Lord's Supper. First, church discipline occurs when the church is assembled.[160] Paul commands the Corinthians to remove the immoral man "when you are assembled in the name of the Lord Jesus and my spirit is present, with the power of our Lord Jesus" (1 Cor 5:4). Because the means by which one comes under the name of Christ into the church is baptism (cf. 12:3, 13), Jesus' and Paul's statements imply that the churches that act to discipline are assemblies of baptized believers.[161] Therefore, second, Jesus' promise to be present to authorize the church's speaking on behalf of heaven (cf. Matt 18:18–20) appears to be applied by Paul to a specific instance of church discipline.[162] Whereas the church acts to affirm a new believer's confession of the gospel through baptism, the church acts to deny the confession of the gospel through church discipline.

Third, the way in which the church renders the verdict that a person is formally and ecclesially not recognized as a kingdom citizen is by removing the person's privilege of participating in the Lord's Supper.[163] The validity

158. Dever, "Baptism," in Schreiner and Wright, Believer's Baptism, 340.

159. For a connection of similar texts to prove this point, see Schreiner, "Biblical Basis for Church Discipline," in Hammett and Merkle, Those Who Must Give an Account, 116.

160. For the relation of the assembled church to Christ's presence and the power of the keys, see Leeman, Surprising Offense, 205–6; Schreiner, "Biblical Basis for Church Discipline," in Hammett and Merkle, Those Who Must Give an Account, 111–12.

161. Leeman claims rightly, "[Paul's] exhortation did not demand a Congregationalist reading, but it at least recommended it" (Leeman, "Church and Churches," 357–58). When combined with Jesus' affirmation of his presence with those gathered in his name (Matt 18:20) and his instruction to "tell [the situation of a professing disciple's unrepentant sin] to the church" (v. 17), the congregational interpretation makes the most sense of the data. Jesus does not appeal to a higher body outside the gathered congregation. Paul calls on the church at Corinth to act with his apostolic authority and with the assumed authority of Christ, given his statement about the power of the Lord being present. Schreiner highlights that the church discipline mentioned in 2 Cor 2:6 was performed by "the majority" of the congregation, signaling a congregational exercise of the keys (Schreiner, "Biblical Basis for Church Discipline," in Hammett and Merkle, Those Who Must Give an Account, 120).

162. Allison, Sojourners and Strangers, 183.

163. Leeman, Surprising Offense, 172. Significantly, because the church's judgment is fallible and Christ does not guarantee infallibility, church discipline renders an authorized verdict by Christ's representatives but it is not a "definitive pronouncement" (184).

of this proposal is implied by the truth that those who receive the Lord's Supper together demonstrate their common identity as belonging to the inaugurated kingdom of Christ (1 Cor 10:16–17; 11:26).[164] Furthermore, the fact that Paul tells the Corinthians "not even to eat" with the unrepentant so-called "brother" strongly suggests that the Lord's Supper is the referent (5:10).[165] Whereas Jesus calls the church to treat an unrepentant person who professes kingdom citizenship as "a Gentile or a tax collector" (i.e., an unbeliever), Paul tells the Corinthian congregation to "expel the wicked person from among you" (1 Cor 5:11 NIV).

Fourth, the realms that church discipline mediates clarify the relationship between exercising the keys and the Lord's Supper. Church discipline formally recognizes a person who claims to belong to the realm of Christ to actually belong to the realm of Satan. That the church is the realm of the kingdom of God is implied by several factors: (1) Jesus promises his presence among assemblies of two or three baptized believers, called churches (Matt 18:17, 20; 28:19–20); (2) those churches function as kingdom embassies; (3) the churches possess authority to open the way into the kingdom through gospel proclamation and to formally recognize kingdom citizens by covenant signs; (4) the church's ongoing affirmation of citizenship in the kingdom of Christ is participation in the Lord's Supper; (5) Paul's call to judge those inside the church but not those outside (1 Cor 5:9–11); and (6) Jesus' promise that all of the churches together cannot be prevailed against by the gates of hell (Matt 16:18). That the action of church discipline declares someone to belong in the realm of Satan rather than the realm of Christ is clear from the ways in which Jesus speaks of those who do not belong to the church as Gentiles and tax collectors.[166] This group, it is implied, do not enjoy his covenantal presence to bless (18:17, 20; cf. 1 Cor 10:16).[167] Several of Paul's statements also verify this conclusion: (1) the call to "deliver this man over to Satan" for the ultimate purpose of his repentance and restoration (1 Cor 5:5) and (2) the implied portrait of those outside the church as

164. Moore and Sagers, "Kingdom of God and the Church," 77–78.

165. Dever, Church, 67. Beale recognizes that only those in the Corinthian church who have the authority to exercise the power of the keys against their sinning "brother" have the ability to obey Paul's exhortation "not even to eat with such a one" (1 Cor 5:11). The linkage of Christ being the Passover lamb and the language of eating (presumably the Lord's Supper; cf. vv. 7–8) in the same context suggests that those who participate in the meal exercise a greater measure of accountability toward one another than is required or possible of Christians from different local churches (Beale, New Testament Biblical Theology, 818).

166. Schreiner, "Biblical Basis for Church Discipline," in Hammett and Merkle, Those Who Must Give an Account, 109, 112.

167. Allison, Sojourners and Strangers, 397.

belonging to Satan (v. 5), inappropriate for churchly association (vv. 9–10), "outsiders" whom God will judge (vv. 11–12), and "evil" (v. 12).[168]

Thus, corrective church discipline is a verdict rendered by the church given Christ's authorization to exercise the keys and formally declare who belongs to Christ and who does not.[169] The verdict serves as a remedial warning, through which the church seeks to display an accurate picture of who will inherit the kingdom.[170] And, the line of demarcation between the church and the world is participation in the Lord's Supper. Through the Lord's Supper the church provides ongoing affirmation of an individual Christian's profession of faith by opening the Table to the Christian. Baptism only happens once, but the Lord's Supper occurs repeatedly. Therefore, "The definitive privilege of church membership is participation in the Lord's Supper, and the definitive act of church discipline is exclusion from the Lord's Supper."[171] Additionally, "Exclusion from the Lord's Supper isn't merely a logical consequence of being excluded from the church's fellowship. Instead, exclusion from the Lord's Supper is exclusion from the church's fellowship."[172]

Reflecting on the relationship of the ordinances to church membership and discipline raises the important question of whom the church should invite to participate in the Lord's Supper and how to fence the Table.

Fencing the Table

Putting close communion into practice requires that those who administer the Lord's Supper on behalf of the church fence the Table. Fencing the Table does not (normally) require those who serve the elements physically to keep individual congregants from picking up the bread and/or cup. Instead, it refers to the words of instruction that the person presiding over the meal (usually pastors/elders) gives to the assembly.[173] Although churches may ad-

---

168. Similar observations are offered by Schreiner, "Biblical Basis for Church Discipline," in Hammett and Merkle, *Those Who Must Give an Account*, 113–17, 125–26.

169. Kimble, *Forty Questions*, 51–55.

170. Moore and Sagers, "Kingdom of God and the Church," 78.

171. Jamieson, *Going Public*, 126; Horton, *People and Place*, 243.

172. Jamieson, *Going Public*, 127. He continues, "the relational consequences of church discipline" follow from this fundamental exclusion. The reason church discipline should be conceived of in this manner is that membership "consists first and foremost in a local church's formal, ongoing permission to participate in the Lord's Supper. All the other privileges and responsibilities of membership flow from this foundational act of inclusion."

173. For more on fencing the Table, see Leeman, *Surprising Offense*, 304.

minister the Lord's Supper in different ways that uphold close communion, the following is offered as an example of fencing the Table:

> We have heard the gospel proclaimed this morning through the preaching of the Word. Now, we will proclaim this gospel by celebrating the Lord's Supper together. If you are a believer in Jesus, who has been baptized by immersion, and are a member in good standing of an evangelical church that preaches this same gospel that you have heard this morning, we invite you to enjoy the bread and cup with us. As we celebrate the Supper, Scripture calls us to examine ourselves in order to consider how our lives reflect Christ and display unity with his body, the church. The forgiveness Jesus gives is a free gift of grace that none of us deserve. Therefore, our goal is not to make ourselves worthy of Jesus, but to renew our submission to Christ and dependence on his grace for our daily lives and our relationships together. We don't want to hold on to any sin that would hinder our relationship to the Lord or each other.
>
> If you are not a baptized believer in Jesus, we are so glad you are here. You are about to witness one of the physical signs that Jesus has given his church that displays our continuing trust in Christ, union with him, and unity together as a church. When the bread and cup come to you, we ask that you let them pass you by. If you have not yet trusted in Christ and followed in believer's baptism, it would be our joy to speak to you more about that afterward. The Lord's Supper is a family meal, and we would love to talk to you about joining the family. Just one other word of instruction, if you will wait until everyone has been served, we will eat at the same time as a sign of our unity together.[174]

At this point, the pastor calls on a server (or other prepared person) to pray with thankfulness for the Lord's broken body. Then, the servers distribute the bread. The pastor then reads or recites Jesus' words of institution to explain the significance of the bread, followed by the cup. Exemplary of the words of institution are the following: "As Jesus gathered in the upper room to celebrate the final Passover with his disciples, at the end of the meal, Jesus took the bread, broke it, gave it to them, and said, 'This is my body, which is given for you. Do this in remembrance of me'" (Luke 22:19). With these words complete, the congregation eats the bread together. Then, after a prayer of thanks for the Lord's atoning blood and the distribution

---

174. The language of this statement is adapted from one of my pastors, John Kimbell, at Clifton Baptist Church, Louisville, KY.

of the cup, the cup is explained as follows: "Likewise [Jesus took] the cup
. . . saying, 'This cup that is poured out for you is the new covenant in my
blood' (Luke 22:20). Take and drink." At the completion of these words, the
congregation drinks the juice or wine together. Although the singing of a
hymn is not a required aspect of the celebration of the Lord's Supper, it is
appropriate to sing the gospel to each other again and close in a benediction
(cf. Matt 26:30).

The pastor's fencing of the Table and the congregant's choice to abstain
from the meal are directly correlated. Clearly, if a person is going through
the process of corrective church discipline, or if the final stage of excommunication has already occurred, fencing the Table serves to warn the unrepentant professing brother not to partake without repentance.[175] At the
same time, a word of caution should be recognized on when to abstain.
Van Neste writes,

> If we have struggled this week and sinned (and we have), that
> is all the more reason we need the Lord's Supper. We need to
> be reminded in a tangible way that Christ has made provision
> for that sin. The only pre-condition for a [baptized] believer is
> that he be repentant. To refuse communion is symbolically to
> refuse the work of Christ. Thus, the only time that one should
> keep himself from the Table is if he refuses to repent. Then, that
> person should realize he is declaring that he refuses to submit to
> Christ and is beginning to show himself an unbeliever.[176]

175. Billings, *Remembrance, Communion, and Hope*, 152. Cheong recognizes that
occasions may arise in which it is appropriate for the elders to withhold communion,
either from one who has been removed from membership or prior to the church's act
of exclusion from membership (Cheong, *God Redeeming His Bride*, 127). While these
categories are legitimate, churches must exercise great wisdom in withholding the
elements in order to keep the church's focus on Christ rather than the unrepentant
attendee.

176. This is a crucial observation. Christians should not wait for the Lord's Supper
to examine themselves and turn from sin. To do so would miss the ongoing role of
confession and repentance in the life of the Christian throughout the week. Earlier
chapters argued that the call to cleanse out the old leaven (1 Cor 5:7), combined with
principle of postponing participation in the meal (Num 9) and the call to self-examination (1 Cor 11:28) suggest the [rare!] possibility that a Christian may find occasion to
abstain from the Supper. At the same time, the warning of v. 28 "does not apply to those
who are struggling with sin but are looking to the cross in repentance, hating their sin
and yearning to be pleasing to God." Van Neste rightly continues, "When the understanding of the people is that you must wait until you have been 'good enough' or have
gotten yourself into a moment of being 'good enough,' we have turned this amazing reminder of grace into an ogre of legalism" (Van Neste, "Lord's Supper," in Schreiner and
Crawford, *Lord's Supper*, 386–87). Similarly, Allison explains that any notion of making
one's self a worthy participant in the Lord's Supper misunderstands that Paul's concern

Abstaining from the Lord's Supper is related to close communion because one reason a person may abstain (within the church in which one is a member) is in the unfortunate case in which a bitter rift has developed between church members. The inherent picture of unity presented in the partaking of the Lord's Supper provide the biblical rationale for this point of abstention.[177] Nevertheless, church members should work toward (at least) an initial stage of forgiveness and determination to be reconciled as soon as possible. Especially in churches where the frequency of communion is monthly or quarterly, allowing divisions to continue without so much as an initial step toward peace is highly unhealthy. Anticipation of the Lord's Supper should provide greater impetus toward relational harmony.[178]

A lesson may be taken here from the Old Testament celebrations of Passover, where the connection between corporate covenant renewal and Passover is often explicit (2 Chr 30; 34–35; Ezra 6:19–22). As a renewing oath sign and covenant ratification meal, the church gathers to corporately reaffirm their repentance from sin and faith in Christ's substitutionary death, participate in Christ's covenantal presence, and be reminded of their reception of all the benefits of the new covenant. Given the covenantal responsibilities for one another, the symbolism of unity, and the need to seek reconciliation with brothers and sisters in the congregation in order to participate in a worthy manner, the Lord's Supper functions as a tangible act of rededication to Christ and (normally) the local body with which one celebrates the meal.[179]

---

is worthy participation, specifically over divisiveness. Allison describes an unfortunate and unbiblical notion of self-examination that is commonly practiced in churches: "A brief pause for self-examination is provided so that those about to participate may confess their personal sins and make themselves worthy participants. This practice is not what Paul meant" (Allison, *Sojourners and Strangers*, 406–7). While the practice of self-examination itself does not inherently bring about the misunderstanding (for indeed, Paul calls for self-examination), those leading the celebration must clearly articulate what is intended by the self-examination and that Christ's own declaration of righteousness (justification!) is the basis upon which one may be reckoned a worthy participant.

177. Paul's instructions to relate to one another with gospel humility, to discern the body, not to encourage divisions or let them grow, and to wait for one another add emphasis to this point.

178. Allison writes, "Churches who encourage their members to prepare for the ordinance ahead of time by acting swiftly to mend divisions do them a great service, for such members may look ahead joyfully and with great anticipation to their worthy participation in the upcoming celebration" (Allison, *Sojourners and Strangers*, 407).

179. If this understanding of the Lord's Supper is grasped, it would seem to preclude many of the public acts of rededication to Christ that occur in some regions of conservative evangelicalism. Furthermore, combined with robust teaching on the meaning of baptism, understanding the Lord's Supper as a corporate covenant renewal would seem

In order to hold the principle of close communion consistently, convictional Baptists may need to abstain from participation in the Lord's Supper in other situations in which they visit a non-baptistic church. If in principle one holds that baptism is Christ's appointed prerequisite to the Lord's Supper, then the pedobaptist church, although a true church with brothers and sisters in it, is not a baptized congregation. For a Baptist to partake of the Lord's Supper in that setting would deny the principle that the sign of entry should precede the sign of participation. For the same reason, plus more substantial theological disagreements over the salvific nature of baptism and the Lord's Supper, Baptists should not participate in communion at a Roman Catholic church.[180] Similarly, if the administering church is baptistic but fails to express any words of institution, explicitly threatens the gospel by their view of either ordinance, or presents a vague to nonexistent theology of the ordinances, the convictional Baptists will need to weigh the appropriateness of participating in the Lord's Supper on a case by case basis.[181]

---

to preclude requests for rebaptism by those who were baptized as professing believers by immersion, experienced a season of waywardness or giving in to sin, and desire to repent. In this vein, Van Neste speaks of offering a "Table call" at the end of each service rather than an "altar call." See Van Neste, "Lord's Supper," in Schreiner and Crawford, *Lord's Supper*, 388. On the Lord's Supper as a meal of rededication and renewal, see Hammett, *Forty Questions*, 276.

180. The Roman Catholic Church itself denies the Eucharist to non-Catholics, e.g., Protestants (*Catechism of the Catholic Church*, 1400).

181. I can imagine situations in which one could know enough about the theology of the church, for example through the statement of faith or a close relationship with long-time members, to participate without theological compromise. However, I do not think that the prospect of offense to the church should usurp theological conviction. In a Pentecostal or Assembly of God church for example, the open communion stance of the church is an important consideration for whether to participate with them as a guest in their church's worship. On this point, the question is raised as to whether it may ever be appropriate to abstain from communion in an open communion Baptist church, even SBC. Although the "Baptist Faith and Message 2000" clearly articulates close communion, the 2012 LifeWay survey found that nearly 70 percent of Southern Baptist churches practice open communion in some form (Pipes, "Lord's Supper"). Therefore, in my view, the prospect of participating with an ecclesially weak SBC church is not a foregone conclusion. Rather, the matter requires discernment. Whether or not to participate should be a prudential matter based upon what exactly the visiting, convictional Baptist knows of the church and what the person presiding over the meal says in the words of instruction and institution. If the administrating minister says nothing to instruct the congregation on who may participate, the visiting Baptist should be wary. If the instruction allows for anyone who desires to participate to join in, the visitor should abstain, because the Supper is not actually functioning as a church identifying meal. If the instruction specifically calls for faith in Christ as the only requirement, then the situation is a little different than visiting a pedobaptist church. Because the church is Baptist, depending on which part of the country one is visiting,

Conclusion

This chapter considers the relationship of the ordinances to Baptist ecclesiology. Whereas the covenantal functions of the ordinances help to explain the covenantal nature of the local church, the relation of the ordinances to the inaugurated kingdom help to explain the role of local churches as embassies of Christ's kingdom. By Christ's authorization of the local church to exercise the keys of the kingdom, local churches act on behalf of heaven to proclaim the gospel and to affirm the identity of those who profess the gospel as kingdom citizens. Thus, baptism and the Lord's Supper give visible and institutional shape to the local church. Furthermore, the themes of kingdom and covenant coalesce in the church's practice of church membership and church discipline. Church membership is a concept that makes explicit what is implicit in the ordinances regarding the horizontal responsibilities of specific groups of Christians toward each other. Close communion is a practice that helps to protect the regenerate nature of the church through membership and discipline, to uphold the covenantal shape of the church, and to recognize the ways in which Christ's kingly authority is exercised through the congregation's practice of the ordinances.

---

it is probably fair to guess that most of the congregation has been biblically baptized (especially in the southern US). However, the principle still exists that the church is celebrating a covenantal sign of participation in Christ without requiring the sign of initiation. Although I would respect close communion advocates who go ahead and participate in the meal, the possibility still exists that the church's membership practices are deficient to the degree that abstaining would be appropriate. For example, an open communion Baptist church that does not practice church discipline carries the structural flaw of institutionally allowing those who are unrepentant of sin and/or may have intentionally avoided baptism to partake of communion.

Chapter 7

Conclusion

THIS WORK HAS ARGUED that believer's baptism by immersion should precede communion as prerequisite to it, due to the explicit example of the New Testament, the assumed pattern that all believers are baptized, and a principle of analogy (continuity) from the necessity of circumcision before Passover. Chapter 1 demonstrated that various Baptists argued for or against close communion based upon an analogous relationship between circumcision and baptism as signs of entry into their respective covenants. Yet, the Baptists surveyed did not formulate a biblical-theological rationale for why the requirement of circumcision before Passover applies to the question of who may take the Lord's Supper. This project is situated within the historical Baptist debate over close communion at precisely this point.

In order to demonstrate sufficient biblical warrant for the principle of continuity (analogy), this book appealed to the significant biblical-theological foundation laid by adherents of progressive covenantalism, especially Gentry and Wellum in *Kingdom through Covenant*. Therefore, chapter 2 surveyed the covenantal functions of circumcision and Passover with respect to the Abrahamic and Mosaic covenants and to each other. Chapter 2 argued that after the Lord mandated circumcision as prerequisite for Passover (Exod 12:43–48), the principle carried through, sometimes explicitly and sometimes implicitly, throughout the Old Testament. Chapter 2 also traced the development of circumcision of the heart as a type that pointed forward to the new covenant.

Chapter 3 surveyed the covenantal functions of baptism and the Lord's Supper in relation to the new covenant and to each other. Two aspects of the thesis appear in chapter 3: (1) that baptism is assumed for every believer and (2) that Acts 2:41 exemplifies baptism as occurring prior to the Lord's Supper in the formation of the church. Chapter 3 argued that baptism and the Lord's Supper each function instrumentally to the believer's union with Christ, the former serving as the means of external appropriation and the latter serving as the means of spiritually deepening union with Christ. Chapter 3 argued that union with Christ is a NT category that refers to all the blessings of the new covenant. In sum, the New Testament data presents baptism as the sign of covenant entry and a pledge of submission and allegiance to Christ as king, and the Lord's Supper as the sign of covenant participation that functions to mark off the inaugurated kingdom community. As new covenant signs, both ordinances signify covenantal obligations to the new covenant community—the church.

Chapter 4 presented continuities and discontinuities between the covenant signs of entry and participation. While certain continuities may be observed between the old covenant and new covenant signs, the chapter grounded the discontinuities in Christ's inauguration of the new covenant. The chapter argued that whereas circumcision points forward typologically to Christ, the true seed of Abraham, and to circumcision of the heart that comes to new covenant members by virtue of union with Christ, baptism externally reflects circumcision of the heart, which occurs when one becomes united with Christ. This covenantal argument for believer's baptism grounds the thesis of the book. When the covenantal role of baptism is combined with the covenantal functions of the Lord's Supper to deepen union with Christ and to enact a horizontal union with others who are united with Christ, close communion is fitting: the sign of entering union with Christ should precede the sign of participating in union with Christ. Thus, the Old Testament requirement that the sign of entry precede the sign of participation yields a biblical-theological principle of continuity (analogy) that believer's baptism should precede the Lord's Supper as prerequisite to it. And, the association of the new covenant signs with union with Christ confirms the principle.

Chapters 5 and 6 defended and applied the thesis. Chapter 5 presented responses to the strongest arguments for open, closed, and ecumenical communion. Chapter 6 applied the theology of the ordinances to ecclesiological doctrine and practice. Chapter 6 began by considering the relationship of the ordinances to the new covenant, the kingdom of Christ, the universal church, and the local church. It closed by delineating the relation of close communion to church membership, church discipline, and fencing the table. While the New Testament does not present an explicit command that baptism precede the Lord's Supper, this book demonstrates that Scripture provides sufficient biblical data to warrant the conclusion. This book presents a biblical-theological constructive argument for close communion in order to promote Christ-focused, gospel loving, healthy churches, rather than to promote sectarianism. It is my hope that all members of the new covenant will benefit from this study, that they will be challenged to unify around the gospel wherever possible, and that they will hold more conscientiously to their denominational distinctives, based on a careful examination of Scripture. A humble submission to and conversation about all that Scripture teaches with respect to the church should promote inter-denominational dialogue, not hinder it. With respect to Baptists, I hope this book helps to undergird the clear affirmation of close communion in Baptist confessional documents and to strengthen the resolve of pastors to follow Christ's design for the local church as a means toward disciple making in the local church to the glory of God.

Bibliography

Akin, Daniel L. *1, 2, 3 John.* New American Commentary 38. Nashville: Broadman & Holman, 2001.

Allen, David L. *Hebrews.* New American Commentary 35. Nashville: Broadman & Holman, 2010.

Allen, Leslie C. *Ezra, Nehemiah, Esther.* New International Biblical Commentary 9. Peabody, MA: Hendrickson, 2003.

Allison, Gregg R. "Baptism with and Filling of the Holy Spirit." *The Southern Baptist Journal of Theology* 16.4 (2012) 4–21.

———. *Historical Theology: An Introduction to Christian Doctrine.* Grand Rapids: Zondervan, 2011. Kindle ed.

———. *Sojourners and Strangers: The Doctrine of the Church.* Foundations of Evangelical Theology. Wheaton, IL: Crossway, 2012.

Armstrong, John H., ed. *The Compromised Church: The Present Evangelical Crisis.* Wheaton, IL: Crossway, 1998.

———. *Understanding Four Views on the Lord's Supper.* Counterpoints. Grand Rapids: Zondervan, 2007.

Augustine. *The Trinity.* Vol. 5 of *The Works of Saint Augustine: A Translation for the Twenty-First Century.* Edited by John E. Rotelle. Translated by Edmund Hill. 2nd ed. Hyde Park, NY: New City, 1991.

Badcock, Gary D. *House Where God Lives: Renewing the Doctrine of the Church for Today.* Grand Rapids: Eerdmans, 2009.

Baldwin, Thomas. *The Baptism of Believers Only, and the Particular Communion of the Baptist Churches Explained and Vindicated in Three Parts.* Boston: Manning & Loring, 1806.

———. *A Series of Letters in Which the Distinguishing Sentiments of the Baptists Are Explained and Vindicated: In Answer to a Late Publication, by the Rev. Samuel Worcester, AM, Addressed to the Author, Entitled Serious and Candid Letters.* Boston: Manning & Loring, 1810.

Barcellos, Richard C., ed. *Recovering a Covenantal Heritage: Essays in Baptist Covenant Theology.* Palmdale, CA: Reformed Baptist Academic, 2014.

Barna, George. *Revolution.* Wheaton, IL: Tyndale, 2005.

Barrett, C. K. *A Critical and Exegetical Commentary on the Acts of the Apostles.* Vols. 1 and 2. International Critical Commentary 34. Edinburgh: T&T Clark, 1998.

Barrett, Matthew, ed. *Reformation Theology: A Systematic Summary.* Wheaton, IL: Crossway, 2017. Kindle ed.

Bartholomew, Craig G. *Where Mortals Dwell: A Christian View of Place for Today.* Grand Rapids: Baker Academic, 2011.

Beale, G. K. *The Book of Revelation.* New International Greek Testament Commentary. Grand Rapids: Eerdmans, 1999.

———. *New Testament Biblical Theology: The Unfolding of the Old Testament in the New.* Grand Rapids: Baker Academic, 2011.

———. *The Temple and the Church's Mission: A Biblical Theology of the Dwelling Place of God.* New Studies in Biblical Theology 17. Downers Grove, IL: InterVarsity, 2004.

Beasley-Murray, G. R. *Baptism in the New Testament.* Grand Rapids: Eerdmans, 1973.

———. *John.* Word Biblical Commentary 37. Waco, TX: Word, 1987.

———. *Revelation.* Rev. ed. New Century Bible Commentary. Grand Rapids: Eerdmans, 1978.

Beckwith, Roger T. "Age of Admission to the Lord's Supper." *Westminster Theological Journal* 38.2 (1976) 123–51.

Benton, Steven S. "Genesis 17:9–14: An Exegetical and Theological Study of the Relation of Circumcision to the Covenant." MTh thesis, Dallas Theological Seminary, 1988.

Billings, J. Todd. *Remembrance, Communion, and Hope: Rediscovering the Gospel at the Lord's Table.* Grand Rapids: Eerdmans, 2018.

Blaising, Craig A., and Darrell L. Bock. *Progressive Dispensationalism.* Wheaton, IL: BridgePoint, 1993.

Block, Daniel Isaac. *The Book of Ezekiel.* Vol. 2. New International Commentary on the Old Testament. Grand Rapids: Eerdmans, 1997.

Blomberg, Craig L. *Matthew.* New American Commentary 22. Nashville: Broadman & Holman, 1992.

Bock, Darrell L. *Luke.* Baker Exegetical Commentary on the New Testament. 2 vols. Grand Rapids: Baker, 1994, 1996.

Bock, Darrell L., and Mitch Glaser, eds. *Messiah in the Passover.* Grand Rapids: Kregel, 2017.

Booth, Abraham. *An Apology for the Baptists.* Philadelphia: Thomas Dobson, 1788.

———. *A Defense for the Baptists: Being a Declaration and a Vindication of Three Historically Distinctive Baptist Principles, Compiled and Set Forth in the Republishing of Three Books.* Paris, AR: Baptist Standard Bearer, 1985.

———. *Pædobaptism Examined: With Replies to the Arguments and Objection of Dr. Williams and Mr. Peter Edwards.* London: Ebenezer Palmer, 1829.

Brack, Jonathan M., and Jared Oliphint. "Questioning the Progress in Progressive Covenantalism: A Review of Gentry and Wellum's *Kingdom through Covenant*." *Westminster Theological Journal* 76 (2014) 189–217.

Brackney, William H. *A Genetic History of Baptist Thought: With Special Reference to Baptists in Britain and North America.* Macon, GA: Mercer University Press, 2004.

Breed, Geoffrey R. *Particular Baptists in Victorian England: And Their Strict Communion Organizations.* Didcot, England: Baptist Historical Society, 2003.

Breneman, Mervin. *Ezra, Nehemiah, Esther.* New American Commentary 10. Nashville: Broadman & Holman, 1993.

Brennan, Sandra. "Musical Bio of Buell Kazee." *Baptist History Homepage,* n.d. Online. http://baptisthistoryhomepage.com/kazee.music.bio.html.

Brewster, Paul. *Andrew Fuller: Model Pastor-Theologian.* Nashville: B&H, 2010.

Briggs, J. H. Y. *The English Baptists of the Nineteenth Century*. Vol. 3 of *A History of the English Baptists*. Didcot, England: Baptist Historical Society, 1994.

Briggs, John. "Two Congregational Denominations: Baptist and Pædobaptist." *International Congregational Journal* 10 (2011) 95–131.

Brooks, James A. *Mark*. New American Commentary 23. Nashville: Broadman & Holman, 1991.

Bruce, F. F. *The Acts of the Apostles: The Greek Text with Introduction and Commentary*. 3rd rev. ed. New International Commentary on the New Testament. Grand Rapids: Eerdmans, 1990.

———. *The Epistle to the Galatians: A Commentary on the Greek Text*. New International Greek Testament Commentary. Grand Rapids: Eerdmans, 1982.

Bruckner, James K. *Exodus*. New International Biblical Commentary 2. Peabody, MA: Hendrickson, 2008.

Budd, Philip J. *Numbers*. Word Biblical Commentary 5. Waco, TX: Word, 1984.

Bunyan, John. *The Works of John Bunyan*. Vol. 2. Edited by George Offor. London: Blackie and Son, 1862.

Burdine, J. T. "English Baptist Ecclesiology from John Smyth to Robert Hall, 1600–1830." PhD diss., Southern Baptist Theological Seminary, 1951.

Canoy, Robert William. "Perspectives on Eucharistic Theology: Luke as Paradigm for an Inclusive Invitation to Communion." PhD diss., Southern Baptist Theological Seminary, 1987.

Carpenter, Eugene E. *Exodus*. Vol. 1. Evangelical Exegetical Commentary. Bellingham, WA: Lexham, 2016.

Carroll, B. H. *Baptists and Their Doctrines: Sermons on Distinctive Baptist Principles*. New York: Revell, 1913.

———. "A Discussion of the Lord's Supper." In *Christ and His Church: Containing Great Sermons Concerning the Church of Christ, Elaborate Discussions of the Baptist View of the Lord's Supper and a Heart-Searching Analysis of the Church Covenant*, edited by J. B. Cranfill, 135–68. Dallas: Helms Printing, 1940.

———. *The Supper and Suffering of Our Lord*. Edited by J. W. Crowder. Fort Worth, TX: Seminary Hill, 1947.

Carson, Donald A. "Evangelicals, Ecumenism and the Church." In *Evangelical Affirmations*, edited by Kenneth S. Kantzer and Carl F. H. Henry, 347–85. Grand Rapids: Academie, 1990.

———. *The Gospel According to John*. Pillar New Testament Commentary. Grand Rapids: Eerdmans, 1991.

———. "Matthew." In vol. 8 of *The Expositor's Bible Commentary*, edited by Frank E. Gaebelein, 3–599. Grand Rapids: Zondervan, 1984.

———. *Showing the Spirit: A Theological Exposition of 1 Corinthians 12–14*. Grand Rapids: Baker, 1987.

———. "Why the Local Church Is More Important than TGC, White Horse Inn, 9 Marks, and Maybe Even ETS." *Themelios* 40 (2015) 1–9.

Cason, Harland James. "The Gathered Community as a Locus of Christ's Presence: A Historical and Theological Analysis of Baptist Sacramentalism in the Lord's Supper." PhD diss., Southwestern Baptist Theological Seminary, 2011.

Chen, Carol. "A Historical, Biblical, and Theological Interpretation of Covenants: Unconditionality and Conditionality in Relation to Justification and Sanctification." PhD diss., Southern Baptist Theological Seminary, 2019.

Cheong, Robert K. *God Redeeming His Bride: A Handbook for Church Discipline*. Fearn, Scotland: Christian Focus, 2012.

Chessman, Daniel. *Memoir of Rev. Thomas Baldwin, DD, Late Pastor of the Second Baptist Church in Boston, Who Died at Waterville, Maine, Aug. 25, 1825*. 2nd ed. Boston: Elder John Peak, 1841.

Ciampa, Roy E., and Brian S. Rosner. *The First Letter to the Corinthians*. Pillar New Testament Commentary. Nottingham, England: Apollos, 2010.

Clarke, Anthony. "Dr Anthony Clarke." *Regent's Park College*, n.d. http://www.rpc.ox.ac.uk/people/dr-anthony-clarke.

———. *For the Sake of the Church: Essays in Honour of Paul S. Fiddes*. Oxford: Centre for Baptist History and Heritage, 2014.

Clarke, Anthony, and Andrew Moore, eds. *Within the Love of God: Essays on the Doctrine of God in Honour of Paul S. Fiddes*. New York: Oxford University Press, 2014.

Clary, Ian H. "Throwing Away the Guns: Andrew Fuller, William Ward, and the Communion Controversy in the Baptist Missionary Society." *Foundations* 68 (2015) 84–101.

Clowney, Edmund P. *The Church*. Contours of Christian Theology. Downers Grove, IL: IVP Academic, 1995.

Cole, Neil. *Organic Church: Growing Faith Where Life Happens*. San Francisco: Jossey-Bass, 2005.

Cole, R. Dennis. *Numbers*. New American Commentary 3B. Nashville: Broadman & Holman, 2000.

"Communion and Baptism." *Christian Church (Disciples of Christ)*, n.d. Online. https://disciples.org/our-identity/communion-and-baptism.

Cooper, Lamar Eugene. *Ezekiel*. New American Commentary 17. Nashville: Broadman & Holman, 1994.

Coxe, Nehemiah, et al. *Covenant Theology from Adam to Christ*. Palmdale, CA: Reformed Baptist Academic, 2005.

Crawford, Matthew R. "'Confessing God from a Good Conscience': 1 Peter 3:21 and Early Christian Baptismal Theology." *Journal of Theological Studies* 67.1 (2016) 23–37.

Crisp, Michael. "B. H. Carroll: Remembering His Life, Expanding His Legacy." *Southwestern Journal of Theology* 58.2 (2016) 159–81.

Cross, Anthony R. *Baptism and the Baptists: Theology and Practice in Twentieth-Century Britain*. Carlisle, England: Paternoster, 2000.

———. "Baptists and Baptism—a British Perspective." *Baptist History and Heritage* 35.1 (2000) 104–21.

———. *Recovering the Evangelical Sacrament: Baptisma Semper Reformandum*. Eugene, OR: Pickwick, 2013.

———. "Revd Dr Anthony R. Cross." *International Baptist Theological Study (IBTS) Centre Amsterdam*, n.d. Online. https://www.ibts.eu/about/info/49.

Cross, Anthony R., and Philip E. Thompson, eds. *Baptist Sacramentalism*. Studies in Baptist History and Thought 5. Eugene, OR: Wipf & Stock, 2007.

———. *Baptist Sacramentalism*. Vol. 2. Studies in Baptist History and Thought 25. Eugene, OR: Wipf & Stock, 2009.

Deenick, Karl. *Righteous by Promise: A Biblical Theology of Circumcision*. New Studies in Biblical Theology 45. Downers Grove, IL: IVP Academic, 2018.

Demarest, Bruce A. *The Cross and Salvation: The Doctrine of Salvation.* Foundations of Evangelical Theology. Wheaton, IL: Crossway, 1997.

Dempster, Stephen G. *Dominion and Dynasty: A Biblical Theology of the Hebrew Bible.* New Studies in Biblical Theology 15. Downers Grove, IL: InterVarsity, 2006.

DeRouchie, Jason S. "Circumcision in the Hebrew Bible and Targums: Theology, Rhetoric, and the Handling of Metaphor." *Bulletin for Biblical Research* 14.2 (2004) 175–203.

——. "Counting Stars with Abraham and the Prophets: New Covenant Ecclesiology in OT Perspective." *Journal of the Evangelical Theological Society* 58.3 (2015) 445–85.

DeRouchie, Jason S., and Jason C. Meyer. "Christ or Family as the 'Seed' of Promise? An Evaluation of N. T. Wright on Galatians 3:16." *The Southern Baptist Journal of Theology* 14.3 (2010) 36–48.

Dever, Mark. "The Church." In *A Theology for the Church*, edited by Daniel L. Akin et al., 603–68. Rev. ed. Nashville: B&H Academic, 2014.

——. *The Church: The Gospel Made Visible.* Nashville: B&H Academic, 2012.

——. *A Display of God's Glory.* Washington, DC: Center for Church Reform, 2001. Online. http://dev.9marks.org/site/wp-content/uploads/2015/08/Display-of-Gods-Glory_CFCR.pdf.

——, ed. *Polity: Biblical Arguments for How to Conduct Church Life.* Washington, DC: Center for Church Reform, 2001.

Dever, Mark, et al. "Church Polity? Really?" *Gospel Coalition National Conference*, October 26, 2017. Online. https://www.thegospelcoalition.org/conference_media/church-polity-really.

Dillard, Raymond B. *2 Chronicles.* Rev. ed. Word Biblical Commentary 15. Waco, TX: Word, 1987.

Doriani, Daniel. "A Redemptive-Historical Model." In *Four Views on Moving Beyond the Bible to Theology*, edited by Gary T. Meadors, 75–120. Counterpoints. Grand Rapids: Zondervan, 2009.

Duesing, Jason G. "A Denomination Always for the Church: Ecclesiological Distinctives as a Basis for Confessional Cooperation." In *The SBC and the Twenty-First Century: Reflection, Renewal, and Recommitment*, edited by Jason K. Allen, 109–25. Nashville: B&H Academic, 2016.

——. *Henry Jessey: Puritan Chaplain, Independent and Baptist Pastor, Millenarian Politician and Prophet.* Mountain Home, AR: BorderStone, 2015.

Dumbrell, William J. *Covenant and Creation: An Old Testament Covenant Theology.* Milton Keynes, England: Paternoster, 2013.

——. *The End of the Beginning: Revelation 21–22 and the Old Testament.* New South Wales, Australia: Lancer, 1985.

——. *The Faith of Israel: A Theological Survey of the Old Testament.* Grand Rapids: Baker Academic, 2002.

——. "Spirit and Kingdom of God in the Old Testament." *Reformed Theological Review* 33.1 (1974) 1–11.

Dunn, James D. G. *Baptism in the Holy Spirit: A Re-Examination of the New Testament Teaching on the Gift of the Spirit in Relation to Pentecostalism Today.* Philadelphia: Westminster, 1970.

Easley, Kendell H., and Christopher W. Morgan, eds. *The Community of Jesus.* Nashville: B&H Academic, 2013.

Edwards, Jonathan. "The Thing Desired in the Sacrament of the Lord's Supper is the Communion of Christians in the Body and Blood of Christ." In *Sermons on the Lord's Supper*, edited by Don Kistler, 1–24. Orlando, FL: Northampton, 2007.

Elwyn, T. S. H. *The Northamptonshire Baptist Association*. London: Carey Kingsgate, 1964.

Emadi, Samuel C., and Aubrey Sequeira. "Biblical-Theological Exegesis and the Nature of Typology." *The Southern Baptist Journal of Theology* 21.1 (2017) 11–34.

Enns, Peter. *Exodus*. NIV Application Commentary. Grand Rapids: Zondervan, 2000.

Episcopal Church, Domestic and Foreign Missionary Society. "Communion." *Episcopal Church*, n.d. Online. https://www.episcopalchurch.org/what-we-believe/communion.

Estes, Douglas. *SimChurch: Being the Church in the Virtual World*. Grand Rapids: Zondervan, 2009.

Evangelical Free Church of America (EFCA). "Statement of Faith." *Evangelical Free Church of America*, June 19, 2019. Online. https://www.efca.org/resources/document/efca-statement-faith.

Farish, Stephen E. "The Open Versus Close Communion Controversy in English and American Baptist Life: An Overview of the History and Evaluation of the Issues." MA thesis, Trinity International University, 2002.

Fee, Gordon D. *The First Epistle to the Corinthians*. Rev. ed. New International Commentary on the New Testament. Grand Rapids: Eerdmans, 2014.

Feinberg, Charles L. "Jeremiah." In vol. 6 of *The Expositor's Bible Commentary*, edited by Frank E. Gaebelein, 355–691. Grand Rapids: Zondervan, 1980.

Feinberg, John S., ed. *Continuity and Discontinuity: Perspectives on the Relationship between the Old and New Testaments: Essays in Honor of S. Lewis Johnson, Jr.* Westchester, IL: Crossway, 1988.

Fensham, F. Charles. *The Books of Ezra and Nehemiah*. New International Commentary on the Old Testament. Grand Rapids: Eerdmans, 1982.

Ferguson, C. Everett. *Baptism in the Early Church: History, Theology, and Liturgy in the First Five Centuries*. Grand Rapids: Eerdmans, 2013.

Ferguson, Sinclair B. *The Holy Spirit*. Contours of Christian Theology. Leicester, England: InterVarsity, 1996.

Fiddes, Paul S. "Baptism and the Process of Christian Initiation." *Ecumenical Review* 54.1 (2002) 49–65.

———. "Covenant and Participation: A Personal Review of the Essays." *Perspectives in Religious Studies* 44.1 (2017) 119–37.

———. *Tracks and Traces: Baptist Identity in Church and Theology*. Studies in Baptist History and Thought 13. Eugene, OR: Wipf & Stock, 2007.

———. "'Walking Together': The Place of Covenant Theology in Baptist Life Yesterday and Today." In *Pilgrim Pathways: Essays in Honour of B. R. White*, edited by William H. Brackney et al., 47–77. Macon, GA: Mercer University Press, 1999.

Finger, Reta Halteman. *Of Widows and Meals: Communal Meals in the Book of Acts*. Grand Rapids: Eerdmans, 2007.

Finn, Nathan. "Baptism as a Prerequisite to the Lord's Supper." White Paper 9. Ft. Worth, TX: Center for Theological Research, Southwestern Baptist Theological Seminary, 2006.

Fowler, Stanley K. *More Than a Symbol: The British Baptist Recovery of the Baptismal Sacramentalism*. Studies in Baptist History and Thought 2. Eugene, OR: Wipf and Stock, 2002.

———. *Rethinking Baptism: Some Baptist Reflections*. Eugene, OR: Wipf & Stock, 2015.

Fox, Michael V. "Sign of the Covenant: Circumcision in the Light of the Priestly 'ōt Etiologies." *Revue Biblique* 81.4 (1974) 557–96.

France, R. T. *The Gospel of Matthew*. New International Commentary on the New Testament. Grand Rapids: Eerdmans, 2007.

Freeman, Curtis W. *Contesting Catholicity: Theology for Other Baptists*. Waco, TX: Baylor University Press, 2014.

Fuller, Andrew, and Michael A. G. Haykin. "The Admission of Unbaptized Persons to the Lord's Supper, Inconsistent with the New Testament." *The Southern Baptist Journal of Theology* 17.2 (2013) 68–76.

Fuller, Andrew Gunton. *The Complete Works of Andrew Fuller*. Vols. 2–3. Edited by Joseph Belcher. Harrisburg, PA: Sprinkle, 1988.

Fuller, Daniel P. *Gospel and Law: Contrast or Continuum? The Hermeneutics of Dispensationalism and Covenant Theology*. Pasadena, CA: Fuller Theological Seminary, 1990.

———. *The Unity of the Bible: Unfolding God's Plan for Humanity*. Grand Rapids: Zondervan, 1992.

Fuller, Richard. *Baptism, and the Terms of Communion: An Argument*. 3rd ed. The Baptist Distinctives 9. Paris, AR: Baptist Standard Bearer, 2006.

Gaffin, Richard B. "Cessationist View." In *Are Miraculous Gifts for Today? Four Views*, edited by Wayne Grudem, loc. 265–1089. Counterpoints. Grand Rapids: Zondervan, 1996. Kindle ed.

Gaines, Darrell Grant. "One Church in One Location: Questioning the Biblical, Theological, and Historical Claims of the Multi-Site Church Movement." PhD diss., Southern Baptist Theological Seminary, 2012.

Garland, David E. *Colossians and Philemon*. NIV Application Commentary. Grand Rapids: Zondervan, 1998.

———. *1 Corinthians*. Baker Exegetical Commentary on the New Testament. Grand Rapids: Baker Academic, 2003.

———. *Luke*. Exegetical Commentary on the New Testament. Grand Rapids: Zondervan, 2011.

Garrett, Duane A. *A Commentary on Exodus*. Kregel Exegetical Library. Grand Rapids: Kregel Academic, 2014.

Garrett, James Leo, Jr. *Baptist Theology: A Four-Century Study*. Macon, GA: Mercer University Press, 2009.

———. "Should Baptist Churches Adopt Open Membership?" White Paper 34. Ft. Worth, TX: Center for Theological Research, Southwestern Baptist Theological Seminary, 2010.

General Conference of The United Methodist Church (GCUMC). *This Holy Mystery: A United Methodist Understanding of Holy Communion*. Nashville: General Board of Discipleship of The United Methodist Church, 2004. Online. http://s3.amazonaws.com/Website_Properties/what-we-believe/documents/communion-holy-mystery-united-methodist-understanding.pdf.

General Council of the Assemblies of God (GCAG). "Sixteen Fundamental Truths." *Assemblies of God*, n.d. Online. https://ag.org/Beliefs/Statement-of-Fundamental-Truths.

Gentry, Peter John, and Stephen J. Wellum. *Kingdom through Covenant: A Biblical-Theological Understanding of the Covenants*. Wheaton, IL: Crossway, 2012.

George, Timothy. "Controversy and Communion: The Limits of Baptist Fellowship from Bunyan to Spurgeon." In *The Gospel in the World: International Baptist Studies*, 38–58. Studies in Baptist History and Thought 1. Waynesboro, GA: Paternoster, 2002.

———. *Galatians*. New American Commentary 30. Nashville: B&H, 1994.

George, Timothy, and David S. Dockery. *Baptist Theologians*. Nashville: Broadman, 1990.

George, Timothy, and Denise George, eds. *Baptist Confessions, Covenants, and Catechisms*. Nashville: B&H Academic, 1996.

Gerrish, B. A. *Grace and Gratitude: The Eucharistic Theology of John Calvin*. Minneapolis: Fortress, 1993.

Gibson, David. "Sacramental Supersessionism Revisited: A Response to Martin Salter on the Relationship between Circumcision and Baptism." *Themelios* 37.2 (2012) 191–208.

Girgis, Sherif, et al. *What Is Marriage? Man and Woman: A Defense*. New York: Encounter, 2012.

Goen, C. C. *Revivalism and Separatism in New England, 1740–1800: Strict Congregationalists and Separate Baptists in the Great Awakening*. New Haven, CT: Yale University, 1962.

Goldingay, John. "The Significance of Circumcision." *Journal for the Study of the Old Testament* 25 (2000) 3–18.

Goodliff, Andy. "Reflecting on Ministry (3) Interview with Ruth Gouldbourne." *andygoodliff: church, world and the christian life*, July 3, 2014. Online. https://andygoodliff.typepad.com/my_weblog/2014/07/reflecting-on-ministry-3.html.

Gould, George. *Open Communion and the Baptists of Norwich*. Norwich, England: Joshua Fletcher, Market Place, 1860.

Gouldbourne, Ruth M. B. *Reinventing the Wheel: Women and Ministry in English Baptist Life*. Oxford: Whitley, 1997.

———. "Revd Dr Ruth M B Gouldbourne." *International Baptist Theological Study (IBTS) Centre Amsterdam*, n.d. Online. https://www.ibts.eu/about/info/50.

Grace, W. Madison, II. "Early English Baptists' View of the Lord's Supper." *Southwestern Journal of Theology* 57.2 (2015) 159–79.

Graves, J. R. *Intercommunion: Inconsistent, Unscriptural, and Productive of Evil*. 2nd ed. Baptist Distinctives 17. Paris, AR: Baptist Standard Bearer, 2006.

Green, Joel B. *The Gospel of Luke*. New International Commentary on the New Testament. Grand Rapids: Eerdmans, 1997.

Greever, Joshua M. "The Nature of the New Covenant: A Case Study in Ephesians 2:11–22." *The Southern Baptist Journal of Theology* 20.1 (2016) 73–89.

Gregory, Olinthus. *A Brief Memoir of the Rev. Robert Hall, AM*. Edited by Olinthus Gregory and Joseph Belcher. Vol. 3 of *The Works of the Rev. Robert Hall, AM*. New York: Harper and Brothers, 1849.

Grudem, Wayne A. "Perseverance of the Saints: A Case Study from the Warning Passages in Hebrews." In *Still Sovereign; Contemporary Perspectives on Election,*

Foreknowledge and Grace, edited by Thomas R. Schreiner and Bruce A. Ware, 133–82. Grand Rapids: Baker, 2000

———. *1 Peter: An Introduction and Commentary*. Tyndale New Testament Commentary 17. Downers Grove, IL: InterVarsity, 2009.

Hafemann, Scott. "The Kingdom of God as the Mission of God." In *For the Fame of God's Name: Essays in Honor of John Piper*, edited by Justin Taylor and Sam Storms, 235–52. Wheaton, IL: Crossway, 2010.

Hall, Chad W. "When Orphans Became Heirs: J. R. Graves and the Landmark Baptists." *Baptist History and Heritage* 37.1 (2002) 112–27.

Hall, Robert, Jr. *On Terms of Communion: With a Particular View to the Case of the Baptists and Paedobaptists*. Boston: Wells and Lilly, 1816.

———. *A Reply to the Rev. Joseph Kinghorn: Being a Further Vindication of the Practice of Free Communion*. 2nd ed. London: Button and Son, 1818.

———. *A Short Statement of the Reasons for Christian, in Opposition to Party Communion*. London: Hamilton, Adams & Co., 1826.

Hamilton, James M., Jr. *God's Glory in Salvation through Judgment: A Biblical Theology*. Wheaton, IL: Crossway, 2010.

———. *God's Indwelling Presence: The Holy Spirit in the Old and New Testaments*. NAC Studies in Bible and Theology 1. Nashville: B&H Academic, 2006.

———. "The Seed of the Woman and the Blessing of Abraham." *Tyndale Bulletin* 58.2 (2007) 253–73.

Hamilton, Victor P. *Exodus: An Exegetical Commentary*. Grand Rapids: Baker Academic, 2011.

Hammett, John S. *Forty Questions about Baptism and the Lord's Supper*. Grand Rapids: Kregel, 2015.

Hammett, John S., and Benjamin L. Merkle, eds. *Those Who Must Give an Account: A Study of Church Membership and Church Discipline*. Nashville: B&H Academic, 2012.

Harmon, Steven R. "Trinitarian *Koinōnia* and Ecclesial *Oikoumenē*: Paul Fiddes as Ecumenical Theologian." *Perspectives in Religious Studies* 44.1 (2017) 19–37.

Harrison, Matthew C., and John T. Pless, eds. *Closed Communion? Admission to the Lord's Supper in Biblical Lutheran Perspective*. St. Louis: Concordia, 2017.

Hawthorne, Gerald F. *The Presence & the Power*. Dallas: Word, 1991.

Haykin, Michael A. G., ed. *At the Pure Fountain of Thy Word: Andrew Fuller as an Apologist*. Studies in Baptist History and Thought 6. Eugene, OR: Wipf & Stock, 2007.

Haykin, Michael A. G., et al., eds. *Ecclesia Semper Reformanda Est: The Church Is Always Reforming: A Festschrift on Ecclesiology in Honour of Stanley K. Fowler on His Seventieth Birthday*. Kitchener, Ontario: Joshua, 2016.

Haymes, Brian, ed. *For the Sake of the Church: Essays in Honour of Paul S. Fiddes*. Oxford: Centre for Baptist History and Heritage, 2014.

———. *A Question of Identity: Reflections on Baptist Principles and Practices*. Macquarie Park, Australia: Greenwood, 2013.

Haymes, Brian, et al. *On Being the Church: Revisioning Baptist Identity*. Studies in Baptist History and Thought 21. Milton Keynes, England: Paternoster, 2008.

Heath, Gordon L., and James D. Dvorak, eds. *Baptism: Historical, Theological, and Pastoral Perspectives*. McMaster Theological Studies 4. Eugene, OR: Pickwick, 2011.

Hicks, John Mark. *1 & 2 Chronicles*. College Press NIV Commentary Old Testament Series. Joplin, MO: College, 2001.

Hilburn, Glenn O. "The Lord's Supper: Admission and Exclusion Among English Baptists." ThD diss., Southwestern Baptist Theological Seminary, 1960.

Hill, Andrew E. *1 & 2 Chronicles*. NIV Application Commentary. Grand Rapids: Zondervan, 2003.

Hill, Christopher. *A Tinker and a Poor Man: John Bunyan and His Church, 1628–1688*. New York: Alfred A. Knopf, 1989.

Himbury, D. M. "Baptismal Controversies, 1640–1900." In *Christian Baptism: A Fresh Attempt to Understand the Rite in Terms of Scripture, History, and Theology*, edited by A. Gilmore, 273–305. London: Lutterworth, 1959.

Holifield, E. Brooks. *The Covenant Sealed: The Development of Puritan Sacramental Theology in Old and New England, 1570–1720*. New Haven, CT: Yale University Press, 1974.

———. *Theology in America: Christian Thought from the Age of the Puritans to the Civil War*. New Haven, CT: Yale University Press, 2003.

Horton, Michael S. *People and Place: A Covenant Ecclesiology*. Louisville: Westminster John Knox, 2008.

Horton, Stanley M. "Spirit Baptism: A Pentecostal Perspective." In *Perspectives on Spirit Baptism: Five Views*, edited by Chad Brand, 47–94. Counterpoints. Nashville: Broadman & Holman, 2004.

Hoskins, Paul M. *Jesus as the Fulfillment of the Temple in the Gospel of John*. Milton Keynes, England: Paternoster, 2006.

Howard, David M. *Joshua*. New American Commentary 5. Nashville: Broadman & Holman, 1998.

Howell, Adam. "The Firstborn Son of Moses as the 'Relative of Blood' in Exod 4:24–26." *The Journal for the Study of the Old Testament* 35 (2010) 63–76.

Isaak, Jon M. "Baptism among the Early Christians." *Direction* 33.1 (2004) 3–20.

Jamieson, Bobby. *Going Public: Why Baptism Is Required for Church Membership*. Nashville: B&H Academic, 2015.

Jeremias, Joachim. *The Eucharistic Words of Jesus*. Translated by Norman Perrin. Philadelphia: Trinity, 1966.

Jessey, Henry. *A Storehouse of Provision, to Further Resolution in Severall Cases of Conscience*. London: Charles Sumptner, 1650.

Jeter, Jeremiah Bell. *Baptist Principles Reset: Consisting of Articles on Distinctive Baptist Principles, a Series*. Baptist Distinctives 1. Paris, AR: Baptist Standard Bearer, 2004.

Jewett, Paul King. *Infant Baptism and the Covenant of Grace: An Appraisal of the Argument That as Infants Were Once Circumcised, So They Should Now Be Baptized*. Grand Rapids: Eerdmans, 1978.

Johnson, Ronald Angelo. "The Peculiar Ventures of Particular Baptist Pastor William Kiffin and King Charles II of England." *Baptist History and Heritage* 44.1 (2009) 60–71.

Jones, Brandon C. *Waters of Promise: Finding Meaning in Believer Baptism*. Eugene, OR: Pickwick, 2012.

Kaiser, Walter, Jr. "Exodus." In vol. 2 of *The Expositor's Bible Commentary*, edited by Frank E. Gaebelein, 285–497. Grand Rapids: Zondervan, 1990.

Kazee, Buell H. *The Church and the Ordinances*. Lexington, KY: Little Baptist, 1965.

Keener, Craig S. *Acts: An Exegetical Commentary*. Vols. 1–2. Grand Rapids: Baker Academic, 2012, 2013.

Kelly, J. N. D. *Early Christian Doctrines*. 2nd ed. New York: Harper & Row, 1960.

Kiffin, William. *A Sober Discourse of the Right to Church-Communion: Wherein Is Proved by Scripture, the Example of the Primitive Times, and the Practice of All That Have Professed the Christian Religion: That No Unbaptized Person May Be Regularly Admitted to the Lord's Supper*. London: George Larkin, 1681.

Kimbell, John Raymond. "The Atonement in Lukan Theology." PhD diss., Southern Baptist Theological Seminary, 2009.

Kimble, Jeremy M. *Forty Questions about Church Membership and Discipline*. Grand Rapids: Kregel Academic, 2017.

Kinghorn, Joseph. *Arguments Against the Practice of Mixed Communion*. London: Wightman and Cramp, 1827.

———. *Baptism a Term of Communion at the Lord's Supper*. 2nd ed. Norwich, England: Bacon, Kinnebrook, and Co., 1816.

———. *A Defense of "Baptism a Term of Communion": In Answer to the Rev. Robert Hall's Reply*. Norwich, England: Wilkin and Youngman, 1820.

Kistemaker, Simon J. *Exposition of the First Epistle to the Corinthians*. New Testament Commentary. Grand Rapids: Baker, 1993.

Klein, Ralph W. *2 Chronicles: A Commentary*. Hermeneia. Minneapolis: Fortress, 2012.

Kline, Meredith G. *By Oath Consigned: A Reinterpretation of the Signs of Circumcision and Baptism*. Grand Rapids: Eerdmans, 1968.

———. "Old Testament Origins of the Gospel Genre." *Westminster Theological Journal* 38 (1975) 1–27.

Klopfer, Sheila D. "Baptists in America (1742–1833) An Historical and Theological Assessment of Baptism with a Corresponding Proposal for Baptist Theology of Baptism in the Twenty-First Century." PhD diss., Southwestern Baptist Theological Seminary, 2006.

———. "The Betwixt and between Baptismal Theology: Of Baptists in Colonial America." *Baptist History and Heritage* 45.1 (2010) 6–20.

Konkel, August H. *1 & 2 Kings*. NIV Application Commentary. Grand Rapids: Zondervan, 2006.

Köstenberger, Andreas. *John*. Baker Exegetical Commentary on the New Testament. Grand Rapids: Baker Academic, 2004.

Köstenberger, Andreas, and Scott R. Swain. *Father, Son, and Spirit: The Trinity and John's Gospel*. New Studies in Biblical Theology 24. Downers Grove, IL: InterVarsity, 2008.

Kynes, Bill. "Why I Am a 'baptist' (with a Small 'b')." *Gospel Coalition* (blog), June 20, 2014. Online. https://www.thegospelcoalition.org/article/why-i-am-a-baptist-with-a-small-b.

Ladd, George E. *A Theology of the New Testament*. Grand Rapids: Eerdmans, 1974.

Lane, William L. *The Gospel According to Mark: The English Text with Introduction, Exposition, and Notes*. New International Commentary on the New Testament. Grand Rapids: Eerdmans, 1974.

Lea, Thomas D., and Hayne P. Griffin. *1, 2 Timothy, Titus*. New American Commentary 34. Nashville: Broadman, 1992.

Leeman, Jonathan. *The Church and the Surprising Offense of God's Love: Reintroducing the Doctrines of Church Membership and Discipline*. Wheaton, IL: Crossway, 2010.

————. *Church Discipline: How the Church Protects the Name of Jesus*. 9 Marks. Wheaton, IL: Crossway, 2012.

————. *Church Membership: How the World Knows Who Represents Jesus*. 9 Marks. Wheaton, IL: Crossway, 2012.

————. *Political Church: The Local Assembly as Embassy of Christ's Rule*. Studies in Christian Doctrine and Scripture. Downers Grove, IL: InterVarsity, 2016.

Leeman, Jonathan, and Mark Dever, eds. *Baptist Foundations: Church Government for an Anti-Institutional Age*. Nashville: B&H Academic, 2015.

Levering, Matthew. *Ezra and Nehemiah*. Brazos Theological Commentary on the Bible. Grand Rapids: Brazos, 2007.

Levine, Baruch A. *Leviticus*. JPS Torah Commentary. Philadelphia: JPS, 1989.

Lints, Richard. *The Fabric of Theology: A Prolegomenon to Evangelical Theology*. Grand Rapids: Eerdmans, 1993.

Longenecker, Richard N. *The Epistle to the Romans: A Commentary on the Greek Text*. New International Greek Testament Commentary. Grand Rapids: Eerdmans, 2016.

Macleod, Angus Hamilton. "The Life and Teaching of Robert Hall, 1764–1831." MA thesis, University of Durham, 1957.

Malone, Fred A. *The Baptism of Disciples Alone: A Covenantal Argument for Credobaptism versus Paedobaptism*. Cape Coral, FL: Founders, 2007.

Marshall, I. Howard. *Last Supper and Lord's Supper*. Vancouver, Canada: Regent College Publishing, 1980.

Martin, Oren R. *Bound for the Promised Land: The Land Promise in God's Redemptive Plan*. New Studies in Biblical Theology 34. Downers Grove, IL: InterVarsity, 2015.

Mathews, Kenneth A. *Genesis 11:27—50:26*. New American Commentary 1B. Nashville: B&H Academic, 2005.

McConville, J. G., and Stephen N. Williams. *Joshua*. Two Horizons Old Testament Commentary. Grand Rapids: Eerdmans, 2010.

McLoughlin, William G. *New England Dissent: The Baptists and the Separation of Church and State*. Vol. 2. Cambridge, MA: Harvard University Press, 1971.

McNutt, Cody Heath. "The Ministry of Robert Hall, Jr.: The Preacher as Theological Exemplar and Cultural Celebrity." PhD diss., Southern Baptist Theological Seminary, 2012.

Meade, John D. "Circumcision of the Heart in Leviticus and Deuteronomy: Divine Means for Resolving Curse and Bringing Blessing." *The Southern Baptist Journal of Theology* 18.3 (2014) 59–85.

————. "The Meaning of Circumcision in Israel: A Proposal for a Transfer of Rite from Egypt to Israel." *The Southern Baptist Journal of Theology* 20.1 (2016) 35–54.

Melick, Richard R., Jr. *Philippians, Colossians, Philemon*. New American Commentary 32. Nashville: Broadman, 1991.

Meyer, Jason C. *The End of the Law: Mosaic Covenant in Pauline Theology*. NAC Studies in Bible and Theology 6. Nashville: B&H Academic, 2009.

Moessner, David P. *Lord of the Banquet: The Literary and Theological Significance of the Lukan Travel Narrative*. Minneapolis: Fortress, 1989.

Mohler, R. Albert, Jr. "A Call for Theological Triage and Christian Maturity." *Albert Mohler* (blog), July 12, 2005. Online. https://albertmohler.com/2005/07/12/a-call-for-theological-triage-and-christian-maturity.

Moo, Douglas J. *The Epistle to the Romans*. New International Commentary on the New Testament. Grand Rapids: Eerdmans, 1996.

―――. *The Epistle to the Romans*. 2nd ed. New International Commentary on the New Testament. Grand Rapids: Eerdmans, 2018.

Moore, Russell D. *The Kingdom of Christ: The New Evangelical Perspective*. Wheaton, IL: Crossway, 2004.

Moore, Russell D., and Robert E. Sagers. "The Kingdom of God and the Church: A Baptist Reassessment." *The Southern Baptist Journal of Theology* 12.1 (2008) 68–87.

Morden, Peter J. *"Communion with Christ and His People": The Spirituality of C. H. Spurgeon*. Oxford: Regent's Park College, 2010.

―――. *The Life and Thought of Andrew Fuller (1754–1815)*. Studies in Evangelical History and Thought. Milton Keynes, England: Paternoster, 2015.

―――. "'So Valuable a Life . . .': A Biographical Sketch of Andrew Fuller." *The Southern Baptist Journal of Theology* 17.1 (2013) 4–14.

―――. "The Spirituality of C. H. Spurgeon 2 Maintaining Communion: The Lord's Supper." *Baptistic Theologies* 4 (2012) 27–50.

Morgan, Christopher. "Baptists and the Unity of the Church." *The Journal of Baptist Studies* 7 (2015) 4–23

Morris, J. W. *Biographical Recollections of the Rev. Robert Hall, AM*. London: George Wightman, 1833.

Morris, Leon. *The Gospel According to Matthew*. Pillar New Testament Commentary. Grand Rapids: Eerdmans, 1992.

Naselli, Andrew David. *Let Go and Let God? A Survey and Analysis of Keswick Theology*. Bellingham, WA: Lexham, 2010.

Naselli, Andrew David, et al. *Forty Questions about Biblical Theology*. Grand Rapids: Kregel Academic, forthcoming.

Nassif, Bradley. "Baptism, Eucharist and the Church—An Eastern Orthodox Synthesis." Paper presented at the Evangelical Theological Society, San Diego, CA, November 2014.

Naylor, Peter. *Calvinism, Communion, and the Baptists: A Study of English Calvinistic Baptists from the Late 1600s to the Early 1800s*. Studies in Baptist History and Thought 7. Waynesboro, GA: Paternoster, 2003.

Nettles, Tom J. *Beginnings in Britain*. Vol. 1 of *The Baptists: Key People Involved in Forming a Baptist Identity*. Fearn, Scotland: Christian Focus, 2005.

―――. *Living by Revealed Truth: The Life and Pastoral Theology of Charles Haddon Spurgeon*. Fearn, Scotland: Mentor, 2013.

Nicholson, Ernest W. "The Covenant Ritual in Exodus 24:3–8." *Vetus Testamentum* 32.1 (1982) 74–86.

Nolland, John. *Luke: 18:35—24:53*. Word Biblical Commentary 35C. Dallas: Word, 1993.

O'Brien, P. T. "The Church as a Heavenly Eschatological Entity." In *The Church in the Bible and the World: An International Study*, edited by D. A. Carson, 88–119. Exeter, England: Paternoster, 1987.

―――. *The Letter to the Ephesians*. Pillar New Testament Commentary. Grand Rapids: Eerdmans, 1999.

O'Donovan, Oliver. *The Desire of the Nations: Rediscovering the Roots of Political Theology*. Cambridge: Cambridge University Press, 1996.

Olive, Dean. "Joseph Kinghorn (1766–1832)." In vol. 2 of *The British Particular Baptists, 1638–1910*, edited by Michael A. G. Haykin, 84–111. Springfield, MO: Particular Baptist, 2000.

Oliver, Robert. *History of the English Calvinistic Baptists, 1771–1892: From John Gill to C. H. Spurgeon*. Edinburgh: Banner of Truth Trust, 2006.

Ostrowski, Ally. "Cyber Communion: Finding God in the Little Box." *Journal of Religion & Society* 8 (2006) 1–8.

Packer, J. I. *Keep in Step with the Spirit: Finding Fullness in Our Walk with God*. 2nd ed. Grand Rapids: Baker, 2005.

Parker, Brent Evan. "The Israel-Christ-Church Typological Pattern: A Theological Critique of Covenant and Dispensational Theologies." PhD diss., Southern Baptist Theological Seminary, 2017.

———. "Paedocommunion, Paedobaptism, and Covenant Theology: A Baptist Assessment and Critique." *The Southern Baptist Journal of Theology* 20.1 (2016) 91–122.

Parsons, Mikeal C. *Acts*. Paideia. Grand Rapids: Baker Academic, 2008.

Patterson, James A. *James Robinson Graves: Staking the Boundaries of Baptist Identity*. Studies in Baptist Life and Thought. Nashville: B&H Academic, 2012.

———. "Participation at the Lord's Table." *SBCLife*, December 1, 2012. Online. http://www.sbclife.net/article/2158/participation-at-the-lords-table.

Patterson, Paige. *Revelation*. New American Commentary 39. Nashville: B&H, 2012.

Payne, Earnest A. *The Fellowship of Believers: Baptist Thought and Practice Yesterday and Today*. London: Carey Kingsgate, 1954.

Peterson, David. *The Acts of the Apostles*. Pillar New Testament Commentary. Grand Rapids: Eerdmans, 2009.

Piper, John. *Andrew Fuller: Holy Faith, Worthy Gospel, World Mission*. Wheaton, IL: Crossway, 2016.

———. "Baptism and Church Membership: The Recommendation from the Elders for Amending Bethlehem's Constitution." *Desiring God*, September 14, 2005. Online. https://www.desiringgod.org/articles/baptism-and-church-membership-the-recommendation-from-the-elders-for-amending-bethlehems-constitution.

Pipes, Carol. "Lord's Supper: LifeWay Surveys Churches' Practices, Frequency." *Baptist Press*, September 17, 2012. Online. http://www.bpnews.net/38730/lords-supper-lifeway-surveys-churches-practices-frequency.

Poe, Harry L "John Bunyan's Controversy with the Baptists." *Baptist History and Heritage* 23 (1988) 25–35.

Polhill, John B. *Acts*. New American Commentary 26. Nashville: Broadman, 1992.

Porter, Stanley E., and Anthony R. Cross, eds. *Dimensions of Baptism: Biblical and Theological Studies*. London: Sheffield Academic, 2002.

Ramsbottom, B. A. *Stranger than Fiction: The Life of William Kiffin*. Harpenden, England: Gospel Standard Trust, 1989.

Ray, Jeff D. *B. H. Carroll*. Nashville: Sunday School Board of the Southern Baptist Convention, 1927.

Reed, Holly G. "Computer-Mediated Communication and Ecclesiological Challenges to and from the Reformed Tradition." PhD diss., Boston University School of Theology, 2011.

Ridderbos, Herman N. *The Epistle of Paul to the Churches of Galatia*. New International Commentary on the New Testament. Grand Rapids: Eerdmans, 1956.

Riddle, Jeffrey T. "Piper's Baptism and Membership Proposal: A Neo-Landmark Response." Paper presented at the Evangelical Theological Society, Glenside, PA, 2006.

Ritchie, Robert H. "Breaking Bread Together: Alexander Campbell's Ecumenical Spirit and the Lord's Supper." PhD diss., Trinity International University, 2012.

Rosner, Brian S. *Paul and the Law: Keeping the Commandments of God*. New Studies in Biblical Theology 31. Downers Grove, IL: IVP Academic, 2013.

Ross, Allen P. *Recalling the Hope of Glory: Biblical Worship from the Garden to the New Creation*. Grand Rapids: Kregel, 2006.

Salter, Martin. "Does Baptism Replace Circumcision? An Examination of the Relationship between Circumcision and Baptism in Colossians 2:11–12." *Themelios* 35 (2010) 15–29.

Sampler, Jason. "Whosoever Is 'Qualified' May Come: Investigating a Connection between Church Membership and Participation in the Lord's Supper in Southern Baptist Theological Writings." PhD diss., New Orleans Baptist Theological Seminary, 2013.

Saucy, Robert L. *The Case for Progressive Dispensationalism: The Interface between Dispensational and Non-Dispensational Theology*. Grand Rapids: Zondervan, 1993.

———. *The Church in God's Program*. Chicago: Moody, 1972.

Schnabel, Eckhard J. *Acts*. Exegetical Commentary on the New Testament. Grand Rapids: Zondervan, 2012.

Schreiner, Patrick James. *The Kingdom of God and the Glory of the Cross*. Short Studies in Biblical Theology. Wheaton, IL: Crossway, 2018.

———. "People and Place: A Spatial Analysis of the Kingdom in Matthew." PhD diss., Southern Baptist Theological Seminary, 2014.

Schreiner, Thomas R. *Commentary on Hebrews*. Nashville: B&H, 2015.

———. *The King in His Beauty*. Grand Rapids: Baker Academic, 2013.

———. *New Testament Theology: Magnifying God in Christ*. Grand Rapids: Baker Academic, 2008.

———. *Paul, Apostle of God's Glory in Christ: A Pauline Theology*. Downers Grove, IL: InterVarsity, 2001.

———. *1, 2 Peter, Jude*. New American Commentary 37. Nashville: Broadman & Holman, 2003.

———. *Romans*. 2nd ed. Baker Exegetical Commentary on the New Testament. Grand Rapids: Baker Academic, 2018.

Schreiner, Thomas R., and Ardel B. Caneday. *The Race Set before Us: A Biblical Theology of Perseverance & Assurance*. Downers Grove, IL: InterVarsity, 2001.

Schreiner, Thomas R., and Matthew R. Crawford, eds. *The Lord's Supper: Remembering and Proclaiming Christ Until He Comes*. NAC Studies in Bible and Theology 10. Nashville: B&H Academic, 2010.

Schreiner, Thomas R., and Shawn D. Wright, eds. *Believer's Baptism: Sign of the New Covenant in Christ*. NAC Studies in Bible and Theology 2. Nashville: B&H Academic, 2006.

Shurden, Walter B., ed. *Baptism and the Lord's Supper*. Proclaiming the Baptist Vision 5. Macon, GA: Smyth & Helwys, 1999.

Smith, Clyde L. "Morehead Baptists Appreciate the Labors of Ex-Pastor Buell H. Kazee." *Western Recorder*, February 26, 1953. Online. http://baptisthistoryhomepage. com/kazee.ltr.apprec.1953.mhd.html.

Snodgrass, Klyne. *Ephesians*. NIV Application Commentary. Grand Rapids: Zondervan, 1996.

Southern Baptist Convention. "The Baptist Faith and Message 2000." June 14, 2000. Online. http://www.sbc.net/bfm2000/bfm2000.asp.

Sprague, William, ed. *Annals of the American Baptist Pulpit or Commemorative Notices of Distinguished Clergymen of the Baptist Denomination in the United States*. Vol. 6. New York: Robert Carter & Brothers, 1860.

Spurgeon, C. H. *The Autobiography of Charles H. Spurgeon*. Vol. 4. Edited by Susannah Thompson Spurgeon and W. J. Harrald. Chicago: Revell, 1900.

―――. *The New Park Street Pulpit*. N.p.: Osnova, 2012. Kindle ed.

Stein, Robert H. "Baptism and Becoming a Christian in the New Testament." *The Southern Baptist Journal of Theology* 2.1 (1998) 6–17.

―――. *Luke*. New American Commentary 24. Nashville: Broadman, 1992.

―――. *Mark*. Baker Exegetical Commentary on the New Testament. Grand Rapids: Baker Academic, 2008.

Stoffer, Dale R., ed. *The Lord's Supper: Believers' Church Perspectives*. Scottdale, PA: Herald, 1997.

Strawbridge, Gregg, ed. *The Case for Covenant Communion*. Monroe, LA: Athanasius, 2006.

―――. *The Case for Covenantal Infant Baptism*. Phillipsburg, NJ: P&R, 2003.

Stuart, Douglas K. *Exodus*. New American Commentary, vol. 2. Nashville: Broadman & Holman, 2006.

Suter, John Wallace, and Lucien Moore Robinson. "Articles of Religion." In *The Book of Common Prayer and Administration of the Sacraments and Other Rites and Ceremonies of the Church*, 591–98. Cambridge ed. Boston: Old Corner Book Store, 1928. Online. http://justus.anglican.org/resources/bcp/1928/Articles.htm.

Thiselton, Anthony. *The First Epistle to the Corinthians: A Commentary on the Greek Text*. New International Greek Testament Commentary. Grand Rapids: Eerdmans, 2000.

Thompson, J. A. *The Book of Jeremiah*. New International Commentary on the Old Testament. Grand Rapids: Eerdmans, 1980.

―――. *1, 2 Chronicles*. New American Commentary 9. Nashville: Broadman & Holman, 1994.

Thompson, James W. *Hebrews*. Paideia. Grand Rapids: Baker Academic, 2008.

Thompson, Marianne Meye. *Colossians and Philemon*. Two Horizons New Testament Commentary. Grand Rapids: Eerdmans, 2005.

Turley, Stephen Richard. *The Ritualized Revelation of the Messianic Age: Washings and Meals in Galatians and 1 Corinthians*. Library of New Testament Studies 544. New York: T&T Clark, 2015.

Turner [Candidus], Daniel. *A Modest Plea for Free Communion at the Lord's Table; Particularly between the Baptists and Paedobaptists in a Letter to a Friend*. London: J. Johnson, 1772.

Turner, Dustin. "Immersed into the Church? A Biblical-Historical Analysis of the Permissibility of Baptismal Modes for Membership in Southern Baptist Churches." PhD diss., New Orleans Baptist Theological Seminary, 2016.

Tyler, John R. *Baptism: We've Got It Right and Wrong*. Macon, GA: Smyth & Helwys, 2003.

Underwood, A. C. *A History of the English Baptists*. London: Carey Kingsgate, 1956.

United States Conference of Catholic Bishops (USCCB). *Catechism of the Catholic Church*. 2nd ed. Washington, DC: Libreria Editrice Vaticana, 2016.

Venema, Cornelis P. *Children at the Lord's Table? Assessing the Case for Paedocommunion*. Grand Rapids: Reformation Heritage Books, 2009.

Vlach, Michael J. "Have They Found a Better Way? An Analysis of Gentry and Wellum's *Kingdom through Covenant*." *Master's Seminary Journal* 24.1 (2013) 5–24.

Vos, Geerhardus, and Danny E. Olinger. *The Teaching of Jesus Concerning the Kingdom of God and the Church*. Middletown, DE: Fontes, 2017.

Walker, Michael. *Baptists at the Table: The Theology of the Lord's Supper amongst English Baptists in the Nineteenth Century*. Didcot, England: Baptist Historical Society, 1992.

———. "Charles Haddon Spurgeon (1834–1892) and John Clifford (1836–1923) on the Lord's Supper." *American Baptist Quarterly* 7.2 (1988) 128–50.

Ware, Bruce A. "The New Covenant and the People(s) of God." In *Dispensationalism, Israel, and the Church: The Search for Definition*, edited by Craig A. Blaising and Darrell L. Bock, 68–97. Grand Rapids: Zondervan, 1992.

Waters, Guy Prentiss. *The Lord's Supper as the Sign and Meal of the New Covenant*. Short Studies in Biblical Theology. Wheaton, IL: Crossway, 2019. Kindle.

Waters, Guy Prentiss, and Ligon Duncan, eds. *Children and the Lord's Supper*. Rev. ed. Fearn, Scotland: Mentor, 2011.

Weaver, Steve. "When Biography Shapes Ecclesiology: Bunyan, Kiffin, and the Open-Communion Debate." *The Journal for Baptist Studies* 9 (2018) 31–54.

Webster, John. *Holy Scripture: A Dogmatic Sketch*. Current Issues in Theology. New York: Cambridge University Press, 2003.

———. "'In the Society of God': Some Principles of Ecclesiology." In *Perspectives on Ecclesiology and Ethnography*, edited by Pete Ward, 200–222. Grand Rapids: Eerdmans, 2012.

Wellum, Stephen J. "Beyond Mere Ecclesiology." In *The Community of Jesus: A Theology of the Church*, edited by Kendell H. Easley and Christopher W. Morgan, 183–212. Nashville: B&H Academic, 2013.

———. *God the Son Incarnate: The Doctrine of Christ*. Foundations of Evangelical Theology. Wheaton, IL: Crossway, 2016.

Wellum, Stephen J., and Brent E. Parker, eds. *Progressive Covenantalism: Charting a Course between Dispensational and Covenant Theologies*. Nashville: B&H Academic, 2016.

White, B. R. "William Kiffin: Baptist Pioneer and Citizen of London." *Baptist History and Heritage* 2.2 (1967) 91–103.

White, Thomas. "James Madison Pendleton and His Contributions to Baptist Ecclesiology." PhD diss., Southeastern Baptist Theological Seminary, 2005.

———. "The Universal and Local Church." In *Upon This Rock: The Baptist Understanding of the Church*, edited by Jason G. Duesing et al., 208–39. Nashville: B&H Academic, 2010.

White, Thomas, et al., eds. *Restoring Integrity in Baptist Churches*. Grand Rapids: Kregel Academic, 2008.

Wilkin, Martin Hood. *Joseph Kinghorn of Norwich: A Memoir*. Vol. 1 of *The Life and Works of Joseph Kinghorn*. Edited by Terry Wolever. Springfield, MO: Particular Baptist, 1995.

Wilkins, Steve, and Duane Garner, eds. *The Federal Vision*. Monroe, LA: Athanasius, 2004.

Williams, Stan. "Buell H. Kazee: Part-Time Banjo Picker; Full-Time Servant of Christ." *Kentucky Baptist Heritage*, May 4, 2004. Online. http://geocitiessites.com/baptist_documents/kazee.buell.bio.html.

Williamson, Paul R. *Sealed with an Oath: Covenant in God's Unfolding Purpose*. New Studies in Biblical Theology 23. Downers Grove, IL: InterVarsity, 2007.

Wills, Gregory A. "The Ecclesiology of Charles H. Spurgeon: Unity, Orthodoxy, and Denominational Identity." *Baptist History and Heritage* 34.3 (1999) 67–80.

Wilson, Douglas. *To a Thousand Generations: Infant Baptism: Covenant Mercy for the People of God*. Moscow, ID: Canon, 1996.

Worcester, Noah. *A Friendly Letter to the Reverend Thomas Baldwin*. Concord, NH: Hough, 1791.

Worcester, Samuel. *Serious and Candid Letters to the Rev. Thomas Baldwin, DD, on His Book, Entitled, "The Baptism of Believers Only, and the Particular Communion of the Baptist Churches, Explained and Vindicated."* Salem, MA: Haven Pool, 1807.

———. *Two Discourses on the Perpetuity and Provision of God's Gracious Covenant with Abraham and His Seed*. 2nd ed. Salem, MA: Haven Pool, 1807.

Wright, Christopher J. H. *Knowing the Holy Spirit through the Old Testament*. Downers Grove, IL: IVP Academic, 2006.

Wright, David F. *Baptism: Three Views*. Downers Grove, IL: IVP Academic, 2009.

———. *Infant Baptism in Historical Perspective*. Studies in Christian History and Thought. Milton Keynes, England: Paternoster, 2007.

Wright, N. T. *The Last Word: Beyond the Bible Wars to a New Understanding of the Authority of Scripture*. San Francisco: HarperSanFrancisco, 2005.

Scripture Index

Old Testament

Genesis

Leviticus

Jeremiah

Ezekiel

John

Acts

Acts (continued)

Romans